# THE ROUGH GUIDE TO

# Shakespeare

**ROUGH GUIDES**

www.roughguides.com

## Credits

**Editor:** Joe Staines
**Series editor:** Mark Ellingham
**Design and layout:** Katie Stephens
**Production:** Katherine Owers
**Picture research:** Kathy Elgin
**Proofreading:** Carole Mansur

## About the cover

The cover is a montage of four portraits, all thought – with varying degrees of plausibility – to depict Shakespeare. Top left is an eighteenth-century engraving based on the "Chandos" portrait, an anonymous painting now in London's National Portrait Gallery. Top-right is a detail from Martin Droeshout's engraving, which fronts the First Folio of 1623. Though not taken from life, the Droeshout engraving is infinitely more likely to resemble Shakespeare than the beautifully worked miniature by Nicholas Hilliard of an unidentified young man (bottom-left), now in the Victoria and Albert Museum. Ingenious scholars have seen in the painting clues identifying the sitter as Shakespeare, but the connection remains highly dubious. Bottom-right is an anonymous nineteenth-century print, taken from an edition of the *Works*. It's based on Droeshout, but in this version the author's hair is freshly crimped, his beard is spruced up, and the notorious bags under his eyes appear to have been surgically removed.

## Publishing Information

This first edition published April 2005 by Rough Guides Ltd, 80 Strand, London WC2R 0RL
375 Hudson Street, New York 10014

Distributed by the Penguin Group
Penguin Books Ltd, 80 Strand, London, WC2R 0RL
Penguin Putnam USA Inc., 375 Hudson Street, New York 10014
Penguin Books Canada Ltd, 10 Alcorn Avenue, Toronto, Ontario MV4 1E4
Penguin Books Australia Ltd, PO Box 257, Ringwood, Victoria
Penguin Books (NZ) Ltd, 182–190 Wairau Road, Auckland 10

Printed in Italy by LegoPrint S.p.A
Typeset in Minion and Helvetica to an original design by Henry Iles

All photographs copyright of credited photographers and agencies
544 pages; includes index
A catalogue record for this book is available from the British Library
ISBN 1-84353-518-1

# THE "ROUGH GUIDE TO

# Shakespeare "

## THE PLAYS · THE POEMS · THE LIFE

Written by

**Andrew Dickson**

/

Edited by

**Joe Staines**

# Contents

## Part I ▷ The Plays

## Part II ▷ The Poems

## Part III ▷ Contexts

## Feature boxes

# Introduction

There are many different Shakespeares. As the years pass, they multiply: theatre is a restless and inquisitive medium, and Shakespeare, the world's most revived playwright, keeps on mutating and evolving. Close to four centuries after his death, his plays continue to be seen by millions of people in thousands of locations across the globe. His words enrich the English language, rippling through casual, day-to-day speech and at the same time propping up the very notion of "high" culture. His works have generated a major publishing industry and been translated into hundreds of different languages. His name has been pressed into the service of convictions and ideologies he could never have dreamed about, and he has become an icon in countries that didn't even exist when he was alive. His image decorates banknotes, tea towels, police badges; it appears on road signs, exam scripts and beer mats. Some grumble that Shakespeare is now global big business – an immoveable heritage fixture, a hefty slice of cultural capitalism. *The Rough Guide to Shakespeare* celebrates the many sides of Shakespeare, and tries to unravel what it is that makes the man and his works so continually compelling.

Just as there are many Shakespeares, there is no single way of explaining what makes his work so appealing. His plays and poems aren't just astonishing works of literary art, but gripping pieces of drama. They're remarkable social documents, but often touched with magic and fantasy. They're full of optimism and comedy about the human condition, yet also shot through with pain, anger and despair. And although they're of their historical moment, they touch something that seems truly universal. Few others writers achieve all that, and it doesn't take long to realize that Shakespeare is the most exciting, challenging and addictive writer in the language.

In spite of this, getting to know Shakespeare can be a bewildering business. At least twenty major editions of the *Complete Works* are currently in print, hundreds of academic articles and critical studies pile up each year, and more films than ever take their cue from his work. Many of these offer something different, something new, and in all likelihood something worth thinking about. But you can't read or see the lot: few people will want to watch the more than fifty screen versions of *Hamlet*, or trudge their way through the countless books devoted to Shakespeare's life and work. *The Rough Guide to Shakespeare* cuts a path through the jungle.

The book is designed to be of use to as many different people as possible. Theatregoers can scan synopses and stage histories. Students can check reference information, browse critical essays and chase up book and Web links. Cinephiles can cut straight to the most rewarding and absorbing film adaptations. Anyone interested in the broader context can go straight to the chapters on Shakespeare's life and stages. And unlike many critical works published on Shakespeare, the aim of this book isn't to show off extravagant new theories; neither is it to tell you what you *should* think about Shakespeare and his writing. The starting point of this book is just that – that it is a starting point.

# How this book works

*The Rough Guide to Shakespeare* is designed to be easy to use. It divides into three sections: PLAYS, POEMS and CONTEXTS. Each of the 38 plays gets a chapter to itself, and, for ease of reference, chapters are arranged alphabetically. All conform to the same pattern, beginning with a short **introductory paragraph,** accompanied by a **synopsis,** a **list of major characters** and information about the play's approximate **date, sources** and **textual history.** This is followed by an **interpretative essay** – the heart of the chapter – that guides you through the play and introduces its crucial themes and ideas. The essay is followed by a **stage history,** describing the play's life in the theatre from the earliest years to the present day, concentrating on the most significant productions in the UK and US. At the end of the chapter are a series of **reviews.** First listed are **screen** and **audio** productions, highlighting the best and most interesting adaptations around and the format they are currently available in. Then it's on to books, with a recommendation of the best individual **edition** of the play in question, followed by selected works of **literary criticism** for readers who want to study or think about a particular play in more detail.

The **Poems** section follows almost exactly the same pattern as the plays, with individual chapters on *A Lover's Complaint, The Rape of Lucrece,* the Sonnets and *Venus and Adonis.* The obvious difference is that there are no performance histories or film recommendations, and only the Sonnets and *Lucrece* have audio versions currently available.

**Contexts** is the final section of the book. It begins with a chapter outlining **Shakespeare's life,** focusing on the documented historical facts but also examining the many myths about him. It's followed by an account of the **stages** on which Shakespeare worked, with specifics about the major acting companies and playhouses, along with details of Shakespeare's colleagues and rivals. A summary of **Shakespeare's canon** – what he wrote and when – precedes a list of recommended **books** covering everything from music in Shakespeare to the works that he himself read; it's supplemented by a comprehensive list of the best **websites,** reflecting the fact that for Shakespearians the Internet has added an exciting new dimension to the field – from checking quotes to renting DVDs. Finally there's a selective **glossary,** defining some useful terminology common to this book and others in the area.

# Quotes and symbols

Quotations from the plays and poems are found throughout *The Rough Guide to Shakespeare.* Each one is followed by a **numerical reference** identifying precisely where it's taken from. The plays are nearly always broken down into acts and scenes, and modern editors usually number the lines too. Following the standardized system, this book cites act numbers first, then the relevant scene number, and finally the line number – so "5.2.23–32" indicates that the quotation in question is taken from Act Five, scene two, and covers lines 23 to 32 ("SD" indicates that the text appears in a stage direction). When referring to the poems, citations provide line numbers. The text used throughout is *William Shakespeare: The Complete Works,* edited by Stanley Wells and Gary Taylor (Oxford University Press, 1988); other editions, including those recommended at the end of each chapter, will in all likelihood number things slightly differently. Text quoted from other writers is in modernized spelling throughout.

In the review sections of each chapter, publishing information for **film** and **audio** versions appears as follows. Films are listed in date order, with cast and director details appearing first, followed by country and date of origin, then current distributor (in the order UK / US where the distributor is different in each territory):

**Hamlet**
E. Hawke, J. Stiles, K. MacLachlan; Michael Almereyda (dir.)
US, 2000 ▷ Cinema Club / Miramax **DVD** ▭

**Macbeth**
S. Dillane, F. Shaw, D. Conlan; Fiona Shaw (dir.)
UK, 1998 ▷ Naxos ⊙ ▭

| | |
|---|---|
| **DVD** | DVD |
| ▭ | VHS |
| ⊙ | CD |
| ▭ | Audio cassette |

**Book details** follow a similar format throughout, listing author/editor, date of original publication, then current publisher (in the order UK / US where publishers are different). "UP" stands for "university press":

**Arden Shakespeare (third series)**
T.W. Craik (ed.); 1995 > Thomson

**The Structure of Complex Words**
William Empson; 1951 > Penguin / Michigan UP [o/p]

Every effort has been made to indicate when books are currently out of print ("o/p"), but with the advent of online bookstores the distinction between titles that are available and those that aren't has become increasingly blurred. It's not impossible that a secondhand book ordered through a specialist retailer will be easier to find – and reach you faster – than something published the previous week. And availability changes continually, so if you're having difficulty locating a particular title it's worth checking with a good bookseller or one of the large Internet stores (see p.499 for reviews and recommendations).

## Author's Acknowledgements

I owe a large debt of gratitude to the many people who have helped with this book. For theatre tickets during the research stage, special thanks must go to Gerry Halliday at the Globe, Brendan Winslow at the National and Dean Asker at the RSC. For review copies, thanks especially to Sue Young at Arden, Bill Shepherd at Arkangel, Rosie Whittam at BBC Audiobooks, Lorena Verdes at Cambridge University Press, Robert Marshall at Heritage Theatre, Roz Hall at Naxos, Claire Prentice at Oxford University Press, and Sarah Allchin and Claire Reeks at Penguin. Thanks too to staff at the British Library; Cambridge University Library; the Cambridge English Faculty Library; Gonville and Caius College Library, Cambridge; Helen Hargest at the Shakespeare Centre; and the wonderful people at Prime Time Videos in Blackheath. I'm also grateful to Susan Clark and Sheila Mühlemann for their advice on Shakespeare in schools, Rebecca Meitlis for her horticultural knowledge, and to Professor Harry Rusche of Emory University for the generous use of his postcards of Shakespearian actors.

At Rough Guides, I'd like to thank Jonathan Buckley, for making it happen; to Mark Ellingham, for Pynchon and encouragement; to Andrew Lockett, for cool handling of alarums and excursions; to Joe Staines, for superlative editing, unbounded enthusiasm and plentiful theatrical arcana; to Katie Stephens and Henry Iles, for elegant design and typesetting; to Kathy Elgin, for her erudite picture research; to Peter Dyer, for an eye-catching cover; to Carole Mansur, for meticulous proofreading; to Miles Irving, for the fine map of Shakespeare's London; and to Duncan Clark, plus the rest of the Reference crew, for the usual.

Friends, flatmates and relations have put up with it (and me) for an extended period of time, and have offered encouragement and ideas aplenty: thanks most especially to Gemma, Siân and Trevor; to Rachel, Femke, Des and assorted Cambridge Dylanites; to Liz and the Davidson clan; and especially to my own family.

## About the author

Andrew Dickson was born in 1979 and grew up in Yorkshire. He studied English at Cambridge University, later returning to specialize in Shakespeare and Renaissance Literature, and now works as a freelance writer and journalist. This is his first book.

# The Plays

# All's Well That Ends Well

The central story woven by *All's Well* seems at first glance more socially optimistic than any other Shakespeare wrote: a poor physician's daughter finds her prince and eventually succeeds in wedding him. But the uncomfortable truth exposed by this bittersweet play is that fairytale endings rarely mesh with real human needs. Helen, the play's questing heroine, needs only to convince her idol that she is worth marrying, but she ends up blackmailing him into it: a finale that the play's sardonic title renders profoundly disquieting. Some have wondered whether *All's Well* is an alternative title for the mysterious *Love's Labour's Won* (see p.186), but although Helen labours to win her love, the play's own ambiguous "end" is worlds away from those of earlier, brighter comedies. George Bernard Shaw compared the play to Ibsen's *A Doll's House* for the way that the "sovereign charm" of Helen is set against "a perfectly ordinary young man, whose unimaginative prejudices and selfish conventionality make him cut a very mean figure". Despite its considerable dramatic strength, *All's Well* and its small cast are not often given the chance to win over audiences; nevertheless, a handful of twentieth-century productions have demonstrated the special intensity and charm of this neglected play.

[DATE] Though considered by some to be the lost *Love's Labour's Won* (see p.186), most scholars believe that *All's Well* dates from 1604–05, after *Othello* – making it the last "problem play".

[SOURCES] Giovanni Boccaccio's *Decameron* (1353), a collection of tales told by a group of Florentines, passes on the basic story, though Shakespeare would have taken it from William Painter's translation *Palace of Pleasure* (1566); see p.5. He adds several characters.

[TEXTS] Though only the Folio text (1623) survives, it is unusually messy and error-strewn, possibly set from the dramatist's foul papers.

## Interpreting the play

Like *Twelfth Night* before it, *All's Well* – though ostensibly a comedy – begins in mourning. The stage is filled with characters clad in black; bereavement hangs in the air. The King of France is gravely ill and has commanded his young ward Bertram to attend him, while in the very first lines of the play Bertram's own departure is likened by his widowed mother, the Countess of Roussillon, to "burying a second husband" (1.1.1–2). Helen, too, is adjusting to the recent loss of her father – a man, moreover, whose medical expertise is now sorely missed at court. The Countess reflects that if only he were here, the King's prognosis would be incalculably improved. Noting that Helen's father's "skill … would have made nature immortal", she plays wistfully with the reality of his loss:

> Would for the King's sake he were living. I think it would be the death of the King's disease.
> **[1.1.20–22]**

## Major Characters & Synopsis

**Countess of Roussillon**, a widow
**Bertram**, Count of Roussillon, the Countess's son
**Helen**, a doctor's daughter and the Countess's servant
**Lavatch**, a clown in the Countess's service
**Reynaldo**, the Countess's steward
**Paroles**, a companion of Bertram
**King of France**
**Lafeu**, an old lord and friend of the Countess
**First** and **Second Lords Dumaine**, brothers
An **Interpreter**
**Duke of Florence**
**Widow Capilet** and **Diana**, her daughter
**Mariana**, a friend of the Widow

**ACT 1** The King of France is dangerously ill and has summoned his ward Bertram (the son and heir of the late Count of Roussillon) to be with him during his last hours. As Bertram leaves his home in Roussillon, the Countess his mother notices that her gentlewoman Helen is upset, and realizes why – Helen secretly loves him. Giving Helen her blessing, the Countess encourages her to follow Bertram on the pretext of offering the medical skills that she has inherited from her father to the King.

**ACT 2** The King agrees to Helen's treatment, promising that if she succeeds he will guarantee her any husband she wants. He rapidly improves under her care and summons all his lords so that she can make her choice. When she picks Bertram, however, he scornfully turns her down, refusing to touch a low-born doctor's daughter. Even though the King forces them to wed, Bertram decides to leave the marriage unconsummated and escape to the Italian wars with his disreputable companion Paroles.

**ACT 3** The Countess's delight at news of the marriage sours when she receives a letter from Bertram declaring that he has fled. Helen announces that she has also received a letter in which Bertram states that he will agree to be her husband only if she removes the ancestral ring from his finger and bears his child – both, he boasts, impossible. Helen reflects that her only option is to disappear, and heads to Italy disguised as a pilgrim. She arrives to mixed news: Bertram has proved himself a brilliant soldier, but has been trying to seduce Diana, daughter of the Widow Capilet. Revealing her identity to Diana's mother, Helen suggests a bed-trick: Diana will agree to sleep with Bertram but be replaced at the last minute by Helen. Meanwhile, Paroles's boastfulness has irritated the other soldiers so much that the Dumaine brothers decide to humiliate him in public.

**ACT 4** The two plots swing into action. Disguised as enemy soldiers, the Dumaines ambush Paroles and interrogate him. When he blithely slanders his comrades, they remove his blindfold and unmask themselves. In the meantime Diana has persuaded Bertram to swap his ring for one of her own (actually Helen's), on the agreement that he will visit her chamber at midnight. All goes to plan, and Helen – who has by now spread rumours of her own death – leaves for France with Widow Capilet and Diana, intending to tell the King everything. Believing Helen to be dead, however, Lafeu has negotiated with the Countess for Bertram to marry his own daughter.

**ACT 5** Bertram returns to France and is pardoned by the King. When he offers an engagement ring for Lafeu's daughter, however, the King recognizes it as one he has given Helen and arrests Bertram on suspicion of having killed her. At that moment a letter arrives from Diana, revealing Bertram's promise to marry her on Helen's death; Diana and her mother appear, and produce his ring. Bertram admits to knowing them but denies offering to marry Diana, who he claims is a whore. Paroles does his best to confuse matters, but everything is resolved when the pregnant Helen makes her appearance. In a neat irony, Bertram has managed to fulfil his own contract without even knowing it. He has no choice but to accept Helen.

But once Bertram is gone, the subject of Helen's own "sorrows" proves more complicated than her companions think. "I think not on my father," she weeps. "My imagination / Carries no favour in't but Bertram's." Her description of him sounds strikingly like a remembrance:

> 'Twas pretty, though a plague,
> To see him every hour, to sit and draw
> His archèd brows, his hawking eye, his curls,
> In our heart's table – heart too capable
> Of every line and trick of his sweet favour.
> But now he's gone, and my idolatrous fancy
> Must sanctify his relics.

**[1.1.91–7]**

Sounding somewhere between Hamlet and the anonymous maid in *A Lover's Complaint* (see p.413), Helen sighs that her heart is only too "capable of" (able to suck in) Bertram's beauty. His departure for the social whirl of the French court might as well be from life itself; she is left behind, an "idolatrous" disciple, to "sanctify his relics".

## Doctor She

Pregnant with religiosity as Helen's words are, what happens next sounds as if it comes out of a fairy story. Under pressure, she "confesses" her love to Bertram's mother, but instead of being appalled that her gentlewoman wants to marry her son, the Countess gives Helen her blessing and advises her to make a dash for Paris. Arriving at court, Helen gains access to the King and promises to use her father's wisdom on him. Though at first he is suspicious, not "credulous of cure", when she offers to submit herself to death if her powers fail, he becomes convinced.

While his medical advisers have informed him that "labouring art" has little chance against the course of nature, Helen seems to promise something different, the kind of "immortal" power that the Countess claims was invested in her father. There is something undeniably magical about this "Doctor She", as Lafeu wonderingly remarks to the King:

---

**KEY SOURCE** Boccaccio's *Decameron*

For both *All's Well That Ends Well* and *Cymbeline* Shakespeare drew upon a renowned collection of stories by the Italian humanist **Giovanni Boccaccio** (1313–75). Boccaccio's *Decameron* (1353) brings together a hundred popular tales, told over a period of ten days by ten people (hence the title, which means "ten days"). The occasion for their telling is the plague that ravaged Florence during 1348, which killed up to half the city's population. Boccaccio's aristocratic cast is safe, but only just: quarantined in a country retreat while the disease rages in the city, they are forced to recount stories to each other in order to pass the time and distract from the gruesome events outside. (Chaucer would borrow the tale-telling framework for his *Canterbury Tales*, begun a few decades later.)

Despite its grim setting, the *Decameron* is largely a collection of love stories, told in an atmosphere of insouciant flirtation between the female and male guests, and many of them stray into bawdy territory – Boccaccio's relaxed and enthusiastic view of sex often embarrassed later commentators. Indeed, the first English translation of the tales, William Painter's *Palace of Pleasure* (1566) was, despite its juicy title, a heavily expurgated version containing just sixteen of Boccaccio's politer stories (John Florio's complete English translation did not appear until 1620). It was from Painter, not the original, that Shakespeare borrowed the stories of Gilette of Narbonne (who cures the King of France and marries Bertrand of Roussillon) and Bernabò of Genoa (tricked into believing that his wife has been unfaithful). Painter's version – which was among Shakespeare's favourite reading – also supplied source material for *Romeo and Juliet*, *The Merry Wives*, *Timon* and *Lucrece*.

> I have seen a medicine
> That's able to breathe life into a stone,
> Quicken a rock, and make you dance canary
> With sprightly fire and motion …

[2.2.71–4]

But one man refuses to succumb to her powers. When the King grants her "power to choose" a husband from among his lords as reward for her magic, Bertram obstinately refuses to take part:

BERTRAM
> My wife, my liege? I shall beseech your highness,
> In such a business give me leave to use
> The help of mine own eyes.

KING                           Know'st thou not, Bertram,
> What she has done for me?

BERTRAM                        Yes, my good lord,
> But never hope to know why I should marry her.

[2.3.107–11]

Bertram's disgusted explanation, that he will not debase his nobility by being forced to marry a "poor physician's daughter", is unappealing, and has earned him a consistently bad press; but, as ever, Shakespeare muddies the moral waters. His is also the honest response of a man being forced to play along with someone else's bizarre fairy tale. Though Helen has brought life to the King, in Bertram's eyes what faces him is a life sentence: marriage to a woman he does not love.

Bertram has little choice but to consent, though no sooner is the ceremony over than he announces his intention to escape France and head to the Tuscan wars. He leaves the marriage unconsummated, a state of affairs that he intends to preserve, vowing in a letter to the Countess that "I have wedded her, not bedded her, and sworn to make the 'not' eternal" (3.2.21–2). His callous pun ("not eternal" for "knot eternal") does not impress his mother, but his crowing message to his wife proves altogether more fateful. "When thou canst get the ring upon my finger, which shall never come off," he writes, "and show me a child begotten of thy body that I am father to, then call me husband" (3.2.57–9). Helen's quest to make those words come true will exercise all her intelligence and ingenuity, but she never swerves from her goal.

## Wicked meaning

Wittily diverting Paroles's obscene attack on the idea of virginity back in Act One, Helen had asked him, coyly, "How might one do, sir, to lose it to her own liking?" (1.1.149). Her determination to do just that, to take responsibility for losing her own virginity and that of Bertram too (as seems likely, he is a virgin too) drives the second phase of the plot. Like Rosalind in *As You Like It*, she dons disguise in order to get what she wants, but unlike Rosalind remains a woman throughout – her cover, in a rather poignant gesture to her "sanctifying" of Bertram at the play's outset, being the cloak of a pilgrim.

> *I cannot reconcile my heart to Bertram; a man noble without generosity, and young without truth; who marries Helen as a coward and leaves her as a profligate; when she is dead by his unkindness, sneaks home to a second marriage, is accused by a woman whom he has wronged, defends himself by falsehood, and is dismissed to happiness.*
>
> Samuel Johnson, commentary to *The Plays of William Shakespeare* (1765)

But her stratagem requires that she wear that devout costume rather ironically. Once arrived in Italy, she rapidly finds that Bertram has been attempting to seduce the beautiful Diana – and though Diana has so far resisted his advances, she is clearly tempted to give in. Pointing out Bertram in the passing parade of soldiers, she sighs, "'Tis a most gallant fellow,"

> I would he loved his wife. If he were honester
> He were much goodlier.
>
> [3.5.79–81]

To which it might be replied that Bertram's problem is too much honesty, not too little – far from pretending to be in love with a wife forced upon him, he takes the first opportunity to flee the country and look elsewhere.

"Honest", a destructive and dangerous word in *Othello*, resonates loudly at this point in Shakespeare's career, and in *All's Well* it is put under unusual pressure. Helen, still in disguise, describes how Bertram's "poor lady" has a "reservèd honesty" (guarded chastity); the Widow speaks of Diana's "honestest defence" against Bertram's advances. But Helen's solution to the problem that afflicts them both will involve not honesty but calculated betrayal. Suggesting that Diana agree to sleep with Bertram (after demanding that he gives her his precious ring), Helen advises a covert assignation with him – for which she, not Diana, will turn up. In the dark Bertram will be none the wiser, and before he knows it he will have consummated his marriage, given his wife a child and surrendered the ring. His scoffing challenge to Helen will have been met, point by point. "Let us essay our plot," Helen urges the Widow after paying her off,

> which if it speed
> Is wicked meaning in a lawful deed
> And lawful meaning in a wicked act,
> Where both not sin, and yet a sinful fact.
>
> [3.7.44–7]

As the Duke pronounces in *Measure for Measure*, "the doubleness of the benefit defends the deceit from reproof" (3.1.59–60); or as Helen (and the play's title) repeatedly expresses it, "All's well that ends well; still the fine's the crown. / Whate'er the course, the end is the renown" (4.4.35–6).

The paradoxes Helen describes – that a deed can be both "lawful" and "wicked", both "sinful" and virtuous, that something so morally questionable can yet "end well" – are brought into unpleasant proximity in the bed-trick. *All's Well* is the second and only other comedy in which Shakespeare uses the device, though numerous other plays, among them *Much Ado*, *Othello*, *The Winter's Tale* and *Cymbeline*, dwell on apparent sexual deceit by women. The difference here, of course, is that the deceit – though accomplished with what are for Helen the best of intentions – is fully real. Commonplace in the tales that were Shakespeare's sources for *Measure for Measure* and *All's Well*, on stage the bed-trick is an unrealistic and uneasy technique, an unsettling combination of intimacy and distance. It implies that sex – even love – is dizzyingly unspecific, so much so that Bertram will fail even to realize that he has slept with the wrong woman. Some critics have defended it along the line that (roughly speaking) Helen takes: that it aligns her "liking" with his, encourages Bertram back to the marital straight-and-narrow despite himself. But for most audiences it remains an immense stumbling-block, the crowning problem in a play replete with them. It is so not least because Helen's own love for Bertram raises more questions than it answers. Is her contentedness to let her husband sleep with (what he thinks is) someone else a good thing or not? Is her unwavering devotion a sign of strength or weakness? Is she open-eyed to her husband's many flaws or wilfully blind to them? Will her hoped-for triumph over Bertram alter Diana's recognition that "'Tis a hard bondage to become the wife / Of a detesting lord" (3.5.64–5)?

## The name and not the thing

Before any of these questions can be answered, though, *All's Well* swerves away from its main subject. It has a minor subplot, invented by Shakespeare, in which the "gallant militarist" Paroles (a bragging soldier straight out of Greek comedy) is shown to be as untrustworthy towards his apparent friends as we, the audience, have realized he is towards everyone else. His fellow soldiers conceive a ruse whereby, disguised as Russian troops, they will capture Paroles, blindfold him and, threatening execution, expose him as a lying coward. All goes to plan: Paroles gives up all the military secrets he has sworn to keep without pausing for breath, and is equally forthright with his opinions on his fellow officers – much to their private displeasure. They then discover that he is carrying a letter addressed to Diana, warning her of Bertram's intentions. Still fooled, Paroles freely explains all:

> My meaning in't, I protest, was very honest in the behalf of the maid, for I knew the young Count to be a dangerous and lascivious boy, who is a whale to virginity, and devours up all the fry it finds.
>
> **[4.3.223–6]**

The irony is, naturally, that the inveterate liar Paroles is nothing other than "honest" here, as Bertram well – and furiously – knows. Though at first sight this scene seems to sit outside the main curve of the play, as the action develops it becomes apparent how closely it informs on the central plot: in this topsy-turvy world a professional con-artist can as easily tell the truth as a woman can guarantee her husband's virtue by arranging him an affair.

By this time, moreover, Bertram has proved himself false to his word, and abandoned Diana to return home – to which Helen compounds her own dishonesty by arranging for a priest to put out word in France that she has died. As Bertram returns to the French court, all seems resolved: his wife is apparently dead, he is forgiven by the King and he is on the point of marrying Lafeu's daughter. But then the King spots that the ring he is about to give his new bride is the same one that he gave Helen. The plot accelerates. Suspecting foul play, the King is about to accuse Bertram of her murder when a note arrives from Diana, swiftly followed by Diana herself. The court becomes a kind of courtroom as the King tries to ascertain precisely what is going on. Rejecting Diana's paradoxical evidence, he roars, "To prison with her." But then her "bail" appears:

> KING                  Is there no exorcist
> Beguiles the truer office of mine eyes?
> Is't real that I see?
> HELEN            No, my good lord,
> 'Tis but the shadow of a wife you see,
> The name and not the thing.
>
> **[5.3.307–10]**

Helen's final miracle is to raise herself, as she raised the King, from the dead, but to do so she has had to divorce her "name" as wife from her real identity.

Her next question, to Bertram, reunites them: "Will you be mine," she asks, "now that you are doubly won?" He has little choice but to acquiesce, but it is striking – and somehow strikingly sad – that he does not even reply directly. "If she, my liege, can make me know this clearly," he addresses the King, "I'll love her dearly, ever ever dearly" (5.3.316–8). The audience is left to work out the consequences of that "if"; the play refuses to resolve it for us.

# Stage history and adaptations

Beyond its likely date of 1604–05 – placing it as one of Shakespeare's first Jacobean plays – there is no evidence of *All's Well*'s initial life on stage. Though there is nothing unusual about that, some have conjectured that it was as unpopular then as it has been until recently. The first performance on record took place in 1741, put on by **Henry Giffard**, who advertised the play as "written by Shakespeare and not acted since his time". Giffard himself acted Bertram and his wife Helen, but a few weeks into the run the young David Garrick joined the company and the comedy was axed so that Garrick could concentrate on more "serious" Shakespeare.

This faltering start cast a pall over many subsequent productions. The Drury Lane version of 1742 was cut short when **Peg Woffington**'s Helen fell ill and her King, **William Milward**, died (despite jokingly professing faith in Woffington's "Doctor She"). Even **Theophilus Cibber**'s Paroles – audiences were reputedly moved to laughter just by the sight of his face – failed to save it, the company rapidly nicknamed *All's Well* "the unfortunate comedy" and it soon closed. A Covent Garden attempt in 1746, with **Henry Woodward** as Paroles to **Hannah Pritchard**'s Helen, fared no better, achieving just one performance before Woodward jumped ship. **David Garrick** decided that *All's Well*'s only redeeming feature was Paroles (described by the actor and writer Thomas Davies as "inferior only to the great master of stage gaiety and mirth, Sir John Falstaff") and penned an adaptation, premiered in 1756, which focused almost exclusively on him. Though Woodward took the role and would continue doing so for the next twenty years, the prompter recorded that "the play went off dull". Garrick doggedly mounted a revival in 1762 and Covent Garden replied the same year with a more popular version starring Woodward and **Maria Macklin**.

Another adaptation, this time by **Frederick Pilon**, was mounted at the Haymarket in 1785 to a warm reception – perhaps because it cut the first three acts. Yet another was staged at Drury Lane in 1794 at the behest of **John Philip Kemble**. Instead of concentrating on Paroles, however, Kemble saw potential in sentimentalizing *All's Well*, with himself as Bertram to **Dorothy Jordan**'s hoydenish Helen. John Philip's brother **Charles** mounted another production in 1811, again with himself as Bertram and **Nanette Johnston** as Helen, and although some reviewers made positive noises about the play itself, by general consensus it disgraced Kemble's Covent Garden. An operatic version by the industrious **Frederick Reynolds** appeared in 1832 – enlivened with lyrics nabbed from other Shakespeare plays – but had a mixed reception, as did **Samuel Phelps**'s version at Sadler's Wells two decades later. Despite Phelps's attempts to refine the behaviour of **Fanny Cooper**'s heroine, played alongside Phelps's own Paroles and **Frederic Robinson**'s Bertram, *All's Well* was savaged by the critics. *The Athenaeum* derided the "rude nature of the plot" and its "exceedingly gross" manners.

This was to be a familiar refrain during the Victorian era, Helen's behaviour frequently being condemned as brazen and indecent, and *All's Well* received precious few stagings. George Bernard Shaw's was a lone voice of support, but as late as 1928 he wrote that the public was unprepared for its unsettling, Ibsenesque qualities. By the time **Frank Benson** came to the play in 1916, only it and *Titus* had failed to be produced at the Stratford Memorial Theatre. But once again fate intervened – Benson had just been knighted, and applause whenever he appeared onstage all but swamped the play. The iconoclastic **William Poel** put on an "Elizabethan" production at Bayswater in 1920, but audiences were puzzled by his decision to cross-cast many of the parts and some were incensed by his overtly political reading, which cast Helen as a Suffragette figure, demanding love as others did the vote.

Helen (Irene Worth) works her magic on the King (Alec Guinness). A scene from the 1953 Stratford Festival of Canada production of *All's Well That Ends Well*

**Robert Atkins** emphasized the play's comedy rather than its problems in the first of his three productions in 1921, but his efforts were panned for lacking depth and the *Observer* concluded that *All's Well* was "very nearly the worst play its distinguished author ever wrote". The Poel disciple **William Bridges-Adams** experienced more success in his Stratford version the following year, but though critics praised **Baliol Holloway**'s Paroles, **Maureen Shaw**'s Helen was considered "too beautiful to be taken seriously" (as the *Birmingham Post* puzzlingly put it). The decade's final performance in 1927 was more innovative, set in modern-day France by **Barry Jackson**'s Birmingham Rep and with a teenage **Laurence Olivier** as Paroles.

In 1953 **Tyrone Guthrie** launched at Stratford, Ontario what was probably the first production of *All's Well* on the North American continent since a fleeting Bostonian appearance in 1799. Edwardian in setting, it starred **Irene Worth** as Helen and **Alec Guinness** as the King, and became a watershed production, adeptly balanced between tragedy and comedy. Guthrie repeated his success at the English Stratford six years later, this time with **Zoe Caldwell** as Helen, **Edward de Souza** as Bertram and **Cyril Luckham** as Paroles. **Edith Evans** played the Countess, the first *grande dame* to take what Shaw called "the most beautiful old woman's part ever written". **Michael Benthall**'s Old Vic production of 1953 was attacked for whimsy (**Claire Bloom**'s Helen merely ornamental and Benthall's Paroles stealing the show); and **Noël Willman**'s Stratford staging, with **Joyce Redman**'s Helen and **Keith Michell**'s Paroles also received criticism for prettifying the play's difficulties with Louis XIV picturesque.

**John Barton** took the play's contrast between youth and age as the keynote of his 1967 RSC production, with **Estelle Kohler**'s schoolgirlish Helen and **Ian Richardson**'s sympathetic Bertram, and opted for a Caroline setting. Also historically conservative was **Jonathan Miller**'s version at the Greenwich Theatre in 1975 which presented a stripped-down Elizabethan *All's Well*. Following **David Jones**'s Stratford, Ontario version in 1977 – once more Louis XIV in design – the play's most sympathetic 1980s production was directed at the RSC by **Trevor Nunn**

in 1982. As with Guthrie, Nunn's Edwardian setting and Chekhovian inflections made sense of the play for reviewers, not least because it was clouded by premonitions of World War I. **Harriet Walter** appeared as Helen to the Bertrams of **Mike Gwilym** and **Philip Franks,** but most audiences were entranced by **Peggy Ashcroft**'s Countess, full of worldly-wisdom and compassion. A recent reawakening of interest in the play is evidenced by its appearance at Stratfords both Canadian and English in 2003: the Ontario version was directed by **Richard Monette,** with **Lucy Peacock** as Helen and **David Snelgrove**'s Bertram; while in **Gregory Doran**'s RSC production (firmly set in the seventeenth century) **Judi Dench** brilliantly conveyed the Countess's split emotions, torn between her affection for **Claudie Blakley**'s sympathetic Helen and her gradual realization that **Jamie Glover**'s narcissistic Bertram has feet of clay.

*All's Well* does not feature largely in Shakespearian filmographies: only the Miller-produced BBC/Time-Life version of 1980, directed by **Elijah Moshinsky,** was purpose-built for TV.

## Screen

### All's Well That Ends Well
**A. Down, C. Johnson, I. Charleson, P. Jeffery; Elijah Moshinsky (dir.)**
UK, 1980 ▷ Ambrose Video (BBC) `DVD`

Does it say something about the BBC/Time-Life Shakespeare project that the plays it excels at are the problem comedies? As with Desmond Davis's 1979 *Measure*, this *All's Well* from the following year receives a gloomy, slightly stifling treatment that captures the play's essence well. David Myerscough-Jones's designs resemble the interiors of seventeenth-century Dutch painting (transforming studio-bound necessity into a kind of virtue), though there is little Vermeerian tranquillity here as Angela Down's steely and solid Helen attempts to ensnare Ian Charleson's peevish Bertram. Donald Sinden is hammy as the King, but on the whole this production is one of the most satisfactory in a famously uneven series. Recently rereleased in the US by Ambrose Video Publishing.

## Audio

### All's Well That Ends Well
**C. Bloom, J. Stride, E. Portman**
UK, 1963 ▷ HarperCollins (Caedmon) 🔊

Like others in the Caedmon series, this 1965 *All's Well* casts a nostalgic glow – a refugee from another Shakespearian era – but, doing so, somehow gets to the heart of the play's poignant ambiguity. It is dominated by Claire Bloom's measured but wonderfully rich Helen and John Stride's callow but not entirely unsympathetic Bertram. Flora Robson (herself a Dame) is a suitably stately and august presence as the Countess, but Robert Stephens's somewhat over-saturated Paroles might try the patience of some.

## Editions

### Oxford Shakespeare
**Susan Snyder (ed.); 1993** ▷ Oxford UP

In the preface to her edition, Snyder relates how she was fortunate to have first come across *All's Well* not as a dry text in a dusty classroom, but via Noël Willman's 1955 version at the RSC, and her book is illustrated with production shots that take up interpretative points she raises. All the more bizarre, then, that she includes a mere paragraph of performance history – a frustrating omission in what would otherwise be a near-flawless edition. That said, Snyder's intellectual savvy is considerable and the attention she pays to the uncomfortable roles played by Helen is adroit. The introduction concludes, neatly, with an in-depth examination of every single element in the play's problematic title.

## Some criticism

### The Unfortunate Comedy
**J.G. Price; 1968** ▷ Liverpool UP / Toronto UP [o/p]

Price's work has the distinction of being the first book devoted to *All's Well*, a comedy that has often struggled to make its voice heard (the title refers to the nickname attached to the play after an ill-fated 1742 production). Price's study breaks down into two main parts, looking at the play's often troubled stage history and contrasting that with its critical reception. He concludes with an impassioned "Defence" of the play, one of the most sympathetic pieces of criticism around.

### Reading Shakespeare Historically
**Lisa Jardine; 1996** ▷ Routledge

Lisa Jardine first sprang onto the academic scene with her 1983 *Still Harping On Daughters: Women and drama in the age of Shakespeare* and has been a highly visible part of it ever since. *Reading Shakespeare Historically* adopts some of the feminist concerns of her earlier Shakespeare book but groups together eight separate essays that form an engaging commentary on the "new historicist" practice of reading literature through its engagement with social and cultural history. The piece that covers *All's Well*, "Cultural Confusion and Shakespeare's Learned Heroines", is Jardine at her best – insightful, sympathetic and astute.

# Antony and Cleopatra

D ramatically adventurous, richly characterized, linguistically gorgeous, *Antony and Cleopatra* is one of the surging triumphs of Shakespeare's late career. It sits closer than anything else he wrote to the Romantic ideal of sublimity – something so magnificent it inspires reverence and awe – and received corresponding praise from Samuel Taylor Coleridge, who extolled its "fiery force" and "giant power", and commented that there are probably no other works by the playwright in which "he impresses the notion of angelic strength so much". In its depiction of the titanic conflict between Rome and Egypt, the play is one of Shakespeare's most ambitious political dramas, but in every way the grand passion of the two lovers lies at the heart of its action, and is ultimately the impetus behind its tragedy. For all its vastnesses the play is also disarmingly domestic in scale, and with their middle-aged squabbles and tantrums Antony and his Egyptian Queen embody something touchingly and fragilely human at the centre of global politics.

[DATE]  First recorded in May 1608, the play is likely to have been composed a few years before: Christmas 1606–07 is possible.

[SOURCES]  Sir Thomas North's translation of Plutarch, *Lives of the Noble Grecians and Romans* (1579), is the main source – Shakespeare lifts some passages from it verbatim. Samuel Daniel's *Cleopatra* (1594) and Barnabe Barnes's *The Devil's Charter* (1607) were also influences as was, to a lesser extent, the Countess of Pembroke's tragic *Antonius* (1592).

[TEXTS]  Although the publisher Edward Blount registered the right to print *Antony and Cleopatra*, it seems he never actually did. The only surviving text is that in the 1623 First Folio; numerous quirks suggest that it was probably copied from Shakespeare's manuscript.

## Interpreting the play

Sublime though it may be, *Antony and Cleopatra* is well-nigh unstageable – and seems frequently at risk of falling apart. Despite a mere handful of main roles (and no crowd scenes) there are around forty characters in the play, with some 220 entrances and exits, many involving significant groups of people. The stage empties over forty times (scenes are not marked in the only surviving text) and as the action builds, everything gets progressively faster. Even in the fluid, rapid-fire theatre of Shakespeare's time the effect must have been dazzling, even disconcerting – a constant procession of people across the stage; cross-cutting, filmic scenes that finish practically as they've begun.

In contrast to Shakespeare's earlier historical Roman play, *Julius Caesar*, *Antony and Cleopatra* wilfully refuses to be Roman in tone – even though it has good grounds to be considered a sequel, picking up political events as the post-Caesar triumvirate of Antony, Octavius and Lepidus explodes under the pressure of clashing personalities. Whereas the action of *Julius Caesar* moves most often through reasoned debate, via persuasion and counter-persuasion, *Antony and Cleopatra* delights in ornament, fancy, excess. Shakespeare

## Major Characters & Synopsis

**Mark Antony**, a triumvir (one of three co-rulers) of Rome

**Octavius Caesar**, triumvir

**Lepidus**, triumvir

**Cleopatra**, Queen of Egypt and Antony's lover

**Domitius Enobarbus**, companion to Antony

**Octavia**, Caesar's sister (later Antony's wife)

**Sextus Pompey (Pompeius)**, rebel against the triumvirs

Antony's followers: **Demetrius**, **Philo**, **Ventidius**, **Silius**, **Eros**, **Camidius**, **Scarus** and **Decretas**

Caesar's followers: **Maecenas**, **Agrippa**, **Taurus**, **Dolabella**, **Thidias**, **Gallus** and **Proculeius**

Pompey's followers: **Menecrates**, **Menas** and **Varrius**

Cleopatra's followers: **Charmian**, **Iras**, **Alexas**, the eunuch **Mardian**, **Diomed** and **Seleucus**

A **Soothsayer**

A **Clown**

**ACT 1** Antony, Rome's finest general, idles away his days far from home. Seduced by the good life in Egypt – the feasting, the parties, and above all by Cleopatra, his lover and Egypt's queen – he is a shadow of the man he was. Such at least is the view of Caesar and his councillors, who are eager to have Antony back in Rome to deal with the threat of rebellion from Pompey, all to no avail. But when Antony hears of his wife Fulvia's death, he realizes that he can delay no longer. Cleopatra is dismayed that he is returning to Rome, and although she eventually agrees, cannot get him out of her mind. In the meantime, though, a soothsayer has predicted that the fortunes of the world's most glamorous couple are on the wane.

**ACT 2** At Pompey's camp, the news that Caesar has assembled an army is not well-received; worse, Antony has returned. Meanwhile, Rome's three rulers are locked in argument: Antony is criticized for Fulvia's erstwhile rebellion but denies undermining Caesar. Agrippa suggests that in order to strengthen their alliance and be reconciled, Antony should marry Caesar's sister Octavia. Both agree, but it isn't long before Antony longs to return to Egypt. News of Antony's conduct has already reached Cleopatra, however, and she is devastated. And although the threat of civil war is averted when Pompey agrees to cease his campaign, it becomes clear at the peace dinner that his intentions are far darker than anyone realizes.

**ACT 3** Rome's campaign against the Parthians has been successful, but old wounds rapidly re-open as Antony, on the way to Athens with his new wife, criticizes Caesar's renewal of hostilities against Pompey. Octavia is sent to Rome to mediate, but it is soon reported that Antony has made his way back to Egypt without Octavia's knowledge, and that he has promised the eastern empire to Cleopatra. Caesar, fresh from his trouncing of Pompey, intends to fight. And Antony, accompanied by his lover, is showing dangerous lapses of judgement: spurning the advice of their military advisers, they prepare for an ill-fated sea assault. As predicted, they lose. Caesar rejects their peace terms, in which Antony is permitted to retire into private life with Cleopatra, and attempts to turn them against each other.

**ACT 4** Having had his challenge of single combat derisively rejected by Caesar, Antony prepares for a decisive second battle. Though the omens are not good – his soldiers are convinced that Hercules has deserted them and Enobarbus has defected – the first day's fighting goes well for Antony and he returns to Cleopatra in triumph. But catastrophe strikes the next day when the Egyptian ships suddenly surrender. Antony, watching from land, blames Cleopatra and threatens to murder them both. When Cleopatra responds by sending news of her own feigned suicide to Antony, he takes it seriously and attempts to kill himself. Fatally wounded, he is carried off to see her one last time.

**ACT 5** When Antony dies Cleopatra sees death as the only option, but she is prevented from stabbing herself by Caesar's soldiers. When Dolabella reveals that Caesar intends her to be paraded through Rome, Cleopatra is appalled and resolves to die at once. Placing asps to her breast and arm, she predicts reunion with Antony in the afterlife. Caesar, discovering her body, arranges for the lovers to share a tomb.

has sometimes been accused of indulging his love of language in this late play: there may be some truth in the charge, but then this tragedy is all about showing off. Its most famous speech, Enobarbus's rapt description of Cleopatra's arrival in her barge – the entrance that puts Antony fatefully under her spell – appeals to the heart, not the head. "The barge she sat in," he declares, "like a burnished throne / Burned on the water."

> The poop was beaten gold;
> Purple the sails, and so perfumèd that
> The winds were love-sick with them. The oars were silver,
> Which to the tune of flutes kept stroke, and made
> The water which they beat to follow faster,
> As amorous of their strokes. For her own person,
> It beggared all description. She did lie
> In her pavilion—cloth of gold, of tissue—
> O'er-picturing that Venus where we see
> The fancy outwork nature. On each side her
> Stood pretty dimpled boys, like smiling Cupids,
> With divers-coloured fans whose wind did seem
> To glow the delicate cheeks which they did cool,
> And what they undid did.

**[2.2.198–212]**

In this almost impossibly sensual scene, life comes to a halt: the oars and the waves beat time, but to little impression of movement, just as the "dimpled boys" fan the Queen's cheeks and yet make them glow, doing "what they undid". Nothing happens – beautifully.

For all *Antony and Cleopatra*'s bustle, it is often observed that in the wider play, too, little happens. Shakespeare streamlines the material in Plutarch's *Life* of Antony, compressing or deleting many of its events and dwelling instead on their personal and emotional implications. When the play begins, Antony has already fallen under Cleopatra's spell, and whatever happens we sense that he will be unable to stay away from "his Egyptian dish" (2.6.126), as Enobarbus harshly describes her, for long. The on-off affair between the protagonists persists in its maddeningly unsettled state for nearly all the play. Much the same happens with the global events that *Antony and Cleopatra* ostensibly spans: the political match with Octavia, designed to hold Antony and her brother Octavius "in perpetual amity", breaks down almost as soon as it is agreed, while it is only too characteristic that the play's defining political turn-point, the sea battle between the Egyptian forces and the Roman army of Octavius at Actium, ends in chaos.

## Pleasure now

The Romans themselves are only too sure that Antony, formerly their greatest captain, the towering example of Roman values, is now an ageing joke. Plutarch, Shakespeare's source, often comments on the morality (or otherwise) of his subjects, and in *Antony and Cleopatra* those juicy comments often find their way into the mouths of Antony's former colleagues. "He fishes, drinks, and wastes / The lamps of night in revel," Octavius acidly observes (1.4.4–5), and even earlier in the play Philo and Demetrius, supposedly Antony's followers, join him in condemnation. "Nay, but this dotage of our General's / O'erflows the measure," Philo insists:

> Those his goodly eyes,
> That o'er the files and musters of the war
> Have glowed like plated Mars, now bend, now turn

The office and devotion of their view
Upon a tawny front. His captain's heart
Which in the scuffles of great fights hath burst
The buckles on his breast, reneges all temper,
And is become the bellows and the fan
To cool a gipsy's lust.

[1.1.1–10]

Sexually enslaved to Cleopatra, the titanic Antony is a mere automaton: a killing machine now on the scrapheap. While on campaign with his Roman men, Octavius laments, Antony would "deign [accept] the roughest berry on the rudest hedge ..." (1.4.64); now he wastes his time in "lascivious wassails", the endless round of banquets that constitute life at the Egyptian court.

Egypt is, of course, the key to Antony's decline and the storehouse for his "pleasure". For Jacobeans no less than Greek historians Egypt held a seductive, exotic appeal – a land of desert yet dominated by the mysterious, all-delivering Nile; the repository of wise yet alien ancient civilizations. In Shakespeare's play, Egypt most often appears in melting, fluid language, a direct challenge to the chiselled certainties of Rome. Attempting to rid himself of his Roman responsibilities near the opening of the play, Antony snarls, "Let Rome in Tiber melt, and the wide arch / Of the ranged empire fall" (1.1.35–6). These words receive a resonant echo in Cleopatra's curse a few scenes later, confronted with a recalcitrant messenger:

Melt Egypt into Nile, and kindly creatures
Turn all to serpents!

[2.5.78–9]

Decadent, death-risking excess characterizes life in Egypt – the twelve wild boars slaughtered for a single breakfast, the "Alexandrian feast" and "Egyptian bacchanals" with which Antony and his followers entertain the shocked Romans after his fateful marriage to Octavia.

Egypt, sensual and sexual, also poses a subversive threat to the uncomplicated world of Roman masculinity. The only Roman woman in the play is Octavia herself, whose "holy, cold, and still conversation" (2.6.122–3) will, Enobarbus predicts, soon tire Antony. In rich contrast, Cleopatra is surrounded by swarms of handmaidens and attendants, who when Antony departs for Rome amuse themselves by gossiping about sex. Even the eunuch Mardian, though "unseminared" (emasculated), indulges in the occasional risqué fantasy. "I can do nothing / But what indeed is honest to be done," he informs his mistress, his words thick with puns,

Yet I have fierce affections, and think
What Venus did with Mars.

[1.5.15–18]

Little wonder that the militant Octavius, serving the Roman god of war in a more straight-forward sense, insists coldly at Antony's Egyptian feast that, given the choice, he would "rather fast from all" for four days than become dangerously drunk in one. He has no desire to suffer Antony's – or indeed Mardian's – fate and become "not more manlike / Than Cleopatra" (1.4.5–6).

> *Antony and Cleopatra can be read as the fall of a great general, betrayed in his dotage by a treacherous strumpet, or else it can be viewed as a celebration of transcendental love.*
>
> A.P. Riemer, *A Reading of Shakespeare's "Antony and Cleopatra"* (1968)

# No more

In the hyperbolic world of Egypt it is not surprising, either, that for Antony there is no world outside his love. It is boundless, illimitable:

CLEOPATRA
  If it be love indeed, tell me how much.
ANTONY
  There's beggary in the love that can be reckoned.
CLEOPATRA
  I'll set a bourn how far to be beloved.
ANTONY
  Then must thou needs find out new heaven, new earth.

**[1.1.14–17]**

The lovers can conceive of no "bourn" (limit) to their love other than of what they themselves are capable. Cleopatra later accuses Antony of forgetting that "eternity was in our lips and eyes, / Bliss in our brow's bent; none our parts so poor / But was a race of heaven" (1.3.33–7).

Cleopatra herself, perhaps Shakespeare's greatest female role, seems eminently capable of constructing new worlds should she so desire. She is attended in the ceremony she jointly holds with Antony to celebrate her hold on power by the pick of the world's kings. She makes a habit of dressing in "th'habiliments of the goddess Isis" (3.6.17), and in Enobarbus's rapt description appears almost immortal: "Age cannot wither her," he cries, "nor custom stale / Her infinite variety" (2.2.241–2). To many characters in the play she is also infinitely unknowable: on the one hand "great Egypt", "most sovereign creature", a "triumphant lady"; on the other, a "foul Egyptian", a "witch", a "cow in June". That shimmering variety is the key to her appeal – for audiences as well as Antony – but is also frequently a source of frustration. She fishes for his commitment even as she makes herself impossible to love. "See where he is, who's with him, what he does," she orders her servants as soon as her lover disappears from the room:

        If you find him sad,
  Say I am dancing; if in mirth, report
  That I am sudden sick.

**[1.3.2–5]**

The moment is comic, but also comically human. Cleopatra is capable of astounding changes of temper, and like the great actress she is ranges from comedy to tragedy in an instant. Struck by Shakespeare's portrayal, the seventeenth-century poet Margaret Cavendish exclaimed, "One would think that he had been Metamorphosed from a Man to a Woman," in order to create a character herself so consistently changeful.

The scene in which she discovers that Antony has betrayed her by marrying Octavia is a glorious set piece for Cleopatra and the actor who plays her: after receiving one of the play's many messengers ("twenty several" of hers alone pursue Antony to Rome), she is so frantic for news that she will not even allow him to speak. Responding to his guarantee that her lover is "well", she barks:

CLEOPATRA                    But, sirrah, mark: we use
  To say the dead are well. Bring it to that,
  The gold I give thee will I melt and pour
  Down thy ill-uttering throat.

MESSENGER

    Good madam, hear me.

CLEOPATRA                Well go to, I will.

    But there's no goodness in thy face. If Antony

    Be free and healthful, so tart a favour

    To trumpet such good tidings! If not well,

    Thou shouldst come like a Fury crowned with snakes,

    Not like a formal man.

MESSENGER           Will't please you hear me?

CLEOPATRA

    I have a mind to strike thee ere thou speak'st.

**[2.5.30–42]**

Though the scene becomes still more broadly comic – particularly when she "hales him up and down" in a rage, as the stage directions have it – it is also coloured by a lingering pathos. As we watch Cleopatra fight her urge to hear Octavia's beauty described (albeit by a messenger now too terrified to tell her anything remotely unpalatable), it seems clear that she feels the loss of what she touchingly calls her "salad days" keenly.

In their solipsistic, self-magnifying obsession with themselves and each other, Antony and Cleopatra resemble Shakespeare's other headlining lovers, Romeo and Juliet. But whereas the young lovers are torn apart by a strife that they cannot hold back, their middle-aged counterparts are fatefully implicated in the events that are their undoing. "These strong Egyptian fetters I must break, / Or lose myself in dotage," mutters Antony just two scenes into the play (1.2.109–10), but Shakespeare makes his task far more muddled, and by the play's end he is still floundering. As his commanders fear, Antony's military instincts have blunted, and against their advice he confronts Caesar at Actium by sea. After losing disastrously he dares Octavius to single combat, only for Octavius to scorn the challenge, and though the subsequent battle goes well for Cleopatra and her forces, their apparent betrayal is Antony's undoing. When news arrives that the Egyptian Queen has committed suicide, it is the end. Preparing for a valiant Roman suicide, Antony muses to Eros that

    Sometime we see a cloud that's dragonish,

    A vapour sometime like a bear or lion,

    A towered citadel, a pendent rock,

    With trees upon't that nod unto the world

    And mock our eyes with air.

**[4.15.2–7]**

"My good knave Eros," he continues, "now thy captain is / Even such a body." It isn't

Constance Collier was Herbert Beerbohm Tree's leading lady from 1901 to 1906. Cleopatra (to Tree's Antony) was one of her finest achievements.

just Antony's reputation that has dissolved – he sees himself disappearing before his own eyes.

In the event, somehow fittingly, Antony bungles his suicide – a suicide initiated by news that Cleopatra is dead. It is the play's bitter joke (and again testament to her "infinite variety") that she is nothing of the kind: Cleopatra put out the news in an attempt to defuse his anger after battle. The truth arrives only once Antony has tried, and failed, to kill himself; and he is doomed to die a lingering death, trying to get her to listen even in his last moments. Although (unlike Romeo and Juliet) they are given a last chance to see each other, Antony and Cleopatra do so at the cost of conventional tragic dignity: Antony's last words are "no more" as his beloved begs, characteristically, "hast thou no care of me?" (4.16.62).

The play does not end with Antony, however, and in its drawn-out final scene, located throughout at Cleopatra's monument as the Romans close in, *Antony and Cleopatra* proves that it is after all a double tragedy. Some of Cleopatra's most passionate speeches about her lover occur once he is dead, and point to the fantasy that sustained their relationship. "I dreamt there was an Emperor Antony," she exclaims to Dolabella. "His legs bestrid the ocean; his reared arm / Crested the world … Realms and islands were / As plates dropped from his pocket." The image is deliberately unreal, and when Cleopatra asks, "Think you there was, or might be, such a man / As this I dreamt of?", Dolabella's only reply is "Gentle madam, no" (5.2.81–93).

Aside from fantasy, however, the only other option for Cleopatra is the grim reality of life under Roman control – and control is not something she is prepared to relinquish. She will not live to be paraded through Rome like a "strumpet", jeered at by the multitude; she cannot bear the thought that "quick comedians" will put them on stage, that

> Antony
> Shall be brought drunken forth, and I shall see
> Some squeaking Cleopatra boy my greatness
> I'th' posture of a whore.

**[5.2.214–7]**

The dramatic irony is powerful: on Shakespeare's stage Cleopatra was already being played by a "boy", possibly the same talented actor who created the roles of Lady Macbeth and Volumnia. But Cleopatra wants to star in her own tragedy, and as she puts on her queenly garments for the last time, expressing her "immortal longings" (5.2.276), she arranges her death like the great actress she is.

## Stage history and adaptations

We don't know for certain at which theatre *Antony and Cleopatra* was first produced, though the indoor **Blackfriars** has been suggested – partly due to the play's surprisingly intimate theatrics, which, unlike the other Roman dramas, need no crowd scenes. No records survive, though the appearance of two other Cleopatra plays, **Fletcher** and **Massinger's** *False One* (1619–23) and **Thomas May's** *Cleopatra, Queen of Egypt* (1626) might hint that Shakespeare's subject matter (if not necessarily his script) had come into vogue a few years after his death.

Although **John Dryden** claimed to "imitate" the Bard in his well-known neoclassical adaptation, *All for Love, or, The World Well Lost* (1678), in fact his version deviates more markedly from Shakespeare than any other Restoration reworking. Cleopatra's skimpy role barely compares with its predecessor, and the focus is firmly on our hero's moral dilemmas as he struggles to balance various calls on his energies – one of whom, Caesar, even fails to make it on stage. In 1759, **David Garrick** bravely attempted a revival of Shakespeare at Drury Lane, but the text was cut and conflated in all but the final act, Garrick relying instead on moveable scenery and his own powers as Antony. That the former dwarfed the latter may account for the production's failure – a fellow actor complained that Garrick was "not sufficiently important and commanding".

Throughout the nineteenth century, the scenery just kept getting larger. Despite the anxieties of his leading lady, **Sarah Siddons**, that playing the "foul Egyptian" might injure her reputation, **John Philip Kemble** went ahead in 1813 with a version that set the tone for years to come. Designed for the vast new Theatre Royal at Covent Garden, it boasted a sea fight complete with galleys, and an elaborate funeral procession with a massed choir. Again, though, it was a flop, and William Hazlitt publicly attacked Kemble's decision to retain some of Dryden's text. **William Charles Macready** revived Kemble in 1833 still more spectacularly, but ironically enough **Clarkson Stanfield**'s magnificent painted scenery attracted the only positive reviews.

Shakespeare himself, now divested of Dryden, was judged the winner in **Samuel Phelps**'s 1849 production at Sadler's Wells. The *Illustrated London News* thought its treatment of the Egyptian scenes "exceedingly *vraisemblable*", though Isabella Glyn as Cleopatra still looked very stately and Victorian. Perhaps it was only inevitable that archeological accuracy would predominate in **Frederick Chatterton**'s 1873 Drury Lane staging, which advertised the fact that its costumes were modelled on the British Museum's Egyptian collection. Though Chatterton achieved sour notices, the critical horror that greeted **Lewis Wingfield**'s unwieldy production at the Princess's Theatre in London seventeen years later was revealing: a soporific four and a half hours long, it was panned by *The Times* as an "Oriental pantomime". Even **Lillie Langtry**, the Prince of Wales's lover, failed to enliven proceedings as Cleopatra. Arrigo Boito's Italian translation of the play had three performances at the Lyric Theatre in 1893, it starred the great Italian actress **Eleonora Duse**, but it was not one of her successes and was attacked by leading critic William Archer.

Nor were things much better with **Herbert Beerbohm Tree**'s 1906 production, headlined with deadening banality as a "Magnificent Spectacle" by the *Daily Telegraph*, although it did boast the formidable beauty of **Constance Collier** as Cleopatra. In fact, it took **Harley Granville-Barker**, influenced by **William Poel**, to call a halt to Orientalist megalomania. Though neither man had the chance to put on *Antony and Cleopatra*, Granville-Barker's *Preface* on the play celebrated its "old fluidity" and argued for sensitive staging. **Robert Atkins** complied at the Old Vic in 1922, using cut-out scenery and a practically bare stage. In 1951 **Michael Benthall** staged a rather more opulent production at the St James's Theatre for the husband-and-wife team of **Laurence Olivier** and **Vivien Leigh**. But it was **Glen Byam Shaw**'s somewhat cooler 1953 Stratford production that really defined the play for the mid-century. Supposedly cast against type, **Peggy Ashcroft** triumphed as a Cleopatra who was sharply intelligent rather than merely capricious while **Michael Redgrave** brought a poetic world-weariness to the role of Antony. **Trevor Nunn**'s 1972 Stratford production marked something of a return to epic luxuriousness, but did so in order to underscore the play's exaggerated view of imperialism. **Richard Johnson** was a robust Antony and **Janet Suzman** a coolly calculating Cleopatra, although some commentators complained that she failed to achieve the requisite grandeur. For **Peter Brook** in 1978 (yet again at Stratford) **Glenda Jackson**'s haughty Cleopatra battled with **Alan Howard** as a petulant and preening Antony, in a designer-chic setting that managed to be both minimalist and sensuous.

The debate about whether the leading couple live up to their roles has dominated responses to most productions of recent times. While **Tony Richardson** (1973) diverted the audience's attention with offbeat iconoclasm (a red-haired **Vanessa Redgrave** vamped it up in a white silk pantsuit), in 1987 **Peter Hall** played it straight, casting a grizzled **Anthony Hopkins** against **Judi Dench**'s earthy queen. Both actors gave their all in what is usually regarded as the most satisfying modern-day staging, one in which the lovers had a tangible sexual chemistry. **Adrian Noble** also went for big names with **Helen Mirren** and **Michael Gambon** in 1982, but with less success. Mirren – an ideal actress for the part – repeated the role at the National Theatre in 1998 but this time a sadly undercharged **Alan Rickman** as Antony meant that the production failed to take off. More subversive modern interpretations have included an all-male production directed by **Giles Havergal** at the Citizens' Theatre in Glasgow in 1972 and **Michael Kahn**'s version of 1988, which cast the black actor **Franchelle Stuart Dorn** as Cleopatra (much of her court was also black, in a studied statement about the play's interest in ethnicity). The 1999 production at Shakespeare's Globe in London attempted an even more radical approach, trying to present the play as a kind of comedy. In this all-male version, **Mark Rylance** played for laughs as Cleopatra but also brought out much of the character's sadness. Opposite him, in a Jacobean-style staging by **Giles Block**, were **Paul Shelley** as Antony and **John McEnery** as Enobarbus.

*Antony and Cleopatra* proper has reached the screen several times in the last half-decade. The only full-scale movie version was that undertaken by **Charlton Heston** in 1972, which saw the actor-director make abundant alterations to Shakespeare's text in the best nineteenth-century tradition; never released in the US, it was widely regarded (like Heston's Antony) as a noble failure. **Trevor Nunn**'s more convincing TV adaptation two years later, like his later *Macbeth* and *Othello*, reworked his stage production and retained the services of Johnson and Suzman. **Jonathan Miller**'s 1981 BBC/Time-Life production in Elizabethan costume, in which **Jane Lapotaire**'s coquettish Cleopatra played against the down-to-earth ruggedness of **Colin Blakely**, was comparably intimate, though here the constraints seemed financial rather than artistic.

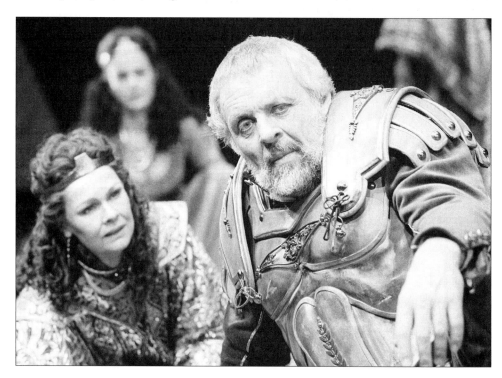

Judi Dench and Anthony Hopkins in the National Theatre's 1987 production of *Antony and Cleopatra*. Hopkins envisaged Antony as a "battered old tomcat; scarred, bruised, raucous, drunken, but a great spirit".

# Screen

## Antony and Cleopatra
**C. Heston, H. Neil, J. Castle; Charlton Heston (dir.)**
UK/Spain/Switzerland, 1972 ▷ Film Classic 📼

After acting Antony in Stuart Burge's *Julius Caesar* (see p.158), Heston became convinced that he was the man to take on the headline role in Shakespeare's grandest – but most stage-unfriendly – Roman play. Orson Welles declined to be involved, so Heston took the director's chair and put everything together himself, cutting and re-ordering most of the text along the way. It was a brave decision, and the film is certainly not as bad as its slimline budget might have so easily ensured, but is damaged (as in so many stage productions) by the limitations of the lead couple. Heston makes a valiant attempt not to sink into self-parody, but Hildegard Neil is simply not up to the job.

## Antony and Cleopatra
**R. Johnson, J. Suzman, C. Redgrave; John Scoffield (dir.)**
UK, 1974 ▷ Fox 📀 📼

One complaint about Trevor Nunn's 1972 staging of the play was that Janet Suzman failed to scale Cleopatra's monumental heights. On video you get a ringside seat as the leading couple slug it out, and it's true that neither is overly imposing – Suzman sometimes too skittish, Johnson's Burtonesque bluffery occasionally false. But deflation is among the play's obsessions, and what they bring to this production – captivating, chameleonic humanity – is of supreme value, and in the end almost unbearably sad. Elsewhere in the cast Corin Redgrave's sub-zero Octavius has passed into legend (it's all in the lips), and even Patrick Stewart's gruff Enobarbus isn't as irritating as at first he seems. Despite it being a production filmed for TV (like Nunn's *Macbeth*; see p.204), Scoffield's camerawork is always inventive, suggestively employing an enforced studio-bound setting to recreate the play's overlapping and often mirage-like spaces. Among the best Shakespeare television has produced.

# Audio

## Antony and Cleopatra
**A. Quayle, P. Brown, P. Daneman**
UK, 1965 ▷ HarperCollins (Caedmon) 📼

Any *Antony and Cleopatra* is made, or unmade, by its lead couple, and despite a dramatic style that might strike some listeners as old-fashioned (this recording dates from 1965) both Anthony Quayle and Pamela Brown are more than up to their shared task. Quayle presents a small-scale yet utterly persuasive Antony, convincingly irritated that he is going to seed, while Brown does her matriarchal best as Cleopatra, a *grand dame* permanently conscious of her audience – and

ultimately who refuses to go gently. Other members of the cast are also first-rate, among them Jack Gwillim's oaky Enobarbus and Paul Daneman's curt Octavius. Ultimately, though, it's this recording's fast pace, which makes convincing sense of the play's boundless energy – not to mention its Egyptian revels – that makes it a top choice. Only its boxy sound, which sometimes makes the lovers seem as if they're quarrelling in a bedsit, lets it down.

# Editions

## Oxford Shakespeare
**Michael Neill (ed.); 1994** ▷ Oxford UP

Neill's edition is probably the most comprehensive currently available – particularly useful for this, one of Shakespeare's densest and richest works. His book-length introduction is suggestive and astute, and probes some interesting thematic links within the play. Neill also deals with performance history in some detail, and usefully includes relevant excerpts from Thomas North's translation of Plutarch, one of Shakespeare's main sources. One slightly idiosyncratic editorial decision, to spell "Anthony" with an "h", receives learned backup, and a notoriously messy text is cleaned up well.

# Some criticism

## Scenic Form in Shakespeare
**Emrys Jones; 1971** ▷ Oxford UP [o/p]

Jones is intrigued by Shakespeare's use of what he calls "the primary dramatic unit", the scene, and shows that understanding this aspect of the playwright's craft illuminates many of the broader intellectual questions about his work. About a third of *Scenic Form in Shakespeare* looks at the general function of scenes in Shakespeare before moving on to specific examples – the culmination of which is *Antony and Cleopatra*, more fluid and adventurous scenically than anything else the playwright wrote, and a play that conveys (in Jones's words) "the day-to-day, even minute-to-minute, feel of experience".

## The Common Liar
**Janet Adelman; 1973** ▷ Yale UP [o/p]

*The Common Liar* modestly subtitles itself "an essay on *Antony and Cleopatra*", but at some 235 pages long that's something of an understatement. It's one of the best places to start: Adelman provides readable, sane and intelligent commentary to many of the play's main concerns, brought together under her overall argument that its compound uncertainties are a measure of its explorative nature. The book also contains appendices on Plutarch, Virgil and Cleopatra's ethnicity – the last still infrequently discussed, but something deliberately provoked by the play.

# As You Like It

Though written during the same period as *Twelfth Night*, *As You Like It* has little of the obvious darkness of the other mature comedies. Perhaps that is because it spends so much time in the Elizabethan "green world" of the Ardenne forest, a rejuvenating environment that allows all the play's erotic entanglements to untie themselves with ease, preparing for a barnstorming finale in which no fewer than eight characters are paired off simultaneously. The play's take-it-or-leave-it title makes that conclusion all the more light-hearted, and perhaps excuses the playwright from the accusation, levelled by some, that its plot is paper-thin. The comedy's genius lies not in its happenings, but its characters who include Shakespeare's most engaging heroine, Rosalind, one in a line of confident and appealingly witty women who dominate the middle comedies. Though it is by no means frivolous, as Helen Gardner, one of the comedy's most engaging critics, writes, *As You Like It* is "the last play in the world to be solemn over".

[DATE] *As You Like It* was entered in the Stationers' Register on August 4, 1600, alongside *Henry V*, *Much Ado* and Ben Jonson's *Every Man in His Humour*. It was presumably written either that year or just before.

[SOURCES] Thomas Lodge's hugely popular *Rosalynde* (1590), a slender but eventful prose tale written while the author was en route to the West Indies, provided Shakespeare with the substance for *As You Like It*, though he refashions its plot and renames its characters.

[TEXTS] Despite being entered in the Register, the play wasn't to reach print until the 1623 Folio, meaning that its entry there was probably a "staying order" – a device to prevent piracy or forestall censorship. The Folio text was perhaps typeset from a promptbook rather than Shakespeare's own papers.

## Interpreting the play

Shakespeare's characters in *As You Like It* have it easy – at least compared to those in his main source, Thomas Lodge's Elizabethan classic *Rosalynde* (1590). Forsaking treachery at court for the wildness of the forest, Lodge's female characters have to confront outlaws, rape and even the threat of incest before they are permitted to reach the story's end; while his male hero, Rosader (Shakespeare's Orlando), faces up to the wrestling challenge knowing that all the previous combatants have died horribly in the attempt. Shakespeare's characters, by contrast, lead lives which can only be described as blessed. As numerous critics have observed, *As You Like It* is the only Shakespearian comedy in which death is kept at arm's length, Oliver's doomed attempts to get rid of Orlando being just that – doomed. It is not altogether surprising that the adjective "fairytale" is often applied to the play. Though its "good" characters are depicted in rounded human complexity, evil has a distinctly two-dimensional presence, ultimately evaporating with near-implausible ease.

That is not to say that all is well in the court of Duke Frederick, Senior's usurping brother, in which we initially find ourselves. In another change to his source, Shakespeare creates a set of neat symmetries between the play's good and bad sides. Just as Duke Frederick has usurped

**Duke Senior**, deposed and living in banishment in the forest of Ardenne

**Rosalind**, Duke Senior's daughter (later disguised as **Ganymede**)

**Amiens** and **Jaques**, Lords attending on Duke Senior

**Duke Frederick**, Duke Senior's brother, the usurper

**Celia**, Duke Frederick's daughter and Rosalind's companion (later disguised as **Aliena**)

**Le Beau**, a courtier attending Duke Frederick

**Charles**, Duke Frederick's wrestler

**Touchstone**, a clown in Duke Frederick's service

**Oliver**, the eldest son of Sir Rowland de Bois

**Jaques** and **Orlando**, Oliver's younger brothers

**Adam**, an old servant of Sir Rowland

**Denis**, Oliver's servant

**Corin**, an old shepherd and his companion **Silvius**, a young shepherd in love with the shepherdess **Phoebe**

**William**, a countryman, in love with **Audrey**, a goatherd

**Sir Oliver Martext**, a country clergyman

**Hymen**, the god of marriage

**ACT 1** Ever since Orlando's father's death, his brother Oliver has kept him in poverty and denied him an education. When the two argue, Oliver plots how he can be rid of him: hearing that Orlando intends to fight in the forthcoming wrestling competition, he orders Charles the wrestler to kill him. At court, Rosalind is dejectedly reflecting on her father's banishment by Duke Frederick when she and Celia are cheered by news of the wrestling match. Both are struck by the brave appearance of a young man taking part – Orlando – and his surprising defeat of Charles. The cousins congratulate him, but Orlando is so smitten by Rosalind that he cannot speak. Duke Frederick, however, is fearful his niece will betray him and banishes her, but Celia secretly arranges for them both to escape in disguise and join Duke Senior in the forest of Ardenne.

**ACT 2** Rumour quickly spreads of the cousins' disappearance, and Duke Frederick recruits Oliver to join the search. Hearing that his brother intends to kill him, Orlando flees. In the forest, Duke Senior and his companions are about to eat when Orlando rushes in with Adam close

behind, both faint with hunger. Realizing who Orlando is, the Duke tells of his respect for Orlando's father and invites both Orlando and Adam to dine.

**ACT 3** Orlando is pining for love, leaving poems about Rosalind throughout the forest. When Rosalind appears with one such poem, Celia teasingly reveals who the author is; when he enters, Rosalind hits on a plan. Disguised as Ganymede, she interrogates Orlando about his love before prescribing a possible cure – to be administered by her. Later, the cousins come across Phoebe who falls immediately in love with Ganymede – despite being wooed by Silvius.

**ACT 4** Rosalind/Ganymede has convinced Orlando to take a more realistic view of love, but complicates things still further by taking on the personality of Rosalind while still dressed as Ganymede, and persuading Celia/Aliena to "marry" them in a mock ceremony. Phoebe has meanwhile addressed a love letter to Ganymede, but Rosalind returns it scornfully. Oliver bursts in, clutching a bloodied cloth, and narrates how he has been saved from a lioness by Orlando's valour, and the two brothers have been reconciled. Rosalind/Ganymede faints.

**ACT 5** Touchstone, meanwhile, has decided to marry Audrey, and rejects William, her current suitor. For his part, Oliver has fallen for Celia/Aliena, and agrees to marry her in front of Duke Senior the next day, leaving his estate to Orlando. Rosalind – still in the guise of Ganymede – promises Orlando that she will make his beloved appear by magic, and they will be married too. She also guarantees success to Silvius if he turns up with Phoebe. The big day arrives, and while everyone prepares, the disguised Rosalind and Celia slip out, before returning in their own clothes and accompanied by Hymen. Loose ends are tied and weddings finalized – Rosalind to Orlando, Celia to Oliver, Audrey to Touchstone and, lastly, Phoebe (who realizes she cannot marry Ganymede) to Silvius. All are leaving joyfully when news arrives that Frederick has become a hermit, leaving the kingdom in Duke Senior's rightful hands.

Duke Senior, Orlando has been disinherited by his elder brother Oliver – a device that will recur in Shakespeare's final solo play, *The Tempest*. But Oliver's villainy – like that of Don John in *Much Ado* – is essentially motiveless, as he himself admits while plotting to have Orlando removed from the frame:

> I hope I shall see an end of him, for my soul—yet I know not why—hates nothing more than he. Yet he's gentle; never schooled, and yet learned; full of noble device; of all sorts enchantingly beloved; and, indeed, so much in the heart of the world, and especially of my own people, who best know him, that I am altogether misprized. But it shall not be so long.
>
> **[1.1.154–61]**

It won't be "long" because Oliver has prepared for Orlando to meet his end in a wrestling bout with his henchman Charles, a contest he is confident that Orlando can never win. It is precisely the kind of capricious cruelty that Frederick's court, which has banished Rosalind's father but not Rosalind herself, delights in – indeed, as Touchstone notes, the women will be encouraged to watch ("It is the first time that ever I heard breaking of ribs was sport for ladies," he tartly notes (1.2.128–9)). But Oliver's grudging litany of Orlando's heroic qualities alerts us to the fact that evil will not prevail. Playing the part of the wandering knight to perfection, Orlando wins the contest against all the odds and captures the greatest prize of all – Rosalind's affection.

## Let the forest judge

But the malevolent world of court does not prove a propitious location for love, and both Rosalind and Orlando soon find themselves banished from its boundaries, catapulted into the forest of Ardenne (spelt "Arden" in the First Folio and many subsequent editions; see box opposite). Ardenne provides the setting for the majority of the play's scenes, if not most of its plot; and in the forest, with the initial rush of actions completed, time slows down to a near-standstill. Ardenne is, as its name seems to indicate, a cross between Arcadia and Eden, the rustic "Golden World" imagined by pagan poets and the biblical garden all in one. Yet it can also be a perplexing – even menacing – location, as the characters from court discover when they enter it for the first time. Orlando describes it as an "uncouth forest", "bleak", a "desert"; and even Rosalind's bright exclamation, "this is the forest of Ardenne", does not impress Touchstone, who acidly replies, "Ay, now am I in Ardenne; the more fool I. When I was at home I was in a better place" (2.4.14–16).

Ardenne occupies the boundary between barbarity and civility. Duke Senior and his lords make what they can of the forest, but the mixed nature of life there is somehow epitomized in Amiens's song, performed as the company sits down to dinner in the wood:

> Blow, blow, thou winter wind,
> Thou art not so unkind
>     As man's ingratitude.
> Thy tooth is not so keen,
>     Because thou art not seen,
> Although thy breath be rude.
> Hey-ho, sing hey-ho, unto the green holly.
> Most friendship is feigning, most loving, mere folly.
>     Then hey-ho, the holly;
>     This life is most jolly.
>
> **[2.7.175–84]**

It is "ingratitude" of sorts that has banished the Duke and lords to Ardenne – proof that the court is a brittle world in which "most friendship is feigning". Yet the song, celebrating the

> *Some sage critics have discovered as a great geographical fault in Shakespeare that he introduces the tropical lion and serpent into Arden, which it appears they have ascertained to lie in some temperate zone. I wish them joy of their sagacity. Monsters more wonderful are to be found in that forest; for never yet, since water ran and tall tree bloomed, were there gathered together such a company as those who compose the dramatis personae of As You Like It.*
>
> William Maginn, writing in *Bentley's Miscellany* (1837)

rustic life, finds a kind of liberation in adversity, like the Duke who, as Amiens earlier says, "can translate the stubbornness of fortune / Into so quiet and sweet a style" (2.1.18–20). "Let the forest judge," Touchstone comments (3.2.119–20), and here it grants the Duke and his men respite from the world's troubles.

Not everyone is convinced by that transformation, however. The Duke's gloomy companion Jaques takes every opportunity to expound bad grace, for as he himself boasts, "I can suck melancholy out of a song as a weasel sucks eggs" (2.5.11–12). Despite the Duke's optimism about their condition, Jaques – with one of the most famous metaphors in literature – remains cynical:

DUKE SENIOR
    Thou seest we are not all alone unhappy.
    This wide and universal theatre
    Presents more woeful pageants than the scene
    Wherein we play in.
JAQUES               All the world's a stage,
    And all the men and women merely players.
    They have their exits and their entrances,
    And one man in his time plays many parts,
    His acts being seven ages.

**[2.7.136–43]**

The miserabilist "ages" that Jaques goes on to sketch – all the way from the "infant, / Mewling and puking in the nurse's arms" to the "second childishness and mere oblivion, / Sans teeth,

## Arden or Ardenne?

"Shakespeare, when he wrote this idyllic play," declared Edward Dowden in 1881, "was himself in Arden." Though Dowden meant these words metaphorically – the forest, he suggested, was a kind of rest-cure – the bond between Shakespeare and the real-life **forest of Arden**, which lay to the north of Stratford-upon-Avon, was strong. The poet's mother even took her maiden name from the wood ("Mary Arden's House", in nearby Wilmcote, was one of the area's tourist hot spots until recently, when another dwelling in the village was discovered to have been her childhood home); and the farmhouse that Anne Hathaway inherited, her "Cottage", stood close to its boundary. As well as providing the title for a respected edition of Shakespeare's works, tradition also holds that *As You Like It* is set – and has often been performed as if it were set – in the Warwickshire Arden, deep in the English countryside.

Why, then, does this book call it "Ardenne"? The answer lies in Shakespeare's source, Lodge's *Rosalynde*, which locates the scene not in England, but France. Pointing towards the numerous French names in *As You Like It* and drawing attention to the great continental forest of the Ardennes, which now borders France, Belgium and Luxembourg, the *Oxford Shakespeare* restores "Ardenne" as its preferred spelling and this guide, following that text, does likewise. In truth, Shakespeare's play – which features both palm trees and lionesses – seems to have a less geographically circumscribed (and more imaginatively exotic) location in mind than either.

From left to right: Touchstone (Nicky Henson), Celia (Fiona Shaw) and a disguised Rosalind (Juliet Stevenson) stride purposefully towards Ardenne in Adrian Noble's RSC production, which opened in 1985.

sans eyes, sans taste, sans everything" – make rich capital from the human comedy, but his laughter is hollow.

His comedy, furthermore, is decisively rejected by the play. The all-inclusive forest delivers the antidote to Jaques's maudlin satire, as Rosalind discovers when she finds Orlando's love poems pinned to the trees. She does so not as herself but in male camouflage, the unravelling of which takes up much of the rest of the play. Although she is forced to dress as a man in order to travel into the forest, Rosalind's initial panic about how to approach her lover in disguise ("Alas the day, what shall I do with my doublet and hose!" (3.2.214–5)) turns into a realization that in fact she can use it to advantage. Dressing as a man liberates her to explore the quality of her love – and her lover – as she would never be able to do as a woman.

Whereas the gender of Lodge's disguised Rosalynde is always clear (even to Rosader), Shakespeare's Rosalind takes full advantage of the sexual ambiguity of her costume. With breathtaking cheek, she even proposes to Orlando an outrageous scheme whereby she will stop him pining for love by imitating Rosalind herself. She explains, breezily, that she has already tried out the "cure" on another man:

> He was to imagine me his love, his mistress; and I set him every day to woo me. At which time would I, being but a moonish youth, grieve, be effeminate, changeable, longing and liking, proud, fantastical, apish, shallow, inconstant, full of tears, full of smiles; for every passion something, and for no passion truly anything, as boys and women are for the most part cattle of this colour—would now like him, now loathe him; then entertain him, then forswear him; now weep for him, then spit at him, that I drave my suitor from his mad humour of love to a living humour of madness, which was to forswear the full stream of the world and to live in a nook merely monastic. And thus I cured him …

**[3.2.392–405]**

Though Celia will later claim, angrily, that "you have simply misused our sex in your love-prate" (4.1.191–2), Rosalind wittily disengages herself from the battle of the sexes by satirizing both sides. The infuriatingly changeable "mistress" she acts is the stuff of male stereotype, but Rosalind manages to blur the boundaries, concluding that "boys and women" are as bad as each other.

Paradoxically, disguise enables Rosalind to be entirely herself – quizzical, interrogative, scurrilous, irrepressible. It has often been thought that she outshines Orlando, her supposed equal, entirely; indeed, the exchanges between them frequently have an air of pupil and teacher. Discussing the strategies by which Orlando might best woo his beloved, she decides that they will rehearse what to do if she refuses him:

## Clowning about (and fooling around)

Like any nervous amateur director, Hamlet does not trust the professionals to get it right. "And let those your clowns," he anxiously advises the players, "speak no more than is set down for them" (3.2.38–9). The fear that a company's fools (as they were also known) might run amok and swamp what the Prince soberly calls the "necessary question of the play" must have been an occupational hazard for Jacobethan playwrights, though Shakespeare characteristically makes his comedians work for their laughs in esoteric and unusual places – as the "antic" Hamlet, wisecracking in Ophelia's grave, knows full well.

Professional fools were for a long time the real stars of the stage, and were instrumental in making sixteenth-century secular theatre the rowdy and irreverent thing it became. The most famous clown of the generation immediately before Shakespeare was **Richard Tarlton** (d.1588), so idolized that the Queen's Men, set up by royal command in 1583 to tour the nation, was built around him; and so funny that Elizabeth reputedly ordered him to stay away because he made her laugh too much. Tarlton's talents extended far beyond comedy: he was an adept dancer, fencer and his "wondrous" witticisms spawned a minor publishing industry; but most importantly he never failed to steal the show, whichever part he took (the root, perhaps, of Hamlet's anxiety). Tarlton's close rival was the more refined **Robert Wilson**, though in Shakespeare's own company **William Kempe** (d.1603) would later challenge both by dint of physical athleticism: he once danced a jig all the way from London to Norwich, a feat which lasted nine days. Kempe's replacement, **Robert Armin** (c.1568–1615), took a more thoughtful approach to his work, and published a book about his experiences in the profession, entitled *Fool upon Fool*. He also inspired most of Shakespeare's great clowning roles, including those of Touchstone in *As You Like It* and Feste in *Twelfth Night*.

For in Shakespeare's plays clowns – rather like the satirical comics who are their closest modern equivalents – also have serious jobs to perform. *Twelfth Night*'s Olivia comments that "there is no slander in an allowed fool" (1.5.89–90), and as Enid Welsford's classic 1935 study of the subject reveals, throughout the middle ages and into the Renaissance fools were a social as well as theatrical reality. Many were employed in courts and wealthy households not only to provide entertainment, but were also "allowed" to speak about whatever they wanted – the idea being that someone outside normal social conventions could say what flattering advisers dare not. The **"Feast of Fools"**, a carnivalesque festival in which life became topsy-turvy during the twelve nights of Christmas immortalized in Shakespeare's play, lasted well into the seventeenth century on the European continent; and none other than the humanist Desiderius Erasmus expounded the necessity of foolery in his satirical *Moriae Encomium* ("Praise of Folly") from 1511.

Touchstone's very name alludes to a truth-revealing trait Erasmus would condone, while Feste's skittish experiments with language frequently undercut the wider events of the play and ridicule its characters even more than they ridicule themselves. But by the time Shakespeare reaches the emotional wilds of *King Lear*, the jokes have become caustically bitter. "I am better than thou art, now," Lear's nameless Fool tells his master. "I am a fool; thou art nothing" (1.4.175–6). In the late tragedy *Antony and Cleopatra*, the final, cruel joke of the play – after Antony has botched his suicide – is that Cleopatra's attempts to satisfy her "immortal longings" are entrusted to a rustic clown, who delivers the fatal asps with the solemn assurance that "those that do die of it do seldom or never recover" (5.2.242–3).

ROSALIND  Well, in her person I say I will not have you.

ORLANDO  Then in my own person I die.

ROSALIND  No, faith; die by attorney. The poor world is almost six thousand years old, and in all this time there was not any man died in his own person, videlicet, in a love-cause. Troilus had his brains dashed out with a Grecian club, yet he did what he could to die before, and he is one of the patterns of love. Leander, he would have lived many a fair year though Hero had turned nun if it had not been for a hot midsummer night, for, good youth, he went but forth to wash him in the Hellespont and, being taken with the cramp, was drowned, and the foolish chroniclers of that age found it was Hero of Sestos. But these are all lies. Men have died from time to time, and worms have eaten them, but not for love.

**[4.1.86–101]**

Rosalind calls cheerily upon the great lovers of antiquity to illustrate her point – Troilus and Cressida, whose tragic love affair was caught across the battle lines of Troy (dramatized by Shakespeare a few years later); and Hero and Leander, separated when Leander drowned while swimming the Hellespont to see his lover. Despite the flippancy of her tone, though, there is good sense in what she says: it is all very well for men to moon over their mistresses, but there is more to life than star-crossed love. This sturdy pragmatism reveals that she sees exactly what Jaques sees, but is not deterred by the prospect.

## Fathom deep

But Rosalind is not impregnable. She confides in Celia that, for all her sardonic words on the subject, she is already sunk "fathom deep" in love, so outright that she "cannot be out of the sight of Orlando" (4.1.195, 206). Her emotions towards him are frequently close to the surface: she has already been reduced to the point of tears by his casual inability to turn up on time, and it isn't long before she comes close to giving the game away by swooning, in a dangerously unmanly fashion, at the news that he has been hurt by a lioness.

By this stage in *As You Like It*, falling in love has become infectious. Following Oliver's lightning conversion to the side of good (inspired by Orlando's nobility in saving him from the lioness), he rapidly proposes to Celia – a match that some critics have found hard to defend, but which is as least a guarantee that his redemption is authentic. And love becomes so prolific in Ardenne that even Touchstone longs to leave the incurably single life of a Shakespearian fool and develops a crush on Audrey. The unlikely pairing of the professional man of words and the tongue-tied goatherd somehow exemplifies not just the range of love accommodated in the play, but its power to draw even the most unusual of couples together. Touchstone's reasons for marrying at least have the merit of being honest, as he tells Jaques:

As the ox hath his bow, sir, the horse his curb, and the falcon her bells, so man hath his desires; and as pigeons bill, so wedlock would be nibbling.

**[3.3.72–4]**

A rather different perspective on love is offered by the shepherd Silvius, who first enters the play in the company of his "true labourer" colleague Corin. Given that Silvius sounds like he's never been near a sheep in his life, it is difficult at first to imagine what they have to talk about – until, that is, Silvius begins a lament about the cruelty of his mistress, Phoebe, which continues unabated for the rest of the play. In a comedy in which falling in love seems implausibly easy, the relationship between Silvius and Phoebe will prove the most tortured of the lot – not least because Phoebe, spurning Silvius, then falls for Rosalind/Ganymede. This is a neat twist on the theory of scornful mistresses outlined by Rosalind earlier in the play, but nonetheless creates the only barrier to love that *As You Like It* presents.

Fittingly, Rosalind herself, having created the problem, resolves it. Gathering everyone together – promising to Orlando that she will produce Rosalind as if by magic and guaranteeing to Phoebe that "I will marry you if ever I marry woman" (5.2.107–8) – she orchestrates what proves to be a flurry of weddings officiated over by no less a presence than that of the god of marriage, Hymen. Yet Rosalind is not permitted to end the play, just as its characters know they cannot remain in Ardenne for ever. Addressing the lovers, Hymen insists, "'Tis I must make conclusion / Of these most strange events":

> Whiles a wedlock hymn we sing,
> Feed yourself with questioning,
> That reason wonder may diminish
> How thus we met, and these things finish.

**[5.4.135–8]**

However our "wonder" diminishes, it will not disappear entirely. *As You Like It* deliberately teases its audience with the highest marriage-count of any Shakespearian comedy, yet asks us to believe in each and every one.

## Stage history and adaptations

There is no hard evidence that *As You Like It* was acted during Shakespeare's lifetime, but the eighteenth-century editor George Steevens reported that the playwright played Old Adam and it may have been performed during Christmas 1603 for James I at **Gillingham House** in Kent. Though **Thomas Killigrew** won the rights to act the play after the Restoration, no production ensued and it was an adaptation – **Charles Johnson**'s *Love in a Forest* (1723) – that introduced *As You Like It* to the eighteenth century. Johnson's version bore little resemblance to the original, extraneous characters being cut and chunks from other Shakespeare plays inserted instead, and his most surprising innovation was to marry off **Colley Cibber**'s Jaques to the play's Celia. It flopped.

The way lay open for **Charles Macklin**, who restored the original play at Drury Lane in 1740 and launched a taste for Shakespearian comedy (ignored by David Garrick, who preferred the serious works). Macklin was blessed in **Kitty Clive**'s Celia and the orotund **James Quin**'s Jaques, but above all in **Hannah Pritchard**'s superlative Rosalind, bursting with "genuine, sprightly, unaffected Nature" (as one witness put it). Pritchard's success encouraged others to follow, and Rosalind became a favourite of such long-standing luminaries as **Peg Woffington** (who acted her from 1741 to 1757, when she collapsed mid-performance); **Ann Barry** (1766–78); and **Dorothy Jordan** (1787–1817). Even **Sarah Siddons**, famous for her Lady Macbeth, had a go in 1785 – albeit to little enthusiasm.

Eagerness for breeches roles ensured *As You Like It*'s near-continual success into the nineteenth century. **William Charles Macready**'s production (Drury Lane, 1842) had Macready himself as Jaques and, initially, **Ada Nesbitt** as Rosalind. But the young **Helen Faucit** soon took over and made a career of Rosalind, the radiance and honesty of her performances winning hearts along the way – among them Ellen Terry's, who spoke admiringly of her "deep and true emotion" in the role. To her great regret Terry herself never got to play Rosalind; when the work was staged at the Lyceum in 1890 it was the Irish-American **Ada Rehan** who took the role, which subsequently became something of a calling-card. **Madge Kendal**, who played opposite her husband **W.H. Kendal**'s Orlando, was another outstanding Rosalind of the 1870s and 80s. But by the time Faucit retired in 1879, the Victorian taste for hyper-realistic staging had become endemic. That year, performances at Stratford featured a freshly culled deer from Charlecote in Warwickshire – a descendant of the flock reputedly poached by Shakespeare – and a turnip from Anne

Vanessa Redgrave as Rosalind in the 1961 RSC production of *As You Like It*.
"A creature of fire and light" was how the *Daily Express* described her.

Hathaway's garden. (The stuffed deer appeared regularly until 1919, though presumably the same is not true of the turnip.) In a similar vein was **Oscar Asche**'s production at His Majesty's Theatre in 1907, in which **Lily Brayton**'s blithe Rosalind and Asche's Jaques roamed around a forest created from two thousand ferns, copious amounts of bamboo and plentiful leaves from the previous autumn.

**Nigel Playfair** turned his back on this over-literal approach with his lively and controversial Stratford production in 1919, distinguished by **Claude Lovat Fraser**'s "futurist" sets. Esme Church directed a Gainsborough-inspired production at the Old Vic in 1936 with **Edith Evans** as Rosalind and **Michael Redgrave** as Orlando. Though Evans was twenty years older than Redgrave, their partnership convinced the critics – perhaps because they were having an affair at the time.

Redgrave's daughter, **Vanessa**, launched the play's most famous postwar production under **Michael Elliott**'s direction at the RSC in 1961. Her gamine Rosalind, often barefoot and sporting a cute cap, received lustrous reviews and added a tangible sparkle to the forest scenes which became the imaginative focus for Elliott's production. Redgrave was supported by **Ian Bannen** as a serious-minded Orlando and **Max Adrian** as a sardonic, fur-coated Jaques. The homoerotic undertow hinted at by Redgrave was more stridently voiced by **Clifford Williams** in 1967 at the Old Vic, with an all-male cast (including **Ronald Pickup**'s Rosalind, **Charles Kay**'s Celia and **Jeremy Brett** as Orlando) acting what some would see as an *As You Like It* way ahead of its time in its exploration of gender and identity – others as camp, drag-act Shakespeare. **Buzz Goodbody**'s RSC rendering of 1973, with **Eileen Atkins** as a denim-clad Rosalind, advertised the play's gender issues, but struggled to communicate its grace.

The year 1977 saw three wildly different versions of the comedy, indicating not just its appeal to directors but its kaleidoscopic opportunities. **Trevor Nunn**'s outlandish version at the RSC nearly drowned out its cast – among them **Kate Nelligan**'s Rosalind and **Peter McEnery**'s Orlando – in Purcellian opera, but after complaints the musical content was scaled back. No such compromises for **Peter Stein** at the Schaubühne am Halleschen Ufer in Berlin, who treated his audiences to extravagant and highly stylized theatre, making them process from Frederick's harsh court to a magical forest in a nearby film studio for the Ardenne scenes. **Robin Phillips**'s staging at Stratford, Ontario gazed back decorously at eighteenth-century culture with **Maggie Smith** as a well-bred Rosalind.

Recent stagings, especially British ones, have attempted to find a visual language that suggests the forest as a world outside of the world. In **Adrian Noble**'s RSC version (1985) the designer Bob Crowley presented Ardenne as a landscape swathed in white silk sheeting in which the powerful double-act of **Juliet Stevenson** as Rosalind and **Fiona Shaw** as Celia could come to self-knowledge – not least about their role within patriarchal society. **Declan Donnellan**'s all-male production for his own Cheek By Jowl company had little time for such seriousness (or budget for such designs) when they toured the play six years later. Their performance space was a simple canvas box, their interpretation joyously irreverent – envisioning an affair between **Adrian Lester**'s Rosalind and **Tom Hollander**'s Celia yet preventing **Patrick Toomey**'s straight Orlando from kissing Ganymede. In a riotous and noisy finale even Hymen and Jaques got together. **Lucy Bailey**'s Globe production of 1998 likewise used little by way of sets, but the point this time was historical – the Elizabethan staging attracted attention to Shakespeare's sly (mis)use of theatrical conventions. The play's most recent major British incarnation, courtesy of **Gregory Thompson** and the RSC in 2003, also used staging in enterprising ways: **Nina Sosanya**'s Rosalind found herself in a forest where the trees were made from people rather than timber (the cast also pretended to be sheep when required).

On screen, *As You Like It* has yet to receive satisfactory tribute. **Paul Czinner**'s movie of 1936 (starring **Elisabeth Bergner** as Rosalind and **Laurence Olivier** as Orlando) blended fairytale whimsy with a script from which some of the most exciting moments have been excised. **Basil Coleman**'s BBC/Time-Life version of 1978 was hamstrung by its heritage location shoots but boasted a very good cast, while **Christine Edzard**'s 1992 film boldly attempted to relocate Ardenne to the London Docklands – with varying degrees of success.

# Screen

### As You Like It
**H. Mirren, B. Stirner, R. Pasco; Basil Coleman (dir.)**
UK, 1978 ▷ Ambrose (BBC) DVD

The negative critical reaction to this – the first taping in the BBC Shakespeare – drove several nails into the coffin of producer Cedric Messina, who masterminded the whole series, and he was sacked a few years later. The decision to shoot on location (in the grounds of Glamis Castle in Scotland) seemed to many to be an awkward cross between nineteenth-century stage "realism" and TV period drama. In fact, compared with some later examples in the series, this *As You Like It* positively glows with health. Nevertheless the literalistic setting really doesn't help: nature (in the form of ferocious midges and distractingly in-shot sheep) often seems to be getting in the way of the action rather than enabling it to develop. What saves the production is the quality of its cast. Though some of the details of her performance are lost due to rather vague camerawork, Helen Mirren is alertly feisty throughout and the chemistry with Brian Stirner's earnest Orlando is always convincing. Angharad Rees's bright Celia also deserves mention, but it is Richard Pasco's acidic Jaques who most often steals the show – even if the production's sentimental style makes his bitterness seem more alien than it should.

### As You Like It
**E. Croft, A. Tiernan, C. Bannerman; Christine Edzard (dir.)**
UK, 1992 ▷ Disney

Ardenne? Try London's Docklands. Love poems on trees?

Graffiti on walls. A magical lion? A half-seen mugger. Such are the transformations wrought by Christine Edzard in a deliberately edgy *As You Like It* which sees Emma Croft's Rosalind slip into baggy jeans and hooded tops instead of doublet and hose. Despite the film's commercial failure, its political point is strong. The fractured worlds of Frederick's court and the forest transplant well to early-1990s London (locations are a City bank foyer and a cardboard city somewhere in Rotherhithe), itself locked into ever-widening divisions between rich and poor. But the production is scuttled by a host of problems: Andrew Tiernan is abysmal as both Oliver and Orlando (a doubling which robs the play of much-needed electricity); the wrestling scene is a wimpish cop-out; and the finale is played between bursts of credits.

# Audio

### As You Like It
**H. Bonham-Carter, N. Little, D. Morrissey; Kate Rowland (dir.)**
UK, 2000 ▷ BBC ⊙

Helena Bonham-Carter is – at least on audio – a pretty much perfect Rosalind: fleet-footed and girlish, gloriously witty and possessed of a touching humanity. Kate Rowland's direction sets her very much at the centre of this version with the result that some of the rest of the cast are forced into the shade and seem not so strong (Natasha Little, in particular, could do with more vigour as Celia). On the whole, however, this is a well-rounded and, more importantly, often very funny production. James Fleet's wise-fool Touchstone is the icing on the cake.

# Editions

## New Cambridge Shakespeare
**Michael Hattaway; 2000** ▷ Cambridge UP

Some minor textual slips notwithstanding, Hattaway's edition is superlative, taking account of the pastoral motifs Shakespeare employs (perhaps one of the play's more difficult aspects for modern readers) and giving plentiful background on them. Hattaway's introduction also spends time discussing the politics of *As You Like It*, both the politics of land – Elizabethans experienced a series of bad harvests and property scandals during the 1590s, events dimly reflected by the play – and those of gender and sexuality. Despite this serious matter, though, Hattaway is a lively critic and never loses sight of the comedy's playful dramatic texture, or indeed its multiple meanings on stage, both backed up by an excellent stage history. Lodge's Rosalynde is printed in excerpts at the back, and a short appendix provides some detail on the songs.

# Some criticism

## Essays, Mainly Shakespearean
**Anne Barton; 1994** ▷ Cambridge UP

Anne Barton is one of the most distinguished Shakespearian critics around. From her hugely successful *Shakespeare and the Idea of the Play* (1962; see p.293) to her recent involvement with the Riverside Shakespeare, she has contributed a vast amount to critical understanding of Renaissance drama, and this book collects some of her best articles, originally published in far-flung places. *As You Like It* is a frequent presence in Barton's thinking, and here it features mainly in two essays written three decades apart: one on "Shakespeare's sense of an ending" (1972), the other on "Parks and Ardens" (1992), the latter of which contains many useful nuggets on Shakespearian forests and the social realities behind them. Her essays on the late plays are also particularly acute.

## Impersonations
**Stephen Orgel; 1996** ▷ Cambridge UP

*Impersonations: The performance of desire in Shakespeare's England* takes its cue from recent interest in the idea of gender in the Renaissance – a debate sparked by French theorist Michel Foucault, who famously argued that sexuality as we understand it today is a modern invention, things being both more fluid and less dogmatic four centuries ago. They were certainly more fluid in the transvestite theatre of Shakespeare and his contemporaries, and Orgel argues not only that the English theatre was the odd one out (other countries accepted actresses), but that for native audiences to insist on seeing boys playing female roles involved a complex kind of social doublethink. The significance for *As You Like It* and *Twelfth Night* is obvious enough, and both plays flit in and out of Orgel's book, but *Impersonations* also touches on Dekker's *Roaring Girl*, Marlowe's *Edward II*, Jonson's masques and even the penchant of James I's wife for masculine headgear.

# The Comedy of Errors

The madcap tale related by *The Comedy of Errors* seems, at first, hard to believe. That is very much the point: Shakespeare adopted the story of long-lost twins who are continually mistaken for each other from the Roman playwright Plautus, but surpasses it in complexity. His play has two sets of identical twin brothers with the same name, separated while still young but all of whom end up in the same location by chance, and the bewildering confusion that results – a masterpiece of comic plotting as the four twins ricochet across stage – takes up most of the rest of the play. We know that *The Comedy of Errors* was performed at a London law-inn in 1594, and was perhaps intended to flatter that well-educated audience, but there is also a more poignant side to the play, one that connects this apprentice comedy to Shakespeare's last work for the theatre. Its tale of separation and madness delves into the essence of human identity, while its finale looks forward to the magical reunions of the late romances.

[**DATE**]  A play sounding like *The Comedy of Errors* was performed at the law college of Gray's Inn on December 28, 1594. Internal evidence suggests, though, that it might have been written earlier – perhaps as early as 1591.

[**SOURCES**]  The play's main source is *Menaechmi* by the Roman playwright Plautus (c.250–184 BC). Shakespeare expands this with material from Plautus's *Amphitruo* and the framing narrative derives from Gower's *Confessio Amantis* (1390s), the main source for *Pericles*. George Gascoigne's *Supposes* (acted 1566) has a number of similarities to Shakespeare's play.

[**TEXTS**]  The Folio text of 1623, possibly printed from Shakespeare's papers, is the only one.

## Interpreting the play

"However can you stage such a conglomeration of improbabilities?" exclaimed an exasperated reviewer after seeing Clifford Williams's 1962 production at the Royal Shakespeare Company. On paper as much as on stage, those "improbabilities" loom large: a father and two sets of twins somehow end up in the same place, are consistently mistaken for one another (but never meet their own doubles), are eventually reunited. The question of staging *The Comedy of Errors* has frequently been answered by adaptation, from the eighteenth century well into the twentieth – as Komisarjevsky's 1938 version and Trevor Nunn's in 1976 make clear (see p.40). *Errors* has been widely performed, but rarely as Shakespeare wrote it.

This seems to suggest that at some level there's a deep discontent with the play itself, a reluctance to trust it in its own terms – or at least to believe that people will ever really take to it. The eighteenth-century editor George Steevens declared that "in this play we find more intricacy of plot than distinction of character", suggesting that it simply bored audiences senseless; while Coleridge held that it was "in exactest consonance with the philosophical principles and character of farce". Nor have more recent scholars and directors been, on the whole, much more understanding: most have wanted to reduce it to the status of farce (despite the fact that

## Major Characters & Synopsis

**Duke** of Ephesus
**Egeon**, an old merchant from Syracuse
**Antipholus of Ephesus** and **Antipholus of Syracuse**, Egeon's twin sons
**Dromio of Ephesus** and **Dromio of Syracuse**, twin servants of the two Antipholuses
**Adriana**, Antipholus of Ephesus's wife
**Luciana**, Adriana's sister
**Nell**, Adriana's kitchen-maid
**Angelo**, a goldsmith; and **Balthasar**, a merchant
A **Courtesan**
**Doctor Pinch**, a schoolmaster and exorcist
A **Merchant** from Ephesus, Antipholus of Syracuse's friend
A second **Merchant**, Angelo's creditor
**Emilia**, an abbess from Ephesus

**ACT 1** Ephesus and Syracuse are at war and Egeon (a native of Syracuse) faces the death penalty for having entered Ephesus illegally. Interrogated by the Duke, Egeon reveals that he is on a quest: he and his wife Emilia had identical twin sons (both called Antipholus), but the family was split up for years following a shipwreck, he and the younger Antipholus plus one of the Dromio twins being separated from Emilia and the other two twins. Years later, Antipholus of Syracuse (Antipholus S) went looking for his brother, but never returned – and now Egeon has arrived in Ephesus in search of them both. Touched by Egeon's story, the Duke delays his execution. Coincidentally, Antipholus S has also landed in Ephesus with his servant Dromio. Left alone, Antipholus S bumps into the other Dromio (who of course lives there), and is mistaken for his twin, Antipholus of Ephesus (Antipholus E) – setting up the chain of transposed identities that dominates the rest of the play.

**ACT 2** Incensed that her husband has not arrived for dinner, Adriana hears from Dromio E that his master (the wrong one, naturally) is behaving oddly. They set off to find him and meet Antipholus S, who is understandably perplexed by her insistence that he should come home and eat.

**ACT 3** Meanwhile, Antipholus E has been with his friends Angelo and Balthasar. Realizing he is

running late, he invites them home – only to discover that his wife is already dining and they are locked out. They head off elsewhere, Antipholus E promising to have his revenge by giving the gold chain intended for his wife to a courtesan instead. The house, meanwhile, is in uproar: Luciana (Adriana's sister) cannot understand why Antipholus S pretends not to know his wife, and is horrified when he tries to woo her instead. For his part, Dromio S is appalled to find that he is engaged to a kitchen wench, and leaves to find a ship so that he and his master can escape.

**ACT 4** Antipholus E accuses Angelo of not delivering the gold chain as promised – which Angelo (having given it to Antipholus S by mistake) denies, and instead arrests Antipholus E for non-payment. Dromio S rushes in, having procured a ship, but his master is bewildered by the offer and demands bail instead. Dromio S is sent to fetch cash from Adriana, and meets Antipholus S on the way back; astonished to find his master at liberty, Dromio S gives him the bail money anyway. The pleasant surprise quickly sours, however, when the Courtesan appears and demands the chain from around Antipholus S's neck. Certain that she is a witch, Antipholus S and Dromio S escape. Antipholus E, meanwhile, is still under arrest and his friends are convinced he has gone mad. Fetching an exorcist, they send him home captive – but are terrified when the other twins suddenly appear, having apparently escaped.

**ACT 5** Confronted by a crowd of people attempting to arrest them, Antipholus and Dromio S make a dash for a nearby priory. Demanding her husband back from the Abbess, Adriana is persuading the Duke – who has arrived with Egeon – to intervene when Antipholus and Dromio E appear, having actually escaped. The Duke is struggling to make sense of it all when the Abbess enters with Antipholus and Dromio S. After protracted confusion, the Abbess recognizes Egeon as her long-lost husband and the twins' identities are revealed. The day's events are unscrambled, Antipholus S proposes to Luciana and Egeon is reprieved.

this is the only play of Shakespeare's with the word "comedy" in its title); few have been encouraged to take up the themes it presents with any seriousness. One reason is perhaps its brevity: at just 1800 lines, it is by some distance the shortest work Shakespeare wrote, and has always struggled to avoid being branded as lightweight entertainment.

## The thing I cannot get

Yet *The Comedy of Errors* is also quite brilliant. Largely influenced by the Roman dramatist Plautus, whose witty, unsentimental and rather brittle comedies had a lasting impact on drama in Renaissance England, *Errors* represents an abrupt change of gear from the harsh world of plays like the *Henry VI* cycle and *Titus Andronicus*. Plautus's reputation was largely based on his skill for intricate plotting and diverting devices. *Menaechmi*, upon which *Errors* is based, is a virtuosic example: it concerns a merchant who has twin sons, Menaechmus and Sosicles. When Menaechmus is stolen as a young child, Sosicles is renamed "Menaechmus" in memory of his absent twin, before growing up and resolving to find his brother. Sosicles/Menaechmus eventually arrives in the right place, Epidaurus, but creates understandable confusion there – first the real Menaechmus's mistress, then his wife and father-in-law, mistake him for the man they know and chaos ensues until the twins are eventually reunited and all is resolved.

Shakespeare follows the same basic plot, while heightening the tale's implausibility by creating a matching pair of servants for his Antipholus twins (all four, apparently, born on the same night and in the same place). But where Plautus concentrates solely on the crazy misunderstandings that drive his plot, Shakespeare's characters are fleshed-out people. Antipholus of Syracuse enters the play tormented by grief, convinced that he will never find his long-lost brother. "He that commends me to mine own content," he begins,

> Commends me to the thing I cannot get.
> I to the world am like a drop of water
> That in the ocean seeks another drop,
> Who, falling there to find his fellow forth,
> Unseen, inquisitive, confounds himself.
> So I, to find a mother and a brother,
> In quest of them, unhappy, lose myself.
>
> **[1.2.33–40]**

Like another melancholy Shakespearian twin, Viola in *Twelfth Night*, Antipholus describes the pain of solitariness – and while later in the play Antipholus will indeed "lose himself" more thoroughly than he realizes, here the tone is tragic, not comic.

Sadness often threatens to encroach upon the central narrative: what Egeon movingly describes as "this unjust divorce of us" (1.1.104), the shipwreck that splits apart his family, forces Egeon, like his Syracusan son, to be a wanderer:

> My youngest boy, and yet my eldest care,
> At eighteen years became inquisitive
> After his brother, and importuned me
> That his attendant—so his cause was like,
> Reft of his brother, but retained in his name—
> Might bear him company in the quest of him;
> Whom whilst I laboured of a love to see,
> I hazarded the loss of whom I loved.
>
> **[1.1.124–31]**

The Japanese Mansaku Company's Kyogen-influenced *Errors*, performed at the London Globe in summer 2001, came up with a novel way of representing the play's visual perplexities: the twins wore indistinguishable masks. Mansai Nomura (left) and Yuki Takeyama (right) played energetic Dromios.

"Love" and "hazard" are forced together: love of family condemns Egeon – and Antipholus, and Dromio – to the life of a nomad.

Indeed, Egeon's very existence seems a counterbalance to the comic giddiness of the rest of the play. While in Plautus the twins' father is barely mentioned, Shakespeare drew upon the tale of Apollonius of Tyre, another much-wronged hero forced into a quest for his family (and the main source for *Pericles*), to create a father ready to risk all for his sons. Egeon is in fact prepared to risk death: the play hinges on the fact that he has been given only a few hours to live, and if there is to be a happy ending it has to be secured within that time. Indeed, the concept of "time" much occupies this shortest play: *Errors* contains more references to time – to time swiftly running out – than any other drama of Shakespeare's. But it is there not simply as comic propellant: Egeon's wait on Death Row hangs over the action; it is the ever-present tragedy that threatens to divert this "Comedy".

## Different from the man he was

This sense that the play needs to accomplish an impossible task within a tightly restrictive time-frame is both serious and amusing, and in a similar fashion many of the play's funniest moments flirt with real danger. Initially Antipholus of Syracuse can't believe his luck – Ephesus is a bemusing paradise where everyone seems not just to know him, but to treat him as an old friend. "There's not a man I meet but doth salute me," he exclaims,

> And everyone doth call me by my name.
> Some tender money to me, some invite me,
> Some other give me thanks for kindnesses …

**[4.3.1–5]**

So when a local merchant marches up, presents him with an expensive gold chain and refuses to accept any money, Antipholus grabs the opportunity. But the chain is of course intended for his twin, and before long Antipholus of Ephesus will be in prison for refusing to pay for it (on the entirely reasonable grounds that he has yet to receive the goods). The joke very quickly turns sour, and when Antipholus sends his servant to collect money for his bail, things really start to unravel. Dromio hands it to Antipholus of Ephesus by mistake – another gift he feels he can't refuse – and for a while it looks as if his twin will never be released.

Shakespeare adeptly balances the fates of his Antipholus twins, ensuring that as one rises, the other falls. The comedy is at its keenest when the identities of the pair are closest to collapsing into one another, the central "error" of the comedy, yet again there are real emotions at stake. One of the play's subplots concerns Antipholus of Syracuse's marriage to Adriana, which is apparently experiencing difficulties even before his twin – and all the confusion he brings – arrives in Ephesus. When her husband fails to arrive for dinner, Adriana is quick to round on her "unkind mate" (2.1.38), and the problems only build when Antipholus of Syracuse turns up unwittingly instead. This Antipholus rapidly realizes that, far from being married to Adriana (as everyone tells him he is), he has in fact fallen for her sister:

> She that doth call me husband, even my soul
> Doth for a wife abhor. But her fair sister,
> Possessed with such a gentle sovereign grace,
> Of such enchanting presence and discourse,
> Hath almost made me traitor to myself.

**[3.2.162–8]**

Antipholus of Syracuse's attempts to woo Luciana are farcically counterpointed by Dromio's terrified attempts to escape the clutches of the kitchen wench who is betrothed to his twin, but the point is the same. Arriving on this mysterious foreign shore has, they come to realize, removed, along with their identity, their liberty.

Nor are they the only victims. Hearing that Antipholus has been attempting to seduce Luciana, Adriana is justifiably appalled (she would be even more appalled to discover that her real husband, locked out by his wife, has been spending time with the Courtesan). She confronts him in a passion:

> How comes it now, my husband, O how comes it
> That thou art then estrangèd from thyself?—
> Thy 'self' I call it, being strange to me
> That, undividable, incorporate,
> Am better than thy dear self's better part.
> Ah, do not tear away thyself from me;
> For know, my love, as easy mayst thou fall
> A drop of water in the breaking gulf,
> And take unmingled thence that drop again
> Without addition or diminishing,
> As take from me thyself, and not me too.

**[2.2.122–32]**

Echoing Antipholus's water imagery, she tries to make him explain what has happened to their marriage. Shakespeare gives her words further resonance (one that his earliest audiences would probably have picked up on) by having her echo Saint Paul's Letter to the Ephesians – aptly enough given the play's geographical setting. The moment may in one sense be funny, but it is also painfully touching: while Antipholus of Syracuse is beginning to doubt his sanity, the woman who thinks she is his wife is trying to persuade herself that he still loves her.

As in *The Taming of the Shrew*, the sometimes tortured relationships between women and men are ruthlessly scrutinized in this play. In contrast to her sister, Luciana has a more cynical view of marriage. "If you did wed my sister for her wealth," she begs Antipholus of Syracuse,

> Then for her wealth's sake use her with more kindness;
> Or if you like elsewhere, do it by stealth:
> Muffle your false love with some show of blindness.
> Let not my sister read it in your eye.

**[3.2.5–9]**

*The main action takes place in a time gone crazy, twisted, looped, turning in on itself, not so much the medium of existence as a manifestation of its perplexities, even, at times, of its horror.*

Gāmini Salgādo, "'Time's Deformed Hand': Sequence, Consequence, and Inconsequence in *The Comedy of Errors*" (1972)

From the outside, of course, Antipholus's insistence that he loves Luciana looks like a man attempting to play away from home; only he knows that he is in the right, and Luciana advises him to hide the fact.

## Much, much different

Money and the problems it buys are a recurrent feature in *Errors*, as is the topic of madness (the connection between the two is made much more extensively in *Timon of Athens*). "Lapland sorcerers inhabit here," mutters Antipholus of Syracuse to himself (4.3.11), but in the event it will be his twin who ends up in the madhouse. Desperately trying to straighten everything out, the imprisoned Antipholus of Ephesus is enraged to discover that Dromio has apparently mislaid the money for his bail. Everyone responds, however, by assuming that it is Antipholus that is mad, and he is bound and submitted to the ministrations of the unappealingly named Doctor Pinch. The Doctor's considered verdict – frighteningly reasonable in the circumstances – is that "both man and master is possessed … I know it by their pale and deadly looks" (4.4.93–4), and he begins an exorcism:

PINCH
    I charge thee, Satan, housed within this man,
    To yield possession to my holy prayers,
    And to thy state of darkness hie thee straight:
    I conjure thee by all the saints in heaven.
ANTIPHOLUS OF EPHESUS
    Peace, doting wizard, peace! I am not mad.
ADRIANA
    O that thou wert not, poor distressèd soul.

**[4.4.55–60]**

Antipholus is caught in the same unenviable catch-22 as Malvolio in *Twelfth Night*. Unable to prove that they are in their wits and that everyone else is behaving irrationally, both characters find themselves confronting the prospect of real insanity – because if everyone else thinks you're mad, you might as well be. Adriana's bewildered observation that her husband is "much, much different from the man he was" (5.1.46) is true enough, but at this point it looks as if no one will ever find out why.

Fortunately, however, *The Comedy of Errors* allows itself to resolve these complicated human muddles – not least the muddle of Egeon, waiting patiently all this time for his death sentence to be carried out. But Shakespeare is reluctant to give up the suspense. When Antipholus of Syracuse is spotted on the loose, everyone assumes that his twin has broken free, and after he and Dromio of Syracuse take refuge in a nearby priory, a crowd gathers impatiently outside and demands their release. The Abbess refuses, however, and it is left to the Duke to sort everything out – and with him is Egeon, who immediately recognizes Antipholus and Dromio. The last joke of the play (though again it is a poignant one) is that he too gets it wrong:

EGEON
    Why look you strange on me? You know me well.
ANTIPHOLUS OF EPHESUS
    I never saw you in my life till now.
EGEON
    O, grief hath changed me since you saw me last,
    And careful hours with time's deformèd hand
    Have written strange defeatures in my face.
    But tell me yet, dost thou not know my voice?
ANTIPHOLUS OF EPHESUS  Neither.

[5.1.296–302]

Egeon once more gets his sons muddled up, and it is not until Antipholus and Dromio of Syracuse stumble onstage that the truth begins to dawn. Even as the twins are reunited, the play keeps its most astonishing revelation for last: the Abbess is none other than their mother. Though its "errors" are finally over, the comedy keeps its promise.

# Stage history and adaptations

From the records of **Gray's Inn** in London, we know that a play resembling *The Comedy of Errors* was performed on the night of December 28, 1594 as part of the Christmas festivities. Another gala performance took place a decade later to the day: the accounts of James I's **court** record "The play of Errors" by "Shaxberd", raising the intriguing possibility that some legally trained audience members may have seen both performances. It was also a success on the public stage, at least judging by the fact that **Middleton** and **Dekker**'s *Honest Whore* (1604) cheerfully steals its locking-out scene.

Nonetheless, it was not revived at the Restoration and its eighteenth-century stage history is dominated by a range of adaptations under a variety of madcap titles. The first was the farcical *Every Body Mistaken* (1716), but this was quickly challenged by the anonymous *See If You Like It, or 'Tis All a Mistake* (1734), which interspersed Shakespeare with Plautus and was acted for the next seventy-odd years. **Thomas Hull** got in on the act in 1762 with *The Twins, or The Comedy of Errors*, which aspired to limited seriousness and would be acted with a few tweaks by **John Philip Kemble**, playing Egeon, in 1808; his younger brother **Charles** acted Antipholus of Ephesus. One **W. Woods** had himself adapted it under the title of *The Twins, or Which is Which?* back in 1780, and the two *Twins* competed over stage time for a number of years.

**Samuel Phelps** was more textually dutiful at Sadler's Wells in 1855, and his production was a triumph. Equally successful was the uncut tercentenary performance mounted in 1864 at the Princess's Theatre; this had brothers **Charles** and **Henry Webb** as near-identical Dromios, while **George Vining** and J. Nelson played their masters. The play reached the Stratford Memorial Theatre in a production by **Edward Compton** in 1888, but the Elizabethan revivalist **William Poel** gained full marks for authenticity six years later: his version of *Errors* was staged at Gray's Inn in 1894 – in the same venue as the first recorded performance, precisely 300 years on.

The play was put on several times over the ensuing decades: **Frank Benson** directed and played Antipholus of Syracuse in 1905; **Ben Greet** presented **Sybil Thorndike** as Adriana in 1915. But the play's fortunes were most drastically revived by **Theodor Komisarjevsky** in 1938, whose Stratford production indulged in joyous topsy-turvydom: its set was a huddle of colourful houses dominated by a huge clock which took on a life of its own at several key moments, while costuming ranged freely across the centuries. Though Komisarjevsky's

Theodor Komisarjevsky directed a groundbreaking, and frequently scandalizing, series of Shakespeare plays at Stratford in the 1930s. His *Comedy of Errors* from 1938 made Ephesus into a colourful Toytown – a tongue-in-cheek version of an English seaside resort (the wayward clock became a star in its own right).

liberties with the text incensed some (one critic pronounced that "the one thing it is determined not to be is Shakespeare's play"), on the whole the production was well received.

Somewhat less extreme was the *Errors* directed at Stratford by **Clifford Williams** in 1962, one of its most successful incarnations. Where Komisarjevsky had conjured carnival, Williams depicted pathos: the cast was praised for picking out the "disquieting" elements of the play and included **Ian Richardson** as Antipholus of Ephesus and **Alec McCowen** as his twin; **Ian Hewitson** and **Barry MacGregor** as the two Dromios; and **Diana Rigg**'s Adriana opposite **Pauline Letts**'s Emilia (Letts had played Luciana with Komisarjevsky a quarter-century earlier). The next major UK production was undertaken by **Trevor Nunn** at Stratford in 1976. Nunn imagined Ephesus as a Mediterranean "tourist trap", complete with a "lively crown of tarts, slinky pimps, priests, policemen". An outstanding cast included **Judi Dench**'s pouting Adriana and **Francesca Annis**'s earnest, bespectacled Luciana, as well as **Richard Griffiths**, **Michael Williams** and **Roger Rees**, but many felt that Nunn's decision to enliven the play with musical numbers was a tasteless mistake.

RSC productions over the last twenty years have illuminated the various sides of the play. **Adrian Noble**'s (1983) was a hotchpotch of different comic styles and (some felt) too gimmicky by half; he suspended a large cradle above the stage, serving both as balcony and interior – but when it broke down mid-performance, **Zoë Wanamaker** (Adriana) and **Jane Booker** (Luciana) were forced to improvise stage business on the spot. **Ian Judge**'s gag-filled version of 1990 was largely felt to be a failure: his decision to double the twins with one actor for each, thus obliterating the pathos of their reunion, attracted particular condemnation. Much subtler was **Tim Supple**'s staging six years later, which used the intimate space of The Other Place to provide a fresh and surprisingly dark view of the play; a youthful cast included **Sarah C. Cameron**, **Eric Mallet**, **Simon Coates** and **Maeve Larkin**. Back in the RSC's main house in 2000, **Lynne Parker** put on an energetic and zany production with gimmicks aplenty: an onstage chase at the end of Act Four co-opted a few spare actors, in costume, from the *1 Henry IV* then playing at the Swan. Equally funny was the Mansaku Company's *Kyogen of Errors*, rewritten by **Yasunari Takahashi**, which played at Shakespeare's Globe on Bankside in 2001. This translated English comedy into Japanese Kyogen, and invited audiences to chant *Ya-ya-koshi-ya* ("How complicated!") at key moments in the action.

*Errors* proper has yet to reach the silver screen, though it has made TV twice, both for the BBC – once in an operetta starring **Joan Plowright** (1954), and again in the BBC/Time-Life Shakespeare, with **Michael Kitchen** playing both Antipholuses and **Roger Daltrey** the Dromios.

## Screen

### The Comedy of Errors
**R. Rees, J. Dench, F. Annis; Philip Casson (dir.)**
UK, 1978 ▷ Universal 📼

As his numerous excursions into musical theatre attest, Trevor Nunn has never been averse to making his employees sing and dance as well as act. His RSC *Errors*, which debuted in 1976 and was filmed for TV two years later, is tricked out with plenty of tunes and choreography, not to mention various comic high-jinks absent from Shakespeare's script. A great idea, but badly realized: Nunn's fine cast looks justifiably ill at ease, and after a few minutes Guy Woolfenden's jaunty intro music will have you scurrying for fast-forward. A shame, as the production is otherwise funny and adroit, picturing Ephesus as a kind of Costa del Sol overrun with holidaymakers and ruled by a banana-republic dictator, and into which Judi Dench, Roger Rees and Francesca Annis inject sympathetic performances. It's certainly a lot better than the woebegone BBC version.

## Audio

### The Comedy of Errors
**D. Tennant, B. Coyle, N. Cusack; Clive Brill (dir.)**
UK, 1998 ▷ Arkangel ⊙ 📼

Managing the comic and tragic elements of *The Comedy of Errors* is something most productions find difficult to do, but this Arkangel version generally succeeds, delivering a moving opening scene built around Trevor Peacock's Egeon and plenty of fleet wit afterwards. This Ephesus is dominated by Irish voices – a welcome novelty, especially for Dromios usually played in bad Cockney – among whom are siblings Niamh and Sorcha Cusack (Adriana and Luciana respectively). Both David Tennant (Antipholus of Syracuse) and Brendan Coyle (Antipholus of Ephesus) are excellent, and fortunately they don't sound too similar. The only problem is the continuously cartoonish sound effects, which strive too hard for laughs.

## Editions

### Oxford Shakespeare
**Charles Whitworth (ed.); 2002** ▷ Oxford UP

The newest major edition of *Errors* on the market, Charles Whitworth's Oxford just beats R.A. Foakes's Arden 2 version (1962), now available in a repackaged "playgoer's" series. Both print a version of Plautus's *Menaechmi* as an appendix (it's worth dipping into Plautus just to see how much more interesting Shakespeare makes his version of the story), but Whitworth's has the advantage of appearing in a translation by William Warner (1595), which appeared at about the same time *Errors* was first performed. Whitworth is also in a position to comment on the critical and theatrical re-evaluation the play has experienced in the last few decades, and his account usefully interleaves the play's life on "page" and "stage".

## Some criticism

### Shakespeare and the Traditions of Comedy
**Leo Salingar; 1974** ▷ Cambridge UP [o/p]

Long out of print but one of the best general introductions, Salingar's study helps to elucidate what the word and concept of "comedy" might have meant to Shakespeare and his dramatic colleagues – and of course to audiences too. *Shakespeare and the Traditions of Comedy* ranges fleet-footedly across history (medieval stage romances, classical comedy), geography (Italian *commedia dell'arte* versus English comedy) and themes ("trickster" figures, trial scenes and the role of the Wheel of Fortune) to present a view of its subject that is both nuanced and – more importantly – not as po-faced as some other studies. Alexander Leggatt's excellent *Cambridge Companion to Shakespearean Comedy* (2002) offers some more recent perspectives.

### The Comedy of Errors: Critical Essays
**Robert S. Miola (ed.); 1997** ▷ Garland

As the author of *Shakespeare and Classical Comedy* (1994), Robert Miola is well-placed to offer opinions on *Errors*, Shakespeare's Plautine experiment. His Garland reader is terrific: you'll find an in-depth account of the play's critical history, particularly detailed on its use of sources; some twenty articles on productions spanning 398 years; and many of the most influential essays on the play – among them G.R. Elliott on "weirdness" and Harold Brooks on its themes and structure. The only puzzle is that Gāmini Salgādo's superlative piece on time in the play (*Shakespeare Survey*, 1972) isn't among them.

# Coriolanus

Shakespeare's muscular final tragedy, *Coriolanus* is also his purest expression of a tragic form, Greek in origin, in which a hero meets a sudden and brutal reversal of fate. While researching his earlier Roman tragedies *Julius Caesar* and *Antony and Cleopatra* in Plutarch's histories, the playwright's eye was caught by the glittering but ultimately catastrophic career of Caius Martius Coriolanus, a Roman general whose brilliance on the battlefield was matched only by his failings as a popular politician. The story is a fable however you look at it, but points in different directions: in one reading, Coriolanus is a hero deserted by a fickle populace; in another, he is a villain whose arrogance threatened dictatorship. Shakespeare makes room for both those positions and more besides, drawing on the politics of his own day to press home urgent and thorny questions about how democracy should operate. During its performance history *Coriolanus* has been interpreted, on one extreme, as propaganda for Hitler's Third Reich; on the other, as a communist tract enshrining the power of the people. As the soldier Aufidius, watching Coriolanus's star plummet, balefully notes: "our virtues / Lie in th'interpretation of the time" (4.7.49–50).

**[DATE]**  Uncertain, though the language of *Coriolanus* puts it close to *Antony and Cleopatra*, *Pericles* and *Timon of Athens* in 1608–09. Allusions within the play to historical events, notably the Midlands food riots and "great frost" of 1607–08, seem to support this. As such it is the last of the tragedies, and perhaps the first of Shakespeare's plays intended for indoor performance at the Blackfriars theatre.

**[SOURCES]**  As with the other Roman plays, North's 1595 edition of Plutarch's *Lives* is the central source, and, as in the case of *Antony and Cleopatra*, some passages are lifted almost verbatim.

**[TEXTS]**  The 1623 Folio provides the sole authoritative text, probably set from a transcript of Shakespeare's foul papers.

## Interpreting the play

Rome, the most powerful empire the world has ever known, stalks Shakespeare's career. Four of his plays and one of his poems have Roman settings, and a Roman army even sneaks into the early Britain of *Cymbeline*. In Shakespeare's eyes, the Empire appears in the most varied of places. Henry V's triumphant return from Agincourt becomes, in the Chorus's words, the arrival of a "conqu'ring Caesar". For his part, Macbeth scorns to "play the Roman fool" and die on his sword even as he realizes Macduff's army is upon him. And even Falstaff manages to name-check the most famous Roman victory of all, coolly bagging a rebel prisoner near the close of *Henry IV Part II*: "He saw me and yielded," Sir John boasts to Prince John, "that I may justly say, with the hook-nosed fellow of Rome, 'I came, saw and overcame.'"

*Coriolanus*, almost certainly Shakespeare's final tragedy, takes us inside Rome itself. What we find there is grim. Where *Antony and Cleopatra* counterpoises an oppressive Rome with the wide, luxurious, exotic expanses of Egypt, in this play we are trapped inside the city as the Volscian enemy circles outside. There has been famine, and the people are out on the streets,

## Major Characters & Synopsis

**Caius Martius**, later known as **Coriolanus**, a patrician (aristocrat) of Rome
**Menenius Agrippa**, another patrician
**Titus Lartius** and **Cominius**, generals and patricians
**Volumnia**, Coriolanus's mother
**Virgilia**, Coriolanus's wife
**Young Martius**, Coriolanus's son
**Valeria**, a lady from Rome
**Sicinius Velutus** and **Junius Brutus**, tribunes (representatives) of the Roman people
Roman **Citizens** and **Soldiers**
**Tullus Aufidius**, a Volscian general
Volscian **Lords**, **Citizens** and **Soldiers**
**Adrian**, a Volscian
**Nicanor**, a Roman

**ACT 1**   Struck by famine, Rome is starving and its citizens are in revolt. A mob, on its way to lynch the city's most hated patrician, Caius Martius, is halted in the streets by Menenius, a fellow patrician. Making the most of his fair-dealing reputation, Menenius holds the crowd back, but reckons without Martius's appearance and his announcement that the mob should be hanged. But Rome has worries other than famine: Aufidius's Volscian army is marching on the city, and Martius is soon appointed to join Cominius's retaliatory force. As the city waits for news of the battle, Volumnia boasts to Virgilia of her son's military prowess and notes with satisfaction that her young grandson is taking after his father. At the battlefront, meanwhile, the wounded Martius performs bravely, reversing a Roman retreat and masterminding the occupation of Corioles. Once Roman victory is confirmed, Cominius confers the honorific "Coriolanus" on his brilliant deputy. Aufidius, defeated and humiliated, contemplates revenge.

**ACT 2**   At the Senate, the tribunes are dissecting Martius's personal flaws when Virgilia announces his victorious return. Coriolanus enters the city to an enormous welcome, horrifying Brutus and Sicinius with the thought that he

will be promoted.  Their fears are confirmed when the Senate make him a consul. Coriolanus himself remains aloof, but is eventually encouraged to address the commoners directly and beg for their votes – a process he finds as distasteful as it is democratic. And, though he eventually gets their support, the tribunes soon convince the citizens to reconsider.

**ACT 3**   Coriolanus is about to be invested when the tribunes gleefully inform him that his popularity has evaporated. Incensed, he declares that the people don't deserve him, at which point the tribunes attempt to arrest him. They fail, but Coriolanus is forced to appear in the marketplace and answer the people's objections. Despite Volumnia's entreaties to stay calm, he loses his temper once more, railing at citizens and tribunes alike. This time he is banished for good.

**ACT 4**   Although the tribunes make no secret of their joy at Coriolanus's departure, it isn't long before rumour spreads that the Volscians will take advantage of his absence and launch another attack. For his part, Coriolanus heads directly for enemy headquarters at Antium and offers his services to Aufidius, who gratefully accepts. As their army heads for Rome, Aufidius's agenda becomes apparent: as soon as Coriolanus outlasts his usefulness, Aufidius will destroy him.

**ACT 5**   Rome, meanwhile, is desperate to win back its saviour, and first Cominius, then Menenius, attempt to persuade him to return. Both fail, but Virgilia, Volumnia, Valeria and Young Martius make a final plea, to which Coriolanus at last relents, fully aware of the danger this puts him in. While Rome celebrates the news, Aufidius accuses Coriolanus of treachery and the Volscians demand his head. The end has come. Coriolanus is first stabbed to death, then trampled by the Volscian crowd. Aufidius, weeping at what he has done, orders him to be buried with full military honours.

inflamed by rumours that the city leaders have been (as Menenius delicately puts it) "cup-boarding the viand", storing food for themselves while everyone else starves. Despite Menenius's desperate attempts to make peace, insisting that the patricians have "most chari-table care" for the people, the citizens are scandalized:

> FIRST CITIZEN  Care for us? True, indeed! They ne'er cared for us yet: suffer us to famish, and their storehouses crammed with grain; make edicts for usury to support usurers; repeal daily any unwholesome act established against the rich; and provide more piercing statutes daily to chain up and restrain the poor. If the wars eat us not up, they will; and there's all the love they bear us.
>
> **[1.1.77–84]**

These complaints about the abuse of political power have an eerily modern ring, but few among today's audiences (in the industrialized West at least) know what it is really like to "famish". The same could not be said of Shakespeare's first spectators. At the time *Coriolanus* was premiered, times had been hard, especially in the playwright's home county of Warwickshire. The so-called "Midlands Riots" during the early summer of 1607 had been touched off by a cycle of bad harvests and rampant inflation in food prices, exacerbated by illegal enclosure of common land. Peasants protested, but were brutally suppressed by local gentry – events whose repercussions were witnessed by Shakespeare, who spent some of 1608 in Stratford attending to his mother's funeral.

As a local landowner himself, it has been argued that the playwright must automatically have sided against the rioters. But *Coriolanus* makes that hard to believe. Trying to disperse the starving crowd (Shakespeare conflates his sources' two riots into one for dramatic impact), Menenius insists that there is simply no point in complaining. "For your wants, / Your suf-fering in this dearth," he begins,

> you may as well
> Strike at the heaven with your staves as lift them
> Against the Roman state, whose course will on
> The way it takes, cracking ten thousand curbs
> Of more strong link asunder than can ever
> Appear in your impediment.
>
> **[1.1.64–70]**

Protest is useless; the state simply rolls on regardless. Though Menenius's words have some-times been taken to imply that *Coriolanus* is a politically conservative play, what seems striking here is the way in which the crowd, desperately hungry, is being fobbed off with mere words – words guaranteeing that, far from being at the heart of the city, they have no say in how it is run.

---

*The whole dramatic moral of* Coriolanus *is, that those who have little shall have less, and that those who have much shall take all that others have left.*

William Hazlitt, writing in *The Examiner*, December 15, 1816

---

## The common file

Menenius's clumsy attempts to calm the crowd are upset by the sudden arrival of Caius Martius, the man whose downfall they are really after. His view of the plebs, though hardly palatable, is at least honest. "What would you have, you curs?", he demands,

He that trusts to you,
Where he should find you lions finds you hares,
Where foxes, geese. You are no surer, no,
Than is the coal of fire upon the ice,
Or hailstone in the sun. Your virtue is
To make him worthy whose offence subdues him,
And curse that justice did it. Who deserves greatness
Deserves your hate, and your affections are
A sick man's appetite, who desires most that
Which would increase his evil. He that depends
Upon your favours swims with fins of lead,
And hews down oaks with rushes.

[1.1.168–79]

Caius Martius's words colour what is an otherwise linguistically austere play. The view of Shakespeare's main source, an English translation of Plutarch's *Life* of Coriolanus, that Martius was "choleric and impatient" is made to seem a dangerous understatement here. Irascible and disdainful, Martius hates the crowd, but (in his terms at least) that makes him deserving of "greatness". The Romantic critic William Hazlitt fought against a lifetime's passionately held liberalism to admit that in *Coriolanus* "the language of poetry naturally falls in with the language of power", and indeed there is something almost hypnotic in this unstoppable raging against the mob. Among Shakespeare's heroes, Martius is the only one able to transform instatiable contempt into what seems, almost, like a virtue.

Caius Martius is the ultimate that Rome can offer. Plutarch describes how "valiantness was honoured in Rome above all other virtues", and in Martius's person we see the end result of that philosophy. Combining lofty aristocracy and effortless *machismo* with near-suicidal valour on the battlefield, Martius acquires his familiar title while performing a particularly

## KEY SOURCE   Plutarch's *Lives*

Directly after polishing off the chronicle-based English histories, Shakespeare turned towards the ancient past. His major source for the Roman plays (plus a good few others) was the collection of *Parallel Lives* by Greek historian L. Mestrius Plutarchus (c.50–120), known by the Anglicized name of **Plutarch** well before his biographical works reached English – which they did in 1579 in a big-boned translation, *The Lives of the Noble Grecians and Romans*, by diplomat **Sir Thomas North** (1523–c.1601). Not that things are quite as direct as that: North was working from a French version by his near-contemporary, scholar and bishop **Jacques Amyot** (1513–93), so the text that reached Shakespeare was at some distance from Plutarch's original.

Even so, North's *Lives* are one of Shakespeare's most fertile sources: in places, particularly in *Coriolanus* and *Antony and Cleopatra*, he quotes them almost directly. It's not hard to see why. Instead of writing broad-brush political history, Plutarch compiled compelling biographies of the most powerful men in the ancient world – the 23 that have survived include giants like **Alexander the Great**, **Theseus** and **Romulus** as well as **Coriolanus**, **Julius Caesar** and **Mark Antony**. As Amyot's celebrated preface to his readers explains, "an history is the very treasury of man's life, whereby the notable doings and sayings of men, and the wonderful adventures and strange cases … are preserved from the death of forgetfulness". What that meant in practice was history that did its utmost to make great men live again, and which exposes their vices along with their virtues. Thus it's from the gossipy (and frequently scandalized) Plutarch that we learn some juicy historical titbits: that Antony was once so drunk that he vomited over a council table; that Coriolanus "never left his mother's house" despite taking a wife; and that Caesar was first wooed by Cleopatra when she wrapped herself up in a mattress and had the bundle smuggled into his bedroom.

spectacular piece of derring-do outside the city of Corioles – hence "Coriolanus". Reborn in the fire and smoke of battle, he "cannot in the world", the smooth-tongued politician Cominius suggests, "be singly counterpoised". In war, Cominius continues, Coriolanus has no equal:

> His sword, death's stamp,
> Where it did mark, it took. From face to foot
> He was a thing of blood, whose every motion
> Was timed with dying cries. Alone he entered
> The mortal gate of th'city, which he, painted
> With shunless destiny, aidless came off,
> And with a sudden reinforcement struck
> Corioles like a planet.

**[2.2.107–14]**

Coriolanus is not human, but a machine "timed with dying cries"; nourished by battle, he is prepared to go on forever as if he were "a perpetual spoil", not even pausing to catch his breath.

The admiring portrait Cominius draws is, of course, horrendous: this unstoppable, blood-soaked warrior is a beast. "There is no more mercy in him than there is milk in the male tiger," (5.4.28–9) says Menenius. Still more shocking is the attitude of his mother, the fearsome Volumnia. As the women of Rome wait nervously for news of the battle at Corioles, Virgilia plaintively hopes that her husband has not been injured. It is all Volumnia can to do hold back her disdain: blood "more becomes a man," she scornfully replies, "than gilt his trophy."

> The breasts of Hecuba
> When she did suckle Hector looked not lovelier
> Than Hector's forehead when it spit forth blood
> At Grecian sword, contemning.

**[1.3.41–5]**

The warrior who becomes on the battlefield "a thing of blood" is eerily predicted in these grim words. Volumnia and her son are a kind of nightmare perversion of Roman values: the city's fetish for military prowess approves Coriolanus's brutality in war just as it encourages the kind of sadistic outlook voiced by his mother. Blood is what binds them, yet Volumnia describes not nurturing motherhood but graphic violence. A few moments later she describes approvingingly how Coriolanus's little son shows every sign of following after his father – by tormenting a butterfly, then ripping it apart with his teeth.

## O' me alone

*Coriolanus* depicts, again and again, the madness of life in Rome: though the people have genuine complaints with the way they are ruled, they allow themselves to be bought off with words (Shakespeare confuses his source, which clearly explains that as a result of the grain riots the people won political representation). Though Roman ideas about "valiantness" seem comprehensible enough, in Coriolanus and his mother they reach an apex of inhumanity. And though the crowd detests the man who calls them "curs", they find themselves persuaded that he deserves to wield power over them.

At the urging of politicians eager to capitalize on his military victories, Coriolanus agrees to stand for the Senate – the only catch being that, in order to be elected by the people, he must first beg for their "voices" (votes). A curious tussle ensues: though the commoners can decide whether to elect him or not, most seem to believe that it would be embarrassing to show "ingratitude" to a man who has done so much for their city. In doing so they reveal that they too are entangled in the ideology worshipped by Volumnia and Coriolanus: though Coriolanus personally despises the citizens, they are prepared to vote for him on condition that he shows them his battle scars. But Coriolanus is not even sure he can bring himself to go that far. The irony that he has become the very man he despises, the man who must "depend" on the crowd's "favours", is not lost on Coriolanus as he stands begging votes. "Better it is to die, better to starve," he bitterly exclaims, "than crave the hire which first we do deserve" (2.3.113–7). Longing for the solitary simplicities of the battlefield, Coriolanus simply cannot see the value in democracy.

Even so, he very nearly gets into office – until, that is, the tribunes Sicinius and Brutus succeed in convincing the crowd to turn against him and have him declared a traitor. Like Plutarch, they make much of his supposed "pride", but Shakespeare makes that view seem too simplistic. Coriolanus's reluctance to hear his "nothings monstered" by Cominius after Corioles demonstrates his personal humility; his refusal to wear the gown of humility exhibits his moral probity; his determination to avoid flattering the citizens and showing his scars underlines his loathing of hypocrisy. Yet somehow Coriolanus manages to transform these virtues into fatal weaknesses, undone by his inability to swerve from his own view of the world. Under attack from the Volscians, he is unflappable; under fire from his own people, he is unredeemable. Though he is accused of treachery and banished from the city, he decides he must banish Rome, not the other way around:

> You common cry of curs, whose breath I hate
> As reek o'th' rotten fens, whose loves I prize
> As the dead carcasses of unburied men
> That do corrupt my air: I banish you.

[3.3.124–7]

With those three magisterial words Coriolanus throws himself into the wilderness. Aristotle famously observed that a man who cannot live in the *polis* is either a beast or a god, and we know enough about Martius to sense that the "city of kites and crows" (4.5.42) outside Rome's walls is where he and the play have always been heading. The soldier who cried "O' me alone!" (1.7.76) at the gates of Corioles has, perhaps, nowhere else to go; and though he is not alone for long – he joins with his enemy Aufidius in order to get hold of his army – Coriolanus's terrible vengeance on Rome is a brooding solitary obsession.

As his and Aufidius's forces encamp outside Rome, ready to lay waste to it, the tribunes send out envoys desperately persuading Coriolanus to spare the city. But Coriolanus remains unmoved. "He does sit in gold," Cominius stammers, "his eye / Red as 'twould burn Rome" (5.1.63–4), and the only way the city's elders can see to save themselves is to send out the women closest to Coriolanus: Volumnia, Virgilia and Valeria, accompanied by Young Martius. Despite Coriolanus's insistence that they should not try "t'allay / My rages and revenges with your colder reasons" (5.3.85–6), over the course of an extraordinarily long and moving scene of pleading – in every way the climax of the play – he is eventually persuaded to back down. Though earlier he attempted to claim that he stood isolated, "As if a man were author of himself / And knew no other kin" (5.3.36–7), the hero is forced to recognize that his family cannot so easily be disowned. Yet his acceptance, painfully won, is also dark with foreboding. "O mother, mother!" he cries, holding her hand in an isolated symbol of empathy,

> What have you done? Behold, the heavens do ope,
> The gods look down, and this unnatural scene
> They laugh at. O my mother, mother, O!

You have won a happy victory to Rome;
But for your son, believe it, O believe it,
Most dangerously you have with him prevailed,
If not most mortal to him.

[5.3.183–90]

"But let it come," he concludes, and with that he knows that his fate is sealed. Though he gives in to Volumnia's pleas, her earlier lesson that "Thy valiantness was mine, thou sucked'st it from me" (3.2.128) proves more enduring.

By this time we know Aufidius jealously believes that Coriolanus is, as his own servants snigger, "the greater soldier" (4.5.170), and is plotting his rival's downfall. Characteristically, though, Coriolanus beats him to it. Angrily denying that the tears of his family – what Aufidius sneeringly calls "certain drops of salt" (5.6.95) – have weakened his resolve, Coriolanus angrily turns upon the Volscians once more. Aufidius's taunt that he is nothing but a "boy of tears" proves the end. "Cut me to pieces, Volsces," Coriolanus cries, commanding even his own death:

Stain all your edges on me. 'Boy'! False hound,
If you have writ your annals true, 'tis there
That, like an eagle in a dove-cote, I
Fluttered your Volscians in Corioles.
Alone I did it.

[5.6.112–6]

And the crowd, clutching knives, surges forward. In the crush of people, Coriolanus is "alone" one last time.

## Stage history and adaptations

*Coriolanus* might well have been the first Shakespeare play to be performed at his brand-new winter venue, the indoor **Blackfriars** playhouse. Intriguingly for a play so concerned with the will of the people, this means that it would have been viewed by a far more exclusive audience than at the South Bank amphitheatres. Early productions of this conspicuously noisy play would have been filled with music, and it is almost certain that **Richard Burbage**, the troupe's leading tragedian, took the role of Martius (given that he was about 40 at the time, scholars are divided as to whom played Volumnia, a boy or an older man).

The next we hear is of **Nahum Tate**'s Restoration rewrite, entitled *The Ingratitude of a Commonwealth*, premiered in 1681. The country was then embroiled in anti-Catholic witch-hunts centring on Charles II, and Tate's piece (as its title reveals) was an unapologetic piece of royalist propaganda; in the dedication the author confessed that "I chose rather to set the *Parallel* nearer to sight, then to throw it off at futher Distance". This was the first expressly topical makeover of the play, but it would hardly be the last. **John Dennis**'s version, *The Invader of His Country* – a patriotic (and anti-Catholic) manifesto – reached the stage in 1719. Less contentious were the Lincoln's Inn Fields performances the previous year, possibly with **James Quin** in the title role (plus some comic parts not in the original). Quin might also have played in another adaptation, *Coriolanus: or The Roman Matron*, which amalgamated sections of an original play by **James Thomson** with Shakespeare's at the behest of **Thomas Sheridan** (father of playwright Richard). Debuting in Dublin with Sheridan as Coriolanus and **Peg Woffington** as his mother in 1747, this version successfully transferred to Covent Garden.

"A thing of blood": Greg Hicks's impatient and energetic Caius Martius celebrates a gory victory at Corioles, in David Farr's 2002 production for the RSC.

After **David Garrick**'s flop a few years later, the play might have sunk without trace were it not for the efforts of **John Philip Kemble**, who detected in Coriolanus a fine match for his patrician, declamatory demeanour, and from 1789 until 1817 it was his signature role. Assisted by two-inch lifts in his sandals, Kemble presented a brooding, grave Martius with his celebrated sister **Sarah Siddons** as Volumnia – the only hiccup arriving with the French Revolution, which forced the conservative actor temporarily to suspend performances. The firebrand **Edmund Kean** failed to break Kemble's spell in 1820, lacking his stature (or his heels), and **William Charles Macready**, too, was criticized for lack of gravitas. **Samuel Phelps** gained plaudits at Sadler's Wells thirty years later, but mainly for the quality of his scenery.

In the States, meanwhile, actors were breathing fresh life into the role. US-born **Edwin Forrest** played Martius as a frontier hero in the 1860s (one commentator said he was "not so much patrician by status as by mind"), and **Tommaso Salvini** also toured in 1885 as a likeable and impetuous Coriolanus, performing in Italian while the rest of the cast spoke English. Less interested in novelty was **Frank Benson**, the first man to bring *Coriolanus* to Stratford-upon-Avon: his own boyish interpretation remained unchanged between 1893 and 1919, though the same could hardly be said for contemporary politics. A nod to the fearsome power of the mob was included in 1910, however, when they were instructed to lynch the Tribunes at the end of Act Four. By that time **Henry Irving**'s ill-fated staging had come and gone (Irving, 63 at the time, was too frail for the fight scenes), and the Victorian taste for grandiloquent Roman staging was on the wane. **William Bridges-Adams** had a particularly fierce crowd in 1933, but later did his best to ignore the uncomfortable parallels between *Coriolanus* and events on the continent – his 1939 production at Stratford was studiously Elizabethan.

Companies elsewhere in Europe had no such luxury, as **Hans Rothe** discovered when his translation of *Coriolanus* was banned by Goebbels, and the writer forced into exile in 1934 – whereupon the play itself became a primer for the Nazis, depicting the "true hero and *Führer*, Coriolanus, who desires to lead the misguided *Volk* to restoration" (as one writer eagerly put it). That Shakespeare's work could, however, equally be put to anti-fascist ends became clear in England in 1935, where a production at Manchester's **Royal Exchange** became an anti-Mussolini allegory complete with shiny uniforms and a Sicinius resembling Lenin. **Laurence Olivier** also had *Il Duce* in mind three years later under **Lewis Casson** at the Old Vic, and his death scene for **Peter Hall**'s famous Stratford version of 1959 deliberately aped the dictator's gruesome end, suspended from a meathook by cheering crowds. Olivier's spoilt Coriolanus, clearly in thrall to **Edith Evans**'s Volumnia, set the tone for many later English stagings (most obviously **Tyrone Guthrie**'s at the Nottingham Playhouse in 1963, which saw **John Neville**'s Martius in homoerotic friction with the Aufidius of **Ian McKellen**). **Alan Howard**'s narcissistic, macho and black-leather-clad Martius, directed by **Terry Hands** at Stratford in 1977, was the zenith – for some, the nadir – of this view of the play.

Again, though, continental audiences received more political resonance, notably with **Berthold Brecht**'s Marxist variation, *Coriolan*, which remained unfinished at his death but was premiered by the Berliner Ensemble in 1964. Employing theories already put into practice in **Giorgio Strehler**'s celebrated production in Milan in 1957, Brecht insisted that the play should be read as a tragedy not of the individual, but of the "individual's indispensability". **Anthony Hopkins**'s Coriolanus at London's National Theatre (1971) benefited not just from Brecht's ideas, but the direction of two of his collaborators, Manfred Wekwerth and Joachim Tenschert. **John Osborne**'s *A Place Calling Itself Rome*, though it appeared the same year, folded *Coriolanus* into the drab realities of 1970s Britain in a decidedly right-wing take on the play.

Since then, *Coriolanus*'s political relevance has never been more in fashion, not least in Eastern Europe, where it has had a lively life on stage. **Peter Hall**, returning to the play in 1984 at the National (with a magnetic **Ian McKellen** opposite **Irene Worth**'s matronly Volumnial), seized the opportunity to satirize post-Falklands England with an intriguing blend of medieval costuming and Thatcherite power-suits; while **William Gaskill**'s 1991 production for the Folger Shakespeare Company, in the wake of the Gulf War, had a Desert Storm-ish Coriolanus face down groups of Palestinian-like Volscians. **Tim Supple**'s 1992 production for **Kenneth Branagh**'s Renaissance Theatre Company at Chichester boasted not merely Branagh's supremely sneering Martius and **Judi Dench**'s haughty Volumnia ("a domestic tyrant with the heart and stomach of a lion", commented one reviewer) but also a mob of fifty extras to swell Shakespeare's crowd scenes. And though stylish postmodern interpretations have had their say – notably at the behest of **Stephen Berkoff**, who has staged *Coriolanus* three times, in 1988 with **Christopher Walken** in the lead – many directors have continued to confront the play's politics head-on. For **David Thacker** at the RSC's Swan Theatre in 1994 that meant draping a sketch of Delacroix's painting *Liberty Guiding the People* across the back of the stage (**Toby Stephens**, his Coriolanus, was just 24); for **David Farr** at the same venue in 2002 it involved recreating the distant territory of samurai Japan, where the pre-eminence of the warrior class remained unquestioned. In the latter production, **Greg Hicks** shone as a testy Martius – though perhaps more Roy Keane than Toshiro Mifune (see p.204).

*Coriolanus* has made surprisingly little impact on screen, with just the BBC's complete Shakespeare series (directed by **Elijah Moshinsky** with the pairing of **Alan Howard** and **Irene Worth** as Martius and mother) and a few educational versions making it into production.

# Screen

### Coriolanus
**A. Howard, I. Worth, J. Ackland; Elijah Moshinsky (dir.)**
UK, 1984 ▷ Ambrose Video (BBC) **DVD**

Alan Howard was a famous Coriolanus at Stratford in 1977, and so it was no surprise that he should be invited to take the role for the BBC. Elijah Moshinsky's production is more conservative in both tone and style than Terry Hands's at the RSC, however, and while Howard undeniably has plenty of vocal power this version makes him look mannered and struggles to support him effectively. Moshinsky's impressionistic screenwork – particularly in the battle scenes outside – might have looked effective on film, but on TV too often fails to have any real impact. Yet Irene Worth's Volumnia, another veteran of the Stratford production, brings a surprising warmth to her role and Joss Ackland's fruity Menenius is also worth watching out for. Ultimately, however, this version simply fails to catch fire. Recently rereleased in the US by educational publishers Ambrose Video.

# Audio

### Coriolanus
**P. Jesson, M. Yates, E. Hooper; Clive Brill (dir.)**
UK, 1998 ▷ Arkangel ⊙ ▦

Any *Coriolanus* needs a magnetic lead star, and in Paul Jesson's grizzled and wonderfully scornful hero Arkangel certainly has that. It also has a fine Volumnia (the splendid Marjorie Yates), a fittingly patrician Menenius (Ewan Hooper), vigorously characterized crowd scenes and some very gruesome battle noises. This recording likewise contains good performances from an unusually steely Virgilia (Sarah Woodward) and Martin Marquez's testy Aufidius (though his "northern" accent betrays a few cracks), and the scene in which Jesson's Coriolanus melts for the first and last time – there is no more moving silence in the canon than the moment when he gives in, and it's well-done here – is impressively affecting. What more could you want? (Possibly not the slightly bizarre brass band music which punctuates the action.)

# Editions

### Oxford Shakespeare
**R.B. Parker (ed.); 1994** ▷ Oxford UP

*Coriolanus* is lucky in having two excellent and recent major

editions, this and Lee Bliss's for New Cambridge (2000). Both are full, but Parker's is particularly recommendable because its editor spends so long experimenting with different ways of looking at the play – considering not only its sources, politics and historical background but the psychological and existential interpretations it has spawned. There is also valuable detail on *Coriolanus*'s style and a thematic study of its stage history (Bliss includes information on Thacker's 1994 RSC production, which appeared too late for Parker to mention it).

# Some criticism

### Disowning Knowledge
**Stanley Cavell; rev. 2003** ▷ Cambridge UP

Though not yet two decades old, *Disowning Knowledge in Six Plays of Shakespeare* already has classic status – and indeed has recently been updated with a new essay on *Macbeth*, taking the count up to seven. This book takes as its premise the notion that the philosophical scepticism manifest in the philosophy of the French thinker René Descartes receives some of its most intriguing exposition in Shakespeare. This leads Cavell into a brilliant development of what he terms the "sceptical problematic", touching *Hamlet*, *Lear*, *Othello* and *The Winter's Tale*. In *Coriolanus* Cavell argues that scepticism about politics is integral to the play, and that its multiple images of feeding and starvation present a Rome suffering from a "famine of words". Cavell can be a hard critic to live with – he is a philosopher by trade – and he makes few concessions to readerly comfort, but *Disowning Knowledge* is very much worth the effort.

### Suffocating Mothers
**Janet Adelman; 1992** ▷ Routledge

Janet Adelman's criticism is consistently engaging and challenging, rarely more so than in *Suffocating Mothers: Fantasies of maternal origin in Shakespeare's plays, "Hamlet" to "The Tempest"*. As her title implies, Adelman is deeply committed to psychoanalytic readings of these plays, stimulated by her observation that in his last dramatic works Shakespeare creates a series of powerful (and, yes, suffocating) mothers, figures who have been all but absent since his early work. *Coriolanus* is very much the seed-bed for Adelman's thesis, and in fact her brilliant piece on the hero's troubled masculine identity – one constructed in famously close symbiosis with his mother – dates all the way back to 1975, nearly twenty years before the book finally made it into print.

# Cymbeline

No one is quite sure why *Cymbeline*, one of Shakespeare's final comedies, was included in the list of "Tragedies" in the First Folio, but if it was a mistake it was at least fortuitous. Everyone who has written about – or seen – the play notices its haunting, bittersweet qualities, perhaps more truly tragicomic than anything else Shakespeare wrote. And though its historical background is esoteric and its plot famously labyrinthine – the playwright drew upon a hotchpotch of sources, something that irritated Samuel Johnson – in the right hands *Cymbeline* can be intensely moving as well as theatrically persuasive. The sequence of breathtaking revelations that brings this late comedy to an end reflects a Jacobean vogue for intricate plots (the play was put together in 1610 or 1611), but also demonstrates Shakespeare using the improvisatory qualities of his art more freely and brilliantly than ever before.

[ **DATE** ]   The play was seen by Simon Forman (an astrologer who witnessed several of Shakespeare's works), and it was certainly on the stage before September 1611. It was probably finished by autumn 1610 – shortly before *The Tempest*.

[ **SOURCES** ]   The play's historical substance, concerning Cunobelinus (Cymbeline), derives from Holinshed's *Chronicles*, the major source for his English history plays; while other details of *Cymbeline*'s notably knotty plot derive from Boccaccio's *Decameron* (1353) and the anonymous play *The Rare Triumphs of Love and Fortune* (1589).

[ **TEXTS** ]   The Folio of 1623 provides the sole authoritative text. It describes the heroine as "Imogen", but this is probably a misprint; the Oxford *Complete Works* (which this book follows) prefers "Innogen".

## Interpreting the play

A terse entry in Holinshed's *Chronicles*, describing the reign of "Kymbeline", seems to have caught Shakespeare's eye. At first glance it is difficult to see why: Cunobelinus (Cymbeline) was a relatively obscure British king who ruled over much of southern England at around the time Augustus Caesar was putting the finishing touches to his *Pax Romana*. As Holinshed tells it, about the most remarkable event to happen during Cunobelinus's reign was entirely unconnected to it: the birth of Christ. What history *Cymbeline* does retell is incidental to its main story, at least for most modern audiences – the trials and tribulations of the heroine Innogen (or Imogen, as she is spelt in the First Folio and elsewhere) and her new husband Posthumus Leonatus take centre-stage.

But in this patchwork of a play that story itself is not easy to follow. After Posthumus becomes convinced that Innogen has been unfaithful to him, she runs away in disguise to the forests of Wales, where she undergoes a bizarre series of confusions: first falling into a death-like slumber when she drinks a magic potion by mistake, then waking to discover a headless corpse wearing her husband's clothes. While in the country, she has been taken in by kindly hunters, who are in fact – though none of them yet knows it – her own brothers, stolen years earlier by a disgruntled courtier and raised in ignorance of their royal blood. The truth even-

## Major Characters & Synopsis

**Cymbeline**, King of Britain

Princess **Innogen**, Cymbeline's daughter (later disguised as **Fidele**)

**Posthumus Leonatus**, Innogen's husband, a poor gentleman

**Queen**, Cymbeline's second wife and Innogen's stepmother

Lord **Cloten**, the Queen's son by a former husband, Innogen's suitor

**Pisanio**, Posthumus's servant

**Cornelius**, a doctor

**Helen**, a lady attending Innogen

Two **Lords** attending Cloten

**Belarius**, a banished British lord (going under the name of **Morgan**)

**Guiderius** (known as **Polydore**) and **Arviragus** (known as **Cadwal**), Cymbeline's sons, stolen by Belarius

**Filario**, Posthumus's host in Rome

**Giacomo**, an Italian friend of Posthumus

Posthumus's other friends: a **Frenchman**, a **Dutchman** and a **Spaniard**

**Caius Lucius**, a Roman ambassador, later general of the Roman army

Various Romans: **Senators**, **Tribunes** and a **Captain**

**Philharmonus**, a soothsayer

Apparitions: **Jupiter**, King of the gods; **Sicilius Leonatus**, Posthumus's father; Posthumus's **Mother**; Posthumus's two **Brothers**

**ACT 1** By marrying Posthumus, Innogen has dismayed her father and angered her stepmother, who wanted her son, the doltish Cloten, to marry her. Posthumus is banished and heads for Rome, after exchanging tokens and vows of fidelity with Innogen. Abroad, Posthumus and his friends debate the relative chastity of their countrywomen, and Giacomo wagers Posthumus that he can seduce his wife. Arriving in Britain, Giacomo finds his attempts resisted by Innogen. The Queen, meanwhile, has obtained what she thinks is poison from the doctor, which she presents as a gift to Pisanio, persuading him it is a life-restoring medicine.

**ACT 2** Determined to win his bet, Giacomo asks Innogen to safeguard a large trunk, which he hides in, emerging as she sleeps and stealing her bracelet. Returning to Rome, he presents it to Posthumus as proof that she has slept with him.

**ACT 3** In Britain, Cymbeline has refused to pay the annual tribute to Rome; the Roman ambassador Lucius responds by declaring war. Meanwhile, Pisanio has received a letter from his master telling him to kill Innogen, but informs her instead. Horrified, she begs him to go through with it, but he persuades her to disguise herself as a man and travel to Rome in Lucius's company. In the Welsh countryside, Belarius is out with his two sons (actually Cymbeline's sons, stolen in infancy to avenge Belarius's banishment) when a hungry Innogen/Fidele appears. Back at court, her absence has been noticed, and Cloten decides to hunt her down.

**ACT 4** While out hunting, Belarius and his "sons" meet Cloten and kill him after he challenges them. Innogen, meanwhile, feeling unwell, takes the Queen's "medicine" given her by Pisanio, and falls into a death-like slumber. Assuming she is dead, Belarius's "sons" place her alongside Cloten's headless corpse. She awakens to what she thinks is her husband's body (Cloten is wearing Posthumus's clothes), and despairingly concludes that she has been betrayed. In the meantime, the Romans have invaded. Lucius comes across the mourning Innogen and takes her into his service.

**ACT 5** Persuaded that Innogen is dead, Posthumus repents and joins the British side; disguised as a peasant, he saves Giacomo (who fails to recognize him). Belarius and his "sons" rescue Cymbeline and reverse a British defeat. But Posthumus wishes to die, and dresses as a Roman before being captured. In prison, he has a vision of his dead family, and of the god Jupiter, who leaves a mysterious message. With the British victorious, Belarius and others are rewarded by the King. After news arrives that the Queen is dead and her evil exposed, Lucius, Innogen/Fidele, Giacomo and Posthumus are brought in as prisoners. Seeing Giacomo, Innogen asks about his ring and he reveals that he cheated Posthumus out of it. Pisanio then recognizes Innogen, before Belarius reveals his own identity and those of Cymbeline's sons. Embracing them, Cymbeline decides to resume the payment of Roman tribute as Jupiter's words, prophesying peace, are decoded.

tually outs when all (Posthumus included) are drawn back to Cymbeline's court, and Shakespeare contrives a jaw-dropping finale in which a captivating sequence of revelations and reunions are plucked, hair-breadth, from disaster.

## I'th' eye

To try and wrest kitchen-sink realism from the romance world of *Cymbeline* is obviously a lost cause. Not for nothing has the play frequently been compared to fairy tales such as *Snow-White* and *Goldilocks*, and indeed Cymbeline's cackling Queen (she has no other name) has more than a whiff of Wicked Stepmother. Angling for her moronic son Cloten to seize her stepdaughter from the "poor but worthy" Leonatus, she tries to persuade Innogen that "you shall not find me, daughter, / After the slander of most stepmothers, / Evil-eyed" (1.1.71–3). But Innogen, the Doctor and the audience know that to be false. "I do not like her," the Doctor mutters just out of earshot,

In 1786 the publisher John Boydell planned an edition of Shakespeare to be illustrated by the leading artists of the day. This engraving, after a painting by Richard Westall, shows a scene from Act Three of *Cymbeline* – Innogen outside the cave of Belarius.

> She doth think she has
> Strange ling'ring poisons. I do know her spirit,
> And will not trust one of her malice with
> A drug of such damned nature.

**[1.5.33–6]**

With "poisonous compounds" the Queen intends to murder Innogen and her husband's servant Pisanio, but she is (for the moment) foiled: the "drugs" Cornelius supplies merely tranquillize, not kill. As *Cymbeline* begins, this cheerful resistance to evil seems built into the plot: though the King is furious that his daughter has flouted his wishes by marrying below her station, he has done little to prevent it. Likewise, Cloten is presented as too dim-witted to offer much of a threat. Continually attended by a brace of lords – one sycophantic, the other overtly rude – Cymbeline's stepson is simply "Too bad for bad report" (1.1.17), so hopeless as not to be worth the effort of describing.

But these hard outlines between characters – the wicked queen and her idiot son, the virtuous daughter, the constant husband – begin to blur as soon as Posthumus is banished from Cymbeline's court. His departure seems to do something to the play's optics, hinting that things will change and shift beyond all recognition. First to be deceived is Posthumus himself. No sooner has he met his companions in Italy than Giacomo is goading him into betting on his "unparagoned" and absent wife's fidelity, a segment of the plot that takes its cue from Boccaccio's courtly compendium of tales, the *Decameron* (see p.5). Bragging that "strange fowl light upon neighbouring ponds" (1.4.87), Giacomo successfully riles Posthumus with his insistence that he cannot fail to seduce Innogen. Posthumus's sealing of the bargain strays into the kind of misogyny only too familiar from *The Winter's Tale*. "Only thus far you shall answer," he addresses his rival:

> If you make your voyage upon her and give me directly to understand you have prevailed, I am no further your enemy; she is not worth our debate.
>
> **[1.4.154–7]**

Fortunately, though, Innogen proves herself less willing to be misled than her husband – at least initially. When Giacomo's attempts to sway Innogen with flattery fall on stony ground, he tries a nastier trick, hinting that Posthumus himself has been unfaithful to her. "Are men mad?" he wonders, apparently commenting on their inability to value beauty (and by extension Posthumus's insanity in abandoning his wife):

> It cannot be i'th' eye—for apes and monkeys,
> 'Twixt two such shes, would chatter this way and
> Contemn with mows the other; nor i'th' judgement,
> For idiots in this case of favour would
> Be wisely definite; nor i'th' appetite—
> Sluttery, to such neat excellence opposed,
> Should make desire vomit emptiness,
> Not so allured to feed.
>
> **[1.6.40–7]**

Giacomo is coldly calculating here, trying to perplex Innogen while also intimating that she has been betrayed. In this cruel trick language itself becomes twisted almost beyond recognition, with the thrust of Giacomo's words (that the "eye" of the absent Posthumus prefers the beauty of "shes" other than his own wife, even though "apes and monkeys" or "idiots" would make the right choice) all but disappearing behind sinister insinuation.

In the event, however, Innogen proves more resistant than Giacomo had hoped, and after realizing that his own coarse attempts to win her are foundering, he switches tack, claiming merely to be testing whether her "affiance / Were deeply rooted" (1.6.164–5). Innogen is immediately won over, and falls for his final ploy, agreeing to keep in her chamber a large trunk, supposedly containing a "present for the Emperor" but in fact harbouring Giacomo himself. As soon as she is asleep, he creeps out – the first of the play's many daring moments of visual staging. Reaching for her bracelet (a token from Posthumus), he cackles gleefully that they are both undone. "'Tis mine," he whispers,

> and this will witness outwardly,
> As strongly as the conscience does within,
> To th' madding of her lord. On her left breast
> A mole, cinque-spotted, like the crimson drops
> I'th' bottom of a cowslip. Here's a voucher
> Stronger than ever law could make. This secret
> Will force him think I have picked the lock and ta'en
> The treasure of her honour.
>
> **[2.2.35–42]**

This too-innocent visible evidence – not just the bracelet but the marks on Innogen's own body, voyeuristically noted down – will condemn her to Posthumus. It is difficult not to think, as Shakespeare himself must have thought, back to the early poem *The Rape of Lucrece* and another guiltless heroine who is undone when a man forces himself into her private chamber.

# Mortal joy

Posthumus's inability to trust his feelings rather than his eyes, proves Innogen's undoing. It also introduces another strand of deceit in a play that braids them tightly together. Inventing for her a sequence of "faults" ("For even to vice," he rages, women "are not constant" (2.5.29–30), he sends one letter to her claiming his undying love while simultaneously arranging for Pisanio to murder her in cold blood. But unlike his master Pisanio is unable to lie – he is the closest the play has to a hero – and reveals the truth to Innogen. Hit hard, she responds in pain. "Come, fellow, be thou honest," she cries,

> Do thy master's bidding. When thou seest him,
> A little witness my obedience. Look,
> I draw the sword myself. Take it, and hit
> The innocent mansion of my love, my heart.

**[3.4.64–8]**

Innogen's urgent wish for death does not prevail (Pisanio finds that he cannot go through with the suicide), and tragedy is for the moment averted, but Innogen opts to undergo a metaphorical death instead – "forgetting" her womanly identity and exchanging her clothes, like many a Shakespearian heroine before her, for those of a young man, in order to flee to Wales. The touching pseudonym she chooses, "Fidele", means "the faithful one".

> *In Act V of* Cymbeline *there is a* Vision, *a* Masque, *and a* Prophecy, *which interrupt the Fable without the least necessity, and unmeasurably lengthen this act. I think it plainly foisted in afterwards for mere show, and apparently not of* Shakespeare.
>
> Alexander Pope, *Works of William Shakespeare* (1725)

Yet death proves difficult to charm away, and before long makes its presence more heavily felt. After reaching Wales, Innogen comes across, then is adopted by, a group of men living wild in the forest yet, like Duke Senior and his companions in *As You Like It*, with all the dignity of gentlemen. The two youths, Guiderius and Arviragus, bristle with "sparks of nature" (3.3.79), but neither is aware of their royal identity. This deception also entangles Innogen – herself in disguise, she has no idea that they are her brothers – and the confusion only intensifies when, feeling unwell, she takes the draught that Pisanio had been given by her evil stepmother earlier in the play. In a nightmarish echo of her previous slumber, she immediately falls into a death-like sleep, and Guiderius and Arviragus are left to conclude, sorrowfully, that their newfound companion has died. They address her silent body with one of Shakespeare's simplest but most moving lyrics. "Fear no more the heat o'th' sun," Guiderius sings,

> Nor the furious winter's rages.
> Thou thy worldly task hast done,
> Home art gone and ta'en thy wages.
> Golden lads and girls all must,
> As chimney-sweepers, come to dust.

**[4.2.259–64]**

Yet of course Innogen/Fidele still has much of her "worldly task" to do, and the deathly still-ness that her brothers invoke is yet, fortunately, far in the distance.

Though she is alive, Innogen – with a distant husband still convinced that she has betrayed him – has not been granted peace of mind, still less come "home". The sight that greets her when she awakes, that of a blood-spattered, headless trunk wearing her husband's clothes, could not be more horrible, and makes a ghastly mockery of her desire to be reunited with him. "But soft, no bedfellow!", she starts, lifting the funeral garlands laid by Guiderius and Arviragus from her body,

> These flowers are like the pleasures of the world,
> This bloody man the care on't. I hope I dream,
> For so I thought I was a cavekeeper,
> And cook to honest creatures. But 'tis not so.
> 'Twas but a bolt of nothing, shot of nothing,
> Which the brain makes of fumes. Our very eyes
> Are sometimes like our judgements, blind. Good faith,
> I tremble still with fear; but if there be
> Yet left in heaven as small a drop of pity
> As a wren's eye, feared gods, a part of it!
> The dream's here still. Even when I wake it is
> Without me as within me; not imagined, felt.

**[4.2.297–309]**

Touching the body, Innogen "feels" what she fears: that it is Posthumus lying next to her. Shakespeare condenses an almost untenable mixture of emotions into one theatrical moment. Cloten had dressed in Posthumus's clothes in order to rape her, but, challenging Guiderius to a fight, met an aptly ignoble end. Now Innogen "dreams" (and she will believe it until the play's final few minutes) that the body next to her is her husband's. Stroking his leg, his hand, then grotesquely smearing herself with his blood, she is fooled – like Posthumus himself before her – by the evidence of her "very eyes", a mistaking that has been made all the more likely in performance by using the same actor to play both Posthumus and Cloten. Observing all this, Shakespeare's audiences may well feel – the piercing intensity of this instant makes the cliché seem fresh – that they don't know whether to laugh or cry.

As so often in these late romances, however, recognition is allowed to work itself out, albeit via more jack-knifing of the plot. Having been discovered by Roman soldiers led by Lucius, Innogen invents a story that the body is her master's, "a very valiant Briton" (4.2.371), and begs to be taken into Roman service. Posthumus, meanwhile, has discovered Giacomo's treachery and announced his intention to be killed in battle. "I'll die / For thee, O Innogen," he swears, in an unknowing echo of her earlier suicide attempt,

> even for whom my life
> Is every breath a death; and, thus unknown,
> Pitied nor hated, to the face of peril
> Myself I'll dedicate.

**[5.1.25–9]**

In an apt image of *Cymbeline* itself, that "peril" brings Posthumus close to death but also, ulti-mately, to happiness. Captured by the British forces, he falls asleep in prison, and with breathtaking bravura Shakespeare dramatizes the vision that appears in his hero's sleep. As "solemn music" plays, the stage directions instruct,

> *Enter, as in an apparition, Sicilius Leonatus (father to Posthumus, an old man), attired like a warrior, leading in his hand an ancient matron, his wife, and mother to Posthumus, with music before them.*
>
> *Then, after other music, follows the two young Leonati, brothers to Posthumus, with wounds as they died in the wars. They circle Posthumus round as he lies sleeping*

**[5.5.123 SD]**

These instructions – taken word for word from the Folio text and behind it Shakespeare's manuscript – have given directors free reign to come up with some impressive theatrics, and from *Cymbeline*'s first days in the theatre the apparition will most likely have been spectacular. As Posthumus slumbers on, it becomes even more so: after his dead family complete their round of song, they call on the god Jupiter to reverse Posthumus's "miseries". And when Jupiter himself appears, he announces that "Your low-laid son our godhead will uplift. / His comforts thrive, his trials well are spent" (5.5.197–8).

Jupiter's words indicate that *Cymbeline* will end in joy rather than pain. Even so, it nearly fails to get there. Posthumus is on the point of being executed by the Britons when news arrives that he is to be freed and taken to Cymbeline's court instead. Innogen, meanwhile, is still in disguise and when she too finds herself there it seems that the lovers will be reunited at last. But the grief-stricken Posthumus, thinking that Fidele scorns his sorrow, lashes out – and it is only when Pisanio exclaims, "O my lord Posthumus, / You ne'er killed Innogen till now" that anyone realizes what is going on. "Does the world go round?" exclaims Innogen's father, dumbstruck:

> If this be so, the gods do mean to strike me
> To death with mortal joy.

**[5.6.232–5]**

Fortunately the gods intend no such thing and, as *Cymbeline* comes to a close, death works finally in the service of good. The wicked Queen has died, Cloten is gone, and as Innogen comes round in her father's arms (a reunion cruelly denied Lear), it only waits for her brothers to be revealed.

## Stage history and adaptations

Records of *Cymbeline*'s history in the theatre begin soon after it was written: Simon Forman, doctor and astrologer, saw the play performed around 1610 and noted it down in his diary. He was particularly impressed by the scene in which Giacomo leaps out of the trunk, though did not record where he saw it – possibly at the **Blackfriars** theatre, where Shakespeare will have been able to use stage machinery for the magical descent of Jupiter. Aptly for a play influenced by Stuart masque, *Cymbeline* was performed at **Whitehall** on New Year's Day, 1634, for Charles I, who approved of it despite its portrayal of a scheming, manipulative Queen – a charge often levelled at his wife, who didn't attend.

*Cymbeline* appears to have disappeared from the stage until 1682, when it surfaced in an adaptation by **Thomas D'Urfey** entitled *The Injured Princess, or The Fatal Wager*. To suit the taste of the age, D'Urfey made Innogen a purely passive victim while Posthumus kills the rakish Giacomo in revenge. Another adaptation by **William Hawkins** arrived in 1759, recast in neoclassical fashion, but Shakespeare's text had reappeared on stage back in 1746 and with **David Garrick** came once more into favour. After playing Posthumus first in 1761, Garrick came to specialize in the role, and his successor **John Philip Kemble** acted it from 1785 onwards. Kemble's Innogen was his formidable sister **Sarah Siddons**, marking a trend which would come to dominate the next era: the age of headlining heroines.

The American actress **Nancy Hallam** had scored great success as Innogen (her talent was captured in an impressive painting by Charles Willson Peele) as early as the 1770s, but from 1837 the British **Helen Faucit** came to epitomize the role during the thirty-odd years she played it. Faucit's characterization was placid and virtuous (she was described by a Victorian commentator as "the purest and most womanly of Shakespeare's women … who includes among her virtues aptitude for cookery"), too much so for some. **Adelaide Neilson**, who played Innogen in 1872, presented a more headstrong interpretation when she toured the role in the United States. By the time that the great **Ellen Terry** came to play the part in 1896, aged nearly 50, she had resolved to present a less angelic and more womanly Innogen – a decision influenced by George Bernard Shaw, who corresponded with her throughout rehearsals. Nevertheless, according to Harley Granville-Barker, when Terry spoke, her voice "seemed to fill the Lyceum Theatre with dancing sunbeams". Her Giacomo was **Henry Irving**, the latest in a line of actors from **William Charles Macready** onwards to have seen star potential in the play's antihero rather than in Posthumus.

This production notwithstanding, *Cymbeline* waned in popularity during the latter half of the nineteenth century and it would not be put on in a major British production until 1923, at **Barry Jackson**'s Birmingham Rep. Like his *Hamlet* two years later, this scandalized audiences by opting for modern dress, though **Cedric Hardwicke**'s Giacomo was universally loved by the critics. Innovation continued in 1937, with **Ben Iden Payne**'s Stratford production, which boasted sets based on Jacobean masques and gained good reviews. But it would be another two decades before *Cymbeline* appeared again in Shakespeare's birthplace, this time at the behest of the young **Peter Hall**, who teamed up with Italian painter **Lila de Nobili** to present a visually spectacular production (and one that used an uncut text). Hall's Innogen was **Peggy Ashcroft**, both experienced in the role – she had played it at the Old Vic 25 years

"Hang there like fruit": Posthumus (Damian Lewis) clutches the swooning Innogen (Joanne Pearce) in the dying moments of Adrian Noble's RSC *Cymbeline* (1997).

earlier – and then at the peak of her career. Another Stratford production appeared in 1962 but its director, **William Gaskill**, eschewed Hall's fairytale setting for a set clothed entirely in white in which **Vanessa Redgrave** played a typically impetuous Innogen. A similarly pared-down staging dominated **Jean Gascon**'s production eight years later at Stratford, Ontario.

Other directions have proved less successful: **John Barton**'s attempt to politicize *Cymbeline* at the RSC in 1974, drawing on British angst about the oil crisis and the EEC, flopped (Barton also attempted to readjust the play by introducing a narrator and cutting around a thousand lines). **Robin Phillips**'s decision to set the play in the 1940s at Stratford, Ontario in 1986 won points for novelty; while **Bill Alexander**'s production two years later gained from the intimacy of the RSC's The Other Place and had, in **Harriet Walter**, an Innogen of startling emotional immediacy. In fact 1988 proved something of an *annus mirabilis* for *Cymbeline*, with Alexander's production at Stratford running concurrently with a similarly small-scale version at the National Theatre, directed by **Peter Hall**. Hall's version focused on the tension between **Geraldine James**'s strong-willed Innogen and **Peter Woodward**'s powerful Giacomo. Although Hall opted to put his cast in Jacobean costume, the Cottesloe stage was dominated by a stylized zodiac from which Jupiter descended in full glory.

More recent versions have likewise stressed *Cymbeline*'s eclecticism: **JoAnne Akalaitis**'s production at New York's Newman Theatre in 1989 was inspired by surrealism, while closer to the present day **Bartlett Sher**'s 2001 staging, once more at The Other Place in Stratford, freely blended cowboys and samurai warriors. The 1997 RSC production, directed by **Adrian Noble** in an Oriental-ish setting, faced hostility for his decision to use a narrator to make sense of the plot, but his cast – which included **Damian Lewis**'s Posthumus, **Joanne Pearce**'s Innogen and **Edward Petherbridge**'s King – received praise. The Bankside Globe's fluid production from summer 2001, starkly staged in white by **Mike Alfreds**, attempted to find coherence in a play all too often criticized for lacking it and employed a cast of just six, among them **Mark Rylance**'s impressive Posthumus/Cloten/Cornelius. The most recent mainstream British production, directed by **Dominic Cooke**, was acclaimed as one of the high points of the 2003 season: **Emma Fielding**'s Innogen, **Daniel Evans**'s Posthumus and **Anton Lesser**'s Giacomo shared plaudits for an emotionally rich account of the play in which, according to the *Times Literary Supplement*, "amazement" seized the audience.

*Cymbeline* has yet to make it anywhere near a film set, but various TV versions do exist. The one generally regarded as the best, and a high-quality addition to the BBC/Time-Life series, was screened in 1982 under **Elijah Moshinsky**'s direction; **Helen Mirren** and **Michael Pennington** played the lovers.

## Screen

### Cymbeline

**H. Mirren, M. Pennington, R. Johnson; Elijah Moshinsky (dir.)**
UK, 1982 ▷ Ambrose Video (BBC) [DVD]

Making sense of *Cymbeline*'s many locations – never mind its plot – is a hard task, and probably the most difficult thing for any TV version to bring off. In interior scenes the BBC does well to capture the play's sometimes claustrophobic atmosphere (particularly so at the elaborately Jacobean court of Cymbeline), and the moments at which it excels are also intimate in scale: Helen Mirren's quiet and touching Innogen reaches a moving climax in her awakening scene, grotesquely smearing Cloten's blood on her face. Other moments are less successful: the appearance of Michael Hordern's Jupiter to Michael Pennington's earnest Posthumus makes little attempt to astound, while the play's conclusion struggles to keep up the intensity – despite Richard Johnson's excellent Cymbeline. Recently rereleased in the US by Ambrose Video Publishing.

## Audio

### Cymbeline

**S. Thompson, B. Porter, J. Shepherd; Clive Brill (dir.)**
UK, 1998 ▷ Arkangel ⊙ 📼

One of the distinguishing features of this *Cymbeline* is that the cast speak wonderfully clearly – entirely necessary when the verse is as knotty as this. Sophie Thompson's steely Innogen especially shines, and although Ben Porter's Posthumus is slightly underpowered the scenes between them are effectively done. Stephen Mangan adds welcome comic detail as an impressively doltish Cloten, and Suzanne Bertish is delightful as his cackling mother. The final scene is (perhaps inevitably) baffling, however, and the "solemn music" of the play's masque – along with Jupiter's descent – has the unintended effect of provoking giggles rather than wonder.

# Editions

## Oxford Shakespeare
### Roger Warren (ed.); 1998 ▷ Oxford UP

Co-editor with Stanley Wells on the excellent Oxford *Twelfth Night* (see p.378), Warren does an equally fine job with this later and more troubling comedy, *Cymbeline*'s most recent major edition to date. His introduction works through various ways of seeing the play, confronting its sudden changes of gear head-on with some well-chosen words on its Jacobean theatrical fireworks, and also spending welcome time discussing its role as a historical play. Warren devotes a tightly argued appendix to his decision to reverse the Folio's "Imogen" and "Iachimo" in favour of "Innogen" and "Giacomo".

## Prefaces to Shakespeare
### Harley Granville-Barker; 2 vols, 1946–47 ▷ B.T. Batsford / Princeton UP [o/p]

Granville-Barker's *Prefaces* to various Shakespeare plays were put together over a 25-year period but built upon a theatrical career that began in the final years of the previous century. Heavily influenced by William Poel (see p.475), Granville-Barker has claims to be England's most inspirational prewar director, responsible for a succession of revolutionary productions that changed the face of British theatre and redefined approaches to Shakespeare. The *Prefaces* began

life as introductions to a multi-volume edition of the plays that subsequently foundered, and as a consequence they were published independently. They are all terrific pieces, sometimes eccentric but never dull, and despite their dated scholarly views they have an unnerring habit of illuminating what the plays are really like to experience and stage. *Cymbeline* benefits from Granville-Barker's practical wisdom (particularly his advice on speaking the verse), but so do all the other plays he covers: *Hamlet*, *Lear*, *The Merchant*, *Antony and Cleopatra* (volume 1) and *Othello*, *Coriolanus*, *Romeo and Juliet*, *Julius Caesar* and *Love's Labour's Lost* (volume 2).

# Some criticism

## Shakespeare: The Last Phase
### Derek Traversi; rev. 1965 ▷ Bodley Head / Stanford UP [o/p]

A classic study, Traversi's *Last Phase* was an early attempt to see Shakespeare's last comedies not merely as a group, but connected by deep thematic links that make it "impossible to regard any of them, even the greatest as mere isolated masterpieces". For this reason the book is as recommendable on *The Winter's Tale* and *The Tempest* as it is on *Cymbeline* (curiously, Traversi is slightly less persuaded by the value of *Pericles* within his larger scheme), and the insights it offers are common to all the last plays: a sensitive awareness of the mythic structures underlining their reawakenings and recognitions; a close attention to the rough power of Shakespeare's verse; and a conviction that they exist within a Christian framework. This connective approach is especially pertinent to *Cymbeline*, whose fragmentary qualities have often offended critics.

# Hamlet

The longest of Shakespeare's plays, *Hamlet* is arguably also his very greatest: a pinnacle of Renaissance culture and a forerunner of modernity. Yet in separating *Hamlet* off from the rest of Shakespeare's works is to do it a disservice: this is a sublime work of intellect and art, the most speculative piece of writing Shakespeare ever produced, but it is also the most brilliant – and brilliantly self-aware – of plays. So lengthy in its most extended version that it is near-impossible to perform uncut, *Hamlet* presents such challenges to its performers that it's been thought that Shakespeare was writing simply to please himself. Even if that were so, this product of the most fruitful and inventive period of his career is a theatrical masterpiece, a thrilling drama of revenge and politics that has never been off the stage since it was written. Authored on the cusp of the seventeenth century, the play translates a story of brutal Norse revenge into a sophisticated Renaissance setting. But it is perhaps in the character of Hamlet, the most compelling and fascinating – yet ultimately unknowable – of Shakespeare's creations that *Hamlet* comes most alive. As the Romantic critic William Hazlitt commented, "it is we who are Hamlet", and audiences and readers have never relinquished their fascination with the Prince over the four centuries he has been in existence.

[**DATE**]  Hard to be precise about. The play was registered to be printed in July 1602, but on internal evidence probably postdates *Julius Caesar* (1599); one version was on the stage by 1600.

[**SOURCES**]  An earlier play of the same name (dubbed the "ur-*Hamlet*" by critics) was apparently a key source, but has since disappeared. Another might be the sixteenth-century French writer François de Belleforest's version of the Norse tale of Amleth – which appears in Saxo Grammaticus's *Historiae Danicae* (c.1200) – but it's not clear whether Shakespeare had access to this version or not.

[**TEXTS**]  One version of the play (Q1) was printed in 1603, but seems to have been assembled from memory – most likely by an actor playing bit parts (see p.68). Another (Q2) appeared in 1604, longer and more authoritative. Yet another version (F1) is included in the 1623 Folio, possibly revised by Shakespeare.

## Interpreting the play

Perhaps fittingly for a man whose thoughts echo down Western culture, Hamlet's roots reach back to the cradle of the middle ages. Scholars have been able to trace his story to twelfth-century Scandinavia and a history of the Danish people by a writer known as Saxo Grammaticus. Though even earlier sources have been unearthed, Saxo's Norse saga is the first to treat Prince Amleth, as he is called, as a hero – albeit one less urbane than his Shakespearian ancestor ("Amleth" means "the stupid one"). The tale Saxo tells could hardly be described as sophisticated: Prince Amleth's father, Horwendil, is publicly killed by his jealous brother, the evocatively named Feng, who then marries his erstwhile wife Gerutha. The child Amleth craves revenge, but is too young to act, so decides that the only way he has any chance of gaining it is to pretend to lose his wits, thus convincing Feng that he offers no threat. A suc-

## Major Characters & Synopsis

**Prince Hamlet** of Denmark, son of King Hamlet and Gertrude

**Horatio**, a student friend of Hamlet

**Ghost** of King Hamlet

**King Claudius** of Denmark, King Hamlet's brother

**Gertrude**, King Hamlet's widow and Claudius's wife

**Polonius**, a lord

**Laertes**, Polonius's son

**Ophelia**, Polonius's daughter

**Reynaldo**, Polonius's servant

**Rosencrantz** and **Guildenstern**, old friends of Prince Hamlet

**Valtemand**, **Cornelius** and **Osric**, courtiers

**Francisco**, **Barnardo** and **Marcellus**, soldiers

**Clowns**, a gravedigger and his companion

**Fortinbras**, Prince of Norway

**ACT 1**  At Elsinore castle, the ghost of the recently deceased King is confronted by soldiers. At court, Hamlet – in mourning for his father's sudden death – expresses his disgust that his widowed mother has married his uncle Claudius. Alerted by his friend Horatio, Hamlet meets his father's ghost, who tells of his murder by Claudius and demands revenge. Meanwhile, Laertes, who is leaving to study in France, warns his sister Ophelia not to trust the Prince, who has apparently tried to woo her; their father Polonius agrees.

**ACT 2**  Hamlet decides to feign madness in order to investigate his father's death, and the whole court is thrown into confusion – Ophelia is stunned, Polonius thinks it is because Ophelia has rejected him, and the King and Queen hire Rosencrantz and Guildenstern to spy on him. When the news arrives that a company of actors is about to arrive at Elsinore, Hamlet sees an opportunity. He will get them to perform a play, *The Mousetrap*, one scene of which closely resembles his father's murder, and with Horatio observe Claudius's reaction.

**ACT 3**  Listening in on a meeting between Hamlet and Ophelia – at which Hamlet seems utterly unhinged – Claudius plots to send him to England. The court gathers to watch the players, and at the moment where the murder is re-enacted Claudius starts up in shock and the play is abandoned; Horatio and Hamlet agree that he must be guilty. On the way to speak with Gertrude, Hamlet sees Claudius praying for forgiveness, but puts off killing him. He angrily accuses Gertrude of unfaithfulness, and when he hears Polonius hiding behind the screen in her room, stabs him to death.

**ACT 4**  Realizing the danger he is in, Claudius sends Hamlet to England with Rosencrantz and Guildenstern, but arranges for him to be killed on arrival. Ophelia has meanwhile been driven mad by her father's death, and Laertes has rushed back from Paris; when news arrives that Hamlet has escaped his companions and is returning to Denmark, Claudius promises to help Laertes kill the Prince. Laertes's anger intensifies when it transpires that Ophelia has drowned herself.

**ACT 5**  On his way back to court, Hamlet meets two gravediggers. When Ophelia's funeral procession arrives, Hamlet initially hides before suddenly revealing himself, to Laertes's fury. Claudius announces that the two should duel, but (unbeknown to Hamlet) arranges for the tip of Laertes's sword to be poisoned. He also prepares a back-up plan by poisoning Hamlet's wine. The duel begins: Laertes wounds Hamlet but they exchange swords and Laertes is also cut. Events spiral out of control as it becomes clear that Gertrude has unwittingly drunk from Hamlet's cup and has been poisoned. The dying Laertes blames Claudius and reveals their plan, and Hamlet finally stabs his uncle before himself collapsing. The grisly scene closes as the invading army of Fortinbras, a Norwegian prince who has arrived to restore rightful rule to Denmark, enters. He arranges for Hamlet to have a full military funeral.

cession of close shaves and plot convolutions notwithstanding, Amleth makes it through to adulthood and puts into practice his long-held yearning – with the added twist that he succeeds in running Feng through with the King's own sword. This is politics as the Norse sagas understand the term: brutal, violent, and with power and revenge side by side.

Shakespeare might have come into contact with this tale in a number of ways, but one of the most fascinating possibilities is that the playwright had a personal connection with the windswept castle of Kronborg, near Elsinore (or Helsingør) in Denmark, where he opts to set his play. A troupe of English actors – among them several of Shakespeare's closest colleagues – toured the country and played Kronborg in the late 1580s, and it's more than possible that Shakespeare's interest in writing about Denmark began from hearing stories about his companions' experiences there. At any rate it's unlikely that he read the story of Amleth in the twelfth-century original: his Hamlet is rather more a Renaissance man.

A version of Saxo's saga was translated by the sixteenth-century poet François de Belleforest, but even if Shakespeare didn't have access to this version (or the French to read it), by the early 1590s a play about Hamlet was being performed by the playwright's own company. Though the text has not survived, critics are confident that a drama they call the "ur-*Hamlet*" (the German *ur* meaning "original") was one of a number of gory revenge tragedies of the period, among them Thomas Kyd's *Spanish Tragedy* and Shakespeare's own *Titus Andronicus*. The reputation of its illustrious ancestor notwithstanding, the ur-*Hamlet* itself (possibly Kyd's handiwork) was not well-reviewed by contemporaries. The writer Thomas Lodge had nothing but scorn for it in 1596, describing a play in which a white-bearded ghost – sounding like nothing so much as an "oyster-wife" on the streets of London – screeched, "Hamlet, revenge". Not, perhaps, the most stimulating of origins.

## Remember me

Even so, it's perhaps fitting that *Hamlet*, a story at least four centuries old by the time Shakespeare came to it, constantly finds itself shuttling between different versions of the past. The play has two Hamlets, not one, yet almost no one seems to remember that fact. Amid the pomp of the Danish court, which is fresh from celebrating the marriage of Claudius and Gertrude, the "inky-cloaked" figure of young Hamlet makes a striking contrast; unlike his new father, who proclaims that mourning for the old King Hamlet must be balanced with "remembrance of ourselves" (1.2.7), Prince Hamlet, in the first of his many soliloquies in the play, is tormented by thoughts of suicide:

> O that this too too solid flesh would melt,
> Thaw, and resolve itself into a dew,
> Or that the Everlasting had not fixed
> His canon 'gainst self-slaughter! O God, O God,
> How weary, stale, flat, and unprofitable
> Seem to me all the uses of this world!

**[1.2.129–43]**

Like Antonio's in *The Merchant of Venice*, Hamlet's melancholy is a kind of *Weltschmerz* ("world-weariness"), but unlike Antonio he goes on to diagnose its cause. Recalling with horror his father's death and what his mother later, candidly, calls her "o'er-hasty marriage", Hamlet struggles to unscramble his emotions and sense of self. His tone is distracted, broken, but as his thoughts develop it becomes clear that he is grappling with memory itself ("But two months dead—nay, not so much, not two", he exclaims, as if struggling to pin down the event). He is trapped by the prison of his body, the "too too solid flesh", and his anguished question to himself a few lines later, "Heaven and earth, / Must I remember?", reveals his urgent but painful struggle to hang on to what remains – especially as everyone else in Elsinore, it seems, has forgotten. Claudius chides his new son that his grief is "unmanly", urging him to forget that his father ever existed, to "think of us / As of a father" (1.2.107–8). Gertrude, who has herself demonstrated her capability to move with the times, argues: "all that lives must die, / Passing through nature to eternity" (1.2.72–3). Even Horatio, Hamlet sourly jokes, has visited the court not to pay respects to the old King, but to see the wedding that quickly followed.

Hamlet's savagely disconsolate voice is all the more remarkable because it foreshadows what we already know – that the past is in fact very much alive. T.S. Eliot peevishly complained that Hamlet's emotion is "in *excess* of the facts as they appear", but part of the wonder of *Hamlet* is the way in which the facts themselves are in glorious excess. The play's unforgettable opening scene, the eerie appearance of the old King's ghost on

Wearing a long scarf (cut in subsequent revivals) and a world-weary, slightly puzzled air, David Warner's student prince from 1965 became an icon of the youthful RSC, then under the direction of founder Peter Hall.

the battlements at Elsinore, reanimates – in a frighteningly literal sense – something dead and buried. Hamlet's recollections of his "poor father" are so vivid that they have already burst out on stage:

> HAMLET
> My father—methinks I see my father.
> HORATIO
> O where, my lord?
> HAMLET             In my mind's eye, Horatio.
> HORATIO
> I saw him once. A was a goodly king.
> HAMLET
> A was a man. Take him for all in all,
> I shall not look upon his like again.
> HORATIO
> My lord, I think I saw him yesternight.
>
>                                  **[1.2.183–8]**

Even over the offhand intimacy of the conversation between Hamlet and his close companion – an intimacy Shakespeare or his scribe renders by using "a" instead of "he", a subtle shading that has long since passed out of the language – the Ghost casts its chill.

Hamlet's encounter with the Ghost, when it occurs, forces the Prince to keep on remembering. Echoing the Ghost's urgent promptings to "Remember me", his son responds, "Remember thee?",

Ay, thou poor ghost, while memory holds a seat
In this distracted globe. Remember thee?
Yea, from the table of my memory
I'll wipe away all trivial fond records,
All saws of books, all forms, all pressures past,
That youth and observation copied there,
And thy commandment all alone shall live
Within the book and volume of my brain
Unmixed with baser matter.

**[1.5.95–104]**

Recycling the Ghost's words, Hamlet then incants them once more (repetition is a verbal tic of the play, and one reason among many for its sprawling size), picturing his memory being erased and rewritten by them. "Remembering" is all.

Unfortunately, though, this is where the problems begin. Though Hamlet presents his mind as if it were a commonplace book (Shakespeare, along with many Elizabethan schoolchildren, will have assembled one as a way of developing his memory), the point about scrapbooks is that they can't be erased or rewritten. Despite swearing that "from this time forth, / My thoughts be bloody, or be nothing worth!" (words that are cut from the Folio text), Hamlet's brain cannot stop thinking of other things. It is the hero's defining problem that he cannot translate his thoughts of remembrance into the mechanics of revenge. Though the Ghost casts him in the role of revenger (a role played so well by his long-distant ancestor Amleth), it is a part Hamlet knows he will have great difficulty performing, even as the Ghost disappears:

The time is out of joint. O cursèd spite
That ever I was born to set it right!

**[1.5.189–90]**

Try as he might, Shakespeare's most self-consciously complex character cannot reduce himself to the simplifications required by the role. In startling contrast to Laertes, the play's other key revenger, who coldly vows to "cut [Hamlet's] throat i'th' church" if necessary to avenge his father Polonius, Hamlet has the greatest of trouble negotiating his scruples. First pausing to see if the Ghost's word is accurate, Hamlet then fluffs the opportunity to kill Claudius at his prayers, not wishing to send his father's murderer to heaven. By the time he does achieve his revenge – not at his own initiative, it might be added – events will have spiralled out of control.

Even in its unmanageable length – a length that often sees it trimmed in performance – *Hamlet* is dominated by postponement and hesitancy. As critics since the mid-eighteenth century have commented in their droves, the issue of Hamlet's own delay is perhaps the biggest question of all, not least because its hero spends a good deal of his precious time ruminating on just what it is to act. Furiously protesting that, despite being "Prompted to my revenge by heaven and hell," he "must, like a whore, unpack my heart with words" (2.2.586–8), Hamlet continues to debate the issue almost non-stop – and with over 1500 lines, almost half as much again as Richard III, the Danish prince is the most voluble character in Shakespeare. Some of those "words" are the most renowned not just in the canon but in the language:

To be, or not to be; that is the question:
Whether 'tis nobler in the mind to suffer
The slings and arrows of outrageous fortune,
Or to take arms against a sea of troubles,
And, by opposing, end them. To die, to sleep—
No more, and by a sleep to say we end
The heartache and the thousand natural shocks

That flesh is heir to—'tis a consummation
Devoutly to be wished. To die, to sleep.
To sleep, perchance to dream. Ay, there's the rub,
For in that sleep of death what dreams may come
When we have shuffled off this mortal coil
Must give us pause. There's the respect
That makes calamity of so long life,
For who would bear the whips and scorns of time,
Th'oppressor's wrong, the proud man's contumely,
The pangs of disprized love, the law's delay,
The insolence of office, and the spurns
That patient merit of th'unworthy takes,
When he himself might with his quietus make
With a bare bodkin? Who would these fardels bear,
To grunt and sweat under a weary life,
But that the dread of something after death,
The undiscovered country from whose bourn
No traveller returns, puzzles the will,
And makes us rather bear those ills we have
Than fly to others that we known not of?
Thus conscience does make cowards of us all,
And thus the native hue of resolution
Is sicklied o'er with the pale cast of thought,
And enterprises of great pith and moment
With this regard their currents turn awry,
And lose the name of action.

[3.1.58–90]

Though Hamlet's thoughts are dizzyingly on the wing, they circle around the idea of stasis. What begins as a rational enquiry into the state of being – "To be, or not to be" – transmutes into a speculative meditation on the ways in which humans are persuaded out of "action". Suicide is on the hero's mind, but even this "resolution" (escapist though he argues it is) stumbles and "turn[s] awry", undone by conscience. Despite his determination to answer the "question", a statement that makes him sound like a schoolboy dutifully arguing the point, Hamlet's thinking is spasmodic, broken – a new kind of dramatic style for Shakespeare, and arguably an entirely new dramatic language. One of Shakespeare's greatest German advocates, August Wilhelm Schlegel, regarded the play as a *Gedankentranerspiel*, a "tragedy of thought", and this speech demonstrates just how in one sense that might be true. Even in its prodigious length and complexity, Hamlet's most famous soliloquy exhibits the way in which thoughts – unique, amazing thoughts – can get in the way.

> In Hamlet *the problems the audience thinks about and the intellectual action of thinking about them are very similar.* Hamlet *is the tragedy of an audience that cannot make up its mind.*
>
> Stephen Booth, "On the value of *Hamlet*" (1969)

The soliloquy contains not a single "I" or "me", and its relationship to Hamlet's own situation is complex. Even so, Shakespeare makes us see the tangible as well as philosophical difficulties of the Prince's position. Hamlet is never entirely sure that what the Ghost says is actually true (unlike the audience, who is allowed to witness Claudius's desperate penitence at his prayers), and his options concerning what to do with the knowledge are also sorely limited.

The court at Elsinore, ruled by a usurping murderer, is hardly likely to provide any kind of justice, and Hamlet has little choice but to embark on what the Elizabethan politician and sage Francis Bacon called the "wild justice" of revenge, a course prompted by a Ghost who could also (as Shakespeare's audiences would be well aware) be a demon sent from Hell. That course is wild indeed: in his early political dramas especially Shakespeare shows that the ethic of revenge tears societies apart. In the *King Henry VI* plays it is revenge that finally rips England to pieces during the Wars of the Roses; in Shakespeare's first Roman tragedy *Titus Andronicus*, revenge transforms the city of Rome into a "wilderness of tigers" where horrible violence consumes the world of the play. Knowledge of the political and ethical problems with revenge haunts Hamlet as much as his father's ghost, or indeed his own sense of self.

## Remember me!

The Argentinian writer **Jorge Luis Borges** once wrote a haunting short story entitled "Shakespeare's Memory" (1983), in which the protagonist, a German scholar by the name of Hermann Sörgel, is offered the chance to possess his idol's memory by a man who claims to have access to it. Sörgel jumps at the chance, a mysterious mental transfer occurs – and the academic suddenly becomes aware that he can remember shady, unsettling things belonging to a life other than his own. But the gift ultimately proves a curse: Shakespeare's memory begins to dominate its victim until Sörgel begins to lose his own mind. Reaching for the telephone book, he dials numbers at random until finally someone agrees to try the experiment for themselves.

Borges's eerie story suggests that Shakespeare haunts all of us who have come into contact with him. *Hamlet* is perhaps the most haunting play of all, and in a ghostly kind of way it has always been so. The first printed version of the text to hit the market (1603) was a so-called "**memorial reconstruction**" of the play sold to the printers by an actor who claimed to know the script, almost certainly without the permission of Shakespeare's company. This "pirated" text has become known as the **bad quarto**, mainly because whichever parts the nameless actor took (the best guess so far is Marcellus, Valtemand and Lucellus) he had trouble remembering anything else. He is reasonably accurate in some places – presumably when he was on stage and able to listen properly – but elsewhere forgets massive swathes of the script. In his version, Hamlet's soliloquy, probably the most well-remembered Shakespearian speech of all, gets completely garbled. This is how it comes out (original spelling and all):

> To be, or not to be, I there's the point,
> To Die, to sleepe, is that all? I all:
> No, to sleepe, to dreame, I mary there it goes,
> For in that dreame of deathe, when we awake,
> And borne before an euerlasting ludge,
> From whence no passenger euer retur'nd,
> The vndiscouered country, at whose sight
> The happy smile, and the accursed damn'd.

Unsurprisingly, Shakespeare or his company scrambled to set the record straight: a "newly imprinted and enlarged" version of the play appeared in print the following year.

A more successful attempt to remember *Hamlet* was pioneered nearly two centuries later by the eighteenth-century language expert **Joshua Steele**, whose life work was a study called *An Essay Towards Establishing the Melody and Measure of Speech* (1775), which attempted to set down in writing, with the aid of musical notation, how people actually spoke. Steele attended **David Garrick**'s performances of *Hamlet*, and his records of what must have been an astonishing occasion appear actually in the book – in which Garrick's every intonation, pitch and shade of voice is meticulously transcribed for posterity. If you can work out Steele's notation, you can even reproduce the great man's delivery for yourself.

Even so, as we might guess given that he spends so long riddling with it, "action" is a word Hamlet understands differently from nearly everyone else in the play. In an obvious sense, Claudius, not his nephew, is the great doer of *Hamlet*, as is abundantly obvious on stage: it is he who kills the King, marries the wife, incessantly agitates behind the scenes for the hero's removal from the plot. Hamlet's deeds are, by contrast, secondhand: he stabs Polonius after mistaking his identity, sentences his companions Rosencrantz and Guildenstern to death by rewriting Claudius's commission to England. Even the Prince's death is scripted for him in advance by his uncle, who arranges a duel with Laertes in which the swords and Hamlet's wine are both "envenomed" with poison. Hamlet's two great "acts" in the tragedy – his "antic disposition" of madness and the play he puts on to test his uncle's conscience – are revealing, for they interpret "acting" as theatrical display rather than purposeful achievement.

Hamlet is continually searching for his part, and Shakespeare fills the play with characters who echo or reflect aspects of the hero. The Prince's way with "words" is comically counterpointed by the excruciating verbal excursions of the royal adviser Polonius, whose reluctance to be "brief" (2.2.93) becomes one of *Hamlet*'s verbal tics. (Ironically, Polonius's inability to keep his mouth shut, hidden in Gertrude's bedchamber, will be his downfall.) Also possessed of rather too much art in speaking is the foppish courtier Osric, who surfaces only in the play's closing minutes – he carries the news of Laertes's challenge to the hero – but nevertheless manages to detain the action by his nonsensical and affected speech. Though both Polonius and Osric are apparently harmless, they are nevertheless functionaries of a regime that rests on lies and deceit. Also servants at the slippery world of court are Rosencrantz and Guildenstern, two men who appear on stage only in each other's company and are sometimes even mistaken for one another. As well as being Hamlet's "dear friends", their situation somewhat mirrors that of the Prince, the difference being that they are entirely happy to do what they are told – a model of dutiful service Hamlet wishes to emulate yet is also right to despise. Hamlet's closest companion Horatio is another of the Prince's doubles, stoic and stalwart, as brief in words as his friend is verbally expansive. Unlike Hamlet, Horatio seems innately attuned to the savage politics of Elsinore (politics as dangerous as those in the Norse saga which is the play's ultimate source). "You will lose this wager, my lord," he tells Hamlet as news of the duel arrives (5.2.155), and his instinct is fatally accurate.

But Hamlet's closest living *doppelgänger* is the Norwegian prince Fortinbras, whose father (also named Fortinbras) lost in battle to the old King Hamlet – an indignity the young Fortinbras is eager to revenge. Though he is off stage for nearly all the play, Shakespeare never allows Fortinbras to leave our minds as we watch, dropping in rumours about his conquest in Poland, his marching through Denmark, his gung-ho bravery in battle. Hamlet is only too aware of the difference between the man he calls a "delicate and tender prince" (a character assessment that has rather more Hamlet than Fortinbras in it) and himself, a "rogue and peasant slave" (2.2.552), and is tortured by what he sees as his own limitations in contrast. Fortinbras does well from the comparison: in the last moments of the play it is he to whom Hamlet gives his "dying voice" as the next King of Denmark, a prince far more warlike – and far more like old Hamlet – than the rightful candidate, young Hamlet himself.

## To what base uses

As we can see, Hamlet's tragedy is not exclusively, as Schlegel has it, a tragedy of thought, nor even the tragedy of (just) the hero. Hamlet's musings on the "thousand natural shocks / That flesh is heir to" are interrupted by the arrival of Ophelia, the "Nymph" whose relationship with the hero is as fraught as his relationship with himself. Fevered speculation has attempted to unravel just what lies between them, but the play itself gives little away. Polonius is only too ready to attribute Hamlet's distracted behaviour to frustrated love (particularly after both he and Laertes advise Ophelia to steer clear of him), and it seems that the Prince has indeed sent her love letters, but beyond this there lies little but uncertainty. It does not help that the only time we see the couple alone together, Hamlet's supposedly feigned madness (yet another huge question mark in the play) is beginning to look rather more real. When Ophelia announces that she has "remembrances" from him to return, Hamlet denies even this much, retorting, "No, no, I never gave you aught" (3.1.95–8). What follows is one of the most perplexing episodes in the tragedy, and certainly one of the most distressing to watch:

> HAMLET  I did love you once.
> OPHELIA  Indeed, my lord, you made me believe so.
> HAMLET  You should not have believed me, for virtue cannot so inoculate our old stock but we shall relish of it. I loved you not.
> OPHELIA  I was the more deceived.
> HAMLET  Get thee to a nunnery. Why wouldst thou be a breeder of sinners?
>
> **[3.1.117–24]**

At first claiming that he loved Ophelia, then in the next breath denying it, Hamlet's words are almost wilfully obscure. He may mean that because "virtue" can do nothing to "inoculate" humanity ("our old stock") from its essential sinfulness, his "love" was not authentic; but in practice his language is even more broken than before. Typically, the Prince has transformed the situation into something beyond itself, arguing that humanity is so tainted by sin that love itself is delusive. That does not soften the savagery of his words, though, nor the cruelty of his insistence, repeated five times in this scene, that Ophelia should "get … to a nunnery" (also Jacobethan slang for a brothel) rather than feel as she does.

When Hamlet confronts his mother a few scenes later, his thoughts return to the themes of "breeding" and sinfulness. As the critic Jacqueline Rose notes, Hamlet's bizarre projection onto Ophelia of intemperate lust (the kind that breeds "sinners") seems suspiciously close to his feelings about Gertrude. When he accuses his mother of "compulsive ardour", it seems clear that his feelings about the incurable sinfulness of humanity are magnified by his belief that in marrying her husband's murderer Gertrude has performed a kind of nightmarish adultery:

> HAMLET              Nay, but to live
>     In the rank sweat of an enseamèd bed
>     Stewed in corruption, honeying and making love
>     Over the nasty sty—
> QUEEN GERTRUDE        O, speak to me no more!
>     Those words like daggers enter in mine ears.
>     No more, sweet Hamlet.
>
> **[3.4.81–6]**

Though we don't have to diagnose Hamlet as suffering from a Freudian Oedipal complex (a famous theory initiated by Ernest Jones in his 1949 *Hamlet and Oedipus*), it is interesting to note the connections that complicate his relationships with the play's two female characters, not least the nightmarish links he constructs between sexuality, sin and death. The brute irony is that Hamlet's spiralling obsession with sins of the body is played out while there is a real corpse to be dealt with – that of Polonius, whom he has just stabbed (suddenly and sinfully) behind a wall-hanging.

It is fitting, perhaps, that sooner or later Hamlet will take his thoughts on the human condition to the grave itself – a literal as well as symbolic destination of the play. Freed from Rosencrantz and Guildenstern by a hair's-breadth escape involving pirates on the high seas,

Olivier confronts Yorick's destiny – and his own – in a still from his 1948 film of *Hamlet*, which propelled its star and director to worldwide fame.

Hamlet returns to Denmark and finds himself, with Horatio, in a churchyard. There he comes across a man who has the expertise to answer his inquisitiveness about bodies, one of the gravediggers. Their discussion becomes a kind of grim comic repartee (aptly, for the gravedigger is a "Clown" in the text):

HAMLET  How long will a man lie i'th' earth ere he rot?
FIRST CLOWN  I'faith, if a be not rotten before a die—as we have many pocky corpses nowadays, that will scarce hold the laying in—a will last you some eight year or nine year. A tanner will last you nine year.
HAMLET  Why he more than another?
FIRST CLOWN  Why, sir, his hide is so tanned with his trade that a will keep out water a great while …

**[5.1.159–66]**

Neoclassical thinkers – most famously Voltaire – objected to this scene because it debased Hamlet's tragedy, but what is striking here is that the Prince's blackly comic routine echoes with delicious vulgarity some of the grander ideas of the play. "To what base uses we may return, Horatio!" Hamlet exclaims (5.1.198) – when it comes down to it, we end up in the grave – and as he gleefully explains to Claudius earlier in the play, "a king may go a progress through the guts of a beggar" (4.3.30–1) after he rots and is eaten by worms. But the laughter, bleak though it is, is short-lived: the grave at which Hamlet and Horatio are conversing has been dug for Ophelia, driven mad by her own father's death (a painfully real echo of Hamlet's feigned insanity, itself caused by bereavement) and who has drowned herself. With this news, the tone of the play begins to narrow: death is no longer a subject for speculative enquiry, but a savage reality. Though Polonius's own end was messy and squalid – Hamlet lunges behind the arras for a "rat", unceremoniously lugging the body off stage afterwards – here we sense that even the fate of "intruding fools" like him (or clowns like Hamlet's long-dead jester Yorick) has a terrible tragic dimension.

Death is of course where Hamlet (and *Hamlet*) end, but despite his multiple desires to escape the prison of his flesh the hero does not go gently. Having put up Laertes to challenge the Prince to a duel, Claudius does his utmost to ensure that Hamlet is finally dispatched – Laertes's swordsmanship, a "treacherous" weapon, poisoned wine. Yet Hamlet, newly aware that "the readiness is all" (5.2.168), fails to be compliant. He fights back. Having hung so long in irresolution, *Hamlet* becomes a full revenge tragedy only in its concluding – its dying – moments. But the play never loses its interest in the chaotic, unpredictable nature of death. Laertes is wounded by his own sword, Gertrude drinks the poison intended for her son, Claudius is stabbed only when Hamlet realizes that he himself has been mortally wounded. Shakespeare's pacing of this final scene is astonishing, something only really comprehensible in performance: from Osric's announcement of the duel to the moment where Gertrude collapses occupies nearly two hundred lines, perhaps ten minutes on stage; yet it is only another fifty lines before Laertes, Claudius and finally Hamlet are finished. Quite suddenly, the revenge is complete, the revenger is dying, and everything is very nearly over.

*The poet places [Hamlet] in the most stimulating circumstances that a human being can be placed in. He is the heir-apparent of a throne: his father dies suspiciously; his mother excluded her son from his throne by marrying his uncle. This is not enough; but the Ghost of the murdered father is introduced to assure the son that he was put to death by his own brother. What is the effect upon the son? – instant action and pursuit of revenge? No: endless reasoning and hesitating …*

Samuel Taylor Coleridge, *Table-Talk* (1812)

Though the hero is, characteristically, thinking of his audience as he readies himself for his terminal interruption, the certainty that "the rest is silence" (5.2.310), he is also aware that events have come full circle. The play ends, as it began, with the death of a Hamlet. "You that look pale and tremble at this chance," he addresses the spectators crowding around,

> That are but mutes or audience to this act,
> Had I but time—as this fell sergeant Death
> Is strict in his arrest—O, I could tell you—
> But let it be.

**[5.2.286–90]**

Yet the play will not quite let Hamlet be: just after he is interrupted by death, so starting on that long-overdue journey to the "undiscovered country from whose bourn / No traveller returns" (3.1.81–2), the stage is filled with "warlike noise", drums and trumpets, as the Norwegian army of Fortinbras swarms on. Hamlet's corpse is lifted and carried off, destined for what the new King of Denmark announces will be a soldier's funeral. It is the last misunderstanding, and the hero is no longer around to protest.

# Stage history and adaptations

While there are no surviving records of *Hamlet*'s first years at the Globe (it was first performed there around 1600), there is little doubt that then – as now – the play seized the imagination of audiences. It is almost unique among Shakespeare's works in never having been off the stage, as far as we can make out, since it was written. Here there is barely space to render even the outlines of that history.

**Richard Burbage** created the Prince's role, and the "bad" 1603 quarto presumably appeared in response to popular demand for a text, its title-page claiming that early performances occurred in **Oxford**, **Cambridge** and the city of London. It was also played at court with **Joseph Taylor**, Burbage's successor, in 1619 and 1637, and travelled widely – even reaching the coast of West Africa, where the crew of an East India Company ship called the *Dragon* acted it in 1607 (the first known performance of Shakespeare on the African continent).

Taylor continued acting Hamlet up to the closure of the theatres in 1642, after which time the gravedigging scene was smuggled into a skit entitled *The Gravediggers*, performed by **Robert Cox**'s company. Once Charles II returned from exile in 1660, *Hamlet* swiftly followed, with the young **Thomas Betterton** appearing in the lead the following year (he would act it for another five decades, last playing the Prince in 1709 at the age of 74). Betterton's stamina would be challenged, but never equalled, by the self-anointed king of the eighteenth-century stage, **David Garrick** (1742–76), who developed a painstakingly fleshed-out interpretation (according to one witness, he "preserve[d] every gradation and transition of the passions"). Garrick's decisiveness in the role, played to **Susannah Cibber**'s Ophelia, was assisted by cutting the Prince's more irresolute speeches and eventually most of Act Five – and he employed a special hydraulic wig to make his hair stand on end at the sight of the Ghost. **John Henderson** took over from Garrick in 1777, and imitated his master's style with some success.

*Hamlet*, albeit heavily cut, was Shakespeare's most popular play during the eighteenth century, and under **John Philip Kemble**'s aegis it continued its pre-eminence into the nineteenth. Despite his stately style Kemble illustrated the gnawing melancholy at the Prince's heart, though was too cool for some – especially when compared with his sister **Sarah Siddons**, who also attempted the role. The same criticism could never be levelled at **Edmund Kean**, who acted Hamlet from 1814 in a portrayal that outlined all the character's "turbulent delineations of passion" (*The Stage*) and, doing so, scandalized audiences used to the more classical acting of Kemble. A decade later **William Charles Macready** attempted to combine the best elements of Kean's and Kemble's styles, but only after Kean's untimely death in 1833 did he become the leading Hamlet of his generation. Kean's son **Charles** acted the play from 1838 onwards to a succession of Ophelias including **Eliza Smith** and his wife **Ellen Tree.**

By this time *Hamlet* had become an intercontinental phenomenon. A performance by **Charles Kemble**'s company at the Paris Odéon in 1827 caused a sensation, not least because **Harriet Smithson** as Ophelia mesmerized Romantic artists like Delacroix and Berlioz (so much so in the latter's case that he married her). In America **Edwin Booth**, encouraged to take up the play by his British actor father **Junius Brutus**, became synonymous with the role in New York from the 1860s, described by one eyewitness as "every inch the noble prince". During the following decade several London-based managers would tour in the US. Among them were **Henry Irving**, who acted Hamlet most famously in a sprawling 1878 Lyceum performance that offered a Victorian version of Hamlet's conundrum – torn between duty to his father and love for **Ellen Terry**'s sensitive Ophelia. The great Italian **Tommaso Salvini**, famous for his titanic Othello, also toured as Hamlet in the 1870s, winning plaudits though playing against type. Still more unusual was **Sarah Bernhardt**'s Parisian Prince (1899), who offered a "boyish" interpretation despite being 54 (and, of course, a girl).

Though *Hamlet*'s days as a star vehicle were by no means over, the late nineteenth century witnessed a growing desire to produce the play as it might have been known by Shakespeare. **William Poel** began his adventures with "Elizabethan" staging in 1881 with a first quarto *Hamlet*, and masterminded three subsequent versions. Elsewhere, the play-text came under scrutiny, initially with **Johnston Forbes-Robertson**'s celebrated Lyceum version from 1897, which restored the Fortinbras subplot for the first time in two hundred years; and then with **Frank Benson's** "full text" productions at Stratford from the turn of the century, which lasted a breathtaking six hours. Even more ambitious was an extraordinary production at the Moscow Arts Theatre which opened in January 1912. Designed and directed by the visionary theatrical innovator **Edward Gordon Craig** (who had played the title role in London fifteen years earlier), the production attempted to create a new idiom for Shakespeare – a kind of epic symbolism that would convey the essence of the play without any distracting naturalistic details. Craig's scenery was made up of enormous screens (either cream or gold) that could be arranged in different figurations.

Craig's influence can be seen in the boldly simplified designs that **Robert Edmond Jones** made for a celebrated New York production in 1925. This starred **John Barrymore**, who discarded poetic introspection in favour of a more assertive and physically dynamic portrayal of the Prince ("the realest Hamlet we have known", claimed the *Herald*). In the same year **Barry Jackson**'s Birmingham Rep mounted an infamous modern-dress production – the "plus-fours" *Hamlet* – that infuriated as many as it impressed. Throughout the 1930s and 40s *Hamlet* secured the careers of an astonishing sequence of British stars based at London's Old Vic. **Ernest Milton**, **Laurence Olivier**, **Maurice Evans** and **Michael Redgrave** were all acclaimed Princes, though the most famous of them all was **John Gielgud**, who first played Hamlet in 1930 – aged just 26 – and acted him in four subsequent versions. Though Gielgud attempted to find something new in the character each time – all the way from the early "angry young man" to a hero for whom, as one critic put it, "wickedness is no surprise" – his noble demeanour and impressive verse-speaking were consistently singled out for praise.

Some indication of the tragedy's near-universal appeal during the mid-twentieth century can be gathered from the fact that during World War II it was fighting for both sides: a pared-down wartime *G.I. Hamlet* was put on to rally American troops by **Maurice Evans** (who had played the role at the Old Vic and on Broadway), while across enemy lines Hitler permitted

Gustaf Gründgens to perform an impeccably Aryan Prince. Since then, *Hamlet* has continued to be performed more often than any other play: London has sometimes seen more than three performances running concurrently, and any attempt to describe more than a handful would be impossible here.

In 1953 **Richard Burton**'s swashbuckling performance at the Old Vic was wildly successful (with eighteen curtain calls on the first night); while the same theatre four years later saw **John Neville** in a more poetic reading, complete with Ruritanian costumes and a touching Ophelia from a very young Judi Dench. But for many, it was **Paul Scofield**'s measured, unhistrionic Hamlet – at Stratford in 1948 and for **Peter Brook** in 1955 – that most truly penetrated the character's multifaceted complexity, and best defined the role for his generation.

Ten years later, **David Warner**'s disaffected and nihilistic student Prince effectively captured the mood of the post-nuclear age – leading one

John Gielgud was the twentieth century's most illustrious Hamlet. This promotional shot, with Jessica Tandy as Ophelia, is from the 1934 production at the New Theatre, London.

esteemed critic to comment that "even the oldest of us feel that we are seeing the play for the first time". Elsewhere in **Peter Hall**'s Stratford cast lay further surprises, **Tony Church**'s politico Polonius and **Glenda Jackson**'s feisty Ophelia among them; though Hall's politicized production would have an easier time than **Adolf Dresen**'s subversive East German version of the previous year, which was banned. At London's Roundhouse in 1969 **Tony Richardson**'s production, dominated by **Nicol Williamson**'s savage Prince, divided the critics, not least because of the laid-back Ophelia of **Marianne Faithfull** – better known as a pop singer. **Buzz Goodbody**'s 1975 production performed at The Other Place (a corrugated iron shed down the road from the RSC's main house), was notable for its powerful immediacy and **Ben Kingsley**'s unheroic prince. Five years later, at London's Royal Court Theatre, **Jonathan Pryce**'s Hamlet created a sensation, in a claustrophobic production by **Richard Eyre**, by speaking his father's lines as if physically possessed by the ghost.

**Ron Daniels**'s RSC production of 1989 was hailed as one of that decade's best, with **Mark Rylance**'s little-boy Prince enthusiastically received (Rylance would play an Elizabethan Hamlet in 2000 while artistic director of the London Globe). **Kenneth Branagh**'s various performances, most successfully under **Adrian Noble** in 1992, demonstrated that Hamlet could be physical too, and even something of a film star. This was even truer of **Ralph Fiennes**, who played the Prince for **Jonathan Kent** at the Almeida Theatre in 1995 as an over-sensitive and confused toff. Controversy attended **Matthew Warchus**'s RSC version of 1997, with **Alex Jennings** as a sardonic Prince, because of the director's decision to cut over a thousand lines of text in order to streamline the play and emphasize its familial aspects. Other directors have identified political undercurrents: **Steven Pimlott**'s 2001 version, again at the RSC, stressed the brutalist aspects of Claudius's regime and had **Sam West** as a youthful but edgy Prince. *Hamlet*'s first internationally successful production of the twenty-first century was directed by one of the biggest directorial names of the twentieth, **Peter Brook**, whose adaptation, *The Tragedy of Hamlet* (2001), explored the metaphysical conundrums of the play with **Adrian Lester** in the lead. **Trevor Nunn**, at the Old Vic in 2004, emphasized the gulf between the generations, casting the emaciated **Ben Whishaw**, just 23 and fresh from drama school, as a febrile student prince alongside **Samantha Whittaker**'s teenagey Ophelia.

Of *Hamlet*'s varied life in translation – all the way from Afrikaans (1945) to Zulu (1954) – little can be added here, save perhaps its special popularity in Russia (where "Hamletism", a word that appears in the 1840s, became a familiar concept). Performed as early as 1837 in Moscow by **Pavel Mochalov**, the play was given an innovative production at the Moscow Arts Theatre in 1912 (see p.74), and more recently **Yuri Lyubimov**'s 1971 production, starring **Vladimir Vysotsky**, gained much attention outside its home country. Germany, too – it was once proclaimed that "Deutschland ist Hamlet" – has provided a welcoming environment. The play was performed there as early as 1626, but became massively popular in **Friedrich Ludwig Schröder**'s eighteenth-century performances (Schröder inspired Goethe's Hamletesque *Wilhelm Meister's Apprenticeship* of 1796). In **Heiner Müller**'s *Hamletmachine* (1977) the play became a political protest against the GDR.

People have wanted to film *Hamlet* from the first days of cinema. Although a French short appeared in 1900, the films of **Johnston Forbes-Robertson** (1913) and **Sven Gade** (1920) – the latter starring the great **Asta Nielsen** in an intriguing cross-gender experiment – are perhaps the most celebrated silent versions of the play. In the talkie era, **Laurence Olivier**'s movie of 1948 has dominated, though **Grigori Kosintzev**'s 1964 film, with **Innokenti Smoktunovsky** in the lead, is a masterpiece on a par with his *King Lear*, despite its relative rarity. The 1960s saw the filmed stage versions of **John Gielgud** (1964) and **Tony Richardson** (1969), starring **Richard Burton** and **Nicol Williamson** respectively – the latter shot almost exclusively in close-up. More recently, the play has attracted large budgets – notably those of **Franco Zeffirelli**, who in 1990 cast Hollywood star **Mel Gibson** as a vigorous and heroic (if mother-obsessed) Prince; and **Kenneth Branagh**, who offered a response to Zeffirelli's swingeingly cut version by releasing a full-text version with himself in the lead. **Michael Almereyda**'s 2000 film relocated the play to modern-day New York and starred **Ethan Hawke** as the Prince. TV versions include **Richard Chamberlain**'s Byronic Hamlet in 1970 (with **Michael Redgrave** as Polonius, **Richard Johnson** as Claudius and Gielgud's Ghost); and **Rodney Bennett**'s lengthy BBC/Time-Life version from 1980, with **Derek Jacobi** as a watchful yet capricious Hamlet to **Patrick Stewart**'s domineering Claudius and **Eric Porter**'s bustling Polonius. **Joseph Papp**'s New York Shakespeare Festival version of the play, with **Kevin Kline** in the lead, was recorded for PBS in 1990 and has recently become available on DVD.

## Screen

### Hamlet

**L. Olivier, J. Simmons, P. Cushing; Laurence Olivier (dir.)**
UK, 1948 ▷ Carlton / Criterion 📀 📼

"Mr Olivier does not speak poetry badly," opined one critic of his 1937 debut as Hamlet. "He does not speak it at all." His verbal eccentricities won't trouble you here (in fact they're rather terrific), but then Olivier gets to do a lot more than just use his voice. *Hamlet*, his second Shakespeare film, is probably the most daring and brilliant of the lot, done out in high-contrast monochrome with obvious debts to German expressionism and *film noir*. Equally insistent is Olivier's obsession with Hamlet's Oedipal conundrum, which led him to cast Eileen Herlie as Gertrude (she was in fact thirteen years his junior), though in all other respects his glacial and imperious interpretation of the role is finely balanced. Even if some have criticized the visuals as fussy – the vertiginous camerawork, exploring the murky recesses of the Prince's imagination, invites strong reactions – the film is bolstered by its sure-footed dramatic pacing, some excellent supporting performances and William Walton's atmospheric music.

## Hamlet (Gamlet)
### I. Smoktunovsky, A. Vertinskaya, M. Nazavanov; Grigori Kozintsev (dir.)
USSR, 1964 ▷ Ruscico *DVD* ▭

Though Kozintsev's expressionistic retelling of *Hamlet* sometimes seems to echo Olivier, it is richer in insight and more mature cinematically. Whereas Olivier employs the meandering staircases of Elsinore to represent Hamlet's quest for identity, Kozintsev presents a castle of massy walls and airless spaces: never has the "prison" of Denmark seemed so inescapable as when the drawbridge thunders down during his opening sequence. This subtext must have had a horribly personal resonance for Innokenti Smoktunovsky, a war hero sent to the Gulag by Stalin, and he delivers an inspired performance as a Prince trapped as much by his position (most memorably when he wanders through crowds of courtiers, soliloquies raging in voice-over) as by the cry for revenge. Also ensnared is Anastasia Vertinskaya's girlish Ophelia, almost literally a wind-up toy for her baleful father (Yuri Tolubeyev) and his thickset boss (Mikhail Nazavanov), though via cuts in the text Elsa Radzina's Gertrude becomes a bystander, her death mere misadventure. It's the film's political dimension that makes it most thrilling: this Prince is a genuine threat to stability, and the arrival of Fortinbras heralds a political dawn so defining it's been seen as Kozintsev's nod to Khrushchev. Shostakovich's propulsive music is an organic part of the drama, though some may feel that it's too intrusive.

## Hamlet
### K. Branagh, K. Winslet, D. Jacobi; Kenneth Branagh (dir.)
UK, 1996 ▷ Warner *DVD* ▭

An oft-repeated fact about *Hamlet* is that, from its first days at the Globe, a full performance will have been impossible. Enter Kenneth Branagh, a fat chequebook and an uncut quarto text. His attempt to see if multiplex audiences will run out of patience – or popcorn – by the time Hamlet flings his rapier into Claudius (just past the 3hrs 45min mark) is magnificently brave, but Branagh just doesn't trust the script. He interpolates fussy silent episodes presumably designed to aid comprehension, but which just add to the hair-tearing excess of it all: any director who wastes Judi Dench and John Gielgud on a wordless sequence has more contacts than sense. They are not the only ill-served luminaries: Branagh's capacious cast ranges from the underused (Simon Russell Beale, Ray Fearon), the undercooked (Winslet, Julie Christie, Billy Crystal, Richard Briers) to the downright bizarre (Ken Dodd, Gérard Depardieu). Branagh's own performance is mixed, not to say limited by his habit of welling up each time he approaches an emotional crux. Centred around Blenheim Palace, the sets are great, but Branagh's bid for Viscontian grandeur too often watches like low-grade Hollywood.

## Hamlet
### E. Hawke, J. Stiles, K. MacLachlan; Michael Almereyda (dir.)
US, 2000 ▷ Cinema Club / Miramax *DVD* ▭

For all the millennial modernity – it's set in a contemporary New York of "Denmark Corp", swish limousines and designer apartments – the director presents a drama whose previous incarnations are as inescapable as Sam Shepard's glowering Ghost. Hamlet can't verbalize his emotions without replaying them on his Handicam, and instead of hiring players to tug at his uncle's conscience he montages *The Mousetrap: A Film/Video*. All very wry, but such gimmickry only encourages the film to topple into parody. Despite the semiotic seductions, playing "To be, or not to be" in Blockbuster Video was surely a mistake, and the movie's air-con setting maroons rather than liberates the play. Hawke plays the heir presumptive as a wised-up student rebel who wears his pinstripes with a Peruvian woolly hat and an air of bad grace, while Julia Stiles scowls efficiently as Ophelia (she hasn't opportunity to do much else; the couple's emotional entanglements are drastically ironed out). This *Hamlet* does well to capture the portmanteau layering of the play, but ultimately fails to convince.

# Audio

## Hamlet
### A. Lesser, E. de Souza, E. Fielding; Neville Jason (dir.)
UK, 1997 ▷ Naxos ⊙ ▭

Choosing an audio *Hamlet* is an invidious task, and a long one – this version stretches across four CDs, a total of three-and-a-half hours' listening. Nevertheless Naxos provides the best long-term audio experience, in part because production values are higher here than with some of the competition: the Ghost scenes are actually pretty unnerving, while the music involves real instruments rather than synthesized electronics. All this is incidental compared to the actors, most especially Anton Lesser, who makes a full-blooded, mature Hamlet, never afraid to experiment with both voice and verse (he played the role on stage for Jonathan Miller in 1982). Emma Fielding's Ophelia is attractively ungirlish, and Susan Engel gives her all as Gertrude. Edward de Souza's Claudius is not as oily as he might be, though Peter Jeffery is nicely over-fussy as Polonius, as much a victim of events as the Prince himself.

## Hamlet
### J. Gielgud, B. Kroeger, D. McGuire; John Gielgud (dir.)
USA, 1951 ▷ Pearl ⊙

Taking the dying Hamlet at his word when he begs Horatio to "absent [himself] from felicity awhile" and "tell" the Prince's story, this recording has John Merivale's earnest Horatio acting as narrator. A necessity given that this cut-down version axes a large portion of the script (it lasts just 74 minutes) and edits scenes somewhat in the manner of film, creating short bursts of dialogue and punctuating highlights with music. One effect is to throw even more limelight on John Gielgud's soloistic Hamlet, and the Prince he presents here is not yet corroded by bitterness: despite his introspection, anger lies close to the surface and he seizes upon revenge with real impetuosity. Despite a sense that Gielgud is often singing rather than speaking the lines, this is a captivating reading. Barry Kroeger's surprisingly reasonable Claudius forms a nice duo with Pamela Brown's wonderfully mumsy Gertrude, as do Dorothy McGuire's wide-eyed Ophelia and George Howe's spry Polonius.

## Editions

### Arden Shakespeare (second series)
**Harold Jenkins; 1982** ▷ Thomson

The last Arden 2 to appear, Jenkins's 1982 *Hamlet*, painstakingly assembled over many years, embodies the best of a certain brand of Shakespeare editing and that series in particular – capacious notes, serious treatment of sources, date and so on, a muscular critical introduction unembarrassed about making bold statements about the play. But it's the "Longer Notes", about a quarter of this very bulky book, that make the Arden edition really worth using: this is the place to go if you want to find all about the sources informing Ophelia's insanity (twelve pages), the role of miniature paintings on the Elizabethan stage (three pages) or what on earth a "handsaw" is doing in the play (one page). But Jenkins has no space for *Hamlet*'s performance history and takes a traditionalist view of the text – that the second quarto is the one to follow.

### New Cambridge Shakespeare
**Philip Edwards; 1985** ▷ Cambridge UP

No one edition could do justice to the most incessantly analysed play in the canon, not to mention one with a horribly convoluted textual history, and Edwards's Cambridge version offers different perspectives to Jenkins on a number of key issues – notably the script. In common with recent critical thinking (which argues that the Folio version contains Shakespeare's cuts for performance), Edwards follows the 1623 Folio, but includes in square brackets passages – some 200 lines – unique to the second quarto. The introduction chases up some interesting lines of enquiry, providing a lucid account of the text along with the development of the play as it was written, and notable for its refusal to romanticize the hero. Another gap (Jenkins's lack of stage history) is,

however, left largely unfilled: anyone needing more than the cursory and somewhat one-sided treatment offered here should head straight for Robert Hapgood's Cambridge *Shakespeare in Production* text (1999), which is selective but valuable.

## Some criticism

### Shakespearean Tragedy
**A.C. Bradley; 1904** ▷ Macmillan / Penguin

It was estimated around the turn of the twentieth century that criticism on *Hamlet* exceeded the entire literary output of several European nations. Whether or not this is true, *Shakespearean Tragedy*, written around the same time, has proved more magisterially influential than the entire lot. Bradley constructed what is still known as the "big four" – *Othello*, *Macbeth*, *Lear* and, of course, *Hamlet* – and outlined moments he saw as of climactic significance. His view of the plays is correspondingly narrow in focus: he has little time for the plays' language, treats Shakespeare most often like a novelist and his Victorian morality sometimes proves burdensome. But the readability of Bradley's analysis (though that is a term he scorned), as well as its resilient interest in humanity, wins through. You won't agree with everything he says, but you will be convinced once again that Shakespeare is the *only* writer worth attending to.

### Hamlet Closely Observed
**Martin Dodsworth; 1985** ▷ Athlone

Criticism of *Hamlet* – following Bradley's lead – often aspires to grandiose generalities about the human condition. Good, then, to read something analytical and thought-provoking about the play itself. Dodsworth does occasionally lift his eyes from the text (and when he does, for instance on the Renaissance concept of "honour", is equally brilliant), but for the most part the book is a "close reading" of *Hamlet* able to spend plenty of time unpicking certain moments and speeches yet reinserting them into the whole. Dodsworth doesn't have much interest in the stage life of the tragedy, but he will make you wonder afresh at the sheer completeness of Shakespeare's work.

# Henry IV Part I

f *Richard II* is a play about behind-the-scenes power-broking, and *King John* unsparingly analyses the cynicism of politics, then both *Henry IV* plays examine how fragile a king's authority can be. Just glancing at the list of characters in *Henry IV Part I* reveals how much the play is concerned with rebellion: the King's party is just five men strong; opposing them are over twice that number. The canny and astute Bolingbroke of *Richard II*, who manoeuvred himself into power with almost imperceptible fluency, is beginning to look fatally undermined, and England's future hangs once more in the balance. Despite its weighty subject matter, however, a thick comic vein runs through the play, and Shakespeare is liberated rather than constrained by his historical materials. *1 Henry IV* spends as much of its time in Eastcheap pubs as in the corridors of power, and of course it introduces one of Shakespeare's most famous double-acts: that of Prince Hal, the glamorous but profligate heir to the throne, and his unlikely alter ego Sir John Falstaff – the "fat knight" who has proved one of the playwright's most enduring creations.

**[DATE]** In print by 1598, *1 Henry IV* was most likely first performed in the summer of 1596 (soon after *Richard II*, its chronological predecessor).

**[SOURCES]** As with his other histories, Shakespeare put Holinshed's *Chronicles* (1587 edition) and possibly Halle's *Union* (1548) to good use. It seems likely that he also read Samuel Daniel's verse *Civil Wars* (1595), chronicles by John Stow and the anonymous play *The Famous Victories of Henry V* (c.1580s).

**[TEXTS]** Both highly topical and immediately popular, the play was published in 1598 (a few fragments survive of what is called Q0) and reprinted seven more times (Q1–7) by 1632. An altered version was printed in the First Folio of 1623.

## Interpreting the play

The grand theme of Shakespeare's "second tetralogy", the group of four plays stretching from *Richard II* to *Henry V*, is the so-called "Tudor Myth" (see p.112), which held that the deposition of Richard II by Bolingbroke fatally weakened the English throne and directly instigated the Wars of the Roses – a conflict brought to a close only by the accession of Henry Tudor in 1485. In *1 Henry IV* those abstract arguments, extensively worked over by the Tudor-friendly historiographers who were Shakespeare's reading, acquire a sombre human dimension. Raphael Holinshed's 1587 *Chronicles* make it clear that Henry's "unquiet" rule was caused by his usurpation: "his regiment [reign]", the historian explains, confronted "the hatred of his people, the heart grudgings of his courtiers, and the peremptory practices of both together".

But in Shakespeare's masterful *Part I*, the King's tragedy – which will eventually grow into the tragedy of England, as we already know from the *Henry VI* plays – is less than half the story. The playwright shunts the conflict into another generation, and what results is a kind of competitive comedy between King Henry's wastrel son Hal, Prince of Wales, and his dashing rival Hotspur, son of the King's main foe, Northumberland. Historically spurious

## Major Characters & Synopsis

**King Henry IV** (sometimes known as
  **Bolingbroke**)
**Prince Harry**, Prince of Wales, Henry IV's eldest
  son and heir (known as **Hal**)
**Lord John of Lancaster**, a younger son of
  Henry IV
**Earl of Westmorland** and **Sir Walter Blunt**,
  supporters of the King

### REBELS AGAINST THE KING

Henry Percy, **Earl of Northumberland**, leader of
  the rebels
Thomas Percy, **Earl of Worcester**,
  Northumberland's younger brother
**Sir Henry (Harry) Percy**, Northumberland's son
  and heir (known as **Hotspur**)
**Lord Edmund Mortimer**, Earl of March,
  Hotspur's brother-in-law
**Lady Mortimer**, Mortimer's wife
**Owain Glyndŵr**, a Welsh lord, Lady Mortimer's
  father
Archibald, **Earl of Douglas**, a Scottish lord
**Sir Richard Vernon**, an English knight
Richard le Scrope, **Archbishop of York**
**Sir Michael**, a member of the Archbishop's
  household
**Lady Percy**, Hotspur's wife and Mortimer's sister
  (known as **Kate**)
**Lady Mortimer**, Glyndŵr's daughter and
  Mortimer's wife

### OTHER CHARACTERS

**Sir John Falstaff**, one of Hal's companions
  (called **Oldcastle** in the early printed texts)
Falstaff's followers: **Edward (Ned) Poins**,
  **Bardolph** and **Peto**
**Mistress Quickly**, hostess of an Eastcheap tavern
**Francis**, a barman, and a **Vintner** (tavern-keeper)

**[▶▶ action continued from *Richard II*]**
**ACT 1** Henry Bolingbroke, new to the throne, is
already battling his first rebellion. Mortimer has
been taken prisoner by the Welsh rebel Glyndŵr,
though the King's forces have succeeded in the
north, where Hotspur has defeated the Scots. In
contrast, Henry's wastrel son, Prince Hal, is booz-
ing with cronies rather than fighting for his father.
At an Eastcheap tavern Hal conspires with Poins
to play a practical joke on their friend Falstaff –
who has turned to highway robbery to pay his

bills – by robbing him in disguise. Hotspur, meanwhile, has withdrawn his co-operation until the
King pays Mortimer's ransom. When he refuses –
denouncing Mortimer as a traitor – Hotspur is
enraged and plots rebellion against him.

**ACT 2**  After Falstaff and his crew rob a group
of travellers, Hal and Poins ambush their friends
and steal their booty. They are already in
Eastcheap by the time Falstaff returns, and pretend to believe his account of the attack before
exposing the truth. Falstaff is recovering from
the embarrassment when Hotspur's rebellion is
announced. Recalled to court and convinced
that the King will take the opportunity to condemn his behaviour, Hal briefly plays out the
scene of his father's wrath with his companions
before they are forced to hide from the sheriff
and his men, who are on Falstaff's trail.

**ACT 3**  King Henry is unimpressed with his
son's antics, but is won round by Hal's promise
to prove himself and fight. In Wales, the rebellion
gathers pace: Mortimer has joined forces with
Glyndŵr, Hotspur and Worcester, and war is certain. On his way to battle, Hal calls on the tavern
and persuades Falstaff to join him.

**ACT 4**  Rumours of Hal's unexpected appearance reach the rebels, who have been hit by
sudden bad news about Northumberland (seriously ill) and Glyndŵr's army (badly under-
prepared). Challenged by the King, they squabble among themselves. Falstaff, meanwhile, is
doing his bit for the royal cause by accepting
bribes to dismiss good soldiers.

**ACT 5**  Distrusting the King's offer of clemency,
Worcester is convinced that the rebels must fight.
Battle at Shrewsbury commences. Although Henry
has arranged for several soldiers to impersonate
him in order to confuse the enemy, Douglas discovers the real King and is about to kill him when
Hal bursts in and saves his father. Hotspur appears
and the two fight, Hal finally killing his rival. He then
notices Falstaff's body lying close by, and laments
the death of his old friend – at which point Falstaff
gets up. The battle is won, Worcester and Vernon
are sentenced to death, and King Henry prepares
to rout the remaining rebels.

though it is (the real-life Henry Percy was over twenty years older than Henry), this dynamic story of two young sons competing for supremacy dominates the action of the play, offsetting the political narrative and often threatening to eclipse it altogether.

## So blest a son

At first it seems as if there will not be much in the way of competition: while Hal is content to while away the hours with various low-life types, Hotspur is where any young noble worth his salt should be, on the battlefield – a source of some discomfort to Hal, who wittily, but perhaps nervously, satirizes him as a man "that kills some six or seven dozen of Scots at a breakfast, washes his hands, and says to his wife, 'Fie upon this quiet life! I want work'" (2.5.103–6). Hal's father is altogether less sanguine about the contrast between the two, unable to think about much else. Henry expresses his "envy" that "my lord Northumberland / Should be the father to so blest a son—"

> A son who is the theme of honour's tongue,
> Amongst a grove the very straightest plant,
> Who is sweet Fortune's minion and her pride—
> Whilst I by looking on the praise of him
> See riot and dishonour stain the brow
> Of my young Harry. O, that it could be proved
> That some night-tripping fairy had exchanged
> In cradle clothes our children where they lay,
> And called mine Percy, his Plantagenet!

[1.1.78–88]

Far from fearing that Hal is not his own child, the King actively wishes he were someone else's. Though his frustration is hemmed in by irony – this disregard for the niceties of inheritance is one reason why he is on the throne – it is also agonizingly real: a father's grief that his son simply will not be as he should.

Not that Hotspur's relationship with his own father is any more productive. While Northumberland is a wily politician (wily enough not to turn up at Shrewsbury when it becomes apparent that the rebels have no chance), his son is the polar opposite. Hotspur's brilliance and chutzpah make him a natural in battle – and a fiery figure on stage – but leave him utterly stranded in the messier world of interpersonal politics. Committed to knightly integrity and a strict moral code, he cannot stand "this ingrate and cankered Bolingbroke", "this vile politician", the "king of smiles" who has (in his view) glad-handed himself onto the English throne. While Richard II's usurpation is a matter of political regret for King Henry – a miscalculation, perhaps – Hotspur vows to "empty all these veins, / And shed my dear blood drop by drop in the dust" in order to avenge it. "By heaven," he exclaims imperiously to his father,

> methinks it were an easy leap
> To pluck bright honour from the pale-faced moon,
> Or dive into the bottom of the deep,
> Where fathom-line could never touch the ground,
> And pluck up drownèd honour by the locks,
> So he that doth redeem her thence might wear,
> Without corrival, all her dignities.

[1.3.199–205]

As an angry young man, only Coriolanus comes close – and the parallel does not bode well. As Worcester wearily notes, Hotspur is addicted to his imagination: "he apprehends a world of figures here, / Not the form of what he should attend" (1.3.207–8). Brilliant though his wit

## Zounds!

Shakespeare's gaffes are few but famous; one came close to endangering his career. In the first versions of *1 Henry IV* Sir John Falstaff is nowhere to be seen: his place is taken by "Sir John Oldcastle". All well and good, except that Shakespeare had made the mistake of naming one of his finest comic creations, the "whoreson round man" of the second tetralogy, after an unimpeachably zealous Protestant martyr. Oldcastle's descendants – one of whom was Elizabeth I's influential Lord Chamberlain – were none too impressed, and the playwright was forced not only to rechristen him, along with Russell (Bardolph) and Harvey (Peto), but to insert a grovelling retraction in the epilogue to *2 Henry IV* insisting that "Oldcastle died a martyr, and this is not the man" (Epilogue, 30).

Shakespeare was usually more careful, for Elizabeth I's goverment kept a wary eye on members of the theatrical profession. In 1581 the Queen made **Edmund Tilney**, her Master of the Revels, responsible for approving all plays that were publicly produced, and as Tilney's interventions to tone down the collaborative *Sir Thomas More* (c.1595) demonstrate, he took his role seriously – as did his successor **George Buck**, in the job during the last years of Shakespeare's career. By that stage things had got even harder for the players. With the passing of the notorious "**Act to Restrain the Abuses of Players**" in 1606, a sop to Puritan parliamentary leaders and popular campaigners, they were banned from acting anything that took the Lord's name in vain. An energetic tradition of stage swearing celebrated by Shakespeare's deliciously rude *Henry IV*s was over at a stroke. Those plays and others, among them *King John*, were henceforth purged of irreligious language (outlawed words included "zounds", short for "God's wounds", "'S'blood"/"Christ's blood" and many others).

The Act initiated a (dis)honourable tradition of cleaning up Shakespeare to suit the supposed sensitivities of his audiences. In this curious pantheon the name of the Reverend **Thomas Bowdler** looms large. Bowdler's *Family Shakespeare* (1818), assembled in collaboration with his sisters (who in fact did most of the work), deleted anything that "cannot with propriety be read aloud in a family", though their swingeing cuts to *Othello* rendered the play so nonsensical that they recommended it be hidden from children just in case they realized. Other plays suffered nearly as much, with the result that the verb "to Bowdlerize" was current in the language just a few decades later.

For some, the idea that Britain's national poet could have penned anything remotely off-colour has simply been too much. The cornerstone of **Joseph C. Hart**'s argument in his splendidly eccentric *The Romance of Yachting* (1848), that Shakespeare did not author the plays, is ingeniously simple: no one man could have written all the filth they contain. Having been "purchased or obtained surreptitiously", Hart thundered, "they were first spiced with obscenity, blackguardism and impurities, before they were produced." Nor are those days entirely past. The prize for misplaced prudery must surely go to the film censors employed by the State of Massachusetts exactly a century later, who insisted that references to "The rank sweat of an adulterous bed" be cut from Olivier's version of *Hamlet* before it could safely be screened.

is – and we see it deployed to devastating effect as he vies with the other rebels for supremacy – it will be one reason for his downfall.

## A tun of man

From snatched hints in Holinshed about the "great resort of people" who hung around the Prince, encouraging him to waste time in "such recreations, exercises and sports as he fancied", in the *Henry IV* plays Shakespeare builds an evolving cast of low-life comic characters who are as varied in personality as they are consistent in their determination to shirk, drink and steal – traits that endear them to the "mad wag" Prince. There's Poins, Hal's close companion and his co-conspirator in the plot to fool Falstaff by robbing him in disguise at Gadshill. There's Russell (later renamed Bardolph; see box above), with his grotesque nose, "all bubuncles and knobs and flames o' fire" (*Henry V*, 3.6.103–4); and Harvey/Peto, cowardly but ultimately honest. There's Francis, well-meaning but dim – and disastrously tongue-tied in front of the

Prince. And finally there's Mistress Quickly, a pub hostess with a gift for unwitting double entendres. In later plays Shakespeare adds to their number with Pistol, a braggart soldier who sounds as if he's just stepped off the pages of Marlowe; and his nemesis Nim, whose favourite – and almost only – word is "humour" (an Elizabethan joke lost on us).

> *No play of Shakespeare's is better than* Henry IV *... History as a dramatic form ripens here to a point past which no further growth is possible.*
>
> Mark Van Doren, *Shakespeare* (1939)

The leader of this motley group, and Shakespeare's largest comic creation in every sense, is Sir John Falstaff (or Oldcastle, as he was originally called; see box opposite), who first appears in *1 Henry IV* and irresistibly dominates both play and stage. Even the subject of his size is a major concern of *1 Henry IV* and a rich seam of the play's linguistic texture: he is "fat-witted", "fat guts", "fat rogue", "woolsack", "huge hill of flesh", "as fat as butter". Until relatively recently he was unquestionably Shakespeare's most popular character; in fact there are so many references to him that *The Shakespeare Allusion-Book* (1909) treats him not as a character but as a work in his own right. A.C. Bradley, writing that same year, merely echoed audiences across the centuries when he proclaimed that "no one in the play understands Falstaff fully, any more than Hamlet was understood by the persons around him. They are both men of genius."

Falstaff comes from a long literary pedigree of vast wenchers, eaters and drinkers, but it is his subversive resistance to the historical patterns of the *Henry IV* plays that make him so attractive. Like the Bastard Falconbridge in *King John*, he considers himself outside the main action. While the rest of the King's army readies itself for battle at Shrewsbury, for instance, Falstaff is openly unimpressed. "What is honour?" he enquires,

> A word. What is in that word 'honour'? What is that 'honour'? Air. A trim reckoning! Who hath it? He that died o' Wednesday. Doth he feel it? No. Doth he hear it? No. 'Tis insensible then? Yea, to the dead. But will it not live with the living? No. Why? Detraction will not suffer it. Therefore I'll none of it. Honour is a mere scutcheon.
>
> **[5.1.133–40]**

Falstaff concludes that "honour", so much a central issue for Hotspur (and ultimately for Hal too), is "a mere scutcheon [cheap heraldic emblem]". That Falstaff has little taste for bravery is clear enough following the episode at Gadshill in the first half of the play, where the disguised Hal and Poins rob their companions in order to see what ludicrous stories of derring-do Falstaff will invent – invention is very much his forte – after the event.

Falstaff is, in an obvious sense, a surrogate father for Hal (indeed, the one character who actually calls him "Hal"), albeit one with whom his relationship is as fraught as the real thing. The relationship between the two is gloriously complicated, and Hal frequently takes the opportunity to test its limits. He stage-manages a role-play at Eastcheap in which Falstaff impersonates King Henry grilling Hal about his antics, but they soon exchange roles and Falstaff is left to defend himself. In response to Hal's accusations about "that villainous, abominable misleader of youth ... that old white-bearded Satan," Sir John is moved to respond:

> That he is old, the more the pity ... If to be old and merry be a sin, then many an old host that I know is damned. If to be fat be to be hated, then Pharaoh's lean kine are to be loved. No, my good lord, banish Harvey, banish Russell, banish Poins, but for sweet Jack Oldcastle, kind Jack Oldcastle, true Jack Oldcastle, valiant Jack Oldcastle, and therefore the more valiant being, as he is, old Jack Oldcastle ... Banish plump Jack, and banish all the world.

PRINCE HARRY  I do; I will.

**[2.5.472–86]**

The tone of Hal's response is famously inscrutable – it can be played as a light-hearted joke just as easily as an open threat (and is perhaps both at once). But it is difficult to watch this moment without thinking of Hal's statement only two scenes into the play that he has every intention of disposing of his "loose behaviour". Imitating Richard II's beloved solar imagery, he proclaims "Yet herein will I imitate the sun, / Who doth permit the base contagious clouds / To smother up his beauty from the world,"

> That when he please again to be himself,
> Being wanted he may be more wondered at
> By breaking through the foul and ugly mists
> Of vapours that did seem to strangle him …
> And like bright metal on a sullen ground,
> My reformation, glitt'ring o'er my fault,
> Shall show more goodly and attract more eyes
> Than that which hath no foil to set it off.
> I'll so offend to make offence a skill,
> Redeeming time when men least think I will.

**[1.2.194–214]**

We glimpse here a Prince who is not making excuses for his wayward existence, but calculating and weighing its advantage with the kingly life to come. His language is impersonal – his companions are "base contagious clouds", the "sullen ground" – but there is no mistaking its thrust. Hal hints that his "reformation", when it arrives, will be a show-stealing change from what has come before.

The finale of *1 Henry IV*, then, has all the ingredients for a blockbuster finish: a military showdown between the royal forces and the rebels; the long-awaited combat between Hal and Hotspur; most importantly, perhaps, the moment where we get to see what will happen between father and son – whether Hal will continue as Henry's "near'st and dearest enemy" (3.3.123) or prove himself his father's heir. Masterfully plotted throughout, the play keeps its audience hanging on to the very end. It is not until the rebels begin to falter, lacking Northumberland's support, that it becomes clear that the King will prevail, and that father and son will indeed be reunited. The outcome of the combat between Hal and Hotspur is somewhat simpler, however. Meeting in battle, Hal crisply warns Hotspur that he can no longer tolerate rivalry. "Think not, Percy, / To share with me in glory any more," he announces,

> Two stars keep not their motion in one sphere,
> Nor can one England brook a double reign
> Of Harry Percy and the Prince of Wales.

**[5.4.62–6]**

Slaying his double, stepping out of his shadow, Hal defines himself.

But the play has one more surprise in store. Near Hotspur's corpse, Hal sees Falstaff lying on the ground, and is struck by emotion:

> What, old acquaintance! Could not all this flesh
> Keep in a little life? Poor Jack, farewell.
> I could have spared a better man.

**[5.4.101–3]**

Hal wants his address to Falstaff's corpse to be a defining moment, his attempt at "reformation". The only problem is that reality isn't compliant with Hal's neat ending – Falstaff is only pretending to be dead in order to steer clear of trouble, and his typically obstreperous resurrection from the battlefield (which seems like a burlesquing prequel to the reawakening scenes Shakespeare employs in his late romances) refuses to finish things off. It is clear there is going to have to be a sequel.

## Stage history and adaptations

Bursting with actorly and comic detail, both parts of *Henry IV* have long been favourites, and it's been estimated that *Part I* was Shakespeare's most successful play in his lifetime. **Richard Burbage** seems to have created the role of Hal, and **John Heminges** (future co-editor of the First Folio) Falstaff. Both will presumably have played before the Flemish Ambassador in 1600, and again at court in 1612 to mark the marriage of James I's daughter Elizabeth (*Part I* is called "The Hotspur" in the records), though by then Burbage will have made a rather elderly prince. Other command performances seem to have occurred in 1625 and 1638, and an adaptation of both plays was prepared for performance at the house of antiquarian **Sir Edward Dering**, *Part I* taking the lion's share, but was never finished.

The runaway fame of Sir John Falstaff – there are over a hundred mentions of him in surviving seventeenth-century documents – makes subsequent references to the plays difficult to untangle. *The First Part of Sir John Falstaff* (1635) is most likely *Part I*, but the dramas described as *Sir John Falstaff* in 1635 and *Oldcastle* in 1638 could be any of Shakespeare's Falstaff plays. Sir John's celebrity even protected him from the theatrical ban imposed by Cromwell's government – a skit entitled *The Bouncing Knight, or, The Robbers Robbed* did the rounds in the 1650s. After the Restoration, the *Henry IV* plays were acted by **Thomas Killigrew**'s company with **William Cartwright** as Falstaff, who was much admired by Pepys. Actor-manager **Thomas Betterton** began as Hotspur in 1682 (playing the role with "fierce and flashing fire", according to one observer), but by the end of the century had migrated to the fat knight.

Betterton's change proved prophetic, for in the eighteenth century *Part I*'s story becomes a roll call of career Falstaffs: first the austere **James Quin**, who gave the knight lofty dignity from 1718 (and who inspired **William Kenrick**'s 1760 spin-off *Falstaff's Wedding*); then actors including **James Love** (from 1761), **Francis Gentleman** (1770) and **John Henderson** (1777). **David Garrick** steered well clear, but did play Hotspur. **John Philip Kemble** also tried Hotspur, leaving Falstaff to his brothers **Stephen**, then **Charles** – although Stephen's talents were limited, he had the advantage of requiring no padding. The most famous Hotspur of the age, however, was **William Charles Macready**, who first acted him in 1815 and continued for the next thirty years.

As evidenced by an adaptation by **Charles Short** called *The Life and Humours of Falstaff* (1826), Sir John's heyday lasted well into the nineteenth century. The American **James Henry Hackett** found it difficult to inspire English audiences in the 1840s (he had more success at home), but his rival **Samuel Phelps** kept Sir John's flame alive at Sadler's Wells for over two decades and famously acted him in a tercentenary *Part I* at Drury Lane in 1864. By this stage grand "historical" productions were all the rage, meaning that *Part I*, lacking in opportunities for pageantry (unlike *Part II*), was less frequently mounted – though **Herbert Beerbohm Tree** did introduce an impressive Battle of Shrewsbury into his version of 1896. After staging it at Stratford a few years later, **Frank Benson** did away with *Part I* altogether in his groundbreaking cycle of histories, replacing it with Marlowe's *Edward II* instead.

The heavily padded Anthony Quayle proved a resonant and convincingly full-bodied Falstaff. He also co-directed the 1951 Stratford production, playing opposite Richard Burton's macho Prince Hal (left) – with whom he had a tricky off stage relationship.

*Part I* would not always fare so badly. **Max Reinhardt** put on both plays at the Berlin Deutsches Theatre in 1912, with **Wilhelm Diegelmann** as Falstaff to **Alessandro Moissi**'s Hal, while **Barry Jackson** went one better nine years later at the Birmingham Rep, presenting both parts on Shakespeare's 357th birthday – *Part I* in the afternoon, *Part II* in the evening. A similar arrangement, directed by **William Bridges-Adams**, marked the opening of the new Memorial Theatre at Stratford in 1932. Seven years later **Orson Welles** presented an adaptation called *Five Kings* in Boston: the *Henry IVs* and *Henry V* became a single play, with excerpts from Holinshed filling the gaps, but it flopped early in its tour.

Immediately after World War II, **John Burrell** directed starry productions of both plays at the Old Vic, with **Laurence Olivier** as a memorable Hotspur (complete with speech impediment), **Sybil Thorndike** as Mistress Quickly and **Ralph Richardson** as a particularly nuanced and sensitive Falstaff. **Anthony Quayle**'s cast at Stratford in 1951 was equally impressive, with **Michael Redgrave** as Hotspur, Quayle himself as a gentlemanly Falstaff and **Richard Burton** as a hard-boiled Hal. Quayle placed much emphasis on the divisive relationship between Sir John and his protégé, as did **Douglas Seale** at the Old Vic in 1955, but in the later production **Robert Hardy**'s Hal had a soft spot for **Paul Rogers**'s Falstaff that only political events eroded.

Since **Clifford Williams**'s epochal staging of the *Henry IVs* as part of the Barton–Hall *Wars of the Roses* cycle in 1964, with **Roy Dotrice** as Hotspur, **Hugh Griffith** as a roguish Falstaff and **Ian Holm** as Hal, the tendency has been for both histories to be played as part of the Henriad cycle, and sometimes of both cycles. The RSC has hosted nearly all: first under **Terry Hands** (1975), who directed a cynical second tetralogy, focused on **Alan Howard**'s graceless prince, that divided audiences – some admiring its imaginative unity, others viewing it as too monochrome (especially with *1 Henry IV*, which was played darkly, Hands's staging making Howard dominant over **Brewster Mason**'s Falstaff throughout). Opposite in conception was **Trevor Nunn**'s Barbican version seven years later, relying on the rich resources of **Joss Ackland** as Sir John (see p.96). **Adrian Noble**'s contribution to the debate in 1991, with a two-play *Henry IV* that opened his reign as director of the RSC, was to emphasize *1 Henry IV*'s vivid spectacle, culminating in an impressively staged Battle of Shrewsbury. Not that this production lacked human detail: **Michael Maloney**'s Hal had plenty of restless energy, **Owen Teale**'s Hotspur was roundly portrayed and **Robert Stephens** was impressive as Falstaff, described by the *Observer* as "a bleak Government health warning on the effects of sack". Also at the RSC, 2000 saw a grand two-tetralogy staging of the histories entitled *This England*, which boasted uncut texts and ran for nearly 24 hours in all. **Michael Attenborough** offered a sombre realization of the *Henry IV*s, with a cast including **David Troughton**'s earnest Bolingbroke and **William Houston** as his wayward son; **Desmond Barrit** made a memorable first appearance as an irrepressible Falstaff, clambering through a trapdoor to puncture the power-broking atmosphere.

But not all royal Shakespeare has appeared courtesy of the RSC. **Michael Bogdanov**'s politically confrontational English Shakespeare Company histories toured the UK as *The Wars of the Roses* from 1986, while a more esoteric approach was tried by the Italian **Collettivo di Parma**, who presented "hypnotic" postmodern versions of their *Enrico IV* at London's Riverside Studios in 1983. Equally radical was the staging of *Part I* by **Ariane Mnouchkine** and the Théâtre du Soleil the following year. Over in New York a decade later, a one-evening abridged version of both parts of *Henry IV* debuted at the Lincoln Center in late 2003. It boasted an impressive cast – **Ethan Hawke**'s Hal to **Kevin Kline**'s Falstaff – and received critical acclaim.

The most artistically memorable film version of the *Henry IV*s remains **Orson Welles**'s *Chimes at Midnight* (1966), but variations on the play surface in **Gus Van Sant**'s *My Own Private Idaho* (1991), in which **William Richert**'s Falstaffian Bob joins **Keanu Reeves**'s rentboy Scott/Hal on the road as they traverse the Pacific Northwest. None other than **Sean Connery** played Hotspur to **Robert Hardy**'s Hal in a 1960 BBC adaptation of *Part I*, while the BBC/Time-Life Shakespeare version was directed by **David Giles** (1979).

## Screen

### Chimes at Midnight
**O. Welles, K. Baxter, J. Gielgud; Orson Welles (dir.)**
Spain/Switzerland, 1966 ▷ Suevia DVD

Compared with *Macbeth* (1948) and *Othello* (1952), *Chimes at Midnight* is the most straightforward work of Orson Welles's three Shakespeare adaptations and also one of his greatest films. Half the wonder lies in the patchworking of material from both *Henry IV*s and the supple pacing. While incipient tragedy is never distant (Hal's "yet herein will I imitate the sun" speech is played with Welles's mountainous Falstaff within anxious earshot), Welles still manages to make the Battle of Shrewsbury – filmed in stomach-churning proximity – a truly impressive first climax, despite limitations of budget. Norman Rodway's fiery Hotspur is both genuinely funny and terribly sad, a verdict that perhaps stands for *Chimes* as a whole, which ditches even more of the historical narrative than Shakespeare in order to concentrate on the personal relationships Welles sees at its centre. Rumours abound that

Miramax intends to restore and rerelease *Chimes*, but for the moment this Spanish version by Suevia Films, released as *Campanadas a Medianoche* but with English dialogue on the DVD, does the job – if you can get hold of it.

### Henry IV Part I
**D. Gwillim, A. Quayle, J. Finch; David Giles (dir.)**
UK, 1979 ▷ Ambrose Video (BBC) DVD

If you want to have access to Shakespeare's *1 Henry IV* as it was originally written, a single and self-contained play, this is the only option. All the usual problems with the BBC Shakespeare project plague it – cardboardish sets, conservative staging, poor picture quality – and real comedy is also somewhat thin on the ground (a huge disadvantage in a play like this). Nevertheless Anthony Quayle's well-bred Falstaff reprises one of his most celebrated stage roles and Tim Pigott-Smith puts in a powerful if somewhat sober performance as Hotspur. David Gwillim's boyish Hal is disappointing: there is little sense of the cold-hearted malevolence that will eventually divorce him from Falstaffian Eastcheap. Recently rereleased in the US by Ambrose Video Publishing.

# Audio

### Henry IV Part I
**J. Glover, J. Glover, T. West; Gordon House (dir.)**
UK, 2000 ▷ BBC ⊙ 💻

Casting a real-life father and son as King Henry and Hal is certainly headline-grabbing, but with quality performances like these it is much more than that: Glovers both senior and junior seem truly to inhabit the roles – Jamie does a good line in slightly unsettling levity, while Julian's King is politically efficient but emotionally troubled. Timothy West is persuasively grizzled as Falstaff, and while this performance may be more reflective than some would like (one occasionally wishes for more fireworks), it makes for excellent listening. Jonathan Keeble brings a north-country edge to his surprisingly sober Hotspur.

# Editions

### Oxford Shakespeare
**David Bevington (ed.); 1987** ▷ Oxford UP

Bevington's terrific edition of *1 Henry IV* offers a no-holds-barred critical introduction to the play and plenty of detail on its textual background, which Bevington takes from the 1598 quarto, one of the neatest texts published during its author's lifetime as well as one of his most popular. Bevington looks hard at the literary and popular models feeding Shakespeare's Falstaff, as well as stretching his interest to events far away in *Part II* but hinted at from early on in the first play – notably Sir John's rejection at the hands of a reformed Hal. Although this edition appears in the Oxford series, Bevington elects to retain the names of Falstaff, Bardolph and Peto as they are usually known (see p.82), arguing continuity. Historical phrases in the text are keyed to passages from Halle and Holinshed at the back.

# Some criticism

### Shakespeare's Histories
**Lily B. Campbell; 1947** ▷ Methuen / Huntington Library Press [o/p]

Peter Saccio's *Shakespeare's Kings* (rev. 2000) remains an excellent introduction to the historical background behind all of Shakespeare's history plays, but if you want a study that puts that theory into practice, Campbell's was one of the first. Along with E.M.W. Tillyard, Campbell was a founder of what is now called the school of "old historicism" and her book, subtitled "Mirrors of Elizabethan policy", attempted to reconstruct how Tudor audiences might have thought about the politics of Shakespeare's histories. Deeply conservative and correspondingly unfashionable, *Shakespeare's Histories* nevertheless makes intriguing reading.

### Sodometries
**Jonathan Goldberg; 1992** ▷ Stanford UP

If you're looking for a counterbalance to the conventional pieties of Campbell, Jonathan Goldberg's controversial recent study should do the trick. Basing itself in the expanding field of gay studies, *Sodometries* looks at different presentations of male homosexuality in Renaissance texts, among them Spenser and Shakespeare. In the *Henry IV* plays, Goldberg investigates just why we (and the characters in the *Henry IV* plays) seem to find Hal so attractive, and uncovers some interesting detail about the play's construction of his sexuality. Goldberg has interesting as well as provocative things to say about sexuality in this period – as about sexuality in the late twentieth century – and has another particularly excellent chapter on Shakespeare's rival Christopher Marlowe.

# Henry IV Part II

The two *Henry IV* plays are startlingly different from one another. Whereas *Part I* is dominated by youth – by two glamorous young men locked in rivalry – its follow-up is both older and gloomier. Though the historical record for the decade compressed into *Part II* is packed with incident, that is not true for the play itself, which witnesses just one abortive battle and a lingering royal death. Shakespeare allows the action to become dominated by response to events already past – and soured by reminiscence and regret. With Hotspur dead, young characters recede into the distance, and the cast becomes populated by people who are starting to seem past their best. Repetition, too, is a major concern as we watch King Henry face yet more rebellion and Hal, having promised his father (and us) a "reformation", pointedly reverting to his bad old ways. Though its humour is often as fresh as ever, the play produces a final twist that still has the capacity to shock. It is no accident that *2 Henry IV* has been called Shakespeare's first tragicomedy.

[DATE] Though presumably *Part II* was written soon after *1 Henry IV*, another "Falstaff" play – *The Merry Wives of Windsor* – may have come between the pair. A composition date of late 1597–early 1598 is generally accepted.

[SOURCES] *2 Henry IV* uses the same set of sources as its predecessor (see p.79). Other details may derive from a source itself employed by John Stow, *The Governor* (1531) by the Tudor courtier Thomas Elyot, and another work, John Eliot's *Ortho-epia Gallica* (1593).

[TEXTS] In contrast to *1 Henry IV*, only one quarto printing (Q1, 1600) is recorded before the play appeared in the 1623 First Folio. Some passages appear in F alone.

## Interpreting the play

Many have wondered how exactly the two *Henry IV*s slot together: did the playwright plan a two-part structure, or was he spurred by the success of *Part I* to pen a follow-up? The so-called "structural problem" of *Henry IV* – whether it is one play or two – still vexes scholars, but perhaps that is because it is really both. Dramatically speaking, what really matters is that *2 Henry IV* is dominated by fallout from events that have already happened, particularly events that have occurred in *Part I*. Though Shakespeare gives no suggestion that time has elapsed between the two parts – quite the opposite, in fact – there is an unmistakable sense that things have changed.

*Part II* turns the fact that it is a sequel into a morbid theatrical preoccupation. With Hotspur dead, it becomes starkly apparent that the play's central political argument – Henry Bolingbroke's usurpation of Richard II's throne – is solely an old men's quarrel. The visibly wilting Northumberland is almost a different character from the proactive politician of *Part I*, and the news of his son's demise destabilizes him further. Though he attempts to make light of his sickness, casting away his crutches and claiming that "these news, / Having been well, that would have made me sick, / Being sick, have in some measure made me well" (1.1.137–9),

## Major Characters & Synopsis

**King Henry IV** of England

**Prince Henry** (known as **Hal**), later crowned **King Henry V**

Hal's brothers: **Prince John** of Lancaster; Humphrey, **Duke of Gloucester**; Thomas, **Duke of Clarence**

The King's supporters: **Earls of Warwick, Surrey** and **Westmoreland**; **Harcourt**; **Gower**; **Sir John Blunt**

### REBELS AGAINST THE KING

**Earl of Northumberland** and his wife, **Lady Northumberland**

**Kate**, **Lady Percy**, Hotspur's widow

**Travers**, Northumberland's servant; and **Morton**, a messenger

Rebellious nobles: **Archbishop of York**; **Lord Bardolph**; **Mowbray**; **Lord Hastings**; **Sir John Coleville**

### OTHER CHARACTERS

**Sir John Falstaff**, one of Hal's companions

Falstaff's followers: **Edward (Ned) Poins, Bardolph**, **Pistol** and **Peto**; and his **Page**

**Mistress Quickly**, hostess of an Eastcheap tavern

**Doll Tearsheet**, a prostitute

**Shallow** and his companion **Silence**, elderly country justices

**Davy**, Shallow's servant

Soldiers recruited by Falstaff: **Mouldy, Shadow, Wart, Feeble** and **Bullcalf**

**Rumour**, the Presenter

[▶▶ action continued from *Henry IV Part I*]

**ACT 1** Northumberland is frantic for news of the rebellion. Initial reports seem good, but the truth soon arrives – the rebels are defeated and his son Hotspur is dead. Northumberland is devastated, but Morton and Lord Bardolph assure him that the fight is not over: the Archbishop of York and others are mustering their forces, and the King's position is not as secure as it seems. Falstaff, meanwhile, is being harangued by the Lord Chief Justice for his influence on Hal, the heir to the throne. Unperturbed by the accusations against him, Falstaff asks for financial support – to no avail.

**ACT 2** Mistress Quickly attempts to have Falstaff arrested for fraud, but he manages to

talk his way out of it by renewing his promise to marry her, even persuading her to pawn her silver to raise cash. Hal, meanwhile, worries about his father's illness, but is diverted from state business when Falstaff sends a letter slandering Poins. Poins denies the allegations, and the pair resolve to spy on Falstaff and find out what he is up to. They sneak into the Eastcheap tavern and overhear Falstaff complaining about the Prince while canoodling with Doll Tearsheet. When confronted, Sir John attempts to convince them he has Hal's best interests at heart. The Prince is interrupted by a summons to court.

**ACT 3** The pressures of leadership are taking their toll on King Henry. Unable to sleep, he reflects ruefully with Warwick and Surrey on his betrayal by the very nobles who helped him to power. Falstaff, visiting Warwickshire to recruit soldiers for the royal army, is on the make – taking bribes to turn down good men.

**ACT 4** York, Mowbray and Hastings, commanding the rebel forces in Gaultres Forest, are unimpressed by Northumberland's flight to Scotland. When they outline their grievances to Hal's brother, Prince John, he promises redress – but as soon as they agree, arrests them for treason. Falstaff, surprisingly, has also succeeded in capturing some enemy troops. The King, meanwhile, is in such poor health that news of his victory causes him to collapse. Arriving at court, Hal assumes his father has died and sadly takes up the crown. The awakening King angrily thinks he covets the throne for himself, but Hal convinces him otherwise and the two are reconciled. The old King dies, hoping that his son's reign will be more peaceful than his own.

**ACT 5** As reports spread that Hal has inherited the throne, the courtiers question his ability. Falstaff certainly believes that his friend has no intention of reforming, and rushes to London to be by his side – also hoping to release Mistress Quickly and Doll Tearsheet from prison. But a shock awaits them: the new King Henry renounces his previous life, pointedly refusing to recognize Falstaff and his companions. Henry V promises to be every inch a king and, according to rumour, plans a campaign against the French.

it is clear that he is no longer really in control. Struggling to assert his youthful strength, he finds he cannot; in "robbing" Hotspur of his youth (*1 Henry IV*, 5.4.76), Hal has all but finished off his rival's father.

## The revolution of the times

King Henry is even more obviously on borrowed time; his demise is the long-deferred event on which both plays depend. In *Part I*, Henry was careworn, weighed down by the double yoke of the crown and his machinations in order to secure it; in *Part II*, he is ailing physically, plagued by illness and insomnia. When we first see him (over a third of the way into the play), he makes a more pitiful figure even than Northumberland. Bitterly asking, "How many thousand of my poorest subjects / Are at this hour asleep?", he continues,

> O sleep, O gentle sleep,
> Nature's soft nurse, how have I frighted thee,
> That thou no more wilt weigh my eyelids down
> And steep my senses in forgetfulness? …
> Wilt thou upon the high and giddy mast
> Seal up the ship-boy's eyes, and rock his brains
> In cradle of the rude imperious surge,
> And in the visitation of the winds,
> Who take the ruffian billows by the top,
> Curling their monstrous heads, and hanging them
> With deafening clamour in the slippery clouds,
> That, with the hurly, death itself awakes?
> Canst thou, O partial sleep, give thy repose
> To the wet sea-boy in an hour so rude,
> And in the calmest and most stillest night,
> With all appliances and means to boot,
> Deny it to a king? Then happy low, lie down.
> Uneasy lies the head that wears a crown.

**[3.1.4–31]**

Henry longs for "forgetfulness", craves the amnesia of sleep – perhaps even the sleep of death. Shakespeare makes the most of hints in Holinshed's *Chronicles* that the King found himself unable to "compose or settle himself to sleep for fear of strangling" after an assassination attempt in 1401, but he gives them a broader motive and introduces a heavy note of irony. It is Henry's very kingliness, an office he had no right to expect, that corrodes his well-being.

But the real undertow of the King's small-hours soliloquy is that of regret, distilled in the person of the anonymous "ship-boy", who for all the perils of his existence still leads a quieter life than his monarch. The harsh mechanics of time haunt Henry's thoughts, as he explains to his supporters Warwick and Surrey:

> O God, that one might read the book of fate,
> And see the revolution of the times
> Make mountains level, and the continent,
> Weary of solid firmness, melt itself
> Into the sea; and other times to see
> The beachy girdle of the ocean
> Too wide for Neptune's hips; how chance's mocks
> And changes fill the cup of alteration
> With divers liquors! 'Tis not ten years gone

Since Richard and Northumberland, great friends,
Did feast together; and in two year after
Were they at wars …

**[3.1.44–55]**

Time brings change, and change lays waste to man. Though the span of years in Henry's mind is only small, it dilates into a geological frame, placed alongside the collapse of mountains and the melting of the earth. As in Shakespeare's Sonnets – a portion of which were probably complete by the time he wrote *2 Henry IV* – "this bloody tyrant", "devouring time", dwarfs mere humanity; man's "stay" on this earth is but "inconstant" (as Sonnets 15, 16 and 19 put it). As Warwick rejoins, "such things become the hatch and brood of time" (3.1.81); time will bring all human actions – both bad and good – to light.

The kingdom at large is, Henry frets, poisoned with "rank diseases" and has "danger near the heart of it" (3.1.37–9); and so too are many of its inhabitants (at least as the play sees it). Into *2 Henry IV* Shakespeare introduces two new characters, Justices Shallow and Silence of Warwickshire, the playwright's home county. In many ways irrelevant to the plot, this pair of old men nevertheless enshrine what much of the play is about. While Henry's memory is a burden to him, Shallow and Silence are only too pleased to launch themselves into reminiscence. As they discuss Falstaff, "this Sir John … that comes hither anon about soldiers", their thoughts turn at once to that other country, the distant past:

SHALLOW  The same Sir John, the very same. I see him breaking Scoggin's head at the court gate when a was a crack, not thus high. And the very same day did I fight with one Samson Stockfish, a fruiterer, behind Gray's Inn. Jesu, Jesu, the mad days that I have spent! And to see how many of my old acquaintance are dead.

SILENCE  We shall all follow, cousin.

SHALLOW  Certain, 'tis certain; very sure, very sure. Death, as the Psalmist saith, is certain to all; all shall die.

**[3.2.26–36]**

Lumbering and meandering though their conversation is – further hobbled by Shallow's habit of repeating everything – the subject of their thoughts is definite enough. Death haunts them at least as much as it haunts the King, for they are closer to it than most. The "mad days", like the youthful combats between Hal and Hotspur they echo, are well and truly over.

Even the subject of Shallow and Silence's musings, Falstaff, is feeling twinges of mortality. If his sheer bulk is a major topic of conversation in *Part I*, in its sequel it is that same body's steady breakdown. Falstaff enters the play enquiring what the doctor thinks of his "water" (urine), and learning (in his brand-new Page's words) that "the water itself was a good healthy water, but, for the party that owed it, he might have more diseases than he knew for" (1.2.3–5). The comedy is obvious, but it masks a serious theme. Whereas in *1 Henry IV* Falstaff is gleefully happy to twist the time of day to his own ends – never mind his time of life – in *Part II* even he is striving, and failing, to stave away thoughts of death. "I am old, I am old," he frets to his Eastcheap mistress, Doll Tearsheet, "Thou'lt forget me when I am gone" (2.4.273–80). When she wonders "when wilt thou leave fighting o'days, and foining o'nights, and begin to patch up thine old body for heaven?", Falstaff is terrified. "Peace, good Doll," he urges, "do not speak like a death's-head, do not bid me remember mine end" (2.4.233–7).

## Tears and heavy sorrows

But the one central death that does occur in *Part II* proves more complicated than those repeated dramatic premonitions might suggest. Hal is spending less time than before in

Eastcheap – his main visit is spent with Poins, setting up Falstaff for yet another comedown – and is being drawn more and more to the court. Everyone knows why. Following the news that Prince John has managed to capture the ringleaders of the rebellion, the King is seized not by joy, but sickness, and rapidly worsens to the point where his closest advisers fear for his life. Coming across his slumbering father, Hal assumes the worst – that Henry is dead. "By his gates of breath / There lies a downy feather which stirs not," the Prince exclaims,

> My gracious lord, my father!—
> This sleep is sound indeed. This is a sleep
> That from this golden rigol hath divorced
> So many English kings.—Thy due from me
> Is tears and heavy sorrows of the blood,
> Which nature, love, and filial tenderness
> Shall, O dear father, pay thee plenteously.
> My due from thee is this imperial crown,
> Which, as immediate from thy place and blood,
> Derives itself to me.
> > *He puts the crown on his head*
> > Lo where it sits,
> Which God shall guard; and put the world's whole strength
> Into one giant arm, it shall not force
> This lineal honour from me. This from thee
> Will I to mine leave, as 'tis left to me.

**[4.3.162–78]**

This moment is the climax of the play and fraught with all sorts of meanings – a teasing meta-theatrical moment for an actor feigning deathlike sleep onstage, it is also a resonant reconstruction of a past event, the deposition scene in *Richard II*, in which the very same crown is handed from one monarch to the next, and with it all the power of the throne. It is striking that Hal is every bit as calculating as his father had been; though invoking "God" as he takes up the precious object in his hands, his words are undeniably legalistic in tone. His part of the bargain is "tears and heavy sorrows of the blood"; his father's is far more tangible, "this imperial crown".

But Hal's spontaneous ceremony is premature. The King is still alive – just – and when he wakes he is incandescent with rage, until Hal persuades him of his honest intentions. As the two are finally reconciled, Henry turns once more to reminiscence:

> God knows, my son,
> By what bypaths and indirect crook'd ways
> I met this crown; and I myself know well
> How troublesome it sat upon my head.
> To thee it descend with better quiet,
> Better opinion, better confirmation;
> For all the soil of the achievement goes
> With me into the earth ...

**[4.3.312–9]**

"For all my reign," he goes on, "hath been but as a scene / Acting that argument." The pageant – and Shakespeare's play – will only be halted with his demise.

Just before Henry dies, he comments, "and now my death / Changes the mood" (4.3.327–8), but if we expect a comic conclusion like that in *Part I* we are to be disappointed. Falstaff's own fate, obliquely hinted at throughout the *Henry IV* plays, hastens closer. Prepared by debunkings

> *It seems probable that* 2 Henry IV *was written some three years before* Troilus, *some six before* Measure for Measure, *yet here Shakespeare anticipates the objectivity of manner, fused with a suggestion of deep and personal concern, which is characteristic of these two later plays.*
>
> Clifford Leech, "The Unity of *2 Henry IV*" (1953)

galore and Hal's cool words on the matter, the audience knows that it is only a matter of time before Falstaff is rejected by the Prince – a conclusion even rehearsed at Shrewsbury. Yet Falstaff and his followers have no such expectation as the news breaks that old King Henry is dead. Grabbing the first horses he finds ("The laws of England," he boasts, "are at my command-ment"), Falstaff is sure that "the young King is sick for me". But when he reaches out from the crowd that throngs the new King Henry, his welcome is icy:

SIR JOHN   God save thee, my sweet boy!
KING HARRY
> My Lord Chief Justice, speak to that vain man.
LORD CHIEF JUSTICE   *(to Sir John)*
> Have you your wits? Know you what 'tis you speak?
SIR JOHN
> My king, my Jove, I speak to thee, my heart!
KING HARRY
> I know thee not, old man. Fall to thy prayers.
> How ill white hairs becomes a fool and jester!
> I have long dreamt of such a kind of man.
> So surfeit-swelled, so old, and so profane;
> But being awake, I do despise my dream.

**(5.4.43–51)**

"Presume not that I am the thing I was," Henry continues, "I have turned away my former self." His reformation is over almost before it has begun, even if some critics (notably the great A.C. Bradley) have questioned whether one of Shakespeare's finest comic creations can be disposed of so easily. Yet when Falstaff attempts to make light of the situation, arguing to Shallow that "this that you heard was but a colour [pretext]", the effect is heart-rending. Shallow's response, that it is "a colour I fear that you will die in" (5.3.85), is typically morbid, but in this instance unusually prescient.

Having wasted time with Falstaff, and watched his father serve it, Hal now attempts to redeem his misspent hours. His education as a prince, one of the major strands in the *Henry IV* plays, has been achieved, but Shakespeare does not hide from us its personal cost, nor does he cosset us by insisting that the perfect prince has to be a perfect man. Questions concerning the sacrifices of kingship are at the forefront of *2 Henry IV*, and in the next play in the cycle, *Henry V*, they will loom even larger.

## Stage history and adaptations

The performance history of *2 Henry IV* largely shadows that of *Part I* (see p.85), but judging by the popularity of printed versions the first play seems to have been better known before Shakespeare's death in 1616. *Part I*'s lighthearted approach to its story – and the numerous comic episodes starring Falstaff – must have attracted audiences, while the darker tone of *Part II* and the tragic banishment of Sir John might have appealed to producers less. Even so, both parts were acted at **court** in celebration of the 1612 marriage between James I's daughter Elizabeth and a German prince (*Part II* appears as "Sir John Falstaff" in the paperwork). The bulky **John Lowin**, the King's Men's longest serving actor, probably took over the role from Heminges (see p.85), and was certainly playing it by the 1620s. The papers of **Sir Edward Dering** contain an adaptation of both parts made around the same time, but it was probably never performed.

Aside from various references to plays and adaptations starring Falstaff (see p.85), the first specific mentions of *Part II* occur at the behest of **Thomas Betterton**, who revived it with the other Falstaff plays during the 1690s. It appeared as a separate piece in 1720 at Drury Lane, with

Doll Tearsheet (Jeanne Moreau) snuggles up to Falstaff (Orson Welles) in Welles's introspective retelling of the *Henry IV* plays, *Chimes at Midnight* (1966), his finest Shakespearian film.

**Colley Cibber** as Shallow and his son **Theophilus** a swaggering Pistol. Despite his initial reluctance to stage either *Henry IV* at Covent Garden, **David Garrick** relented and played King Henry from 1758 onwards – staging Hal's coronation with plenty of pomp, not to mention period costume (a recent innovation). A few years later a pastiche entitled *Falstaff's Wedding* by **William Kendrick** appeared, which developed an entire plot from loose ends in *Part II*; and the first recorded Shakespearian production in Australia was a version of *Henry IV*, performed in 1800.

A Falstaff-centred adaptation of *Part II* by **John Philip Kemble** took the boards in 1804, continuing a steady trend towards ever grander spectacle that reached new heights in **William Charles Macready**'s production of 1821 with **Charles Kemble** as Hal. This featured no fewer than four additional coronation scenes, catering for the coronation fever that attended the crowning of George IV that year (George responded by lavishing free tickets for Covent Garden on his subjects). After touring to New York, Macready presented a spiced-up *Part II* at Drury Lane in 1834 complete with musical interludes. Following his triumph as a richly comic Falstaff in *Part I* (he delighted audiences by being unable to sit down without assistance), **Samuel Phelps** turned his talents to both King Henry and Shallow in versions of *Part II* that appeared at Sadler's Wells from 1853.

**Frank Benson** had a preference for *Part II* in the Henriad productions he put on at Stratford from 1894 (*Part I* disappeared entirely in 1906) and played Falstaff himself before **Louis Calvert** took over the role, while his wife **Constance** acted Doll Tearsheet. As **Max Reinhardt**'s versions of both plays wowed audiences in Berlin in 1912, **Barry Jackson** was preparing his own stagings at the pioneering Birmingham Rep in which full-text *Henry IV*s were performed on the same day. **Ben Greet** revived *Part II* at the Old Vic in 1917, following with its predecessor three years later, and **William Bridges-Adams** celebrated the opening of the new main house at Stratford in 1932 with productions of both – **Dorothy Massingham**'s haunting Doll garnered praise, though the rest of the cast was described as "tired out" after an exhausting rehearsal schedule.

After the cessation of hostilities in 1945 **John Burrell** opened twin Old Vic productions of the *Henry IV*s with an impressive cast, many of whom had cut their teeth with the same company before the war. **Ralph Richardson**'s Falstaff was regarded as one of the finest ever – "not a *comic* performance", in Kenneth Tynan's words – and after his extraordinary Hotspur **Laurence Olivier** excelled as Shallow, described by Tynan as "a paltering scarecrow of a man" yet bursting with generosity. At Stratford, in the Festival of Britain season of 1951, **Michael Redgrave** directed *Part II* after playing Hotspur in *Part I*; **Anthony Quayle** remained as a superlative Falstaff, and **Richard Burton** a commanding Hal who really showed his mettle in the second play. Four years later **Douglas Seale**'s Old Vic production headlined the young **Robert Hardy** as Hal and **Paul Rogers** as Falstaff, but also with **John Neville**'s Pistol and **Rachel Roberts**'s Mistress Quickly.

Seale's grand vision of the histories as a unit would influence subsequent directors, most famously **Peter Hall** and **John Barton**, who produced in 1964 a cycle of the English histories into which *2 Henry IV* was slotted under **Clifford Williams**'s control, with **Hugh Griffiths** as a moving Falstaff adrift in the turbulent politics that surrounded him – politics in which **Ian Holm**'s reserved Hal was entirely comfortable. Since then the play has nearly always been produced in company with *Part I*, frequently in large cycles put on by the RSC. **Terry Hands**'s sober version of 1975, presenting the second tetralogy, centred on **Alan Howard**'s sourly calculating prince (according to one observer, the oats he sowed "were never very wild"), who consistently suborned **Brewster Mason**'s patient and dignified Falstaff until the inevitable betrayal – a rejection scene in which Henry appeared, statue-like, clad in gold from top to toe. In thought-provoking contrast **Trevor Nunn**'s staging from 1982 made both parts of *Henry IV* Falstaff's via the talents of **Joss Ackland**, who delivered a rounded interpretation of the role that plumbed its tragic depths alongside its comedy. Nunn's Hal, **Gerard Murphy**, was a bland drop-out ("less hell-raiser than housemaid", said one reviewer), although **Patrick Stewart**'s politically astute King generated positive notices.

**Adrian Noble**'s RSC production in 1991 was applauded by reviewers for its subtle touches of staging, many of which connected both parts of *Henry IV*; **Michael Maloney** played Hal to **Julian Glover**'s Henry with **David Bradley**'s fussy Shallow attracting particular attention. **Michael Attenborough**'s version of the *Henry IV*s, part of the RSC's history extravaganza *This England* in 2000 (see p.87) handled the different styles of the two plays more impressively even than Noble – **Desmond Barrit**'s previously energetic Falstaff was visibly ailing in *Part II*, a hostage to affairs beyond his control, while the manic double-act of **Benjamin Whitrow** and **Peter Copley** as Shallow and Silence captured the bizarre futility of rural escape. **Michael Bogdanov**'s English Shakespeare Company production, which opened in 1986, saw **John Woodvine**'s Falstaff – "sly as a fox and warm as a coal-fire", according to Michael Billington – play against **Jenny Quayle**'s Doll. In 2003 New York, audiences were treated to a one-evening version of *Henry IV*; its glittering cast – **Ethan Hawke**'s Hal to **Kevin Kline**'s Falstaff – was met by equally glowing reviews.

The most interesting cinema adaptation of both *Henry IV*s is **Orson Welles**'s *Chimes At Midnight*, which uses more *Part II* text than *Part I*, and which in turn inspired **Gus Van Sant**'s *My Own Private Idaho* (see p.87). The BBC/Time-Life version, directed like *Part I* by **David Giles**, was aired in 1979; **Anthony Quayle**'s return as Falstaff after playing him nearly thirty years before was the production's most noteworthy aspect.

## Screen

### Chimes at Midnight

**O. Welles, K. Baxter, J. Gielgud; Orson Welles (dir.)**
Spain/Switzerland, 1966 ▷ Suevia 📀 📼

Even in the midst of *1 Henry IV*'s comic highlights Orson

Welles always seems to be thinking of *Part II* – Falstaff's glum observation to Shallow that "we have heard the chimes at midnight" forms part of its opening sequence – and in truth the second play's darkness is closer to his conception of what they are both about. Here the central intimacy between Welles's Falstaff and Keith Baxter's shady Hal is always doomed, and often it seems that only Falstaff's incessant guzzling of sack insulates him from the chilly winds of reality. In *Chimes* that chill is memorably embodied in Gielgud's precise King Henry and even Jeanne Moreau's passionate Doll (a terrific cameo) proves entirely unable to protect her man. But Welles's skill is such that the film's conclusion – a typically deft insertion from *Henry V* – still feels like an appalling shock, the rejection scene played for all it's worth, while even Henry's own death is unexpectedly moving. In the absence of a properly rereleased *Chimes* this version from Spain's Suevia Films, released as *Campanadas a Medianoche* but with English dialogue on the DVD, more than suffices.

## Henry IV Part II
### D. Gwillim, A. Quayle, J. Finch; David Giles (dir.)
UK, 1979  ▷ Ambrose (BBC)  ▭  DVD

Despite a lingering unease that Giles's two-part production is rather too Merrie England for its own good, his *2 Henry IV* does in the end try to remain true to the play's darker tone. Jon Finch relished playing Bolingbroke/King Henry across *Richard II* and the *Henry IVs*, and in an unexpectedly fierce death scene it shows, but David Gwillim lacks the necessary savagery and produces a merely callow Hal. And while Quayle's Falstaff is chillier and more bad-tempered than in *Part I*, he steadfastly refuses to dominate the play – producing a rejection scene that may leave some audiences feeling hard done by. While the BBC version is certainly more faithful to Shakespeare's script than Welles, as an artistic achievement it never comes remotely close. Recently rereleased in the US by Ambrose Video Publishing.

## Audio
### Henry IV Part II
### J. Glover, J. Glover, T. West; Gordon House (dir.)
UK, 1999  ▷ BBC  ⊙  ▭

Continuity is the order of the day with the BBC's *Henry IVs*: a near-identical cast features, and in the director's chair once again is Gordon House. In truth the slightly cool style of this production suits *Part II* better, and the scenes between Prunella Scales's earthy Mistress Quickly, Timothy West's dark-toned Falstaff and Lucy Briers's Doll have a particular poignancy. That said, Shallow (Richard Briers) and Silence (Timothy Bateson) bring some welcome comedy to affairs – though Jamie Glover plays Hal earnestly, a man on a mission and genuinely conscious that time is pressing, while his father Julian genuinely seems wracked by his countless woes.

## Editions
### New Cambridge Shakespeare
### Giorgio Melchiori; 1989  ▷ Cambridge UP

The perils facing any Shakespearian editor are great, greater still when you consider that one of the most banal pieces of text in this play (Bardolph's "Who keeps the gate there, ho!" at

1.1.1) was footnoted in such preposterous detail in the 1923 Arden edition that those notes were once included in an anthology of comic writing. Fortunately Giorgio Melchiori makes no such mistakes for New Cambridge, presenting a brisk (if anything, a little rushed) critical introduction to *2 Henry IV* that deals sensibly with all its major concerns. Much of his time is taken up with stage history, assisted as always in this series by C. Walter Hodges's masterly pen-and-ink impressions of Elizabethan performance. Melchiori's text is taken from the 1600 quarto, but includes various passages unique to the Folio edition. Various sources, including a segment of *The Famous Victories of Henry V*, are included in an appendix.

## Some criticism
### Oxford Lectures on Poetry
### A.C. Bradley; 1909  ▷ Macmillan / Classworks

After his *Shakespearean Tragedy* (see p.78) Bradley's most influential work is this collection of lectures delivered while the author was Professor of Poetry at Oxford. The volume indulges his Romantic tastes (among the contents are articles on Wordsworth, Shelley and "The Sublime") but heads inexorably towards Bradley's great love, Shakespeare – and one of his greatest loves of all, Falstaff. In this classic essay Bradley's thesis is simple: "In Falstaff," he declares, the poet "overshot his mark. He created so extraordinary a being, and fixed him so firmly on his intellectual throne, that when he sought to dethrone him he could not." This sense that Shakespeare simply cannot kill off someone so touched by genius has remained influential, and even Bradley's suggestion that poet and Falstaff are locked into a kind of battle to the death retains a certain appeal. This reading is determined to make *2 Henry IV* into a tragedy in the largest (and most Bradleian) sense, and thus shies away from nearly everything else in the play.

### Henry IV Parts One and Two
### Nigel Wood; 1995  ▷ Open UP [o/p]

The pronouncements of Renaissance critics concentrating on hard-core literary theory can be gnomic to the point impenetrability. *Henry IV Parts One and Two: Theory in Practice* does occasionally veer towards mystification, but it does at least set out to show that readings informed by literary theory can be tied to specific texts and work convincingly – and without implying that Shakespeare had the collected works of Derrida and Bakhtin alongside his Halle and Holinshed. Four essays feature, each introduced by an explanatory editorial piece and followed by a dialogue between Nigel Wood and the contributor. Peter Womack's piece suggesting ways in which the *Henry IV* plays are a kind of Brechtian "epic theatre" and make audiences aware of their problematic design, is perhaps the best of the bunch; but Donald MacDonald's article on the relationship between Bakhtin and the carnival sides of Shakespeare is also persuasive.

# Henry V

With its dramatization of a miraculous English triumph at Agincourt under a glamorous, youthful king, *Henry V* is often thought of as Shakespeare's most overtly patriotic play. Rousing, flag-waving productions have made it into a symbol – even a cliché – of England and English resoluteness. Stirring snippets have passed into the language; politicians regularly cite it as their favourite play; even the history books still seem in thrall to Shakespeare's boyish King. By the same token, *Henry V* has sometimes been treated with wariness by writers and directors embarrassed by its supposedly nationalistic message. Director Michael Bogdanov transformed it into a crudely jingoistic pantomime in the 1980s, and audiences at the National Theatre in London have recently been treated to a production which draws parallels between fifteenth-century France and twenty-first-century Iraq. But there are more complex meanings to Shakespeare's drama than critics sometimes allow. *Henry V* does not shy away from the savage realities of conflict, and though it celebrates martial glory and heroism, those who ignore its complicating counter-currents are deaf to much of what the play is about. Like all great works of art – and unlike propaganda – the play contains the potential to be understood in radically and creatively different ways.

[DATE] Perhaps the easiest play to date because of a reference it makes to the Earl of Essex's campaign in Ireland, *Henry V* was almost certainly first acted in the summer of 1599.

[SOURCES] As with Shakespeare's other histories, the combination of Holinshed's *Chronicles* (1587) and Halle's *Union* (1548) provides the basic narrative. These were bulked out by *The Famous Victories of Henry V* (c.1580s), Samuel Daniel's poem *The Civil Wars* (1595), and John Stow's *Chronicles* (1580) and *Annals* (1592).

[TEXTS] While the Folio text (F1, 1623) was printed from Shakespeare's own papers, the play had already circulated in a "bad" quarto version published in 1600 (Q1) and reprinted twice more.

## Interpreting the play

An old king is dead, his youthful son is on the throne and the internecine wrangling of the two *Henry IV* plays promises at last to recede. *Henry V* is eager to put the past to rest. Shunning the insidious figure of Rumour, who acts as the presenter to *Part II*, Shakespeare's Chorus (who introduces the story at the beginning of each Act) in *Henry V* has an altogether bolder message. Capitalizing on the sense of optimism and excitement that attends the play's opening, he cries, "O for a muse of fire, that would ascend / The brightest heaven of invention:"

> A kingdom for a stage, princes to act,
> And monarchs to behold the swelling scene.
> Then should the warlike Harry, like himself,
> Assume the port of Mars, and at his heels,
> Leashed in like hounds, should famine, sword, and fire
> Crouch for employment.

*[Prologue, 1–8]*

## Major Characters & Synopsis

**Chorus**, introducing the action

**THE ENGLISH**
**King Henry V** of England (known as **Harry**)
**Dukes of Gloucester** and **Clarence**, Henry's
   brothers
**Duke of Exeter**, Henry's uncle
**Duke of York**
**Earls of Salisbury**, **Westmorland** and **Warwick**
**Archbishop of Canterbury**
**Bishop of Ely**
Traitors to King Henry: **Richard**, **Earl of**
   **Cambridge**; **Henry**, **Lord Scrope of**
   **Masham**; **Sir Thomas Grey**
**Pistol**, **Nim** and **Bardolph**, Falstaff's former
   companions
**Boy**, formerly in Falstaff's service
**Hostess**, formerly Mistress Quickly, Pistol's wife
**Captains Gower**, **Fluellen**, **Macmorris** and
   **Jamy**, serving in Henry's army
**Sir Thomas Erpingham**
**John Bates**, **Alexander Court** and **Michael**
   **Williams**, English soldiers

**THE FRENCH**
**King Charles VI** of France
**Queen Isabel**, Charles's wife
**Louis the Dauphin**, their son and heir
**Princess Catherine**, their daughter
**Alice**, a lady attending Catherine
French noblemen: **Constable of France**; **Dukes**
   **of Bourbon**, **Orléans**, **Berri** and **Normandy**;
   **Lord Rambures** and **Lord Grandpré**
**Montjoy**, the French herald
**Governor of Harfleur** and **Ambassadors** to the
   English court

[▶▶ action continued from *2 Henry IV*]
**ACT 1** The relationship between England and
France has sunk to new depths. King Henry's religious advisers are convincing him to claim the
French throne, and the Dauphin has sent a barrel
of tennis balls to the English king, mocking his
youth and his reputation as a wastrel. Stung by
the insult, Henry decides to invade.

**ACT 2** As the country prepares for war, Bardolph,
Nim and Pistol plan to enlist, but end up brawling.
They are interrupted by a summons to Falstaff who,
broken by Henry's rejection, dies soon after their

visit. Embarking at Southampton, the King narrowly
avoids an assassination attempt organized by
Scrope, Cambridge and Grey, who are arrested for
treason. France's leaders are divided, meanwhile:
King Charles is nervous about the English threat,
while the Dauphin refuses to take it seriously.

**ACT 3** Fighting rages outside Harfleur, where
King Henry exhorts his forces to drive through the
town walls. Bardolph is keen to advance, but his
reluctant companions have to be driven on by
Fluellen, who then argues with his fellow captains.
They are interrupted by Henry's address to the
Governor of Harfleur, warning of potential atrocities if the town continues to resist. The Governor
surrenders – a triumph for Henry, whose forces
are flagging. At the French court, where Princess
Catherine is secretly learning English, King
Charles is so shocked by events that he commits
a huge army to engage the invaders. Back
among the English, Bardolph is to be executed
for stealing. King Henry tells the French herald
that though his army is weak he will not avoid an
encounter with the French.

**ACT 4** The night before battle, Henry visits his
demoralized troops in disguise. One soldier,
named Williams, is challenged by the King for
doubting the value of their mission. In the morning,
the English (outnumbered five to one) are glumly
saying farewell to each other when Henry raises
them with an inspiring speech. They head for what
seems certain death at Agincourt, but the battle
unexpectedly turns their way. As the French are
regrouping, Henry orders all enemy prisoners to be
killed, just before news arrives that the French have
murdered the boys guarding the English camp.
Henry's victory finally assured, it is confirmed that
French casualties have topped 10,000 to just 25
English dead. The King goes in search of Williams,
and reveals his true identity before forgiving him.

**ACT 5** At a peace conference in France, the
two sides negotiate terms – one of which is a
marriage between Henry and Catherine. Henry
privately woos her and she relents, at which
peace is concluded and their wedding agreed. All
seems resolved, but the Chorus warns that it
won't remain so – the reign of Henry's son (Henry
VI) will bring only sorrow for England.

"Can this cock-pit hold / The vasty fields of France?" the Chorus enquires, his voice charged with the strong vowel sounds that were the powerhouse of the Elizabethan stage, "Or may we cram / Within this wooden O the very casques / That did affright the air at Agincourt?" Though it's possible that *Henry V* premiered at the Curtain, a temporary home for the Lord Chamberlain's Men (see p.458), it seems more likely that it was the new Bankside Globe – which had room for some three thousand spectators, about one percent of London's total population – that first played host to the Chorus's ironic protestations. His speech brings patriotism and drama into creative alignment. This is to be the moment when history becomes History.

## Warlike Harry

Our first introductions to the new King leave us in no doubt that the "wildness" of his youth is past. When the Archbishop of Canterbury and Bishop of Ely get together to discuss the possibility of a war in France, they are full of praise for a King they consider "full of grace and fair regard", as Canterbury exclaims:

> The breath no sooner left his father's body
> But that his wildness, mortified in him,
> Seemed to die too. Yea, at that very moment
> Consideration like an angel came
> And whipped th'offending Adam out of him,
> Leaving his body as a paradise
> T'envelop and contain celestial spirits.

[1.1.26–32]

---

### KEY SOURCE  Holinshed's *Chronicles*

All of Shakespeare's English history plays – and several others including *Macbeth* and *Cymbeline* – are indebted to one key source, the sprawling **Chronicles of England, Scotland and Ireland**, first printed in 1577. The work's general editor was **Raphael Holinshed**, who began his career as a translator but soon found himself in charge of a unique historical enterprise, an attempt to catalogue the history and topography of "Great Britain" – a term that first appears under Henry VIII, who annexed Wales and had himself declared King of Ireland. Declaring their intention to have "an especial eye unto the truth of things", Holinshed and his team mined many sources to bring to an Elizabethan readership a lively and patriotic account of their nation, starting from its semi-legendary beginnings and providing plenty of engaging detail along the way. The book was hugely successful, and in fact outlived Holinshed himself; he died around 1580 and it was left to his co-authors, among whom were **Edmund Campion**, **William Harrison**, **Richard Hooker**, **Richard Stanyhurst** and **John Stow**, to bring the *Chronicles* up to date. Doing so was politically risky – the second edition covered events as recent as ten years before – and the new edition they published in 1587 came under fire from the censors, who demanded large-scale changes before the book could be distributed. These alterations survive in some extant copies, which have pages curiously misnumbered or lines simply missed out.

It was to this 1587 edition that Shakespeare repeatedly turned, and he also drew directly upon one of Holinshed's key sources, **Edward Halle**'s Tudor-friendly and hyper-moralistic *Union of the Two Noble and Illustrious Families of Lancaster and York* (1548). The only puzzle is how a youthful and probably impoverished playwright could have afforded to buy such expensive tomes in the first place (his earliest history play to use them, probably *2 Henry VI*, dates from 1590–91). One theory is that he simply borrowed them from his friend and fellow Stratfordian, the printer **Richard Field**, but if that is so then the loan might have been more long-standing than either party was expecting – Shakespeare's last play to use Holinshed, *Henry VIII*, dates from over twenty years later.

The reformation is complete – and in explicitly religious terms, with an "angel" purifying the King from his earthly dross. One of Shakespeare's sources, Edward Halle's chronicle, emphasizes that Henry was a monarch "whose life was immaculate and his living without spot … the mirror of Christendom and the glory of his country". This connection between godliness and Englishness might make us think of Gaunt's description of the "blessèd plot" in *Richard II*, but in *Henry V* God's support for the English cause is never in doubt. "O God, thy arm was here," Henry exclaims after his victory at Agincourt and the revelation that the English losses are miraculously (and unhistorically) slight. "Take it God, / For it is none but thine" (4.8.106–12).

Henry is equipped with the lion's share of words in the play (his is Shakespeare's largest role to date), and his skills as an orator have passed into legend. "Once more unto the breach, dear friends, once more," he urges his compatriots outside the walls of Harfleur:

> Or close the wall up with our English dead.
> In peace there's nothing so becomes a man
> As modest stillness and humility,
> But when the blast of war blows in our ears,
> Then imitate the action of the tiger,
> Stiffen the sinews, conjure up the blood,
> Disguise fair nature with hard-favoured rage …
>                      … And you, good yeomen,
> Whose limbs were made in England, show us here
> The mettle of your pasture; let us swear
> That you are worth your breeding—which I doubt not,
> For there is none of you so mean and base
> That hath not noble lustre in your eyes.
> I see you stand like greyhounds in the slips,
> Straining upon the start. The game's afoot.
> Follow your spirit, and upon this charge
> Cry, 'God for Harry! England and Saint George!'

**[3.1.1–34]**

The glamour of Henry's speech, one of the most famous in the Shakespearian canon – and which actually occupies a whole scene – is undeniable, and it has frequently been included in literary anthologies for soldiers heading to war (most recently in Iraq). But the King's rhetoric, though thrilling, is intrinsically euphemistic: war is a "game", the English soldiers "greyhounds", not killers. Even class divisions are erased: the King addresses his subjects as "friends"; the "mean and base" are made "noble" fighting side by side with their countrymen. Henry's equalizing spirit will appear again at Agincourt, where he urges his troops, calling them "We few, we happy few, we band of brothers" (4.3.60).

Meeting stiffer resistance, however, the King offers a less appealing analysis of battle. Faced with the intractable citizens of Harfleur – who have the effrontery to resist the occupying English army – Henry's tone darkens as he threatens the townspeople with the consequences of their actions. "Take pity of your town and of your people," he coldly suggests,

> Whiles yet my soldiers are in my command,
> Whiles yet the cool and temperate wind of grace
> O'erblows the filthy and contagious clouds
> Of heady murder, spoil, and villainy.
> If not—why, in a moment look to see
> The blind and bloody soldier with foul hand
> Defile the locks of your shrill-shrieking daughters;
> Your fathers taken by the silver beards,

Adrian Lester made a dynamic, can-do and believably calculating King in Nicholas Hytner's staging of *Henry V* at the National Theatre in 2003.

And their most reverend heads dashed to the walls;
Your naked infants spitted upon pikes,
Whiles the mad mothers with their howls confused
Do break the clouds, as did the wives of Jewry
At Herod's bloody-hunting slaughtermen.

**[3.3.110–24]**

A threat it may be – and, as it proves, effective enough to prevent its implementation – but there is no disguising the calculated violence in Henry's words, nor the fact that it foreshadows one of *Henry V*'s most obscene actions, the execution by both sides of their prisoners. Though the King will later insist that God's "arm" was at Agincourt, here his own soldiers are compared to King Herod's "bloody-hunting slaughtermen", the biblical soldiers whose grim task it was to hunt down the infant Jesus. In little more than the space of two scenes, we are confronted with the extreme realities of war – its pity along with its glory.

Some of the King's soldiers, many of them conscripts, are openly cynical about his gung-ho spirit. Though the Chorus is eager to describe the restorative effect of Henry's incognito night-time visit to his troops (eagerly promising "a little touch of Harry in the night"), in the event the King's common touch all but deserts him when he encounters a group of English squaddies while disguised as an officer. One, Williams, is not impressed by Henry's unctuous assertion that "methinks I could not die anywhere so contented as in the King's company, his cause being just and his quarrel honourable". Williams angrily retorts:

But if the cause be not good, the King himself hath a heavy reckoning to make, when all those legs and arms and heads chopped off in a battle shall join together at the latter day, and cry all, 'We died at such a place'—some swearing, some crying for a surgeon, some upon their wives left poor behind them, some upon the debts they owe, some upon their children rawly left. I am afeard there are few die well that die in a battle, for how can they charitably dispose of anything, when blood is their argument? Now, if these men do not die well, it will be a black matter for the King that led them to it …

**[4.1.133–44]**

Williams's fears are forceful ones: not to be allowed to "die well", and to put one's earthly and spiritual affairs in order, is a heavy price for serving an earthly king. His nightmarish vision of the "latter day" (the Day of Judgement), awash with truncated body-parts, provides a strong pacifistic argument. But his chief worry is about the justness of this particular conflict – and it is a question Henry evades, preferring to argue merely that "the King is not bound to answer the particular endings of his soldiers" (4.1.154–5). Though the religious justification for Henry's war in France is carefully laid out in the first few scenes of the play, there are jarring notes – among them the fact that the Church is backing it in order to divert attention from a royal inquiry into their coffers. Williams's concerns aired, audiences in the know may well think back to the dying King's advice to his son in *Henry V*'s predecessor, "to busy giddy minds / With foreign quarrels" (*2 Henry IV*, 4.3.342–3). Crusade or smokescreen?

## Entertain conjecture

At least Williams's courage is not under question; that is not true for all the King's troops. The men the Chorus rather hopefully calls "culled and choice-drawn cavaliers" (3.0.24) include some of Henry's erstwhile Eastcheap pals, Bardolph, Nim and Pistol – none of whom is distinguished by their bravery. Though Bardolph is briefly fired up by the King's speech at Harfleur, echoing, "On, on, on, on, on! To the breach, to the breach!" (3.2.1–2), his exhortation to his comrades falls on stony ground. The Boy provides the most astute analysis of all:

> Would I were in an alehouse in London. I would give all my fame for a pot of ale, and safety.
>
> **[3.2.12–3]**

Cowering in their foxhole – a parodic version of *esprit de corps* – until they are chased out by Captain Fluellen (a Welshman), they represent an England which is rather less patriotic in practice than it might like to believe.

The story of the Eastcheap soldiers, sordid and unhappy as it is, is a powerful undercurrent to the "official" view of the action as represented by the Chorus and Henry himself. The kind of vivacious and rumbustious comedy they offer in the *Henry IV* plays is all but silenced in *Henry V*, something first noticed by Samuel Johnson, who commented ruefully that "the comic personages are now dismissed". Before long Bardolph manages to get himself executed for robbing a church (his death underwritten by the King himself), while Pistol leaves the play as a solitary figure, having heard that "my Nell is dead ... of a malady of France" (5.1.77–8), a euphemism for venereal disease which ironically underscores the nature of his own position. King Henry may have adapted winningly to his changed circumstances, but other characters do not have that luxury.

And if the "mad wag" Hal sunk into the grave with his father's corpse, the gaping absence of another father figure – one whose body is a good deal larger – dominates *Henry V*. Falstaff dies during the play, but he does so without once coming on stage. *2 Henry IV*'s Epilogue promised that "If you be not too much cloyed with fat meat, our humble author will continue the story with Sir John in it," going on, "where, for anything I know, Falstaff shall die of a sweat—unless already a be killed with your hard opinions." (Epilogue, 24–8). Given Falstaff's instantaneous celebrity on the Elizabethan stage, that last comment must have seemed like a lighthearted quip, no more, to its first hearers. But Shakespeare turns the joke back on his audiences. Falstaff's sordid rejection by his erstwhile companion in the dying moments of *Part II* turns out, against all expectation, to have been his swansong. There is little doubt as to what lies behind his death. As Mistress Quickly tearfully relates, "The King has killed his heart" (2.1.84).

> *Shakespeare can scarcely have intended that the force of preconception should, hundreds of years after his death, still be preventing the careful, the learned, and the sympathetic from seeing what he so definitely put down.* The play is ironic.
>
> Gerald Gould, "A New Reading of *Henry V*" (1919)

All Elizabethan comedies end with marriage, and *Henry V*, though a history play, is no exception. But the alliance between Henry and Catherine of Valois, frequently acted as a light-hearted coda to the English victory at Agincourt, is not without its own problems – or affected by some of the other questions of the play. As the English and French diplomats meet in order to thrash out how to guarantee what Burgundy calls "gentle peace" for France, Henry insists that they must "buy that peace"; part of his ransom ("our capital demand") is the French princess. But she will not be bought so easily – first reacting with what seems like disgust to the praise he heaps on her head, then recoiling from his mastery as the conquerer of her land. "Is it possible dat I sould love de *ennemi* of France?" she enquires, to which Henry's answer is blunt:

> KING HARRY  No, it is not possible that you should love the enemy of France, Kate. But in loving me, you should love the friend of France, for I love France so well that I will not part with a village of it, I will have it all mine; and Kate, when France is mine, and I am yours, then yours is France, and you are mine.
> CATHERINE  I cannot tell vat is dat.
>
> **[5.2.169–77]**

Catherine's baffled incomprehension, though Shakespeare makes it linguistic, might echo our own. Henry's casual intermingling of the language of love with that of military conquest could be a gruff soldier's attempt to speak well – he claims it is – but from a King as linguistically versatile as Henry that seems to ring false. It is perhaps no accident that his choice of words echoes Richard II's resignation speech ("Your own is yours, and I am yours, and all" (3.3.195)), nor even that it foreshadows the marriage proposal offered to Isabella by the Duke in *Measure for Measure*. Henry's status as the owner of France is above all what concerns him here; he is intent on implementing his particular version of *droit du seigneur*.

Given that this scene is so delicately balanced between comedy and something darker, it offers a thought-provoking conclusion to a drama that continually asks its audiences to consider what kind of play it really is. The Chorus's appearances at the beginning of each act, inviting us to "entertain conjecture" (4.0.1), remind us of Shakespeare's stagecraft, but they also draw attention to the ways in which we are co-opted into events beyond our control. Henry may exclaim at Agincourt that those not present "shall think themselves accursed that they were not here" (4.3.65), but, Shakespeare asks, do we ultimately feel the same way?

## Stage history and adaptations

*Henry V* has enjoyed a rich life on stage, though not in mainland Europe, where it is the only one of Shakespeare's histories to have been virtually ignored. Although it may have premiered in 1599 at the newly erected **Globe** (probably with **Richard Burbage** in the lead), there is little to suggest that it was popular, and the next recorded performance took place in 1605 at James I's **court**. Nor was it revived after the restoration of James's grandson, Charles II, though a spin-off was staged by **Thomas Betterton** in 1664.

Shakespeare's play had to wait until 1738, when it returned to the London stage. It became particularly popular whenever war with France beckoned (as later in the century it often did), one of its most famous appearances being **David Garrick**'s in 1747, the same year as the catastrophic English loss at Lauffeld. **William Smith** frequently appeared as Henry during the 1750s and 60s, but **John Philip Kemble**'s adaptation of 1789 became the standard acting version for many years. **William Charles Macready** acted a restored version exactly a half-century later, but still cut it so as not to distract from **Clarkson Stanfield**'s impressive dioramas. These paled beside **William Telbin**'s extravagant designs for **Charles Kean**'s 1859 production, employing two hundred extras and spectacular even by their own standards. Kean inserted a triumphal entry for Henry after Act Four in which the King was showered in gold by a gaggle of angels, his wife appearing as the choric "Clio", the muse of history.

**Charles Calvert**'s Manchester version of 1879 was the most popular of Victorian revivals; and actor-manager **George Rignold** also won success in the 1870s, touring Henry to wild acclaim as far afield as New York and Sydney. **Lewis Waller**'s 1900 staging typified this heroic, patriotic view of the play: from the moment Waller's Henry bounded on stage, he "radiated power" (according to one observer) and won as many female admirers as critical plaudits. In the same mould were **Frank Benson**'s Stratford productions, which toured from 1897 to 1916 with Benson in the lead. His sheer energy – which included pole-vaulting onto the walls at Harfleur – wowed many, but Max Beerbohm famously described this as a "university cricket" *Henry V*, in which "speech after speech was sent spinning across the boundary".

Others attempted to subvert expectations, most obviously **Tyrone Guthrie**'s Old Vic staging of 1937, in which **Laurence Olivier** tried a bombast-free Henry in a version pushing an overtly pacifistic message. Neither of the productions mounted in 1951 (Festival of Britain year) went that far, but they did locate hitherto hidden qualities. **Glen Byam Shaw**'s emotionally involved Old Vic version had **Alec Clunes** in the lead; while over at Stratford **Richard Burton**'s youthful and wily King (directed by **Anthony Quayle**) demonstrated that there could be more to Henry than boyish charm. Quayle's production placed *Henry V* in the context of its companion plays, a path also trod by **John Barton** and **Peter Hall**, who in 1964, four centuries after Shakespeare's birth, put on a version as part of their two-tetralogy cycle, entitled *The Wars of the Roses*. Following series policy, *Henry V* was cynical about war and focused on the careworn figure of **Ian Holm**'s Henry; though winning approval in some quarters, others felt (with Robert Speaight) that it was too tendentious, and "every moment of every play had been squeezed for the last ounce of meaning it contained". Other 1960s directors went for altogether simpler messages. That same year an overtly anti-war translation ironically entitled *Held Henry* ("Hero Henry") appeared in Bremen, directed by **Peter Zadek**. Four years later, **Michael Kahn** went for outright controversy at Stratford, Connecticut, with an anti-Vietnam *Henry V* in which the King's pre-Agincourt speech was surmounted by a message reading "The Machine Creates The Believable Lie".

**Terry Hands**'s RSC productions of 1975 (once more as part of a "Henriad" cycle) attempted to roughen the play's gloss with Brechtian Alienation-effects – notably a decision to act sections of the play in "rehearsal" clothes – but were nevertheless dominated by **Alan Howard**'s commanding Henry. **Kenneth Branagh**'s King was similarly dominant in **Adrian Noble**'s Stratford version of 1984, and despite the production's brutality it persuaded Charles and Diana to name their second son Harry. The first British production properly to confront the results of the 1982 Falklands campaign – interpreted by some as Thatcher's Agincourt – was that toured by **Michael Bogdanov**'s English Shakespeare Company from 1986, with **Michael Pennington** as Henry. The anti-war message was displayed at some cost to subtlety: the English were portrayed as football hooligans, memorably unfurling a banner proclaiming "FUCK THE FROGS" to the strains of Parry's *Jerusalem*.

Productions since have often turned their backs on such overt politicking and concentrated instead on *Henry V*'s human cost. **Matthew Warchus**'s RSC version of 1994 led with **Iain Glen**'s godly monarch to a poppy-saturated finale, while his Stratford successor **Ron Daniels** (1997) created a set which reminded many of the Veterans' Memorial in Washington DC. **Edward Hall**'s 2000 production, part of the RSC's *This England* jamboree, was closer to the spirit of Bogdanov – it interpolated songs by the left-wing activist Billy Bragg – but many felt short-changed by **William Houston**'s low-key King. Few made the same criticism of **Mark Rylance**'s subtly characterized monarch at the London Globe in 1997, but the rest of the production (directed by **Richard Olivier**, son of Laurence and famous for preaching *Henry V*'s leadership lessons to businesspeople) offered an unabashedly triumphalist reading of the play, rewarded with crowd cheers when the French were executed. The two most recent UK productions demonstrate that there is space in the play for more complicated messages. **Barrie Rutter**'s Northern Broadsides company toured a typically pared-down version in 2003 that ignored overall politics in favour of an emotional message. Altogether different was **Nicholas Hytner**'s debut as director of the National Theatre, which drew pointed parallels between the play's "foreign quarrels" and British involvement in the invasion of Iraq; **Adrian Lester**'s on-message Henry exchanged his tailored suit for combat fatigues for the TV cameras, but in the end it was the squaddies who were left to pick up the pieces.

In addition to the two celebrated movies of *Henry V* by arch-popularizers Olivier (1944) and Branagh (1989), the play has had various outings on the small screen. The BBC/Time-Life production of 1979 was directed by **David Giles**, with **David Gwillim** as Henry.

# Screen

### Henry V

**L. Olivier, R. Asherson, L. Banks; Laurence Olivier (dir.)**

UK, 1944 ▷ Carlton / Criterion 📀 📼

Dedicated to the fighting men who liberated Europe at the close of World War II, Olivier's *Henry V* was regarded by the British authorities as such a boost for morale that schoolchildren were escorted to special mass screenings on its release. Watching it sixty-odd years later, it is indeed the pep-talk patriotism that hits first – along with bewilderment that a movie which caricatures the French so grotesquely can have been made when they were allies. Olivier, as ever, works with broad brush-strokes. Though it is often visually disappointing – the colour garish, the sets winsome (especially the French court's cartoonish battlements) – William Walton's score is arguably his finest and Agincourt, the film's sole location shoot, is breathtakingly done (albeit with help from Eisenstein, whose battle scenes in *Alexander Nevsky* Olivier quotes repeatedly). The acting is uneven, too, and while Olivier is often impressive he can also be irritatingly mannered. But *Henry V*'s intriguing conceit – the main action is framed by a quaintly realized Elizabethan production – is more imaginative and successful than the film's detractors make out.

### Henry V

**K. Branagh, E. Thompson, D. Jacobi; Kenneth Branagh (dir.)**

UK, 1989 ▷ United Pictures 📀 📼

When Branagh's version of *Henry V* premiered it was touted as the darker, messier rival to Olivier; the one that was prepared

to tell war like it is. While there's some truth in that – Branagh restores the second Harfleur speech and emphasizes the ghoulish execution of Bardolph, both cut by Olivier – it's interesting to note that Shakespeare still demands atrocities (such as the massacre of French prisoners) that even latter-day filmmakers can't stomach. And although Branagh's own Henry is more intimately sketched that Olivier's, it is far from antiheroic: appropriating the language of Hollywood, Branagh makes him a troubled Eighties action hero, *Die Hard* rather than *Dam Busters*. *Henry V* was targeted as a mass-market movie, and it succeeds in that role, Oscars and all. Though there are some real errors of judgement – the silent insert of Robbie Coltrane's sweaty death as Falstaff and Derek Jacobi's hammy Chorus are just two – strong performances from Paul Scofield (the French King) and Ian Holm (Fluellen) save the day.

# Audio

### Henry V

**J. Glover, S. Todd, B. Cox; Clive Brill (dir.)**

UK, 1998 ▷ Arkangel ⦿ 📼

Same name, different label – a logical way to follow up the excellent BBC *Henry IV*s is this Arkangel version with Jamie Glover to make the transfer from Hal to Henry. This he does adeptly, with an urgent and serious-minded performance that makes a good case for Henry's heroism. Not that this version shies away from less appealing sides to the play: war is somehow acutely disturbing in audio, and Clive Brill's direction (admirably taut on the whole) captures well the tense hours pre-Agincourt and the seasoned nerves of the English soldiers. Brian Cox puts in a powerful cameo as the Chorus, a role ideally suited to this medium.

Dedicated to the Allied forces who liberated Europe, Laurence Olivier's wartime *Henry V* (1944) closely identified the struggle against Nazism with the English triumph at Agincourt – and won an honorary Oscar for its director, producer and star.

# Editions

### Arden Shakespeare (third series)
**T.W. Craik (ed.); 1995** ▷ Thomson

Gary Taylor's 1982 Oxford edition, one of the first in that series and indeed one of its best, is well worth taking a look at. (Taylor, always polemical, was later to court controversy by writing about *Henry V*'s "shock and awe" tactics just as the US and UK went to war in Iraq in 2003.) But despite the Oxford edition's strengths, Craik's Arden version has just that bit more to offer and is able to discuss two major recent milestones in the play's performance history, Michael Bogdanov's 1986 ESC production and Kenneth Branagh's film three years later. Craik's introduction is organized along traditional Arden lines, with sections on Date, Sources, Texts, Criticism and so forth, but is easily navigable and he includes a facsimile of Q1 at the back along with some useful maps. The text itself is helpfully glossed with liberal quotations from Holinshed and *The Famous Victories*.

# Some criticism

### Shakespeare and the Problem of Meaning
**Norman Rabkin; 1981** ▷ Chicago UP [o/p]

This slender volume unites several of Norman Rabkin's essays from a variety of locations but is held together by its conviction that exploring what Shakespeare *means* can be a process as complicated – and illuminating – as reading or seeing the plays themselves; and that they will wriggle free from whatever we attempt to make them mean. At the heart of this collection is Rabkin's famous piece on *Henry V*, in which he compares the play to one of those two-dimensional optical illusions that seems like a duck one moment and a rabbit the next – and which cannot be both at the same time, however much you want it to. Also included are essays on *The Merchant of Venice* and the Romances.

### Shakespeare Left and Right
**Ivo Kamps (ed.); 1991** ▷ Routledge [o/p]

Few plays have found themselves more caught up in political ideology (or ideologies) than *Henry V*, and in Kamps's confrontational collection the play finds itself under cross-examination several times – notably from Harry Berger (on the Henriad), David Scott Kastan (in an essay exploring New Historicist approaches to the histories) and Chris Fitter (who puts Branagh's film under the microscope and exposes "an establishment cover-up"). *Shakespeare Left and Right* is varied in quality, but the contributors' urgent arguments, from all angles of the political debate, will not leave you on the sidelines.

# Henry VI Part I

istorically speaking, *Henry VI Part I* kicks off what is sometimes called the "first tetralogy" – the sequence of four plays covering the turbulent period in English history through the life and death of Henry VI, his usurpation by Edward IV and the murderous succession of Edward's brother, Richard of Gloucester, as Richard III. If it is the earliest play of the four, it is Shakespeare's first attempt to wrestle with the Wars of the Roses – still uncomfortably recent history when he was writing. But the play is not some abstract treatise, nor a Tudor propaganda piece: it is a vivid and powerful drama about high-stakes international politics, albeit one whose potential has been exploited all too rarely on the modern stage. Dominated by the impressive and terrifying character of Joan la Pucelle (better known as Joan of Arc), one of Shakespeare's first great female roles, it offers plenty of spectacle and excitement – not least in its vivid battle scenes and onstage fights.

[DATE] *1 Henry VI* was a roaring success from 1592 onwards – although a prequel to the two other *Henry VI* plays, it could have been written after them. Thomas Nashe has been suggested as one of at least two other likely collaborators with Shakespeare.

[SOURCES] Raphael Holinshed's 1587 *Chronicles of England, Scotland and Ireland* and Edward Halle's *Union of the Two Noble and Illustrious Families of Lancaster and York* (1548) provide the story's backbone. Some scenes also derive from Robert Fabyan's *New Chronicle of England and France* (1516).

[TEXTS] The 1623 Folio provides the only authoritative text – unlike the other *Henry VI* plays, which were published in quarto.

## Interpreting the play

Though written up to seven years after *1 Henry VI* (a long time for the industrious Shakespeare), the closing lines of *Henry V* give an eloquent and moving description of what will follow the miraculous English victory at Agincourt. The omens are not good, the Chorus comments:

> Thus far with rough and all-unable pen
>   Our bending author hath pursued the story,
> In little room confining mighty men,
>   Mangling by starts the full course of their glory.
> Small time, but in that small most greatly lived
>   This star of England. Fortune made his sword,
> By which the world's best garden he achieved,
>   And of it left his son imperial lord.
> Henry the Sixth, in infant bands crowned king
>   Of France and England, did this king succeed,
> Whose state so many had the managing
>   That they lost France and made his England bleed,
> Which oft our stage hath shown—and, for their sake,
> In your fair minds this acceptance take.

*[Henry V, Epilogue 1–14]*

## Major Characters & Synopsis

**THE ENGLISH**
**King Henry VI** of England and France
**Duke of Gloucester**, Henry's uncle and Protector
**Bishop of Winchester**, Henry's great-uncle, later Cardinal
**Richard Plantagenet** (later **Duke of York**)
**Edmund Mortimer**, Plantagenet's uncle
**Duke of Bedford**, Henry's uncle and Regent of France
**Duke of Exeter**, King Henry's great-uncle
**Duke of Somerset**, Exeter's nephew
**Earls of Warwick**, **Salisbury** and **Suffolk**
**Lord Talbot** (later **Earl of Shrewsbury**) and **John Talbot**, his son
Various English dignitaries, including **Sir William Glasdale**, **Sir Thomas Gargrave**, **Sir John Fastolf** and **Sir William Lucy**

**THE FRENCH**
**Charles**, Dauphin of France
**René**, **Duke of Anjou** (later **King of Naples**)
**Margaret**, René's daughter
**Duke of Alençon**
**Bastard of Orléans**, the Duke of Orléans's illegitimate son
**Duke of Burgundy**, King Henry's uncle
**Countess of Auvergne**
**Joan la Pucelle**, a peasant (also known as **Joan of Arc**)

**ACT 1** Henry V, England's greatest king, is dead. The funeral is interrupted by news that his hard-won legacy – the conquest of France – is under threat: in fact, territory has already been lost to the French. The English nobles squabble among themselves in the absence of the young King, Henry VI; Gloucester and Winchester in particular jostle for political advantage and their hatred spills over into brawling between their followers. Meanwhile, in the battle for Orléans, the French are beaten back. The peasant Joan la Pucelle arrives, however, and presents herself as France's saviour; when she beats the Dauphin in single combat, it seems she is gifted with superhuman powers. Under her direction the French fire on English positions, Salisbury is mortally wounded and Talbot is disarmed. Orléans is once more in French hands.

**ACT 2** The battle turns once again as the English assault Orléans and drive out the French. Back in England, the political infighting reaches new levels as rivals Richard Plantagenet and Somerset face each other in the Temple garden, plucking red and white roses to mark their opposing loyalties. The Wars of the Roses – the battle between the houses of York and Lancaster for control of the crown – have symbolically begun, and when Plantagenet visits his uncle, the dying Edmund Mortimer, the Wars' argument is rehearsed: Plantagenet's claim to the English throne rests on the fact that Richard II (York) was deposed by Henry IV (Lancaster). The hold of the present king, Henry VI (Lancaster), is weak.

**ACT 3** The King appears, struggling to smooth relations between Gloucester and Winchester. Attempting to calm the York–Lancaster quarrel, he makes Plantagenet Duke of York – so alienating his kinsman Somerset. Henry heads to France to be crowned, only to find more strife between supporters of York and Lancaster when he arrives. Joan continues her devilish machinations: she leads the French in disguise to take Rouen and persuades the Duke of Burgundy (Henry's uncle) to switch sides.

**ACT 4** Henry's coronation is interrupted by news of Burgundy's treason, and his problems deepen when he attempts to mediate in another quarrel between York and Lancaster supporters, unwittingly favouring the Lancastrians. It seems barely surprising that the battle for Bordeaux goes spectacularly wrong: Talbot's forces are left stranded and the two English commanders, York and Somerset, blame each other.

**ACT 5** As part of a peace deal with France, Henry agrees to marry the Earl of Armagnac's daughter, but Suffolk has other plans – he woos the beautiful Margaret of Anjou for the King, plotting to keep her as his own mistress. Paris rebels against the Dauphin and Joan, and Joan is captured by York, later being condemned to death. The play closes as Henry accepts Margaret in the face of bitter opposition from his nobles: her dowry is non-existent and England must give up more French territory as part of the

The Chorus's words muse not just on the historical facts – that England will "bleed" with civil strife following Henry V's unexpected death – but give the "bending author" pause to look back at his early work. *Henry VI Part I*, which tells of the origins of the Wars of the Roses, was one of Shakespeare's first triumphs, and part of the series of three plays that made his name. His colleague and possible collaborator Thomas Nashe wrote admiringly of the play and its effect on "ten thousand spectators at least (at several times)" – all were apparently moved to tears by the tragic death of the English soldier John Talbot in Act Four – and the series as a whole did much to cement Shakespeare's reputation as the best, and most adventurous, young dramatist in London. Nashe's figure, by the way, is almost certainly an underestimate: according to the accounts of Philip Henslowe, owner of the playhouse where it was first performed, many more than ten thousand spectators crowded in to see it.

Shakespeare was clearly making a name for himself. No one had written English history plays on this kind of scale before: although Christopher Marlowe's *Tamburlaine* (1587–90) began a fashion for writing multi-decker drama, Shakespeare's *Henry VI* sequence in its final form is the only professional three-part play from this period. That said, many critics think that *1 Henry VI* was in fact the last of the trilogy to be penned, capitalizing on the success Shakespeare had already experienced with *The First Part of the Contention of the Two Famous Houses of York and Lancaster* (now known as *2 Henry VI*) and *The True Tragedy of Richard Duke of York and the Good King Henry the Sixth* (*3 Henry VI*). If this is true, the young playwright's decision to write a prequel dramatizing the origins of the York–Lancaster conflict was logical enough.

John Heminges and Henry Condell, actor-editors of the 1623 First Folio, placed the (numbered) *Henry VI* plays in historical order, directly inviting readers to interpret them as a "real" sequence – a kind of national epic whose interior cohesion reinforces its continuity with the Elizabethan present. Taking that view, some nineteenth-century critics compared it to Aeschylus's *Oresteia* trilogy or Wagner's *Ring* cycle; others have linked it to the medieval mystery plays; still others have made comparisons with TV period drama. It's worth observing that one of Nashe's reasons for picking out *1 Henry VI* is to demonstrate that it had an improving purpose: to make the past live again for the education of its audiences.

## Civil broils

But if *1 Henry VI* is a history lesson, what does it teach? Following the doyen of mid-twentieth-century historical criticism, E.M.W. Tillyard, who declared in 1944 that "throughout the *Henry VIs* and *Richard III* Shakespeare links the present happenings with the past", many commentators have argued that the plays believe in what Tillyard christened the "Tudor myth" (see p.112). This depicts Henry VI's reign as a period of horror-filled instability: the King loses his grip on power, in the process throwing true-bred English heroes like Talbot to the wolves and bringing England to the brink of chaos. In this view, the histories present a stark message: war is bad, peace good. But in recent years Tillyard's position has come under sustained fire from more rebellious critics, who insist that Shakespeare is not complicit with the Tudor regime, but a critic of it. And far from criticizing events such as Talbot's death, Shakespeare is dramatically dependent on them. Both viewpoints have their strengths: on one level, it might be said that the playwright takes an "official" line, and presents arguments that worthily call for peace and civility; on another, his task is complicated by the fact that strife is the life-blood of drama, and that war is both thrilling and stirring.

This latter view receives strong backing in *1 Henry VI*, which vividly animates the two conflicts which dominate its action – war in France and internecine strife at home. There is little doubt that this is one of Shakespeare's most action-packed dramas, for all that it is infre-

## Mything the point

Taken together, eight of Shakespeare's ten history plays – *Richard II*, the two *Henry IV*s, *Henry V*, the three *Henry VI*s and *Richard III* – tell an unbroken tale of English monarchy from the deposition of Richard II to the deposition of Richard III. The man responsible for the latter was **Henry Tudor**, whose triumph at the Battle of Bosworth in 1485 inaugurated the Tudor dynasty, which proclaimed to heal the wounds inflicted by the Wars of the Roses and bring peace and prosperity to an England wracked by civil conflict. As Shakespeare's Henry declares in words that close *Richard III*: "Now civil wounds are stopped; peace lives again. / That she may long live here, God say 'Amen'." (5.8.40–1).

Ironically enough, for critics of Shakespeare's histories, this soothing speech has been tantamount to a declaration of war. One of the opening salvoes was fired by **E.M.W. Tillyard**, whose 1943 study *The Elizabethan World Picture* developed the view that "ordinary" Elizabethans believed solidly what their masters told them to: in the strength of Church, state and monarchy. Developing these ideas in *Shakespeare's History Plays* (1944), Tillyard stated that Shakespeare went along with all this; furthermore, his history plays consistently promote what he called the "**Tudor myth**" – the idea peddled by Tudor historiographers such as Polydore Vergil (c.1470–c.1555), Edward Halle (c.1498–1547) and Raphael Holinshed (d. c.1582), that Henry VII's accession was divinely ordained, and that his granddaughter Elizabeth's reign was, as Tillyard puts it, the "acknowledged outcome" of God's providence. In using Halle and Holinshed, Tillyard's Shakespeare is reassuringly conservative, at his "most individual when most orthodox and of his age".

Subsequent critics would come to radically different conclusions about the lesson(s) the histories offer. The Polish critic **Jan Kott**'s *Shakespeare Our Contemporary* (1964) famously recast the myth as a "Grand Mechanism", a "great staircase on which there treads a constant procession of kings", all of them functions of the same depersonalized system. As opponents have eagerly noted, though, while Kott stressed faceless chaos rather than Tillyardian order, this simply replaces one overriding structure with another. **A.P. Rossiter** suggested that the histories are ambivalent and evasive about the morals of kingship, while **Norman Rabkin**'s *Shakespeare and the Common Understanding* (1967) posited that they were dominated by "illogicality, irregularity, complexity, contrariety, complementarity, polyphony, doubleness, ambivalence, even *discoherence*". This taste for transgressive ambiguity has naturally found favour among latter-day writers unwilling to accept Shakespeare as an establishment lackey – though, intriguingly, so-called "**new historicist**" critics have most often stressed the state-friendly "ideology" of the plays so enthusiastically that they all but accuse him of precisely that.

quently revived. Over twenty fights take place, many of which occur hand-to-hand on stage. Often – as with Joan la Pucelle's breathtaking defeat of the French Dauphin – those combats provide its most stunning effects. And, as recent critics have pointed out, late sixteenth-century audiences (a large proportion of them young men) would hardly have put up with the dull and stylized choreography some present-day directors call "fighting". Real weapons would have been used – and swordsmanship was something in which such audiences took a near-professional interest. Given that the play was first performed at the Rose, whose shallow stage and intimate scale added an added thrill to the fight scenes, it is difficult to avoid the conclusion that *1 Henry VI* was written to show off its writer's ability to create explosive, dangerous drama. While Nashe defends the elevated historical and tragic purpose of the play, it's perhaps more likely that a significant percentage of those "ten thousand spectators" were there for the battle scenes, not the tears.

*1 Henry VI* specializes in depicting grand set-piece occasions that are violently disrupted. Nowhere is this more apparent than with the funeral of Henry V at its very opening. England's lords are grouped around the coffin to pay their last respects when an argument suddenly flares up:

WINCHESTER
> He was a king blest of the King of Kings.
> Unto the French, the dreadful judgement day
> So dreadful will not be as was his sight.
> The battles of the Lord of Hosts he fought.
> The Church's prayers made him so prosperous.

GLOUCESTER
> The Church? Where is it? Had not churchmen prayed,
> His thread of life had not so soon decayed.

[1.1.28–34]

What is so brilliantly dramatic here is the way in which Shakespeare transforms innocent eulogy into naked aggression. *1 Henry VI*'s lords are full-time politicians: even the funeral of their erstwhile monarch turns into an opportunity for point-scoring. Bedford attempts to make peace:

> Cease, cease these jars, and rest your minds in peace.
> Let's to the altar. Heralds, wait on us.
> Instead of gold, we'll offer up our arms—
> Since arms avail not, now that Henry's dead.
> Posterity, await for wretched years,
> When, at their mothers' moistened eyes, babes shall suck,
> Our isle be made a marish of salt tears,
> And none but women left to wail the dead.
> Henry the Fifth, thy ghost I invocate:
> Prosper this realm; keep it from civil broils;
> Combat with adverse planets in the heavens.
> A far more glorious star thy soul will make
> Than Julius Caesar or bright—
> *Enter a Messenger*

[1.1.44–56]

Bedford's attempt to conjure Henry V's "ghost" is abruptly broken off, and his attempt to restore calm is, aptly, left incomplete. In a neat linkage, the messenger interrupting him brings news that the conquest of France, the dead King's greatest success, is under threat – the twin themes, international and domestic war, are sounded simultaneously. Henry's funeral rites are forgotten, and the play's full-time depiction of political fragmentation gets underway – before long, in fact, the servants of Gloucester and Winchester will be brawling openly on stage. Something curiously similar happens in the two other ceremonies that dominate *1 Henry VI*'s action: the new King's coronation is interrupted by news that Burgundy has defected, then by warring supporters of York and Somerset; and the proposed marriage of Henry to the Earl of Armagnac's daughter doesn't even get past the planning stage because Henry changes his mind for factional reasons.

One of the play's most impressive scenes in this vein occurs at the very centre of its action, soon after the English armies have been shown fighting to uproot the French from Orléans. Back in London, the Lancaster and York factions are vying for place at court when they meet in the garden of the Temple Church. Richard Plantagenet (York) believes that Somerset (Lancaster) has wronged him and, as in France, violence is very much on everyone's minds:

RICHARD PLANTAGENET
> The truth appears so naked on my side
> That any purblind eye may find it out.

SOMERSET
> And on my side it is so well apparelled,
> So clear, so shining, and so evident,
> That it will glimmer through a blind man's eye.

RICHARD PLANTAGENET
> Since you are tongue-tied and so loath to speak,
> In dumb significants proclaim your thoughts.
> Let him that is a true-born gentlemen
> And stands upon the honour of his birth,
> If he suppose that I have pleaded truth,
> From off this briar pluck a white rose with me.
>> *He plucks a white rose*

**[2.4.20–30]**

Somerset responds by defiantly choosing a red rose, and with that gesture, the Wars of the Roses (a nineteenth-century name for a conflict first described by the Tudor historians Shakespeare was reading) are shown to have begun.

## So fair a dame

But competition between men is just one of *1 Henry VI*'s many enmeshed conflicts. It is also a play in which war crosses gender boundaries, in which men are seriously threatened by strong women. Talbot, "the terror of the French", a man whose very name strikes fear into the enemy, faces his biggest challenge in outwitting the Countess of Auvergne, a seductress who attempts to ensnare him with her feminine wiles. In a similar way, the entire *Henry VI* sequence comes to rest on Henry's biggest blunder: marrying Margaret of Anjou, possibly one of Shakespeare's most satisfyingly evil female roles, a character whom the Duke of York will memorably describe as a "tiger's heart wrapped in a woman's hide" (*3 Henry VI*, 1.4.138) but who appears in this play as "so fair a dame" that the Earl of Suffolk cannot resist her charms.

Then, of course, there is the "holy maid" Joan la Pucelle, a character who has been described by one critic as "a composite portrait of the ways women are dangerous to men", a character who uproots not just conventions of gender but those of religion, society and politics. Once she has defeated the Dauphin in single combat, it barely seems surprising that she can face down the entire English army; nor that she employs witchcraft in order to do so. While this last might seem to introduce a note of implausible fantasy into Shakespeare's history, in fact the historical Jeanne d'Arc was accused by the English of being "a disciple and limb of the Fiend ... that used false enchantment and sorcery". Joan herself sees her mission as something simpler, to rescue France from English destruction, and Shakespeare gives her plenty of verbal as well as magical power with which to do so. "Look on thy country, look on fertile France," she begs the Duke of Burgundy, who has gone over to the English side:

> And see the cities and the towns defaced
> By wasting ruin of the cruel foe.
> As looks the mother on her lowly babe
> When death doth close his tender-dying eyes,
> See, see the pining malady of France,
> Behold the wounds, the most unnatural wounds,
> Which thou thyself hast given her woeful breast.

**[3.7.44–51]**

Burgundy is soon won over and persuaded to rejoin the French: "either she hath bewitched me with her words," he exclaims, "or nature makes me suddenly relent" (3.7.58–9). Indeed, all three female characters in *1 Henry VI* seek control over men and attempt to suborn them to their ends (which are, needless to say, wicked through and through) – a fact which has led some to caricature the young Shakespeare as a woman-hater, others to claim that this play's stereotypes strike an early blow for feminism by satirizing male anxieties.

> The subsurface, "mythic" war waged in this play is a war against women, identified with sexuality: it is a war against the outlaw feminine principle.
>
> Marilyn French, *Shakespeare's Division of Experience* (1982)

And the male world the play depicts is in serious trouble. For *1 Henry VI*'s male characters – in particular Henry VI himself – things are steadily becoming unstuck: haunted by the triumphs of their fathers' generation, they are struggling to prove themselves worthy heirs. Though Henry is older in the play than his historical counterpart (who was just nine months old at Henry V's death), he is still depicted as dangerously young, both naive and ineffectual. His first words in the play, which attempt to quell the growing argument between Gloucester and Winchester, sound as if his only knowledge of conflict is what he has read in school textbooks:

O what a scandal it is to our crown
That two such noble peers as ye should jar!
Believe me, lords, my tender years can tell
Civil dissension is a viperous worm
That gnaws the bowels of the commonwealth.

**[3.1.70–4]**

Accurate though his words unquestionably are, they are a sign – if any sign were needed – that Henry VI will fail to hold his father's "commonwealth" together. That very failing will rapidly lead to the deaths of another father and child, Talbot and his son, who perish due to the high-level feud between Somerset and York. Their twinned death is in that sense symbolic: it represents the fracturing of a world in which male certainties are being rendered impotent. It is a framing irony in the *Henry VI* plays that the Wars of the Roses are to do with bloodlines, inheritance, family; and yet they remorselessly tear families apart, separate father from son.

# Stage history and adaptations

The early public life of *1 Henry VI* is recorded in unusually precise detail by **Thomas Nashe's** impressionistic description of it in 1592; in the role of Talbot was possibly **Edward Alleyn**. That the play was a staggering success is confirmed by the owner-manager of the Rose theatre, **Philip Henslowe**, who noted receipts totalling over £33 for this, a "new" play – far outstripping other hits of the season such as Kyd's *The Spanish Tragedy* and Marlowe's *The Jew of Malta*. This initial triumph is the first we hear until 1738, when *1 Henry VI* was acted by request at **Covent Garden**, apparently in a performance that featured numerous dance episodes.

Thereafter, as with the other *Henry VI* plays, adaptations provided the only opportunities for airing. The celebrated **Edmund Kean** revived it in December 1817 as part of **J.H. Merivale's** five-act *Richard Duke of York; or the Contention of York and Lancaster*, which also threw gobbets of Chapman and Webster into the brew. Kean shone as Richard, one commentator declaring him (somewhat lukewarmly) "in many scenes, unusually great". Another one-evening adaptation was undertaken by **Charles Kemble**, John Philip Kemble's little brother, later in the century, but that clearly proved a dead end – no performance is recorded. Slightly

Joan La Pucelle (Janet Suzman) is captured by the English, led by the Duke of York (Donald Sinden). A climactic moment from the RSC's condensed history cycle, *The Wars of the Roses*.

more success seems to have occurred on the continent; the play was acted in Germany and a particularly notable performance took place in Vienna in 1873. Back in England, **G. Osmond Tearle** put on *1 Henry VI* in 1889 with himself as Talbot, **Erskine Lewis** as Henry and **Ellen Cranston** as Margaret.

In 1906 **Frank Benson** decided to present all three *Henry VI*s on different evenings. With *3 Henry VI* billed as the "revival play" (none too successfully, at least judging from the takings), Benson cut props down to a minimum and did away with scene changes entirely. Though the intention was to revive the practice of fluid staging, one reviewer's eye was still caught by the sheer atmosphere of the production: "everything … blended with perfect harmony to give the prevailing sentiment of mournful grandeur due precision".

**Robert Atkins** built a thrust stage which jutted out from the London Old Vic's proscenium in his 1923 adaptation, but was textually less radical than Benson – he opted once more to compress three plays into one *Henry VI*. But the ground was laid for several influential English productions, the first of which transferred from Birmingham Rep to Atkins's former haunt, the Old Vic, under the aegis of **Barry Jackson**. Jackson's 1953 version, directed by **Douglas Seale**, was praised for its "clean thrusting style" and featured **Jack May** as King Henry and **Rosalind Boxall** as his wife, in a Gothicky set designed by **Finlay James**. More radical still was an amateur production in 1959 Hovenden, which used an uncut text and presented Joan as sympathetically as possible.

Back in the professional theatre, **Peter Hall** and **John Barton**'s RSC cycle, *The Wars of the Roses* (1963), engineered two plays – *Henry VI* and *Edward IV* – out of Shakespeare's three (with *Richard III* making *Roses* a trilogy) for reasons partly artistic, partly financial. The text was not only cut in numerous places, but, in the best eighteenth-century traditions, Hall and Barton added new material – some of it selected from the chronicles, and some which they wrote themselves. They did so in the belief that the plays were not entirely Shakespeare's work, Barton coolly remarking later that he "wouldn't dream of trying to write bits into *Lear*". John Bury designed an austere metallic set that reinforced the harshness and brutality of the play's world. The result was a huge critical and popular success, with **David Warner**'s Henry, **Peggy**

Ashcroft's lisping Margaret and **Janet Suzman**'s Joan attracting particular enthusiasm. **Terry Hands** played down comparisons with Barton and Hall when he directed the cycle fourteen years later at the Swan, again for the RSC, but could not help but be influenced by their approach. In many ways it was every bit as epic – the set was dominated by an imposing iron bridge – but attempted to be more searching in terms of characterization. **Alan Howard**, who played nearly all Hands's kings in the cycle, saw Henry as simply uninterested in politics, while **Helen Mirren** smouldered as Margaret.

Political relevance was back on the agenda for **Michael Bogdanov**'s ESC versions of 1987, once more cut and spliced as part of a two-tetralogy touring series entitled, yet again, *The Wars of the Roses*. *Part I* came out relatively well, being in the main preserved: **Mary Rutherford**'s Joan made a serene martyr, her death provocatively got up as a South African-style execution with a burning tyre placed around her neck. At the RSC, meanwhile, **Adrian Noble** presented *The Plantagenets* (1988), a two-play adaptation more theatrically conventional than Bogdanov's and certainly more grandiose, which was distinguished by **Ralph Fiennes**'s excellent King. In 2000 the RSC once more put on a cycle of Shakespeare's histories, but unlike previous adaptations the texts remained uncut; the *Henry VIs* were directed by **Michael Boyd** at the small-scale Swan Theatre with **David Oyelowo** as Henry (the first black actor to play an RSC monarch). More recently still, **Edward Hall** presented a two-part version of the *Henry VIs* radically different from that of his father, which toured the UK in 2001–02 under the kitschy title of *Rose Rage*. Hall's youthful, all-male company stressed the plays' needless violence by setting them in a slaughterhouse. Typically, *Part I* was the one to suffer, made to share one evening with a compressed *Part II* and deprived of nearly all its interest.

Influential non-English versions have included **Giorgio Strehler**'s 1965 adaptation, *Il Gioco dei Potente*, influenced by both Barton–Hall and Strindberg; Peter Palisch's stark *Krieg der Rosen* (1967); and **Denis Llorca**'s 1978 French adaptation, entitled *Kings, ou les adieux à Shakespeare*, which attempted to approach the plays from the "enemy" perspective. On screen, the Hall–Barton *Roses* cycle made a strong impact when adapted for TV in 1965, but otherwise the *Henry VI* plays have not proved popular with filmmakers: only one purpose-built production, part of the BBC Shakespeare series and directed by **Jane Howell**, exists. Howell's interpretation, which concentrated on the plays' childish, game-like elements, gained mixed reviews. More warmly received were the tapings of Bogdanov's ESC productions, which were recorded live, preserving something of the excitement and vitality of the original performances.

## Screen

### King Henry VI: House of Lancaster
P. Brennen, B. Stanton, C. Farrell; Michael Bogdanov (dir.)
UK, 1990 ▷ Vision ▭

Though it might seem unflattering to call Bogdanov's *Wars of the Roses* production-line Shakespeare, in turnaround time this seems apt enough: the plays were filmed on consecutive nights at the Grand Theatre in Swansea and the "live" results released on video. Though this didn't allow the luxury of retakes or fine-tuning (witness the occasionally crude editing), the interpretations are slick and have dated surprisingly well (despite the odd dodgy moustache). *1* and part of *2 Henry VI* are here combined with some success: the action is fast-paced and performances are excellent if undemonstrative – Richard Jarvis, who returns in the title role of *Richard III*, is a

strongly characterized exception, sparkling in cameo as the Dauphin. Paul Brennen's earnest Henry looks permanently as if it's his first day at school, and only Brenda Blethyn's spaced-out Joan seems a disappointment.

## Audio

### Henry VI Part I
D. Tennant, N. Rodway, J. Bowe; Clive Brill (dir.)
UK, 1998 ▷ Arkangel ⊙ ▭

Plenty of excitement in the military scenes of this *1 Henry VI*, even if some of it seems excessively shouty (the sound effects, reminiscent of World War I, are equally noisome). Plenty of excitement elsewhere, too: little surprise that David Tennant's kindly Henry has trouble reining nobles as hot-headed as these, while Amanda Root's Joan crackles with righteous aggression. The play's comic energy is somewhat sacrificed to this approach, but with rounded performances from the likes of Norman Rodway, as an earnest Gloucester, and Nigel Cooke, urbane and sly as Suffolk, it's difficult to complain.

# Editions

### Arden Shakespeare (third series)
**Edward Burns (ed.); 2000** ▷ Thomson

Unlike the New Cambridge general editors, who give Michael Hattaway the job of editing all three *Henry VI*s, Arden has decided to separate the task out – laudably regarding them as individual artistic entities. Edward Burns's *1 Henry VI* offers an excellent way into this still undervalued play, and presents a closely argued case for multi-authorship. Whether you're convinced by this or not, Burns's introduction will certainly provide food for thought. His cursory treatment of stage history is the only irritation.

# Some criticism

### Shakespeare's History Plays
**E.M.W. Tillyard; 1944** ▷ Penguin / Athlone [o/p]

Tillyard's study has cast a long shadow over the critical history of the *Henry VI* plays, not least because it became cheaply available to a generation of students after being issued in paperback in 1962. In it Tillyard honed theories from his earlier *The Elizabethan World Picture* (1943), which set out his notion of the "great chain of being", beginning with God's place at the centre of the universe and moving outward and downwards through kings and princes to common people and even lower forms of life. This static image of commonplace assumptions to which all Elizabethans had access is notable chiefly for its emphasis on order and degree, a fearlessly orthodox interpretation. This book has been doggedly attacked from the 1960s onwards, but it remains a key text in the history of Shakespearian criticism.

### The Origins of Shakespeare
**Emrys Jones; 1977** ▷ Oxford UP [o/p]

In the 1970s, the Oxford don Emrys Jones published two influential books whose subtle and sensitive scholarship shed fresh light on Shakespeare's work. One was *Scenic Form in Shakespeare* (see p.21), the other is this one. Shakespeare's "origins" are not just those of his early career, but concern his reading, sources and the late Tudor cultural environment in which he thrived. Jones sees the *Henry VI*s as integral to his development, arguing for their cyclical construction yet presenting subtle and suggestive readings of each and every play; in *1 Henry VI* he focuses on the idea of "fame" and its ramifications, suggesting that hunger for earthly glory is one of the play's main anxieties – one that sentences Talbot to death.

# Henry VI Part II

enry VI Part II begins, appropriately enough, in the thick of things. As events in France fade into the background, the English court begins to fragment more dramatically than ever before – Gloucester's enemies finish him off, the King is pushed onto the defensive and York exposes his own ambition for the crown. But in *2 Henry VI* Shakespeare expands the scene beyond dynastic wrangling: he steps out from the main narrative at several key moments, showing that history means more than quarrels over bloodlines. Among its most celebrated strands is the story of Jack Cade's Kentish rebellion, which comes close to destabilizing the country (and the play) in ways that even England's leaders find impossible to control. In what might have been the first drama in the *Henry VI* sequence to be written, Shakespeare also dwells on some of the stranger aspects of the past: the plot includes a man whose blindness is apparently cured by a miracle, a lurid story borrowed from John Foxe's anti-Catholic collection, the *Book of Martyrs* (1563).

[DATE] If the play was the first of the *Henry VI* sequence to be penned (a currently fashionable view), it most likely dates from 1590–91.

[SOURCES] Halle's *Union* and Holinshed's *Chronicles*, as with the other two plays, provide the substance of *2 Henry VI*. Eleanor's penance may derive from an Elizabethan biographical collection, *The Mirror for Magistrates*, while the miracle scene probably comes from John Foxe's *Book of Martyrs* (1583).

[TEXTS] A quarto version (Q1) entitled *The First Part of the Contention* was printed in 1594, to be followed by others in 1600 (Q2) and 1619 (Q3), though all these texts were probably reconstructed from memory. The 1623 Folio version was almost certainly printed from Shakespeare's papers.

## Interpreting the play

In *2 Henry VI*, Shakespeare takes up the political narrative from King Henry's marriage to Margaret of Anjou, through the Duke of Gloucester's fall and Cade's rebellion, to the Duke of York's long-intended bid for the crown and the clash between his forces and those of the King at St Albans. In contrast to *1 Henry VI*, the focus is shifted decisively from the clash of nations to disputes on the home front – problems in France continue to dog Henry's regime, but they are pushed almost completely off stage. Even the sudden announcement at court that England has lost all its domains in France, the moment where Henry's international star is at its lowest, is remarkably underplayed:

KING HENRY       What news from France?
SOMERSET
    That all your interest in those territories
    Is utterly bereft you—all is lost.
KING HENRY
    Cold news, Lord Somerset; but God's will be done.

### LANCASTRIANS
**King Henry VI** of England and France
**Queen Margaret**, Henry's wife
William de la Pole, **Marquis** (later **Duke**) of
  **Suffolk**, the Queen's lover
**Duke Humphrey of Gloucester**, the King's
  uncle and Protector
**Duchess of Gloucester**, Duke Humphrey's wife
Cardinal Beaufort, **Bishop of Winchester**,
  Henry's great-uncle
**Dukes of Buckingham** and **Somerset**
Old **Lord Clifford** and **Young Clifford**, his son

### YORKISTS
Richard Plantagenet, **Duke of York**
York's sons: **Edward**, Earl of March and
  **Richard**, Earl of Salisbury
**Earl of Warwick**, Salisbury's son

### OTHER CHARACTERS
The combatants: **Thomas Horner** and **Peter
  Thump**, Horner's man
The conjurors: the witch **Margery Jordan**, the
  conjuror **Roger Bolingbroke** and **Asnath**, a
  spirit
**Simon Simpcox**, supposedly cured by the "mir-
  acle", and his **Wife**
The rebels: the Kentishman **Jack Cade** (secretly
  supported by the Duke of York and pretending
  to be John Mortimer) and his supporters
Opponents of the rebels: **Clerk of Chatham**; **Sir
  Humphrey Stafford** and his **Brother**; **Lords
  Saye** and **Scales**
**Alexander Iden**, from Kent, who kills Cade

[**▶▶ action continued from *Henry VI Part I*]**
**ACT 1**  The English court is in uproar. King
Henry is to marry Margaret of Anjou, even though
she has no dowry and the English must renounce
French land as part of the deal. Gloucester, the
King's Protector, is appalled, and his enemies
Winchester and Buckingham demand his
removal from office. York, meanwhile, wants the
crown for himself, but bides his time. Gloucester's
wife is equally ambitious, dreaming of supplanting
the King and Queen, and is tricked by her enemies at court into consulting witches about her
fortune; York and Buckingham are lying in wait at
the séance and arrest her. Political unrest has
also reached the commoners, and a small group

petitions Queen Margaret and her lover Suffolk for
help – to their scorn. Back in council, the bicker-
ing continues: Gloucester denies accusations of
corruption while King Henry struggles to control
the deepening row between York, Somerset and
their respective supporters.

**ACT 2**  Out hawking with the King, Gloucester and
Winchester continue to argue when they are interrupted by a man who claims that his blindness has
been cured by a miracle. King Henry naively believes
him, and, though Gloucester brilliantly exposes the
hoax, news soon arrives of the Duchess of
Gloucester's arrest; Gloucester resigns the protector-
ship in disgrace, and his wife is banished.

**ACT 3**  Gloucester's opponents close in on
him. The Queen denounces him in parliament
and he is blamed for the loss of the remaining
French territories. Arresting his uncle, Henry
announces that Gloucester will be tried fairly, but
Margaret plots with York and Suffolk to have him
killed. York secretly begins his campaign for the
crown, revealing that he has convinced a com-
moner, Jack Cade, to impersonate John
Mortimer (York's dead ancestor) and incite rebellion against the Lancastrian rule of Henry. News
of Gloucester's sudden death reaches Henry,
who accuses Suffolk of murder and has him
exiled. Winchester dies, driven mad by guilt.

**ACT 4**  Suffolk is murdered at sea by the ship's
captain and crew in revenge for Gloucester's
death and because of his affair with the Queen. In
Kent, Cade's rebellion is beginning: his supporters
kill Sir Humphrey Stafford and his brother, who
intervene on the King's side. Cade's rioters attack
London before executing Lord Say and his son-in-
law, but the rebellion falters when Old Clifford and
Buckingham offer to pardon those who will support Henry V's son. Cade flees, a broken man,
and is killed by Iden. Meanwhile it is reported that
York's army is marching towards the King.

**ACT 5**  York and his sons challenge Henry, and
their armies fight at St Albans. York kills Old Clifford
(whose son vows revenge) and Richard kills
Somerset, before Margaret and Henry admit defeat
and escape for London. They are pursued by the
Yorkists, determined to seize the crown itself.

YORK (*aside*)

Cold news for me, for I had hope of France,
As firmly as I hope for fertile England.

[3.1.83–8]

While Henry is content to take the loss of France as part of some divine plan (something, therefore, he is powerless to resist), York's response is wholly selfish: his thoughts focus on how it impinges on his designs on the crown. This moment is crucial not merely because it demonstrates how irrelevant the struggle for France has become, but because it illuminates the extent to which the English court is now factionalized. While *1 Henry VI* depicts nobles so terrified of losing in war that, in Bedford's words, news of it will make the old King Henry "burst his lead and rise from death" (*1 Henry VI*, 1.1.64), in the sequel France is little more than an excuse for political infighting.

In this play dynamic, opportunistic figures such as Richard of York (and of course his son, Richard of Gloucester, later Richard III) leave others standing by the wayside: while Henry fiddles and the lords bicker, York is after power. He speaks one of the play's few soliloquies after his colleagues unwittingly dispatch him to Ireland:

My brain, more busy than the labouring spider,
Weaves tedious snares to trap mine enemies.
Well, nobles, well: 'tis politicly done
To send me packing with an host of men.
I fear me you but warm the starvèd snake,
Who, cherished in your breasts, will sting your hearts.
'Twas men I lacked, and you will give them me.
I take it kindly. Yet be well assured
You put sharp weapons in a madman's hands.

[3.1.339–47]

His language is blunt rather than artful (Shakespeare will give his son, Richard of Gloucester, sharper oratory), but York, toying with the meaning of "politic", knows what ultimately matters.

## Hope of harmony

This kind of brute political philosophy is completely at odds with that espoused by the King. His celebrated address to the arguing nobles in Act Two has been widely commented upon:

The winds grow high; so do your stomachs, lords.
How irksome is this music to my heart!
When such strings jar, what hope of harmony?

[2.1.58–60]

Henry speaks in terms which would have been familiar to his audience – that musical and political discord function alike and are equally unnatural. But Henry's fine words get him nowhere, unlike York's: they are simply a commentary on events of which Henry is no longer in control – and an analogy which is beginning to look rather hopeless. While an Elizabethan audience (parts of it at least) might well have agreed with Henry's well-meaning sentiments, the action of the play is already leaving him behind.

Whereas we now know the play as *Henry VI Part II*, when published in 1594 the King's name was conspicuously absent from the title-page, which described "The First Part of the Contention betwixt the two famous Houses of York and Lancaster, with the death of the good Duke Humphrey: And the banishment and death of the Duke of Suffolk, and the Tragical end of the proud Cardinal of Winchester, with the notable Rebellion of Jack Cade: And the Duke of York's first claim unto the Crown". Almost everyone is present, in fact, apart from Henry: it is the people surrounding him – Gloucester, Suffolk, Winchester, Cade, York – who get top billing. This is symptomatic of the King's creeping irrelevance, an irrelevance he actually seems to invite. As the battle at St Albans begins to turn against the Lancastrian forces, Queen Margaret simply cannot believe that anyone can be so comprehensively inactive:

> KING HENRY
>> Can we outrun the heavens? Good Margaret, stay.
> QUEEN MARGARET
>> What are you made of? You'll nor fight nor fly.
>> Now it is manhood, wisdom and defence,
>> To give the enemy way, and to secure us
>> By what we can, which can no more but fly.

**[5.4.2–6]**

Henry will "nor fight nor fly"; Margaret can describe him only by what he will not do. Where the sources presented the reign of King Henry as a byword for weak governance, in this play Shakespeare develops a character whose inability to act out anything – even run away from his enemies – makes his existence as a dramatic entity somewhat questionable.

Henry's piety might seem to form the moral centre of a conspicuously amoral play, but what events emphasize is that morals are out of fashion in these "dangerous" days. Indeed, Henry has also been described as a medieval character adrift in a Renaissance play: his appeals to divine providence have the ring of sincerity, but they advertise his dislocation from the real business of life. Nowhere is this truer than in the so-called "mock-miracle" scene, when the royal party is visited by a man falsely claiming to have been cured of blindness at the shrine of St Alban. While Henry – ever the believer – takes Simpcox at his word, Gloucester plays the sceptic, fooling him into revealing that the miracle is manufactured. Shakespeare bases this incident not on Halle or Holinshed, his main sources, but on Foxe's *Acts and Monuments*, a virulently anti-Catholic tract and history of Protestant martyrdom better known as the *Book of Martyrs*, which by the time of Elizabeth's reign had become the most significant Protestant work after the Bible. In Foxe's rendering, the tale is simply a demonstration of Duke Humphrey's wisdom – and of course a swipe at miracle-touting Catholics. Shakespeare, however, makes it more than that. The King's Christian credulousness seems not just naive, but horribly outdated; Gloucester's empirical rationalism carries the day. Ominously, this is Henry's first embarrassment at St Albans; his second, in battle with the Yorkists, will endanger his very throne.

> *In Margaret we have a foreshadowing of Lady Macbeth finely contrasted with the meek and holy Henry, whose gentle lowliness of spirit is brought out with a prominence and beauty a good deal beyond what history alone would have suggested to the Poet …*
>
> G.C. Verplanck, *The Illustrated Shakespeare* (1844–47)

Henry is not alone in being out of step with the times. The Duchess of Gloucester attempts to employ witchcraft to control events (like Joan la Pucelle in *1 Henry VI*), but this simply leads her into a trap laid by her enemies. Medieval chivalry, too, does not escape Shakespeare's hard-edged satire. During an argument between the armourer Horner and his man Peter in which Horner accuses Peter of treason, the two men are ordered to fight it out in feudal style, but the knightly trial-by-combat turns into brutal farce when Horner turns up drunk and

Peter bludgeons him to death. Even the ancient rule of law, upheld by Gloucester, is up for grabs, as the plotters against him realize when conspiring how best to dispose of him:

> That he should die is worthy policy;
> But yet we want a colour for his death.
> 'Tis meet he be condemned by course of law.

[3.1.235–7]

"Colour" could translate as "pretext" or "pretence" – a word Shakespeare frequently uses in this dissembling sense (adding a further irony to Gloucester's exposing of Simpcox, which rests on the "blind" man's uncanny ability to spot colours). Equally shifty are words such as "worthy", "policy" and "meet" – which, in Winchester's lexicon, are all about playing the game to best advantage.

## Wild Moriscos

Another inset into the story of the Wars of the Roses throws a different light on its dynastic squabbles. At the beginning of Act Three, York reveals that he has recruited the talents of a dynamic Kentish troublemaker, Jack Cade, and persuaded him to rebel against the King. This uprising comes to occupy most of Act Four, and in it Shakespeare focuses for the first time of his career (but certainly not the last) on politics at the grassroots, from the viewpoint of the common people – who barely feature in *Part I*. It would be hard to describe Shakespeare's portrait of the crowd as sympathetic: his commoners are dim-witted, destructive and fickle, galvanized into revolt by Cade's promises of easy takings but easily dispersed when threatened. This perspective matches that of Shakespeare's sources, Halle and Holinshed, both of whom are critical of the revolt – Holinshed in particular describes Cade as a "villainous rebel" leading an army composed of "idle and vagrant persons". For all that, though, Shakespeare deliberately complicates matters. Cade is one of the most attractive characters in the play, and he promises revolution:

> Be brave, then, for your captain is brave and vows reformation. There shall be in England seven halfpenny loaves sold for a penny, the three-hooped pot shall have ten hoops, and I will make it felony to drink small beer. All the realm shall be in common, and in Cheapside shall my palfrey go to grass … [T]here shall be no money. All shall eat and drink on my score, and I will apparel them all in one livery that they may agree like brothers, and worship me their lord.

[4.2.66–77]

In this alluring jumble of philosophies, communist utopianism, theocracy and decent booze somehow gel. Small wonder, perhaps, that Cade is described by York as a "wild Morisco" (morris dancer), and indeed some theatre historians have suggested that Shakespeare's colleague Will Kempe, the most famous clown of his day, might have taken the part. Whether this is accurate or not, Cade exhibits an anarchic, carnivalesque power. And ironically he might well have gathered popular support among Shakespeare's audiences: his fantasies of low prices exploit anxieties about inflation (a pressing problem in the last years of Elizabeth's reign), and one critic has argued that Shakespeare drew on a reservoir of rebellion-friendly popular debate in constructing this section of the play. In a history otherwise so concerned with the suffocating intricacies of dynastic politics, Cade's own perspective on life can seem like a breath of fresh air.

Attractive though those alternatives might seem at first, as the rebels gather in strength events take a turn for the worse. As soon as they learn that the captured Clerk of Chatham can "write and read and cast account", Cade puts his manifesto to work:

CADE  Dost thou use to write thy name? Or hast thou a mark to thyself like an honest plain-dealing man?

CLERK  Sir, I thank God I have been so well brought up that I can write my name.

ALL CADE'S FOLLOWERS  He hath confessed—away with him! He's a villain and a traitor.

CADE  Away with him, I say, hang him with his pen and inkhorn about his neck.

**[4.2.101–9]**

In depicting this savage attack on literacy, Shakespeare drew not just on the account of Cade's rebellion in Halle and Holinshed, but turned back several chapters to the Peasants' Revolt of Wat Tyler – which was notably more brutal than its latter-day equivalent. Shakespeare is obviously keen to make his audiences think hard about precisely what this kind of unregulated rule can really mean.

Perhaps this suggests the role played by the Jack Cade scenes within the wider action of the play. While the rebellion comes from a different world from the feud between the Lancastrians and Yorkists, in fact the two are closely linked: the revolt is nourished by popular support, but initiated by a shady aristocratic backer. And, just as the scenes at court present a world in which Henry's inertia is outclassed by York's breathtaking dynamism, the rebellion offers an image of power at its most fluid – and its most dangerous. Both York and Cade are arresting figures when compared to the fatally weak King, but the kind of violence and brutality they represent offers a grim premonition of the future.

## Stage history and adaptations

Unlike the other two *Henry VI* plays, there is no direct evidence of early performance – hardly uncommon. The only information we do possess derives from the 1594 quarto, whose unusually detailed stage directions appear to reflect the play as it might have been performed at the **Rose** theatre. Some editors have speculated that the play must also have toured when the city theatres were closed because of plague, though there is no documentary proof for this. In any case, we can infer that *Part II*, like its companions, was popular when first performed.

The next we hear is via **Thomas Crowne**, who in 1681 created an expanded version of Acts One to Three of *Part II*, literalistically – if misleadingly – entitled *Henry the Sixth, the First Part, With the Murder of Humphrey Duke of Gloucester*. The Cade rebellion was excised and moved to the sequel, *The Misery of Civil War* (see p.133), while Crowne, an ardent royalist, boldly made the Cardinal of Winchester into a full-blown Papist villain (Catholicism was particularly unpopular at the time). **Ambrose Philips** attempted something similar in his 1723 *Humfrey Duke of Gloucester*, performed at Drury Lane, but felt confident enough to jettison most of Shakespeare's text – only around thirty lines of the original survive. The wisdom of this decision is rather thrown into question by the quality of Philips's own poetry, which was limp-wristed enough to earn its author the nickname "Namby-Pamby". **Theophilus Cibber**, son of the more renowned Colley, turned his hand to the plays a few months later, this time retaining a good deal more text. His *Henry VI* cobbled together the first few Acts of *Part III* with the last of *Part II*, and dwelt on the pathos-filled death of York's son Rutland (see p.130).

Thereafter, as with the other *Henry VI* plays, adaptations provided the only opportunities for performance. **Edmund Kean** revived it in December 1817 playing Richard in **J.H. Merivale**'s five-act, star-vehicle *Richard Duke of York; or the Contention of York and Lancaster*, which was mainly *Part II* bulked out with a few scenes of *Part I*. In Shakespeare's tercentenary year, 1864, the Surrey Theatre put on a "restoration" of *2 Henry VI* with **James Anderson** as both York and Cade. Slightly more success seems to have occurred on the continent; the play was acted in Germany and Austria. Back in England, **G. Osmond Tearle** put *1 Henry VI* on in 1889 with himself as Talbot, **Erskine Lewis** as Henry and **Ellen Cranston** as Margaret.

In 1906 **Frank Benson** presented all three *Henry VI* plays on successive evenings (he had first acted them at the Shakespeare Memorial Theatre five years earlier), cutting props and doing away with scene changes entirely. This fluid staging was well-received, even if *The Athenaeum* objected that for Benson's death scene as the Cardinal the set was "strewn unaccountably with sheaves of straw, which distracted from his tragic intensity".

Despite a specially erected thrust stage at the Old Vic, **Robert Atkins** reverted to eighteenth-century type by compressing three plays into one *Henry VI*. But the ground was laid for several influential English productions, the first of which transferred from Birmingham Rep to ——— haunt, the Old Vic, under the aegis of **Barry Jackson**. Jackson's 1951 version —— ———— the others following in successive years), directed by ———— enry and **Rosalind Boxall** as Margaret. In 1957, ———— s' entertainment, with **Barbara Jefford** replacing ———— ribing Margaret as "one of the greatest feminine ———— nwhile been acted in the US several times, first in ———— e in California.

———— aking RSC cycle from 1963, *The Wars of the Roses*, ———— to two, *Henry VI* and *Edward IV*, freely cutting – ———— em to *Richard III*. The productions struck a chord

*Franz Kafka*
*Orwell*

*Maya Angelou*

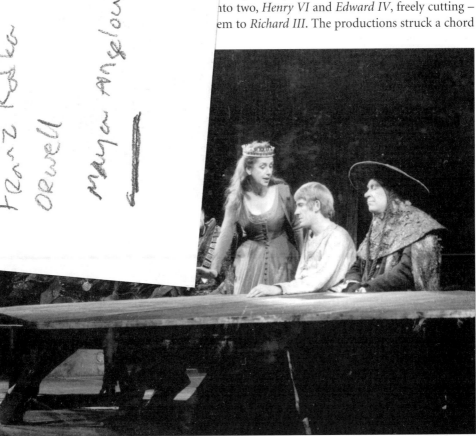

The vast council table at the centre of the RSC's *The Wars of the Roses*, co-directed by Peter Hall and John Barton (1963–64), symbolized the incessant power-broking of the *Henry VI* plays. Peggy Ashcroft's fiery Margaret (standing) and David Warner's vacillating King (in white) became a memorable duo.

with critics and audiences alike, not least for their parallels with contemporary *realpolitik*. They were also terrifically cast with **David Warner** presenting Henry as a kind of "Holy Fool" and **Peggy Ashcroft** letting rip with a chillingly fierce depiction of Margaret. This version established the *Henry VI* plays in the modern theatre and they returned to the RSC (in less mangled form) under **Terry Hands** in 1977, with **Alan Howard**'s thoughtfully characterized King particularly praised. Hands's bare staging received a mixed press, however, as did his tendentious approach to the politics of *Part II*, which some felt robbed the play of its comic humanity.

Thatcherite politics proved the driving force behind **Michael Bogdanov**'s English Shakespeare Company touring version from 1987, which inserted *Part II* into a series entitled (with some unoriginality) *The Wars of the Roses*. **June Watson**'s handbagging Queen Margaret reminded many audiences of a real-life politician of the same name, although **Michael Pennington** came close to stealing the show as a punkish, Union flag-wearing Cade. **Adrian Noble**'s RSC company attempted no such contemporary parallels a year later with their carefully historicized *Plantagenets* adaptation, which (like Barton and Hall before) compressed the three *Henry VIs* into two. Though some felt an opportunity had been missed, **Ralph Fiennes**'s Henry and **David Waller**'s Duke Humphrey gained glowing reviews, and **Anton Lesser**'s dynamic Richard of Gloucester was even now in the ascendant.

The *Henry VIs* have appeared once again at the subsidized RSC, this time under **Michael Boyd** at the intimate Swan Theatre. Though Boyd used uncut texts, his decision to introduce a spurious fiend-like character who mysteriously appeared as characters died was somewhat less authentic. The same criticism could be levelled at **Edward Hall**'s two-evening version from 2001, entitled *Rose Rage*. Hall used a text adapted in collaboration with **Roger Warren**, and *Part II* did well, with the Cade scenes (played by a lively **Tony Bell**) making a great impression.

Influential non-English versions featuring *Part II* have included **Giorgio Strehler**'s 1965 adaptation, *Il Gioco dei Potente*; **Peter Palisch**'s stark *Krieg der Rosen* (1967), which put its characters on Jan Kott's "treadmill of power"; and **Denis Llorca**'s 1978 French adaptation, entitled *Kings, ou les adieux à Shakespeare*. On screen, the Hall–Barton *Roses* cycle (adapted for TV in 1965 by Peter Hall and Robin Midgely) is sadly no longer available on video. The only purpose-built production of the *Henry VI* plays is in the BBC Shakespeare series. Directed by **Jane Howell**, it concentrates on the plays' childish, game-like elements and is decidedly patchy. The filming of Bogdanov's ESC productions are more impressive and preserve much of the vigour of the original performances.

## Screen

### King Henry VI: House of Lancaster
**P. Brennen, B. Stanton, C. Farrell; Michael Bogdanov (dir.)**
UK, 1990 ▷ Vision 📼

Preserved for posterity in front of a live audience at Swansea, Michael Bogdanov's successful *Wars of the Roses* series remains a good way into the *Henry VI* plays (though there aren't many alternatives). This touring production keeps everything pretty basic but crafts virtue from necessity: it's unpretentious stuff, convincingly delivered, and at least the verse drowns out some of the tinniest music you're likely to hear this side of a shopping mall. The first segment of *2 Henry VI* is grafted onto its predecessor to make *House of Lancaster*,

particularly noteworthy are the double-act of Siôn Probert's drawling public-school Somerset and Barry Stanton's blunt York.

### King Henry VI: House of York
**P. Brennen, A. Jarvis, B. Stanton; Michael Bogdanov (dir.)**
UK, 1990 ▷ Vision 📼

*House of York* has all the attractions and minor flaws of its predecessor: punchy, no-nonsense acting in front of a live audience and some appealing production touches. *2 Henry VI* loses some of its coherence in Bogdanov's adaptation, but the Cade scenes are famously lively – Michael Pennington, Bogdanov's co-director, plays the rebel as a punkish yob wearing a Union flag singlet – while Andrew Jarvis's Richard of Gloucester is already dominating the action.

## Audio

### Henry VI Part II
**D. Tennant, K. Hunter, N. Rodway; Clive Brill (dir.)**
UK, 1998 ▷ Arkangel ⊙ 🔲

Arkangel's second instalment in the *Henry VI* cycle retains many of the personnel from *Part I*, and the recording is every bit as well-made. In the opening scenes there's a nagging sense that Kelly Hunter isn't putting her all into Margaret, but as the production develops she adds more fire to the role and produces a fearsome interpretation, but also a persuasively human one – not a sadistic battleaxe, but a woman driven to extreme ends. The scrum of lords at court (and their machinations to get the head of Norman Rodway's forbearing Duke Humphrey) is properly oppressive, with Steve Hodson's Winchester adding grizzled menace. And as the play nears its end Clive Merrison's forthright York and David Troughton's wry Richard of Gloucester, both men of business, already sound like leaders of England.

## Editions

### Arden Shakespeare (third series)
**Ronald Knowles (ed.); 1999** ▷ Thomson

Though it predates Edward Burns's Arden *1 Henry VI* (see p.118) by a year, Ronald Knowles's surprisingly fat version of *2 Henry VI* is even more complete – among its six appendices are a page-by-page facsimile of the first quarto and a chart suggesting doubling for all parts. His coverage of the play's chequered critical history is similarly detailed, distinguished by its even-handedness and its focus on the carnivalesque elements of the play.

## Some criticism

### Shakespeare's History Plays
**E.M.W. Tillyard; 1944** ▷ Penguin / Athlone [o/p]

As ever with the history plays, Tillyard provides a bracing, no-nonsense introduction to *2 Henry VI*, in which he sides with Henry's infamous declaration that "When such strings jar, what hope of harmony?", interpreted here as a serious statement that the rest of the play is in consonance with. Though it's easy to disagree with him, Tillyard does have an uncanny knack of getting to the heart of things – in this case identifying that supposedly "incidental" scenes such as the combat between Horner and Peter are in fact integral to *Part II*'s construction.

### Shakespeare and the Popular Voice
**Annabel Patterson; 1989** ▷ Blackwell

Patterson has no time for those who would deify the "Bard", or even (as the nineteenth century was fond of doing) promote him socially: for her he is a glover's son, actor and theatrical shareholder, man of business – and, most importantly, someone whose work often finds itself speaking in the "popular voice". Her larger project, of locating Shakespeare's "social assumptions" and his attitude to "the ordinary working people inside and outside his plays" might strike some as foolhardy, but for the fresh light this sheds on the political postures of his drama it seems worth it. *2 Henry VI* is an obvious text on which to focus – even though the "ordinary" people in it are conspicuously not working – and Patterson clarifies the contemporary significance of Cade's revolt by drawing attention to some Elizabethan experiences of rebellion.

# Henry VI Part III

f ever a play provided evidence of what Jan Kott called the "constant procession of kings" in Shakespeare's histories, it is *Henry VI Part III*. The action, which follows Queen Margaret's fleeting triumph at Wakefield to the Lancastrians' last stand at Tewkesbury and Henry's subsequent murder, sees no fewer than three characters claiming the throne – with one more, Richard of Gloucester, poised to make his bid as the curtain falls. But *Part III* is also Shakespeare's clearest exposition yet of the horrors of civil war. For critic M.M. Reese, it presents "a dreadful example of what happened when God's kindly watchfulness was turned to wrath by the crimes, ambition and misgovernment of men"; for other commentators it radically undermines all of those assumptions. The play was originally known as *The True Tragedy of Richard, Duke of York*, and York's messy end forms one of its most traumatic images – after being captured by Margaret's forces, the Duke is mockingly crowned with a paper coronet and taunted with the murder of his own son, before being stabbed to death by Margaret herself. There is no denying that *3 Henry VI*, which draws extensively on the revenge dramas then popular on the Elizabethan stage, is one of Shakespeare's most violent plays. It is perhaps the darkest history of all.

[DATE] On the theory that the play was written after *Part II*, probably 1591 – it was definitely completed by 1592.

[SOURCES] As with the two other *Henry VI* plays, Shakespeare used Edward Halle's *Union* (1548) and Raphael Holinshed's 1587 *Chronicles* to provide the narrative basis of *3 Henry VI*. Thomas More's *History of King Richard III* (c.1513) influences some scenes, as does work by Kyd and Marlowe.

[TEXTS] An octavo edition (O), possibly reconstructed from memory, was published in 1595 and was followed by various printings (Q2, 1600; Q3, 1619) based on the same text. The Folio version (1623) is thought to derive from Shakespeare's manuscript.

## Interpreting the play

*3 Henry VI* has sometimes struggled to win friends. After his cagey approval of the other two parts, the British critic E.M.W. Tillyard thought *Part III* was uneven at best, postulating that Shakespeare was "either tired or bored" with his material and remarking that "there are indeed splendid things in it, but they are rather islands sticking out of a sea of mediocrity than hills arising from the valleys or undulations of an organic landscape". Shakespeare's younger contemporary, Ben Jonson, expressed contempt for the *Henry VIs* more generally when he sneered in the Prologue to *Every Man In His Humour* (1601) about plays that "with three rusty swords, / And help of some few foot-and-half-foot words, / Fight over York and Lancaster's long jars: / And in the tiring-house bring wounds to scars". *3 Henry VI* has inspired even nastier criticism, too. The playwright and poet Robert Greene, older than both Shakespeare and Jonson, addressed part of his 1592 pamphlet, *Greene's Groatsworth of Wit, bought with a million of Repentance*, supposedly composed on his deathbed, to his colleagues in the theatre. He warned them to watch out for one man in particular:

## Major Characters & Synopsis

### LANCASTRIANS

**King Henry VI** of England and France
**Queen Margaret**, Henry's wife
**Prince Edward**, Henry and Margaret's son
**Dukes of Somerset**, **Exeter** and
  **Northumberland**
**Earl of Westmorland**
**Lords Clifford** and **Stafford**
Somerville
**Henry, Earl of Richmond** (later **Henry VII**)

### YORKISTS

Richard Plantagenet, **Duke of York**
York's sons: **Edward, Earl of March** (later
  **Edward IV**), **George** (later **Duke of Clarence**)
  and **Richard** (later **Duke of Gloucester**), **Earl
  of Rutland**
York's uncles: **Sir John** and **Sir Hugh Mortimer**
**Lady Gray**, a widow (later Edward's wife)
**Earl Rivers**, Lady Gray's brother
Rutland's **Tutor**
Other Yorkists: **Earl of Pembroke**, **Duke of
  Norfolk**, **Sir John Montgomery** and **Sir
  William Stanley**

### THE NEVILLES

**Earl of Warwick**, first a Yorkist, then a Lancastrian
**Marquis of Montague**, Warwick's brother, a
  Yorkist
**Earl of Oxford**, Warwick and Montague's brother-
  in-law, a Lancastrian
**Lord Hastings**, Warwick and Montague's brother-
  in-law, a Yorkist

### THE FRENCH

**King Louis** of France
**Lady Bona**, Louis's sister-in-law

[**▶▶** action continued from *Henry VI Part II*]
**ACT 1**  After their success at the Battle of St
Albans, the Yorkists force King Henry to compro-
mise: he will remain in power, but after his death
Richard, Duke of York, will inherit the throne.
Queen Margaret is outraged that her son, Prince
Edward, has been disinherited and prepares to
fight. In the meantime, York has decided to break
his oath and seize the crown. His forces meet
Margaret's at Wakefield, where his young son,
Rutland, is killed and he himself is captured and
murdered by Clifford and the Queen.

**ACT 2**  Despite his father's death, Edward
Plantagenet is proclaimed rightful king. In the
royal camp Henry knights his own son, but
declines to fight. When Edward appears and
repeats his claim to the throne, Margaret and her
supporters reject it and the two armies fight at
Towton. Henry ponders on the country's suffering
but is interrupted by news that Margaret's army
has lost. Clifford is killed, and Edward heads to
London to be crowned.

**ACT 3**  Edward (now King Edward IV) desires
the widow Lady Gray and blackmails her into marriage. Once alone, Richard Plantagenet (now
Duke of Gloucester) reveals that he wants the
crown for himself. Henry, meanwhile, has been
captured and sent to the Tower. Margaret appeals
for help from King Louis of France, only to find that
Warwick is trying to arrange a marriage between
King Edward and Louis's sister, Lady Bona. When
he discovers that Edward has already married
Lady Gray, Warwick angrily switches his allegiance
to Margaret and King Henry.

**ACT 4**  In England unrest continues as Richard
and George Plantagenet criticize their brother's
choice of wife. George (now Duke of Clarence)
deserts for Warwick's camp; the two men capture
Edward and remove his crown, only for Richard
to free him once more. Henry is in turn released
from the Tower by Warwick and George, whom
he appoints protectors, but shortly after is recap-
tured by the Yorkists. Edward is back in control.

**ACT 5**  Warwick's forces meet the Yorkists at
Coventry, but the Lancastrians are dealt a series
of heavy blows: George rejoins his brother
Edward, Warwick's brother Montague is killed,
and Warwick himself dies from his wounds. The
victorious Edward sets off to face Margaret, who
is struggling to rally her war-weary troops at
Tewkesbury. Margaret and her son Prince Edward
are soon in Yorkist hands, and despite his mother's pleas the young Prince is murdered. In the
commotion, Richard slips away to the Tower and
enters Henry's cell. Guessing his motives, the
deposed King predicts that the evil omens at
Richard's birth foretell more bloodshed; Richard
responds by stabbing him and declaring that
nothing will keep him from the throne.

There is an upstart crow, beautified with our feathers, that with his *tiger's heart wrapped in a player's hide* supposes he is as well able to bombast out a blank verse as the best of you; and, being an absolute *Johannes Factotum* [Jack-of-all-trades], is in his own conceit the only Shake-scene in a country.

This bitter denunciation contrasts Greene's own poverty and struggle for fickle success with that of a mystery dramatist whose identity is obscured, none too subtly, behind an allusion to "the only Shake-scene". It also contains a good deal of snobbery: what seems to incense Greene most is the fact that he and his colleagues – university "scholars" to a man – are being upstaged by a mere "upstart crow" who has stolen their "feathers". That this can only refer to Shakespeare is confirmed by Greene's twisting of a line from *3 Henry VI*, "O tiger's heart wrapped in a woman's hide!" (1.4.138), into a professional insult. What is less frequently commented upon is that Greene steals the line from Shakespeare's Duke of York, who is himself railing against Queen Margaret just before his execution – so Greene, similarly near death, actually offers a kind of back-handed compliment to the power of Shakespeare's verse and its dramatic context. He had clearly been listening attentively: none of Shakespeare's plays was yet in print.

## Heavy times

Whatever Greene's intentions, in terms of reputation alone *3 Henry VI* is integral to the story of Shakespeare's career; at the very least, it confirms that by the early 1590s he was making waves as a dramatist. And, in some ways, the fact that Greene picked out a fragment from a grand set-piece speech is fitting: this play demonstrates Shakespeare exploring the possibilities of rhetoric more widely than ever before. Quoted more fully, York's speech shows the character (perhaps the playwright himself) straining at the leash to express hatred for the Queen who has murdered Rutland, his youngest son:

O tiger's heart wrapped in a woman's hide!
How couldst thou drain the life-blood of the child
To bid the father wipe his eyes withal,
And yet be seen to bear a woman's face?
Women are soft, mild, pitiful, and flexible—
Thou stern, obdurate, flinty, rough, remorseless.
Bidd'st thou me rage? Why, now thou hast thy wish.
Would'st have me weep? Why, now thou hast thy will.
For raging wind blows up incessant showers,
And when the rage allays the rain begins.

**[1.4.138–47]**

York seems to go through a kind of mental thesaurus in attempting to slander Margaret and contrast his perception of her with his perception of what women should be – he is, quite literally, struggling to find the words. His speech is also remarkable in its dramatic self-consciousness: York draws attention to his own actions, his raging, his weeping, in terms that make him sound like an actor emphasizing the skill of his own spectacle.

If the dying York is attempting to make sense of inhuman actions, some critics have suggested that the play as a whole represents the final stage in Shakespeare's representation of moral anarchy. The whole action is spread over four tremendous battles – at Wakefield, Towton, Barnet and Tewkesbury. In real life some 50,000 men fought at Towton, and over half were killed, more than in any conflict on British soil before or since. Unable to call upon anything like that number of extras, Shakespeare crystallizes the slaughter into one poignant scene. A man enters lugging a body which he hopes to rob, but, removing the helmet, he makes a grim realization. "Who's this?" he cries,

> O God! It is my father's face
> Whom in this conflict I, unawares, have killed.
> O, heavy times, begetting such events!

[2.5.61–3]

As if this irony were not enough, from the other side of the stage another man enters, this time a father carrying the body of his son. Shakespeare seems to have taken the cue for this entire scene (which has no other obvious source) from a chance remark by one of his sources, Halle, who states that "this conflict was in manner unnatural, for in it the son fought against the father, the brother against the brother, the nephew against the uncle, and the tenant against his lord, which slaughter did sore and much weaken the puissance [power] of this realm".

> *In* Henry VI *the sacrificial idea, which makes catastrophe a consequence of sin, is sharply challenged by the "machiavellian" idea that makes it a consequence of weakness.*
>
> Philip Brockbank, "The frame of disorder – *Henry VI*" (1961)

Shakespeare deepens the irony still further by centring the scene on the presence of King Henry, the man whose own inability to hold things together is responsible for the chaos that surrounds him. He enters longing for an existence away from regal cares ("O God! Methinks it were a happy life / To be no better than a homely swain" (2.5.21–2)), but the folly of this fantasy is exposed when he witnesses the dead sons and fathers. He cries out:

> Woe above woe! Grief more than common grief!
> O that my death would stay these ruthful deeds!
> O, pity, pity, gentle heaven, pity!
> The red rose and the white are on his face,
> The fatal colours of our striving houses …

[2.5.94–7]

The savage beauty of this description shows Shakespeare using the formal resources of the Elizabethan stage – ritualized scenes, powerful laments – to intensify his audience's sense of the characters' suffering. Where the other *Henry VI* plays allow Shakespeare to show off his skill in reportage, here he uses highly patterned devices to depict the breakdown of moral order.

## Revenge sufficient

It's been said, too, that the play brings into serious question exactly what we think of as "moral order". In a further development of the father-son theme that occupies Shakespeare first in *1 Henry VI* and then in that scene at Towton, one of *Part III*'s dominant figures is the revenger Young Clifford. Clifford's father is killed by York in *Part II* and the son swears to avenge his death – but in doing so, his actions become worryingly dubious. Moments before killing the young Rutland, he boasts that he will stop at nothing:

> Had I thy brethren here, their lives and thine
> Were not revenge sufficient for me.

> No—if I digged up thy forefathers' graves,
> And hung their rotten coffins up in chains,
> It could not slake mine ire nor ease my heart.
> The sight of any of the house of York
> Is as a fury to torment my soul.
> And till I root out their accursèd line,
> And leave not one alive, I live in hell.

**[1.3.26–34]**

Clifford's love for his father and wish to see justice done is here twisted into unjust vengeance; it is gruesomely apt that he declares his intention to root up York's entire family in order to avenge the murder of one of his own. The cycle of bloody retaliation is deeply ingrained in the play's fabric: York is killed for his crimes; Clifford (one of the architects of York's death) is tormented by Warwick, Edward and Richard as he lies dying; even the mighty Warwick gets his comeuppance. It scarcely seems surprising that among Shakespeare's plays *3 Henry VI* is second only to *Titus Andronicus* in the number of times it uses words with the root "venge": both plays dwell on unstoppable cycles of violence. Where in *Part II* the seductive dangers of power are fully on display, *Part III* depicts the moral repercussions – that war is not simply a matter of personal loss or individual action, but corrodes the foundations of society itself.

And where in *Part II* Gloucester's enemies were eager to hide their Machiavellian actions behind the "colour" of legality, few of *Part III*'s characters have such scruples. Nearly all the central players go back on their word at some point in the action, setting up another kind of cycle – this time of untrustworthiness. Edward breaks his compact with Warwick over the marriage to Lady Bona, Warwick responds by changing sides to fight for the Lancastrians, George follows by switching to Henry's cause (and then back again in the latter stages of the play). But the play's most important oath occurs at the climax of the very first scene, when Henry brokers a deal with York enabling him to hold onto the throne:

> KING HENRY                I here entail
> The crown to thee and to thine heirs for ever,
> Conditionally, that here thou take thine oath
> To cease this civil war, and whilst I live
> To honour me as thy king and thy sovereign,
> And nor by treason nor hostility
> To seek to put me down and reign thyself.
> YORK
> This oath I willingly take and will perform.

**[1.1.195–202]**

Though York later claims to mean what he says – in sharp contrast to his sons, who do their best to persuade him that the oath is "vain and frivolous" – it isn't long before he resolves to turn once again against Henry. But, as it turns out, he needn't have bothered: news arrives that Margaret has broken Henry's side of the oath for him. While Samuel Johnson was keen to draw "moral instruction" from this tale – pointing to the irony that, if only York had waited, he would have kept his hands clean – it might be said that the lesson is, if anything, conspicuously amoral: this turn of events demonstrates that oaths have no value whatsoever. The die is cast: far from being "part of God's service and commanded by him" (as the Elizabethan *Brief Treaty of Oaths* puts it), oaths and loyalties can be manipulated – just like anything else – by the new breed of power-brokers. Richard of Gloucester, who flatly states that "But for a kingdom any oath may be broken. / I would break a thousand oaths to reign one year" (1.2.16–17), is their persuasive spokesman.

Indeed, if anyone can prosper in the ethical vacuum around him, it is Richard. It is perhaps not too extreme to say that the horrors of the play give birth to a character who is as morally twisted as (he boasts) he is physically distorted. Pondering on his "indigested and deformèd shape", Gloucester rejoices in his demonic capabilities:

> Then, since the heavens have shaped my body so,
> Let hell make crooked my mind to answer it.
> I had no father, I am like no father;
> I have no brother, I am like no brother;
> And this word, 'love', which greybeards call divine,
> Be resident in men like one another
> And not in me—I am myself alone.

**[5.6.78–84]**

Richard is isolating himself from the conflicts around him – the wars fought by two great families – by claiming to be author of himself. He even distances himself from his father, whose sole ambition it was to restore the House of York to the throne. Richard is interested in power simply for its own sake, and – in a crucial development – he is prepared to murder his own immediate family to seize it.

If there is a continuity to the *Henry VI* plays, perhaps it's that they demonstrate an unremitting breakdown of values: *Part I* begins as a patriotic adventure but ends with its nobles ranged against one another; *Part II* depicts the fragmentation of society, with different sections of English society in conflict; *Part III* shows a country in breakdown as fathers murder their own sons and sons their fathers. But Richard is prepared to turn against not merely his own country, nor even his political enemies, but his own family – and it is his bloody path to power which occupies *Richard III*, the next and final play in the historical sequence.

## Stage history and adaptations

Like its brethren, the stage history of *3 Henry VI* is a tale of initial success followed by a struggle (dogged by doubts about authorship) to be performed in anything approaching its early form. Though there is no other sixteenth-century record of it on the stage, **Robert Greene**'s coded reference to the play in 1592 (see p.129) doesn't merely catalogue the author's resentment at a younger rival, but confirms that *Part III* was popular when initially acted. All goes quiet until 1681, when **Thomas Crowne** put on the first of many adaptations. *The Misery of Civil War*, based on *3 Henry VI*, was a Restoration reworking whose title baldly states its main concerns. Evidently not nervous about labouring the point, Crowne added Cade's rebellion from *Part II* to underscore the horrors of civil conflict, and employed painted scenery depicting grisly scenes of soldiers on the rampage. In a more domestic touch, Crowne also provided King Edward with a mistress (killed in battle, in delightfully cod Shakespearian fashion, while disguised as a boy). The play's political resonances were clearly too strong for others – in 1700, **Colley Cibber** was refused permission to stage the murder of Henry VI in his version of *Richard III*, lest it stir Jacobite sympathies for the exiled King James II. Cibber's son **Theophilus** was luckier 23 years later, his version grafting Acts One to Three of *Part III* onto the final act of *Part II*.

Nineteenth-century dramatists set out on a different tack. **J.H. Merivale**'s *Richard Duke of York; or the Contention of York and Lancaster* (1817) compressed all three parts into an evening's entertainment and utilized the electrifying talent of **Edmund Kean**, already a star as Richard III, in the central role. Another one-evening adaptation was apparently undertaken by **Charles Kemble** later in the century, but seems not to have made it onto the boards.

The English Shakespeare Company brought Shakespeare's histories to audiences across the land during the late 1980s. In its two-play remake of the *Henry VI*s, Paul Brennen was a bright but fatally naive Henry, while June Watson's steely Margaret reminded many of the then Prime Minister, Margaret Thatcher.

Historicizing then took over. Following **James Anderson**'s lead – Anderson celebrated 1864, the year of Shakespeare's tercentenary, by staging an unexpanded *2 Henry VI* – in 1906 **Frank Benson** bravely put on all three plays. In this, the first time that *3 Henry VI* had been performed in its entirety since the 1590s, Benson attempted to restore some sense of the Elizabethan theatre – though his efforts were not to everyone's liking, one critic cavilling that "there was an unnecessary amount of fighting, never very effective on the stage". Shouldering the role of Richard of Gloucester himself, following one performance Benson even spoke to the audience as soon as the applause had died down, expounding his own (patriotic) views about the cycle. In the end, though, *Part III* brought in the smallest houses of the week.

After **Robert Atkins**'s 1923 production of *Henry VI* (which, like Merivale's a century before, squeezed three plays into one), several twentieth-century performances have restored the reputation of Shakespeare's earliest histories. The first was undertaken in 1951 by **Barry Jackson**, who had seen Benson fifty years before. He made the most of the tiny space offered by the Birmingham Repertory Theatre and built a strong, cohesive company in which doubling was used to great effect. **Peter Hall** and **John Barton** did things differently in their RSC cycle, *The Wars of the Roses* (1963), which consisted of three plays (*Henry VI*, *Edward IV* and *Richard III*), the first two derived from Shakespeare's work plus other material. As with Peter Brook's infamous *King Lear* of the previous year, the radical politics and bleak worldview of Jan Kott's *Shakespeare Our Contemporary* held sway, and the set was dominated by an intimidatingly massive conference table. **David Warner** played Henry as a boyish martyr, **Peggy Ashcroft** made an impressive Margaret (terrifyingly intense in her murder of York) and a young **Ian Holm** appeared as Gloucester. More politically reticent was the widely praised production mounted in 1977 by **Terry Hands** at the Swan in Stratford, in which the director used near-uncut texts and focused on characterization rather than ostentatious thematic gestures. A seasoned **Alan Howard** played the King to **Helen Mirren**'s Margaret – despite her conspicuous success in the role, Mirren still suffered from physical nausea every time York's death scene was performed.

Political relevance was back on the agenda for **Michael Bogdanov**'s ESC versions of 1987, once more cut and spliced as part of a two-tetralogy series entitled, yet again, *The Wars of the Roses*. In this pared-down touring production, Thatcherite power politics wrestled with yob culture in an ultimately cynical reading. At the RSC, meanwhile, **Adrian Noble** presented *The Plantagenets* (1988), a two-play adaptation whose imaginative designs (by **Bob Crowley**) and intellectual breadth were enthusiastically received; **Ralph Fiennes** played the King to **Anton Lesser**'s (sometimes literally) satanic Richard Gloucester. In 2000 the RSC once more put on a cycle of Shakespeare's histories entitled *This England*, this time with uncut texts; the *Henry VIs* were directed by **Michael Boyd** at the small-scale Swan Theatre. More recently still, **Edward Hall** presented a two-part version of the *Henry VIs* drastically different from that of his father, which toured the UK in 2001–02 under the kitschy title of *Rose Rage*. Hall's youthful, all-male company offered a vigorous interpretation of the plays set in a slaughterhouse, in which cartoon-like violence, butcher's off-cuts and Victorian hymns formed an unlikely melange.

Influential non-English versions have included **Giorgio Strehler**'s 1965 adaptation, *Il Gioco dei Potente*, influenced by both Barton–Hall and Strindberg; **Peter Palisch**'s stark *Krieg der Rosen* (1967); and **Denis Llorca**'s 1978 French adaptation, entitled *Kings, ou les adieux à Shakespeare*, which attempted to approach the plays from the "enemy" perspective. In the absence of the Hall–Barton *Roses* trilogy (adapted for TV in 1965), the only purpose-built production to see release is one directed by **Jane Howell** for the BBC in 1983. Howell's interpretation, which imagined the plays as a public-school brawl, gained mixed reviews, delighting some but appalling others. More warmly received were the tapings of Bogdanov's ESC productions, which were recorded live.

# Screen

### King Henry VI: House of York
**P. Brennen, A. Jarvis, B. Stanton; Michael Bogdanov (dir.)**
UK, 1990 ▷ Vision [cassette]

Adapting the *Henry VI*s into a two-part play emphasizes Richard Gloucester's hold on the plot, and with Andrew Jarvis in the role, Bogdanov has a star worthy of the attention: his gleeful, toothy and bald-pated Richard is frankly irresistible (and someone the live audience obviously appreciates). Also impressive is June Watson's Queen Margaret, who bears an uncanny and rather chilling resemblance to Margaret Thatcher. Some of the ESC's theatrical techniques – khaki battle scenes contrasted with black-tie cocktail parties – now seem like clichés and don't always capture *3 Henry VI*'s subtler resonances, but they get near its combination of warring brutality and power politics. And Bogdanov's is very much a sequence: Jarvis utters the famous first lines of *Richard III* as the lights come down.

# Audio

### Henry VI Part III
**D. Tennant, K. Hunter, J. Bowe; Clive Brill (dir.)**
UK, 1998 ▷ Arkangel ⊙ [cassette]

*3 Henry VI* sees Shakespeare exploring the language of brutality more fully than ever before, and on audio there's little to insulate against it: the scene in which Jamie Glover's fierce Clifford murders the boy Rutland (a very convincing Jay Barrimore) is in some ways more horrible to listen to than see, but it is just one of a series of vicious moments in this disturbingly violent play. Much of that violence is captured in Clive Brill's excellent Arkangel trilogy, and like its predecessors *3 Henry VI* has an excellent cast with some genuinely terrific performances (Kelly Hunter's Margaret comes into her own here, while David Troughton's strongly characterized Richard of Gloucester is as restlessly energetic as ever).

# Editions

### Arden Shakespeare (third series)
**John D. Cox & Eric Rasmussen (eds); 2001** ▷ Thomson

John D. Cox has a reputation as a card-carrying new historicist

– his *Shakespeare and the Dramaturgy of Power* (1989) is a classic of the movement – but this collaborative edition is gratifyingly unbiased in its appraisal of the play's critical history. Although Michael Hattaway's Cambridge version offers strong competition, Arden is the one to have, pushed into pole position by its vivid historical information – a photo of the mangled skull of a soldier from Towton, one of 24,000 dead, is a salient reminder that the Wars of the Roses weren't mere play-acting. If your curiosity is pricked by the play's contorted textual history the 1595 octavo *True Tragedy* is reproduced in facsimile as an appendix.

# Some criticism

### Shakespeare's History Plays
**E.M.W. Tillyard; 1944** ▷ Penguin / Athlone [o/p]

Though Tillyard's unflattering comments concerning *Part III*'s unevenness have already been relayed (see p.128), his view of the play as "chaos itself, the full prevalence of civil war, the perpetration of one horrible deed after another", given his reservations, seems surprisingly near the mark. Though he does not spend a great deal of time discussing the play, his account of it should be read in the context of his overall argument about the cyclical nature of the early histories. Tillyard interprets the brutal twists of *Part III* as divine retribution for events ultimately dating back to the deposition of Richard II, as the Tudor chronicles themselves had done. While this reading has limits (it's notable how *rarely* characters in these plays make reference to Richard II, for instance), it is a good place to start.

### Shakespeare's Histories
**John W. Velz (ed.); 1996** ▷ Medieval & Renaissance Texts and Studies

Subtitled "a quest for form and genre", this collection of essays covers new and unusual approaches to the history plays and is particularly helpful in the case of *3 Henry VI*, criticism of which is especially thin on the ground. Among them is Naomi Conn Liebler's excellent essay on "ritual and play in the shaping of *3 Henry VI*", which offers a lighter way to look at the play from that which usually prevails. It isolates Richard as a spoilsport, "the antithesis of game" – game being, in this instance, the rules of dynasticism, war, government and legitimacy.

# Henry VIII

Written with John Fletcher, *Henry VIII* (or *All Is True*) is one of Shakespeare's most ostentatiously spectacular works – Coleridge called it a "show play". But though it may have added to the playwright's reputation among his contemporaries, it was also responsible for burning down his playhouse. During a performance on June 29, 1613, material from a cannon fired in Act One ignited the Globe's roof and within hours the theatre was destroyed. This event foreshadowed an even larger loss: Shakespeare's imminent retirement to Stratford following *The Two Noble Kinsmen*, his final collaboration with Fletcher. *Henry VIII* itself, however, gives little hint of departure, slotting tightly into the mould of the early history plays. Picking up events a generation after the close of *Richard III*, it redeploys the kind of court chicanery and high-level politics familiar from the *Henry VI* cycle – albeit with a more jaundiced eye than ever before. But, like *Antony and Cleopatra*, it also deals with the personal suffering that goes hand in hand with political events – most touchingly the humiliating treatment of Queen Katherine, stripped of her position as King Henry's first wife. The fact that her successor, Anne Boleyn (the mother of Queen Elizabeth I), was executed three years later makes *Henry VIII*'s unsparing reflections on the ever-turning wheel of fortune seem utterly prescient.

[DATE] According to evidence describing the Globe fire on June 29, 1613 (see below), *Henry VIII* – or *All Is True*, as it was probably first known – was a new play when the incident occurred, probably written by Shakespeare and Fletcher earlier that year.

[SOURCES] As with the other history plays, the *Chronicles* by Raphael Holinshed and others (1587) and Edward Halle's *Union of the Two Noble and Illustrious Houses of Lancaster and York* (1548) provide *Henry VIII*'s main sources. Other details derive from John Foxe's anti-Catholic *Book of Martyrs* (1563) and Samuel Rowley's play *When You See Me, You Know Me* (1603), as well as George Cavendish's 1592 *Life* of Wolsey.

[TEXTS] Only one text, that in the 1623 First Folio, survives. It was probably typeset from a scribe's copy of the play.

## Interpreting the play

One reason the Globe burnt down so quickly was that its audience was too engrossed in the play to notice. While their eyes were "more attentive to the show," wrote the diplomat Sir Henry Wotton to his nephew, the flames "kindled inwardly, and ran round like a train, consuming within less than an hour the whole house to the very grounds". The authors may thus have had cause to rue the success of *Henry VIII*, only in its third or fourth performance at the time: perhaps if some of the spectators had allowed their attention to wander, the theatre might have been preserved. The very fact that a cannon was being fired to welcome King Henry – not as the more usual shorthand for a battle scene – speaks volumes. *Henry VIII* was intended to astound its first audiences.

## Major Characters & Synopsis

**Prologue** and **Epilogue**

**King Henry VIII** of England

**Katherine** of Aragon, Henry's wife, later his divorcée

**Anne Boleyn**, Katherine's maid-of-honour and Henry's second wife

**Cardinal Wolsey**

**Thomas Cranmer**, later Archbishop of Canterbury and his colleague the **Bishop of Lincoln**

**Stephen Gardiner**, Henry's new secretary, later **Bishop of Winchester**

**Cardinal Campeius**, ambassador of the Pope

**Lord Caputius**, ambassador of Emperor Charles V

**Thomas Cromwell**, Henry's adviser

**Duke of Buckingham**

**Lord Abergavenny** and the **Earl of Surrey**, Buckingham's sons-in-law

Nobles, gentlemen and officials at the English court: **Dukes of Norfolk** and **Suffolk**, **Lord Sands**, **Sir Thomas Lovell**, **Sir Anthony Denny**, **Sir Henry Guildford**, **Sir Nicholas Vaux**, the **Lord Chamberlain** and the **Lord Chancellor**

Three **Gentlemen** at the court

Buckingham's **Surveyor**

**Griffith**, Katherine's usher

**Patience**, Katherine's waiting woman

**Old Lady**, Anne Boleyn's companion

**Doctor Butts**, Henry's physician

**ACT 1** The English court is abuzz with news from the Field of Cloth of Gold, a spectacular peace conference between England and France. But the influence wielded by Cardinal Wolsey (Lord Chancellor and the mastermind behind the event) is the source of much jealousy among certain lords. Sneering at his ambition and low birth, Buckingham, Abergavenny and Norfolk grumble that the peace deal with the French is already falling apart. But Wolsey is one step ahead of his enemies, and Buckingham is arrested. The Cardinal seems unstoppable: though news of his damaging taxes reaches the King, no sooner are they repealed than Wolsey craftily puts out word that it is he who has called for the changes. Though suspicions are high, the King has other matters on his mind: namely the beautiful Anne Boleyn, his wife's maid-of-honour, whom he dances with and kisses at the Cardinal's palace.

**ACT 2** As Buckingham heads to his execution, rumours begin to circulate that Henry intends to divorce his wife Katherine at Wolsey's behest, and in fact Cardinal Campeius has travelled from Rome especially to arrange matters. Meanwhile, Anne Boleyn expresses her qualms about queenship to the Old Lady. At the divorce court in Blackfriars Katherine puts up strong resistance, however, and refuses to be intimidated by Wolsey and his henchmen.

**ACT 3** The case stalls until Katherine decides to relent following a visit from Wolsey and Campeius. But a further hold-up occurs when deceitful letters sent by Wolsey to the Pope are revealed to the King. With his career in ruins, Wolsey is replaced as Chancellor by Sir Thomas More.

**ACT 4** The coronation of Anne has taken place with great ceremony, but her triumph cruelly coincides with Katherine's decline. Lying sick at Kimbolton, Katherine has a vision of angels and celestial spirits before receiving a visit from Lord Caputius. She dies after commending her daughter to the King's care.

**ACT 5** The new Queen is soon pregnant, but the news only antagonizes the King's secretary Gardiner, who vows to attack her and Cranmer, Henry's virtuous Archbishop of Canterbury (and latest confidant). But the King is not to be outplayed: when Gardiner and his cronies turn against Cranmer in council, Henry's support is steadfast. Amid scenes of wild public rejoicing, Anne's newborn daughter Elizabeth – the future queen – is christened. Cranmer predicts that her reign, and that of her successor, will be blessed.

Even in its four-hundred-year-old play-script, *Henry VIII* gives a vivid impression of its visual punch. Many of the play's pivotal moments are attended by grand theatrical set pieces, all described with unusually detailed stage directions. The first big moment, Wolsey's banquet in Act One – the first scene that hints the King, dancing with Anne Boleyn, will stray from his marriage – requires several tables on stage, copious guests and plenty of music. In Act Two, the aftermath of the Duke of Buckingham's trial is designed to seize our attention with his ignominious entrance, flanked by "halberdiers" (armed soldiers) and a throng of noblemen and commoners.

But these pale compared to the visual splendours later in that same Act when Queen Katherine herself is tried. As scene four begins, both "trumpets" and "cornetts" sound as the court proceeds majestically into session, led by a train of twenty-four named personnel, ranging from functionaries, such as "two vergers with silver wands" and "two gentlemen bearing two great silver pillars", all the way up to a gang of some five bishops – not to mention the estranged King and Queen themselves, each attended by numerous flunkies (2.4.0.SD). As is attested by the extravagant 1520 peace conference between England and France known as the Field of Cloth of Gold (with which the play begins), Henry VIII's real-life court was acutely conscious of the political value of majestic ceremonial trappings – and *Henry VIII* does its best to reproduce them. Following that court scene, three other spectacular events map out the course of the rest of the play: Anne's coronation, represented by an extensive "royal train"; Queen Katherine's dream vision, featuring "six personages in white robes" who dance around her to the accompaniment of music; and finally the christening of the young Princess Elizabeth (Anne Boleyn's daughter and the future Queen) that brings the play to its conclusion.

## The very persons

The play itself urges audiences to take this kind of realism seriously. From Wotton's letter describing the fire we gather that "The Life of King Henry the Eight", as it was printed in the 1623 First Folio, was more usually known by a jaunty alternative title, *All Is True*. There was a brief Jacobean fad for colloquial, playful titles – Samuel Rowley's play *When You See Me, You Know Me* (revived in 1613) was also about King Henry, while Thomas Heywood's *If You Know Not Me, You Know Nobody* (1605) appears to have been a source for Shakespeare and Fletcher. Shakespeare's own taste for tongue-in-cheek names appears in the comedies as *Much Ado About Nothing* and *What You Will*, the latter better known as *Twelfth Night*. But "All Is True" is more outrageously daring than any of these: it suggests not merely that "all" will be "true" in the end, but insists that what the playwrights are putting on stage really did happen. As we have seen, the play's taste for spectacular staging makes it quite apparent that reproducing the visual realities of Henry's court is a major concern. And as the Prologue himself puts it,

> To rank our chosen truth with such a show
> As fool and fight is, beside forfeiting
> Our own brains, and the opinion that we bring
> To make that only true we now intend,
> Will leave us never an understanding friend.
> Therefore, for goodness' sake, and as you are known
> The first and happiest hearers of the town,
> Be sad as we would make ye. Think ye see
> The very persons of our noble story
> As they were living; think you see them great,

And followed with the general throng and sweat
Of thousand friends; then, in a moment, see
How soon this mightiness meets misery.

**[Prologue, 17–30]**

This is no knockabout farce, no "fool and fight" show, but a drama to feed the mind. Furthermore, it is drama intended to be indistinguishable from the "truth" of real life: unlike *Henry V*'s Chorus, who urges spectators to "piece out our imperfections with your thoughts" (Prologue, 23), there is no apology here for the limitations of the Globe. And there would have been an even more heightened sense of "truth" at the King's Men's new venue, where the play may have transferred after the fire. Located in the upmarket Blackfriars area north of the river, their recently refurbished indoor theatre occupied the site of an old Dominican monastery and contained the very hall in which Queen Katherine's divorce case was tried, eighty-odd years earlier. When the trial occurs on stage in Act Two, it must have been difficult to avoid a sense that events were being played out as, once upon a time, they had been for real. "The very persons of our noble story", it seems, had stood almost on the same spot as the actors.

## Many hands

Given that Shakespeare is often regarded as the greatest writer in the English language, it can be a substantial disappointment to discover that we possess practically no examples of the great man's hand – no manuscripts, no printed books with his jottings. All that remain are six scratchy but authenticated signatures on various legal documents (the infamous will was written out by a professional scribe, the client simply signing in the appropriate places).

That isn't quite the end of the story, however. Many believe that at least some of the handwriting in a unique surviving copy of a text entitled "**The Booke of Sir Thomas Moore**" (c.1603), preserved in the British Library, is Shakespeare's. This manuscript is a play-text (in this instance "book" equals "promptbook") based on the life of the eponymous politician, writer and Catholic martyr – executed on the orders of Henry VIII – but it seems never to have been acted or published. One reason for that might have been the involvement of Elizabeth I's Master of the Revels, Sir Edmund Tilney, who apparently rejected the play and refused to allow it to be performed. Perhaps in response to this censorship, various rewritings and additions seem to have been made to the text – and some of those changes are in handwriting subsequently (and somewhat unromantically) described as "**Hand D**". Since the nineteenth century scholars have argued that this hand is Shakespeare's and excerpts from the text are included in many *Complete Works* and have even been performed on stage.

If Hand D *is* Shakespeare's – watertight identification is difficult – it prompts fascinating questions about his involvement in collaborative playwriting. The hands of dramatists **Anthony Munday**, **Henry Chettle**, **Thomas Dekker** and possibly **Thomas Heywood** also feature in the More manuscript, indicating that in this instance at least the work was shared. Heywood later claimed to have had "a entire hand or at least a main finger" in over two hundred plays, and in recent years theatre historians have argued that writing plays in collaboration was the rule for Elizabethan dramatists rather than the exception. *Sir Thomas More* also provides tantalizing hints about Shakespeare's creative process: the insertions ascribed to Hand D have plenty of false starts and crossings-out, suggesting that the playwright's patterns of work were both messy and fairly rapid. And the fact that these insertions include a powerful speech by More addressed to the citizens of London, in which he successfully quells a riot against foreigners, also implies that Shakespeare had become well known among his contemporaries for producing emotive work – and work that showed an affinity with what the text calls "wretched strangers", the minority victims of mob violence.

If you feel like dipping into the sections of *Sir Thomas More* usually ascribed to Shakespeare, the *Oxford Complete Works* (1988) prints the relevant excerpts. The full text is edited by Vittorio Gabrieli and Giorgio Melchiori and published as part of the Revels Plays series (1990).

Even if the play's early audiences were unaware of the location of Katherine's downfall, the dizzying sense that history was intimately entwined with the present must have been inescapable if they paused to "think" about the monastery itself, whose change-of-use was instigated by Henry VIII's most wide-reaching political act: the split with the Catholic hierarchy, the foundation of the Church of England and the dissolution of religious houses. Indeed, the fact that *Henry VIII* hinges on the momentous events of the English Reformation – a schism instigated by Henry's wish to divorce Katherine despite being refused by the Pope – has been taken by many to argue that Fletcher and Shakespeare's play is Protestant propaganda dressed up as history. After all, it climaxes with the birth of Princess Elizabeth, a Protestant monarch who will preside over a country in which "God shall be truly known", as Archbishop Cranmer puts it in the play's closing minutes (5.4.36). Writing a full decade after that same Elizabeth's death, the playwrights were freed from the Queen's injunction not to perform plays touching "either mat-

*Henry VIII*, as illustrated in Nicholas Rowe's 1709 edition of Shakespeare. Despite its "modern-dress" setting (the gossiping courtiers sport periwigs and breeches), both Henry and Wolsey appear in Tudor garb.

ters of religion or of the governance of the estate of the common weal", and took the opportunity to retell some of the events of her father's reign, events that were only just beyond living memory for some of their spectators.

In one sense the play's overall trajectory does seem to confirm a Protestant message: it also pivots on the downfall of Cardinal Wolsey, the lord chancellor historically sacked by Henry as soon as it became clear that he would be unable to broker the King's "great matter" and arrange a divorce. During his time as chief royal adviser, many were appalled at Wolsey's influence over Henry: all-powerful, vainglorious and with a larger household even than the royal one (the magnificent royal palace at Hampton Court was in fact originally his), the Cardinal was seen to embody everything that was wrong with England. By the time that Wolsey had outlasted his usefulness, Protestant commentators rejoiced that he would be rejected alongside the devilish Roman Church he represented. The play itself makes the reason for Wolsey's downfall more specific, and more ironic. Wolsey's bitter enemy Suffolk gleefully narrates the ins and outs:

> The Cardinal's letters to the Pope miscarried,
> And came to th'eye o'th' King, wherein was read
> How that the Cardinal did entreat his holiness

To stay the judgement o'th' divorce, for if
It did take place, 'I do', quoth he, 'perceive
My king is tangled in affection to
A creature of the Queen's, Lady Anne Boleyn'.

[3.2.30–6]

And with these words Wolsey signs what will eventually prove his death sentence as well as his ejection from office. The complicating factor is of course that, at least in this instance, he has done absolutely nothing wrong: in fact the Cardinal has simply told the truth. The difficulty is that this truth is rather too sensitive to bear – it makes the King's actions seem somewhat grubbier than he would prefer. By this stage everyone knows that Henry has tired of Katherine and fallen for Anne Boleyn (after dancing with her in Wolsey's house, ironically enough). Even so, Henry is hasty to claim that he desires a divorce not because his eye has been caught by another woman, but because Katherine has been unable to give him a male heir. It is a curse that has resulted, the King claims, because the match between them is actually void: Katherine was initially married to his older brother Arthur, but Arthur died soon afterwards and rather than break the political alliance with Spain, she was handed to Henry instead. "Hence I took a thought," Henry heatedly explains to the papal legate Campeius,

This was a judgement on me that my kingdom,
Well worthy the best heir o'th' world, should not
Be gladded in't by me.

[2.4.190–3]

If Campeius is unimpressed by these arguments (as Henry suspects he is), it is a cynicism only encouraged by the play. The King has often been portrayed as the play's out-and-out hero, a Protestant monarch who finally banishes the arch-tempter Wolsey (as a previous King Henry banished Falstaff) and takes control of England for himself. Yet that exemplary image is hardly to be found in *Henry VIII*. Whereas in real life Henry wed Anne Boleyn some four years after the rift with Katherine, in the play the marriage follows with indecent haste. Likewise, for all the King's bluster about his "wounded conscience", his courtiers have little doubt as to the reality:

LORD CHAMBERLAIN
It seems the marriage with his brother's wife
Has crept too near his conscience.
SUFFOLK                              No, his conscience
Has crept too near another lady.

[2.2.16–18]

The rib-nudging tone of the exchange – and its unfussy language, somewhat characteristic of the play – speaks volumes. And though Henry publicly undertakes to stay with his wife if the cardinals prove the marriage "lawful", Katherine sadly reveals that he has long since banished her from his bed.

## A glist'ring grief

If Henry isn't a spotless hero, neither is Wolsey an out-and-out villain. Eager though the play might seem to offer a tale of regal redemption – the kind of tale that Shakespeare's earlier romances had created a taste for – its commitment to historical "truth" among the web of Tudor politics (even the unpalatable truth about Henry's sexual interests) opens up plenty of other options. The play began with a grim demonstration of the Cardinal's malevolence: the downfall of the Duke of Buckingham, whose error is to criticize too openly Wolsey's domi-nance, and who pays the price soon afterwards. But as we watch Wolsey's snarling enemies turn on the former lord chancellor himself, Buckingham's earlier words on the fickleness of power seem more acute than ever. Heading to his execution, Buckingham grimly warns anyone within earshot that the court is a dangerous place to eke out a career. "You that hear me," he calls,

> This from a dying man may receive as certain—
> Where you are liberal of your loves and counsels,
> Be sure you be not loose; for those that you make friends
> And give your hearts to, when they once perceive
> The least rub in your fortunes, fall away
> Like water from ye, never found again
> But where they mean to sink ye.

**[2.1.125–32]**

It is the kind of counsel given weight by the speaker's proximity to death: like John of Gaunt in *Richard II*, who insists that "the tongues of dying men / Enforce attention" (2.1.5–6), Buckingham hopes that his stark message will be taken for truth. Power is slippery, he warns: anyone can suffer a fall, and friends inevitably become enemies, "fall[ing] away / Like water" (a vivid and surprising poetic image) before they turn against you. In the treacherous world of the sixteenth-century court – *Henry VIII* is the only one of Shakespeare's histories to be set in the Renaissance – the only person you can trust to be true is yourself.

> *In architectural elevation there may not be anything very imposing in* Henry VIII. *It is no towering edifice, based and buttressed, one substructure resting upon another. But everything is meshed, consequential, and more subtly interrelated than one may suspect at first.*
>
> Kristian Smidt, *Unconformities in Shakespeare's History Plays* (1982)

In time Wolsey too has good reason to rue these realities (his fine speech acknowledging his weaknesses has been much anthologized), and the insistent parallels between Buckingham and Wolsey's respective downfalls – both tell the truth, both are undone by omnipresent ene-mies – overcome the differences between them. The play begins to look less like the straightforward story it seems at first, and more like a satire on the ever-rumbling treadmill of power. But like *King John*, another play that looks unsparingly at the messy business of pol-itics, in its next depiction of a downfall *Henry VIII* presents a properly tragic aspect: the suffering of the blameless Queen Katherine, who forms another and more pitiful embodiment of truth – the kind of truth hinted at by Buckingham, the commitment to absolute constancy. Initially the play sets her up (ahistorically) as a kind of heroine, ranged against Wolsey in a fight for the people. In the play's second scene we see her kneeling in front of Henry and exclaiming that his subjects are "in great grievance" because of what she earnestly calls "exac-tions" – ruinously high taxes set by Wolsey in defiance of his royal master (1.2.20–6). As soon as the matter comes to light, Henry rescinds them and the royal couple are confirmed in their strength. But Katherine's next involvement with power politics will not be so fortunate: after the banquet at Wolsey's, rumours begin to circulate of the King's eagerness to seek a divorce, and when we next see the Queen it is at her trial. Ritually kneeling once more to her husband, she movingly describes what it is like to be outmanoeuvred politically (in a speech probably written by Shakespeare, who might have contributed around half of the play, around two scenes per act). "Heaven witness / I have been to you a true and humble wife," she addresses Henry,

> At all times to your will conformable,
> Ever in fear to kindle your dislike,
> Yea, subject to your countenance, glad or sorry
> As I saw it inclined. When was the hour
> I ever contradicted your desire,
> Or made it not mine too? Or which of your friends
> Have I not strove to love, although I knew
> He were mine enemy?
>
> **[2.4.20–9]**

These are questions for which Henry cannot provide answers – he will not even speak until much later in the scene – and in fact Katherine's "enemies" are already gaining the upper hand. The Queen eloquently attempts to clear her name of any taint of suspicion, but she had little idea until now that being "true" could harm her. "Have I lived thus long," she cries, "a wife, a true one?"

> A woman, I dare say, without vainglory,
> Never yet branded with suspicion?
> Have I with all my full affections
> Still met the King, loved him next heav'n, obeyed him,
> Been out of fondness superstitious to him,
> Almost forgot my prayers to content him?
>
> **[3.1.124–31]**

"Truth loves open dealing," she earlier warned the scheming Wolsey (3.1.39), and as she finds herself gambled out of her throne, truth has never seemed more isolated among the chicanery at court. Before the play is out Katherine will be dead – but not before experiencing a miraculous vision in which "spirits of peace" crown her with garlands in a symbol of divine innocence.

Katherine's prominently unlovely fate makes it difficult to accept in simple terms the role of her successor as Queen, Anne Boleyn, who is crowned even before Katherine's death. The play leaves Anne's motives and experience largely in shadow, and although it ends with yet another spectacular occasion celebrating the birth of Elizabeth (a daughter Henry is desperate to avoid in his eagerness for a male heir), the Queen's silent presence at the ceremony of thanksgiving seems almost foreboding. Though everyone else present looks towards the future, to the "thousand thousand blessings" of Elizabeth's reign as Queen (5.4.19), from the perspectives enabled by the play it is hard to avoid the sense that before that comes to pass Anne herself will be accused of adultery and beheaded, Henry will have remarried another four times and England will have been plunged into bitter religious turmoil. Anne's own words on the subject much earlier in the play, though they dissolve amid the pomp and ceremony of the closing scene, seem uncannily accurate. Discussing the sorry state of Katherine with her companion the Old Lady, Anne's opinion is strongly – truthfully – held. "Verily, I swear," she declares,

> 'tis better to be lowly born
> And range with humble livers in content
> Than to be perked up in a glist'ring grief
> And wear a golden sorrow.
>
> **[2.3.19–22]**

"Our content / Is our best having," the Old Lady agrees; wanting any more is incalculably dangerous. That message is one of the truest things *Henry VIII*, or *All Is True*, contains.

# Stage history and adaptations

Though the **Globe** fire of June 1613 proved devastating, a rebuilt replacement was up and running withing twelve months and performances of *All Is True* no doubt continued at the indoor **Blackfriars**, probably with the corpulent **John Lowin** as Henry. Another performance was commissioned in 1628 by the widely reviled **Duke of Buckingham**, apparently as a device to increase his popularity (he pointedly left the performance after his namesake's unjust execution), but satirists wondered why he failed to spot the play's more obvious message – the downfall of a hugely unpopular courtier.

This is all we know until the 1660s, when *Henry VIII* (as it became known in this period) was put on by **William Davenant** at Lincoln's Inn Fields. Sponsored by the newly restored Charles II, Davenant emphasized the play's propagandistic purposes, employing impressive Tudor pageantry and employing the talents of **Thomas Betterton**'s noble Henry and **John Verbrugger**'s Wolsey. Pepys was one of many satisfied customers – he saw it twice, thinking it "better than I ever expected", and the production became a watchword for lavish production values. **John Banks** mounted a strongly Protestant adaptation entitled *Virtue Betrayed, or Ann Bullen* in 1682, **Barton Booth** playing Henry in both this and Shakespeare's play (itself much curtailed).

Brushes with literal royalty continued in the next century. *Henry VIII* was played at **court** in front of George I in 1717 (his English being limited, the jokes had to be explained), and then a decade later to coincide with George II's coronation. **Colley Cibber** was responsible for the latter, the royal connections paying off handsomely in 1728 when George announced he would attend a performance: people responded by breaking into Drury Lane in order to procure seats with a good view of him. Cibber's productions starred **Peg Woffington** and **Hannah Pritchard** from the 1740s, and **James Quin** also played redoubtable Henrys. Coronation fever in 1761 again inspired stagings of *Henry VIII*, this time in a showdown between **David Garrick** at Drury Lane and **John Rich** at Covent Garden (Garrick's performances were accused of being shabby by comparison). Near the century's end the play would receive new life in the hands of **John Philip Kemble** – or, more accurately, his sister **Sarah Siddons**. Renowned as a tragic actress, Siddons was recommended to play Queen Katherine by none other than Dr Johnson, and the results were apparently spectacular: one actor reputedly refused to go on stage with her, so searing was her performance; and audiences commonly refused to applaud, out of respect, until her body had left the stage.

But it was the historical realism of Kemble's production that would influence directors throughout the nineteenth century, perhaps *Henry VIII*'s most popular period. **William Charles Macready** and **Samuel Phelps** put on competing performances at their respective houses, but in 1848 came together at Drury Lane to perform (yet again) in front of royalty, this time Queen Victoria and her consort Albert. Their Katherine was the impressive American actor **Charlotte Cushman**, who later toured the role in the States (building upon the success of **Charles** and **Fanny Kemble**, who had taken the play to New York in 1834) and even, in 1859, played Wolsey. By that time **Charles Kean**'s 1855 performance in London was infamous, if only because of its vast scale and cutting-edge technology. Pioneering the use of spotlighting and so-called "raking flats" (backcloths set at an angle to give the impression of distance), Kean's version employed a cavalcade of angels to represent Katherine's vision and built up to a "Grand Moving Panorama" of Tudor London scrupulously copied from a 1543 drawing. Unsurprisingly, the text was severly cut – Kean reasoning, perhaps accurately enough, that there simply wasn't space for everything.

His production would seem restrained compared to those mounted by **Henry Irving** in 1892 and **Herbert Beerbohm Tree** in 1910, both of which broke extravagant new ground. Though Irving called upon the services of **Ellen Terry** (Katherine) and **William Terriss** (Henry), with Irving himself as Wolsey, he cut most of the final two acts and surrounded them with lavish "historical" scenery. As did Tree, constructing monumental fan-vaulted sets and filling the stage with extras in the belief that the period required "great sumptuousness". But his obsession with detail rebounded when he toured to the US in 1916, shipping over some

Henry Irving as Cardinal Wolsey dominated the 1892 production of *Henry VIII* at London's Lyceum Theatre. His performance won high praise for what the *Saturday Review* called "…the soul struggle which rends the heart and intellect of the great statesman."

375 costumes and 135 items of furniture in the process: having little else to comment on (half the play was cut), critics simply accused it of looking scruffy.

The Victorian and Edwardian taste for "authenticity" was passing, and ripe for satirizing – which is precisely what happened at the Cambridge Festival Theatre under **Terence Gray** in 1931. Instead of Holbein, Gray took inspiration from the topsy-turvy worlds of Lewis Carroll, creating weirdly modernist designs that ended up dominating the action, culminating in a baptism scene in which a cardboard infant Elizabeth I was shown to have a sixty-year-old face before being tossed blithely to the audience. **Tyrone Guthrie**'s *Henry VIII* at the Old Vic two years later was much more traditional and had in **Charles Laughton** the epitome of the "bluff King Hal" approach to the role. Guthrie's 1949 staging at Stratford won him even warmer reviews. Using a full text, he filled the stage not with vast sets but bustle and colour, and also emphasized the play's comedy. **Diana Wynard**'s Katherine and **Anthony Quayle**'s Henry were well-received, and the production was subsequently revived in the coronation year of 1953.

Since then the play has appeared only infrequently, most often at the behest of the state-subsidized RSC (which can afford to make a loss). By general consent the most satisfying postwar production was put on by **Trevor Nunn**, who largely ignored *Henry VIII*'s politics in favour of its psychological drama, with **Donald Sinden**'s tormented Henry and **Peggy Ashcroft**'s fine Katherine much praised (Ashcroft, for one, seems to have taken her role every bit as seriously as Siddons did). **Howard Davies**, again at the RSC, reacted against this by putting on an aggressively radical production in 1983 (almost unique in the play's performance history) that underscored its power politics with all manner of directorial conceits – most notoriously a coronation scene which was tauntingly "rehearsed" on stage. **Ian Judge**'s insipid Chichester Festival production of 1991 was likewise condemned, but **Gregory Doran**'s efforts at the RSC's Swan Theatre in 1996 received positive notices for its attempt to combine the play's pageantry with its political and personal realism; **Paul Jesson**'s Henry and **Jane Lapotaire**'s conspicuously Spanish Katherine were both sensitively performed. In a pointed reference to the play's original title and its contemporary resonances, "All Is True" was emblazoned across the back of the stage.

Sections of **Beerbohm Tree**'s 1910 production were captured on silent film – making *Henry VIII* one of the first Shakespeares to make it onto celluloid – but the prints were destroyed a few weeks later and nothing survives. The BBC/Time-Life production of 1979 is the only other screen version; it was directed by **Kevin Billington**.

## Screen

**Henry VIII**
J. Stride, C. Bloom, T. West; Kevin Billington (dir.)
UK, 1979 ▷ Ambrose Video (BBC) DVD

Billington's decision to shoot *Henry VIII* on location might seem like a much-needed liberation, or it could be seen as the inevitable conclusion of a nineteenth-century aesthetic (epitomized by Irving and Tree) of staging the plays in as historically "realistic" a manner as possible. But although the great Tudor rooms it lives in are undeniably more impressive than anything cobbled together by the props department, the play's subversive ironies are perhaps stifled as a result. The cast are mixed: John Stride's Henry is attractive but lacks depth while Timothy West plays Wolsey efficiently yet with a touch of perfunctoriness. Claire Bloom produces a moving performance as the betrayed Katherine, however. Recently rereleased in the US by Ambrose Video Publishing.

## Audio

**King Henry VIII**
P. Jesson, J. Lapotaire, T. West; Clive Brill (dir.)
UK, 1998 ▷ Arkangel ⊙ ▭

This Arkangel *Henry VIII* potters along pleasingly enough, though it's slightly lacking in vividness – but perhaps that's inevitable for a play so inescapably visual. Paul Jesson's Henry is ill-advisedly bluff at times (the banqueting scene is annoying in this respect), but Jane Lapotaire's Katherine is appropriately dignified, as in her stage performance for Doran and the RSC a few years earlier, and the other parts are thoughtfully cast: Anton Lesser makes a rounded Duke of Northumberland and Timothy West gets the opportunity to reprise the role of Wolsey, this time with greater conviction. *Henry VIII*'s gossipy character, too, comes across well: intimate recording (particularly of the two gentlemen who repeatedly murmur about the ins and outs at court) takes you to the very centre of the action.

# Editions

### Arden Shakespeare (third series)
### Gordon McMullan (ed.); 2000 ▷ Thomson

R.A. Foakes's Arden edition of *Henry VIII* (1957) was the first to take the play, and its place in the Shakespearian canon, seriously, and his third-series successor Gordon McMullan does a fine job of bringing things up to date. As with other recent Ardens (notably the three *Henry VI* editions, published around the same time), McMullan's text is chunky, bulked out by no fewer than seven appendices, among them a handy historical chronology and a doubling chart rationalizing the play's extensive *dramatis personae*. At the other end of the book, McMullan's sizeable introduction makes spirited – though sometimes tendentious – reading, exploring various spins on the play's concern with "truth", and he makes a neatly argued case for co-authorship between Shakespeare and Fletcher.

# Some criticism

### King John and Henry VIII: Critical essays
### Frances A. Shirley; 1988 ▷ Garland

*King John* and *Henry VIII* have little obvious in common other than their relative isolation in the Shakespearian canon (neither forms part of a historical sequence), but this collection's handy presentation of reading on both plays makes it invaluable. Slightly over half the book is devoted to *All Is True*, and there are some excellent pieces here – theatre reviews of early productions alongside conventional academic essays. Among the latter, Lee Bliss's piece on Fortune in the play (1975) and an excerpt from Kristian Smidt's *Unconformities in Shakespeare's History Plays* (1982) are particularly full of insight into the play's thematic patterns.

### Stages of History
### Phyllis Rackin; 1990 ▷ Routledge / Cornell UP

What the word "history" meant to Shakespeare and his contemporaries is a fascinating question, and the best recent approach to the subject – written from the angle of a professional historian – is D.R. Woolf's *The Idea of History in Early Stuart England* (1990). Phyllis Rackin's contemporaneous *Stages of History: Shakespeare's English Chronicles*, which attempts to "historicize Shakespeare's historical practice", offers a connected but more literary approach. While Rackin is especially good on Renaissance historiography – the processes that produced texts such as Halle and Holinshed – she also has an eye on feminist concerns and there is an stimulating chapter on the role of women within predominantly male histories. *Henry VIII* has little more than a walk-on part here, but Rackin's remarks on the role of the infant Elizabeth (Shakespeare's one representation of her, well after her death) is intriguing.

# Julius Caesar

hough in many ways a drama of ideas, *Julius Caesar* is probably Shakespeare's tautest study of political intrigue. It is also one of his leanest plays: nearly half the size of *Hamlet*, with the action compressed into just sixteen high-voltage scenes – the result of deft dramaturgy that shows the playwright had learnt from the experience of his recently completed English histories, which distilled sprawling chronicle narratives into punchy popular theatre. This tragedy is also the first to employ the Greek historian Plutarch's richly characterized (and racily written) *Lives of the Noble Grecians and Romans*. It has often been called the most Roman play in the canon: as critic Frank Kermode puts it, Shakespeare's cast "speak like Romans" throughout, and the measured, cool style of the play – in which even private conversations take on the tone of public oration – can seem monochrome at first glance. But the closer you look, the stranger and more intriguing *Julius Caesar* gets, not least in its thrilling self-consciousness about performance and rhetoric – fittingly enough, for it was one of the first plays to be acted at the new Globe. And as a play whose ostensible protagonist dies early in Act Three, it probes not only the ancient debate of whether Caesar is a tyrant or the greatest of men, and thus whether his assassination is defensible or disastrous, but questions whether anyone's actions can be called heroic amid the cross-currents and riptides of history.

[DATE] The play was seen at the Globe by a Swiss tourist in autumn 1599, and other evidence suggests that it was written that year for the opening season of the new theatre.

[SOURCES] For *Julius Caesar* Shakespeare turned for the first time to a massive book that would dominate his subsequent career – Thomas North's translation of Plutarch, *Lives of the Noble Grecians and Romans* (1579). In addition to freely plundering North, he may well have been influenced by the anonymous drama, *The Tragedy of Caesar and Pompey* (1595).

[TEXTS] *Julius Caesar* was treated well in the 1623 Folio, where it was first printed – the text is unusually free of errors.

## Interpreting the play

Understood as a unit, the so-called "Henriad" – *Richard II*, the *Henry IV*s and *Henry V* – explores, along with much else, the big questions of government. Is it better for a monarch to be rightful (like Richard II) or effective (like Henry IV)? Can there be such a thing as a perfect king? The play that Shakespeare wrote almost immediately afterwards turns to those imperatives once again, but with a stark difference. Using for the first time Sir Thomas North's English translation of Plutarch's *Lives*, Shakespeare was free to explore more fundamental questions of kingship and legitimacy. *Julius Caesar*, set in classical Rome at the moment it became the most important and powerful city in the world, asks whether we need monarchs at all.

It begins as the story of a man whose ambition, military success and unparalleled popular support put him within reach – quite literally – of the Roman crown. Yet Caesar's career

## Major Characters & Synopsis

**Julius Caesar** (later a **Ghost**)
**Calpurnia**, Caesar's wife
The conspirators against Caesar: **Marcus Brutus**, **Caius Cassius**, **Casca**, **Trebonius**, **Decius Brutus**, **Metellus Cimber**, **Cinna** and **Caius Ligarius**
**Portia**, Brutus's wife
**Lucius**, Brutus's servant
The triumvirs (three co-rulers) after Caesar's death: **Mark Antony**, **Octavius Caesar** (Julius Caesar's great-nephew) and **Lepidus**
Tribunes of the people: **Flavius** and **Murellus**
Senators: **Cicero**, **Publius** and **Popillius Laena**
**Cinna**, a poet
A **Soothsayer**
**Artemidorus**, a Doctor of Rhetoric
**Pindarus**, Cassius's servant
**Titinius**, an officer in Cassius's army
Offers and soldiers in Brutus's army: **Lucillius**, **Messala**, **Varrus**, **Claudio**, **Young Cato**, **Strato**, **Volumnius**, **Flavius**, **Dardanius** and **Clitus**
Another **Poet**
Plebeians: a **Cobbler**, a **Carpenter** and others

**ACT 1** Julius Caesar has triumphed over Pompey in the civil wars, and Rome celebrates with him – to the annoyance of the tribunes Flavius and Murellus. Caesar prepares to address the people, ignoring the warnings of the Soothsayer that he should beware. While Caesar speaks off stage, Cassius and Brutus discuss his increasing power and popularity. Casca relates to Cassius and Brutus how, during his speech, Caesar was offered the crown but felt obliged to turn it down. That night, panic spreads as fearful portents appear. Cassius interprets the signs as omens against Caesar, and encourages Brutus to join a conspiracy against him.

**ACT 2** Brutus privately resolves that Caesar's ambition means he must die. Joined by Cassius and other conspirators, he agrees to kill Caesar, but Brutus vetoes the suggestion that Antony should also be killed. Portia has noticed that her husband is troubled but reluctant to explain why. Caesar is also nervous about the portents, and when a sacrifice goes wrong Calpurnia begs him not to leave home, revealing that she has dreamt of his death. Caesar initially agrees, but changes his mind when Decius (a conspirator) tells Caesar how the Senate

wish to make him king. Other conspirators, and Antony, arrive to escort him to the Capitol. Artemidorus, meanwhile, plans to warn Ceasar by giving him a letter as he walks by.

**ACT 3** At the Capitol, Caesar rejects Artemidorus's letter but instead listens to a petition requesting the banishment of Metellus's brother be repealed. When he refuses, the conspirators stab him to death. Antony arrives at the scene and mourns Caesar's death but promises to delay judgement until the murderers have explained themselves at Caesar's funeral, at which Antony intends to speak. At the funeral all goes well for the conspirators when the popular Brutus speaks, but Antony's address to the crowd wins them round. Convinced of their treason, the crowd begins to bay for the conspirators' blood, but they have already fled. In the ensuing riot, citizens murder a poet called Cinna, mistaking him for a conspirator of the same name.

**ACT 4** Antony, Octavius Caesar and Lepidus have assumed the leadership of Rome. Meanwhile Brutus and Cassius combine their forces at Sardis, but the two men quarrel when Brutus accuses Cassius of accepting bribes. Though momentarily reconciled (just as news arrives that Portia has killed herself), they clash again over tactics. Receiving information that Antony and Octavius's army is heading towards Philippi, Cassius wants to remain where they are, while Brutus is for marching to meet them. Brutus's decision prevails, but left alone he is disturbed by the ghost of Caesar, who tells him that they will meet again at Philippi.

**ACT 5** As news reaches Antony and Octavius that the enemy is approaching, the two leaders quarrel. As battle commences, Brutus attacks Octavius's troops but Cassius, believing that his own forces are surrounded, commits suicide with the help of his servant Pindarus. Titinius arrives from Brutus with news of imminent victory but when he sees Cassius's body he too kills himself. Brutus and Young Cato resolve to fight on, but Cato is killed and Brutus realizes that the cause is lost. Brutus begs his colleagues to kill him and finally dies by falling on Strato's sword. When the victorious Antony and Octavius find his corpse, they swear to bury him with honour.

climaxes not in coronation but assassination: he is brutally cut down by a coalition who cite the defence of Rome's republican ethic as justification. Some Renaissance thinkers agreed, arguing that Caesar was a dangerous tyrant; for others, he was a blameless hero. Dante put Brutus and Cassius, ringleaders of the conspiracy, in the lowest circle of Hell in his *Inferno*, while the English historian John Stow, arguing that Caesar was "the most ambitious and greatest traitor that ever was to the Roman state", presumably thought he should take their place. But often Elizabethan writers have difficulty coming to a final opinion: the courtier Sir Thomas Elyot, whose book *The Governor* influenced a number of Shakespeare's plays, admired Caesar's leadership while deploring his pride; while the anonymous *Mirror for Magistrates*, a source for *Richard II*, came to much the same (lack of) conclusion.

## There's the question

*Julius Caesar* throws its audiences immediately into the turbulent debate about Caesar. As the play gets underway Rome is in ferment: the crowds are out on the streets, "rejoicing" at Caesar's defeat of his rival (and former co-ruler) Pompey by declaring a holiday. But the tribunes Flavius and Murellus are aghast at their fickleness. Murellus cries out:

> Wherefore rejoice? What conquest brings he home?
> What tributaries follow him to Rome
> To grace in captive bonds his chariot wheels?
> You blocks, you stones, you worse than senseless things!
> O, you hard hearts, you cruel men of Rome,
> Knew you not Pompey?

[1.1.32–7]

Caesar, Murellus witheringly notes, has done nothing to deserve Rome's rejoicing; its citizens are "worse than senseless" to think he has. Recalling the days when Caesar returned from victory in some far-flung corner of the empire with "tributaries" (captives) in tow, Murellus insists that his political domination is not a triumph: it is a tragedy.

> *How too could Brutus say he finds no personal cause, i.e. none in Caesar's past conduct as a man? Had he not passed the Rubicon? Entered Rome as a conqueror? Placed his Gauls in the Senate? Shakespeare (it may be said) has not brought these things forward. True! and this is the just ground of my perplexity. What character does Shakespeare mean his Brutus to be?*
>
> Samuel Taylor Coleridge, *Marginalia on "Julius Caesar"* (1818)

The man himself makes an appearance in the next scene, but the atmosphere surrounding him remains tense and uneasy. As Caesar enters, thronged by citizens, a Soothsayer is pushed out from the crowd, warning sinisterly that Caesar should "beware the ides of March" (1.2.25) – the "ides" being the midpoint of the month and the next day in the play. Despite the heavy dramatic irony, however – we know only too well the risk Caesar is in – the Soothsayer is not given the opportunity to elaborate and Caesar moves on. As the crowd passes by, another pair of men are left on stage, and again they have little good to say about Caesar. The fluctuating bond between Brutus and Cassius will become crucial to the play, but here it's enough to notice how brilliantly Shakespeare manages to conjure up the different currents of emotion in Rome. As the two men earnestly talk, their conversation is punctuated by cries from the crowd nearby, shouts of adulation as "new honours", Brutus comments, are "heaped on Caesar" (1.2.135). And though their business is private, it has everything to do with what is going on outside, as Cassius rancorously explains:

Why, man, he doth bestride the narrow world
Like a Colossus, and we petty men
Walk under his huge legs, and peep about
To find ourselves dishonourable graves.
Men at sometime were masters of their fates.
The fault, dear Brutus, is not in our stars,
But in ourselves, that we are underlings.
Brutus and Caesar: what should be in that 'Caesar'?
Why should that name be sounded more than yours?
Write them together: yours is as fair a name.
Sound them: it doth become the mouth as well.
Weigh them: it is as heavy. Conjure with 'em:
'Brutus' will start a spirit as soon as 'Caesar'.
Now in the names of all the gods at once,
Upon what meat doth this our Caesar feed
That he is grown so great?

**[1.2.136–51]**

Cassius's caustic analysis of the mystique of power refuses to admit that Caesar is anything other than a man, but it does so by grotesquely magnifying him – he is a "Colossus" that looms over Rome, a city whose "wide walls", he continues, "encompa[ss] but one man" (1.2.156). The nightmare he conjures is of complete tyranny: a leviathan Caesar whose shadow eclipses the figures of men who are in every way his equal.

Caesar himself soon expresses unease that Cassius "looks / Quite through the deeds of men" (1.2.203–4), but his skill is not merely that of an observer. *Julius Caesar* is Shakespeare's most subtle analysis of the power of oratory, and Cassius's words form the first big speech of the play. They work on us as much as on the stoic Brutus, making us hear the word "Caesar" – the most frequently uttered name in the drama – in new and unsettling ways. It is much to the point, likewise, that Cassius's words to Brutus are allowed to eclipse the political crux going on in the wings, which sees Caesar being offered the crown by an increasingly enthusiastic people. Shakespeare allows us to hear about this scene only through the words of Casca, who narrates that Caesar collapsed in front of the crowd (historically he probably suffered from epilepsy) – an event which seems, if anything, to have increased their leader's popular standing. "Three or four wenches where I stood cried 'Alas, good soul!' and forgave him with all their hearts," Casca waspishly observes:

But there's no heed to be taken of them: if Caesar had stabbed their mothers they would have done no less.

**[1.2.273–5]**

Caesar's collapse is made to seem like a strategy to win favour, and for all we know it is.

Caesar's actions, in fact, remain mostly in shadow. He is on stage for just three scenes, and it is no accident that Shakespeare emphasizes the human failings of this world-conqueror – his indecision, his physical frailty (the playwright even makes him deaf). Persuaded to join the conspirators against him, Brutus seems only too aware that the arguments for assassinating this man also leave plenty of unanswered questions. Even so, "it must be by his death," he resolves,

And for my part
I know no personal cause to spurn at him,
But for the general. He would be crowned.
How that might change his nature, there's the question …
Th'abuse of greatness is when it disjoins

An indomitable Mark Antony (Marlon Brando) begins to woo the crowd over the body of the slain Caesar. From the 1953 Hollywood fim of *Julius Caesar* directed by Joseph Mankiewicz.

Remorse from power. And to speak truth of Caesar,
I have not known when his affections swayed
More than his reason. But 'tis a common proof
That lowliness is young ambition's ladder,
Whereto the climber-upward turns his face;
But when he once attains the upmost round,
He then unto the ladder turns his back,
Looks in the clouds, scorning the base degrees
By which he did ascend. So Caesar may.

[2.1.10–27]

"May" is very much the operative word in this masterfully ambiguous speech; the question of how Caesar would really behave as king is one the play is never permitted to answer. Likewise Brutus, for all his show of logic, starts from a presumption that Caesar's "death" is necessary. His words are a remarkable example of someone preventing themselves being argued out of a case.

## Lend me your ears

So is Caesar a "Colossus" who threatens to swallow up Rome, or an ill man who struggles to get through a public meeting without collapsing? Is he unmoved, "as constant as the Northern Star" (as he claims to the Senators), or fatally swayed by impulse? Are the citizens right to hail him as their leader, or does he represent a danger to their city? In short: will his death be defensible assassination (what Brutus calls "the even virtue of our enterprise" (2.1.132)) or cold-blooded murder? One answer is that Caesar is all of these things and more: he is the great paradox at the centre of the play. Another answer is that Shakespeare doesn't let us make up our minds – or rather, doesn't allow us to hold to just one view. And while we sit by in indecision, the conspirators have forced events to a head. Surrounding Caesar in the Senate while he hears Cinna's plea to reverse the banishment of his brother, they suddenly surge forward and unsheath their knives.

But when Caesar is dead the conspirators, too, cannot make up their minds. Against Cassius's instincts, Brutus decides that, lest their course "seem too bloody", Antony should not be killed along with his master:

> For Antony is but a limb of Caesar.
> Let's be sacrificers, but not butchers, Caius.

**[2.1.165–6]**

With these words Brutus demonstrates that he has little capacity for dealing with the reality of what he is about to unleash; that reality includes a knife-riddled body and a live Antony who has every intention of doing something about it. As soon as the assassins are out of earshot, Antony exclaims movingly to the corpse, "O pardon me, thou bleeding piece of earth, / That I am meek and gentle with these butchers," (3.1.257–8), as if turning Brutus's feeble words back on him. In the long term, he prophesies, "Domestic fury and fierce civil strife / Shall cumber all the parts of Italy" (3.1.266–7). In the shorter term, he does everything possible to ensure that the conspirators' triumph rapidly turns into a disaster.

The contest between those views becomes the centrepiece and climax of the play. Brutus announces his intention to "appeas[e] / The multitude" almost as soon as Caesar is dead, and sets to work convincing the restless crowd of his good intentions. "Romans, countrymen, and lovers," he begins,

> Hear me for my cause, and be silent that you may hear. Believe me for mine honour, and have respect to mine honour, that you may believe. Censure me in your wisdom, and awake your senses, that you may the better judge.

**[3.2.13–17]**

So he continues, arguing calmly by stages that his hands are bloody not because "I loved Caesar less, but that I loved Rome more" (3.1.21–2). And the strategy works: as Brutus prepares to leave, the people are behind him, promising to "give him a statue with his ancestors".

But it does not last. In another well-meaning yet deadly mistake – again against Cassius's better judgement – Brutus allows Antony to speak to the crowd. The results are both infamous and, for the conspirators, fatal. "Friends, Romans, countrymen, lend me your ears," Antony begins, reusing Brutus's words in an attempt to reclaim the crowd. Then he begins to work them:

> I come to bury Caesar, not to praise him.
> The evil that men do lives after them;
> The good is oft interrèd with their bones.
> So let it be with Caesar. The noble Brutus
> Hath told you Caesar was ambitious.
> If it were so, it were a grievous fault,
> And grievously hath Caesar answered it.
> Here, under leave of Brutus and the rest—
> For Brutus is an honourable man,
> So are they all, all honourable men—

Come I to speak in Caesar's funeral.
He was my friend, faithful and just to me.
But Brutus says he was ambitious,
And Brutus is an honourable man …

[3.2.74–88]

And so it goes on, each clanging "honourable" another nail in their collective coffin. In this extraordinary speech Antony employs many rhetorical techniques – the most insistent being one that Shakespeare would have learnt at school whereby as phrases are repeated they grow in intensity, the words gradually shifting from apparent straightforwardness to biting sarcasm. The persuasive rhythms of Antony's speech aptly recreate what Plutarch called Antony's "study of eloquence" and, with devastating irony, he conforms entirely to the brief agreed with the conspirators, but effectively depth-charges their whole operation.

Antony has his way, and the crowd immediately revolt. The terrible dangers unleashed by his words are underlined when a poet whose name happens to be Cinna is torn apart by citizens under the impression that he is one of the conspirators, and soon Rome slides – as predicted – into a bitter civil war. But Shakespeare focuses tightly on the personal consequences of these grand actions. Brutus is at the centre of them all – so much so that he, not Caesar, has sometimes been taken as the play's real tragic hero. Persuaded into action by dire warnings of tyranny, he is alone among the conspirators in his belief that he is fighting for "peace, freedom and liberty", and his inability to keep the crowd on his side begins to seem symptomatic. As he and Cassius take sides against the combined forces of Antony, Lepidus and Caesar's great-nephew Octavius, quarrels with Cassius over strategy take centre-stage. As they all prepare for war, Brutus is tormented by a vision of Caesar's ghost, arrived to remind him that "thou shalt see me at Philippi" (4.2.335). And after Cassius's senseless death (in a tragic mistake he becomes convinced that Brutus's camp has been overrun by the enemy), Brutus is left to fight a final, futile battle, one that ends in his suicide. Coming across his corpse, Antony is generous but even-handed. "This was the noblest Roman of them all," he says:

All the conspirators save only he
Did that they did in envy of great Caesar;
He only in a general honest thought
And common good to all made one of them.
His life was gentle, and the elements
So mixed in him that Nature might stand up
And say to all the world 'This was a man.'

[5.5.67–74]

But if this is so, Antony's audiences might feel prompted to ask, what does this say about the state of the world? If it is politicians like Antony who end up on top, the ethics of your cause don't come into it; presentation is everything. As Cassius said, standing over the newly slain Caesar's body,

How many ages hence
Shall in this lofty scene be acted over
In states unborn and accents yet unknown!

[3.1.112–4]

In this boldly metatheatrical gesture, the actor playing Cassius – and the audience in front of him – together know what Brutus and the others do not. Yet though he is unquestionably right that the interest in Caesar's death will touch "states unborn", this scene will not always be "lofty", any more than its agents will be hailed as "the men that gave their country liberty" (3.1.119).

# Stage history and adaptations

In the diary of one Thomas Platter, a Swiss tourist visiting Elizabethan England, we have a description of a very early performance of *Julius Caesar*. Platter records that in September 1599 he and some friends crossed the Thames to the new **Globe** and "saw the tragedy of the first Emperor Julius Caesar, very pleasingly performed … at the end of the play they danced together admirably and exceedingly gracefully, according to their custom". The play may have been on the stage for a few months by then, and it remained popular into the next century: "Caesars Tragedye" was performed for the court at **Whitehall** in 1612, and again at **St James's Palace** in 1637 – an irony, perhaps, given that Charles I had proclaimed several years earlier that he would rule without parliament, an act that saw him accused of Caesar-like tyranny.

*Julius Caesar* resurfaced after the Restoration and reopening of the theatres, when it was allotted to **Thomas Killigrew** and the King's Company. But its emphasis had changed: Caesar's role was reduced to that of petty tyrant, while Brutus – especially in the hands of **Thomas Betterton** – became the stoic, philosophical hero of the piece. Betterton acted him until 1708, often in the company of **Colley Cibber**'s Cassius and **Edward Kynaston**'s Antony. After Betterton's retirement, **Barton Booth** took up the role, followed in 1728 by **James Quin**. All three acted in a version of the play prepared by **John Dryden** and **William Davenant**, which made Brutus into a genuine tragic hero by cutting any lines that distracted from his moral nobility and commitment to liberty, and had him commit suicide by his own hand. The play was further simplified by transforming the mob into a comic turn, but even so it's probably no coincidence that Shakespeare's tale of tyrannicide received no London productions after George III began suffering mental illness amid demands that he be removed from power. On the other side of the Atlantic, however, *Julius Caesar* became something of a rallying cry for the restive colonies. A 1770 production in **Philadelphia** advertised it as depicting "The noble struggles for Liberty by that renowned patriot Marcus Brutus", launching an enthusiasm for the play in the post-Independence US that culminated in the enormously popular nineteenth-century productions of **Lewis Hallam** and **Edwin Booth** among others. In 1864 Booth gave a single performance of the play in New York, playing Brutus opposite the Cassius of his older brother **Junius Brutus Booth Jr.** Ironically, the part of Antony was played by their younger brother, **John Wilkes Booth**, who five months later lived out what he presumably saw as the play's libertarian ideals by assassinating the US President, Abraham Lincoln.

Back in London, **John Philip Kemble** brought the "noble drama" (as the *Times* called it) out of mothballs in 1812, near the end of his career. His own Brutus was acclaimed, as was his brother **Charles**'s Cassius, but the production's main draw was its scale, enhanced by seventy-odd supers. The German playwright Ludwig Tieck sneered that Kemble's stylized stagecraft was merely "clever ballet", but the die was cast and immense, unwieldly productions soon became the norm. **William Charles Macready** and **Samuel Phelps** put these on at Covent Garden and Sadler's Wells respectively throughout the 1830s, 40s and 50s, playing together in 1838 (Macready's Brutus to Phelps's Cassius), both in Kemble-sized productions but attempting to inject more life into the drama than he had managed. The **Duke of Saxe-Meinigen**'s company brought a German version to London in 1881, resplendent in historically researched costumes, but with a new emphasis on ensemble work rather than star perform-ances – though **Ludwig Barnay**'s Antony and **Paul Richard**'s Caesar were praised. **Herbert Beerbohm Tree**'s staging at Her Majesty's Theatre from 1898 was the apogee of the Victorian tradition: Tree pruned the text into three acts, each emphasizing his own Antony; recruited a cast of hundreds; and invested heavily in gargantuan Roman sets from **Lawrence Alma-Tadema**, a painter who specialized in luxurious classical subject matter. **Charles Fulton**'s powerful Caesar played to **Lewis Waller**'s Brutus, and the production remained in the repertoire for the next fifteen years.

Though Tree's staging was grander than anything previously seen, it also sounded the death knell of Victorian theatrics, and subsequent performances tried hard to find new things to say. **William Bridges-Adams** used an uncut text and "Elizabethan" stagecraft in his Stratford production of 1919, but a more significant revolution in the understanding of *Julius Caesar* appared with political developments in the 1930s. *Wunderkind* **Orson Welles** opened his Mercury Theatre in New York with an adaptation of the play subtitled "Death of a Dictator", set in Mussolini's Italy and which saw Welles's own Brutus defeating the fascistic Caesar of **Joseph Holland**; the *Washington Post* thought that "the touch of genius is upon it". **Henry Cass**'s Old Vic version, back in London, employed similar techniques in 1939 on the eve of World War II, but to less critical success.

"Et tu, Brute?" John Gielgud's imperious Caesar collapses for the last time, moments after the dagger clutched by Brutus (Brian Cox, right) strikes home. The assassination scene from John Schlesinger's 1977 National Theatre production.

Postwar productions have, perhaps understandably, rarely been that overt, but equally the play's echoes of recent history have rarely been ignored. That co-directed at Stratford in 1950 by **Anthony Quayle** and **Michael Langham** was admittedly not one, relying instead on the enviable quality of its cast, which included **John Gielgud**'s Cassius, **Harry Andrews**'s Brutus and **Alan Badel**'s Octavius. **Glen Byam Shaw**'s version at the same venue seven years later attempted to understand *Julius Caesar*'s ideas by concentrating on its all-too-human titular hero, played by **Cyril Luckham** with **Alec Clunes** as Brutus and **Geoffrey Keen**'s Cassius. **John Barton** once more found fascistic overtones at the RSC in 1968, but **Brewster Mason**'s Caesar invited many reviewers to think of de Gaulle rather than Mussolini or Hitler. **Trevor Nunn**'s Stratford production of 1972, as part of a sequence of Roman plays, was quite literally built around **Mark Dignam**'s Caesar – or rather a vast statue of him that remained insistently on stage long after its model's death. The spirit of **John Gielgud**'s authoritative Caesar was similarly unquenchable under **John Schlesinger** at the National Theatre in 1977, with **Brian Cox**'s Brutus tormented at Philippi by a ghost eerily represented by four face masks.

Several recent productions have struck vital political nerves. **David Thacker**'s staging at RSC's The Other Place in 1993 invited audiences to compare its actions to events then occurring in Bosnia, while a year earlier **Peter Stein**'s acclaimed version with his Schaubühne Theatre filled the stage with a yobbish crowd that threatened to overrun the theatre itself. The libertarian message of *Julius Caesar* made it particularly resonant in apartheid South Africa (though under Thabo Mbeki's government it has risked being banned from schools for being "sexist"); a multilingual adaptation by the South African **Yael Farber**, *SeZaR*, toured in 2002.

On screen, the play has experienced several reworkings, led by the big-budget versions of **Joseph L. Mankiewicz** (1953) and **Stuart Burge** (1970). Both had impressive casts, but Mankiewicz's is usually thought the finer achievement. The BBC/Time-Life version (1978) was directed by **Herbert Wise**, starring **Charles Gray** as Caesar, **Richard Pasco** as Brutus and **David Collings** as Cassius.

## Screen

### Julius Caesar

M. Brando, J. Gielgud, J. Mason; Joseph L. Mankiewicz
US, 1953  ▷  United Artists 📼

Mankiewicz's *Caesar* has gone down in Hollywood legend as the film that got everything right – impressive cast, impressive staging, impressive filming – but watching it a half-century later it's difficult not to feel, well, a bit stupefied. The exception, of course, is Brando, who gives an electrifying performance as Mark Antony, particularly compelling in his rendition of the funeral oration. But John Gielgud seems miscast as a rather pallid Cassius while James Mason is fatally underpowered as Brutus. The pacing is leaden, and ultimately the whole production is rather too cool, dominated by monumental Roman sets and bleakly monochrome visuals (Roland Barthes, in a famous essay, noted how every character in the film, from principals to extras, sported a fringe as a sign of their Roman-ness). After Brando does his stuff outside the Senate it's just too tempting to switch off. If you do, you won't miss a great deal: Mankiewicz's Battle of Philippi strays too deep into Cowboy-and-Injun territory to be taken entirely seriously.

### Julius Caesar

J. Gielgud, C. Heston, R. Johnson; Stuart Burge (dir.)
UK, 1970  ▷  Fox 📀 📼

Widely known as a stage and TV director in the UK, Stuart Burge never shone on film, despite some big projects – Olivier's hotly contentious *Othello* (see p.270) being one. The other is his 1970 *Julius Caesar*, his second foray into the play (his first, from 1959, is all but forgotten now). Though it holds little by way of surprise and tends towards the over-literal – Cassius's bitter "what should be in that 'Caesar'?" speech is conducted in front of a wall helpfully covered with graffiti – it is ably done and has some quality touches. These chiefly stem from casting, Burge's great strength: Richard Johnson grumbles effectively as Cassius, Heston makes a nobly shaggy Antony, a glacial Gielgud is more at home as Caesar than as Cassius, and Jason Robards quietly falls apart as Brutus. Aficionados of classic TV spy drama will have a ball: Robert Vaughn (Casca) and Diana Rigg (Portia) share screen time.

# Audio

## Julius Caesar
**M. Feast, J. Bowe, A. Lester; Clive Brill (dir.)**
UK, 1998 ▷ Arkangel ⊙ 📼

In common with many of the Arkangel series, the pace of this *Julius Caesar* feels rapid, even if it's actually a full ten minutes longer than the BBC version below. There are other differences, too, and some excellent solo performances make this recording an interesting contrast. Adrian Lester's Antony is perhaps the star of the piece, delivering a convincing mix of political self-interest and genuinely righteous anger that seems as effective in private as in the tumult of the Forum, though Estelle Kohler's urgent and womanly Portia makes you wish that the play gave them an opportunity to meet. Cassius seems to lack energy (Geoffrey Whitehead makes him an embittered civil servant rather than the lean and hungry man we might expect), however, and Brutus himself, a slightly plodding John Bowe, rarely hints at his character's interior conflict.

## Julius Caesar
**G. Murphy, N. Farrell, J. Firth; Eoin O'Callaghan (dir.)**
UK, 1999 ▷ BBC ⊙ 📼

This BBC offering is perhaps a little too cool and relaxed to be genuinely gripping, but it contains some excellent moments: among them the scene of the assassination itself, which leaves you in no doubt of the conspirators' personal enmity towards Caesar. The bustle of the play's many public scenes comes across well – this Rome is convincingly busy – and Nicholas Farrell's measured Brutus particularly shines, as does Gerard Murphy's irascible Caesar (Colin McFarlane's Cassius may not be edgy enough for some, and Jonathan Firth's youthful Antony is perhaps too lightweight for this role). The 1920s setting advertised in the booklet doesn't really make a great deal of aural impact, though, and portentous music often distracts from the tension that the play conjures perfectly well on its own.

# Editions

## Arden Shakespeare (third series)
**David Daniell (ed.); 1998** ▷ Thomson

This is the most recent major edition of *Julius Caesar*, and the fullest. Daniell is undeterred by its school-play image and keen to play up its strengths, which he takes to rest in Shakespeare's dispassionate eagerness not to "endorse anyone", still less come down on one side of the play's incessant debates. While this view of the tragedy can leave it looking more diffuse than some may be happy with – an impression not aided by Daniell's sometimes gnomic prose style – it does have the merit of leaving readers to make up their own minds. There is plentiful detail on the historical background to Shakespeare's drama, and extended excerpts from Plutarch's *Lives* are included at the back. The text itself is cleanly and helpfully presented.

# Some criticism

## Shakespeare: The Roman plays
**Derek Traversi; 1963** ▷ Stanford UP

Long a standard work on the "standard", Plutarch-based Roman plays (*Julius Caesar*, *Antony and Cleopatra* and *Coriolanus*) Traversi's book remains a useful and humane companion, seeing in Shakespeare's continued engagement with Roman materials the development of his mature tragic art. Traversi's work on *Julius Caesar* in particular is excellent, escorting readers through the play and paying close attention to the text while never losing sight of its larger complicating themes. Some might find it hard to agree with Traversi that Shakespeare's tragedies are almost exclusively about their heroes, but the force of his arguments is still difficult to resist.

## Roman Shakespeare
**Coppélia Kahn; 1997** ▷ Routledge

This is part of the Routledge "Feminist Readings of Shakespeare" series, and there are no prizes for guessing where the focus of Kahn's interest lies. Nevertheless its extended exploration of Shakespeare's Roman work – all the way from *Lucrece* and *Titus* to *Cymbeline*, via more familiar stopping-points *Julius Caesar*, *Antony and Cleopatra* and *Coriolanus* – shows that this book is interested in asking bigger questions and has a broader view of its subject than a study like Traversi's. Kahn's reading of *Julius Caesar* looks carefully at the paradoxes within the play's presentation of Rome, and what emerges is a closely nuanced reading of masculinity and the idea of the state (in England as much as Italy). Kahn also has some interesting words on Portia's "voluntary wound", inflicted to prove her scorn for womanish weakness.

# King John

**K**ing John is the chronicle play that got away. Set in an earlier period of medieval English history than the two "tetralogies", it is even less well known than that other isolated history play, *Henry VIII*. Despite a vivid life on stage during the nineteenth century – mainly because of its potential for pomp and pageantry – it escaped the theatrical revival of interest in the histories during the twentieth century, and until recently has rarely figured in scholarly debates about Shakespeare's political writing. In *King John* even more than in the earlier plays, politics is depicted as cynical, hard-edged and ultimately corrosive. The plot ranges across the defining events of John's reign – though it leaves out the most famous of them all, Magna Carta – but continually takes risks with its material, representing the chaotic and messy workings of reality in unsparing (and frequently unflattering) detail. Though located furthest from the present day, from a twenty-first-century perspective *King John* seems one of Shakespeare's most modern works, as well as his boldest experiment with making drama out of history.

[DATE] No records of early performances survive, but stylistic evidence indicates 1595–97, close to *Richard III*, *The Merchant of Venice* and *1 Henry IV*.

[SOURCES] An anonymous play, *The Troublesome Reign of King John* (printed 1591), is strikingly close in certain respects to Shakespeare's – the relationship between the two is still disputed. Holinshed's 1587 *Chronicles* is the main printed source.

[TEXTS] *King John* was first printed in the 1623 Folio in a text purged of profanities, suggesting that it was prepared after a clampdown by the authorities (see p.82).

## Interpreting the play

Though much is made of *King John*'s isolation from the rest of Shakespeare's "histories", it is the links between them, not the differences, that are striking. The *Henry VI* plays, written a few years before in the early 1590s, are much concerned with the problems of a monarch who is unable to hold together the fragile coalition that sustains him in power, and who is eventually ejected from the throne. *Richard II* (1594–95), though dating from later in Shakespeare's career, uncovers the root of those problems, dramatizing the terrible conundrum of a rightful but inept king removed from his throne by a man who is the polar opposite – effective and convincing, but undeniably illegitimate. As the *Henry IV* plays are worked out, we see the corrosive effects of past indiscretions: Henry is first weighed down by worry and constant rebellion, then ultimately killed by it. For its part, *Henry V* asks us to look at a king who is both glamorous and morally beyond reproach – and then square that image with his response to the squalid realities of war.

These themes also surface in *King John*, probably written soon after *Richard II* but before its sequels. Like that of Bolingbroke, Richard II's usurper, King John's claim to the English throne is disputed – in this case because he inherited the crown from his brother, Richard I (known as *Coeur de Lion*, "Lion-heart") rather than giving it to Arthur, son of their brother Geoffrey. This

## Major Characters & Synopsis

**King John** of England, brother of the deceased Richard I

**Queen Eleanor**, their mother

**Prince Henry**, John's son (later **King Henry III** of England)

**Lady Blanche** of Spain, John's niece, later married to Louis the Dauphin

**Hubert**, a follower of King John

Rebellious English nobles: **Earls of Essex**, **Salisbury**, **Pembroke** and **Lord Bigot**

**Lady Falconbridge**

**Philip Falconbridge**, also known as the **Bastard**, her illegitimate son by King Richard I

**Robert Falconbridge**, her legitimate son

**James Gurney**, her servant

**King Philip** of France

**Louis the Dauphin** of France, Philip's son

**Arthur**, later Duke of Brittaine, King John's young nephew (the son of his elder brother Geoffrey)

**Lady Constance**, Arthur's mother

**Duke of Austria**

**Châtillon**, ambassador from France to England

**Count Melun**

**Citizen** of Angers

**Cardinal Pandolf**, a legate from the Pope

**Peter Pomfret**, a prophet

**ACT 1** At the English court Châtillon challenges King John's right to the English crown and declares France's support for the claim of his nephew Arthur. The two nations face war. John then hears a dispute between the two Falconbridge brothers. Robert, the younger, accuses Philip, the elder, of being the bastard son of Richard I and claims his inheritance. Presented with a choice – accept bastardy and become Sir Richard Plantagenet, or keep the land – Philip ("the Bastard") chooses the former and swears allegiance to Queen Eleanor. Lady Falconbridge arrives to defend her name but eventually admits the truth.

**ACT 2** The two armies confront each other at Angers. The French claim the city for Arthur; King John demands it as his. A citizen, acting as spokesman, vows loyalty to the King of England, but insists that the battle will determine who that is. The armies fight and both claim victory but still the city denies them entry. Infuriated, the enemy kings are about to join forces against Angers when the citizen suggests a solution: the warring sides will be united by a marriage between the Dauphin Louis and Lady Blanche (John's niece). The parties agree and, in addition, John gives the city to Arthur. All are happy except Constance, who is horrified that the French have abandoned her son's cause.

**ACT 3** After the wedding, Constance berates King Philip and the Duke of Austria for their weakness but is interrupted by the arrival of Cardinal Pandolf, the papal legate. The Cardinal tells John that he must accept the Pope's candidate for Archbishop of Canterbury. John refuses and is excommunicated by Pandolf, who then threatens the same for King Philip unless he turns against John. Philip reluctantly agrees and prepares to fight once more. In the ensuing battle the Duke of Austria is killed and Arthur is captured. King John then commissions Hubert to murder Arthur. Meanwhile in the French camp, Cardinal Pandolf exhorts the Dauphin to continue the fight against John and claim the English throne for himself.

**ACT 4** Back in England, Hubert visits the cell where Arthur is held, but cannot bring himself to kill him. At court, the support of Salisbury, Pembroke and Bigot – already weakened by John's decision to be crowned a second time – is further damaged by news of Arthur's apparent death. The situation worsens as John hears of the arrival of a huge French army, and that both Eleanor and Constance are dead. Rumours circulate, stirred up by Peter of Pomfret, of John's imminent downfall. In alarm, he blames Arthur's death on Hubert, who reveals that the boy is still alive. Neither knows, however, that Arthur has been killed in a fall when escaping from captivity. When his body is discovered by Salisbury, Pembroke and Bigot, they assume it is murder and join the Dauphin's army.

**ACT 5** John accedes to the Pope's wish, but Pandolf fails to call off the Dauphin. As war breaks out, news arrives that the French reinforcements have been shipwrecked. Suffering from fever, John cannot celebrate but is forced to take refuge in Swineshead Abbey. The English receive a further boost when Salisbury, Pembroke and Bigot leave the French, but the situation collapses with the news that John has been poisoned and half the English army drowned at the Wash. John dies just as peace is being negotiated.

dilemma, and the political machinations that surround it, launch the action. Only seven lines in, the French ambassador Châtillon presents the case that will dominate the rest of the play:

> CHÂTILLON
>
> Philip of France, in right and true behalf
> Of thy deceasèd brother Geoffrey's son,
> Arthur Plantagenet, lays most lawful claim
> To this fair island and the territories,
> To Ireland, Poitou, Anjou, Touraine, Maine;
> Desiring thee to lay aside the sword
> Which sways usurpingly these several titles,
> And put the same into young Arthur's hand,
> Thy nephew and right royal sovereign.
>
> KING JOHN
>
> What follows if we disallow of this?
>
> CHÂTILLON
>
> The proud control of fierce and bloody war,
> To enforce these rights so forcibly withheld—
>
> KING JOHN
>
> Here have we war for war, and blood for blood,
> Controlment for controlment: so answer France.

**[1.1.7–20]**

The language of legitimacy rings out clearly: Philip's cause is "right" and "true"; Arthur's claim is "lawful" and, again, "right". But John is uninterested in words. His curt question demands outcomes. What translates is simple: "war for war", "blood for blood", "controlment [restraint] for controlment". That's politics.

This question receives a new colouring just moments later, with the entry of the Falconbridge brothers. They, too, are engaged in a battle over rights, this time over which sibling is their father's rightful heir – Robert accusing Philip of being illegitimate, and therefore not entitled to his land. The man claimed as Philip's real father is Richard I, who is supposed to have had an affair with Lady Falconbridge while her husband was away. For the King this question is close to home in more ways than one. His opinion that "your brother is legitimate" is not unconnected to his own determination to hang onto the English throne:

> My mother's son did get your father's heir;
> Your father's heir must have your father's land.

**[1.1.128–9]**

This fudge will seem even more suspicious in the next meeting with the French, when Eleanor accuses Arthur of being a "bastard", and therefore unable to claim the crown. In the wider perspective, the quarrel between the brothers Falconbridge over their father's "fair five hundred pound" of inheritance points up the argument over who should be king of England for what it is: a tussle over property.

The story of the Bastard Falconbridge (as he becomes known) could not be more crucial to the play. He has been called Shakespeare's first real hero, for he demonstrates that it doesn't much matter whether you're legitimate or not – it is what you make of it that counts. Given the opportunity to choose between his two identities, he decides to spurn his father's inheritance, admit illegitimacy and become Sir Richard Plantagenet. In so doing he represents a spirit of opportunism that animates the play – a forerunner, perhaps, of Shakespeare's more famous bastard, Edmund in *King Lear*. Reflecting on "new-made honour", the Bastard rejoices in his recent promotion into a higher social class. "This is a worshipful society," he neatly observes:

And fits the mounting spirit like myself;
For he is but a bastard to the time
That doth not smack of observation ...

[1.1.205–8]

Flexing the meaning of his identity, the Bastard claims that, for "the time", he is utterly legitimate. So is anyone with "observation", or the ability to watch for changing opportunities and make the most of them. Often stepping out of the action and speaking directly to the audience, the Bastard acts as a chorus to the play, commenting on – and often smirking at – events as they scroll past. If we're complicit with anyone in *King John*, it's him.

## Mad world, mad kings

The opportunistic principles the Bastard embodies reach a climax in Act Two at Angers, in which the French and English armies attempt to face each other down. Both need to win the town in order to claim victory, but, with an interest in self-preservation entirely characteristic of the play, Angers' citizens decline to declare their colours until they know who will win. Though one of those citizens admits that "we are the King of England's subjects", that King's appeals go unheard:

KING JOHN
    Acknowledge then the King, and let me in.
CITIZEN
    That can we not; but he that proves the king,
    To him will we prove loyal; till that time
    Have we rammed up our gates against the world.

[2.1.267–72]

Their demand for "proof" stays. Yet proof is not swift in arriving: the battle fought between the English and the French ends inconclusively, and, when the citizens again defer judgement, both kings decide to join forces – and, as John bluntly puts it, "lay this Angers even with the ground" (2.1.399). The irony of this situation is staggering: instead of coming together in the interests of their people, the two rulers unite to obliterate them. This is a novel spin on John's desire to match his enemy "war for war" and "blood for blood".

Aptly, the town is only saved through a still more staggering political ploy, a speedily concluded marriage between Dauphin Louis and Lady Blanche. As John resigns areas of France as part of the deal, it isn't hard to agree with the Bastard that it is all a pointless charade:

Mad world, mad kings, mad composition!
John, to stop Arthur's title in the whole,
Hath willingly departed with a part;
And France, whose armour conscience buckled on,
Whom zeal and charity brought to the field
As God's own soldier, rounded in the ear
With that same purpose-changer, that sly devil,
That broker that still breaks the pate of faith,
That daily break-vow, he that wins of all,
Of kings, of beggars, old men, young men, maids—
Who having no external thing to lose
But the word 'maid', cheats the poor maid of that—
That smooth-faced gentleman, tickling commodity;
Commodity, the bias of the world ...

[2.1.562–75]

Falconbridge (Lewis Waller, left) squares up to a French lord (Norman McKinnell) in Beerbohm Tree's grandiose London production of 1899.

John's impassioned defence of his realm, France's religious fervour; all are undone by "commodity" (self-interest). Given the Bastard's wisecracking speech, it will be little surprise to learn that, just a few scenes later, the brief peace is over. Cardinal Pandolf – having excommunicated John – puts pressure on King Louis to reconsider his self-interest, and turn against the "cursed" John instead.

Many acts in *King John* are cynical, some are brazenly so. One of its most unappealing events is the plot concocted by King John to rid himself of his nephew Arthur, who has been captured from the French. The tone of their exchange, one of the most remarkable in the play, is as spine-tinglingly sinister as anything in *Richard III*. John coos, "Good Hubert, Hubert, Hubert, throw thine eye / On yon young boy,"

> I'll tell thee what, my friend,
> He is a very serpent in my way,
> And wheresoe'er this foot of mine doth tread,
> He lies before me. Dost thou understand me?
> Thou art his keeper.
> HUBERT            And I'll keep him so
> That he shall not offend your majesty.
> KING JOHN
> Death.
> HUBERT    My lord.
> KING JOHN      A grave.
> HUBERT           He shall not live.
> KING JOHN                Enough.

**[3.3.59–66]**

Strung across one line of verse, Hubert's and the King's thoughts are all of a piece: curt, evasive, euphemistic. John concentrates on Arthur's eventual destination, not the act of killing him; Hubert puts it all safely in the negative. Everything is read between the lines. The aim, of course, is deniability, and indeed as it turns out the King will attempt to refute that he ever ordered Arthur's death – which, strictly speaking, is accurate enough.

Arthur will be saved, however, and for a while it looks as if the play will redeem itself from cynicism. Moved by the boy's eloquent appeals to his "heart", Hubert undergoes an astonishing conversion from henchman to saviour and spares him. Wrongly persuaded that Arthur has been murdered, King John undergoes a transformation that is no less striking: he tries to blame Hubert for persuading *him* into "bloody villainy" and frets that the boy's death will blot his copybook at the "last account", the Day of Judgement (4.2.217). But his sorrow is as nothing compared to that of Arthur's mother Constance, likewise convinced since his capture that her young son is dead. Her words are heartbreaking in their simplicity. "Grief fills the room up of my absent child," she cries,

> Lies in his bed, walks up and down with me,
> Puts on his pretty looks, repeats his words,
> Remembers me of all his gracious parts,
> Stuffs out his vacant garments with his form …

**[3.4.93–7]**

Constance lives up to her name, providing – as do other female figures in the history plays – a strong ethical centre in a world otherwise amoral. Shakespeare's only son Hamnet was buried in August 1596, around the same time that *King John* was premiered, and it is tempting to read into these plain but moving words the feelings of a man who knew her kind of "grief" only too well.

But the play itself makes little further attempt to spare our feelings. Though Arthur has survived the King's plotting, it is only to face death a few scenes later, jumping from a wall while disguised as a ship-boy. This is just the kind of senseless event that *King John* frequently delivers – a chaos reflecting what the Bastard describes as the "tug and scramble" of the world (4.3.147). For all that, though, as territorial intrigues and political chicanery continue, our eyes are caught by the fate of the King. Already ill by the time he engages one last time with the French in Act Five, John travels to the monastery at Swineshead for relief, but – in a bizarre final twist – is poisoned there by a monk. As he lies on his deathbed, the monarch's mind wanders around the consequences of his actions. "Ay marry, now my soul hath elbow-room," he says, riddlingly,

It would not out at windows nor at doors.
There is so hot a summer in my bosom
That all my bowels crumble up to dust;
I am a scribbled form, drawn with a pen
Upon a parchment, and against this fire
Do I shrink up.

[5.7.28–34]

There is a macabre irony in John's words: just as he attempted to have Arthur eliminated by means of a note passed to Hubert, so his very body has become a "scribbled form" shrinking into the fires of Hell.

*The problem is less history's meaninglessness than its excessive meaningfulness: the plot promises more coherence than it delivers. The apparent trajectory of events repeatedly proves illusory; seemingly decisive moments turn out to be mere episodes in the open-ended, ironic, unpredictable movement of history.*

Walter Cohen on *King John*, in *The Norton Shakespeare* (1997)

Although the King is meted out a form of just deserts – in the manner of the moralized history books that Shakespeare often used – the play nevertheless teases its audience right up to the end. No sooner is King John dead and Prince Henry on the throne than news arrives, in another sudden reversal, of a French offer of peace. All of a sudden, the play is over. Allowed the final word, the Bastard Falconbridge makes of these events what he can, but his attempt to end things on a rousing patriotic note cannot but sound a little hollow. Reflecting that "England never did, nor never shall, / Lie at the proud foot of a conqueror," he attempts to turn a lucky escape into a national triumph:

Now these her princes are come home again,
Come the three corners of the world in arms
And we shall shock them. Naught shall make us rue
If England to itself do rest but true.

[5.7.112–8]

Whether we allow ourselves to believe that this is *King John*'s ultimate message is as open-ended as the play itself.

## Stage history and adaptations

We know practically nothing about *King John*'s first years in the theatre. It might have been written after an anonymous play entitled *The Troublesome Reign of King John* which was published in 1591 but performed by the Queen's own company several years earlier. Shakespeare's version didn't reach print until the 1623 First Folio and there is no indication of when – or even whether – it was acted. It is possible to guess, however, that the boy role of Arthur would have been a gift for a young actor, and the part of Constance (also acted by a man in Shakespeare's all-male company) would have provided opportunities for virtuoso acting.

Although it was allotted to **Thomas Killigrew**'s company after the Restoration, there is no other record of *King John* until 1737. In that year it was performed under the aegis of **John Rich** in London, possibly with the support of the Shakespeare Ladies' Club – a mysterious organization led by the Countess of Shaftesbury and dedicated to reviving the plays. Also in

1737 the celebrated dramatist **Colley Cibber** prepared a revised adaptation entitled *Papal Tyranny in the Reign of King John*, which (as its title baldly states) was strongly anti-Catholic. Because of political sensitivities Colley's version stayed off the stage, however, and would not appear until 1745, the same year that **David Garrick** began performing an abbreviated version of Shakespeare's text at Drury Lane. As usual, Garrick transformed the play into a star vehicle for himself as John (the scene in which he received the news of Arthur's death particularly impressed spectators), and for the next few years *King John* became an integral part of the London scene.

It would be popular again in the era of **John Philip Kemble**, who first acted the play at the request of George III in 1783 and played it intermittently thereafter. Kemble made a fittingly villainous King, but as ever his sister **Sarah Siddons** won hearts as Constance – her "eagle-like power" in the role was particularly remarked on. Kemble's son **Charles**, who had played the Bastard Falconbridge under his father, took on *King John* in 1823 and toured it to America two decades later in a production, designed by the antiquarian **J.R. Planché**, which broke new ground for the historical accuracy of its staging (the US tour carted around no fewer than 170 costumes and 150 actors). **William Charles Macready**'s 1842 version was again led by pictorial design, this time by **William Telbin**, but Macready's thoughtfully presented King John also attracted comment. Later in the 1840s, **Samuel Phelps**'s productions at Sadler's Wells gained some success, while **Charles Kean**'s 1852 staging was another lavishly detailed extravaganza.

*King John* escaped the notice of most other producers and it was left to **Herbert Beerbohm Tree** to mount a large-scale revival in 1899. Large it certainly was: Tree introduced silent tableaux representing battle in Act Five and, unimpeded by Shakespeare's script, the signing of Magna Carta (one historical episode the playwright leaves well out of his play). *The Athenaeum* commended this approach, commenting that "a play such as *King John* is to be regarded as a vehicle for stage pageant". In the end Tree's version ran for 114 performances.

In the twentieth century, the play's popularity began to dwindle. **Frank Benson** put it on at Stratford several times before World War I, but it never rivalled his larger productions, and at the same venue **William Bridges-Adams** produced it in 1925 but met with failure. Nevertheless, during this era **Sybil Thorndike**'s monumental Constance became well known in a variety of productions, as did **Ralph Richardson**'s gung-ho Bastard under **Harcourt Williams** in 1931. **Paul Scofield** played the Bastard at Birmingham Rep under **Peter Brook** in a well-received staging from 1945, while at Stratford three years later **Robert Helpmann**'s sinister John was supported by a sternly resolute **Anthony Quayle** as the Bastard. At the Old Vic in 1953, **George Devine** was lucky in having as his Bastard the swashbuckling **Richard Burton**, and although there were some problems with the production (audiences tended to laugh in the wrong places) the *Times* commented that it was "unusually satisfying".

Apart from a politically cynical German translation by **Friedrich Dürrenmatt** (which opened at Basle in 1968) and a celebrated production in 1964 by Northampton Repertory Players, *King John* has had little opportunity to be seen anywhere but the state-supported RSC in the later twentieth century. **Buzz Goodbody**'s low-tech 1970 production cut large swathes of the script and introduced a Brechtian slant, but undeniably the decade's most tendentious reading was provided by **John Barton**'s company four seasons later. As in his *Cymbeline* of the same year (see p.60), Barton stressed the play's political resonance and erased much of the script in what was described as "a parable for our times", but was again slated by the critics – one of whom was sufficiently angered to write a full-scale academic article about the fiasco.

A 1980 production by the **Weimar National Theatre** received much warmer reviews (its unsparing view of war was particularly commended), as did **Deborah Warner**'s RSC production eight years later. Warner received plaudits for not shying away from the play's multiple shifts of tone, with her English and French sides brawling in front of Angers before the niceties of diplomacy took hold. **Nicholas Woodeson**'s short-statured King John brought out the comedy of his role, as did **David Morrissey** as the Bastard. *King John* surfaced once more ten years later at the Globe Theatre, but for one night only: **Patrick Tucker**'s Original Shakespeare Company performed it in summer 1998 after just a day's rehearsal in an attempt to reconstruct Elizabethan theatre conditions. And despite the play's comparative neglect, 2001 saw no fewer than two major productions in the UK: **Barrie Rutter**'s Yorkshire-based Northern Broadsides came first with a touring production whose clarity and verve impressed the critics; Rutter himself starred as a wily Cardinal Pandolf, while **Marie Louise O'Donnell** made a plangent Constance. Soon afterwards **Gregory Doran**'s RSC production opened in Stratford to considerable acclaim: **Guy Henry**'s flippant John was well-received, as was **Jo Stone-Fewing**'s Bastard. The *Guardian* described Doran's interpretation of the play's politics as like "a series of playground games played for high stakes".

Although the chances of *King John* being produced as a modern motion picture remain slim, scenes from **Beerbohm Tree**'s staging are the earliest surviving Shakespeare on film, dating all the way back to 1899. Closer to the present day, it has seen little interest: **Donald Wolfit** played John for TV in 1952 but the most recent production is the BBC/Time-Life version from 1984, directed by **David Giles** and starring **Leonard Rossiter** (John) and **Claire Bloom** (Constance).

## Screen

### King John
**L. Rossiter, C. Bloom, J. Thaw; David Giles (dir.)**
UK, 1984  ▷ Ambrose Video (BBC) **DVD**

Leonard Rossiter is probably best-known as a TV sitcom actor, but in fact he had an extensive stage career – he was a notable Richard III in 1980 – and makes a robustly characterized and precisely spoken King John. Also worth mentioning is Claire Bloom's touching Constance, while the Hubert of John Thaw, another notable TV actor, is appropriately gritty. Unfortunately the production itself has few attractions: its staging is frequently ludicrous – a two-dimensional Angers is perhaps intended to resemble Olivier's *Henry V* but simply looks cheap – while the pacing isn't smart enough to retain much interest. George Costigan's Bastard is fine, but the part seems emaciated without an audience. Recently rereleased in the US by Ambrose Video Publishing.

## Audio

### King John
**M. Feast, E. Atkins, M. Maloney; Clive Brill (dir.)**
UK, 1998  ▷ Arkangel ⊙ 🎞

Finding harmony between *King John*'s warring sides – caustic political satire versus startling depictions of personal suffering – must be hard, arguably impossible. Here Clive Brill tries to have it both ways, ramping up the camp and the comedy (most of all in Michael Maloney's crazed and, it has to be said, somewhat overplayed Bastard), but also gives his cast plenty of emotional space – Eileen Atkins is unbearably tender as Constance, mother rather than matriarch, and in a quiet performance Michael Feast illuminates King John's progress from cynicism to devouring and pathetic paranoia. Things

sound slightly imbalanced as a result (sudden switches of mood, emphasized by Brill's rapid editing, can startle), but as a view of the play it's persuasive, and the cast clearly believe wholeheartedly in what they're doing. A welcome addition to the series.

## Editions

### Oxford Shakespeare
**A.R. Braunmuller (ed.); 1989**  ▷ Oxford UP

Braunmuller's Oxford *King John* is as easy to recommend as his more recent Cambridge *Macbeth* (see p.206) – both present strong and involving arguments about the plays' meanings couched in wider critical debates but not coerced by them. This is especially welcome in the case of *King John*, which until recently had few defenders and languished in the obscurer corners of the canon. Braunmuller's handling of a sometimes tricky text is well done, and he makes a good case that it was revised before printing in the Folio. A reasonably detailed stage history covers the play's mixed fortunes in the theatre.

## Some criticism

### Shakespearean Meanings
**Sigurd Burckhardt; 1968**  ▷ Princeton UP [o/p]

A collection of essays on various Shakespearian topics left very nearly finished at its author's death, *Shakespearean Meanings* starts from two bold assertions: that Shakespeare should be *read* (the italics are Burckhardt's) rather than performed; and that we can uncover what he intended his plays to *mean* (ditto). There is much to disagree with in this, to be sure, but in the instance of *King John* Burckhardt does a persuasive job – perhaps because in this play, he argues,

Shakespeare shows himself becoming restless with the kind of "Elizabethan World Picture" described by E.M.W. Tillyard (see p.112) and allows himself to send it up remorselessly.

### King John: New Perspectives
**Deborah Curren-Aquino (ed.); 1989** ▷ Delaware UP

In our cynical age, interest in *King John* has reached an all-time high, and as the editor of this collection comments, "Shakespeare creates in *King John* a play provocatively charged with the urgency, anguish and relevance of 'now'". Several of the pieces collected here take up that sense of latter-day political anxiety – most clearly Virginia M. Vaughan's argumentative reading of the history as "A Study in Subversion and Containment" and Larry S. Champion's suggestion that it simply defies "artistic form". Also highly recommended is Phyllis Rackin's article on the play's eloquent but trapped women. One of the best things about *King John: New Perspectives* is its sense that the theatre, not the study, holds the key to many of the play's most interesting problems – several essays probe its life in performance. Another anthology, Frances Shirley's Garland essay collection (1988), is reviewed on p.148.

# King Lear

King *Lear* has long had a reputation as the ultimate in tragedy: this harrowing tale of an irascible father driven mad by the cruelty of his children asks more searching questions of its audiences than many commentators have felt equipped to answer. A.C. Bradley thought *Lear* to be "Shakespeare's greatest achievement"; William Hazlitt declared it "the best of all Shakespeare's plays"; G. Wilson Knight was so in awe that he spoke of "the *Lear* universe". But many have found the darkness, brutality and sheer imaginative scale of this rawest of tragedies too much to handle – Tolstoy called it "unnatural"; Charles Lamb complained that "the Lear of Shakespeare cannot be acted"; Bradley went on to qualify his praise by saying that "it seems to me *not* his best play". This overwhelming bleakness helps explain why Shakespeare's version of the play disappeared from the stage for nearly two centuries, being replaced by a sentimental rewrite by Restoration dramatist Nahum Tate, who somehow contrived a happy ending from the brutal wreckage of the original. Even so, three centuries after Tate, *Lear* seems more in tune with the pessimism and emptiness of the modern era than any other Shakespeare play: Jan Kott radically compared it to Beckett and Ionesco's theatre of the absurd, commenting that in *Lear* "the abyss, into which one can jump, is everywhere".

[DATE] Probably written in 1605, although *Lear*'s first recorded performance took place on December 26, 1606, at the court of King James I.

[SOURCES] Shakespeare's most obvious source was an anonymous play performed by the Queen's company, *The Chronicle History of King Leir and His Three Daughters* (not published until 1605). The Duke of Gloucester subplot is taken from Philip Sidney's *Arcadia* and some of Poor Tom's language derives from a viciously anti-Catholic pamphlet (1603) by Anglican cleric Samuel Harsnett. Michel de Montaigne's *Essays* also seem to have been fresh in Shakespeare's mind at this point.

[TEXTS] Two distinct versions of the play exist (see p.172). The first was printed in quarto in 1608 and seems to represent an early version; the 1623 First Folio includes a different text, possibly revised by Shakespeare after performance.

## Interpreting the play

Looked at one way, *King Lear* is all about politics. It begins with a ruler's casual resignation from power, and ends in catastrophe when rival factions tear his country apart. There's reason to think that Shakespeare's earliest spectators would have seen at once the relevance of this fable – particularly on St Stephen's Night 1606 (December 26, the day after Christmas), when the audience for this new play included King James I, a ruler who had brought Scotland and England into uneasy political union for the first time. Read as a warning to princes, *King Lear*'s message is stark: power is yours, it says, but so are the gravest of responsibilities. People's lives, the lives of what the play calls the "poor naked wretches" who make up the commonwealth, matter (3.4.28). It is only by being driven mad that King

## Major Characters & Synopsis

**King Lear** of Britain
**Goneril**, Lear's eldest daughter
**Duke of Albany**, Goneril's husband
**Regan**, Lear's second daughter
**Duke of Cornwall**, Regan's husband
**Cordelia**, Lear's youngest daughter
**Duke of Burgundy**, Cordelia's first suitor
**King of France**, Cordelia's second suitor
**Earl of Kent**, a follower of Lear (later disguised as
    **Caius**, a servant of the King)
**Earl of Gloucester**
**Edgar**, Gloucester's legitimate son, and his eldest
    (later disguised as "Poor Tom")
**Edmund**, Gloucester's illegitimate and younger son
**Old Man**, a tenant of Gloucester
**Curan**, a courtier
**Fool** in Lear's service
**Oswald**, Goneril's steward

**ACT 1** King Lear wishes to divide his kingdom among his three daughters, according to whoever loves him most. Goneril and Regan speak sycophantically and are rewarded, but his youngest and favourite daughter, Cordelia, refuses to flatter him. Angered by her response, Lear rejects her and gives her share to her sisters – with whom he now intends to spend his time. Despite Cordelia's loss of favour, the King of France agrees to marry her, but when Kent defends her, Lear banishes him. Meanwhile, Gloucester's illegitimate son Edmund is planning to frame his brother Edgar and steal his land; he shows Gloucester a forged letter revealing Edgar's plans to kill him. At Goneril's castle, the new domestic arrangements are not working: Lear and his retinue are accused of being too rowdy, so he departs in a rage for Regan's palace, along with the Fool and a disguised Kent.

**ACT 2** Edmund tells Edgar of their father's anger and persuades him to flee, whereupon Edgar resolves to disguise himself as a beggar. Meanwhile Kent has attacked Goneril's steward Oswald and is put in the stocks by Regan and Cornwall; Lear and the Fool discover him there and demand to know why he has been punished, and although Regan and Cornwall release him they refuse to accommodate the King unless he dismisses his retinue. When Goneril arrives and also refuses her father access, Lear leaves in a fury, bitterly vowing to contend with the wilderness instead.

**ACT 3** Lear appears with his Fool, raging against the storm and his daughters' cruelty. Kent arrives and tries to persuade them to shelter in a nearby hovel, where the Fool finds Edgar, disguised and feigning madness. Lear, now genuinely mad, takes pity on him. Gloucester – though forbidden to do so – seeks out Lear and offers to house him. Meanwhile Edmund has informed Cornwall of his father's contact with France. Gloucester is captured and his eyes gouged out, but a servant who defends him fatally wounds Cornwall.

**ACT 4** Edgar finds his blinded father who – ignorant of Edgar's identity – asks to be taken to Dover to commit suicide. Edmund, Goneril and Oswald enter, discussing Albany's inaction; Goneril gives Edmund a love token; Albany appears and accuses Goneril of cruelty towards her father. Meanwhile Cordelia, heading a French army, has landed in Britain. Goneril's and Regan's armies separately prepare for battle. Near Dover, Gloucester attempts to throw himself off a cliff but Edgar arranges it so that his father is in fact on level ground. When Gloucester fails to die Edgar pretends to be a stranger, and convinces him that he has in fact jumped and survived. When Oswald appears, delivering a message from Goneril to Edmund, Edgar kills him. At the French camp Cordelia and Kent are reunited and Lear is carried in, asleep; he awakes and recognizes Cordelia.

**ACT 5** Regan, also in love with Edmund, demands to know whether he has feelings for Goneril but he denies everything. As Goneril and Albany plan war with France, the disguised Edgar hands Albany Goneril's love letter and demands to fight Edmund in single combat after the battle. The British forces rout the French, and Lear and Cordelia are captured and imprisoned. Albany having read Goneril's letter accuses Edmund of treason, and Edgar, disguised as a mysterious knight, fights his brother, only revealing his identity (and that Gloucester has died) after Edmund is mortally wounded. Just as news arrives that Goneril has poisoned Regan and killed herself over Edmund, Edmund confesses that Lear and Cordelia are to be executed on his orders. Albany orders their immediate release, but the message arrives too late. Lear enters, carrying Cordelia's body, and dies, demented by grief.

Lear realizes that truth, but one of the play's many tragedies is that by then it is too late: his kingdom has already gone.

*King Lear* pushes the political and the personal into massive conjunction, and it addresses not just politicians but ordinary mortals too: it shows that who has power matters, and that problems afflicting a country's rulers can have terrifying consequences. Shakespeare makes the story of what happens "when majesty falls to folly", as King Lear's Kent bluntly puts it (1.1.148), the epicentre of his tragedy. It famously opens with the King's declaration that it is only by displaying "love" towards him (a love that has to find its way into polished words) that his daughters can be rewarded with political power, a share in the kingdom he is so recklessly breaking up. The court attentively crowded round, King Lear begins, "Tell me, my daughters—"

> Since now we will divest us both of rule,
> Interest of territory, cares of state—
> Which of you shall we say doth love us most,
> That we our largest bounty may extend
> Where nature doth with merit challenge?

> **[1.1.48–53]**

Lear's first mistake is to divide his realm; his second is to mix "love" with politics, and to misinterpret speeches describing love for the real thing. Two of his daughters, the devious Goneril and Regan, effortlessly perform as required, declaring their commitment "beyond what can be valued", as Goneril sycophantically puts it (1.1.57). But Lear's third child, Cordelia, is not prepared to flatter her father, and her treatment is severe. Her inheritance is cut off and she is left no dowry to attract a husband.

## Lear or Lears?

As if the existential pain of the script weren't enough, for students of *King Lear* there's a further headache: the texts. "Texts" plural, because there are in fact three separate versions of the play. One is known as the **first quarto** (Q1), for the simple reason that it is the earliest edition of *Lear* to have been printed (it appeared in 1608) and is in the small-format "quarto" size (see p.485). A slightly different **second quarto**, Q2 for short, was published eleven years later in 1619; and the 1623 First Folio (F1) also includes a text of "The Tragedie of King Lear" quite different from either of its predecessors.

For a long time it was assumed that all three derived from a lost authorial manuscript, and editors from the eighteenth century onwards cobbled them together as best they could. But it's now thought that the Q texts correspond to an early version of the play, with F1 representing a **revision** made a few years later. The Folio loses around three hundred lines and adds another hundred, and because it is dramatically punchier it's been argued that these changes were made post-performance. Linguistic evidence suggesting Shakespeare made the additions, it is likely that he was behind the cuts too – so what these two sets of texts seem to offer is a precious insight into the ways he wrote and rewrote for the theatre.

Around half of Shakespeare's plays exist in multiple texts – *Hamlet* has three, while the problems reconciling *Othello*'s two versions are notorious – but because of the extreme divergences in *Lear* many have been tempted to treat the Folio and quarto versions separately, ones with a good claim to be considered, and performed, as distinct entities. *The Oxford Shakespeare* caused a storm in 1988 by doing just that, calling the quarto text **The History of King Lear** and the Folio the **Tragedy**. *The Norton Shakespeare* (1997) prints these side by side, making the differences obvious, though it also (confusingly) offers a conflated edition "so that readers can encounter the tragedy in the form that it assumed in most editions from the eighteenth century until very recently".

For the purposes of this book, the *King Lear* cited is the Folio *Tragedy* as it appears in *The Oxford Shakespeare*.

King Lear, with Stonehenge in the background, bewails the death of Cordelia. An engraving after the painting by James Barry (1786).

The 40-year-old Shakespeare, by this stage a veteran of at least thirty major plays, probably found the skeletal story of *Lear* buried in his early career. He seems to have had links with an Elizabethan company who were performing a play called *The Chronicle History of King Leir and His Three Daughters* in the early 1590s, when he was most likely training as an actor. This old play is different from the new one in countless ways – Shakespeare prunes some of its plot and makes innumerable changes – but it contains the story of a father and his daughters and the breakdown of the relationship between them, ingredients that the playwright would use to construct one of the most disturbing and shocking tragedies ever written.

## The bond cracked

For it isn't only politics that makes *King Lear* a masterwork: it is the appalling story of a man driven to madness that gives this tragedy its unique intensity. The King is often reminded that he is too old, that as Regan callously puts it, "Nature in you stands on the very verge / Of his confine" (2.2.320–1), and as the play develops Lear begins to fret that he will topple over into madness. Though at first it is simply his political actions that are described as "mad" (Kent forces the point in the very first scene), it becomes clear that the threat to the King's sanity is quite real.

Shakespeare makes madness in multiple forms one of the biggest concerns of the play. At first it is rooted in Lear's terrible anger, which foreshadows his mental collapse. Lear's infamous rant against the storm, delivered as Goneril and Regan make it clear that they are no longer prepared to house the ageing King and his rowdy knights, brings his bitter wrath to a head. Declaring his intention to "abjure all roofs" and confront "the enmity o'th' air" (2.2.381–3) rather than stay with such heartless children, Lear rages at the cosmic forces in one of the play's most memorable images. "Blow, winds, and crack your cheeks!" he cries,

> Rage, blow
> You cataracts and hurricanoes, spout
> Till you have drenched our steeples, drowned the cocks!
> You sulph'rous and thought-executing fires,
> Vaunt-couriers of oak-cleaving thunderbolts,
> Singe my white head; and thou all-shaking thunder,
> Strike flat the thick rotundity o'th' world,
> Crack nature's moulds, all germens spill at once
> That makes ungrateful man.

**[3.2.1–9]**

Lear makes the storm raging around him into a symbol of his suffering, but though addressing these elemental forces he is not in control of them, and the destruction they wreak will in the end seem directed against him alone.

The storm scene is Shakespeare's invention, as is Lear's companion on the heath, his faithful but in some ways equally mad Fool. Lear's Fool (he has no other name) is, like his equivalents in *Twelfth Night* and *All's Well*, a wry commentator on events, "licensed" by his position – as many Fools were in the households of real-life nobles – to ridicule those in authority and say things that others could not. In *King Lear* the humour is bleak, and the wisecracks of Lear's Fool, bizarre as they are, never stray far from the subject of his master's own folly. "Canst tell how an oyster makes his shell?" the Fool enquires, mock-innocently:

LEAR   No.
FOOL   Nor I neither; but I can tell why a snail has a house.
LEAR   Why?
FOOL   Why, to put 's head in, not to give it away to his daughters and leave his horns without a case.

**[1.5.26–32]**

"If thou wert my fool, nuncle," the Fool continues, "I'd have thee beaten for being old before thy time … Thou shouldst not have been old till thou hadst been wise" (1.5.40–4). His bitter punchline echoes Regan's curt conclusion early on that for all her father's advancing years, "he hath ever but slenderly known himself" (1.2.292–3), but the Fool's counsel is ignored by the King, who seems perpetually unable to hear those who have most concern for his welfare.

> *There are no longer kings and subjects, fathers and children, husbands and wives. There are only huge Renaissance monsters, devouring one another like beasts of prey … All that remains at the end of this gigantic pantomime is the earth – empty and bleeding.*
>
> Jan Kott, *Shakespeare Our Contemporary* (1964)

Lear's progress to self-knowledge is halting, and before he gains any further insight he will become, through madness, an utterly different person. His distress – like ours, watching it – is intense. And he is far from the only character to suffer during the course of the play: in *King Lear* terrible pain touches nearly everyone. Lear's experience is shadowed by that of one of his courtiers, the Duke of Gloucester, who falls prey to a plot by his illegitimate son Edmund to disinherit his brother Edgar, who as Gloucester's lawful offspring stands to inherit his father's land. The parallels with Lear and his children are obvious, and when the machiavellian Edmund manages to convince Gloucester that it is Edgar who has turned against *him*, Gloucester frets that the world itself is coming to pieces. Reflecting on the King's own behaviour, Gloucester anxiously exclaims, "These late eclipses in the sun and moon portend no good to us:"

Love cools, friendship falls off, brothers divide; in cities, mutinies; in countries, discord; in palaces, treason; and the bond cracked 'twixt son and father. This villain of mine comes under the prediction: there's son against father. The King falls from bias of nature: there's father against child. We have seen the best of our time.

[1.2.101–10]

Gloucester correctly sees that if families are wrenched apart, the state itself will follow, and he notes that what he delicately calls the King's "bias of nature" (his temperament, though we might think of his developing insanity) has the capacity to destroy everything in its path. Yet Gloucester fails to understand how his own "bias" towards Edgar has been overcome by Edmund, who resembles *Othello*'s Iago (and of course Shakespeare's sometime Duke of Gloucester, Richard III) in his ability to convince others of his goodness while plotting to ensnare them all. And in this play Gloucester will be made to suffer terribly for his error: when Edmund informs on his father, revealing that he has been in contact with the forces of Cordelia and the King of France, plotting to invade Britain and recapture it, Gloucester is captured by Goneril, Regan and Cornwall and as punishment his eyes are gouged out. He pays for his metaphorical blindness in the most grotesquely literal of ways. In this his plight resembles that of his son Edgar, who is forced onto the run and decides that his only chance of survival is to disguise himself as an insane beggar, a refugee from the "Bedlam" madhouse. The irony of his disguise becomes starkly obvious when the pretend madman meets Lear, the real one, on the heath. *King Lear* has a way of turning the most lurid of nightmares into reality.

## Joy and grief

This sense that the most horrific things imaginable are being acted out for real dominates the experience of seeing or reading *King Lear*, but as ever Shakespeare retains the ability to surprise his audiences. One of the tragedy's most poignant but strangest moments occurs in the final third of the play, when Gloucester decides that, now blind, his only option is to commit suicide. Encountering a man calling himself "Poor Tom" (in fact his disguised son Edgar), he asks to be led to a cliff at Dover so that he can throw himself off. And instead of revealing himself, Edgar agrees to show him the way: it is as if the play will not let them be reconciled so easily, and so the two undergo a bizarre charade in which Edgar persuades his father that they have arrived at Dover, then tells him to jump. As Edgar well knows, Gloucester is nowhere near a cliff, and ends up throwing himself merely onto the ground. But this is not the end of Edgar's charade: now pretending to be a passer-by, he attempts to convince his father that he has in fact fallen, and has only survived by the unlikeliest of miracles. "Hadst thou been aught but gossamer, feathers, air," he tells the incredulous Gloucester,

> So many fathom down precipitating
> Thou'dst shivered like an egg. But thou dost breathe,
> Hast heavy substance, bleed'st not, speak'st, art sound.
> Ten masts a-length make not the altitude
> Which thou has perpendicularly fell.
> Thy life's a miracle.

[4.5.49–55]

Yet the "miracle" is entirely of Edgar's doing, and it is also cruelly absurd, a unreal pre-echo of the mystical transformations and revelations that close Shakespeare's final plays, and – some have thought – the playwright's mocking exposé of the triviality of his craft. "Why I do trifle thus with his despair / Is done to cure it," Edgar says (4.5.32–3), but it is not clear that performing this ritual has done anything of the kind, or granted Gloucester any touch of happiness. Later on Edgar finally reveals himself, and father and son are reconciled, but it is tragically fitting that the joy of reunion – the joy of discovering love – ends tragically. "I asked his blessing," Edgar tells Albany long after the event,

> and from first to last
> Told him our pilgrimage; but his flawed heart—
> Alas, too weak the conflict to support—
> 'Twixt two extremes of passion, joy and grief,
> Burst smilingly.

**[5.3.187–91]**

## New and improved

With the death of Oliver Cromwell in 1658 and the subsequent collapse of his son's government, the path opened for King Charles II to return from French exile and take up the English throne. Among the many changes initiated by his **Restoration**, those in the theatre were both immediate and profound: before 1660 was out Charles had rescinded the ban on drama brought in by parliament eighteen years earlier. London could once again become the hub of a thriving entertainment industry.

But the theatres desperately needed material. While playwrights busily set about writing new scripts, managers plundered the pre-Civil War repertoire for ideas. Among their finds were the plays of Shakespeare. When King Charles licensed two playwrights, **Sir William Davenant** and **Thomas Killigrew**, to recruit theatrical companies in August 1660, they split Shakespeare's work – along with Ben Jonson's and Beaumont and Fletcher's – between them. The well-connected Davenant (who liked to claim that he was Shakespeare's love-child) got the slightly better deal – among his haul were *The Tempest*, *Lear* and *Hamlet* – though Killigrew gained the much-loved English histories and *Othello*.

Shakespeare would have found the Restoration theatres bewildering, however. As part of the new licensing arrangements King Charles announced that professional actresses were to be allowed, while the new indoor theatres built by Davenant and Killigrew boasted cutting-edge design, including proscenium arches and "flats" for three-dimensional sets. If Shakespeare's plays were to survive, they too needed drastic surgery – and at the hands of Restoration rewriters, they got it. Davenant was himself involved with an adaptation of *The Tempest* in collaboration with the youthful **John Dryden**, which debuted in 1667 and saw astounding success. In addition to pruning Shakespeare's knottier language (felt to be a constant problem), they took advantage of the presence of female actors by inserting another set of lovers to keep Ferdinand and Miranda company. Dryden's solo work *All For Love* (1677) was a freer version of *Antony and Cleopatra* and retained practically none of the original script, but it too catered for the neoclassical tastes of Dryden's audiences, setting the action after the Battle of Actium and transforming the play into the story of Antony's tragic failure to pull himself together.

Both these versions pale, though, alongside **Nahum Tate**'s reworking of *King Lear*. His 1681 adaptation removes the Fool entirely and cuts Gloucester's suicide attempt, but saves its most swingeing alterations for the very end. In Tate's own words, "the tale conclude[s] in a success to the innocent distressed persons": King Lear is allowed to live out his last years in peace, while Cordelia survives in order to marry Edgar in the joyful closing moments. While Tate has rarely been forgiven for this perceived abomination ("Tatefication" became a dirty word in the Victorian era), his younger colleague **Colley Cibber** has largely escaped vitriol: lines from his version of *Richard III* (1700) even made it into Laurence Olivier's infamous 1955 film (see p.303).

Texts of these wayward gems are available not only in Sandra Clark's handy anthology *Shakespeare Made Fit: Restoration adaptations of Shakespeare* (1997) but the more wide-ranging *Adaptations of Shakespeare: A critical anthology of plays* (2000), edited by Daniel Fischlin and Mark Fortier.

It is not true to say that *King Lear* is loveless or cold, as some critics have insisted: the problem it explores is the difficulty of communicating that love. Lear mistakes Cordelia's love for arrogance; Kent has to pretend he is someone else in order to convince his lord of his faithfulness; Gloucester's misplaced love ends in his physical torture; and both Goneril and Regan fall for Edmund, a doomed passion that he chillingly betrays. Even so, when Cordelia and France's army finally arrives in Britain, it seems as if further tragedy might somehow be averted. Lear is found and taken in, and – in contrast to the fractured meetings between Edgar and Gloucester – father and daughter are movingly reunited. Kneeling in front of Lear, Cordelia prays, "O look upon me, sir,"

> And hold your hands in benediction o'er me.
> You must not kneel.
> LEAR                   Pray do not mock.
> I am a very foolish, fond old man,
> Fourscore and upward,
> Not an hour more nor less; and to deal plainly,
> I fear I am not in my perfect mind.
> Methinks I should know you, and know this man;
> Yet I am doubtful, for I am mainly ignorant
> What place this is; and all the skill I have
> Remembers not these garments; nor I know not
> Where I did lodge last night.

**[4.6.50–61]**

Though confused, Lear does eventually recognize Cordelia and for the moment his insanity dissolves. Touching her weeping eyes and finding them "wet", he is brought into physical contact with his child – a moment echoed in *The Winter's Tale*, when it is touch that alerts Leontes to his wife's survival – as well as with his own plight. It might be said that just as his experiences on the heath teach him what it is to suffer, in this reconciliation the King learns for the first time what it is to love.

> *I was many years ago so shocked by Cordelia's death, that I know not whether I ever endured to read again the last scenes of the play till I undertook to revise them as editor.*
>
> Samuel Johnson, commentary to *The Plays of William Shakespeare* (1765)

The moment is so precious that it is difficult not to interpret it as a sign of Lear's redemption, but if that is true Shakespeare does not grant him any lasting peace. The long-awaited battle between the French army and those of Edmund and the two sisters is both rapid (it is placed almost entirely off stage) and brutal: the invading forces are crushed, and Cordelia is captured with her father. At this point Shakespeare's audiences – at least those who knew the old *King Leir* and were expecting a happy ending – would probably be disconcerted, but not for long. After Edmund is fatally wounded by Edgar in single combat, it looks as though the play will right itself one last time: overtaken by a last-minute conversion to good, the dying Edmund reveals that his "writ / Is on the life of Lear and on Cordelia" (5.3.220–1) and a messenger is sent to save them before it is too late. The question of whether it *is* too late is one that Shakespeare refuses at first to answer, and the suspense is perhaps more horrific than anything else in the play. Clutching Cordelia's apparently lifeless body as he limps on stage, Lear at first thinks she is dead – but grief soon gives way to frantic hope:

Howl, howl, howl, howl! O, you are men of stones.
Had I your tongues and eyes, I'd use them so
That heaven's vault should crack. She's gone for ever …
She's dead as earth. Lend me a looking-glass.
If that her breath will mist or stain the stone,
Why, then she lives.

[5.3.232–8]

"Is this the promised end?" Kent asks (5.3.238), and we are surely intended to share his bewilderment. Holding a "looking-glass" to the mouth of the living, breathing actor playing Cordelia can only intensify the confusion, and despite Lear's initial certainty ("She's dead as earth") a few seconds later he becomes convinced that she is still breathing. When it becomes apparent that this hope is mere fantasy, the shock of her loss, strung out until the final moment, is almost unspeakable. Lear puts it into plain monosyllables, among the last words he has:

No, no, no life?
Why should a dog, a horse, a rat have life,
And thou no breath at all?

[5.3.281–3]

"Never, never, never, never, never," he concludes, an empty jangle that says both everything and nothing. Nothing makes sense, and it's with that terrifying thought that King Lear dies – and *King Lear* ends.

## Stage history and adaptations

The early life of *King Lear* is mysterious. It was successful enough to be played in front of James I at court, probably with **Richard Burbage** in the lead role and **Robert Armin** as the Fool (that performance, on December 26, 1606, is the first on record), but only one other seventeenth-century reference to it being acted survives. Perhaps this was why Shakespeare was encouraged to tinker with it (see p.172); at any rate, the existence of an anonymous **ballad** called "A Lamentable Song of the Death of King Lear and his Three Daughters" indicates that the story was well-known enough to be a popular song.

Then came **Nahum Tate**'s 1681 adaptation with the great **Thomas Betterton** as Lear, which introduced a happy ending (see p.176) and was still performed in preference to Shakespeare until the 1830s. **David Garrick** – who first played Lear in 1742 at the age of 25 and continued until retirement 34 years later – progressively restored Shakespeare's text (while still clinging to Tate's ending), and did much to turn the role into a star vehicle: apparently his final performance reduced even Goneril and Regan to tears. Nevertheless, forty or so years later, the tragedy disappeared from the stage altogether: during the illness of what Shelley memorably called "an old, mad, blind, despised, and dying King" (George III), it was out of the question even to think of putting on *Lear*.

After much hesitation, **William Charles Macready** took the plunge and used a shortened version of Shakespeare's play – and its ending – in 1838, which eventually proved a success. But nineteenth-century audiences proved hard to win over, despite heavy cuts to the text and spectacular, high-tech staging. **Ernesto Rossi** and **Tommaso Salvini** toured Europe in the 1870s and 80s, both performing in their native Italian, but Henry James, writing in 1883, couldn't imagine "a drama that accommodates itself less to the stage". **Henry Irving**'s 1892 production, which boasted elaborate sets with Druidical and Viking costuming, flopped.

Rasping, granitic and with a bitter inner anger, Paul Scofield was for many audiences a near-perfect Lear. The desolate 1962 production of the play, directed by Peter Brook for the RSC, was adapted for film nine years later.

Only with **William Poel**, and his turn-of-the-century attempts to revive fluid "Elizabethan" staging, did *Lear* regain lost ground. Since then, the play has become a core part of the repertoire and once again a test of the expressive potential of designers as well as actors. **Theodor Komisarjevsky** led the way in 1936 with an expressionistic staging that used lighting to gain most of its effects, although in **Randle Ayrton** he had an old-fashioned, declamatory actor as the King. One of Poel's actors, **Harley Granville-Barker**, directed an outstanding version at the Old Vic in 1940, with **John Gielgud** in the central role, which stressed what he saw as the play's mythic, fairy-tale dimension. Four years later the maverick actor-manager **Donald Wolfit** triumphed in his own production of at London's Scala Theatre, giving a performance that brought out both the grandeur and the frailty of Lear's character. James Agate in the *Sunday Times* said that Wolfit "opened abysses at our feet", but the fact that the actor continued to tour the same production for years to come rather took the shine off its reputation. At the New Theatre in 1946 the 39-year-old **Laurence Olivier** also directed and played the title role; his performance, if not the production, is widely regarded as one of his greatest achievements. Critics were particularly struck by Olivier's power and vocal brilliance: Harold Hobson felt that "the cries and the lamentations … that are torn out of his breast are like the crash of thunder and the stab of lightning. They are not the whimpering of a weak old man: they are the groaning and the weeping of the universe."

Gielgud's second attempt at the role, at Stratford in 1950, was distinguished in particular by the tenderness of his scenes with **Peggy Ashcroft**'s Cordelia; while his third, for **George Devine** five years later, became infamous for the bold abstract designs of sculptor **Isamu Noguchi**, which ultimately overwhelmed the play. At Stratford in 1959 **Charles Laughton** was thought to be stronger on pathos than rage: indeed, some found his performance in the play's post-storm scenes almost unbearably moving. But it was **Peter Brook**'s influential 1962 RSC production, with **Paul Scofield** as the King, that marked a real sea-change for the play. Brook pitched *Lear* in bleak postwar terms, with bare staging and minimal costuming – all much influenced by the critic Jan Kott, whose comparisons of the play with Samuel Beckett's *Endgame* had caused a critical storm. The approach would become one of the defining motifs of twentieth-century performance, as directors attempted to represent the alienation and cynicism of a nuclear and post-nuclear age. **Adrian Noble** also reached for his Beckett in a bleakly comic RSC production from 1982, dominated by **Antony Sher**'s energetic Fool, but with Sher's death (killed by **Michael Gambon**'s Lear in Act Three) the comedy leached out of the play and it became solely tragic.

For all that, more recent productions – of which there are too many to attempt to list here – have avoided obvious approaches to the play. **Peter Zadek**'s 1974 version caused controversy by pitching *Lear* in circus tents and depicting the King sexually assaulting Cordelia. Equally experimental was a version directed by **J.A. Seazer** at the Tokyo Globe in 1991, which interpolated mime scenes to draw out underlying themes. The previous year had seen two major British productions running concurrently: those by **Deborah Warner** at London's National Theatre and **Nicholas Hytner** at the RSC. Critics found themselves divided: some preferred Hytner's sheer theatricality, embodied in **John Wood**'s craggy Lear; others went for Warner's inventiveness, which saw **Brian Cox**'s King enter on a wheelchair sporting a celebratory (but also symbolic) red nose.

Another year in which British productions competed, 1997, again saw contrasting approaches: **Peter Hall**'s Old Vic staging opted for carefully researched Jacobean dress, but in **Alan Howard** had a vocally mannered and unsympathetic Lear; at the National Theatre **Richard Eyre** found something more timeless in the play, with **Ian Holm** presenting an often child-like King who was nevertheless capable of bouts of terrifying, uncontrollable anger. Rather more radical was a production by **Helena Kaut-Howson** at the Leicester Haymarket; the versatile **Kathryn Hunter** took the title role, and everything was presented as a literal nightmare – the play opening and closing in a run-down nursing home. At the other end of the imaginative scale was **Jonathan Miller**'s

2002 production at Stratford, Ontario (revived in New York in 2004), which offered a claustro-phobic seventeenth-century setting instead of cosmic open spaces, emphasizing *Lear*'s brutal comedy and Hobbesian pessimism. In the lead was **Christopher Plummer,** who produced what some described as the best performance of his lengthy career (*The New York Times* commenting that his was a finely shaded "portrait for the ages, drawn in self-consuming fire"), though **Barry MacGregor**'s music-hall cockney Fool and **Claire Jullien**'s somewhat priggish Cordelia (clearly her father's daughter) were also singled out for praise.

The story of *Lear* on film begins with a 1909 silent version directed by **William Ranous,** and continues through **Kozintsev**'s 1970 Russian adaptation, translated by Boris Pasternak; **Peter Brook**'s of the following year (derived from his stage production); and **Kurosawa**'s epic *Ran* (a 1985 feudal interpretation in Japanese). The 1980s saw two disappointing TV productions. **Jonathan Miller,** who had directed a fine *Lear* with **Michael Hordern** at the Nottingham Playhouse in 1969, filmed a version for the BBC in 1982, again with Hordern as the King and **Frank Middlemass** as an elderly Fool; unfortunately Miller's decision to film his excellent cast almost exclusively in close-up dissipated any sense of tension. The next year, Granada wheeled on **Laurence Olivier,** by now far too frail for the role, in a rather earnest and literal produc-tion directed by **Michael Elliot.**

## Screen

### King Lear (Korol Lir)
**Y. Yarvet, O. Dal, E. Radzin; Grigori Kozintsev (dir.)**
USSR, 1970 ▷ Ruscico **DVD** 🔲

At about the same time Peter Brook was struggling to keep warm in Jutland (see below), Grigori Kozintsev was putting the finishing touches to his Russian film of *Lear*. The two versions have similarities (among them bleak locations and morose black-and-white texture), but it's the differences that make Kozintsev's version stand out – and a more rewarding cinematic experience. While Brook concentrates unremittingly on the central characters, Kozintsev's opening sequence, which tracks a crowd of peasants limping up to Lear's castle, reveals that this tragedy will shake an entire population. This socialist interpretation is further stressed by the Fool, who remains until the very end – when he is kicked out of the way by one of the King's retinue. At its centre is the Estonian Yuri Yarvet (Kozintsev cast him even though he couldn't speak a word of Russian), whose small frame and imploring eyes make his Lear childish rather than regal; where Scofield is stony, Yarvet is pathetic, conveying perhaps a more rounded impression of the role. And if you're bilingual you get the best of both worlds: Pasternak's masterly Russian spoken, Shakespeare's text in subtitles.

### King Lear
**P. Scofield, J. McGowran, I. Worth; Peter Brook (dir.)**
UK, 1971 ▷ Warner 🔲

Brook writes approvingly in his book *The Empty Space* (1968) of the cinema's "mobility" versus the static qualities of theatre, and it's tempting to regard his film of *Lear*, released three years later – though distilled from his 1962 Stratford production – as the director's conclusive view of the play. It's a bleak vision: the film's grim, Beckettian no-man's-land (actually Jutland) is permanently snowbound; no human love, it seems, will melt the permafrost. On stage, Scofield's Lear was widely acclaimed as among the finest of its time; on celluloid, it's his face, etched with inexpressible pain and bewilderment, that does all the work – and is sometimes too painful to watch. In fact the whole film presents challenges to its audience: it contains not a note of music; is sufficiently uninterested in narrative flow that onscreen plot summaries become a necessity; and Brook's meandering camera alienates and unsettles – particularly in the "mad" scenes, when the choppy jump-cuts make it feel like you're watching unedited film. This isn't a reading which reflects the complex multifariousness of the play (it cuts Edmund's dying speech, along with much else), but for sheer force it remains unequalled.

### Ran
**T. Nakadai, A. Tereo, J. Nezu; Akira Kurosawa (dir.)**
Japan, 1985 ▷ Warner / Wellspring **DVD** 🔲

Akira Kurosawa's second homage to Shakespeare builds on the techniques of his 1957 *Throne of Blood* (see p.204) – translating the story of *Lear* to feudal Japan and freely adapting its contents. The Gloucester subplot is gone, and Hidetora (Lear) has sons, not daughters (Mieko Harada provides the obligatory demonic woman as Lady Kaede, wife of one). This interpretation, which alternates stretches of remarkable tranquillity with scenes of luridly colourful violence, won't be for everyone – but it is thought-provoking viewing. Inflected by Kurosawa's pessimism about global politics, the entire film seems poised on the brink of the civil "chaos" its title describes.

## Audio

### King Lear
**C. Redgrave, J. Waddell, D. Troughton; Cherry Cookson (dir.)**
UK, 2001 ▷ BBC ⊙ 🔲

Getting Lear right – even getting just some of him right – is a fearful task, one that actors often compare to mountaineering without the security of ropes. Corin Redgrave does formidably well, rapidly ascending from cosy indulgence and childish whimsy to howling irascibility: his is a truly astonishing performance. Though the rest of the cast have their work cut out attempting to compete, they manage impressively: also deserving of mention are David Troughton's gruff Kent and Justine Waddell's earnest Cordelia, while William Houston's gleefully mocking Edmund makes an excellent foil to Robert Glenister's quiet and affecting Edgar. Geraldine James is perhaps not haughty enough as Goneril (Kika Markham's part-kittenish, part-wolvish Regan leads the way), though Paul Copley does his utmost to make the Fool's role play convincingly on audio – and very nearly succeeds. A few touches of music aside (and the obligatory rumbles of canned thunder), the soundscape is restrained but atmospheric – some of it was recorded in a chapel – making the whole production a remarkably intense experience.

## King Lear
**P. Scofield, A. McCowen, K. Branagh; John Tydeman (dir.)**
UK, 2002 ▷ Naxos ⊙ ▭▭

Of Paul Scofield's many Shakespearian roles, his Lear under Peter Brook has passed most firmly into legend, an early summit in a sixty-year career on stage and among the century's finest. His return to the role on audio forty years later (at 80, he is at last the right textual age) is more measured than earlier incarnations, and takes time to warm up: this Lear is solid granite to Redgrave's seething lava. If Scofield's collapse into despair is surprisingly quiet, his puzzled insanity feels disconcertingly real – though the creaking sound effects that recreate the storm all but ruin his carefully shaded performance. Still, this production is directed by one of the most experienced names in radio drama and the cast is to die for: Alec McCowen rejoining Scofield as a twinkling Gloucester (his successor as the Fool, Kenneth Branagh, displays an under-exploited gift for this kind of comedy), Harriet Walter as a nervy Goneril to Toby Stephens's urbanely malevolent Edmund and David Burke's deep-hearted Kent. The text follows Jay Halio's Folio-based edition (see below).

# Editions

## New Cambridge Shakespeare
**Jay L. Halio (ed.); 1992** ▷ Cambridge UP

Halio's edition (one of the fattest in the New Cambridge series) is based on the 1623 Folio version of King Lear (see p.172), and it's an impressive way into this version of Shakespeare's text. Halio's introduction is a model of its kind – if sometimes a little prolix – and provides an exhaustive survey of the play's thematic concerns and its various spin-offs, paying welcome attention to its life on screen as well as in the theatre. Halio also includes an extensive analysis of Lear's textual history, defending his choice of text with vigour but providing plenty of

detail on the issues at stake, including parallel passages drawn from both quarto and Folio. The notes will be erudite and detailed enough for even the most enquiring of readers, and the editor also presents some sensible suggestions for further reading. A terrific achievement.

## King Lear: A Parallel Text Edition
**René Weiss (ed.); 1993** ▷ Longman

If your interest extends to the variant texts of Lear, René Weiss's ingenious edition presents Folio and quarto side by side, allowing you to see just what the differences (and similarities) are. His notes are helpful, and the introduction takes readers through the suggestive – if slightly technical – opportunities offered by a two-text Lear. Stanley Wells's recent Oxford edition (2001), based solely on the quarto version, is also well worth looking up.

# Some criticism

## Shakespearean Negotiations
**Stephen Greenblatt; 1988** ▷ Oxford UP

Authored by the founding member of the "new historicist" movement, this book is idiosyncratic, dense and often downright bizarre. But it's a virtuosic display, and Greenblatt's essay on Lear, "Shakespeare and the Exorcists", showcases the insights that can result from approaching a canonical text via contemporaneous, non-"literary" documents – in this case a Catholic-bashing pamphlet that provided Shakespeare with a key source for Lear. Though Greenblatt and the entire new historicist movement have come under fire for their sometimes formulaic ways of reading texts (Greenblatt freely admits that he is most interested in "what can only be glimpsed, as it were, in the margins", and what he finds there doesn't change a great deal), Shakespearean Negotiations is one of the most persuasive studies of its kind. The book also contains provocative approaches to several other plays, including Twelfth Night, the Henry IVs and Henry V, and The Tempest.

## The Wheel of Fire
**G. Wilson Knight; rev. 1960** ▷ Routledge

This collection of Shakespearian essays, two of which focus on King Lear, is as readable and as thought-provoking in its fourth edition as when it first appeared in 1930. The first piece looks at the play's grotesque comedy, the second focuses on what the author memorably christens "the Lear Universe", its larger-than-life philosophical scope and deployment of apparently cosmic forces (Knight insists that "mankind's relation to the universe is [the play's] theme"). Though critical fashions may have moved on, Knight's eloquent analysis of the contradictions at the heart of Lear is a persuasive example of the image-based and thematic readings he pioneered. The play seems large enough for this brand of interpretation, which further has the advantage of appearing less fatalistic (or indeed less black and white) than some other approaches.

# Love's Labour's Lost

L ove's Labour's Lost has sometimes been compared to the "curious-knotted garden" that the Spanish braggart Don Armado rhapsodizes early in the play: a winding comic maze, filled with interesting corners and delightful patterns but little else. Though a drama of love, it has been said to lack the romantic intensity of *Romeo and Juliet*, while its plot (which seems to be the playwright's own) has been criticized for its farcical qualities. But it can be one of Shakespeare's most fleet-footed and funniest plays, and it is above all a transitional work – a comedy which dares to end unconventionally, with a conclusion that keeps both critics and audiences guessing as to what it might ultimately mean. The first of the "lyrical" plays, to be followed by *A Midsummer Night's Dream* and *Richard II*, it showcases the pleasures of delighting in language, but also the dangers: the social worlds of the play collide with sometimes prickly hostility; and beneath the extravagant verbal sparring enjoyed by everyone there lies a vein of lingering pathos.

[DATE]  Most likely 1594 or 1595, around the same time as *A Midsummer Night's Dream*, *Romeo and Juliet* and *Richard II*.

[SOURCES]  No direct sources survive, though given that the real-life Henri of Navarre (1553–1610) had two lords named Biron and Longueville, it has been conjectured that the play derives from a lost account of them. Other possible analogues include Pierre de la Primaudaye's *L'Académie Française* (1577) and Robert Wilson's play *The Cobbler's Prophecy* (c.1594), and there are clear debts to the Italian *commedia dell'arte* tradition.

[TEXTS]  Two: the quarto of 1598 (Q) – actually unactable due to its confusing speech-prefixes, probably the result of foul-ups by Shakespeare – and the 1623 Folio (F1).

## Interpreting the play

*Love's Labour's Lost* relishes games – games with words, games of acting, games of love. It opens in apparent seriousness, with a resolution by the King of Navarre and his three lords to devote themselves to stern pursuits: for three whole years they will study, fast, be celibate, sleep for three hours a night – all in the name of what Dumaine proudly calls "philosophy" (1.1.32). But the joke of the first half of the play is that they haven't the remotest chance of achieving it. Biron, the most cynical of the lords as well as by far the wittiest, is reading the agreement among them aloud when he realizes there are problems:

'Item: if any man be seen to talk with a woman within the term of three years, he shall endure such public shame as the rest of the court can possibly devise.'
This article, my liege, yourself must break;
   For well you know here comes in embassy
The French king's daughter with yourself to speak—
   A maid of grace and complete majesty—
About surrender-up of Aquitaine
   To her decrepit, sick and berid father.
Therefore this article is made in vain …

[1.1.128–37]

## Major Characters & Synopsis

**King Ferdinand** of Navarre
**Biron**, **Longueville** and **Dumaine**, lords
  attending the King
**Princess of France**
**Rosaline**, **Catherine** and **Maria**, ladies attend-
  ing the Princess
**Boyet**, a French lord attending the Princess
**Don Adriano de Armado**, a braggart from
  Spain
**Mote**, Don Armado's page
**Mercadé**, a French messenger
**Costard**, a clown
**Jaquenetta**, a dairymaid
**Sir Nathaniel**, a curate
**Holofernes**, a schoolmaster
**Anthony Dull**, a constable

**ACT 1** King Ferdinand has proclaimed a new moral order. Persuading his lords to sign an agreement renouncing women and dedicating themselves to three years of study, he hopes to turn the court into the academic envy of the world. But aristocrats aren't alone in feeling the effects: the countryman Costard is brought before the King and punished for pursuing Jaquenetta. The insufferably pompous Don Armado, who has informed against Costard, reveals why – he covets Jaquenetta for himself.

**ACT 2** But the King's plan hits an unexpected obstacle. The Princess of France has arrived in Navarre with three ladies, announcing that her father will repay an outstanding loan – but Ferdinand disputes the figures, claiming he is owed more. While the legalities are clarified, Ferdinand is forced to accommodate the party (much to the secret delight of his lords). Each clandestinely asks for details about their female guests: Longueville likes Maria, Dumaine fancies Catherine, while Biron is keen on Rosaline. Even King Ferdinand seems to have a crush on the Princess.

**ACT 3** Don Armado makes a move for Jaquenetta by employing Costard to send her an impassioned love letter. Thinking along the same lines, Biron recruits Costard to deliver his own letter to Rosaline.

**ACT 4** Finding the ladies out hunting, Costard produces Don Armado's letter by mistake. Without realizing his error, Costard then delivers the other letter to Jaquenetta and they ask the pretentious schoolmaster Holofernes to read it out. Biron, meanwhile, has overheard the King composing love poems in private, and they both hear Longueville doing the same. Dumaine then walks by, trying out his own poetry, at which point Longueville emerges from hiding and accuses him of breaking their agreement. The King follows, crit-icizing them both, but Biron waits until last and accuses all three of hypocrisy. Unluckily for him, though, Jaquenetta and Costard arrive, brandish-ing his own letter to Rosaline. The four men agree to forget their pact and set about wooing the ladies in earnest.

**ACT 5** Don Armado greets Holofernes, Nathaniel and Dull with news that he has been commanded by the King to provide an entertain-ment for the Princess. The four suitors, mean-while, disguise themselves in order to win their ladies; having been forewarned, the ladies mask up and pose as each other in order to embarrass their visitors. When the lords reappear, this time as themselves, the ladies pretend not to have recognized them, but Biron realizes that they have been duped. Renouncing all stratagems, the lords promise to woo honestly from now on and all prepare to watch the entertainment per-formed in their honour. Don Armado and the oth-ers boldly attempt to present a pageant of the nine most famous people in history (the "Nine Worthies"), but the result is predictably risible, Don Armado's own self-important impersonation of Hector coming unstuck when Costard announces that Jaquenetta is pregnant by the Spaniard. Don Armado and Costard are scuffling when Mercadé suddenly arrives with a message that the Princess's father has died. Despite entreaties to stay and agree to marriage, the Princess resolves to return home and mourn for her father. However, she will reconsider the King's proposal one year on – subject to his good behaviour. The other ladies make the same demand of their respective suitors.

And with that, in one sense, much of the play is over. From the speed with which their compact breaks down, Shakespeare drops a large hint that it won't be long before the King and his lords have fallen further, in fact fallen head over heels for the French Princess and her three ladies. The King is "shamed" by his own ridiculous edict, and with the entry of the women the real game of the play – the game of love – can begin.

For all that it seems inevitable, the process by which the lords come to the realization that love has ensnared them occupies over half of the play's action. It approaches its comic climax near the end of Act Four in a gloriously witty scene in which the lords are forced to admit that, far from keeping to their vow of chastity, each and every one intends to dispose with it. The entire plot hinges on this event, and yet what might be the tensest moment in the comedy is also its most tongue-in-cheek: in a wonderfully daring piece of stagecraft, Shakespeare sets up a scene whose outcome is as predictable as its sheer improbability. Safely hidden up a tree, Biron overhears first the King, then Longueville, then Dumaine, all rehearsing love poems. At its most complicated, there are no fewer than three lords hidden from view (invisible to each other but visible to Biron) while the unfortunate Dumaine reads out a halting "sonnet" for his lover. Intricately constructed though it is, the scene is patently ridiculous. As Biron gleefully exclaims, "All hid, all hid—an old infant play."

> Like a demigod here sit I in the sky,
> And wretched fools' secrets heedfully o'er-eye.
>
> **[4.3.75–7]**

As the scene builds up formulaically, so it unravels: Longueville appears, accusing Dumaine of hypocrisy; the King steps in, rounding on them both; and finally Biron descends from his hiding-place, reproaching them all and exclaiming with breathtaking self-righteousness that "I that am honest, I that hold it sin / To break the vow I am engagèd in" (4.3.175–6). Except, of course, that he has broken the vow, too, as everyone realizes when Jaquenetta and the clownish Costard burst in with Biron's own missive to the "celestial" Rosaline.

The scene never becomes too serious: the lords' progress towards self-awareness is constructed through a series of comic blunders – first believing that they are alone in love, then that they can hide it from the others, then that they have exposed someone else. Though they are transformed, they are transformed into the same thing. As Biron declares:

> Sweet lords, sweet lovers!—O, let us embrace.
>   As true we are as flesh and blood can be.
> The sea will ebb and flow, heaven show his face.
>   Young blood doth not obey an old decree.
> We cannot cross the cause why we were born,
> Therefore of all hands must we be forsworn.
>
> **[4.3.212–7]**

The chiming rhymes and jaunty pulse of Biron's speech confirm that all's well that ends well: everyone is in love (as we, the audience, knew they were all along), and there's no more to say.

## Obscene and most preposterous

There is in fact plenty more to say, for *Love's Labour's Lost* is also one of Shakespeare's most talkative plays. According to one count, it uses more "new" words (words the playwright hadn't used before) than any other work of Shakespeare's. In his recent book on the poet's language, Frank Kermode notes that as its characters adore wordplay and fast-talking quibbles, so over sixty percent of the comedy's lines are rhymed, a figure unrivalled by any other Shakespearian play. But what those figures don't indicate is that in *Love's Labour's Lost* language is often wildly out of control. While the King and his lords are in the process of repenting their hasty words, also resident in Navarre are two characters, the schoolmaster Holofernes and his curate sidekick Nathaniel, who provide an extreme example of what it is like to have too much language. Their speech is peppered with obscure literary allusions and classical tags, while mere conversation provides the opportunity for rhetorical one-upmanship and grammatical point-scoring. The Princess's killing of a deer while out hunting furnishes the schoolmaster with an excuse to put his linguistic virtuosity to the test. Promising to "something affect the letter" (use alliteration in the manner of old-fashioned verse), he launches into an "extemporal epitaph" celebrating the occasion:

> The preyful Princess pierced and pricked a pretty pleasing pricket.
> >   Some say a sore, but not a sore till now made sore with shooting.
> The dogs did yell; put 'l' to 'sore', then 'sorel' jumps from thicket—
> >   Or pricket sore, or else sorel. The people fall a-hooting.
> If sore be sore, then 'l' to 'sore' makes fifty sores—O sore 'l'!
> Of one sore I an hundred make by adding one more 'l'.

**[4.2.56–62]**

## Lost en route

Quite apart from the messy debates concerning Shakespeare's real identity, other questions nag editors and students about his work – not least how many works he actually wrote (see p.486). There is another problem, too: some texts have apparently disappeared for good.

The oldest mystery concerns **Love's Labour's Won**, a play mentioned by Elizabethan writer Francis Meres in a gushing catalogue of Shakespeare's early works. No play by that name survives, and some have even argued that the search for one is futile – the title being merely an alternative for a canonical work such as *As You Like It* or *All's Well That Ends Well*. But that hasn't dampened speculation. The eminent Shakespearian Cedric Watts recently attempted to conjure up a plot – commenting gleefully that "to do so is a temptation that it seems sinful to resist" – and the fictional discovery of a missing manuscript even formed the basis for a 1948 detective story by high-class thriller writer Edmund Crispin. Real life has proved almost as exciting (at least for scholars): five years after Crispin's novel was published, a bookseller's inventory from 1603 was unearthed, recording a work named "loves labours won" and thus implying that a separate play really did exist. If this is indeed the case, the puzzlingly dark ending of *Love's Labour's Lost* – where marriage between the main characters is left hanging in the air in a most un-Shakespearian fashion – might make more sense. Perhaps the playwright decided on a multi-part comedy to rival his experiments with the histories of *Henry VI*.

Question-marks also hang over a play from the other end of Shakespeare's career. In 1613 the King's Men performed at court a drama the records call "Cardenno" or "Cardenna", but the play (attributed to Shakespeare and John Fletcher) didn't surface again until 1653, well after the republican closure of the theatres, and appears never to have made it into print. **Cardenio**, as it's now known, was apparently based on Cervantes's *Don Quixote*, and if it was new when the King's Men performed it was probably Fletcher and Shakespeare's first collaboration. Heminges and Condell failed to feature it in the First Folio (but probably not on the grounds of co-authorship; they included *Henry VIII*), and it passed into obscurity. Notwithstanding, a spin-off entitled *Double Falsehood; or, The Distressed Lovers*, "Written Originally by W. SHAKESPEARE", appeared courtesy of playwright **Lewis Theobald** in 1728 and was performed successfully at Drury Lane. But the original script – Theobald claimed to have access to three separate copies – has long since vanished, perhaps in one of the numerous theatre fires that plagued the eighteenth-century stage.

Trevor Nunn's National Theatre production (2003) relocated the French court of Navarre to Edwardian England. Innocent of future cares, the King (Simon Day, standing) waxes philosophical to his Lords.

It's tempting to think that this speech has lost something in historical translation, but in fact Elizabethan audiences would probably have been as puzzled by it as we are. This monstrous exercise, rather like Holofernes himself, is amusing but socially dysfunctional: it fails to make language useful. Congratulated by Nathaniel on his "rare talent", Holofernes, flattered, replies: "This is a gift that I have, simple, simple—a foolish extravagant spirit, full of forms, figures, shapes, objects, ideas, apprehensions, motions, revolutions …" (4.2.66–8). The more he cycles through synonyms, the less he means.

Where Holofernes and Nathaniel are content to impress each other, yet another resident at court, the Spaniard Don Armado, has grander ambitions – to cement a friendship with the people he tries to regard as equals, King Ferdinand and his intimates. The problem is that Don Armado's addiction to what he calls the "sweet smoke of rhetoric" (3.1.61) illustrates some of the social dangers of saying the wrong things. Blissfully unaware that even his page, Mote, sneers at him, he writes to the King, informing on Costard's illegal liaison with Jaquenetta. He aims to impress: addressing the King somewhat implausibly as "Great deputy, the welkin's viceregent and sole dominator of Navarre, my soul's earth's god, and body's fostering patron", he continues in awkwardly grandiose style:

> So it is, besieged with sable-coloured melancholy, I did commend the black-oppressing humour to the most wholesome physic of thy health-giving air, and, as I am a gentleman, betook myself to walk. The time when? About the sixth hour, when beasts most graze, birds best peck, and men sit down to that nourishment which is called supper. So much for the time when. Now for the ground which—which, I mean, I walked upon. It is yclept thy park. Then for the place where—where, I mean, I did encounter that obscene and most preposterous event that draweth from my snow-white pen the ebon-coloured ink which here thou viewest, beholdest, surveyest, or seest …
>
> **[1.1.216–39]**

Though searching desperately for a courtly tone, Armado gets it stunningly wrong. Rather like his performance as Hector in the pageant of the Nine Worthies near the end of the play – which ends in even greater fiasco than the artisans' play in *A Midsummer Night's Dream* – Armado's incapacity to judge how he appears, and how he speaks, renders him an ignominious figure of fun. A similar fate meets Holofernes, whose own impersonation of Judas Maccabeus is destroyed by heckling, and who wretchedly exclaims that his treatment is "not generous, nor gentle, nor humble" (5.2.622). In moments such as these, it is possible to see Shakespeare hinting at what will become increasingly apparent in his later comedies: that words really can bruise.

## Well mocked

For, while the characters in *Love's Labour's Lost* are frequently playing games with one another, the stakes are sometimes perilously high. While the King and his lords indulge in ivory-tower fantasies, the Princess and her three ladies, in the critic Anne Barton's words, "come from a world outside the confines of Navarre that is colder and more realistic than the playground of the park". They arrive on financial business, and from the first they refuse to indulge the niceties of *politesse* – or insist on seeing through it. Meeting the party outside the court, the King nobly declares them "welcome to the court of Navarre". But the Princess does not hide her disapproval that they are to be left camping outside. "'Fair, I give you back again,'" she indignantly exclaims,

> and welcome I have not yet. The roof of this court is too high to be yours, and welcome to the wide fields too base to be mine.
>
> **[2.1.91–4]**

Her skill at deflation is even sharper in the scene where the lords decide to dress up as "frozen Muscovites" in order to represent their enslavement to love. Tipped off beforehand and with Boyet as go-between, Rosaline and her companions set to work on wilfully misinterpreting their suitors' claim to have "measured many miles" in pursuit:

BOYET
> If to come hither you have measured miles,
> And many miles, the Princess bids you tell
> How many inches doth fill up one mile.

BIRON
> Tell her we measure them by weary steps …

ROSALINE        How many weary steps
> Of many weary miles you have o'ergone
> Are numbered in the travel of one mile?

BIRON
> We number nothing that we spend for you.
> Our duty is so rich, so infinite,
> That we may do it still without account.
>
> **[5.2.190–9]**

Biron survives what Boyet later calls "the tongues of mocking wenches", but only just – and, anyway, the game is already lost. The disguised ladies have baffled their suitors, and when Biron later realizes that they have all been duped, the Princess has succeeded in doing what she declared at the outset, "To make theirs ours,"

> and ours none but our own.
> So shall we stay, mocking intended game,
> And they well mocked depart away with shame.
>
> **[5.2.153–5]**

*The disruptions perpetrated by the characters eventuate in the destruction of the romantic form, the form which is ideally the literary celebration of the wedding of individuals, sexes, and classes. The King's last-minute plea for the Princess's hand has already been disgraced by death.*

Louis A. Montrose, "'Sport by sport o'erthrown': *Love's Labour's Lost* and the politics of play" (1977)

It's for these kind of reasons that *Love's Labour's Lost* has sometimes been interpreted as a reply to the male-supremacist attitudes prevalent in *The Taming of the Shrew*. But the play is about more than the battle of the sexes: it is ultimately cynical about the ability of any of its characters to transcend reality. Far from concluding as Biron and the others expect it will, *Love's Labour's Lost*, as its title suggests, ends unhappily. Just as the comedy is at its sharpest, news arrives that the Princess's father has died, the "scene begins to cloud" (5.2.714) and the ladies refuse – for the moment – to wed their suitors. Biron is sent by Rosaline to use his wit on the "speechless sick", and similar trials are constructed for his colleagues. The lords will need to do more than say they are in love if their lovers are to believe them. As Biron ruefully comments, "Our wooing doth not end like an old play":

> Jack hath not Jill. These ladies' courtesy
> Might well have made our sport a comedy.
> KING
> Come, sir, it wants a twelvemonth an' a day,
> And then 'twill end.
> BIRON                That's too long for a play.

**[5.2.860–4]**

"Too long" indeed – the playing has come to an end. Some have interpreted this dark ending as a forcible growing-up; others have read into it Shakespeare's unhappiness with comic form itself; still others have suggested that he is preparing for a now-lost sequel (see p.186). Whatever the truth, *Love's Labour's Lost* gives its audiences plenty of serious things to think about.

## Stage history and adaptations

Though the 1598 **first quarto** loudly proclaims that *Love's Labour's Lost* was "presented before her Highness [Elizabeth I] this last Christmas" (presumably the winter of 1596–97, though possibly a year earlier), it was also popular on the public stage – as the publication of a poem by one Robert Tofte, in which the poet describes taking his girlfriend to see the play, testifies. The year 1598 also saw the publication of **Francis Meres**'s *Palladis Tamia*, a pioneering work of literary criticism that set out to compare "our English poets, with the Greek, Latin and Italian poets" and spoke glowingly of twelve of Shakespeare's plays, among them *Love's Labour's Lost*.

At any rate, it was clearly worth keeping the play in repertoire. It was performed for Queen Anne at the **Earl of Southampton**'s house during an extended bout of festivity over Christmas 1604–05. (Though Richard Burbage apparently recommended the comedy for its "wit and mirth", he hadn't much choice – the Queen had already seen every new play they were offering.) We also know that *Love's Labour's Lost* was played at the **Blackfriars**, the permanent winter home of Shakespeare's company from about 1609 onwards, but what we don't know is how they performed the extended final act – which is longer than candles of the time could cope with without guttering and filling the theatre with smoke.

It wasn't the candles, though, that kept *Love's Labour's Lost* off the stage for nearly two hundred years. Regarded as the least revivable play in the canon, it was the only one of Shakespeare's dramas not to be performed in the eighteenth century. An anonymous adaptation entitled *The Students* (1762) seems never to have been acted, and even the dogged **David Garrick** failed to get the "musical" version he commissioned in 1771 onto the boards – suggesting that others producers shared John Dryden's view that *Love's Labour's Lost*, *The Winter's Tale* and *Measure for Measure* were "either grounded on impossibilities, or at least, so meanly written, that the Comedy neither caus'd your mirth, nor the serious part your concernment".

In fact, *Love's Labour's Lost* had to wait until 1839 and the redoubtable **Elizabeth Vestris**, one of the great actress-managers of the period, to see the inside of a theatre again. Her production was lavish, with gorgeous costumes by **J.R. Planché**, but on the opening night at Covent Garden the audience was more concerned by the fact that the shilling seats had recently been axed and came close to rioting. The next staging came in 1857 under the industrious **Samuel Phelps** in an Arcadian setting which won some plaudits, but the play failed to catch on and was infrequently acted for the rest of the century (though it reached the US in 1874). It was performed on Shakespeare's birthday at Stratford-upon-Avon in 1885 – apparently its sheer obscurity singled it out for attention – but soon afterwards George Bernard Shaw wondered whether it was "worth viewing at this time of day".

Despite **Harley Granville-Barker**'s assumption that *Love's Labour's Lost* was an apprentice piece, his influential *Preface* (1927) to the play claimed that all a successful production needed was "style in the acting". At the Westminster Theatre five years later, his advice was heeded by **Tyrone Guthrie**, who employed eighteenth-century costumes and staging, and even per-

Peter Brook's brilliant Stratford production of *Love's Labour's Lost* (1948) did much to re-establish the play's reputation.

suaded the arch-sceptic editor John Dover Wilson to change his mind. Guthrie directed the play again in 1936, this time at the Old Vic with a strong cast (but rather threadbare set) that included **Alec Clunes** as Biron and **Michael Redgrave** as the King of Navarre. But it was the next major production of *Love's Labour's Lost* that proved to be a watershed: it was the 1946 Stratford debut of the 21-year-old *wunderkind* **Peter Brook**, who – like Guthrie – raided the early eighteenth century, this time in imitation of the wistful Rococo paintings of Jean-Antoine Watteau. Brook presented the play elegiacally, with **Paul Scofield** as a mournful, Don Quixote-like Armado. **Hugh Hunt** put it on just three years later, with Redgrave this time as Biron and **Diana Churchill** as Rosaline (this time in Elizabethan costume), and also saw success. **Laurence Olivier** staged the play at the National Theatre in 1969, but offered it in starker terms – unlike Brook, who gradually dimmed the lights towards the end, Olivier's Mercadé appeared suddenly, "as if from nowhere".

Since then, *Love's Labour's Lost* has become a solid favourite, being mounted four times in major British productions during the 1970s and frequently in the US. **David Jones** at the RSC was well received in 1978, with **Estelle Kohler** as Rosaline opposite **Ian Richardson**'s show-stealing Biron. **John Barton**, again at Stratford, told his actors to "think Chekhov" four years later, exploring the painful side of love. Barton attempted to be deliberately anti-romantic, with **Richard Griffiths** as a distinctly podgy King and **Carmen Du Sautoy**'s spectacles-wearing Princess; **Michael Pennington** played Biron to **Jane Lapotaire**'s Rosaline. Over at Stratford, Ontario, in the same year **Robin Phillips** further underscored the play's sense of doom by setting it in 1914 to the rumbling of distant guns. **Trevor Nunn** deployed a similar strategy with his 2003 National Theatre version in London, which emphasized the play's icier elements by opening it with a tableau of the Western Front to which **Joseph Fiennes**'s consummately sarcastic Biron and **Kate Fleetwood**'s mischievous Rosaline were destined to be sent.

There have been no fewer than five silent films from 1912 onwards, but **Kenneth Branagh**'s 1999 version has been the only film on the modern big screen; though lukewarmly reviewed, its intriguing decision to present Shakespearian conceits through the prism of golden-age musicals was at least novel. **Elijah Moshinsky** directed the BBC Shakespeare version in a Regency staging in 1984, but this production (despite **Maureen Lipman**'s mature Princess) was generally considered a flop.

## Screen

### Love's Labour's Lost
K. Branagh, A. Silverstone, N. Lane; Kenneth Branagh (dir.)
UK, 1999 ▷ Fox Pathé **DVD**

Undemanding and slightly naive it may be, but this version of *Love's Labour's Lost* is not without charm. In uncritical homage to the heyday of Hollywood musicals, Branagh sets the action in a kind of soundstagey Oxbridge (wittily designed by Tim Harvey) and at crucial moments has his cast spin on their heels and croon American songbook standards by Porter, Kern, Gershwin and company instead of launching into sonnets and masques. This cleverly translates the play's own stylization into something cinematically more approachable, even if most of its linguistic crossfire ends up on the cutting-room floor (and it has to be said that Branagh's own singing voice, along with others in his cast, wouldn't have made it past Irving Berlin). In the end, though, you can't help thinking that it would all look so much better with the colour turned down.

## Audio

### Love's Labour's Lost
A. Jennings, E. Fielding, S. Bond; Clive Brill (dir.)
UK, 1998 ▷ Arkangel

Perhaps it's only in audio that you can get the true measure of the wordiest play in the canon, but *Love's Labour's Lost* needs careful handling: done too slowly it fails to take flight, too fast and it becomes a blur of wordplay. Generally speaking this production gets the mix just right, and it's helped along the way by a genuinely terrific cast, one that must make Clive Brill the envy of many a stage director: Alex Jennings as a homely Biron, Samantha Bond's delightfully pointed Princess and Emma Fielding's sprightly Rosaline are just some of the highlights. Alan Howard rather hams it up as Don Armado, but it's the kind of role in which you can get away with it.

# Editions

### Arden Shakespeare (third series)
**H.R. Woudhuysen (ed.); 1998** ▷ Thomas Nelson

Despite strong competition from John Kerrigan's insightful Penguin edition (which is a bargain, too), Woudhuysen's more complete and up-to-date Arden 3 just pips it to the post. The text is intelligently and helpfully glossed – particularly worthwhile in a play so obsessed by language in all its colourful permutations – and Woudhuysen presents the literary and publication background succinctly. There's plenty here on stage history, and two appendices deal with textual issues in more detail, the second providing lines Shakespeare appears to have tweaked and which were published by mistake in the early editions (probably a foul-up by one of the printer's compositors).

# Some criticism

### Shakespeare's Happy Comedies
**John Dover Wilson; 1962** ▷ Faber [o/p]

John Dover Wilson edited *Love's Labour's Lost* for the New Shakespeare in 1923 and again in 1962 – and, between the two, utterly changed his view of it. The production responsible for this change of heart was directed by Tyrone Guthrie (see p.190), and the essay included in this volume, subtitled "the story of a conversion", is as much a personal account as a critical study – though it is that, too, and from one of the twentieth century's most respected editors and writers. Wilson looks at the play's life in the theatre rather than on the page, describing it as a "kaleidoscope" and comparing it to Mozart's *Così fan Tutte*; he is also keen to stress its darker sides, suggesting that "tragedy is always there, *felt*, if not seen". The book also contains essays on the middle comedies and some enthusiastic general observations on Shakespeare's comic skill – still an undervalued topic when Wilson was writing.

### The Great Feast of Language
**William Carroll; 1976** ▷ Princeton UP

Even a few moments spent watching or reading *Love's Labour's Lost* makes it clear that Mote is only too accurate to remark on "the great feast of language" in the play (a feast from which Holofernes and company have merely "stolen the scraps"). There is so much to say on the subject that the reader might seem at risk of being swamped, but Carroll's approach is clear, presenting various different aspects of the play's language – linguistic style, theatrical devices, self-conscious "poetry" – before moving on to link these with its larger themes. *The Great Feast of Language* is a welcome rehabilitation of a comedy which has often been (as Carroll puts it) "the darling of the Shakespearean lunatic fringe", and it is one of the first examples of the language-based analyses that have done so much to revive interest in Shakespeare's comedies. Keir Elam's *Shakespeare's Universe of Discourse* (1984) goes even further, taking the comedies and testing them against recent linguistic theory.

# Macbeth

M acbeth, Shakespeare's shortest and darkest tragedy, still retains its ability to shock. "The Scottish play", as it is nervously known in the theatre, is attached by longstanding tradition to all manner of unlucky occurrences – quite apart from those dictated by the script, which are brutal enough. It was more than likely written to honour King James VI of Scotland, who in 1603 took over the English throne and whose ancestor Banquo appears as the most honourable of Macbeth's victims. But the tragedy itself refuses to be cast in black and white: whereas *Othello* distils its evil into the tempter Iago, in *Macbeth* the hero steadily becomes the villain, and our ethical compass is forced to recalibrate as a result. So it is, too, with the merciless Lady Macbeth, who despite being in many ways the most fearsome character of all (far more so, in fact, than her husband) ends up a victim of the play, her sanity shattered by the terrifying march of events. Though many fine productions – such as Trevor Nunn's famous 1976 version at the RSC – have responded sensitively to the otherworldly, eerie aspects of this unique tragedy, *Macbeth* never forgets that the demons we conjure ourselves are the ones we should fear. As the clergyman George Gifford wrote in his *Dialogue Concerning Witches and Witchcraft* (1593), "the power of devils is in the hearts of men".

[DATE] From internal evidence – notably a cryptic reference to the trial of the Gunpowder Plot conspirators – *Macbeth* was probably first performed in 1606, around the time that *Antony and Cleopatra* was written.

[SOURCES] Raphael Holinshed's massive *Chronicles* (revised 1587) provided Shakespeare with the story of Macbeth and Duncan, as well as other material. George Buchanan's *Rerum Scoticarum Historia* (1582) possibly offered further leads, and Matthew Gwynne's Latin pageant *Tres Sibyllae* (performed for James I in 1605) has been tenuously linked with *Macbeth*.

[TEXTS] Only the Folio version (1623) survives. This was probably derived from a playhouse script, thought to be an adaptation by Shakespeare's younger colleague Thomas Middleton.

## Interpreting the play

*Macbeth* is, quite literally, a murky play. The great critic A.C. Bradley put on paper what is obvious to audiences from its very first moments. "Darkness, we may even say blackness, broods over this tragedy," he wrote. "It is remarkable that almost all the scenes which at once recur to memory take place either at night or in some dark spot." Those dark corners – Macbeth's vision of the dagger, Duncan's murder, Banquo's murder, Lady Macbeth's tormented sleepwalking – provide at a glance a synopsis of the play, as it travels from the Macbeths' ambition for power, the savage murders they perform to secure it, and the steady erosion into nothingness of everything they hold dear.

But one major component is missing from Bradley's scheme, and it is far more memorable to audiences:

## Major Characters & Synopsis

**King Duncan** of Scotland
**Malcom**, Duncan's elder son
**Donalbain**, Duncan's younger son
A **Captain** in Duncan's army
**Macbeth**, Thane of Glamis
**Lady Macbeth**, Macbeth's wife
**Porter** at Macbeth's castle
**Seyton**, servant of Macbeth
**Banquo**, a thane, and his son **Fleance**
**Macduff**, Thane of Fife
**Lady Macduff**, Macduff's wife
**Lennox**, **Ross**, **Angus**, **Caithness** and
  **Menteith**, thanes
**Siward**, Earl of Northumberland, and his son
  **Young Siward**
**Hecate**, Queen of the Witches
Six **Witches**

**ACT 1** War divides Scotland as the rebellious Macdonald fights against King Duncan. But Duncan has the resolute Thane of Glamis, Macbeth, on his side and the battle goes their way. Returning from the war, Macbeth and his fellow general Banquo encounter three Witches, who prophesy that Macbeth will be rewarded and one day become king, while his companion's ancestors will prosper. As the Witches vanish, a party from Duncan arrives, announcing that – as predicted – Macbeth is now Thane of Cawdor. Reeling from the news, Macbeth writes to his wife, who resolves that her husband needs to be helped on his way to power. So when news arrives that King Duncan intends to stay at their castle, she persuades the reluctant Macbeth to murder him.

**ACT 2** As Macbeth steals towards Duncan's chamber, his resolve weakens as he comes across Banquo and then is troubled by strange hallucinations. Nonetheless, as Lady Macbeth waits and Duncan's drugged guards sleep, he kills the King. Shortly afterwards Macduff arrives at the palace and discovers Duncan's corpse. Feigning horror, Macbeth murders the guards, who Lady Macbeth has attempted to frame by smearing them with blood. Fearing for their own

lives, Donalbain and Malcom flee – thus arousing suspicion of their involvement. Macbeth is now king: the Witches' prophecy has come true.

**ACT 3** Although Banquo harbours doubts about his friend's role in events, he agrees to celebrate the coronation at a banquet. But Macbeth wants Banquo dead, and arranges for assassins to murder him and his son Fleance. The attempt is botched, however, and Fleance escapes. That night at the banquet, Macbeth alarms his guests when he sees what he thinks is Banquo's ghost. The dinner breaks up in disarray. Lennox and another Lord discuss their misgivings about Macbeth and how Macduff is trying to raise an army against him.

**ACT 4** Macbeth visits the Witches, desperate for information about his future. He is warned about Macduff but also told that "none of woman born / Shall harm Macbeth". Hearing that Macduff has escaped to England, Macbeth orders the deaths of his wife and children. In England, Malcom falsely describes himself to Macduff as dissolute and unfit to be King; when Macduff recoils, Malcom knows him to be loyal to Scotland. The two men are discussing the campaign against Macbeth when news arrives that Macduff's entire family has been slaughtered.

**ACT 5** Back in Scotland, Lady Macbeth has been sleepwalking and raving about the various murders. By this time Malcom's forces are marching on the King's castle, Dunsinane, carrying branches to disguise their approach. Macbeth – convinced that the Witches have predicted his invincibility – refuses to acknowledge the threat until he hears that Lady Macbeth is dead and that Birnam Wood is moving towards them. He fights on, eventually coming face to face with Macduff, whom he learns was delivered by Caesarian section. Macduff succeeds in killing him and presents his head to Malcom, hailing him as the new King of Scotland.

FIRST WITCH
When shall we three meet again?
In thunder, lightning, or in rain?
SECOND WITCH
When the hurly-burly's done,
When the battle's lost and won.
THIRD WITCH
That will be ere the set of sun.
FIRST WITCH
Where the place?
SECOND WITCH          Upon the heath.
THIRD WITCH
There to meet with Macbeth.
FIRST WITCH
I come, Grimalkin.
SECOND WITCH
Paddock calls.
THIRD WITCH          Anon.
ALL
Fair is foul, and foul is fair,
Hover through the fog and filthy air.

**[1.1.1–11]**

Though centuries of familiarity and theatrical tradition have done a good job of stripping the Weird Sisters of their capacity to inspire terror, Shakespeare's audiences, brought up on lurid tales about the potency of witchcaft (and who might have witnessed first-hand the persecution of women believed to be witches), would not have been so relaxed. Though it is unclear whether this brief scene, the very first in the play, takes place at night, it deserves to appear in any list of *Macbeth*'s eeriest moments. If played convincingly, the Witches unleash something genuinely terrifying into the play, bridging the gap between the world that we know and comprehend, and the wild, chaotic space beyond it. The Sisters "look not like th'inhabitants o'th' earth," Banquo exclaims, "and yet are on't" (1.3.39–40).

The oldest meaning of the word "weird" refers to the magical ability to govern fate, and the message the Witches deliver to Macbeth (that he will be "king hereafter") confirms that they live up to their name – as he himself realizes once their first prediction, that he will be made Thane of Cawdor, comes true. "This supernatural soliciting," he murmurs, "cannot be ill, cannot be good."

If ill,
Why hath it given me earnest of success
Commencing in a truth? I am Thane of Cawdor.
If good, why do I yield up to that suggestion
Whose horrid image doth unfix my hair
And make my seated heart knock at my ribs
Against the use of nature?

**[1.3.129–36]**

One man who took witches sufficiently seriously to publish a book about them was the monarch for whom, in all probability, *Macbeth* was written: James I. Many scholars believe that Shakespeare's Scottish play was composed to honour the Edinburgh-born king who had recently taken control of the English throne, uniting the two nations for the first time and also extending his patronage to Shakespeare's company. Shakespeare repaid his and his colleagues'

David Garrick as Macbeth and Hannah Pritchard as Lady Macbeth, roles they played regularly between 1748 and 1768. As Johann Zoffany's depiction indicates, it was customary to perform Shakespeare in contemporary dress in the eighteenth century.

debt in fine style, returning to the main source for his English histories, the sprawling *Chronicles* (1587) published by Raphael Holinshed and others, and drawing out from the "History of Scotland" the tale of the eleventh-century thane Banquo, believed to be the ultimate ancestor of all Scottish monarchs, James included. Yet in concentrating on the story of Macbeth, Banquo's sometime companion and ruler, Shakespeare allowed himself the freedom to construct a play in which witchcraft could play a forceful role (according to Holinshed, Macbeth relied on supernatural advice to govern Scotland). As well as further flattering King James's interest in such matters, in so doing Shakespeare created a dramatic world in which witchcraft and humankind become dangerously – and tragically – entangled. In a strange kind of way (and the play is nothing if not strange), the Witches are, as critic Terry Eagleton puts it, intended to be "the heroines of the piece".

## Unsex me here

It would be interesting to know what James – or his contemporaries – made of another rogue female that dominates *Macbeth*, the hero's wife. From a few hints in Holinshed, chiefly the bald statement that Lady Macbeth was "very ambitious", Shakespeare conjured a character who, despite the many things about her that remain enigmatic (not least her first name, which is never mentioned, not even by her doting husband), has exercised a powerful influence over the imagination of audiences and critics alike – to the extent that she has become a kind of cultural shorthand for the ambitious, threatening, ruthless figure of woman. Shakespeare had already created malevolent females who literally wrestle with demons (Joan la Pucelle in

*Henry VI Part I* is the clearest example), but never ones who, like Lady Macbeth, attempt to turn their sex inside out. Receiving the news that Duncan is to stay that night at their castle, she calls upon "you spirits / That tend on mortal thoughts" to

> unsex me here,
> And fill me from the crown to the toe top-full
> Of direst cruelty. Make thick my blood,
> Stop up th'access and passage to remorse,
> That no compunctious visitings of nature
> Shake my fell purpose, nor keep peace between
> Th'effect and it. Come to my woman's breasts,
> And take my milk for gall, you murd'ring ministers …

**[1.5.39–47]**

Lady Macbeth imagines "stopping up" her sensitivity to "remorse" as if it were menstrual blood; being "unsexed" and inhuman are, to her, one and the same thing. But she draws power from her femaleness, too: her "woman's breasts" both give out "gall" (bile) and take it in. Elsewhere she makes the connection between maternal nurture and destructive power horribly clear. Mocking Macbeth's last-minute nerves before he heads off to kill Duncan, she boasts, "I have given suck,"

> and know
> How tender 'tis to love the babe that milks me.
> I would, while it was smiling in my face,
> Have plucked my nipple from his boneless gums
> And dashed the brains out, had I so sworn
> As you have done to this.

**[1.7.54–9]**

> *[T]hough in Macbeth the strife of mind is greater than in his wife, the tiger spirit not so awake, and his feelings caught chiefly by contagion from her,—yet, as both were finally involved in the guilt of murder, the murderous mind of necessity is finally to be presumed in both.*
>
> Thomas De Quincey, "On the Knocking at the Gate in *Macbeth*" (1823)

Lady Macbeth stops at nothing in driving her husband on to murder Duncan – at first taunting his manliness ("Was the hope drunk / Wherein you dressed yourself?" she scoffs), then claiming that she would "dash the brains out" of their own child had she undertaken to do so. Though the question of whether the Macbeths actually have children – they are not mentioned elsewhere – remains a puzzling gap in the play (a gap some critics have spent a great deal of energy attempting to fill), what is important here is that Lady Macbeth's ghastly words make her sound still more like the Witches: both mother and murderer, good and evil, fair and foul.

## The word of promise

The play would be meaningless, however, if witchcraft had sole sway: it would be over before it began. The Sisters may ordain, but they do not perform the many "horrid deed[s]" Macbeth and his wife take upon themselves on their bloody path to the throne. Yet they do make the hero's grip on events seem disturbingly slippery. While it may be difficult to notice in performance (things move too fast), what is striking when reading *Macbeth* is that the idea of killing Duncan, the play's all-important point of no return, seems to originate from nowhere. The Witches insinuate that Macbeth will be King of Scotland, but not how he should go about achieving it. Even Lady Macbeth, after hearing of their prophecies, skirts coyly around the subject, noting astringently that though her absent husband is "not without ambition", he is "too full o'th' milk of human kindness / To catch the nearest way" (1.5.16–18) – "the nearest way" meaning, of course, murdering their ruler (and guest) in cold blood. Though the milk she has eradicated from herself apparently lingers in her husband, ironically it is she who can't quite bring herself to spell out death.

Macbeth, by contrast, does his utmost to confront the complexity of his situation. Though initially comforting himself with the thought that "if chance will have me king, why chance may crown me / Without my stir" (1.3.142–3), it soon becomes apparent that Fate will require some urgent prompting. By the time that Duncan has entered the castle and a feast prepared in his honour, Macbeth is already imagining in a kind of jumpy doublethink past his murder to what lies beyond:

> If it were done when 'tis done, then 'twere well
> It were done quickly. If th'assassination
> Could trammel up the consequence, and catch
> With his surcease success: that but this blow
> Might be the be-all and the end-all, here,
> But here upon this bank and shoal of time,
> We'd jump the life to come.

**[1.7.1–7]**

The extraordinarily choppy texture of these lines, and their tongue-tripping quality for actors, show that Macbeth is trying to think through what seems unthinkable. His language is thick with euphemisms – "assassination" is a chilly coinage for "murder" (this is its first appearance in the English language); "his surcease" means "Duncan's death" – and Macbeth seems to be arguing, or at least hoping, that this one killing will be the last, that it will be the "be-all and the end-all". He imagines cause and effect being "trammelled" (bundled up) together into one instant, feverishly plotting far beyond the immediate moment ("this bank and shoal of time") into "the life to come". "The meanings cannot be remembered all at once, however often you read it," William Empson commented on this speech. "It remains the incantation of a murderer, dishevelled and fumbling among the powers of darkness."

Despite Macbeth's best hopes, however, Duncan's murder isn't by any means the "be-all and the end-all"; it is only the beginning. "Blood," as the hero anxiously remarks later on, "will have blood" (3.5.121), and the lurid vision of a dagger stained with "gouts of blood" that led him to Duncan's chamber proves an apt symbol of what Macduff calls the "bloody-sceptred" tyrant who wrests control of Scotland. Just after the deed is done, Macbeth gazes at his blood-stained hands, imagining them polluting the visible world:

> Will all great Neptune's ocean wash this blood
> Clean from my hand? No, this my hand will rather
> The multitudinous seas incarnadine,
> Making the green one red.

**[2.2.58–61]**

Macbeth's terror is more than the fear that their crime will be discovered: it is that he has unleashed forces that will ultimately tear him apart. The vision of the oceans stained crimson by Duncan's assassination is too gruesomely extravagant to be true, but when Macbeth's coronation supper is interrupted by the "gory" ghost of the recently murdered Banquo (the Macbeths' second major victim), it seems that anything is possible. "The time has been / That, when the brains were out, the man would die, /And there an end," Macbeth cries out, to his wife's horror, "But now they rise again …" (3.4.77–9).

Baffled and panicked by Banquo's ghost, Macbeth heads once again to the Sisters. What he finds there, instead of the appealing certainties of before, is a series of dark riddles. Though "none of woman born / Shall harm Macbeth" (4.1.96–7), the Witches chant, Macduff is still a threat; though Macbeth has nothing to fear until "Great Birnam Wood to high Dunsinane Hill … come against him", the last vision he sees depicts a sequence of Banquo's descendants stretching out "to th' crack of doom", as Macbeth shouts out, aghast (4.1.133). From these mixed assurances, equivocal as anything in the play, Macbeth constructs a kind of comfort – after all, if you can't conceive of your forest rising up against you, what have you to be scared of? What is a talisman protecting you against anyone "of woman born" if not a guarantee of immortality? What the Witches offer Macbeth is the certainty that his mind is the only limit: he only need imagine it for it to be true.

> Suicide is either a protest or an admission of guilt. Macbeth does not feel guilty, and there is nothing for him to protest about. All he can do before he dies is to drag with him into nothingness as many living beings as possible.
>
> Jan Kott, *Shakespeare Our Contemporary* (1964)

But Macbeth's brain is, as he anxiously reflects to his wife, "full of scorpions" (3.2.37), and, like her – as the Doctor later comments to a servingwoman – he has known what he should not. Although he isn't the first casualty of this knowledge (Lady Macbeth, discovered sleepwalking and guiltily washing her hands of Duncan's blood, is that), the sudden announcement that his wife is dead – presumably suicide, though the play leaves the verdict open – initiates a speech in which Macbeth pictures himself gazing into the abyss. "She should have died hereafter," he mutters,

> There would have been a time for such a word.
> Tomorrow, and tomorrow, and tomorrow
> Creeps in this petty pace from day to day
> To the last syllable of recorded time,
> And all our yesterdays have lighted fools
> The way to dusty death.

**[5.5.16–22]**

Life is, he concludes, "a tale / Told by an idiot, full of sound and fury, / Signifying nothing" (5.5.25–7). Endlessly repetitive, it is also ultimately futile, a stuttering sequence of tomorrows, an empty riff on the biblical assurance that life has value as "a tale that is told".

As the tragedy hurtles towards its conclusion, the sequence of horrors Macbeth has performed – Duncan's murder, Banquo's death, the slaughter of Macduff's wife and children – turn is decisively against him. In a bizarre spin on the perversion of nature for which he is responsible, Birnam Wood does indeed rise up against Macbeth, in the form of Malcom's and Macduff's soldiers carrying branches in the hope of confusing enemy scouts. But *Macbeth* reserves its biggest twist for last. Confident of immortality, Macbeth vows to fight until "from my bones the flesh be hacked" (5.3.33), slaying Young Siward and facing Macduff undaunted. When the pair finally meet in combat, Macbeth taunts, "Thou losest labour … I bear a charmèd life" (5.10.8–12). But Macduff's reply stops him dead:

Lady Macbeth (Judi Dench) tries to persuade her husband (Ian McKellen) to return the daggers to the scene of Duncan's murder – exactly the same moment as depicted in the Zoffany painting on p.196.

> Despair thy charm,
> And let the angel whom thou still hast served
> Tell thee Macduff was from his mother's womb
> Untimely ripped.

[5.10.8–16]

Macduff boasts that he was delivered via Caesarean section – a dangerous last-ditch operation in seventeenth-century England, let alone feudal Scotland, and one that invariably resulted in the death of the mother. The revelation is fittingly unreal (a word that appears for the first time in the play), and in it Macbeth recognizes a bitter irony. "Accursed be the tongue that tells me so," he gasps,

> For it hath cowed my better part of man;
> And be these juggling fiends no more believed,
> That palter with us in a double sense,
> That keep the word of promise to our ear
> And break it to our hope.

[5.11.17–22]

By his "better part" Macbeth means his courage; we know as well as he that anything good has long since drained away. The circumstances of Macduff's birth have sentenced him to death; the Witches' "promise" proves worthless. And like so much else in the play, Macbeth realizes that his "hope", too, signifies absolutely nothing.

# Stage history and adaptations

It's likely that *Macbeth* was popular when it reached the **Globe** in around 1606, probably with **Richard Burbage** as Macbeth and **Robert Armin** as the Porter. The astrologer Simon Forman saw it there in 1611 and was impressed by the "3 women fairies or nymphs" and Lady Macbeth's sleepwalking scene. **Thomas Middleton** (possible collaborator on *Timon*) overhauled the play a few years later, adding Hecate and some dance scenes for the Witches. But the most famous seventeenth-century adaptation was **William Davenant**'s (1664), which beefed up the Macduffs' roles while underscoring Macbeth's similarities to the hated Cromwell and adding some spectacular flying witches (achievable with Restoration stage technology). **Thomas Betterton** and his wife **Mary** acted, to triumphant receptions: Pepys saw them no fewer than eight times, and one night his own wife walked out rather than suffer Betterton's understudy.

James Quin succeeded Betterton from 1717, but in 1744 was eclipsed by **David Garrick**, which he announced would be performed "as written by Shakespeare" and alongside **Hannah Pritchard**. The next great Macbeth, **Charles Macklin**, didn't dare challenge Garrick's signature role until his seventies, and outdid him only sartorially – with "authentic" Highland costume. Later in the 1770s **John Philip Kemble** turned his attention to the play, and, despite his own impressive performance in the lead, had the mixed fortune to be acting alongside his remarkable sister, **Sarah Siddons**, perhaps the greatest of all Lady Macbeths. Pre-empting Stanislavskian techniques by over a century, Siddons observed sleepwalkers in order to get inside the role, and was acclaimed for a "womanly" interpretation that nonetheless led her to seem almost "above nature", as Hazlitt breathlessly exclaimed.

*Macbeth* also became popular in Germany in this era, with **Friedrich von Schiller**'s adaptation of 1800 and **Ferdinand Fleck**'s celebrated acting leading the way. **Edmund Kean** was perhaps Fleck's English equivalent, and he guided the play into the Romantic era, but compared to his

## The Scottish Play

Perhaps inevitably for a tragedy that lends witchcraft such a major role (let alone one that takes place almost entirely at night), *Macbeth* has long been associated with malign theatrical forces. Legend has it that its curse began during an early run when a boy actor named **Hal Berridge** died while playing Lady Macbeth. Although the story is probably apocryphal – no Berridge appears in the theatrical records – his ghost has proved difficult to exorcize: scholars have recently discovered a child who was christened "Henry Berredge" in July 1593, making him just the right age for the part.

Even so, it's unlikely that *Macbeth* acquired its reputation for woeful luck until 1772 and the great Irish actor **Charles Macklin**. Macklin's characteristically innovative approach – he studied the text in unprecedented detail, stripping out comic roles and imposing "authentic" Scottish costume – caused friction in rehearsals and the resulting production was anxious. It became even more so during the fourth performance, when the audience, stoked up by supporters of Macklin's rival Garrick, began to riot. Although he soldiered through to the end, Macklin was sacked soon afterwards. An even worse riot – the most violent in New York's history – occurred in 1849 when the English tragedian, **William Charles Macready**, attempted (for the second time) to appear as Macbeth at the Astor Place Opera House. Opposing him were the supporters of his former friend, but by now arch-rival, the American **Edwin Forrest**. Whipped up by rabble-rousing nationalists, an estimated 20,000 people hit the streets and, as the play began, hurled paving stones and other debris at the theatre. Eventually the National Guard were called, and in the ensuing chaos some thirty people were shot dead and over four times that number were injured.

In the twentieth century the curse has gained a number of high-profile victims. An early casualty was the Russian pioneer of "method" acting, **Konstantin Stanislavsky**: when his Macbeth suffered a memory lapse during the dress rehearsal, the prompter failed to deliver his cue – and was found dead in his box, a grim omen that closed the show. Likewise, **Laurence Olivier**'s 1937 staging at the Old Vic was beset by a catalogue of woes including sets that didn't fit, a director who had to be replaced at the last minute after a car crash, and a near-miss for Olivier himself, who narrowly escaped being crushed by a stage weight. When Lilian Baylis, the Old Vic's redoubtable founder, died during final preparations, it seemed that the curse had truly taken hold.

**Peter Hall**, staging the play at Stratford thirty years later with Paul Scofield and Vivien Merchant, urged his actors to ignore the superstition – and was rewarded when he caught a vicious case of shingles during rehearsals. The show had to be postponed, and when it finally reached the stage, was judged a failure despite its wonderful cast. But these disasters pale in comparison to **Oldham Rep**'s revival of *Macbeth* in 1947. A few nights into the run, the climactic fight between Antony Oakley's Macduff and Harold Norman's Macbeth seemed to audiences to be more realistic than usual, and as the curtain fell it became obvious why – Norman had been stabbed in the chest. He died soon afterwards.

Unwilling to take on the curse, many actors simply obey its dictums. They never refer to *Macbeth* by name in a theatre or quote from the text, except when performing it (acceptable euphemisms include "The Scottish Play"). If these rules are broken, the offender must leave the building, turn around three times, then spit or swear. But the curse surfaces in the oddest of places, as the ever-industrious actor-manager **Donald Wolfit** discovered to his cost during a touring version of *Macbeth* in the 1940s. Disgruntled about his low wages, a young actor playing a Messenger decided to make a few last-minute adjustments to the script in order to register his feelings. So instead of announcing Lady Macbeth's sudden death to Wolfit's expectant King, he coolly walked on stage and declared: "My lord, the Queen is much better … and is even now at dinner." It may have been the only time in his lengthy career that Wolfit was lost for words.

sensational Richard III, his Macbeth hit the heights only in bursts. **William Charles Macready,** who played him constantly from 1821 to 1848, was more successful and Macbeth soon became one of his most celebrated roles: critics singling out the terrifying way he recoiled at the sight of Banquo's ghost. By 1847, when **Samuel Phelps** put on *Macbeth* at Sadler's Wells, the fashion for extravagant staging had begun to take over. Phelps's productions indicated witchcraft by spreading green gauze across the front of the stage, but as ever **Charles Kean**'s vast sets and massive reserves of extras stole a march on his rivals, in this instance when his ultra-"Scottish" *Macbeth* debuted in 1853.

The American **Charlotte Cushman**, famed for her Romeo (see p.311), was Macready's leading lady for a time, and during the latter end of the nineteenth century the play became more than ever Lady Macbeth's drama. The remarkable Italian actress **Adelaide Ristori** toured an adaptation by **Giulio Carcano** (later used as the basis for **Giuseppe Verdi**'s celebrated opera) in the 1850s, yet the most celebrated Lady Macbeth of the era was probably **Ellen Terry** – though several critics felt she was just too nice for the role. First seen in **Henry Irving**'s Lyceum production of 1888, Terry was unforgettable in an incandescent red wig and a dress covered with glittering beetle-cases, and outshone not merely Irving's Macbeth but also his gargantuan Pre-Raphaelite sets. Yet not all Macbeths would be so easily outdone – the towering Italian **Tommaso Salvini** toured the play during the 1870s and 80s, and the virtuosic German **Friedrich Mitterwurzer**, who acted it from 1877 onwards, did his utmost to upstage everything else (even Banquo's ghost, which he attacked in a frenzy).

**Herbert Beerbohm Tree**'s staging, though it premiered in 1911, was virtually the last gasp for overblown Victorian *Macbeth*s: within twenty years **Barry Jackson**'s Birmingham Rep had put on a modern-dress version, and by 1933 the avant-garde **Theodor Komisarjevsky** was directing it at Stratford as an Expressionist nightmare, with an aluminium set dominated by a large staircase. Even more radical was the version mounted in Harlem, New York by the 21-year-old **Orson Welles** three years later: known as the "voodoo" *Macbeth*, it was set in nineteenth-century Haiti and had an all-black, mainly amateur, cast. **Donald Wolfit** provided a momentary throwback to Victorian times with his blood-and-thunder touring production, which began life in 1937. Employing such devices as a change of wig for the hero (red in the first half, white in the second), it was loved by the public but the critics were merciless, James Agate describing it as a "ranting, raving, Saturday night melodrama". **Margaret Webster**'s production at New York's National Theatre in 1941 was conventional but rather less corny, and it boasted two outstanding performances – from **Maurice Evans** as Macbeth and **Judith Anderson** as Lady Macbeth.

*Macbeth*'s difficulty – or curse – is such that most critics list just a handful of defining postwar productions. **Glen Byam Shaw**'s at Stratford in 1955 remains a touchstone, partly because of its glamorous leading couple, **Laurence Olivier** and **Vivien Leigh**. Despite his idiosyncratic way with the verse, Olivier's hero received almost unanimous praise ("he radiates a kind of brooding sinister energy," wrote one critic, "a dazzling darkness …"), perhaps because he took the unusual step of building his character towards the end of the play; and even Leigh, long dismissed as a pretty face and little else, won plaudits. By contrast, the critics savaged **William Gaskill**'s modish Royal Court production eleven years later, partly because **Alec Guinness** as Macbeth was too low-key and **Simone Signoret** as Lady Macbeth largely unintelligible, but also because with its pared-down sets it refused to glamorize the play.

That reluctance to approach *Macbeth* as a heroic work also characterized what has been for many its most powerful recent incarnation, that directed at the RSC by **Trevor Nunn** from 1976 onwards. Audiences at Stratford's intimate The Other Place (and later in London) were exposed to an interpretation that magnified the play's unnerving darkness. Restricted originally by a budget of just £250, all the action took place within a small chalk circle – which Macbeth traversed anticlockwise, a demonic device – and gave unusual prominence to the Witches. Yet it was also psychologically gripping, notably in the compelling relationship between **Ian McKellen**'s gangly but magnetic Macbeth and **Judi Dench**'s powerhouse of a wife.

Only **Gregory Doran**'s 1999 RSC production, with **Antony Sher** as a bluff soldier and **Harriet Walter** as his wild-eyed spouse, gained anything like Nunn's effusive reviews, but in recent times *Macbeth* has received a number of innovative non-English reworkings – particularly in places where its political or philosophical content has acquired resonance. A translation by **Xu Xiaozhong** made many think of the tyrannical Mao Ze Dong when it appeared in Beijing in 1980, and elsewhere on the globe *Macbeth* has been grafted successfully onto folk drama, notably in India, with **B.V. Karanth**'s *Barnam Vana* (1979) from the south-western state of Karnataka; and **Lokendra Arambam**'s well-regarded *Stage of Blood*, which premiered in 1997 at Imphal in the northeast of the subcontinent. The UK has seen a number of touring foreign-language productions, notably **Yukio Ninagawa**'s picturesque but powerful Japanese version, which arrived in 1985; and **Welcome Msomi**'s popular Zulu reworking *uMbatha*, which appeared most recently at the London Globe in 2000.

Though often regarded as theatrically difficult, *Macbeth* has received considerable attention on screen, most clearly with big-budget movies such as those by **Akira Kurosawa** (1957) and **Roman Polanski** (1971); but also with smaller projects developed from stage productions – notably **Orson Welles's** typically idiosyncratic 1948 film; Hall of Fame's 1960 TV version with **Maurice Evans** and **Judith Anderson**; and **Trevor Nunn**'s TV adaptation (1978). It has also occasioned several spin-offs, among them gangster movies by **Ken Hughes** (*Joe Macbeth* from 1955) and **William Reilly** (*Men of Respect*, 1991). The 1982 BBC/Time-Life production was directed by **Jack Gold**, starring **Nicol Williamson** and **Jane Lapotaire**. The Beeb returned to the play in 1997 with **Penny Woolcock**'s *Macbeth on the Estate*, set on Birmingham's Ladywood estate and featuring a mostly non-professional cast drawn from the local area.

# Screen

### Throne of Blood (Kumonosu-Jo)
**T. Mifune, I. Yamada, M. Chiaki; Akira Kurosawa (dir.)**
Japan, 1957 ▷ BFI / Criterion **DVD** 📼

Akira Kurosawa had long aspired to transplant Shakespeare's own retelling of distant Scottish history to the screen, but, hearing that Orson Welles planned likewise, delayed doing so. Yet *Throne of Blood* (*Kumonosu-Jo*, "The Castle of the Spider's Web", in Japanese) is in an entirely different league from most films of Shakespeare. Set amidst a painstakingly realized warrior aristocracy of medieval Japan, it retains practically none of Shakespeare's language, thins out his characters (though the lead couple are powerfully played by the ever-fierce Toshiro Mifune and a chilling Isuzu Amada) and removes several key components of his plot. But what *Throne of Blood* lacks in linguistic texture it recreates through vibrant visual poetry and an impressive command of atmosphere, all marshalled by typically expert editing. Kurosawa has an innate grasp of what makes inspirational film, even if that means ignoring Shakespeare – so Tsusuki/Duncan's murder is handled wordlessly, while Washizu/Macbeth dies not in single combat but under a storm of arrows in a truly astonishing final sequence. Quintessential *auteur* cinema, and the most perfect Shakespearean movie in existence.

### Macbeth
**J. Finch, F. Annis, J. Stride; Roman Polanski (dir.)**
UK, 1971 ▷ Columbia Tristar **DVD** 📼

Immediately notorious because it was part-funded by Playboy mogul Hugh Hefner, this violent *Macbeth* also attracted

scandal because it seemed to draw on the director's own personal experiences – notably the brutal murder of his wife by followers of Charles Manson's cult. Behind the headlines, though, there lies a fine movie, co-scripted with drama critic Kenneth Tynan and filmed with thoroughgoing realism in a moody medieval Scotland (actually Wales). Polanski's emphasis is heavily on the lead couple, Jon Finch and the gamine Francesca Annis – both young, sexy and credible, if somewhat raw. Things fall apart, however, when it comes to audio: Polanski redubbed a large percentage of the film, and the results are mixed – partly because soliloquies are frequently done in voice-over, partly because it is clearly difficult to muster wit's-end terror in a sound booth. Two nuggets of trivia: contrary to popular rumour, Hefner did not insist that Annis's sleepwalking scene should be done in the nude (that was Polanski's idea); and fans of British low-end TV might enjoy spotting a youthful – and jowly – Keith Chegwin vamping it up as Fleance.

### Macbeth
**I. McKellen, J. Dench, J. Woodvine; Philip Casson (dir.)**
UK, 1978 ▷ Fremantle **DVD** 📼

Trevor Nunn's innovative 1976 RSC production stressed the play's suffocating claustrophobia by locking the action within a small circle, emphasizing its demonic qualities and deploying Ian McKellen's histrionic powers in the title role to devastating effect. Collaborating with Philip Casson in this reworking for Thames TV, Nunn determined to "photograph the text", nothing more, attempting to preserve what McKellen has called the "intimate horror" of the whole experience. In many ways video is the ideal medium for what is sometimes regarded as the finest of all TV Shakespeare adaptations, and it features particularly impressive performances from Judi Dench (Lady Macbeth) – her unearthly scream near the end of the play will have you cowering into the cushions – and John Woodvine as a granitic Banquo. McKellen himself occasionally risks overdoing it, but in a scenario this terrifying who could blame him?

## Audio

### Macbeth

**S. Dillane, F. Shaw, D. Conlan; Fiona Shaw (dir.)**
UK, 1998 ▷ Naxos ⊙ 🎞

Your ears prick up at the very opening of this *Macbeth*: over Stephen Warbeck's eerie music Fiona Shaw places the sound of shallow and anxious breathing – even before the Sisters begin their incantation. Shaw's taste for aural theatricality permeates this version: the spaces it creates are hallucinatory rather than sound-effects realistic, an adventurous strategy that works surprisingly well. Excellent performances, too, notably Shaw's own (unhistrionic, but all the better for it) Lady Macbeth alongside Stephen Dillane's soft-spoken hero, and there's a terrific cameo from Bill Paterson as the Porter. Some

might feel this production could be swifter, but it does at least emphasize *Macbeth*'s reflective qualities.

### Macbeth

**A. Guinness, P. Brown, A. Cruikshank**
UK, 1953 ▷ Pearl ⊙

Alec Guinness's one major shot at the role of Macbeth, at the Royal Court in 1966, was largely rubbished and he never attempted it again. That makes this 1953 recording his definitive version, and despite its dated air – most evident in some rather excitable sound effects – it has its attractions. Guinness himself sounds quiet and even weary in the role ("If it were done when 'tis done ..." has the air, rather brilliantly, of a middle-ranking civil servant planning a memo), and his attempts at tyrannical command ring increasingly false as the play progresses. Opposite him is Pamela Brown's caustic Lady Macbeth, never more alive than when scolding her low-performing husband yet able to raise hairs with the merest of whispers. Andrew Cruikshank is an aristocratic and resonant Banquo, more of a genuine power-broker than Macbeth will ever be, and the auld-world partnership of Macduff (Robin Bailey) and Malcom (Anthony Service) signal that Scotland will be more firmly ruled from now on.

The final moments of Lord Washizo (Toshiro Mifune) in *Throne of Blood* (1957), Kurosawa's brilliant film adaptation of *Macbeth*.

## Editions

### New Cambridge Shakespeare
**A.R. Braunmuller (ed.); 1997** ▷ Cambridge UP

Braunmuller's admirably full edition makes a clear first choice, distinguished by its habit of coming up with fresh angles on a play so critically worked over that editors sometimes struggle for new things to say. Thus here you'll find an engraving illustrating precisely what the Captain means when he describes Macbeth hacking into an enemy "from the nave to th' chaps"; plentiful information on the eerie context of Shakespeare's Witches; and historical detail on contemporary practice regarding the nursing of children. Nor does Braunmuller avoid the play's core issues: his thoughts are subtle and intelligently argued, drawing a useful distinction between "*Macbeth* in the mind" and "*Macbeth* in performance", the latter providing a detailed stage history. There is an intriguing appendix on "casting Macbeth", a perennial problem for directors and actors alike.

## Some criticism

### The Well Wrought Urn
**Cleanth Brooks; 1947** ▷ Harvest

This methodical, calm but brilliant account of *Macbeth*'s unsettling poetic qualities might seem a perverse recommendation were it not that many of the play's finest poetic moments seem in performance to be gone in a flash, such is the breakneck pace of its plot. Brooks was one of the shapers of the so-called "New Criticism" movement that appeared in the US during the 1940s and his essay on *Macbeth* is a classic, launching itself from the incandescent (if near-indecipherable) speech in which the hero compares the "pity" released at Duncan's death to "a naked new-born babe" (1.7.21) and hitching it to the submerged symbols that run throughout the play's language. Brooks refuses to give up on its difficulties, and what emerges is a reading of the play's imagery that will transform your understanding of Shakespeare's writing – even if it leaves your theatrical awareness none the wiser.

### King Lear, Macbeth, Indefinition, and Tragedy
**Stephen Booth; 1983** ▷ Yale UP

Stephen Booth is a superlative critic whose tenacious refusal to settle for easy answers is what most strongly characterizes his work. In *King Lear, Macbeth, Indefinition, and Tragedy* he spends much of his time worrying away at the (in)definitions of tragedy, taking his cue from Aristotle's ruminations in the *Poetics*. His conclusions in the case of *Macbeth* is that the play's brilliance lies in its restless reluctance to be defined *as* tragedy – despite being among Shakespeare's most celebrated uses of the tragic mode. Another section of the book suggests that our puzzled first responses to works of art often persist longer than we care to think (Booth admits that whenever he sees *Othello* he hopes against hope that Desdemona's apparent revival in Act Five will last).

# Measure for Measure

T
hough it's set in Vienna, *Measure for Measure*, Shakespeare's unsettling comedy of sex in the city, reflects more closely than anything else he wrote the
Jacobean London the playwright knew. Saturated with moral decline – something that all but killed its chances in the Victorian theatre – it moves between
court-room, prison, nunnery and brothel as the old tale of a corrupt judge
who propositions the sister of a defendant is worked through to a newly troubling conclusion. Coleridge thought it "the most painful – say rather the only painful"
play of Shakespeare's, and it is most often known as the first of his "problem comedies", a
group of plays whose hard-edged and cynical tone often seems to preclude fantasies of
lasting happiness. Yet this fable of justice, morality and power, perhaps intended for performance in front of the new King James I, is by no means clinical. The rich but scabrous
humour of the play's Viennese fleshpots has a kind of raw energy that frequently threatens
to overwhelm the main business of the plot, while the moral ambiguity of nearly every
character on stage (impossible to ignore in performance) makes it difficult to track the
course of *Measure for Measure* on a straightforward ethical spectrum.

[ DATE ]  Played at court on December 26, 1604, *Measure for Measure* was probably written up to a year before.
That performance, coupled with its thematic interest in Puritanism, law and governance, suggests that it draws
topical parallels with James I's rule (he acceded in 1603).

[ SOURCES ]  The play's chief sources are Giraldi Cinthio's Italian novella *Hecatommithi* (1565) and an English
play along similar lines, George Whetstone's *Promos and Cassandra* (1578). Other elements derive from dramas
by Shakespeare's contemporaries – Middleton's *The Phoenix*, Marston's *The Malcontent* and Jonson's *Sejanus*.

[ TEXTS ]  The Folio of 1623 provides the sole authoritative text, probably set from a promptbook.

## Interpreting the play

Hearing of a play named *Measure for Measure*, Shakespeare's contemporaries would in all likelihood have thought of one thing: God. More specifically, they would have thought of the
biblical injunction, contained in Matthew's gospel, about how a good Christian should behave
towards others. "Judge not, that ye be not judged," Christ advises his followers during the
Sermon on the Mount,

> With what judgement ye judge, ye shall be judged: And with what measure ye mete, it shall be
> measured to you again. Seest thou a mote in thy brother's eye, but perceivest not the beam that
> is in thine own eye? Or, how sayest thou to thy brother: Suffer me, I will pluck out a mote out of
> thine eye: and behold, a beam is in thine own eye? Thou hypocrite, first cast out the beam out
> of thine own eye: and then shalt thou see clearly, to pluck out the mote out of thy brother's eye.

**[Matthew 7:1–5]**

Christ's famous words insist that we should think before judging others; before presuming to
criticize another person (noticing the "mote" or speck in their eye) we should be careful not

## Major Characters & Synopsis

**Duke Vincentio** of Vienna
**Angelo**, the Duke's deputy
**Escalus**, an old councillor
**Claudio**, a young gentleman
**Juliet**, Claudio's betrothed
**Isabella**, Claudio's sister, a novice in a nunnery
**Lucio**, a "fantastic" (extravagant young man)
**Froth**, another gentleman
**Mistress Overdone**, a brothel-keeper
**Pompey**, Mistress Overdone's servant
**Elbow**, a constable
**Abhorson**, an executioner
**Barnadine**, a condemned prisoner
**Mariana**, Angelo's ex-fiancée
**Friar Peter**
**Francesca**, a nun
**Varrius**, a lord and friend of the Duke
A **Provost**, a **Justice** and others

**ACT 1**  Vienna is lawless and morally corrupt. Its ruler, the Duke, has decided to leave the city in the care of his puritanical deputy, Angelo, in the hope that he will reintroduce order while the Duke is away. But the Duke has an ulterior motive: instead of leaving town, he disguises himself as a friar in order to observe Angelo's actions. Angelo immediately announces that brothels are to be pulled down and the city's laws to be strictly applied. At one such brothel Pompey and Mistress Overdone discuss the proclamation when they are interrupted by Claudio, who has been arrested for getting Juliet, his betrothed, pregnant. Under the new regime Claudio faces execution, and in desperation sends Lucio to find his sister Isabella (who has just entered a nunnery) so that she can plead with Angelo on his behalf.

**ACT 2**  The practical problems of the clampdown are exposed when the doltish constable Elbow attempts to have Pompey and Froth tried for corrupting his wife. Isabella is then brought before Angelo to plead for her brother. The deputy is initially unmoved by her arguments, but gradually becomes touched by her virtue and courage. But he is also attracted to her, and when they meet again declares that he will save

her brother's life on one condition – that she sleeps with him. She is horrified and threatens to tell everyone, but realizes that she will not be believed. At the prison, meanwhile, the Duke reappears in disguise and lectures a penitent Juliet on her sinfulness.

**ACT 3**  The Duke (still in disguise) visits Claudio, and prepares him for death. Isabella arrives at the prison, and reluctantly tells her brother about Angelo's proposition. When he begs her to agree and save his life, she is outraged. The Duke has overheard their conversation, however, and suggests a solution: Isabella must trick Angelo into sleeping with his ex-fiancée, Mariana, in the belief that she is actually Isabella.

**ACT 4**  The bed-trick works, but the Duke discovers that Angelo has failed to keep his side of the bargain: Claudio still faces execution. Invoking the Duke's authority, he persuades the Provost that another prisoner – also under sentence of death – should be executed early, and that his head be sent to Angelo as proof of Claudio's death. He hides this from Isabella, however, who believes her brother is dead. The Duke then sends word to Escalus and Angelo that he is ready to return to Vienna.

**ACT 5**  At the city gates, the Duke (no longer disguised) meets Escalus and Angelo. Isabella is brought before him – unaware that he and the friar are the same – and denounces Angelo for his corruption. The Duke demands evidence and Mariana enters, claiming that she and Angelo are betrothed and have consummated their marriage. The confusion deepens as the Duke re-enters in disguise and backs up her story. But when he is accidentally unmasked, Angelo realizes that the truth is out and begs to be executed. Mariana then pleads for him and, as Claudio is revealed to be alive, Angelo is pardoned on condition he marries Mariana. The play closes with a final twist, however: the Duke asks Isabella whether she will marry *him* ...

to be blinded by our failings (the "beam" or block in our own). It has been suggested that Shakespeare might have faced censorship from the authorities for alluding so directly to the Bible: a few years after it was written, Puritan campaigners succeeded in pushing through a parliamentary Act banning the use of religious words or phrases on stage (see p.82).

Nor does he avoid the confrontational aspects of the parallel: while Jesus warns against the perils of passing judgement because we ourselves are fallible, *Measure for Measure* dramatizes an Italian tale about a corrupt official who falls into precisely that trap. In Giraldi Cinthio's *Hecatommithi*, a collection of tales that also provided the inspiration for *Othello*, Shakespeare found the story of a strict judge named Juriste who falls in love with Epitia, the younger sister of a man Juriste has condemned for rape, when she comes to plead for his life. Under pressure from her brother, the young woman relents to Juriste's demands, but no sooner has he taken her to bed than he orders that the brother be beheaded anyway. Epitia finds out and demands justice from the city's ruler, but finds that his punishment is to marry her to none other than Juriste. Fortunately, however, she realizes that she has fallen in love and everything ends happily.

Shakespeare made the story both richer in texture and even more replete with problems. His Isabella is not merely virtuous, she is a nun; her brother Claudio is guilty not of rape, but has merely slept with his betrothed. And Shakespeare makes a major role for the shadowy figure of Vienna's Duke, who leaves his deputy Angelo ruling in his absence and yet stays in the city disguised as a friar, safeguarding the comic resolution of a play which frequently threatens to be anything but. The Duke's motivation for involving himself in the lives of his subjects may be mysterious, but it does divert the play from outright tragedy. And yet the conclusion of Shakespeare's *Measure for Measure* is for most audiences its most surprising and perplexing aspect: having saved Isabella and her brother from the depredations of Angelo, Duke Vincentio decides that he wants the nun for himself.

## Most biting laws

The first words of *Measure for Measure* are "Of government", and the dominant action of the play concerns an experiment to see how best the people of Vienna can be governed – whether, in fact, they *can* be governed. The initial evidence is not promising. Having ruled Vienna leniently, Duke Vincentio has decided to try a stricter approach, but instead of implementing the crackdown himself he leaves his puritanical deputy Angelo (a man "whose blood / Is very snow-broth", according to the libertine Lucio (1.4.56–7)) in charge. As the Duke explains to Friar Peter, the city needs harsh measures, and fast:

> We have strict statutes and most biting laws,
> The needful bits and curbs to headstrong weeds,
> Which for this fourteen years we have let slip;
> Even like an o'ergrown lion in a cave
> That goes not out to prey. Now, as fond fathers,
> Having bound up the threat'ning twigs of birch
> Only to stick it in their children's sight
> For terror, not to use, in time the rod
> More mocked becomes than feared: so our decrees,
> Dead to infliction, to themselves are dead;
> And Liberty plucks Justice by the nose,
> The baby beats the nurse, and quite athwart
> Goes all decorum.

**[1.3.19–31]**

Just as the Duke has been struggling (and failing) to maintain his power for all those years in office, here it his language that runs riot. He manages to say "headstrong weeds" rather than "headstrong steeds", so making nonsense of his own figure of speech, and the jumble of metaphors he calls on to describe the way in which "decorum" has been thwarted sounds every bit as chaotic as the city he describes. Though he does his best to speak like a Puritan zealot, the Duke's analysis sounds only troubled in its attempt to keep things under control.

At least Vincentio is no longer having to deal with the real business of government; Angelo, on the other hand, is confronted in the first scene of Act Two with the gravest threat yet to his new regime – people themselves. Despite his insistence to Escalus that "we must not make a scarecrow of the law" (2.1.1), Angelo has reckoned without officials like Constable Elbow, who manages to transform the task of making the law look ridiculous into a full-time occupation. Elbow has arrested the pimp Pompey on the basis that Pompey has done something to Elbow's wife (quite what Pompey has done Elbow never gets round to explaining), and the comic routine between the two – Elbow's malapropisms versus Pompey's rambling answers – lasts the rest of the scene. Angelo survives only a few minutes before storming off, leaving Escalus to deal with the mess. Though the scene is funny, it soon hits some of the bigger questions investigated by the play. When Escalus demands, "What do you think of the trade [prostitution], Pompey? Is it a lawful trade?", Pompey's reply is disarmingly simple:

> POMPEY  If the law would allow it, sir.
> ESCALUS  But the law will not allow it, Pompey; nor it shall not be allowed in Vienna.
> POMPEY  Does your worship mean to geld and spay all the youth of the city?
> ESCALUS  No, Pompey.
> POMPEY  Truly, sir, in my poor opinion they will to't then.
>
> **[2.1.215–23]**

In other words, until such time as there is no call for sex (because Escalus and his colleagues would "geld and spay", or sterilize, the city's young people), illicit sexual activity will thrive. The comedy here is double-edged: though Pompey's interpretation of "lawful" wouldn't stand up in court, it suggests the futility of banning something which, however morally repugnant, is a constant of human nature – Pompey's "trade" is, after all, the oldest trade there is. And though these issues vex lawmakers today as much as ever, they would have had a special resonance for Jacobean audiences visiting a theatre located in Southwark, part of the so-called "liberties" outside city jurisdiction. Prostitution thrived just outside the Globe's doors, and the playwright's Vienna is pointedly similar to the London he knew so intimately.

Early audiences would also have had sympathy with another victim of Angelo's new moral order, Claudio. He has been arrested for sleeping with his fiancée, Juliet, before they are officially married – technically fornication, but a common offence in early modern England, and one that Shakespeare knew only too well (when he married Anne Hathaway in 1582, she was several months pregnant). To make matters more complicated, Claudio claims that "upon a true contract, / I got possession of Julietta's bed" (1.2.133–4), in effect that they are engaged – in this era often interpreted as serious a commitment as marriage itself. And yet he faces the death penalty.

*Almost all that is here worthy of Shakespeare at any time is worthy of Shakespeare at his highest: and of this every touch, every line, every incident, every syllable, belongs to pure and simple tragedy.*

A.C. Swinburne on *Measure for Measure*, in *A Study of Shakespeare* (1879)

Isabella's predicament is different, but it is no less morally difficult. Dragged from the convent in which she is about to become a nun, Isabella has the unenviable task of pleading for a brother whose "vice" (as she admits to Angelo) she "abhors". Unlike Portia in *The Merchant of Venice*, Isabella – on the point of cutting herself off from male company for good – has no masculine disguise behind which to hide. Quite the contrary: it is her womanliness that Claudio is relying upon ("in her youth," he remarks, "There is a prone and speechless dialect / Such as move men" (1.2.170–2)). Those persuasive gifts are undeniable: arguing in front of Angelo that "it is excellent / To have a giant's strength, but it is tyrannous / To use it like a giant," she draws upon the full rhetoric of Christianity to argue her position:

> Merciful heaven,
> Thou rather with thy sharp and sulphurous bolt
> Split'st the unwedgeable and gnarlèd oak
> Than the soft myrtle. But man, proud man,
> Dressed in a little brief authority,
> Most ignorant of what he's most assured,
> His glassy essence, like an angry ape
> Plays such fantastic tricks before high heaven
> As makes the angels weep, who, with our spleens,
> Would all themselves laugh mortal.

[2.2.117–26]

Though Isabella's impassioned words are not easy to untangle (she pictures apish, "proud man" laughing at sins that make angels "weep", but also those angels laughing themselves to death at our weakness), their argument – that "merciful heaven" should be reflected here on earth – is impossible to misunderstand.

## Th'offence pardons itself

But Isabella's speech has a disconcerting effect on its auditor, Angelo. He is smitten, and – stunned by these new feelings – soon offers her the deal that we have been expecting all along. This is the lurching crux on which *Measure for Measure* will turn – whether Isabella should allow herself to be raped by him in order to save her brother, or allow Claudio to die and hold onto her convictions. Her response to this, which is to decide that "more than our brother is our chastity" (2.4.185) has attracted violent disagreement: she has been attacked as a "vixen" and "self-absorbed" (by male critics, perhaps unsurprisingly); but also defended as "saintly", utterly committed to ideals few of us have the courage to face. For his part Claudio is initially convinced that she must save herself, but, confronting the logical outcome, soon changes his mind. "Death is a fearful thing," he reminds a horrified Isabella:

ISABELLA  And shamèd life a hateful.
CLAUDIO
> Ay, but to die, and go we know not where;
> To lie in cold obstruction, and to rot;
> This sensible warm motion to become
> A kneaded clod, and the dilated spirit
> To bathe in fiery floods, or to reside
> In thrilling region of thick-ribbèd ice;
> To be imprisoned in the viewless winds,
> And blown with restless violence round about
> The pendent world; or to be worse than worst
> Of those that lawless and incertain thought
> Imagine howling—'tis too horrible!

[3.1.116–28]

Though he is hardly a Hamlet, Claudio takes up the Prince's musings on "the undiscovered country" and argues, mapping it out in fearful detail, that it must be more horrific than anything life can offer. Though nearer to it than most, he articulates the main problem repeatedly posed by the play: whether it is preferable to allow life, in all its flawed corruption; or cut it off.

In *Measure for Measure* we are forced to see every point of view, and to ask every question. Claudio has sinned, but should he die? Is it right that his sister should submit to Angelo in order to save him? Can the end (saving a life) ever justify the means (rape)? Can "measure" answer for "measure"? The play, following its title, places these incommensurable ethical issues side by side and demands that they be resolved.

Its proposed solution is, if anything, yet more fraught. Disguised as a friar, the Duke has observed Isabella's predicament. Revealing the fact that Angelo has all this time been "affianced" to another woman (and thus uncomfortably resembles Claudio), Vincentio improvises a plan – Mariana sleeping with Angelo instead of Isabella – that will solve everything at a stroke. The so-called "bed-trick" is Shakespeare's addition to the story, as theatrically elegant as it is morally suspect. "Th'offence pardons itself," as the Duke breezily observes later in the play (5.1.533), opting to evade the full implications of those words.

Though deceit and disguise are familiar enough in Shakespearian comedy, the Duke's actions as *Measure for Measure* heads towards its denouement put comic ideals under almost impossible strain. As in *All's Well*, the play's climax is extended over a breathtakingly tense final scene. Here Vincentio virtuosically shuttles between his multiple personae, staging a grand return to Vienna as the Duke while also maintaining his friar's disguise. First Isabella arrives, unaware that Claudio has been spared and hysterically demanding "justice, justice, justice, justice" (5.1.25); then Mariana appears, claiming to have slept with Angelo as strongly as Isabella claims that he raped her. The mystery deepens:

DUKE  What, are you married?
MARIANA  No, my lord.
DUKE  Are you a maid?
MARIANA  No, my lord.
DUKE  A widow then?
MARIANA  Neither, my lord.
DUKE  Why, you are nothing then; neither maid, widow, nor wife!

**[5.1.170–7]**

The Duke puts himself in a position where only he can solve the conundrums Mariana speaks of, and, after further delay, he does so, theatrically emerging from disguise to the disbelief of everyone present.

The punishments and rewards he produces, however dazzling, leave many of the play's characters stunned into silence. Angelo is married to Mariana, but promptly sentenced to death – until, that is, Claudio is produced, apparently back from the dead. For his impertinence to the Duke, Lucio is initially threatened with the hangman's noose, then told to marry a prostitute (whom he got pregnant) instead. Though it is impossible to take it entirely seriously, the ferocity of Lucio's response to his apparently lucky escape nevertheless hangs in the air:

Marrying a punk, my lord, is pressing to death, whipping, and hanging.

**[5.1.521–2]**

And the Duke's insistence that his comedy must end in marriages goes even further. "Dear Isabel," he calls,

I have a motion much imports your good,
Whereto, if you'll a willing ear incline,
What's mine is yours, and what is yours is mine.

[5.1.533–6]

These words all but finish the play, and Isabella is given no opportunity to respond. Unlike Shakespeare's earlier comedies, marriage here does not grow organically from its characters, even if it is a neat conclusion to events. As *Measure for Measure* ends, Shakespeare makes it seem as if happiness has never seemed further away.

# Stage history and adaptations

A play recorded as "Mesur for Mesur" by one "Shaxberd" was acted at **court** in front of James I on December 26, 1604 – the first performance we know of, probably with **Richard Burbage**, the company's star actor, as the Duke. In 1621, **Thomas Middleton**, possibly a collaborator on *Timon of Athens*, adapted *Measure*; in his version the city comedy aspects of the plot are beefed up to suit late Jacobean taste.

Shakespeare might well have approved, but it's difficult to imagine that he would have felt the same for **Sir William Davenant**'s *The Law Against Lovers*, staged in 1662. This excised most of the play's underworld characters and replaced them with Beatrice and Benedick from *Much Ado*, while Angelo became a Cromwellian Puritan. Another adaptation, this time premiered in 1700 by **Charles Gildon**, sounds, if anything, even odder: breezily entitled *Measure for Measure, or Beauty the Best Advocate*, it interspersed stretches of Shakespeare with Purcell's *Dido and Aeneas*. Gildon's Angelo and Mariana are already married, presumably to give the bed-trick a sheen of respectability.

Neither Davenant nor Gildon's versions enjoyed popularity, and it wasn't long before Shakespeare's play returned. During the eighteenth century and into the next, the star roles of Isabella and the Duke became much-prized vehicles for leading actors: **James Quin** first played Vincentio in 1720, and was joined by **Susannah Cibber**'s Isabella in 1731; **John Henderson** and **Mary Yates** stepped into their shoes in the 1770s and 80s. But it was the pairing of **John Philip Kemble** and his sister **Sarah Siddons** from 1794 onwards that defined this phase in the play's history. Kemble's version of *Measure* was typically conservative, with sexual and subversive overtones airbrushed out, emphasis being placed instead on Siddons's Isabella and her brother's patrician Duke. Siddons dominated the role so effectively that she was still playing it in 1812 at the age of 57, creaking joints notwithstanding.

Doubts about *Measure*'s morals had become widespread by the first decades of the nineteenth century, and it was produced with declining frequency. New York audiences were first given the chance to see it in 1818, but versions in London fared badly. Though **Samuel Phelps** at Sadler's Wells employed a text from which all indecorous language had been rooted out ("not an offensive phrase left", applauded *The Athenaeum*), it failed to take off and the play languished in the doldrums during the rest of the Victorian era.

Its fortunes were to change, however. **William Poel** chose *Measure* as the first play on which to attempt his experiments in historicist staging, and his production of 1893 was hailed as revolutionary. Though Poel constructed an "Elizabethan" stage for the play, his interpretative ideas were less radical: the text was still heavily cut and the *Leamington Courier* felt able to proclaim that it was a "great purifying influence" when Poel brought it to Stratford in 1908 (admittedly to resistance from the local vicar). Poel's disciple **William Bridges-Adams** risked an uncut text at the same venue in 1923, leading the *Birmingham Post* to suggest that, if Shakespeare were still alive, he would certainly be censored. **Tyrone Guthrie**'s fine Old Vic

From left to right: the Duke (David Troughton), the Provost (Angus Wright) and Escalus (Mike Grady) discuss the imminent execution of Angelo. A Complicite/National Theatre co-production, 2004.

production ten years later was notable for the sinister Angelo of **Charles Laughton** ("a lustful black bat" was how the *Daily Telegraph* described him), but it still failed to attract audiences – despite supportive letters by T.S. Eliot and John Gielgud.

Gielgud's enthusiasm for the play proved prescient: he was to play Angelo in a Stratford production of 1950 mounted by the young **Peter Brook** (one of several Shakespearian comedies he rescued from relative obscurity), in what turned out to be *Measure*'s defining postwar staging. A foreboding fixed set looming throughout, Brook caught the play's darkness and, bravely, its comedy (many thought of Bruegel, but to the director it was "Dostoevskian"). But he still pushed a conformist line: the script was skewed to flatter **Harry Andrews**'s benevolent Duke, and **Barbara Jefford** brought to Isabella all the innocence of her 19 years – though in the final scene she was instructed to pause for as long as she thought the audience could stand before deciding to plead for Angelo's life. Kenneth Tynan thought this production "a perfect marriage of shrill imagination and sober experience".

Brook's advocacy – along with a burgeoning interest in its audacious blend of repression, power and sexuality – saw *Measure* more popular postwar than ever before. **Berthold Brecht**'s Berliner Ensemble acted their version in 1952, and two years later **James Mason**, who had played Claudio in Guthrie's Old Vic production, played Angelo for the same director at Stratford, Ontario. But in British theatre the play's equivocal view of politics was stressed most persuasively by **John Barton** at Stratford in 1970, with **Sebastian Shaw** playing a capricious Duke to **Ian Richardson**'s icy Angelo. Barton also made the comedy's conclusion truly problematic – following the Duke's marriage offer, **Estelle Kohler**'s Isabella simply turned to the audience in despair. **Keith Hack**'s staging at the same venue four years later proved notorious, not least because in the closing scene the Duke was flown in on a bar labelled "Deus ex machina".

Charles Marowitz penned a typically fierce adaptation in 1975 at the Open Space, which restored much of Cinthio's narrative yet added new material to create a satire on power – most jarringly when Isabella (**Ciaran Madden**) was denied justice by the Duke (**Geoffrey Staines**). Since then two different kinds of *Measure* have predominated in English-language productions. The first was launched in 1974 by **Jonathan Miller**, who set the play in a pre-Nazi Austria steadily overtaken by fascism – an approach echoed by **Nicholas Hytner** at the RSC in 1988 and **Michael Boyd** with the same company a decade later. The other tendency has been to portray another kind of Vienna, that inhabited by Sigmund Freud. **Robin Philips** tried this at Stratford, Ontario in 1975, but for many critics **Trevor Nunn**'s 1991 version at the studio-scale The Other Place has been the most revealing attempt to date to view the play through its intimate psychology: **David Haig**'s fussy, nervous Angelo became coldly brutal when confronted by **Claire Skinner**'s schoolgirlish Isabella.

Other directors have brought out the contemporary relevance of the play, notably **Declan Donnellan** in his 1994 Cheek By Jowl production, which witnessed Isabella becoming an increasingly isolated figure in a world of slippery moral relativism. Ten years on **Simon McBurney** emphasized the symbiotic relationship between the world of politics and the world of the brothel, dovetailing their respective scenes in a fast and fluid Complicite production at the National Theatre. TV monitors were employed both for the surveillance of political prisoners (dressed in Guantánamo Bay orange) and for the projection of pornography. The moral ambiguity of the Duke's actions – powerfully conveyed by **David Troughton** – culminated in the chilling image of him coaxing a stunned Isabella (**Naomi Frederick**) towards a vast double bed that had suddenly been illuminated at the back of the stage.

Despite its recent popularity, there is no film of *Measure for Measure*. Only one TV version exists, part of the BBC/Time-Life complete Shakespeare and widely regarded as one of the best in that series. It was directed by **Desmond Davis**, with **Tim Pigott-Smith**, **Kenneth Colley** and **Kate Nelligan** as Angelo, the Duke and Isabella respectively, and aired in 1979.

## Screen

**Measure for Measure**
K. Colley, K. Nelligan, T. Pigott-Smith; Desmond Davis (dir.)
UK, 1979 ▷ Ambrose Video (BBC) **DVD**

The BBC/Time-Life Shakespeare series was always a bit hit-and-miss, and has not worn the years well: this seventeenth-century *Measure*, recently rereleased in the States by Ambrose Video, is as close as the project has to a jewel in the crown. The budgetary and creative restrictions that torpedoed others in the series – flimsy sets, tawdry costuming, woeful picture quality – here become a kind of virtue, with gloomy interior spaces and a down-at-heel feel adding to the play's subterranean atmosphere (an atmosphere only occasionally punctured by over-zealous sound effects). The cast, too, is excellent: Kate Nelligan's Isabella is a *tour de force* of righteous (but sympathetic) virtue; Kenneth Colley's Duke can twinkle when he wants, but has plentiful reserves of shadiness; Tim Pigott-Smith's Angelo has unsettling menace; John McEnery's pompous Lucio has it coming to him. Despite the sometimes painfully literal camerawork, the only real flaws surface in the underworld scenes – difficult enough on stage, never mind in a studio. And how do they handle the end? Well, that would be telling …

## Audio

**Measure for Measure**
R. Allam, S. Russell Beale, S. Gonet; Clive Brill (dir.)
UK, 1998 ▷ Arkangel ⊙ [▭]

The contrasting worlds of *Measure for Measure* – its schizoid splits between the room of state, the brothel, the jail and the confessional – are convincingly conveyed in this production. It is all too clear that decisions made at the clipped and somewhat sterile court (memorably embodied in Roger Allam's nicely anxious Duke and Christopher Benjamin's sober Escalus) have little hope of restraining life elsewhere in the city (as becomes clear in the wild exchange between Desmond Barritt's irrepressibly Welsh Pompey and Simon Russell Beale's fatefully precise Angelo). Russell Beale is perfectly cast, capable of evoking sympathy yet deploying an undertow of megalomania that makes his resignation to "our evils" both inevitable and shocking. As Isabella Stella Gonet communicates well the character's unwitting sexuality as well as her fierce rage when cornered, and the intense scenes between her and Angelo are in many ways the highlight of this recording.

## Editions

### New Cambridge Shakespeare
**Brian Gibbons (ed.); 1991** ▷ Cambridge UP

There is no shying away from the challenges of *Measure for Measure*, and the play has produced some of the best editions of Shakespeare in existence. J.W. Lever's scrupulous and engaging Arden 2 edition (1965) was one of the best in that series, and is still well worth consulting. But Brian Gibbons's version for New Cambridge (he is the current series editor) is even better, aided by a stage history which takes into account the late-twentieth-century revival of interest in the play and providing a decent amount of space on the critical dogfights it has spawned. Gibbons's notes are also exemplary, and his treatment of a quirky text, while more invasive than some would prefer, is subtle and intelligent.

## Some criticism

### Speechless Dialect
**Philip C. McGuire; 1985** ▷ California UP [o/p]

Isabella's notorious wordlessness at the end of *Measure for Measure*, as McGuire shows, is just one of many Shakespearian "open silences" whose meaning is as debatable – and significant – as any of the words in the script. Though it dates from the same year as *Political Shakespeare*, McGuire's

approach could not be more different, focusing closely on performance history and text to develop a study into the "silences that Shakespeare's words impose upon characters who remain alive". His results suggest the complex and suggestive possibilities offered by plays as rich as *Twelfth Night*, *The Tempest*, *Lear* – and of course *Measure for Measure*.

### Political Shakespeare
**Jonathan Dollimore and Alan Sinfield (eds); rev. 1994** ▷ Manchester UP / Cornell UP

A play as perennially provocative as *Measure for Measure* demands confrontational reading, and Dollimore and Sinfield's collection, now in its second edition, has raised many hackles since it appeared in 1985. Published as a kind of manifesto for "cultural materialism" – a term coined by Raymond Williams which came to characterize a Marxist-inflected school of critics – *Political Shakespeare* remains the best way to grapple with the benefits (and pitfalls) of applying recent critical "-isms", among them feminism, post-structuralism and post-colonialism, to Shakespeare. Though some of the essays here have dated badly, both of those dedicated to *Measure for Measure* are as fresh and engaging as ever – Kathleen McLuskie on the "patriarchal Bard" and Jonathan Dollimore on "transgression and surveillance". Could be best read in conjunction/argument with a more traditionalist approach, such as that offered by G. Wilson Knight in *The Wheel of Fire* (see p.182).

# The Merchant of Venice

V iewed one way, *The Merchant of Venice* is anti-Semitic propaganda: a Christian merchant becomes indebted to a rapacious Jewish moneylender, Shylock, who seizes on the merchant's bankruptcy to demand repayment in the grisly form of a pound of the debtor's flesh. Viewed another way, the play's most tragic character is Shylock himself: a man abused by the Christians of Venice, robbed and deserted by his own daughter, and finally humiliated by being forced to abandon his own religion and convert to Christianity. Both sides of the story are there in this brilliant and troubling play, and it's easy to feel that they're irreconcilable: what Keats called Shakespeare's "negative capability" – his capacity for making audiences see things from multiple angles – here makes for disturbing viewing. Shylock may be descended from the devilish Jewish villains that were a staple of Christian storytelling, but Shakespeare makes it impossible to view him as simply evil; while the Christians of the play, for all their apparent civility, are racist, fixated by money and in the end brutally vicious. Yet *The Merchant*, which contains so much hatred, is also a comedy of love, and it's in this – in the collision between the two folk stories that were Shakespeare's sources – that the play throws up its most searching questions, in particular the involvement of the wealthy heroine Portia in the grubby battle for money and life at the centre of the plot. It is impossible to sit on the fence when watching *The Merchant*, and the issues it raises about religious intolerance and conflict seem more pressing now than ever before.

**[DATE]**  Certainly in existence by July 1598, the *Merchant* was possibly being acted 1596–97.

**[SOURCES]**  Barabas, the antihero of Marlowe's *The Jew of Malta* (c.1589), looms large, but a more specific source is Giovanni Fiorentino's fourteenth-century tale collection *Il Pecorone* ("The Dunce"). Myriad other analogues include an anonymous play, *The Jew* (c.1578), though the major plot elements – the flesh-bond and the story of the three caskets – may derive from folk roots.

**[TEXTS]**  The play's most important text is its first quarto printing, Q1 (1600), probably set from a scribal copy of Shakespeare's manuscript; both the second quarto (Q2, dated 1600 but in fact 1619) and the First Folio versions are based upon it.

## Interpreting the play

Given its deliberately flat title, the plot of *The Merchant of Venice* can seem strange, even bizarre. It meshes two great folk stories – the story of the creditor who attempts to secure a pound of flesh instead of repayment; the tale of the lover who wins his lady through a riddle game and three caskets – and works them out in painstaking detail. Though hardly the only comedy of Shakespeare's to use folk motifs, critics have frequently been struck by the *Merchant*'s fantastical, even improbable qualities: the director Harley Granville-Barker infamously declared it a "fairy tale", adding that "there is no more reality in Shylock's bond and the Lord of Belmont's will than in Jack and the Beanstalk".

## Major Characters & Synopsis

**Antonio**, a merchant from Venice
**Bassanio**, Antonio's friend, suitor to Portia
**Lorenzo**, a friend of Antonio and Bassanio, in
    love with Jessica
**Graziano**, another friend
**Saliero** and **Soliano**, acquaintances
**Leonardo**, Bassanio's servant
**Shylock**, a Jewish moneylender
**Jessica**, Shylock's daughter
**Tubal**, another Jewish moneylender
**Lancelot**, Shylock's clownish servant, later
    Bassanio's
**Gobbo**, Lancelot's father
**Portia**, an heiress from Belmont (later disguised
    as **Balthasar**, a lawyer)
**Nerissa**, Portia's gentlewoman (later disguised as
    Balthasar's clerk)
**Balthasar** and **Stephano**, Portia's servants
**Princes of Morocco** and **Aragon**, Portia's
    suitors
**Duke of Venice**

**ACT 1** Bassanio needs a favour from his close
friend Antonio – money in order to woo the
wealthy heiress Portia. Though Antonio's capital is
tied up overseas, he gladly agrees to let Bassanio
borrow the money in his name. Bassanio
arranges a loan with the moneylender Shylock,
who spots an opportunity to be revenged on his
old foe Antonio – jokingly suggesting a contract
stipulating that if the money is not repaid on time,
Shylock can have a pound of Antonio's flesh.
Confident that his cash flow will improve, Antonio
consents. In Belmont, meanwhile, Portia reviews
her father's will, which insists that she must marry
the suitor who correctly chooses among three
caskets of gold, silver and lead. Unfortunately, the
candidates so far – excepting Bassanio – do not
look promising.

**ACT 2** Lancelot informs his old father that he
has decided to leave Shylock's service and the
pair ask Bassanio if Lancelot can serve him
instead. Shylock's daughter, Jessica, is also planning to desert her father, in order to elope with
Lorenzo, a Christian. Back in Belmont, the Prince
of Morocco agrees to take part in the contest for
Portia's hand but loses when he opens the gold

casket. The Prince of Aragon, who chooses the
silver one, fares no better.

**ACT 3** Shylock is incensed by his daughter's
flight and the fact that she has stolen money from
him, but is cheered by news that one of Antonio's
merchant ships has sunk, and bankruptcy looks
likely. In Belmont, Portia tries to dissuade Bassanio
from choosing a casket, in order to prolong his
company. Undeterred, he chooses the leaden casket, and is rewarded with a message granting him
Portia's hand. Inspired, Graziano announces that
he and Nerissa (Portia's gentlewoman) also wish to
marry. But the two couples' joy is soured by news
that Antonio's business has indeed collapsed and
Shylock is after his flesh. While Bassanio rushes
back to Venice with the money, Portia has another
plan: she and Nerissa will follow him undercover
and see how they can help.

**ACT 4** Though Bassanio has arrived back in
Venice and offers to repay Antonio's debt twice
over, Shylock demands nothing less than his legal
rights. The Duke is stalling for time when a young
lawyer, "Balthasar" (Portia in disguise), arrives with
Nerissa (also disguised) acting as her clerk. When
their appeals to Shylock's mercy fail, Antonio's
fate seems sealed and Shylock prepares to make
the fatal incision. Suddenly, however,
Balthasar/Portia stops him, stating that although
he is entitled to a pound of flesh he may shed not
a drop of blood. Stunned by this brilliant legal
technicality, Shylock agrees to take the money
after all. But the judgement is not over: she also
informs him that, as an alien attempting to take
the life of a Venetian, he faces the death penalty.
Though Shylock is immediately pardoned by the
Duke, he is forced to give up half his wealth and
convert to Christianity.

**ACT 5** Returning in triumph to Belmont, the
men are met by their wives, who are not
impressed to learn that Bassanio and Graziano
have given away their wedding rings to the
"lawyers" who defeated Shylock. Portia and
Nerissa make them squirm for as long as possible – before, brandishing the rings, they gleefully
relate their coup.

But if the play seems at times like a fairy tale, it does not shirk the everyday messiness of human psychology. At its centre is Antonio, the merchant of the title, who begins the action with famous words dwelling on the shortcomings of rational explanation. "In sooth," he complains to his acquaintances Saliero and Soliano, "I know not why I am so sad,"

> It wearies me, you say it wearies you,
> But how I caught it, found it, or came by it,
> What stuff 'tis made of, whereof it is born,
> I am to learn;
> And such a want-wit sadness makes of me
> That I have much ado to know myself.
>
> [1.1.1–7]

Antonio is not on speaking terms with his "sadness", and though many critics have tried to explain it, the answer eludes them too. Noting that Antonio travels through the play as an outsider – never more clearly than in the last scene, where he is a solitary figure surrounded by couples – some have suggested that he is a kind of scapegoat in the play, the "tainted wether of the flock" (4.1.113), as he puts it, who will inevitably suffer for his friends' sake. Less complicatedly, perhaps, his melancholy has been called a kind of *Weltschmertz* ("world-weariness"), and in a play where happiness is as much a commodity as anything else he is not the only sufferer.

## And now worth nothing

It is revealing of Shakespeare's Venice, however, that Antonio's companions do not hesitate to speculate what they think is the matter. "Your mind is tossing on the ocean," Saliero suggests, among the "argosies" (merchant ships) Antonio's trade relies on. "Should I go to church," Saliero continues,

> And see the holy edifice of stone
> And not bethink me straight of dangerous rocks
> Which, touching but my gentle vessel's side,
> Would scatter all her spices on the stream,
> Enrobe the roaring waters with my silks,
> And, in a word, but even now worth this,
> And now worth nothing?
>
> [1.1.29–36]

The thought of religion does not inspire religious thoughts in Saliero – or at least only makes him think on Mammon. Though capital is all, its perilous instability is part of the bargain: worth "this" one moment, "nothing" the next. And though Antonio rejects Saliero's diagnosis, the merchant is not about to deny the significance of money.

> *For the Venetians, money is a medium of exchange representing not the goods and services of academic economists, but the passions of love and hate.*
>
> Alexander Leggatt, *Shakespeare's Comedy of Love* (1974)

Historically infamous as a centre of European commerce, Venice in Shakespeare's play oozes conspicuous consumption: its citizens organize masques, music and revels, and spend a great deal – as the moneylender Shylock realizes, quite literally to his cost, when his daughter Jessica splurges in "one night fourscore ducats" after running off with Lorenzo (accompanied by much of her father's wealth). This leads, of course, into the play's central issue, which dwells heavily on borrowing and debt. Shakespeare wishes his audience to be under no illusions that consumption costs; Bassanio's own taste for the high life has left him in dire financial straits, as he explains to Antonio early on:

> 'Tis not unknown to you, Antonio,
> How much I have disabled mine estate
> By something showing a more swelling port
> Than my faint means would grant continuance,
> Nor do I now make moan to be abridged
> From such a noble rate; but my chief care
> Is to come fairly off from the great debts
> Wherein my time, something too prodigal,
> Hath left me gaged.
>
> **[1.1.122–30]**

Though Bassanio expresses his indebtedness somewhat coyly, it is clear that in Venice money talks. His solution is to get more of it, by launching an expedition to woo the "richly left" heiress Portia, which he hopes will secure his long-term economic future.

There are shades here of Petruccio in the *Shrew*, but the tone is more serious, not least because money actually delineates the friendship between the two men. "To you, Antonio, / I owe the most in money and in love," Bassanio insists, and Antonio urges him in turn not to doubt their relationship:

> You know me well, and herein spend but time
> To wind about my love with circumstance;
> And out of doubt you do me now more wrong
> In making question of my uttermost
> Than if you had made waste of all I have.
>
> **[1.1.153–7]**

Backed by Antonio's coffers (or rather a debt made to refill them), Bassanio travels from Venice to Belmont in order to woo Portia and, in the climax of the plot's first phase, takes part in the bizarre game laid out in her father's will: selecting from three caskets by working out the riddles inscribed on them. Her first suitor, the Prince of Morocco, chooses the golden casket and loses out; as does the Prince of Aragon, who opts for the silver. It is left to Bassanio – inevitably – to choose the leaden casket (paradoxically the most valuable, as Bassanio adeptly realizes) and with it win Portia's hand. Lest we should ignore this com-modification of the play's heroine, Shakespeare makes Portia herself sketch its terms. Taking Bassanio's hand, she explains, "myself and what is mine to you and yours / Is now converted,"

> But now I was the lord
> Of this fair mansion, master of my servants,
> Queen o'er myself; and even now, but now,
> This house, these servants, and this same myself
> Are yours, my lord's.
>
> **[3.2.66–71]**

This verbal balance sheet is, as she describes it a few lines earlier, the "full sum of me", and the lot is now in her lover's possession.

# The means whereby I live

The first and most comic phase of the play is over. But, as we already know, it has always been underpinned by more unsettling forces. "When I told you / My state was nothing," Bassanio tells Portia soon after their marriage is agreed,

> I should then have told you
> That I was worse than nothing, for indeed
> I have engaged myself to a dear friend,
> Engaged my friend to his mere enemy,
> To feed my means.
>
> [3.2.256–61]

Antonio's "mere enemy", as Bassanio calls him, is Shylock, the moneylender who stands as close to the centre of the play as his real-life counterparts were integral to the Elizabethan economy. Usurers were hated as a matter of course, but in Shakespeare's Venice that loathing takes on a specific racial shading. Shylock is Jewish, and in *The Merchant* he is never allowed to forget it. Most often the Venetians simply call him "the Jew" and, for those content to borrow from him while simultaneously despising his religion and people, he may as well have no other identity (in Shakespeare's source, an Italian tale entitled *Il Pecorone*, he is not even given a name).

Shylock himself continually asserts his exclusion from those who make no attempt to hide their hatred for him. Angered and grief-stricken by his daughter's elopement, he savagely turns on the Venetians Saliero and Soliano when they jokingly assert that he has nothing against Antonio. "He hath disgraced me, and hindered me half a million," Shylock cries,

> laughed at my losses, mocked at my gains, scorned my nation, thwarted my bargains, cooled my friends, heated mine enemies, and what's his reason?—I am a Jew. Hath not a Jew eyes? Hath not a Jew hands, organs, dimensions, senses, affections, passions; fed with the same food, hurt with the same weapons, subject to the same diseases, healed by the same means, warmed and cooled by the same winter and summer as a Christian is? If you prick us do we not bleed? If you tickle us do we not laugh? If you poison us do we not die? And if you wrong us do we not revenge?
>
> [3.1.50–62]

We have no reason to doubt a word, for even when taking his money Antonio made no secret of his distaste for Shylock, his willingness to "spit" on the usurer (1.3.129).

It's hard to know how Shylock's impassioned speech would have been heard by Shakespeare's first audiences. Some Jews did live in Elizabethan London, working mostly as merchants, and sixteenth-century Venice was notorious for its Ghetto, into which all of the city's large Jewish community was demeaningly and squalidly crammed. On the English stage, meanwhile, Jews were unremittingly caricatured as villains, and Marlowe's *The Jew of Malta* (c.1589) – a play that Shakespeare certainly knew – has an antihero called Barabas who, however striking, snugly fits the archetype of a Jew who is both miserly and gleefully murderous. Shakespeare's Shylock is not nearly as crude as audiences would have expected, though, and the play makes it difficult to demonize him – one reason among many why *The Merchant* has had such a varied and rich stage history, witnessing performances in which the Jew has been played as anything from out-and-out villain to nobly tragic hero. Though the play does not make him seem attractive, Shakespeare is careful to imply (like Marlowe before him) that the mercenary Christians are not much more appealing: and they, unlike the Jew, have the luxury of appearing otherwise. And for all that Shylock and his co-religionists seem integral to the economy of Venice and its

Henry Irving's 1879 performance of Shylock was notable for its haunting intensity and the high degree of sympathy he brought to the character.

reputation for tolerance, the city's Christian community never permits the moneylender to forget that he exists there only on sufferance – the moneylender is socially as well as legally alien in Venice. More than that, in this play he is quite literally alone: his servant and daughter both desert him during its course, and his wife, the fleetingly mentioned "Leah", is long in her grave. It is not too much to say that Shylock's loneliness – an isolation confirmed and strengthened by jarring religious and cultural differences from those around him – is the ground for his tragedy.

But it is also the ground for his gruesome revenge. It is unlikely that Elizabethan audiences would have felt much sympathy for Shylock's position, and soon enough his ruminations on the body take on a darker aspect. When news arrives that Antonio's ships have miscarried, the merchant is plunged into bankruptcy and events take a sickening twist. Determined not to squander his opportunity for "revenge", Shylock demands that his "merry jest" with Antonio must stand. Refusing to be bought off, the moneylender insists that he is owed a pound of the merchant's flesh, nothing less. While this grisly detail usually strikes modern viewers as savage and bewildering, for Elizabethan audiences living in a period of heavy inflation and soaring debt (Shakespeare's own father fell into heavy arrears in the 1570s), Antonio's looming sacrifice must have seemed a vivid metaphor for those real-life debtors who were sent by bloodsucking creditors to notorious London jails such as Newgate and Ludgate. And the insistent sacrificial metaphors of Shakespeare's play begin to seem frighteningly real as Shylock's demand reaches fever pitch. Hamstrung by Venice's need for Jewish investment, the Duke cannot persuade Shylock to provide a "gentle [gentile] answer", as he ill-advisedly warns the usurer (4.1.33). The Jew's insistence for "a weight of carrion flesh" (4.1.40) looks unstoppable.

Shylock's mistake, however, is to rely on the legal literalness of his claim. As the final strand of his plot, Shakespeare introduces a device that will become familiar in his later comedies, that of the disguised heroine. Despite giving Bassiano all the cash he needs, Portia itches to be involved in the plan to free Antonio, and as soon as he is gone arranges for her and Nerissa to dress up as lawyers and send word to Venice that they are legal experts. They enter the court just as Shylock is sharpening his knife. Portia's pleas for (Christian) mercy falling on deaf ears, she prepares to deliver her verdict. "A pound of that same merchant's flesh is thine," she tells Shylock, examining the bond while the flummoxed Venetians sit by:

SHYLOCK
    Most learnèd judge! A sentence: (*to Antonio*) come, prepare.

PORTIA
    Tarry a little. There is something else.
    This bond doth give thee here no jot of blood.
    The words expressly are 'a pound of flesh'.
    Take then thy bond. Take thou thy pound of flesh.
    But in the cutting it, if thou dost shed
    One drop of Christian blood, thy lands and goods
    Are by the laws of Venice confiscate
    Unto the state of Venice.

**[4.1.299–309]**

With that, Shylock's case falls apart. A technicality it may be, but – at least in this court – it is enough to free Antonio. Portia's triumph is a victory for women (and it is capped by a ruse in which she and Nerissa humiliate their new husbands by persuading them to relinquish their wedding rings), and ostensibly for humanity too.

But Shylock sees little of the latter, and this strand of the comedy – it is officially that – ends bitterly. Initially taunted by his eagerness to take the money and run, Shylock finds that he has been snared in a catch-22. Another law unearthed by Portia states that if an "alien … seek the life of any citizen", his goods and money have every right to be confiscated (4.1.346–8). For all that his comeuppance is inevitable, Shylock is keenly aware of the singular nature of his treatment. "Nay, take my life and all, pardon not that," he desperately exclaims,

    You take my house when you do take the prop
    That doth sustain my house; you take my life
    When you do take the means whereby I live.

**[4.1.371–4]**

Shylock's words don't redeem him – they are those of a man unable to see anything beyond money – but in the Venice of the play that is hardly unique. And the Christians are so far from caring that, though "pardoned", he is stripped of half his income before being (in the play's most notorious action) forcibly converted to Christianity. *The Merchant* ends, like other comedies, with its community brought together. But rarely does Shakespeare make us so sensitive to the cost.

# Stage history and adaptations

Practically all our knowledge about the early performance history of the *Merchant* arrives from its only text, the 1600 quarto, which states that "it hath been divers times acted by the Lord Chamberlain his Servants", presumably at the **Theatre** in Shoreditch, the company's main home until 1597. The question of personnel is likewise uncertain: some have proposed that Shakespeare's lead comedian, **William Kempe**, took the part of Shylock; others that it was created by the tragedian **Richard Burbage**. Knowing the answer might help us understand how Shakespeare conceived the role – but perhaps it is better that we don't.

An early performance took place in front of James I at **court** on Shrove Tuesday, 1605, and was repeated two days later. *The Merchant*'s celebrity in the Jacobean theatre is also suggested by various plays containing Jewish characters – among them *The Travels of the Three English Brothers* (1607) by **John Day**, **William Rowley** and **George Wilkins**. Nonetheless, we have no records of any other seventeenth-century performance of Shakespeare's text: although it passed into the hands of **Thomas Killigrew** and the King's Company in 1669, it was never acted.

Just into the new century, the Tory politician **George Granville** remedied this deficiency by putting it under the Marlovian title of *The Jew of Venice* and putting it on at Lincoln's Inn Fields in London. Reworking the play for the neoclassical taste of his day, Granville deleted much of Shakespeare's text and replaced it with his own (introducing, according to critic John Gross, "a note of wearisome vulgarity"). He also thinned out Shylock's role to that of a conventional villain, played by a well-known comedian, **Thomas Doggett**. Though never hugely popular, *The Jew of Venice* held the stage until 1741, when **Charles Macklin** put on a triumphant revival of Shakespeare's *Merchant* at Drury Lane. Macklin's portrayal of Shylock was a revelation: in place of the conventional comic characterization, he presented a fully rounded figure – touched by pathos as well as embittered and malevolent. Despite first-night jitters, this was one the most successful productions of the period and made Macklin's career – he was still acting Shylock at 89 and stopped only when his memory failed completely.

Though the *Merchant* reached the United States in 1752 – courtesy of **Lewis Hallam** and his English company, who staged it at Williamsburg, Virginia in 1752 – most eighteenth-century performances occurred back in England. It was produced a number of times by **David Garrick** (with whom the great **Sarah Siddons** debuted as Portia in 1775), **George Colman**, **George Frederick Cooke** and **John Philip Kemble**, but audiences had to wait until 1814 and **Edmund Kean** for an interpretation of the central role as ground-breaking as Macklin's – Shylock as hero. Though the auditorium at Drury Lane was three-quarters empty, Kean's tragic portrayal was to propel him into superstardom (he celebrated by buying a stallion and naming it "Shylock"). As importantly, it resonated with Romantic critics headed by William Hazlitt – who, borrowing from *Lear*, reverently described Kean's Jew as a man "more sinned against than sinning". G.H. Lewes later wrote that it was impossible to watch him "without being strangely shaken by the terror, and the pathos, and the passion of a stormy spirit uttering itself in tones of irresistible power".

**William Charles Macready** acted the play from 1823 onwards, but was never entirely comfortable in the role. **Charles Kean** (Edmund's surviving son) followed him at the Princess's Theatre in 1858 but distracted attention from the actors by evoking all the fun of the *Carnevale*, complete with colourful crowds, gondolas and "real" canals. In the US, meanwhile, the *Merchant* had flourished, not least among companies who toured the frontiers of the burgeoning nation. One of the most successful Shylocks of the century was **Edwin Booth**, the first American talent to make a name for himself in Europe. His performance at New York's Winter Garden in 1867 was enthusiastically acclaimed, but turned its back on Kean's sympathetic interpretation – in Booth's view, Shylock was obsessed by money and malice (the text was cut to emphasize that). The African-American **Ira Aldridge** (see p.264) added him to his extensive list of roles in the 1850s, but the most influential exponent of a sympathetic Shylock in the late nineteenth century was **Henry Irving**, who based his 1879 characterization on a "Moorish Jew" he had seen while travelling. Acting opposite **Ellen Terry**'s Portia at the Lyceum in the conviction that Shylock was "the type of a persecuted race; almost the only gentleman in the play, and the most ill-used", Irving didn't stint on pathos, even to the point of adding an emotive wordless scene in which the Jew returned home to discover Jessica fled. Though Henry James thought Irving "rigid and frigid", most agreed with F.J. Furnivall, who declared in a fan letter that "one longs Shakespeare could be here to see you".

Irving's designs – like his dramatic approach – were elevated and spectacular, but they invited a backlash. The first stirrings were masterminded by **William Poel** (see p.475), whose "authentic" approach encouraged him to play a villainous Shylock in his own 1898 production. The year 1932 saw conservative and radical forces meet at Stratford-upon-Avon. **Frank**

Benson's company played a well-worn *Merchant* in his farewell outing, while in a portent of things to come **Theodor Komisarjevsky** put on his brand-new version later in the summer. As in his later *Comedy of Errors* (see p.40), the director's vision was eclectic: his higgledy-piggledy Venice was populated with mimed *commedia dell'arte* episodes and clowning galore. The sub-text, though, was satirical: his Christians were dissolute wastrels, while **Randle Ayrton**'s Shylock was a "twisting, comic devil". Given what was then happening in Germany, though, Komisarjevsky's critique now looks naive – as **Max Reinhardt**, a Jewish director who had reg-ularly staged the *Merchant* since 1905, discovered when he was forced to flee the country the following year. One of Reinhardt's colleagues, **Werner Krauss**, would later act in Nazi-spon-sored productions of the play, Shakespeare being exempted from Hitler's ban on foreign writers.

Though the horrors of Hitler's "Final Solution" became widely apparent in the last months of World War II, this was not initially reflected in productions of the *Merchant* – at least in England. Following **Donald Wolfit**'s success in the role, Shylock was acted as a stage villain well into the 1950s, and even **Michael Redgrave**'s sensitive performance at Stratford in 1953 was notable mainly for its brooding intensity and rage. It was only in 1960, in **Michael Langham**'s Stratford version with the young **Peter O'Toole**'s heroic Shylock, that some kind of response was formulated. Perhaps the most searching postwar production in England was **Jonathan Miller**'s, at the National in 1970. **Laurence Olivier** played Shylock as a Jew trying hard – too hard – to assimilate in a Venice of the 1880s, Miller's aim being to demonstrate that economic forces lay at the root of anti-Semitism. His cast – **Joan Plowright**'s Portia and **Jeremy Brett**'s Bassanio among them – suggested the *froideur* and emptiness at the heart of the play.

Successive productions in both the UK and US have dealt with its ethnicity in different ways, but all have paid close heed. **John Barton**'s 1978 version at The Other Place cast **Patrick Stewart**'s Shylock as a mean-spirited miser, but above all a bad Jew; directing it again in 1981, Barton used the Jewish **David Suchet**, who kept his character's religion at the centre of his interpretation but faced corresponding anxieties from reviewers. Much the same difficulties faced **Antony Sher** (again of Jewish origin) when he essayed the role at the RSC in 1987 under **Bill Alexander**'s direction: Sher adopted a Turkish accent and was equipped with flowing Oriental robes in an attempt to reconstruct Jacobean exoticism. This self-consciously "for-eign" Shylock faced outright hostility from the play's Christians, as he did in **Barry Edelstein**'s 1995 production in New York; **Ron Liebman** donned yarmulke and beard in a visual state-ment of Shylock's heritage. A few years earlier **Peter Hall** directed **Dustin Hoffman** in London and once again the Christians were portrayed as unappealing racists. **Peter Zadek**'s 1995 pro-duction, originating in Germany but later touring internationally, stressed the capitalist problems at the root of the play – even bringing Shylock to Belmont to advise on the casket wager. By contrast, the Holocaust was never very distant from **Trevor Nunn**'s 1999 National Theatre production, with **Henry Goodman** playing Shylock in a setting reminiscent of 1930s Berlin. Goodman spoke Yiddish to his daughter and played up his character's Jewishness in what the *Guardian* described as "a challenging and disturbing production" and the *Times* acclaimed as "the best *Merchant* for many years". Also excellent was **Barrie Rutter**'s searching production with Northern Broadsides in 2004, which had at its centre Rutter's sympathetic Shylock in a reading that brought out the clash of personalities at the play's centre.

Things were understandably different for the play in Israel, where it had first been per-formed in 1932 under the great German director **Leopold Jessner**, with **Aharon Meskin** in the lead. **Tyrone Guthrie** was the next to direct in 1959, a generation later and well after the for-mation of the State of Israel – as well as after the Holocaust. He felt free to experiment, introducing modern dress but bringing back Meskin to play Shylock, this time as a capitalist financier. The production had other problems, however, and failed – as did **Yossi Yzraeli**'s version in 1972, which risked a deeply unsympathetic Shylock, the comedian **Avner Hyskiahu**, and paid the price at the box-office. Money problems also finished another recent Israeli production of *The Merchant*, this time directed by **Yossi Alfi** in a translation by **Avraham Oz** (well-known as an academic and specialist on the play). This failed even to make the stage of the Bet-Lessin Theatre, pulled because of financing difficulties.

*The Merchant* debuted on the modern big screen in December 2004. Directed by **Michael Radford**, and starring **Al Pacino** as Shylock, **Jeremy Irons** as Antonio and **Joseph Fiennes** as Bassanio, the film looked magnificent but failed to generate much narrative tension. There have been numerous silent versions, however, and (in addition to the adapatation of Jonathan Miller's 1970 *Merchant*) various well-regarded TV productions. The BBC/Time-Life version was directed by **Jack Gold**, with **Warren Mitchell** as Shylock.

## Screen

### The Merchant of Venice
**L. Olivier, A. Nicholls, J. Plowright; John Sichel (dir.)**
UK, 1973 ▷ Universal / Artisan 📼

Produced by Jonathan Miller and based on his celebrated 1970 production for the National Theatre, this *Merchant* is certainly slick. Set in 1880s Venice, the staging brings to mind the damasked interiors of Freud's Vienna as well as mid-century London – all gloomy tapestries and thin-lipped *politesse*. The problem is that the sheer physical horror of the play feels worlds away: the flesh-bond is just too incredible to believe, and Anthony Nicholls's Antonio barely has to remove his frock coat before Plowright's immaculate Portia steps in. But then Antonio isn't the emotional centre here: it's Olivier's Shylock, cast as tragic hero in true Irving style (the "I hate him for he is a Christian" speech is cut, for instance). His is a big performance, perhaps a bit too big, though it's persuasively finessed and doesn't duck controversy – some critics thought Olivier was impersonating the Rothschilds, others Trollope's Augustus Melmotte, still others Hitler. Though partial, Miller's is a consummately intelligent reading of the play, and there isn't a weak performance to be found.

### The Merchant of Venice
**H. Goodman, A. Hanson, D. Crotty; Trevor Nunn (dir.)**
UK, 2000 ▷ Metrodome / Image 📀

Henry Goodman's searing, masterful performance was reason enough to record Trevor Nunn's award-winning 1999 National Theatre production. His mild-mannered Shylock seems utterly benign at first, but clearly possesses a groundswell of torment he does not fully understand – he flinches even as he draws the knife, as if unable to comprehend quite what prompts his ghastly revenge. But Shylock's decision to turn his back on "mercy" here sunders him from his religion (and in a brilliant touch his kinsman Tubal stalks out of the court in disgust), a moment of critical importance and one echoed in a tremendously moving finale, which sees Gabrielle Jordan's anguished Jessica break tearfully into Yiddish song as she is handed her father's wealth. The production, set in a Venice artfully reminiscent of interwar Berlin, bristles with attentive

detail, and rarely have the play's intimate psychological shadings seemed so freshly real. Every character travels into uncomfortable and irredeemable emotional territory – not least David Bamber's careworn and pallid Antonio, Alexander Hanson's thoughtful Bassanio and a highly strung (and utterly brilliant) Portia from Derbhle Crotty.

## Audio

### The Merchant of Venice
**W. Mitchell, M. Jarvis, S. West; Peter Kavanagh (dir.)**
UK, 2000 ▷ BBC ⊙ 📼

A twinkling-eyed Warren Mitchell squints out from the cover of this BBC *Merchant*, and given that his most famous role was that of the comical bigot Alf Garnett in the 1960s sitcom *Till Death Us Do Part*, some listeners might approach this recording with trepidation. Mitchell's cackling cockney Shylock does surprise after Olivier's assimilative tones (see above), but he has both history and ethnicity on his side: the East End was for many years the centre of London's Jewish community (Mitchell himself grew up there) and his interpretation sparkles with life. It also marks him off aurally from the drawling world of Sam West's Bassanio and Martin Jarvis's Antonio, a class distinction that lies at the heart of this version. Juliet Aubrey's Portia is excellent, but after her humiliation of Shylock amid jeering and spitting Christian crowds it's difficult to think there is much harmony in the play's conclusion.

## Editions

### New Cambridge Shakespeare
**M.M. Mahood (ed.); rev. 2003** ▷ Cambridge UP

Though the core of Mahood's edition of the *Merchant* dates back to 1987, it has just been revamped with new information on recent critical and theatrical debates. These bring up to date what was already an excellent title: Mahood's introduction explores a variety of intellectual approaches but never loses sight of what "experiencing the play" in the theatre is like. While some might quibble with her assertion that "first and foremost *The Merchant of Venice* is a romantic

Softly spoken and eminently reasonable, Henry Goodman's Shylock (complete with yarmulke and *tallit*) formed a striking contrast with David Bamber's spiteful Antonio, in Trevor Nunn's brilliant National Theatre production (1999).

play", she makes a persuasive case and Charles Edelman's contributions, taking into account recent books by James Shapiro and others, finesse it. Only a shame that the quality of printing – as in other updated Cambridge texts – has taken a nose dive.

## Some criticism

### Shakespeare's Comedy of Love
**Alexander Leggatt; 1974** ▷ Routledge / Methuen [o/p]

Alexander Leggatt is the recent editor of *The Cambridge Companion to Shakespearean Comedy* and author of much else besides, but his most celebrated book is probably his early *Shakespeare's Comedy of Love*. It remains one of the most sympathetic, suggestive and humane studies of Shakespearian comedy around, consistently alive to the wistful and even tragic qualities present in these plays, yet celebrating their diverse and inventive explorations of comic romantic love. His essay on *The Merchant* is superlative, demonstrating how love (and not just romantic heterosexual love) seems here as much a part of the commercial environment as anything else, a thematic link that yokes together its two contrasting plots; Leggatt's final conviction that the play shows "a larger world than it can finally bring into harmony" seems about as fine a

description of the play as it's possible to write. Alongside *The Merchant*, the book also contains chapters on each of the major comedies: the *Dream*, *Much Ado*, *The Merry Wives*, *As You Like It* and *Twelfth Night*.

### Shylock
**John Gross; 1992** ▷ Pocket Books / Simon & Schuster

When *The Merchant* was first printed in 1600, its title-page drew attention to the "extreme cruelty of Shylock the Jew towards the said merchant", and the moneylender has, undersandably enough, rarely been absent from discussion about the play. Literary and theatre critic John Gross refuses to close off debate, instead providing information along with further questions: why is Shylock forcibly baptized when Church policy went against it? How does the legal substance of the play stand up? Why "Shylock", even? The book is really a cultural history of attitudes to Jewishness brought into focus by versions of Shakespeare's play, and its range – extending from medieval Jewry to T.S. Eliot's Bleistein – is impressive. Attending to the complexity of his task in our post-Holocaust world, Gross senses a "permanent chill in the air" in *The Merchant*. Also well worth looking at in this context is James Shapiro's more recent *Shakespeare and the Jews* (1996).

# The Merry Wives of Windsor

T
he only comedy of Shakespeare's to be located in England from first to last, *The Merry Wives of Windsor* takes rich delight in its social and geographical setting, eschewing the verbal artfulness of earlier comedies for an earthy, prosy texture. In this subtly crafted and often genuinely funny play, Shakespeare removes Sir John Falstaff and several of his followers from the world of *Henry IV* and transplants them to the alien territory of Elizabethan Windsor – perhaps in order to keep a pact with the audience, who were promised at the end of *Part II* that the playwright would "continue the story with Sir John in it". Further background for its genesis is provided by the (possibly apocryphal) theory that it was performed in front of Queen Elizabeth in March 1597 in order to celebrate the knightly Order of the Garter. Whatever the exact reasons behind its creation, though, its generic affinities are easily defined. The story of two wives who gain the upper hand over their husbands and the interloping Falstaff borrows elements from the folktale tradition, and the play is a sharp and pointed social comedy, one in which the good people of Windsor – in particular the "wives" – emerge gloriously triumphant.

[**DATE**]  It seems likely that an entertainment performed in front of Elizabeth I in April 1597 was *The Merry Wives of Windsor*, or at least part of it. The play was probably finished by 1598 (when the cycle of history plays starring Falstaff was completed).

[**SOURCES**]  This spin-off from the *Henry IV–V* cycle has no direct sources, and is the only play of Shakespeare's to be wholly set in England – a fact that has encouraged critics to detect any number of Elizabethan in-jokes.

[**TEXTS**]  A quarto version, perhaps reconstructed from an actor's memory of the play, appeared in 1602 (Q1), and was popular enough to be reprinted in 1619 (Q2). A more authoritative text was included in the 1623 Folio, but it was cleansed of "profanities" in response to new legislation (see p.82).

## Interpreting the play

Written only a year or two after *The Merchant of Venice*, another play with markedly middle-class credentials, *The Merry Wives* is set among the provincial milieu of Windsor – then, as now, a well-to-do satellite of London – and portrays a bustling, vivid tapestry of small-town life. Shakespeare steered clear of so-called "city comedy" (a hard-bitten, satirical genre pioneered by younger colleagues like Thomas Dekker, John Marston and Thomas Middleton), and *The Merry Wives* might best be described as suburban in tone. Among its population are a parson, a doctor and an innkeeper – not to forget the "wives" of the title and the network of servants who surround and support them. Unusually for a Shakespearian comedy, the play also depicts family life in some detail; it even includes a scene set in a schoolroom, hardly a conventional setting for comedy (though via Mistress Quickly's impromptu involvement, even young William Page's Latin lesson becomes a convincing comic routine). No direct

## TOWNSPEOPLE OF WINDSOR

**Margaret Page** (the first "wife")
**George Page**, Margaret Page's husband
**Anne Page**, their daughter
**William Page**, their son, a schoolboy
**Alice Ford** (the second "wife")
**Frank Ford**, Alice Ford's husband (later disguised as **Brooke**)
**John** and **Robert**, the Fords' servants
**Sir Hugh Evans**, a Welsh parson
**Doctor Caius**, a French physician
**Mistress Quickly**, Dr Caius's housekeeper and Anne Page's confidante
**John Rugby**, Dr Caius's servant

## AT THE GARTER INN

**Sir John Falstaff**, lodging at the Garter Inn
**Bardolph**, **Pistol** and **Nim**, Falstaff's followers
**Robin**, Falstaff's page
The **Host** of the Garter
**Robert Shallow**, a justice of the peace
**Master Abraham Slender**, Shallow's nephew
**Peter Simple**, Slender's servant
**Master Fenton**, a young gentleman

**ACT 1** Justice Shallow is complaining to Sir Hugh Evans about the presence in Windsor of the unruly Sir John Falstaff, who has been poaching his deer. Also present is the doltish Slender, who hopes to marry the Pages' daughter Anne. When Falstaff appears, Shallow denounces him, but trouble is averted, and all dine together at Page's house. Back at the Garter Inn, Falstaff, convinced that Mistress Ford and Mistress Page fancy him, intends to seduce them both and get hold of their husbands' money. Pistol and Nim, however, reveal all to Ford and Page. At Dr Caius's house, meanwhile, Simple has arrived with a letter from Evans to Mistress Quickly enlisting her support in Slender's cause. When Caius unexpectedly returns, he is incensed (he also hopes to win Anne's hand) and challenges Evans to a duel. Finally, another suitor, Fenton, turns up seeking Mistress Quickly's advice.

**ACT 2** Mistresses Page and Ford have been sent identical love letters by Falstaff. The two plot revenge: they will pretend to play along but bankrupt Falstaff in the process. Ford – aware of Falstaff's scheme and consumed with jealousy – decides to disguise himself as Brooke, an invent-ed suitor of Mistress Ford who wishes Falstaff to seduce her on his behalf. Falstaff willingly agrees, boasting that he's already arranged to meet her.

**ACT 3** The duel between Caius and Evans fails to occur when the Host of the Garter sends them to different places; reconciled, the two men agree to be revenged on him instead. In the meantime, Ford grows more jealous, unaware that the wives plan to humiliate Falstaff by hiding him in a laundry basket (on the pretext of Ford's sudden arrival) and dumping him in the Thames. When Ford does indeed arrive home, expecting to find Sir John, this is precisely what happens. Recovering at the Garter, Falstaff is persuaded by Mistress Quickly that the whole thing was a mistake and that Mistress Ford wants another meeting. Unfortunately, Ford (as Brooke) finds out about it. Meanwhile Fenton has been competing for Anne's hand, and though she is tempted by his offer, her father still favours Slender.

**ACT 4** At Ford's house, Falstaff's renewed seduction of Mistress Ford is stalled once again by the arrival of Mistress Page, warning that an angry Ford is on the prowl. The two women disguise Falstaff as an old woman before Ford enters; again, he is baffled to have missed his wife's supposed lover. But Mistress Ford soon reveals the truth, and the two reconciled couples plot Falstaff's final humiliation – which will occur that night in Windsor Park. On top of this, Page has secretly arranged for Anne to elope with Slender, while his wife (not knowing her husband's plan) plots the same, but with Caius.

**ACT 5** At midnight, Falstaff waits in the Park disguised, as instructed, as Herne the Hunter – an ancient woodland spirit. Just as Mistresses Ford and Page arrive, the forest is filled with noise. To Falstaff's disbelief, a group of fairies suddenly materializes (local children in costume, shepherded by Evans and Anne Page). Falstaff panics, but they drag him from his hiding place and condemn his sinfulness. At a prearranged signal they are replaced by the Pages and Fords, and Falstaff realizes that it has all been a hoax. Just as the entire party is about to leave for Windsor, however, Slender runs in, followed by Caius. Anne has evaded everyone and married Fenton instead.

sources for the play appear to exist: it seems that Shakespeare assembled it from venerable English folktale traditions, as certain threads – the jealous husband, the game of suitors – imply.

> *The first act of the* Merry Wives *alone contains more life and reality than all German literature.*
>
> Friedrich Engels, writing to Karl Marx (1868)

All this, however, is to ignore the man who, in an early printed text, shares top billing with the "wives": Sir John Falstaff. The roguish "fat knight", who first took a bow in *1 Henry IV*, seems to have been so popular that Shakespeare decided to write a spin-off featuring the comic characters from the history plays. Unruly, fractious and funny, Falstaff and his cronies always threaten to overwhelm (and undermine) the epic kingly narrative played out in the histories. Though caught up in its events, they are gleefully resistant to their historical role, preferring – if at all possible – to while away their lives in Eastcheap taverns, surrounded by cheap booze and women of questionable repute. And *The Merry Wives*, in which they get a play all to themselves, is barely grazed by the courtly and military world of *Henry IV* and *Henry V*. At times this is puzzling: though it imports characters from the histories, this comedy has an open-ended relationship with its predecessors. The action must presumably take place before Falstaff's broken-hearted death in *Henry V*, but Shakespeare has no intention of making the linkages neat. Mistress Quickly, for instance, behaves exactly like her namesake in the *Henry IV* plays but seems not even to know Falstaff, still less be desperate to marry him (as she is in *Part II*). Forcibly relocating his historical cast to the provinces, Shakespeare gives us characters who are – and are not – the same as those we know.

## Ashore at Windsor

We are not the only ones striving to make sense of Falstaff's arrival in town: the good folk of Windsor – or at least some of them – are having trouble with the unexpected (and unwelcome) new arrivals. As the play gets underway, Justice Shallow is heatedly threatening to "make a Star Chamber matter" of Falstaff's none-too-neighbourly taste for poaching Shallow's deer and attacking his men. Though the idea of a local magistrate attempting to seek justice in the highest court in the land is amusing enough (located at Westminster, the Star Chamber was responsible for dealing with the most high-profile of cases), it is Shallow's horror that some metropolitan upstart should be allowed to throw his weight around in Windsor that is most striking. "If he were twenty Sir John Falstaffs, he shall not abuse Robert Shallow, Esquire" (1.1.2–11), Shallow fumes to his dimwit nephew Slender, his rage fuelled by the unpalatable fact that, as a knight, Falstaff actually outranks him socially. But "abuse" is precisely what he gets, as becomes clear when Falstaff eventually appears:

SIR JOHN  Now, Master Shallow, you'll complain of me to the King?
SHALLOW  Knight, you have beaten my men, killed my deer, and broke open my lodge.
SIR JOHN  But not kissed your keeper's daughter?
SHALLOW  Tut, a pin. This shall be answered.
SIR JOHN  I will answer it straight: I have done all this. That is now answered.

**[1.1.102–9]**

Punning on "answer" ("legal redress"/"reply"), one of Shakespeare's most verbally dextrous characters demonstrates that he is more than a match for rural folk of this stripe. It has long been suspected that in allowing Falstaff to run rings around Shallow and Slender, with all their petty snobberies, the playwright is poking fun at minor gentry around Stratford – one hoary tale is that Shakespeare spent his youth poaching deer, just like Falstaff (see p.454) – but we don't need to know that to enjoy the put-down. The age-old tension between city and country is integral to this scene – and the play.

As with many of his real-life knightly counterparts, Falstaff's claims to social superiority are offset by his permanent hunger for hard cash, and Windsor, he thinks, offers a solution. It isn't long before he hits on a sure-fire money-making scheme that involves seducing both Mistresses Page and Ford and thereby gaining access to their husbands' wealth. Concocting a plan to woo them via letter, he boasts to Nim and Pistol that it will be an easy job to bend Mistress Ford to his will. "I spy entertainment in her," he smirks,

> She discourses, she carves, she gives the leer of invitation. I can construe the action of her familiar style; and the hardest voice of her behaviour, to be Englished rightly, is 'I am Sir John Falstaff's'.
>
> PISTOL He hath studied her well, and translated her will: out of honesty, into English.
>
> **[1.3.39–45]**

Falstaff intends to let his skill with language earn him some money, banking on the certainty that the wives will be star-struck by his knighthood. After all, having an affair is as simple as a cheerful exchange of words – the kind of relaxed attitude to infidelity (and the kind of plot for making a fast buck) that dominates contemporary city comedy.

But this is not the city. Though the town is content to let its visitor poach deer, poaching housewives is assuredly off-limits, as Mistress Ford insists, scandalized, when she reads her love letter from the "greasy knight":

> What tempest, I trow, threw this whale, with so many tuns of oil in his belly, ashore at Windsor? … Did you ever hear the like?
>
> **[2.1.61–6]**

"Perceive how I might be knighted," she exclaims, turning what Falstaff presumes is his key attraction smartly back on him. When it transpires that the letters are duplicates, Mistress Page is even more shocked, and the pair immediately agree to be "revenged" on Falstaff by any means that "may not sully the chariness of our honesty", as Mistress Ford puts it (2.1.94–5).

The rest of the main plot tracks the progress of that richly deserved comeuppance, but Shakespeare introduces a twist. Where Sir John appears to believe that one woman can be treated much like another, Master Ford is obsessed with the idea that his wife is being unfaithful behind his back. The playwright, naturally, brings them together. Driven on by reports that Falstaff has his eye on her, Ford goes to the unlikely lengths of disguising himself as one "Master Brooke" and paying Sir John to attempt to seduce her. Once Falstaff assures him that it will be an easy task to lure Mistress Ford away, her husband thinks he has all the evidence against his wife he needs. "Who says this is improvident jealousy?" he seethes, alone on stage:

> My wife hath sent to him, the hour is fixed, the match is made. Would any man have thought this? See the hell of having a false woman! My bed shall be abused, my coffers ransacked, my reputation gnawn at … I will rather trust a Fleming with my butter, Parson Hugh the Welshman with my cheese, an Irishman with my aqua-vitae bottle, or a thief to walk my ambling gelding, than my wife with herself.
>
> **[2.2.280–95]**

Twisted by misogyny, the little-Englander Ford regards his "woman" as a commodity, like so much home-churned butter or cheese. The extent to which his rage is directed at characters such as Sir Hugh Evans, the Welsh parson, marks his distance from a community that has taken outsiders such as Evans and the French Dr Caius to its heart (for all that the play itself gives them what appear to be "funny" foreign accents). And although Ford's speech is comic because we have the confidence that his wife's good sense will win through, it hints at jealousy's destructive force. While on one level he is undeniably the "poor cuckoldly knave" that Falstaff later describes, what appears comic in *The Merry Wives* will have altogether darker ramifications in *Othello* and, later still, *The Winter's Tale*.

## Sinful fantasy

Fortunately Mistresses Page and Ford never allow affairs to become that serious: they are as well equipped to deal with Ford's jealousy as they are to neutralize Sir John. The process of the two men's re-education, via a mounting sequence of comic emasculations, takes up the rest of the play. While allowing Ford's ludicrous suspicions to build, they first engineer a scene in which both men are shown up to be the fools they really are. Scheduling a romantic tête-à-tête between Mistress Ford and Falstaff, both wives arrange for Master Ford to make a surprise entrance, forcing Falstaff to hide in a conveniently placed washbasket – which is then emptied into the nearby Thames (exposing him to household drudgery first-hand, as it were, as well as administering a well-deserved soaking). Satisfyingly, all goes to plan: Ford is duped, Falstaff dumped and neither are any the wiser. But this is just the start of his sufferings, as Falstaff discovers to his dismay when he reschedules a meeting with Mistresses Ford and Page. Hearing

Gossiping beneath twin beehive hairdryers, Mistress Page (Janet Dale) and Mistress Ford (Lindsey Duncan) plot Falstaff's humiliation in Bill Alexander's "new Elizabethan" *Merry Wives* at the RSC (1985).

that Ford is threatening to burst in once again, his wife has an inspirational idea – to disguise Falstaff as her maid's aunt and smuggle him out. Unfortunately for Sir John, Ford loathes Mother Prat, the "fat woman of Brentford", with a passion unique even for him. "I'll prat her!" he exclaims and lunges, howling:

> Out of my door, you witch, you rag, you baggage, you polecat, you runnion! Out, out! I'll con-
> jure you, I'll fortune-tell you! … Hang her, witch!
>
> [4.2.170–8]

Though the comedy is broad, it is not without depth. There is a gratifying aptness in seeing Ford's misogyny addressing itself to one of Shakespeare's most resolutely masculine charac-ters; the pleasure is compounded by the irony that this is the only time in all of Shakespeare's plays that a man appears on stage dressed as a woman (an irony not without force, given the transvestite theatre in which he operated). Ford's own response to the situation is unwittingly to ridicule himself. "Come hither, Mistress Ford!" he yells,

> Mistress Ford, the honest woman, the modest wife, the virtuous creature, that hath the jealous
> fool to her husband. I suspect without cause, mistress, do I?
>
> MISTRESS FORD  God be my witness you do, if you suspect me in any dishonesty.
>
> [4.2.117–22]

Following this incident, the wives decide that Ford has suffered enough and let him into their big secret.

But Falstaff's final disgrace is yet to come. After the robust comedy of his earlier treat-ment, his final humiliation, in which he is persuaded into Windsor Great Park in the dead of night and attacked by malicious fairies (in fact local children), can seem bewildering. It makes rather more sense, as critics have repeatedly emphasized, when understood in rela-tion to the folktale ancestry of *The Merry Wives*. Drawing attention to the ancient rituals that underpin the final scene, Jeanne Addison Roberts suggests that the townspeople of Windsor treat Falstaff as a scapegoat who must be slaughtered because his sexual aggres-sion threatens the community of the play. The fairies' chant, which intones, "Fie on sinful fantasy! / Fie on lust and luxury!" (5.5.92–3) draws this out. It's also worth observing that Shakespeare's comedies frequently end by isolating single characters as everyone else is paired off around them: in *As You Like It* it's Jaques, in *Twelfth Night* it's Malvolio, in *Much Ado* it's Don John. If the comic community of *The Merry Wives* is to heal its wounds, Shakespeare suggests, Falstaff needs not just to be thrown out but to be utterly humiliated, crowned with horns like a cuckolded husband. If the wives are to prove themselves "merry, and yet honest too" (4.2.95), the duper needs to be duped.

Thus the play's finale concerns more than Falstaff: it is about the wives' reassertion of con-trol over their community. But in the dying moments of the comedy they, too, are taught a lesson. While the rest of the plot has been working satisfyingly away, the Pages' daughter Anne has been pursued by a variety of suitors. The stultified Slender has ambitions, and despite his inability to string together a cogent sentence is secretly supported by Anne's father. Mistress Page, meanwhile, has her hopes pinned on Dr Caius, the town's irascible and near-nonsensical French physician. But Anne has other dreams, and in making them reality she outwits both parents. While everyone else is busy fooling Falstaff in the wood, Anne manages to get herself married to young Fenton instead. As Fenton tells it, the climax of *The Merry Wives* is nothing less than a victory for love. "Hear the truth of it," he addresses his new parents-in-law:

You would have married her, most shamefully,
Where there was no proportion held in love.
The truth is, she and I, long since contracted,
Are now so sure that nothing can dissolve us.
Th'offence is holy that she hath committed,
And this deceit loses the name of craft,
Of disobedience, or unduteous title,
Since therein she doth evitate and shun
A thousand irreligious cursèd hours
Which forced marriage would have brought upon her.

**[5.5.212–23]**

The wider movement of the play suggests that we – and the people of Windsor – would do well to take Fenton's grave words seriously. It is a lesson Master Ford, recently reconciled with *his* wife, would do well to observe.

## Stage history and adaptations

Until recently it was believed that *The Merry Wives* was written specifically for **Queen Elizabeth I** (there is an apocryphal tale that she commanded Shakespeare to write a play showing Falstaff "in love"), or perhaps for a 1597 feast celebrating the **Order of the Garter**, but in the absence of hard evidence it's thought that the comedy was intended for public performance from early on and it seems it did well. Among its first casts will have been **Richard Burbage** (Ford), **Robert Armin** (Evans) and **John Heminges** (Falstaff). "A Play of the Merry Wives of Windsor" was played at **court** in 1604; and another performance is recorded in 1638 at Inigo Jones's Cockpit-at-Court Theatre, this time with the excessively portly **John Lowin** as Falstaff.

It was one of the first Shakespeare plays to be resurrected following the Restoration, initially at the Vere Street Theatre (where Pepys saw it on several occasions, liking it less each time), and though **John Dennis** launched an adaptation he entitled *The Comical Gallant: or The Amours of Sir John Falstaff* in 1702, claiming that "all those men of extraordinary parts, who were the Ornament of that Court … were in love with the Beauties of this Comedy", it failed to dislodge the original from the repertoire of **Thomas Killigrew**'s King's Company. **Thomas Betterton** performed *The Merry Wives* at court in 1705, with **Anne Bracegirdle** and **Ann Barry** playing the leads; and it appeared at **John Rich**'s Lincoln's Inn Fields fifteen years later, with **James Quin** as Falstaff. Though novelist Tobias Smollett notoriously likened Quin's declamatory style to "heaving ballast into the hold of a ship", Quin continued to play the part successfully until his retirement in 1751. Nearer the century's end **Charles Kemble** was another famous Falstaff (he acted in a heavily cut version of the play), and his brother **John Philip** first staged it at Covent Garden in 1803.

The period also saw one of the few non-native successes for the play – a Russian adaptation by none other than **Catherine the Great**, which debuted in 1786. And in addition to frequent English performances during the eighteenth and nineteenth centuries (some thirty or so at major venues), during this era *The Merry Wives* also reached the continental operatic stage in versions set by **Antonio Salieri** (1799), **Otto Nicolai** (1849) and, most famously, **Giuseppe Verdi**, whose much-loved *Falstaff* premiered in 1893. The best that England could come up with, meanwhile, was an "operatized" adaptation by **Frederick Reynolds** from 1824, incorporating lyrics from other Shakespearian plays and with **Eliza Vestris** starring (and singing) as Mistress Page. Vestris took Reynolds's version to Covent Garden with her in 1839, this time with a cast including **Louisa Nisbett** as Mistress Ford and **George Bartley**'s Falstaff, and it was also performed at the Haymarket under **Benjamin West** five years later.

Bartley transported the role to the Princess's Theatre when **Charles Kean** put on the original play in 1851, where Kean acted Ford with his wife **Ellen Tree** as his onstage spouse. **John Hollingshed**'s 1874 production at the Gaiety Theatre was notable not merely for the experienced actor-manager **Samuel Phelps** in the role of Falstaff, but incidental music by **Arthur Sullivan**. Close to the century's end, **Herbert Beerbohm Tree** would mount several versions of *The Merry Wives*: the first, in 1889, was also his first Shakespeare (it starred his wife, **Helen Maud**, as Anne Page); while the second was a lavish and painstakingly historicized spectacle mounted in 1902 to celebrate the coronation of Edward VII. Alongside **Madge Kendal**'s and **Ellen Terry**'s middle-aged Wives, Tree was widely acclaimed as "the finest Falstaff of them all".

*The Merry Wives* continued to be acted every few years, though after Tree's grand fifteenth-century treatment, it wasn't wholly suprising that **Oscar Asche**'s production of 1911 at the Garrick Theatre, featuring spare and snowbound sets, was not well-received – yet his subsequent Haymarket staging (1929), boasting modern-dress and a motorcycle upon which Anne Page rode pillion, did better. Outrage greeted **Theodor Komisarjevsky**'s colourfully Viennese production of 1935, though traditionalist sympathies would be assuaged by **Donald Wolfit**'s patriotic performances at the Strand Theatre in 1940 and 1942.

As with other less popular plays, *The Merry Wives* has found the Stratford Memorial Theatre (and its state-subsidized troupe, the Royal Shakespeare Company) its most eager postwar advocates. Numerous productions have appeared at their behest, beginning with **Glen Byam Shaw**'s 1955 version – in which **Anthony Quayle** injected a dose of melancholy into Sir John – and continuing with **Terry Hands**'s staging of 1968, with **Brewster Mason** as Falstaff, **Brenda Bruce** and **Elizabeth Spriggs** tackling the role of the Wives, and **Ian Richardson**'s Ford. Hands revived the play seven years later with a similar cast (the sole novelty being **Barbara Leigh-Hunt**'s Mistress Ford), this time as part of a cycle of the *Henry IV–V* plays. Though **Trevor Nunn** and **John Caird**'s RSC version of 1979, with **John Woodvine** as Falstaff and **Ben Kingsley**'s Ford, was well-received, by common consent the most memorable recent RSC production was put on by **Bill Alexander** in 1985. Set in "new Elizabethan" 1950s suburbia, this saw **Janet Dale** and **Lindsey Duncan**'s Wives plotting under adjacent beehive hairdryers how to ensnare **Peter Jeffrey**'s raffish Falstaff, and featured memorable design touches including a Herne's Oak cut down by the Ministry of Works and replaced by an "Ancient Monument" sign. **Rachel Kavanaugh**'s 2002–03 touring version, again for the RSC, opted to retread this route with **Richard Cordery**'s towering but gentle knight attempting to lord it over a postwar, demobbed Windsor.

## Screen

### The Merry Wives of Windsor
**J. Davis, P. Scales, R. Griffiths; David Hugh Jones (dir.)**
UK, 1982 ▷ Ambrose Video (BBC) `DVD`

Comedy is something the BBC Shakespeare project always struggled with, straitjacketed by a conservative series policy that left directors little option but to emphasize the verbal wit of the plays (notoriously difficult to bring off on screen) over any other kind of humour. That restriction all but sinks David Hugh Jones's Elizabethan *Merry Wives* in comic terms – the cast simply cannot make the laughs work – though apparently the director preferred instead to concentrate on the social dynamics that drive the play. To this extent the Wives are counterpointed as petit bourgeois (Judy Davis's Mistress Page) and nouveau riche (Prunella Scales), while Ben Kingsley attempts a properly paranoiac Ford. But Richard Griffiths makes little apparent effort as Falstaff, robbing the play of much of its interest, and in general Jones's straight-faced interpretation fails to hold together – neither persuasively serious nor honestly funny. It almost goes without saying that the staging (plenty of Tudor beams and cardboard trees, complete with a sealed-down model of Windsor for distance shots) does not do this production any favours. Recently rereleased in the US by Ambrose Video Publishing.

## Audio

### The Merry Wives of Windsor
**J. Redman, J. Jago, A. Quayle**
UK, 1966 ▷ HarperCollins (Caedmon) 🔲

Despite some suspicions that this 1966 *Merry Wives* might prove insufferably old-fashioned, its cast is enviable and in many ways its character-led approach makes the play seem freshly minted. Quayle was one of the century's most famous Falstaffs and his performance here is absolutely magisterial, though he has plenty of competition: Ronnie Stevens is poignantly wonderful as Slender, Hazel Hughes is ideal as Mistress Quickly and even Dr Caius comes alive in the hands of Micheál MacLiammóir. Almost the best thing about this recording is that everyone sounds as if they're doing it for fun.

## Editions

### Arden Shakespeare (third series)
**Giorgio Melchiori (ed.); 2000** ▷ Thomson

Melchiori's edition of the companion play *2 Henry IV* for the New Cambridge Shakespeare comes highly recommended, so it's little surprise that his version of *The Merry Wives* is every bit as good. Although often treated as a mere spin-off, the comedy is not without its critical difficulties – among them the matter of its date and provenance. Melchiori steers a controversial line, arguing that the Garter entertainment presented in front of Elizabeth I could not possibly have been the play, and is thus free to date it after *2 Henry IV*. On less vexed topics Melchiori is informative and argumentative, arguing that the play is Falstaff's as much as the Wives'. The main text is helpfully glossed, and a facsimile of the 1602 first quarto is included in appendix.

## Some criticism

### Shakespeare's English Comedy
**Jeanne Addison Roberts; 1979** ▷ Nebraska UP [o/p]

Roberts's interest in the "Englishness" of *The Merry Wives* relates mainly to its use of native folk and ritual motifs – such as those used to humiliate male adulterers – going back many hundreds of years, analogues (or, in her term, "contexts") she employs to construct a persuasive defence of its dramatic techniques as well as its place in the Shakespearian canon. As well as providing a thorough symbolic analysis of the play – one that has a good deal to recommend it – Roberts also offers information on textual history and critical reception.

### The Metamorphoses of Shakespearean Comedy
**William Carroll; 1985** ▷ Princeton UP [o/p]

Carroll's engaging exploration of metamorphosis and its place within Shakespearian comedy from the *Shrew* to the romances finds a natural midpoint in *The Merry Wives*, in which both Falstaff and Ford find their worlds turned upside down by the play: Falstaff (until now, Carroll remarks, "like Frankenstein's monster … still on the loose") is conquered, Ford apparently reformed. While covering some of the same ground as Roberts, Carroll suggests that the play's final trick may be on its audiences, and perhaps that we too are meant to be chastened by its conclusion – a conclusion leading inexorably towards Falstaff's death in *Henry V*.

# A Midsummer Night's Dream

O ne of the most enduringly popular of Shakespeare's comedies and the playwright's first mature masterpiece, *A Midsummer Night's Dream* is probably the most widely acted play in the canon. Curiously, that's been a mixed blessing: mined by Victorian producers for its spectacular potential and indelibly associated with hosts of fluttering fairies, it's arguably only in the last few decades that the *Dream* has been acknowledged as the dangerous, high-wire piece of theatre it really is. Though Shakespeare's cast of sprites could have been recruited from any number of Elizabethan masques – there's a long-standing theory that he drew upon boyhood recollections of royal festivities held in Warwickshire – in this play his fairies influence, and subvert, mortal life and love with mischievous and often unsettling power. Indeed, audiences and critics have often thought that the emotional tussles between Oberon, Puck and Titania are the most dramatic of all, nearly eclipsing those of Shakespeare's Athenian lovers as they wander in the forest at night-time. But perhaps it's the collisions between the *Dream's* varied social worlds that most surprise and enchant. During the course of the comedy, unexpected transformations and translations occur aplenty; and in the pseudo-tragedy that brings things to a halt, performed for the Athenians by a troupe of local artisans, Shakespeare even sends up the business of theatre itself.

[DATE] Probably 1595–96, towards the end of a group of plays including *Love's Labour's Lost*, *Richard II*, *Romeo and Juliet* and *The Merchant of Venice*.

[SOURCES] Shakespeare amplifies Chaucer's "Knight's Tale" (c.1388), which provides the wedding narrative, with classical sources including Ovid's *Metamorphoses* in Arthur Golding's 1567 translation and Apuleius's *The Golden Ass* (trans. 1566). Myriad other sources have also been detected – more than in any other play.

[TEXTS] The *Dream* is relatively pain-free: a quarto version (Q1) typeset from the dramatist's papers appeared in 1600, and was reprinted in 1619 (Q2). The Folio edition (1623) suggests that Shakespeare tinkered with Act Five.

## Interpreting the play

One of the reasons that *A Midsummer Night's Dream* is so popular, perhaps, is that it offers so much to so many. It is a romantic comedy, a comedy of love and lovers in the lyrical vein of *Love's Labour's Lost*. It is festive, too: framed by a wedding which is to be celebrated, as Theseus promises his bride, "with pomp, with triumph, and with revelling" (1.1.19), it also has close resonances with the ancient festival of midsummer, traditionally a celebration of fertility and fecundity. It is a comedy that dwells extensively in the Elizabethan "fairy land", which interacts – and collides – with the human world of the play to an extent unparalleled in any other drama of the period. And it is a comedy in the more modern sense of that word. In his glorious rendering of the entertainment mounted earnestly but misguidedly by Bottom and his pals, Shakespeare doesn't just succeed in sending up the labours of the poet Arthur Golding

## Major Characters & Synopsis

**Theseus**, Duke of Athens

**Hippolyta**, Queen of the Amazons, engaged to Theseus

**Philostrate**, Theseus's master of revels

**Egeus**, an Athenian gentleman, Hermia's father

**Hermia**, Egeus's daughter, in love with Lysander

**Lysander**, loved by Hermia

**Demetrius**, also in love with Hermia (with Egeus's support)

**Helena**, in love with Demetrius

**Oberon**, King of the Fairies

**Titania**, Queen of the Fairies

**Robin Goodfellow** (known as **Puck**), Oberon's fairy attendant

**Fairies**, among them **Peaseblossom**, **Cobweb**, **Mote** and **Mustardseed**

The artisans: **Peter Quince**, a carpenter (acts **Prologue** in the play *Pyramus and Thisbe*); **Nick Bottom**, a weaver (**Pyramus**); **Francis Flute**, a bellows-mender (**Thisbe**); **Tom Snout**, a tinker (**Wall**); **Robin Starveling**, a tailor (**Moonshine**); **Snug**, a joiner (**Lion**)

**ACT 1** At the Athenian court, preparations are underway for the marriage of Theseus and Hippolyta. The royal couple is discussing arrangements when an angry Egeus storms in: his rebellious daughter Hermia refuses to marry Demetrius as arranged, but instead prefers Lysander. Although Demetrius formerly courted Helena (who still loves him), Theseus decrees that Hermia should obey her father, and announces that she has until the day of his own marriage (in four days' time) to decide. Left alone, Hermia and Lysander resolve to elope, and arrange to meet in the forest. But they reveal as much to Helena – who reflects that alerting Demetrius might be the way to win him back. Elsewhere, a group of workers led by Peter Quince are making their own plans: they hope to perform their play, *Pyramus and Thisbe*, at the royal wedding celebrations.

**ACT 2** In the woods, Oberon and Titania bicker over a boy in Titania's service, whom Oberon wants as an attendant. When Titania refuses, Oberon plots revenge, sending Puck to find him a magic flower, the juice of which (when dropped on the eyelids of a sleeping person) makes them fall in love with whatever they see first. Oberon applies it to Titania's eyes. By this time,

Demetrius and Helena have entered the forest on Hermia and Lysander's trail, and Oberon orders Puck to bewitch Demetrius, too, hoping that he will fall for Helena. But Puck gets the wrong man, applying the juice of the flower to Lysander's eyes by mistake. When he is woken by Helena, Lysander immediately falls in love with her and abandons Hermia.

**ACT 3** When Puck sees the artisans rehearsing their play, he mischievously changes Bottom's head to that of a donkey, causing his companions to flee in horror. Slumbering nearby, Titania awakes and, as intended, immediately falls for the puzzled (but flattered) Bottom and leads him to her bower. Puck gleefully relates this to Oberon, but when Lysander and Demetrius appear, it becomes apparent that something has gone appallingly wrong. Attempting to resolve the situation, Puck applies the juice to Demetrius's eyes, but when he falls in love with Helena too, she merely concludes that it is all a cruel joke. Matters worsen when the women turn on each other, just as the men are deciding to duel. All eventually fall asleep, exhausted, and Puck sets about fixing affairs.

**ACT 4** Oberon takes pity on Titania and decides to undo the spell. She is appalled to find Bottom in her arms, but when Oberon removes Bottom's ass-head, the fairy couple is reconciled. Meanwhile, Theseus and Hippolyta are out hunting with Egeus in the forest, when they discover the sleeping lovers. Waking them, Theseus overrules Egeus and commands that Hermia should marry Lysander and Demetrius Helena.

**ACT 5** Following the weddings of all three couples, Theseus demands entertainment, which the artisans provide – to the court's mounting bemusement. The plot concerns Pyramus and Thisbe, divided lovers, who arrange to meet and communicate through a chink in a wall. Later, Thisbe sees a lion and flees, dropping her mantle, which Pyramus picks up, woefully concluding that his lover has been eaten. He kills himself just before Thisbe reappears, finds the dead Pyramus, and does likewise. The court struggles to hold back its laughter as Theseus orders everyone to bed.

(from whose translation of Ovid's *Metamorphoses* the tale of Pyramus and Thisbe derives), but produces effects so richly comic that audiences still laugh out loud, four centuries on.

Perhaps it is Shakespeare's skill in synthesizing and shaping all these materials (and this is a play which has more sources than any other in the canon) that is most impressive. Though drawing his three groups of characters – the lovers, the fairies and the artisans – from utterly different walks of life, their experiences and fates are bound up in surprising and illuminating ways: for some critics, a demonstration of Shakespeare's optimism about the human condition, if only that when it comes down to it we're all as ridiculous as each other.

## O strange!

Despite the play's multifariousness, Shakespeare often makes us notice the linkages between the different elements in his drama rather than the things that make them distinct. One common thread is his interest in the ways in which people change – or, rather, the tension between the ways in which they change and yet remain the same. In part this is a continuing dialogue with Shakespeare's sources, in particular Ovid, whose *Metamorphoses* ("Transformations") provide patterns of transformation that dominate the play. Most obvious is the case of the pugnacious weaver Nick Bottom, who, like Ovid's Midas, is given an ass's head by the mischievous spirit Puck. This unfortunate transformation occurs while the "hempen homespuns", as Puck calls them, are rehearsing a play for Theseus's wedding in the forest. Bottom is about to make his grand entrance as the hero Pyramus, completely unaware of his asinine makeover, when chaos ensues:

BOTTOM (*as Pyramus*)
    If I were fair, Thisbe, I were only thine.
  QUINCE  O monstrous! O strange! We are haunted. Pray, masters; fly, masters: help!

**[3.1.99–100]**

The artisans dash for cover, terrified by an apparition that is half-man, half-beast. As we might guess given its distinguished literary pedigree, this transformation is more than an excuse to use a comic prop – though eager directors have often equipped the transmogrified Bottom with a mechanical head, complete with rolling eyes and wagging ears. On one level, Bottom's new appearance literalizes what the audience have known all along: that he is an ass (indeed, his name points to another meaning of the word). On another, the joke is that he simply doesn't realize that he is any different – much as, the rest of the time, he is unable to connect his own elevated view of himself with what others inevitably think. He simply cannot understand why his colleagues address him in fear:

SNOUT  O Bottom, thou art changed. What do I see on thee?
  BOTTOM  What do you see? You see an ass-head of your own, do you?
  QUINCE  Bless thee, Bottom, bless thee. Thou art translated.
  BOTTOM  I see their knavery. This to make an ass of me, to fright me, if they could …

**[3.1.110–5]**

Bottom, though it would pain him to realize it, is already an "ass". Except that his own transformation into an animal is stuck awkwardly in the middle – further emphasizing what his limited abilities as an actor make clear, that he is fundamentally unable to be anyone but himself. Despite the terror expressed by the other artisans and the apparent seriousness of the transformation – as critic Stanley Wells observes, Quince's "translated" could mean, among other things, "carried to heaven without death" – Bottom more or less stays as he is. He may develop a bemused taste for "good dry oats" and "great desire to a bottle of hay" (4.1.31–2),

"Ovidius Naso," sniffs Holofernes in *Love's Labour's Lost*, "was the man." That this supreme compliment issues from a pompous windbag of a schoolteacher is a sly joke – Ovid was by some distance Shakespeare's favourite classical poet, perhaps even his favourite author in any language.

**Publius Ovidius Naso** was born in 43 BC at Sulmo (Sulmona), among the Apennines, and was educated in Rome. After making a few reluctant stabs at a government career, he devoted himself to a life of poetry. He enjoyed conspicuous success until 8 AD, when he was suddenly banished by Augustus Caesar for reasons partly connected with his licentious *Ars Amatoria* ("Art of Love"), which fell foul of the emperor's severe moral taste. Settling unhappily in Tomis, on the bleak western shores of the Black Sea, he set about recording his despair in works such as *Tristia* (9 AD) and *Epistulae ex Ponto* (13 AD), and died a few years later. Ovid's work was highly esteemed by medieval readers – **Chaucer** and **Gower** among them – and his fame continued into the Renaissance, where his works became a backbone of the humanist curriculum. Shakespeare will almost certainly have discovered Ovid at school, and been required to rehearse his Latin by memorizing sections of the poetry – thus initiating a intense dialogue with the Roman author that continued throughout his working life.

Jonathan Bate, a recent writer on the subject, points out that Shakespeare was at his most Ovidian at both ends of his career: his early narrative poems "demand to be read side by side with the narratives upon which they improvise", while *The Winter's Tale* and *The Tempest* both betray strong links with the *Metamorphoses* ("Transformations"), a compendium of myths and tales that Ovid himself transformed into an epic poem prior to his banishment. Something like ninety percent of Shakespeare's allusions to classical mythology refer to narratives contained in this volume: the tale told in *Venus and Adonis* uses Book 10, where it appears amid a sequence of stories relating frustrated love; *Titus Andronicus* turns to Book 7's rape of Philomel and her subsequent transformation into a nightingale – so knowingly, in fact, that the play's Lavinia, herself raped and tongueless in a queasy echo of Ovid, brings the *Metamorphoses* on stage in order to relate her plight. With other plays (in particular *Cymbeline*, *The Merchant of Venice* and *Twelfth Night*) the playwright's debt is more muted, but in *A Midsummer Night's Dream* Shakespeare allowed himself an extended riff on the possibilities – and impossibilities – of Ovidian transformation.

Characteristically, Shakespeare points up differences as much as similarities. Bottom's fate resembles Midas's in *Metamorphoses* Book 11 (after failing to praise Apollo's musical abilities highly enough, Midas is given ass's ears), but the fact that the weaver has to appear "translated" in the flesh and on stage – usually with an obviously fake head – only highlights the fragile realities of theatrical illusion. Likewise, when Shakespeare introduces the tragic tale of Pyramus and Thisbe from Book 4 to the play, he plays it entirely for laughs – and even sends up the sometimes lumbering translation of *Metamorphoses* by **Arthur Golding** (1564). While Francis Meres was right to declare in 1598 that "the sweet witty soul of Ovid lives in mellifluous and honey-tongued Shakespeare", Shakespeare was not above debunking his classical predecessor once in a while – as Holofernes's eulogy testifies.

but the overriding comedy of the situation cushions it. When Bottom comes round, he is impressed by his "rare vision … past the wit of man to say what dream it was" (4.1.202–3), and not distressed.

We might feel more disturbed, however, by other ambiguous transformations in the play. The Athenian lovers are forced to confront bewildering changes as they traverse the wild, sometimes frightening, territory of the moonlit forest. They end up there partly by accident: after Hermia's father threatens her with death for refusing to marry Demetrius, she elopes with Lysander, but Demetrius and Helena quickly pursue, and all four lovers find themselves in the wood. Once there, they find it near-impossible to leave: the fairy king Oberon (a father figure often doubled successfully with Theseus) attempts to resolve the love triangle by casting a spell on Demetrius, but his messenger Puck blunders and anoints the slumbering Lysander with a "love juice" distilled from a magical flower of the forest by mistake. Lysander awakes, falls promptly in love with Helena, and very immediately everything begins to go wrong. Though the wood offers liberation from the stifling oppressiveness at court – a symbol since ancient times of sexual freedom and fertility – here it complicates rather than resolves the lovers' experience.

This initial confusion sets up a chain of other transpositions, and the lovers turn against each other with alarming rapidity. The effect is terrifying for those who have to deal with it – which is to say, not those who are actually transformed (Lysander and Demetrius remain oblivious), but those around them. The troubling issues at stake are anxiously expressed by Hermia as she struggles to deal with the fact that Lysander has apparently changed from her devoted lover to a man who claims to "hate" her and adore Helena instead:

> Hate me—wherefore? O me, what news, my love?
> Am I not Hermia? Are not you Lysander?
> I am as fair now as I was erewhile.
>
> **[3.2.273–5]**

Hermia cannot believe that Lysander looks the same, yet behaves so differently – and demands whether she, too, has visibly changed. (Lysander, though drugged, has already introduced the issue to Helena, crying: "Who will not change a raven for a dove?" (2.2.120)).

Nor are they the only ones caught up in the confusion. Demetrius, recently anointed by Puck in order to straighten things out, has just announced that he once again loves Helena (as apparently he did before the play began). But instead of accepting him gladly, she switches her position, believing – rather like Bottom – that her erstwhile friends are "bent / To set against me for your merriment" (3.2.146). The irony of this turnaround is sharp: just a few scenes before, she had lamented that she was not as "fair" as Hermia, and that all would be well if only they could switch identities:

> Demetrius loves your fair—O happy fair!
> Your eyes are lodestars, and your tongue's sweet air
> More tuneable than lark to shepherd's ear
> When wheat is green, when hawthorn buds appear.
> Sickness is catching. O, were favour so!
> Your words I catch, fair Hermia; ere I go,
> My ear should catch your voice, my eye your eye,
> My tongue should catch your tongue's sweet melody.
> Were the world mine, Demetrius being bated,
> The rest I'd give to be to you translated.
>
> **[1.1.181–91]**

Yet, being "translated", as the whole situation has been translated, Helena finds that she cannot adjust – something hinted at, too, by the straitened and forced texture of her language, all the more obvious in a play which is otherwise so rich and imaginative linguistically.

> *What matters in the end is not whether characters "really" love each other or not – since anyone after all can love anyone else – but whether their illusions interlock.*
>
> Terry Eagleton, *William Shakespeare* (1986)

This unnerving sense of familiarity and alienation is climactically expressed in the mock fight between Demetrius and Lysander in Act Three, orchestrated throughout by the magic of Puck. Their rivalry goes back to the play's opening – except Helena, not Hermia, is now being

At the Old Vic in 1937 Vivien Leigh proved both a beautiful and a beguiling Titania in Tyrone Guthrie's Victorian-style production of the *Dream*.

fought over. Like the farcical combat between Sir Andrew Aguecheek and the disguised Viola in *Twelfth Night*, this fight is all in the mind; but, as the *Dream* repeatedly demonstrates, the deluded mind can be a terrifying place to be. Yet again, the situation is neither one thing nor the other. Though both men are at being led "so astray / As one come not within another's way" (3.3.359–60), their aggression is desperate – and desperately personal. Having boasted of the ease with which he shifts shape, "Sometime a horse I'll be, sometime a hound, / A hog, a headless bear, sometime a fire" (3.1.103–4), Puck is the perfect symbol of what Demetrius and Lysander are both fighting and fighting over: as the critic Terry Eagleton puts it, he is the "delusive space", both everything and nothing, that represents their whole experience in the forest.

## But with the mind

Shakespeare teasingly suggests that love itself may be at fault. While Demetrius and Lysander blunder around the forest, all too neatly symbolizing what Helena calls "winged Cupid painted blind", the fairy queen Titania is experiencing her own variation on the theme. At Oberon's behest she too has been drugged, and sweetly calls her love to "sit thee down upon this flow'ry bed,"

> While I thy amiable cheeks do coy,
> And stick musk-roses in thy sleek smooth head,
> And kiss thy fair large ears, my gentle joy.

[4.1.1–4]

The object of her deluded affection is Bottom, but again she experiences a simple transposition of identity. She is not convinced that he is an ass, merely that those facets of him that are ass-like are suddenly attractive: love makes her an ass by making her fall in love with one. These instances upend Helena's early assertion that "Things base and vile, holding no quantity, / Love can transpose to form and dignity" and unflatteringly gloss her belief that "Love looks not with the eyes but with the mind" (1.1.232–4). In *A Midsummer Night's Dream* love does indeed transpose, but rarely does it dignify. As the Polish critic Jan Kott phrases it, in this play "the world is mad and love is mad": something Titania will realize only when she recovers and find that she has been sleeping with a donkey (not entirely innocently, the play hints, characteristically tongue in cheek).

Another approach to love is put forward by the Mechanicals, whose performance of their drama *Pyramus and Thisbe* at the long-deferred royal marriage celebrations strives for literary seriousness (it is based on the omnipresent *Metamorphoses*) but, "very tragical mirth", unwittingly sends up all the conventions of its genre. Still more, it plays motifs which until now have been serious – lovers meeting by moonlight, the threat of death – as comedy, allowing them to be purged in laughter and revelling. Bottom's *tour de force* as Pyramus is supremely funny in its own terms, but opens out beyond them:

> O grim-looked night, O night with hue so black,
>    O night which ever art when day is not;
> O night, O night, alack, alack, alack …

[5.1.168–71]

Taken seriously – which of course they are not meant to be – Pyramus's words echo those spoken by Helena ("O weary night, O long and tedious night" (3.3.19)) just a few scenes ago: the entertainment is not as distant from real life as the lovers like to imagine (and, notably, it is surprisingly close to the denouement of *Romeo and Juliet*, perhaps written concurrently with the *Dream*). Burlesque though it is, *Pyramus and Thisbe* sends up the kind of melodramatic behaviour we have already seen acted out for real.

There is perhaps a rich joke here. Despite being more or less incidental to the plot (Bottom is characteristically the exception), the artisans are not only the most realistic characters in the *Dream* – they are beautifully observed, certainly when compared to the interchangeable lovers – but provide a wryly accurate commentary on its main action. Though the aristocrats find themselves chortling at the homespun play offered in their honour, that is only because they fail to see how prescient and humane it is. Shakespeare encourages us to think otherwise. Far from being "nothing, nothing in the world" (as Egeus snootily describes it), it might be said that the artisans' play, in Hippolyta's apt expression, like the *Dream* itself, "grows to something of great constancy; / But howsoever, strange and admirable" (5.1.26–7).

## Stage history and adaptations

We don't know anything concrete about the earliest years of the *Dream*; the first recorded performance took place on New Year's Day at **Hampton Court** in front of James I (scholars presume that the "play of Robin good-fellow" in the records was Shakespeare's). Its transgressive power is perhaps attested by another seventeenth-century staging, which took place around 1631 at **Buckdale** in Huntingdonshire: it broke the Sabbath and the actor playing Bottom ended up in the stocks for twelve hours – still wearing his ass's head. Restoration audiences were unimpressed by the *Dream*'s strangeness, however: Pepys saw a performance in 1662 and, though he noted some "handsome women", described it as "the most insipid ridiculous play that ever I saw"; and a year before it had been truncated into a playlet entitled *The Merry Conceited Humours of Bottom the Weaver*.

This taste for cherry-picking continued in the eighteenth century with versions including **Richard Leveridge**'s *Comic Masque of Pyramus and Thisbe* (1716) and **John Frederick Lampe**'s *Pyramus and Thisbe – a Mock-opera* (1745). By then, another way of dealing with this troublesome drama had appeared: the musical adaptation. **Henry Purcell**'s *Fairy Queen*, commissioned by **Thomas Betterton** and first performed in 1692, was the first and best. This kept the spoken play (heavily reworked) and inserted separate musical masques at the end of each act. Another musical attempt was masterminded by **David Garrick**, whose *Fairies* (1755) inserted songs with music by **John Smith** (Handel's pupil), cut three-quarters of the text and eliminated the Mechanicals. Garrick was uncharacteristically coy about the finished result – Horace Walpole described the libretto as "forty times more nonsensical than the worst translation of any Italian opera-books" – and left a revised version in the hands of **George Colman**, whose initial performance in November 1763 was so catastrophic that he rewrote it in three days as a two-act afterpiece entitled *A Fairy Tale*. This unhappy story didn't deter the last of the large-scale musical adaptors, **Frederick Reynolds**. As with Reynolds's *Comedy of Errors* three years later, the production was antiquarian in style and spectacular in scope, retaining some of Garrick's lyrics but utilizing new music. Popular though it was, it nearly put William Hazlitt off theatre for life.

Shakespeare's play, meanwhile, hadn't seen the stage for nearly two centuries by the time **Elizabeth Vestris** followed up the success of her *Love's Labour's Lost* of the previous year (see p.190) by resurrecting the *Dream* with something like its original text. She played Oberon herself, with **J.R. Planché**'s Athenian designs featuring a spectacular entrance for Puck, who ascended on a giant mushroom. While in Germany **Ludwig Tieck** was directing groundbreaking "authentic" stagings of the play in Schlegel's translation (**Mendelssohn**'s sparkling incidental music was written for a Tieck production at Potsdam in 1843), in England directors were seeing fairies: **Charles Kean**'s 1856 production had no less than ninety tutu'd sprites on stage for the finale, while Oberon and Puck were both played by actresses (the latter was the 8-year-old **Ellen Terry**). Still more spectacular were **Augustine Daly**'s Broadway production of 1888, which employed an onstage pleasure-barge and scrolling dioramic scenery; **Frank Benson**'s version the following year, which was particularly commended for its "mirth-provoking ass's head" and employed the services of 24 dancing girls; and **Herbert Beerbohm Tree**'s 1900 staging, which *The Athenaeum* described as having reached "the limits of the conceivable". But the reviewers reckoned without **Max Reinhardt**, whose Berlin productions (1905 onwards) represented the apotheosis of grandiose staging – his stage productions used real trees, while his 1935 film used no less than 600,000 yards of Cellophane.

But a revolt was underway. In 1914 **Harley Granville-Barker** ditched a half-century of theatrical tradition and mounted a futuristic production which used just two sets, an uncut text and folk song instead of Mendelssohn. No corps de ballet here: in the words of one spectator, **Norman Wilkinson**'s menacing adult fairies "look[ed] like Cambodian idols and posture like Nijinsky". Reviewers were hostile, and when Wilkinson designed the *Dream* again – for **William Bridges-Adams** in 1932 – he was noticeably less radical. Bridges-Adams had directed the play at Stratford as early as 1920, and there too had deliberately avoided controversy: his Puck was female, his fairies children, and the *Observer* commended it for being "not freakish, or futurist, or rebellious". The 1937 productions of **Tyrone Guthrie** also stuck resolutely with tradition: taking his inspiration from the world of Pollock's Toy Theatres and Victorian children's books, Guthrie created a magical – but safe – fairyland of muslin-clad fairies (choreographed by **Ninette de Valois**) and offered the glamorous partnership of **Robert Helpmann** as Oberon and **Vivien Leigh** as Titania (although most critics singled out **Ralph Richardson**'s endearing Cockney Bottom). **George Devine**, directing in 1954, aimed to avoid such "conventional prettinesses" and achieved something like the shock value of Granville-Barker (his fairies were harsh and birdlike). Again, though, reviewers were unhappy – as they were with **Peter Hall**'s 1959 production at Stratford, which aimed for novelty by playing the lovers unsympathetically as stroppy, over-sexed teenagers, and the fairies as near-feral.

Among the vast number of postwar productions, perhaps the most revelatory was, typically, the most controversial: **Peter Brook**'s at Stratford in 1970. Designed by **Sally Jacobs**, this set the action in a three-sided white box hung with trapezes; Brook claimed that it celebrated "the theme of theatre", but many detected a darker undertow. **Alan Howard** and **Sara Kestelman** doubled Theseus and Hippolyta with Oberon and Titania, suggesting the tense continuities between the couples; and the nature of Titania's relationship with **David Waller**'s Bottom was obviously far from innocent. Though audiences loved it, some critics felt that Brook's sexualized interpretation was too dogmatic.

Much the same accusation dogged the Canadian **Robert Lepage**'s visually spectacular production at the National Theatre in 1992: his set was dominated by a large muddy pond around and into which the fairies and lovers periodically slithered. Puck was played by the Francophone contortionist **Angela Laurier** – who, despite her brilliant acrobatics, was described as negotiating "English verse with all the nimbleness of Inspector Clouseau". Reviewers were less hostile to **Timothy Spall** as Bottom, though the rest of Lepage's cast attracted criticism for their flat delivery of the text. The Halifax-based Northern Broadsides under actor-director **Barrie Rutter** took a similar, though more well-received, route: their touring version of 1994 erased discrimination towards the Mechanicals (who are usually given "regional" accents in British productions) because the entire cast spoke in Yorkshire accents. Even more linguistically experimental was **Karin Beier**'s German production (1995), which employed fourteen actors from nine countries and had them all speak in their own languages – the result was apparently "a UN meeting without simultaneous translation". One of the best-

Titania (Sara Kestelman) orders her fairies to lead a priapic Bottom (David Waller) "to her bower". A scene from Peter Brook's ground-breaking RSC production of 1970.

regarded recent British stagings was that of **Edward Hall** (2003), which emphasized the play's different worlds and its erotic entanglements, with the innovation of an all-male cast: the *Guardian* commented that this *Dream* was "put together by a magician".

The *Dream* has proved irresistible to directors on film as well as stage. **J. Stuart Blackthorn** and **Charles Kent**'s silent film (1909) uses an open-air setting, while **Max Reinhardt** and **William Dieterle**'s talkie of 1935 visited all the places his stage version couldn't quite reach – owls, deer and unicorns included. Reinhardt's desired cast of Greta Garbo as Titania and Charlie Chaplin as Bottom unfortunately didn't come off, but the final line-up did include **James Cagney** as Bottom, **Olivia de Havilland** as Hermia and **Mickey Rooney** as Puck. An equally starry cast was assembled by Peter Hall for the 1968 film (based on his RSC production): **Helen Mirren, Ian Holm, Diana Rigg, Ian Richardson** and a near-naked **Judi Dench** all frolicked gamely in a muddy Warwickshire wood, but it's questionable whether the deliberately rough filming – choppy editing, jarring close-ups – really did them justice. **Adrian Noble**'s 1996 version was likewise based on his colourful RSC production, while **Michael Hoffman**'s Hollywood rendering tried to replicate the appeal of Branagh's *Much Ado* (see p.256). Eight TV productions have been made in all; the BBC/Time-Life version of 1981 was directed by **Elijah Moshinsky** and produced by **Jonathan Miller**.

## Screen

### A Midsummer Night's Dream
**W.V. Ranous, M. Costello, J. Swayne Gordon; J. Stuart Blackthorn & Charles Kent (dirs)**
USA, 1909  ▷ On Silent Shakespeare (BFI) V DVD

One of the pre-eminent American silent film houses, Vitagraph specialized in what are nowadays called art-house productions. Shot in a gorgeous sun-dappled setting, this ten-minute *Dream* (1909) is charming: the stylized perambulations of the lovers make excellent sense, while Gladys Hulette's girlish Puck effortlessly zips in and out of the frame, aided by the magic of cinema (one adventurous shot has her putting "a girdle round about the earth" suspended over a giant rotating globe).

Vitagraph's decision to replace Oberon with a female character called "Penelope" is mystifying, but William V. Ranous's strongly characterized Bottom more than makes up for it. Even Laura Rossi's music – which elsewhere may have you reaching for the mute button – doesn't cast too much of a pall. This *Silent Shakespeare* video from the BFI also features versions of *Lear, The Tempest* (see p.335), *Twelfth Night* (see p.378), *The Merchant of Venice* and *Richard III* (see p.303).

### A Midsummer Night's Dream
**A. Jennings, L. Duncan, D. Barrit; Adrian Noble (dir.)**
UK, 1996  ▷ Cinema Club / Buena Vista DVD V

Capturing the theatrics of the *Dream* on celluloid has proved an elusive art, arguably never really achieved. Noble's adaptation of his RSC production at least confronts the play's anti-filmic qualities head-on: it is obviously filmed in a studio, with lots of good old-fashioned stage magic (trapdoors, cradles aloft, invisible wires) jazzed up by the occasional sprinkle of digital effects. As a filmed play it is excellent, with assured ensemble performances (Desmond Barrit's large-framed Bottom and Barry Lynch's Puck/Philostrate deserve special mention) and an attractively quirky jumble of visual styles. As a movie it is rather less so, hobbled by Noble's bizarre introduction of a crisply pyjama'd young boy as a kind of wordless spectator, through whose wondering eyes we are presumably supposed to encounter events (combined with Howard Blake's chocolate-box score, he's redolent of nothing so much as *The Snowman*). Perhaps too much *Poppins* or *Potter* to be seriously convincing.

### A Midsummer Night's Dream
**R. Everett, M. Pfeiffer, K. Kline; Michael Hoffman (dir.)**
USA, 1999  ▷ Fox  `DVD`  `▭`

The full title, *William Shakespeare's A Midsummer Night's Dream*, makes you wonder if it's possible to sue for defamation four hundred years on. Someone clearly told Michael Hoffman (perhaps it was Kenneth Branagh) that filming Shakespeare was a doddle: select quaint Tuscan backdrop – don't forget a smattering of picturesque rural poor, bless their worn-out socks – assemble starry cast, cut in a few seconds of Mendelssohn. It's tempting to say that the result is vacuous, but that seems unnecessarily hostile towards vacuums. The best that can probably be said is that Kevin Kline brings some pathos to a hen-pecked Bottom, while perma-pout Calista Flockhart makes the persuasive – if not wholly unexpected – case that Helena is actually Ally McBeal. Both Anna Friel (Hermia) and Michelle Pfeiffer (Titania) flounder in attempting to keep their heads above water, and the ever self-sacrificing Rupert Everett (Oberon) does a fine job of making everything else look more charismatic (buildings included). Come back, Ken – all is forgiven.

## Audio

### A Midsummer Night's Dream
**W. Mitchell, M. Maloney, S. Woodward; Neville Jason (dir.)**
UK, 1997  ▷ Naxos  `⊙`  `▭`

Interspersing Purcell's glorious music for *The Fairy Queen* makes it very hard for a director to go wrong, and fortunately the rest of this *Dream* lives up to the soundtrack. The scenes between the lovers overcome what can sometimes seem like perfunctoriness in less well-cast productions (those between Emily Raymond's Helena and Jamie Glover's Demetrius are impressive), and in the fairy world too this performance very nearly retains its magic: only some slightly cheap sound effects and Michael Maloney's slightly overblown Oberon endanger things. The Mechanicals are alike impressive, though the Bottom played by Warren Mitchell (also a fine Shylock; see p.226) dominates – as perhaps he should.

## Editions

### Oxford Shakespeare
**Peter Holland (ed.); 1994**  ▷ Oxford UP

This, the most recent major edition of the *Dream*, has many attractions. One is Holland's extensive discussion (surprisingly uncommon) of the meanings of "dream" to Renaissance thinkers and writers, drawing on a long inheritance of dream-science extending all the way back to classical writers such as Artemidorus of Daldis and Macrobius. The rest of the introduction is divided among the different groups of characters, neatly reconstructing its competing social strata, and the editor provides sensible and sane commentary on many of the play's major themes (perhaps too sensible for some – Holland has no truck with radical theories about the play's interest in sexuality). Shakespeare's revisions to Act Five – some speeches are apparently reworked – are printed as an appendix.

## Some criticism

### Something of Great Constancy
**David Young; 1966**  ▷ Yale UP [o/p]

Young begins his study of *A Midsummer Night's Dream* with a disarming declaration: "a work of criticism that exceeds its subject in length", he notes, "is rightly regarded with suspicion." No such worries here, though: Young's account seems so in tune with the play's varied spirit that it would be churlish to complain about its size. And in fact *Something of Great Constancy* is slender and feels even smaller, made up of a set of brief points on pertinent themes (folklore, the idea of transformation, the play's imagery, the use of "art") that together illuminate the tapestry of influences that make up the play. Young never condescends to the reader, nor – best of all – to the play itself, seeming somehow to preserve its atmosphere of mystery and magic.

### Shakespeare's Festive Comedy
**C.L. Barber; rev. 1972**  ▷ Princeton UP

Barber's landmark study asserts on its opening page that "Much comedy is festive – all comedy, if the word festive is pressed far enough", and goes on to demonstrate that the word is indeed sufficiently flexible to describe not only Shakespeare's comedies but various other Renaissance entertainments and pageants. Though Barber's approach seems somewhat innocent, even conformist nowadays – it's difficult to agree wholeheartedly with his orthodox views on *Twelfth Night* – in *A Midsummer Night's Dream*, which dwells so much in a world of festivity that many have assumed it to be written for a special occasion, this kind of reading remains influential and has much to recommend it. François Laroque's excellent *Shakespeare's Festive World* (1991) takes up many of Barber's insights and puts them in the context of subsequent work in the area, inspired by the theoretician of all things carnivalesque, Mikhail Bakhtin.

# Much Ado About Nothing

Set in the Sicilian town of Messina, *Much Ado About Nothing* fizzes with holiday spirit. Its rich humour was singled out early on by Elizabethan writer Francis Meres, who included it in a 1598 list of plays demonstrating that Shakespeare was "most excellent" in comedy, and it is every bit as concerned with verbal wit as an earlier work mentioned by Meres, *Love's Labour's Lost*. The lead couple in that play, Biron and Rosaline, may well have inspired Shakespeare to create the feisty Beatrice and Benedick, whose battle to out-talk each other dominates *Much Ado* – at least until they are tricked into falling in tongue-tied love, raising suspicions that their verbal jousting was all along a kind of repressed flirtation. Technically, however, their romance forms the comedy's subplot, grafted on to an Italian tale concerning another pair of lovers (in *Much Ado* they're named Hero and Claudio) who fall prey to a sinister scheme to separate them. In connecting the two stories of deception, Shakespeare forces both sets of lovers to rethink their understandings of love and each other; and for all of them, painful loss precedes resolution. For an uncomfortable amount of time in *Much Ado* genuine tragedy clouds the scene, and (ironically enough) the device by which comedy is restored puts the sunny atmosphere of the play under greatest strain of all.

[**DATE**]  Between mid-1598 and early 1599 – flanked by *2 Henry IV* and *Henry V*.

[**SOURCES**]  Ariosto's *Orlando Furioso* (1516) is a possible source for the Hero–Claudio plot, possibly filtered through Matteo Bandello's *La Prima Parte de le Novelle* (though the tale occurs in multiple versions). The Beatrice–Benedick story is most likely Shakespeare's own, as is the clownish Watch.

[**TEXTS**]  The 1600 quarto *Much Ado* was set from Shakespeare's working papers; some of the speech prefixes mistakenly use actors' names rather than characters. This text was reprinted in the 1623 Folio with a few amendments.

## Interpreting the play

Shakespeare's penchant for throwaway titles is often commented on, and in his middle period, around the turn of the sixteenth century, he seems to have been especially fond of choosing names with a kind of cheeky, take-it-or-leave-it quality. *As You Like It* and *What You Will* (the latter better known as *Twelfth Night*) tease their audiences not to take things, or their author, too seriously; while later comedies such as *Measure for Measure* and *All's Well That Ends Well* dare spectators to take *their* titles – and the contortions of their plots – at face value.

*Much Ado About Nothing* sits squarely in the middle of this period, and its title plays multiple games with readers and audiences alike. On one level the phrase seems to deny that there's anything worth getting fussed about: there may well be "much ado" as the lovers sort themselves out, but things will be all right in the end. The well-known song sung by Balthasar to Benedick midway through the play picks up on just this sentiment. "Sigh no more, ladies, sigh no more," he croons,

## Major Characters & Synopsis

**Don Pedro**, Prince of Aragon
**Benedick**, a young lord from Padua
**Claudio**, Benedick's companion, a young lord from Florence
**Balthasar**, a singer attending Don Pedro
**Don John**, Don Pedro's illegitimate brother
**Borachio** and **Conrad**, followers of Don John
**Leonato**, governor of Messina
**Hero**, Leonato's daughter
**Beatrice**, Leonato's niece, an orphan
**Antonio**, Leonato's brother, an old man
**Margaret** and **Ursula**, Hero's attendants
**Friar Francis**
**Dogberry**, a parish constable in charge of the **Watchmen**
**Verges**, Dogberry's partner, a lower-ranking constable
A **Sexton** (church officer)

**ACT 1** Accompanied by his daughter Hero and niece Beatrice, Leonato, governor of Messina, awaits the return of Don Pedro, fresh from victory over his disaffected brother Don John. Don Pedro arrives along with Claudio and Benedick, the latter an acquaintance of Beatrice – with whom he has a relationship of mutual mockery. When, after Leonato's party has left, Claudio reveals that he is in love with Hero, Don Pedro offers to help win her by impersonating Claudio at a masked ball that evening. When the plan reaches Leonato, he advises Hero to accept. Casting a shadow over events, however, is Don John – still determined to create mischief.

**ACT 2** At the ball, Don Pedro successfully woos Hero for Claudio, but the latter is persuaded by Don John that he has actually done so for himself. After Don Pedro convinces Claudio of the truth and marriage is agreed, he outlines a further plan: the sparring Beatrice and Benedick will be tricked into falling in love. To this end, Don Pedro arranges for Benedick to overhear a staged conversation in which he and Leonato discuss Beatrice's supposed love for him. Benedick is taken in and resolves to respond. Elsewhere, Don John continues to scheme: his man Borachio will court Margaret (Hero's gentlewoman), who will disguise herself as Hero, thus suggesting to Claudio Hero's infidelity.

**ACT 3** Don Pedro's plan continues to work when Beatrice overhears Hero and Ursula describing Benedick's secret passion for her. At this point Don John arrives and announces that Hero has been unfaithful. Claudio and Don Pedro refuse to believe him, but Don John claims to have evidence: that night they will see her with another man. Sure enough, when they spy on Margaret and Borachio, Claudio is convinced that the woman is Hero. By a freak chance, though, the dim-witted Watch (newly recruited by Dogberry and Verges) catch Borachio bragging about his success to Conrad soon afterwards, and arrest them both. They inform Leonato, but he is preoccupied with the impending marriage.

**ACT 4** As the wedding ceremony begins, Claudio savagely denounces Hero, backed up by Don Pedro and Don John. Hero faints, thus convincing her father of her guilt. Friar Francis stands by her, however, and advises that her death be announced while she hides away till her innocence can be proven. Benedick tells Beatrice that he does not believe the accusations; when he then admits that he loves her, she reciprocates but urges him to kill Claudio. The Watch, meanwhile, have taken their prisoners to the Sexton, who realizes that Hero has been framed.

**ACT 5** Leonato and Antonio angrily confront Claudio and Don Pedro and accuse them of killing Hero, but they refuse to be drawn, and are surprised when Benedick enters and challenges Claudio to a duel. They are even more shocked when Dogberry and Verges reveal the truth about Don John's plan. Appalled, Don Pedro and Claudio beg Leonato's forgiveness, and he instructs them to write an epitaph that will clear his daughter's name, and tells Claudio that he must marry Antonio's daughter. Claudio agrees. Benedick, meanwhile, has been struggling to write Beatrice love poems. Next morning, as Claudio is about to marry Antonio's daughter, she lifts her veil and reveals herself to be Hero. Beatrice and Benedick realize that they have been tricked soon afterwards, but when his poems and her love letters are revealed, they bow to the inevitable and admit their love. All are reconciled – with the exception of the captured Don John, whose punishment is postponed until another day.

> Men were deceivers ever,
> One foot in sea, and one on shore,
> To one thing constant never.
> Then sigh not so, but let them go,
> And be you blithe and bonny,
> Converting all your sounds of woe
> Into hey nonny, nonny.

**[2.3.61–8]**

Whatever happens, the song insists – jealousy, bitterness, betrayal – you have to keep on singing, converting "sounds of woe" into nonsense like the old refrain "hey nonny, nonny". "These are very crotchets [trivialities] that he speaks," says Don Pedro to Balthasar just beforehand, reaching for a musical pun. "Note notes, forsooth, and nothing!" (2.3.55–6).

Shakespeare's audiences would also have heard a bawdier joke in the play's title. "Nothing" was risqué Elizabethan slang, usually referring to the female sex organs, but in practice pretty much all-purpose. In this light the play's concern with love and sex seems a little more cynical (where does all that "ado" get you?), but the playfulness remains. Yet another possible meaning of "nothing" can be obtained by removing the "h", as Elizabethan pronunciation often did. The comedy and tragedy of the play rest alike on observation and overhearing, whether it's Benedick and Beatrice listening in to reports of the other's frenzied love or Claudio being persuaded that Hero has been unfaithful to him. When tempted, the title implies, people "note" things that are in fact "nothing".

## Talk themselves mad

The play itself is as witty as its title. Most of *Much Ado*'s impressive verbal fireworks appear courtesy of Beatrice and Benedick, Shakespeare's infamously talkative couple (and his sole addition to a story sourced from several Renaissance romances). Though in some ways they resemble the *Shrew*'s Katherine and Petruccio, who likewise spend much of their time together fighting, Beatrice and Benedick prefer to wage what Leonato calls their "merry war" with words alone. But what words they are. Though Don Pedro and his gentlemanly retinue have only just arrived in Messina, it is not long before Beatrice and Benedick renew their acquaintance. They do so, as ever, by being – verbally speaking – at one another's throats:

BEATRICE   I wonder that you will still be talking, Signor Benedick. Nobody marks you.

BENEDICK   What, my dear Lady Disdain! Are you yet living?

BEATRICE   Is it possible disdain should die while she hath such meet food to feed it as Signor Benedick? Courtesy itself must convert to disdain if you come in her presence.

BENEDICK   Then is courtesy a turncoat. But it is certain I am loved of all ladies, only you excepted. And I would I could find in my heart that I had not a hard heart, for truly I love none.

BEATRICE   A dear happiness to women. They would else have been troubled with a pernicious suitor. I thank God and my cold blood I am of your humour for that. I had rather hear my dog bark at a crow than a man swear he loves me.

BENEDICK   God keep your ladyship still in that mind. So some gentleman or other shall escape a predestinate scratched face.

BEATRICE   Scratching could not make it worse an 'twere such a face as yours were.

BENEDICK   Well you are a rare parrot-teacher.

BEATRICE   A bird of my tongue is better than a beast of yours.

BENEDICK   I would my horse had the speed of your tongue …

**[1.1.110–35]**

And so it continues. It is practically impossible to quote Beatrice and Benedick's verbal fencing in short; they often sound as if they could simply go on for ever, thrusting and parrying relentlessly, each trying to dispatch the other with yet more spectacular linguistic flourishes. Even the masked ball, set up once Don Pedro and his lords arrive in town and providing a suggestive opportunity for the lovers to woo in disguise, gives Beatrice the chance to insult her counterpart. Encountering the masked Benedick, she announces that the very same man is "the Prince's jester, a very dull fool" (2.1.127).

Despite Leonato's warning to his niece that "thou wilt never get thee a husband if thou be so shrewd of thy tongue" (2.1.16–17), Beatrice has already met her match – in every sense of the word. Or at least that is what the other characters think, plotting to bring them together by a stratagem somewhat more complicated than a masked ball. Promising to "undertake one of Hercules' labours, which is to bring Signor Benedick and the Lady Beatrice into a mountain of affection th'one with th'other" (2.1.341–5), Don Pedro first stage-manages a meeting with Claudio and Leonato in which they are to discuss – within earshot of Benedick – the news that Beatrice has been pining for him all this time. Immediately convinced, Benedick decides that "this can be no trick", and resolves at once to be "horribly in love with her" (2.3.209, 223) in response. Beatrice is "limed" soon afterwards – this time by Ursula and Hero, who pretend to have discovered that Benedick is "wast[ing] inwardly" for *her* and make sure to say so while she is within eavesdropping range. The effect is more sudden than anyone can have hoped for:

> BEATRICE (*coming forward*)
>     What fire is in mine ears? Can this be true?
>         Stand I condemned for pride and scorn so much?
>     Contempt, farewell; and maiden pride, adieu.
>         No glory lives behind the back of such.
>     And Benedick, love on. I will requite thee,
>         Taming my wild heart to thy loving hand.
>
> **[3.1.107–12]**

Beatrice is so taken in that she promises to "tame" herself – the *Shrew*'s Katherine makes no such concessions – and even forsakes her usual prose to launch into an abbreviated sonnet saying as much.

Lest such immediate conversions ring false, Shakespeare is careful to hint that Beatrice's apparent antagonism towards Benedick stems from a long-past affair which has never healed. And he creates a good deal of comedy from their creaking attempts to go through the motions of love once again. Despite his ear for language, Benedick is soon forced to admit, frustratedly, that he is having the greatest of trouble compressing his feelings into "rhyme":

> I have tried. I can find out no rhyme for 'lady' but 'baby', an innocent rhyme; for 'scorn' 'horn', a hard rhyme; for 'school' 'fool', a babbling rhyme. Very ominous endings. No, I was not born under a rhyming planet …
>
> **[5.2.35–9]**

As Benedick "suffer[s] love" for Beatrice (5.2.60), his wit is brought low – to a recycling of nonsensical vowel sounds. Contrary to Leonato's amused insistence that "if they were but a week married they would talk themselves mad" (2.1.330–1), in fact the effort of wooing has them both tied up in verbal knots. And when Beatrice and Benedick do eventually find out that they have been duped, it is the evidence of their "halting" letters and poems to each other that persuades them to go through with the marriage.

Drenched in Tuscan sunlight, Kenneth Branagh's feel-good *Much Ado* (1993) paved the way for Shakespeare's re-entry into Hollywood. Branagh played Benedick himself, opposite the Beatrice of his then-wife Emma Thompson.

## The wonder of her infamy

Before the lovers can get to the altar, however, more malign deceptive forces make their presence felt in Messina. Don Pedro's bastard brother Don John realizes that the play's other new couple, Claudio and Hero, can be forced apart. Again, visual and aural deception are the key. Arranging for his henchman Borachio to woo Hero's gentlewoman Margaret, Don John escorts Claudio and Don Pedro to a dark spot from where they can see Borachio conversing with her. Persuaded that the woman they see is Hero, Claudio immediately swears (as Borachio cacklingly tells it) to "meet her as he was appointed next morning at the temple, and there, before the whole congregation, shame her with what he saw" (3.3.152–5). Instead of formalizing the marriage in front of the whole of Messinan society, Claudio will turn the ceremony into one of ritual humiliation.

And as soon as Leonato gives her away, Claudio does just that. "Give not this rotten orange to your friend," he furiously cries:

> She's but the sign and semblance of her honour.
> Behold how like a maid she blushes here!
> O, what authority and show of truth
> Can cunning sin cover itself withal!
> Comes not that blood as modest evidence
> To witness simple virtue? Would you not swear,
> All you that see her, that she were a maid,
> By these exterior shows? But she is none.
> She knows the heat of a luxurious bed.
> Her blush is guiltiness, not modesty.

**[4.1.32–42]**

In his obsession with female hypocrisy Claudio echoes Master Ford, but in *Merry Wives* no one doubts for a moment that Ford's jealousy exists solely in his mind. Here even Leonato, Hero's good-natured father, is immediately convinced of her guilt, crying, "O she is fallen / Into a pit of ink, that the wide sea / Hath drops too few to wash her clean again" (4.1.140–2).

This is the very darkest moment in the play, and it should be noted that the only evidence behind Claudio's wild accusations is that, as Don Pedro explains, she talked "with a ruffian at her chamber window" – an act they witnessed at night and with only Borachio's word to confirm it. This bond of trust between men, which is able to erase at a stroke an entire heterosexual relationship, seems to confirm what some commentators have claimed, that Messina is a less tolerant society than might at first appear. In this respect it points forward to the anguished world of *Troilus and Cressida*, whose heroine becomes guilty (if guilty is the word) of what Hero is not when she is observed flirting with a rival wooer. In both plays, it is women who bear the brunt of restrictive social codes that delineated behaviour between the sexes in the Renaissance, and in presenting Hero's suffering so powerfully *Much Ado* pointedly suggests that it doesn't much matter whether a woman deserves "dishonour" or not: it's what society thinks that counts. When Hero is condemned not merely by her suitor and his comrades but her own father, a rigid culture of shame and honour turns in full force against her, a catastrophe caused by the flimsiest of fabrications.

It is the ferocity of this culture that most appals in *Much Ado*: stung by Hero's stunned inability to reply (she has in fact fainted), Leonato is terrifyingly quick to believe his daughter's accusers rather than Hero herself, and so frantic with rage that he several times threatens to "tear her" with his own bare hands. Shakespeare does indeed make her die as a result of her shame, but fortunately not as literally as Leonato demands – the resourceful Friar suggests that Hero should fake her own decease, arguing that "the supposition of the lady's death / Will quench the wonder of her infamy" (4.1.240–1), in effect that everyone (especially Claudio) will be so overcome by grief that they will forget all about the scandal. It is a desperate measure, but Hero's plight is extreme – so extreme, it seems, that social reputation outweighs life itself. It is left to Beatrice to voice the corollary, that Claudio too should not escape the consequences of his actions. She demands from an unsuspecting Benedick a real sign of love:

> BEATRICE  I love you with so much of my heart that none is left to protest.
> BENEDICK  Come, bid me do anything for thee.
> BEATRICE  Kill Claudio.
>
> **[4.1.287–90]**

Called upon to act as a revenger, Benedick is confronted by a situation which demands that he place his affection for Beatrice above loyalty to his closest friend. The comic world of *Much Ado* seems a long way away at this emotion-filled crux, not least because, having been pushed finally to fall in love, it now seems possible that circumstances will drive Benedick and Beatrice apart.

Fortunately, however, the play does not allow that to happen. Claudio and Don Pedro are not the only characters to have been eavesdropping. The conversation between Borachio and Conrad, in which Borachio boasted about his "villainy", has been overheard by members of Messina's comically useless Watch, led by constable Dogberry and his sidekick Verges. By

---

*It is here [in the church scene] that the social abnormality of aristocratic society in Messina is exposed once and for all for what it is – a shallow and perverse application of a standard of behaviour that is both automatic and uncharitable.*

Walter N. King, "Much Ado About Something" (1964)

rights the Watch should be too hopeless to achieve anything at all, but somehow a couple of its members succeed in arresting Borachio and Conrad, thereby setting in motion events that will expose Don John's malicious hoax. The well-meaning Verges attempts to inform Leonato about their recent coup, but Dogberry – doing his level best to impress – wants to have the governor all to himself. Urging Verges to stop waffling, he takes it upon himself to criticize his companion's way with words:

> VERGES  Yes, I thank God, I am as honest as any man living that is an old man and no honester than I.
> DOGBERRY  Comparisons are odorous. Palabras, neighbour Verges.
> LEONATO  Neighbours, you are tedious.
> DOGBERRY  It pleases your worship to say so, but we are the poor Duke's officers. But truly, for mine own part, if I were as tedious as a king I could find in my heart to bestow it all on your worship.
>
> **[3.5.13–21]**

Enumerating Dogberry's linguistic limitations has proved an engaging pastime for editors, but it is the spontaneous felicity of his errors that really stands out – the Duke is "poor" indeed to have such "tedious" officials (clearly Dogberry interprets the word as a compliment) on his side.

Dogberry makes an unlikely fairy godmother, but he turns out to hold all the means for a happy ending. *Much Ado*'s final scene is characterized by relief as various truths are outed, but the conclusion is not facile. Persuaded that Hero was innocent after, the guilt-stricken Claudio agrees to Leonato's offer to marry his niece instead. Even Leonato's assurance that she is "almost the copy of my child that's dead" (5.1.281) does not prepare Claudio for her unveiling at the ceremony:

> CLAUDIO
> Another Hero!
> HERO               Nothing certainer.
> One Hero died defiled, but I do live,
> And surely as I live, I am a maid.
>
> **[5.3.62–4]**

"She died, my lord, but whiles her slander lived," echoes Leonato, pointing to the kind of mythic rebirth that will so inspire Shakespeare in his last plays. For the moment, though, the comic community of Messina is allowed to heal its wounds and gather once more (as the script puts it) in a "Dance".

## Stage history and adaptations

The title-page of the 1600 quarto claims that *Much Ado* was "sundry times publicly acted" by the **Chamberlain's Men**. The text also helpfully includes some speech prefixes telling us who took various roles – among them were **Will Kempe**'s Dogberry and **Richard Cowley**'s Verges. Subsequent references to the comedy indicate its steady popularity, and it was one of fourteen plays provided by **John Heminges** and the King's Men (as they were now known) at **court** for the festivities celebrating the marriage of James I's daughter in 1613. It appears in the records as "Benedicte and Betteris", suggesting that even then its lead couple had become dominant; for his part, Charles I renamed it "Benedik and Betrice" in the royal copy of the 1632 Second Folio.

William Davenant took on the play following the Restoration, and promptly squeezed it into his 1662 *Law Against Lovers*, a version of *Measure for Measure* that stole the Beatrice–Benedick subplot (and much else; see p.213). But it flopped, and the unadapted *Much Ado* bounced back in 1721 at the behest of theatre manager **John Rich**. Though elements of the comedy found their way into other reworkings (among them **Charles Johnson**'s 1723 *Love in a Forest* and **James Miller**'s 1737 *The Universal Passion*), the play itself prospered during the eighteenth century, most spectacularly under **David Garrick** at Drury Lane from 1748. Garrick's Benedick was one of the few comic parts in which he excelled, and he played it over a hundred times to a roll call of lively Beatrices including **Hannah Pritchard**, **Elizabeth Pope** and **Frances Abbington**. Abbington herself continued with the role for twenty years after Garrick's retirement, and **Sarah Siddons**, **Elizabeth Farren** and **Dorothy Jordan** also tried their hand before the century's end.

Siddons's younger brother **Charles Kemble** challenged Garrick's longevity, performing *Much Ado* from 1803 with actresses including **Anne Brunton**, his daughter **Fanny** and **Louisa Nisbett**. By the time of his farewell appearance in 1836, his leading lady was the 19-year-old **Helen Faucit** and there was a 42-year age gap between the two. Faucit did more than any other to convert Beatrice from fire-breathing vixen into rounded human being; a review from 1846 describes the "rare beauty" of her performances. **Henry Irving**'s co-star **Ellen Terry** took the role in 1882, a few years after Faucit's retirement, and produced a Beatrice who was "buoyant, winsome, merry, enchanting" (in Bram Stoker's words). Though she outclassed Irving's Benedick, their Lyceum production notched up nearly 250 performances and toured to the US. It was no less famous for its lavish sets, designed by **William Telbin**: Hero's denunciation took place in an exquisite Italianate church with columns thirty feet high.

**Herbert Beerbohm Tree**'s 1905 version, equally grand, was the end of an era: an Ellen Terry revival two years earlier, designed by her son **Edward Gordon Craig**, featured stripped-down sets, and in 1904 **William Poel** put on a reconstructive "Elizabethan" production boasting period music. Through the first decades of the twentieth century *Much Ado* became once again a star vehicle, chiefly at the Old Vic. **Sybil Thorndike** and **Edith Evans** both played Beatrice pre- and interwar, joined by the Benedicks of **Lewis Casson** and **Baliol Holloway**. **John Gielgud** acted opposite **Dorothy Green** in 1930, and returned to the play at Stratford in 1949 in what became its first successful postwar production. Gielgud initially directed **Anthony Quayle**'s Benedick and **Diana Wynard**'s Beatrice, but during three subsequent revivals took the lead himself, first with **Peggy Ashcroft**, then **Margaret Leighton**.

*Much Ado* has remained one of Shakespeare's most popular comedies, as the bewildering variety of its subsequent stagings suggests. Within a few years it would appear in guises ranging from Tex-Mex (Stratford, Connecticut in 1957) to Regency-Risorgimento (at Stratford, UK in 1958 under **Douglas Seale** with **Michael Redgrave** and **Googie Withers**). **Michael Langham**'s Stratford incarnation of 1961 also returned to Regency England, but **Geraldine McEwan**'s Beatrice was apparently "a modern young woman" nonetheless. **Franco Zeffirelli**'s National Theatre version (1965) and **Trevor Nunn**'s Stratford staging (1968) both attempted to historicize the play: Zeffirelli in a typically operatic nineteenth-century Sicily; Nunn in one of the few Elizabethan settings to have made it into performance. Both had up-and-coming stars (**Maggie Smith** with **Robert Stephens** and **Janet Suzman** with **Alan Howard** respectively), in contrast to one of the most famous twentieth-century UK productions, **John Barton**'s Stratford version of 1976, which struck an autumnal tone with a mature **Donald Sinden** and **Judi Dench**. Barton set the play in colonial nineteenth-century India, focusing on the officers' mess posturing of Don Pedro and his men and undercutting the low comedy by making the Watch into a "native" force.

Beatrice was the Shakespearian role closest to Ellen Terry's own lively personality, and one she excelled in. Her Benedick at the Lyceum Theatre was Henry Irving, whom she described as "too deliberate, though polished and thoughtful."

Among recent versions, a handful have succeeded in bringing innovation to *Much Ado* without trampling on its sensibilities. **Terry Hands**'s 1982 RSC production, starring **Sinead Cusack** and **Derek Jacobi**, was dominated by **Ralph Koltai**'s mirrored sets, representing the play's shifting representations of truth and falsehood. **Judi Dench** directed **Kenneth Branagh**'s Renaissance Theatre Company in 1988 (in another Regency setting) with Branagh's Benedick well matched by **Samantha Bond**'s feisty Beatrice. **Declan Donnellan**'s irreverent Cheek By Jowl company took it on in 1993 in a downbeat production that emphasized the characters' mutual shabbiness, while the following year **Mark Rylance** and **Janet McTeer** proved a particularly effective pairing in **Matthew Warchus**'s lively West End production – he slightly diffident with a soft Ulster accent, she tall and domineering. Outside the UK it has continued to be widely performed, with myriad productions in English-speaking territories such as North America and Australia (where it debuted in Melbourne, courtesy of **Edwin Booth**, in 1843). Foreign-language versions range all the way from **Stanislavsky**'s Russian performances in 1893 to **Jiang Weigon**'s translation, which debuted in China in 1986 and soldered *Much Ado* onto the Huangmeixi folk tradition.

As well as **Kenneth Branagh**'s film of 1993, *Much Ado* has appeared in various screen incarnations. **Franco Zeffirelli**'s production was adapted for TV in 1969, and the BBC/Time-Life Shakespeare has seen not one version but two: **Donald McWhinnie**'s of 1978 (with **Michael York**, **Penelope Keith** and **Ian Richardson**), originally designed to open the series; and **Stuart Burge**'s replacement from six years later, with **Robert Lindsey** and **Cherie Lunghi** in the leads.

## Screen

### Much Ado About Nothing

K. Branagh, E. Thompson, D. Washington; Kenneth Branagh (dir.)

UK, 1993 ▷ MGM **DVD**

Indisputably the most-watched recent Shakespeare movie, this Tuscan *Much Ado* persuaded Hollywood producers that having the Bard as co-screenwriter didn't necessarily entail commercial suicide. The patented Branagh formula has since become both familiar and imitated – Hollywood stars alongside British talent, period settings, plenty of sentiment and chortling – but back then it was a novelty. A decade later? Well, it still looks fresh (if you discount the carcinogenic perma-tans) and contains some pleasing moments. Branagh's Benedick is as spry – and intermittently fatuous – as ever, but it's Thompson's womanly Beatrice who is scripted to win our sympathy, and that she does with a performance that Helen Faucit and Ellen Terry (so one guesses) would be proud of.

Just as well, really, as Michael Keaton's Dogberry is godawful – practically impossible to comprehend – and Keanu Reeves's monochrome Don John succeeds as eye-candy and precious little else.

## Audio

### Much Ado About Nothing
**D. Tennant, S. Spiro, D. Swift; Sally Avens (dir.)**
UK, 2001 ▷ BBC ⊙ ▦

On tape as much as on stage, it's the casting of Beatrice and Benedick that decides whether *Much Ado* sinks or swims. This version emphatically does the latter, with some gloriously fast-paced scenes between the Scot David Tennant's cynical Benedick and Samantha Spiro's wry Beatrice (the gulling scenes come across surprisingly well with some adept sound balance). Elsewhere among the cast Chiwetel Ejiofor brings a sombre sympathy to Claudio – a character who might not seem to deserve it – and David Haig's Dogberry thankfully avoids overdoing things, a trap other actors do not always resists. Sally Avens does not avoid tinkering with the text, however, and there are some transpositions and excisions.

## Editions

### Oxford Shakespeare
**Sheldon P. Zitner (ed.); 1993** ▷ Oxford UP

While A.R. Humphreys's 1981 Arden 2 edition, much reprinted, is highly recommended – not least because Humphreys seems so in tune with *Much Ado*'s spirit – Zitner's Oxford version capitalizes convincingly on recent insights into the play, chiefly a more cynical view of its gender politics than is offered by more traditional interpretations. Zinter's introduction abounds with pithy thoughts, and his notes to the text, while doing an excellent job, are less invasive than Humphreys's. There is an appendix on "Music, Song, and Dance" along with a particularly detailed index.

## Some criticism

### Shakespeare's Comedies
**Bertrand Evans; 1960** ▷ Oxford UP [o/p]

Bertrand Evans is a sympathetic and lucid guide to the varied worlds of Shakespearian comedy, but this book has a bolder thesis than its name implies: it argues that the playwright's skill rests in his deft marshalling of what Evans calls "awareness" – whether (or to what extent) the audience knows what the characters don't. The interplay between relative awareness is obviously of pressing concern in *Much Ado*, and for Evans the "mutually complementing alacrities in deceiving and being deceived" are what make the play come alive. He covers the full range of comedies, from *Errors* to *The Winter's Tale*, and though the pages on *Much Ado* are relatively few, they are full of insight.

### Shakespeare's Comedies of Play
**J. Dennis Huston; 1981** ▷ Columbia UP [o/p]

Though initially concerned with the earliest comedies, *Shakespeare's Comedies of Play* revels in the honing of Shakespeare's dramatic powers. Huston interprets "play" in a rich variety of ways, arguing that, in *Much Ado*, "playing" – in the sense of social performance – becomes more serious than ever before. Huston's overall thesis, that Shakespeare's work radically changes between the earlier comedies and plays such as *Much Ado*, sometimes feels strained, but he is an observant and interesting reader of these works, constantly illuminating new connections between them. And while noting *Much Ado*'s unsettling qualities, Huston maintains that Dogberry is its saving grace, "unaccountably tied to the spirits of goodness".

# Othello

A lthough it may not have the cosmic or philosophical resonance of *Hamlet* or *Lear*, the playwright's second great tragedy, *Othello*, is often felt to be his most gripping – and tormenting – play. The story of a soldier propelled into murderous fury by his wife's apparent unfaithfulness first appears in a sensationalist Italian novella, but Shakespeare transforms this small-scale, somewhat domestic drama into a maelstrom of turbulent emotion, and he produces the most heart-stopping of tragic finales. *Othello* is, importantly, also about race: its hero is a black man in a society governed by whites, and from its first days on the stage audiences have been forced to confront the complex ethnic issues it presents. Othello is a hero, not a devil – Shakespeare's contemporaries would have assumed the reverse – and ends the play an isolated and tragic figure. The calculating killer of an innocent white girl, he might easily have been the lurid villain of racist stereotype, but instead, crucially, he becomes another victim. For we in the audience see what Othello does not: the demonic nature of the play's real villain, the white Italian Iago, who, unbeknown to everyone on stage, directs every moment of the action. It is impossible not to respond strongly to *Othello*, and passionate reactions also dominate the play's history in the theatre: there are numerous stories of audience members fainting or screaming – or even begging the cast not to go through with it because events are too painful to watch. The tragedy of *Othello* draws us in like no other, and for that reason it is one of Shakespeare's very greatest achievements.

[**DATE**] Possibly as early as 1601–02; perhaps as late as 1603–04 – any decision rests on a number of resemblances to *Hamlet*. At any rate, *Othello* was composed during the period when Shakespeare wrote his major tragedies.

[**SOURCES**] Shakespeare's greatest debt is to a novella from Giraldi Cinthio's *Hecatommithi* (1565), which he read in either the original Italian or a French version by G. Chappuys (1583). Facts about the Turkish invasion may come courtesy of Richard Knolles's *History of the Turks* (1603), while the *History and Description of Africa* by Leo Africanus (1600) is another possible source.

[**TEXTS**] Famously problematical. A quarto printing (Q1) was published in 1622, just a year before the First Folio text, but is different in many details (and 160 lines shorter).

## Interpreting the play

Elizabethan and Jacobean plays featuring black characters were a rarity; ones in which they took centre-stage were unheard of. In England there was a long tradition of blacking-up in order to represent evil or exotic characters for the medieval mystery and morality cycles, and in courtly entertainment acting "black" became briefly fashionable – as in Ben Jonson's *Masque of Blackness* from 1605, during which female courtiers amused themselves by dressing as "blackamoors". Yet in real life, even with the expansion of colonial trade involving far-flung corners of the globe,

## Major Characters & Synopsis

**Othello**, a black soldier, the "Moor" of Venice
**Desdemona**, Othello's new wife
**Michael Cassio**, Othello's lieutenant
**Bianca**, a courtesan in love with Cassio
**Iago**, Othello's ensign (a low-ranking officer)
**Emilia**, Iago's wife
**Brabanzio**, Desdemona's father, a Venetian senator
**Graziano**, Brabanzio's brother
**Lodovico**, a relation of Brabanzio
**Roderigo**, a Venetian gentleman in love with Desdemona
The **Duke of Venice**
**Montano**, Governor of Cyprus
**Senators** of Venice
A **Clown** in Othello's employment

**ACT 1** Roderigo and Iago are on their way to inform Brabanzio that his daughter has eloped with Othello – the black commander of Venice's military forces. Roderigo is in love with Desdemona, while Iago claims to be angry at being passed over for promotion by Othello in favour of Cassio. Brabanzio is appalled by the news of his daughter's marriage and sets off with his kinsmen to confront Othello. But the Duke of Venice has already summoned his senators and advisers to discuss the sighting of a hostile Turkish fleet advancing towards Cyprus, a Venetian colony. Othello arrives and is ordered to defend Cyprus, while Brabanzio's wild claim that his daughter has been bewitched is dismissed when Desdemona enters and confirms her love, after which the couple immediately leave for Cyprus. But their problems are only beginning: Iago, who has the general's absolute trust, is plotting Othello's downfall.

**ACT 2** Though battered by storms, the Venetians arrive safely in Cyprus to news that the Turkish fleet has dispersed. Roderigo is also in Cyprus, and Iago is quick to exploit his jealousy. Persuading him that Desdemona is now in love with Cassio, he encourages him to pick a fight with Cassio later that evening. To make this more likely, Iago gets Cassio drunk and in the ensuing brawl Cassio strikes a fellow officer. Dragged from his bed, Othello demands an explanation, which Iago gives in such a way that – without directly blaming him – Cassio is dismissed. Iago then

advises Cassio to win back Othello's favour via Desdemona's influence; but his own secret plan is to convince Othello that Cassio is having an affair with her.

**ACT 3** When Desdemona intercedes on Cassio's behalf, Iago suggests to Othello that she does so out of more than mere friendship. Othello is resistant at first, but as Iago gradually works on him, the idea of her adultery comes to seem more and more feasible. When Desdemona reappears, she tries to soothe her husband's obvious disquiet by binding his head with her handkerchief. Iago's wife Emilia later finds the handkerchief on the floor and gives it to Iago, who seizes the opportunity to play on Othello's suspicion. Told by Iago that Desdemona has given it to Cassio as a love-token, Othello demands it back from his wife – who, innocently, tries to turn the subject back to Cassio. By now convinced of her infidelity, Othello decides on revenge.

**ACT 4** Iago continues to fuel Othello's jealousy, to the point where he collapses in a fit. When he recovers, Iago arranges for him to overhear a meeting with Cassio, during which Othello becomes even more certain that Desdemona is unfaithful. He resolves to kill her, while Iago undertakes to murder Cassio. When a deputation arrives from Venice recalling Othello, he publicly abuses Desdemona (to everyone's horror) and later, in private, accuses her of being a whore.

**ACT 5** At Iago's bidding, Roderigo attacks Cassio but only wounds him, and in the confusion that follows Iago stabs Roderigo to death. Othello, meanwhile, is about to kill the sleeping Desdemona when she awakens; despite her anguished denials, he smothers her in their own bed. Discovering them both, Emilia insists on her mistress's innocence, and when Othello mentions the handkerchief the extent of Iago's villainy is finally revealed. Iago has arrived in the meantime, but when Othello attacks him, he escapes after killing Emilia. Returning under arrest, he refuses to give any reason for his actions. Othello finally realizes the truth and, after asking Cassio's forgiveness, stabs himself. He dies clutching his dead wife.

there were few black people resident in England itself (some had been expelled by Elizabeth) during Shakespeare's lifetime. The world-revealing public theatres must have been one of the very few means by which the public, at least in London, experienced such "exoticism" first hand.

Shakespeare himself had introduced a "Moor", Aaron, into the Roman world of *Titus Andronicus*, and another, the Prince of Morocco, makes an appearance in *The Merchant of Venice*, itself a play massively concerned with the idea of an ethnic outsider living in the metropolis. Neither character makes much of a positive precedent: Morocco is a pompous bore, while Aaron is as close as the young playwright got to evil incarnate, a fearsome yet thinly sketched villain – both characterizations doing little to challenge commonplace Elizabethan assumptions about the moral or intellectual qualities of men who were black, let alone lurid fears about miscegenation (both men are involved with white women). Yet in *Othello* everything changes. A black man is the tragic hero, the noble "Moor of Venice" for whom the play is named; it is a white Italian, Iago, who is the villain.

That apparent contradiction must have struck *Othello*'s first audiences hard, and indeed the Duke of Venice admits to feeling it too, hearing that Desdemona, daughter of one of his senators, has done the unthinkable and married a black soldier. "Noble signor," he addresses her fuming father,

> If virtue no delighted beauty lack,
> Your son-in-law is far more fair than black.

[1.3.289–90]

The division between outward appearance and inner reality will prove a crucial – and increasingly malignant – idea in *Othello*, but for the moment it seems that at least some Venetians recognize that a man who happens to be black need not be a savage.

This realization appears hard won. In opening scenes of unparalleled bitterness and brutality, we have watched as Iago and Roderigo – Othello's ensign, and his rival for Desdemona's hand – do their utmost to slander his name. Before the first scene is out, and before he even appears on stage, "the Moor" (as Iago sneeringly calls him) is described as a "thick-lips", a "Barbary [Arab] horse", a "lascivious Moor". Attempting, and succeeding, to drive Desdemona's father insane with anger at the news that she has eloped with Othello, Iago puts it in the basest terms he can think of. "'Swounds, sir, you're robbed," he taunts Brabanzio,

> Your heart is burst, you have lost half your soul.
> Even now, now, very now, an old black ram
> Is tupping your white ewe.

[1.1.86–9]

What we are soon to see described (in Othello's rapt words) as a love "too much of joy" (2.1.198), a love upon which the play will hinge, is here reduced to brute animal lust – and crude racist stereotype.

Over the four centuries *Othello* has been upon the stage, actors and audiences have likewise struggled with the idea that Othello could be both black and the hero of the piece – one commentator, writing in the southern United States only a few years after the Civil War had brought an end to slavery, declared that, in her view, "Shakespeare was too correct a delineator of human nature to have coloured Othello *black* … Othello *was* a *white* man." Such colour blindness (in the worst sense of that phrase) was hardly at a premium. Though there were occasional exceptions, notably the nineteenth-century African-American star Ira Aldridge, Othellos were played by white actors in makeup right up to the 1960s. Critics have fussed – some, incredibly, still do – over his precise ethnicity, as if by being proved not to be a "veritable negro" (as Coleridge argued), he could more easily be understood.

## Shakespeare's "Moors"

At least three "Moors" appear in Shakespeare's plays: Aaron in *Titus Andronicus*, the Prince of Morocco in *The Merchant of Venice*, and of course the most famous of all, Othello, the "Moor of Venice" (though a fourth, a nameless Moorish girl made pregnant by Lancelot Gobbo in *The Merchant*, also surfaces briefly). The word **"Moor"** has its roots in ancient Mauretania in North Africa, approximately modern-day Algeria and Morocco, but shifted northwest during the eighth century when people of mixed Arab and Berber descent, called *Moro*, conquered Spain and made it part of the Islamic empire.

However, Shakespeare's use of the term, like that of many of his contemporaries – indeed, people much later – is generic at best, and in *Othello* still causes confusion. On the one hand Iago describes the hero as a "Barbarian" (hinting that he is from Barbary in North Africa, perhaps having lighter skin); on the other, Othello calls himself "black", and Roderigo tauntingly refers to him as "the thick-lips", implying that he is negroid and perhaps therefore from sub-Saharan Africa. But Roderigo and Iago's crude racist insults don't exactly make for trustworthy evidence – and the debate would have had little practical value for Shakespeare, still less the white actor blacking up for the part (see p.264). "Moor", "Blackamoor" and "Muslim" were often interchangeable in this period (all three thought to portray an exotic, godless and brutish people), and even if the playwright's sensitivity to his hero's ethnicity were more sophisticated than his countrymen's, this play reminds us that apparently reliable facts about appearance are often anything but. Othello himself relates some more crucial reasons why he feels like an alien: his age, military background and social status all make him an awkward guest in Venice, and Jacobethan audiences would have been quick to observe the strangeness of his marriage to a young society girl. In *Othello*, of all plays, we have to do more than look skin deep.

The surprising thing is, those shocking first few scenes aside, *Othello* is not a play that explores racism in any real detail – *The Merchant*, also set in the racial melting-pot of Venice, is far more analytical in that respect. As Othello himself testifies, he is employed as a general by the Venetian state and has every reason to expect his position to be respected. And in a sense, it is: though Brabanzio is inflamed by racist slander, his real irritation is that his daughter has flouted his wishes; likewise, Roderigo's grudge against Othello is simply that Desdemona prefers her new, more exciting, suitor to the drab Venetian.

## Enmesh them all

Othello has, it seems, not the slightest clue that there is anything at work against him. But Iago's racist insults, delivered while Iago successfully pretends to be Othello's closest companion, take on a more frightening aspect when the action relocates to the far-flung island of Cyprus. Posted there in order to confront the encroaching Turks, the party of Venetians – Othello, his wife and Cassio, plus soldiers – arrives to the welcome news that the Turkish fleet has been broken up by the storm. But though the military threat has evaporated, Iago has not. Trapped as he is in this suffocating outpost, his plot to devastate the fragile colony and Othello, the man at its centre, develops and builds strength uninterrupted.

We might wonder why Iago is so desperate to destroy Othello, but the play has no real answer – or rather, presents too many to believe. Samuel Taylor Coleridge famously commented on Iago's "motive-hunting of motiveless malignity", and though more literal-minded commentators have taken up the scattered, often preposterous, clues Iago tosses to the audience (which include anything from professional envy to the belief that Othello has, in Iago's grim expression, "leapt into my seat" by sleeping with his wife), Coleridge comes closer than most to defining the sense of absolute evil Iago represents. There is a terrifying void at the centre of his character, something that simply cannot be rationalized. In one of Iago's most chilling soliloquies, he even plays tricks with the one thing that is certain about him – his insatiable wickedness. "And what's he then that says I play the villain?" he taunts,

> When this advice is free I give, and honest …?

[3.1.327–8]

Dispensing "advice" to all and sundry under the cover of plain-speaking honesty, Iago's devilishness, as he goes on to boast, lies in his ability to produce "heavenly shows" while all the time plotting the "blackest sins" imaginable – a triumphant duplicity that will see Othello calling his ensign "honest Iago" until practically the last moment of the play.

> *Iago knows that an identity that has been fashioned as a story can be unfashioned, refashioned, inscribed anew in a different narrative: it is the fate of stories to be consumed or, as we say more politely, interpreted.*
>
> Stephen Greenblatt, *Renaissance Self-Fashioning* (1980)

Once the Venetians are settled in Cyprus, Iago sets to work. He does so by telling stories – more specifically a single story, that Desdemona has been unfaithful with Cassio. Here the power to transform is entirely in the service of evil, as Iago reflects, outlining his plan to ensnare Desdemona:

> So will I turn her virtue into pitch,
> And out of her own goodness make the net
> That shall enmesh them all.

[2.3.351–3]

Relying on Desdemona's open-heartedness and Othello's absolute trust, Iago deftly turns each and every "virtue" into a flaw, and each character into their own most destructive enemy. In this sense he rewrites *Othello* itself, which begins like a comedy, with a marriage achieved against all odds by a rebellious daughter (like, say, *The Merry Wives* or the *Dream*), followed by a storm that presents deliverance, not evil – and yet which turns into monstrous tragedy, one that, as Iago boasts, does indeed trap everyone.

Shakespeare gives Iago nearly a third of the lines in the play, many more than Othello, and he has sometimes been seen as almost a surrogate playwright. His control of the plot and his willingness to improvise is masterly, a work of malign genius. On their first night in Cyprus, Iago arranges for Cassio to get drunk and start a fight with Roderigo (who has accompanied Iago, goaded on by Iago's promise that it's only a matter of time before Desdemona is his). As Iago well knows, that night is also the wedding night, and Othello is so unimpressed at being disturbed that he strips Cassio of his post on the spot. Cassio is mortified and desperate to recover his "reputation", so Iago persuades him that the quickest way to the general's heart is to appeal to his wife. With all this in place, Iago begins to work Othello. When the two men are alone, Iago innocently asks, "Did Michael Cassio, when you wooed my lady, / Know of your love?"

OTHELLO
　　He did, from first to last. Why dost thou ask?
IAGO
　　But for a satisfaction of my thought,
　　No further harm.
OTHELLO　　　　　　Why of thy thought, Iago?

IAGO
    I did not think he had been acquainted with her.
OTHELLO
    O yes, and went between us very oft.
IAGO  Indeed?
OTHELLO
    Indeed? Ay, indeed. Discern'st thou aught in that?
    Is he not honest?
IAGO  Honest, my lord?
OTHELLO  Honest? Ay, honest.
IAGO
    My lord, for aught I know.
OTHELLO                What dost thou think?
IAGO  Think, my lord?
OTHELLO
    'Think, my lord?' By heaven, thou echo'st me
    As if there were some monster in thy thought
    Too hideous to be shown! Thou dost mean something.

**[3.3.96–112]**

While what Iago wants Othello to think he "means" is already becoming clear, the plain truth, that the whole thing is a monstrous fiction, will not be exposed until it is far too late. Iago uses his control over language to run rings around his master – hinting and insinuating, never stating. Deniability is a key component of Iago's subterfuge, as is his technique of ensuring that Othello is left to construct his own nightmare, breed his own "monsters". And it works, horribly. "By the world," Othello rages at Iago soon afterwards, "I think my wife be honest, and think she is not."

    I think that thou art just, and think thou art not.
    I'll have some proof. My name, that was as fresh
    As Dian's visage, is now begrimed and black
    As mine own face. If there be cords, or knives,
    Poison, or fire, or suffocating streams,
    I'll not endure it.

**[3.3.388–95]**

Once Othello's feelings are aroused they will not be assuaged, and over the next scenes of the play his doubts about Desdemona's faithfulness (and Cassio's "honesty") will harden into certainty. Iago, typically, is the first to mention the word "jealousy", warning his master with apparent concern that "it is the green-eyed monster which doth mock / The meat it feeds on" (3.3.170–1). For his part Othello is already becoming convinced that his "name" is destroyed and that murderous violence is inevitable.

## Confirmations strong

Othello persuades himself that he is acting rationally by demanding "some proof", but he reckons without Iago's skill – or the workings of chance. As Iago had planned, Othello's is "a jealousy so strong / That judgement cannot cure" (2.1.300–1), and he will be convinced by the flimsiest of grounds. That "proof", almost farcically, is a handkerchief, "spotted with strawberries", that Desdemona happens to drop. Seized on by Emilia, who hands it to her husband, the handkerchief makes its way to Cassio's chamber and thereby becomes the sum total of the physical evidence proving Desdemona's guilt. As Iago jubilantly remarks, "trifles light as air /

## A veritable negro

Samuel Taylor Coleridge's notorious assertion that "it would be something monstrous to conceive this beautiful Venetian girl falling in love with a veritable negro" speaks of the anxieties many nineteenth-century audiences felt confronting *Othello*'s views on race. On the one hand, Othello was black (though Coleridge tried hard to prove he wasn't); on the other, he was the hero – and some had trouble reconciling the two. The striking thing about Coleridge's angst is its newness: the few surviving seventeenth-century references to the play simply admire the power of the role, and even in the eighteenth century *Othello* seems to have been understood as a play about jealousy rather than race.

It's interesting to counterpoint this with its performance history. When *Othello* first appeared around 1604, there would have been no question of a black man taking the lead – apart from anything else, few were resident in London. Shakespeare's theatre (as its critics continually fulminated) was well practised at illusion: just as boys played girls, white actors played black roles such as those in the anonymous *Lust's Dominion* (1599) as well as in Shakespeare's own *Titus Andronicus*, *The Merchant of Venice* and *Othello*. The same remained true into the nineteenth century and far beyond – the Moor was too good a part to give up. The last white Othello at the RSC, **Donald Sinden**, appeared as recently as 1979, while **Jonathan Miller**'s BBC 1981 television production cast Anthony Hopkins as a blacked-up hero (admittedly to widespread outcry).

Miller argued that the play was not really about ethnicity, but the first great black Othello, the nineteenth-century actor **Ira Aldridge**, felt differently: *Othello* became a symbol of his struggle to win over audiences unwilling to see a "negro" act Shakespeare. Having found little success in the United States but some in Britain, Aldridge embarked on a wide-ranging European tour in the 1850s, reaching as far as Russia and winning ecstatic praise wherever he went. As the anti-slavery movement was gathering pace, a Russian liberal, K. Zvantsev, wrote fervently that Aldridge's Othello voiced "the far-off groans of his own people, oppressed by unbelievable slavery, and more than that – the groans of the whole of suffering mankind". Not until **Paul Robeson**'s performances in the 1930s and 40s would *Othello* again have such passionate resonance with the politics of racial oppression.

Later in the twentieth century, directors have been wary of underplaying Othello's ethnicity, perhaps fearful of being accused, ironically enough, of racism (this does not seem to be an issue in opera, where

A portrait of the actor Ira Aldridge (1807–67) as a visibly agitated Othello. Painted by James Northcote in 1826, it was the first picture to be purchased for the then new Manchester City Art Gallery.

it is still the norm for white singers to black up for the title role in Verdi's *Otello*). A bold experiment by Jude Kelly at the Washington Shakespeare Theater in 1997 – a so-called **"photonegative" production** – attempted to re-evaluate the racial dynamics of the play, but many felt that by employing Patrick Stewart's white Othello amid an otherwise African-American cast Kelly had simply pandered to the box-office and made things even harder for black actors trying to secure lead roles. Something of the same anger makes itself felt in the novelist **Ben Okri**'s account of watching Ben Kingsley play a Moorish Othello at the RSC in 1985. Okri remarks in *A Way of Being Free* (1997) on feeling like "the only black person in the audience" and insists that the play is unavoidably about colour: "any black man who has gone out with a white woman", he argues, "knows that there are a lot of Iagos around". For all that Kingsley is of Indian descent, "colour-blind" casting was never going to be easy for a play like *Othello*.

Are to the jealous confirmations strong / As proofs of holy writ" (3.3.326–7). The eighteenth-century dramatist Thomas Rymer famously belittled *Othello* as a "bloody Farce", irreverently suggesting that it should be called "the *Tragedy of the Handkerchief*", and though few have felt brave enough to defend him, Rymer does put his finger on the sheer horror of what the play presents: a husband persuaded into murderous jealousy by mere gossip, a wife sent to her death by a "little napkin" – even if, as Othello later claims, the handkerchief was woven for his mother and has "magic in the web of it" (3.4.69). But perhaps that's the point: even the tiniest or apparently most insignificant details are put under huge pressure by this play, and when they fail to take the weight, the tragedy collapses with spectacular force. Desdemona's well-meaning eagerness to help Cassio rebounds terribly against her; Emilia's desperate efforts to earn her husband's love makes her an unwitting accessory to his plot.

The play's greatest perversity, though, is built into its very structure. *Othello* is the site of one of Shakespeare's most virtuosic theatrical coups, the so-called "double time-scheme". Othello and Desdemona have, on one level of the play, almost implausibly little time together: their new marriage is threatened by her father's wild intervention, then by the news that Othello must be sent to Cyprus; likewise, their wedding-night is disturbed by Cassio's brawl (leading some critics to infer that the match remains unconsummated), then by the witless group of musicians he pays to play outside their window in a misguided attempt to curry favour. It has been calculated from internal references that, once in Cyprus, the action of the play occupies no more than 33 hours – just under a day and a half. On stage, of course, *Othello* feels much longer, apparently lengthened by Shakespeare's scattered gestures to more extended time periods. The effect is of a play at once too long and too short: long enough for Othello and Desdemona's marriage to feel convincing, yet short enough for it to be insecure; short enough for Iago's plot to remain secret, yet long enough for it to work its way to completion. Though he is ignorant of it, Othello himself picks up on this impossible, torturing tension. "What sense had I of her stol'n hours of lust?" he cries,

> I saw't not, thought it not; it harmed not me …
> He that is robbed, not wanting what is stol'n,
> Let him not know't and he's not robbed at all.

> [3.3.343–8]

Those "stol'n hours" are, of course, an impossibility; there is simply no time in the action of the play (even if there were reason) for Desdemona to be unfaithful. Shakespeare steals time from us too, just as Iago steals from Othello his mind. Time is just another ingredient of Iago's plot.

Nor does Shakespeare give us opportunity to draw breath. Just a few minutes after beginning to suspect Desdemona, Othello is racked by doubt; another few minutes after that, he is swearing "capable and wide revenge" with Iago's gleeful help (3.3.462), convinced by the evidence and resolved not to go back. After the handkerchief makes its appearance and Cassio is framed, the effect on the hero is devastating. "Lie with her? Lie on her?" Othello cries desperately,

> We say 'lie on her' when they belie her. Lie with her? 'Swounds, that's fulsome! Handkerchief—confessions—handkerchief. To confess and be hanged for his labour. First to be hanged and then to confess! I tremble at it. Nature would not invest herself in such shadowing passion without some instruction. It is not words that shakes me thus. Pish! Noses, ears, and lips! Is't possible? Confess? Handkerchief? O devil!

> *He falls down in a trance*

> [4.1.33–42]

Though Othello will rapidly recover from this fit, the mental turmoil it represents will stay with him until his death.

> *In the first half of the play the main conflict is merely incubating; then it bursts into life, and goes storming, without intermission or change of direction, to its close.*

A.C. Bradley, *Shakespearean Tragedy* (1904)

But first the blameless Desdemona must die. Although Iago plants the idea of her infidelity in Othello's mind, the notion of killing her in revenge is all her husband's. "O, blood, blood, blood!" he rages just moments before his wife appears, as innocent of the knowledge as she is in character. She assumes that state business has distracted Othello, made him unwell, but her ministrations do nothing but infuriate him. The terrible cycle of jealousy does its work. After a horrific public shaming during which Othello hits her in front of guests from Venice, the lovers have a tearful final argument. Othello taunts her with his own certainties, refuses to listen to her denials. "What, not a whore?" he cries incredulously,

DESDEMONA                No, as I shall be saved.
OTHELLO  Is't possible?
DESDEMONA  O heaven forgive us!
OTHELLO  I cry you mercy then.
    I took you for that cunning whore of Venice
    That married with Othello.

**[4.2.89–94]**

There is something infinitely moving about Othello's lingering torment, but of course he is not its main victim. Instructing Desdemona to prepare for bed, he readies himself for an execution in cold blood. Even so, the testimony of her sleeping body almost persuades him not to go through with it. "It is the cause, it is the cause," he murmurs, stepping silently into her bedroom,

Let me not name it to you, you chaste stars.
It is the cause. Yet I'll not shed her blood,
Nor scar that whiter skin of hers than snow,
And smooth as monumental alabaster.
Yet she must die, else she'll betray more men.

**[5.2.1–6]**

He will not "scar" her alabaster skin, but he will kill her before the scene is out. This is perhaps the most chilling of Iago's many malicious victories: as well as robbing Othello of his sanity, he makes him into the villain imagined by crude racist fantasy – a black murderer stealing into a white girl's bedchamber. Worse still, Othello seems aware of the fact, drawing attention to her "whiter" complexion rather than his "foul", "filthy" murder. Emilia informs Othello what many seventeenth-century audiences will have suspected all along: "O, the more angel she, and you the blacker devil!" (5.2.140).

With that, the play is very nearly over – but not quite. Though it is too late for Desdemona (and indeed for Othello), in the dying moments the truth does out. Following Emilia's furious testimony – like her namesake in *The Winter's Tale* she is a fierce guardian of the truth – the real story emerges. "O thou dull Moor," she yells, "that handkerchief thou speak'st of / I found by fortune and did give my husband…" (5.2.232–3). Realizing that his fictions are collapsing, Iago makes a last attempt to rewrite the conclusion and lunges brutally at his wife, mortally wounding her. Othello, meanwhile, begins the slow and tragic journey to realization. He, too, is desperate to be understood. "When you shall these unlucky deeds relate," he tells the assembled throng, as it gathers around the corpses on stage,

> Speak of me as I am. Nothing extenuate,
> Nor set down aught in malice. Then must you speak
> Of one that loved not wisely but too well,
> Of one not easily jealous but, being wrought,
> Perplexed in the extreme; of one whose hand,
> Like the base Indian, threw a pearl away
> Richer than all his tribe …

**[5.2.350–7]**

For Iago, however, the story-telling has come to an end. "Demand me nothing," he sneers. "What you know, you know." (5.2.309–10). There will be no other answers.

# Stage history and adaptations

The first performance of *Othello* on record is at James I's **court** on November 1, 1604. After his death **Richard Burbage** was applauded for his playing of the "grieved Moor"; opposite him as Iago was possibly **John Lowin**, better known for his Falstaff. Fifteen or so years later Burbage's heir **Ellyaert Swanston** took on Othello and **Joseph Taylor** Iago. Another early staging was recorded at **Oxford** in 1610, where the performance apparently moved spectators to tears, and the play was being performed in London right up to the Civil Wars.

It soon returned, almost unique among Shakespeare's output in not being adapted for the Restoration stage: Desdemona was one of the first roles to be taken by a professional actress. **Michael Mohun** was a celebrated Iago in the 1670s and the play was possibly performed at Dublin's Smock Alley Theatre soon afterwards, but from 1682 *Othello* became indelibly associated with **Thomas Betterton**'s magisterial Moor, much commended for his "Rage and Jealousy" in the role. Those words came from **Colley Cibber**, who played a smirking Iago to **Barton Booth**'s heroic and noble Othello from 1710 to 1727. Booth's reputation was so great that **James Quin** struggled when he attempted the role in 1720 (again to Cibber's Iago), and when **Charles Macklin** turned to the play in 1734 he opted for Iago instead, producing one of the subtlest interpretations of the century. Eleven years later **Garrick**, too, was defeated by the Moor (Quin came along to barrack from the stalls) and performed him only three times. **Spranger Barry**'s electrifying Othello – so passionate that female audience members shrieked whenever he came on stage – offered too much competition, so Garrick joined forces with Barry at Drury Lane in 1747 while still attempting to dominate as Iago. Barry's Desdemona was the excellent **Susannah Cibber**, and a generation later it was **Sarah Siddons** who transformed Desdemona into a central role, acting her alongside the stately Othello of her brother, **John Philip Kemble**, from 1785. Soon afterwards the play became known in French via **Jean-François Ducis**'s translation, its Parisian audiences so stunned by the play that Ducis reportedly had to scribble an emergency happy ending in case they rioted.

**Edmund Kean** seized upon *Othello* in 1814, and his mercurial hero was received with adulation. Opting for lighter makeup than usual, and emphasizing the facial expressions and the emotional extremes that were his hallmark, Kean downplayed the first two acts of the play, but came into his own during Othello's breakdown, producing, according to Hazlitt, "the finest piece of acting in the world". In his first season, Kean played the role of Iago – equally successfully – on alterate nights, before establishing the precedent of hiring rival tragedians to

"Peace, and be still." Othello (Paul Robeson) moves to kill Desdemona (Peggy Ashcroft). A scene from the 1930 production of *Othello* at London's Savoy Theatre.

play Iago, virtually in competition to his Othello. **Junius Brutus Booth** was humiliated this way in 1817, the Kemble disciple **Charles Mayne Young** fared slightly better in 1822, but by the time Kean took on **William Charles Macready** in 1832 he was a broken man. A year later, during his final performance, he collapsed into the arms of his son **Charles Kean,** who was playing Iago, and died two months later. By this time the brawny **Edwin Forrest** had become well known in the US (he played Othello for the next half-century) at around the same time that the black actor **Ira Aldridge** was struggling to make his name. Aldridge would eventually succeed in the 1850s with a European tour that turned him into a folk hero, but in Britain and the States audiences were often openly racist (see p.264). His pan-European success would be replicated a few decades later by the Italians **Tommaso Salvini** and **Ernesto Rossi**, both playing impressive Othellos in their native language; Salvini won praise for being "supremely, paralyzingly real" in the role.

English actors failed to match the grandeur of these foreign stars, and during the late Victorian era *Othello* became more than ever Iago's play. **Henry Irving** attempted the Moor in 1876, but even his leading lady **Ellen Terry** (herself an impressive Desdemona) admitted that watching him was "painful" in the worst sense, and when they revived it in 1881 Irving took Iago to **Edwin Booth**'s Othello. By the end of the decade **Giuseppe Verdi**'s grand opera had become known in England and Shakespeare's play suffered as a result. *Othello* became a problem for producers struggling to make it visually impressive, and so different directions were required: **Baliol Holloway** took the risk of performing an egotistical Othello in 1922, while in 1929 **H.K. Ayliff**'s Birmingham Rep gave the play modern-dress. But the most famous Othello of the era was **Paul Robeson**, who closely associated the role, like Aldridge before him, with the struggle against racist oppression. He appeared at London's Savoy Theatre in 1930 opposite a young **Peggy Ashcroft** as Desdemona (audiences were audibly shocked when the lovers kissed); again in a 1943 production directed by **Margaret Webster**, which still retains the record for longest run on Broadway; and finally at Stratford in 1959 with **Sam Wanamaker** as Iago and **Mary Ure** as Desdemona. Though Robeson was sometimes accused of being expressionless, he brought to the part (according to one witness) a "tranquil dignity and a melancholy infinitely sad".

Back in England directors tried hard to compete, but **Ralph Richardson**'s Othello under **Tyrone Guthrie** at the Old Vic in 1938 was underpowered – in contrast to **Laurence Olivier**, who played Iago as a repressed homosexual and stole the show. **Donald Wolfit** took the role in his many touring productions during the 1940s, while over in the States **Orson Welles** acted in the 1951 production that would eventually become his film. By this time black actors had become more familiar in the role: **Earle Hyman** played Othello in the 1950s, but it was **James Earl Jones**'s resonant 1964 New York Shakespeare Festival performance that became most celebrated (he repeated the role on Broadway in 1982, but this time **Christopher Plummer**'s Iago got the rave reviews). The year 1964 also saw was also the year of **John Dexter**'s National Theatre production, which had **Laurence Olivier** attempt an anti-heroic Othello in deference to the critic F.R. Leavis, who had criticized the character's self-absorption. Olivier's efforts to act against type (and to be as "black" as possible) upset many and risked swamping an otherwise appealing production, marked by **Maggie Smith**'s reserved Desdemona and **Frank Finlay**'s icy Iago.

The 1970s saw more experimentation. **Charles Marowitz**'s *An Othello* (1972) made both hero and villain black and ditched much of Shakespeare's language, while in Hamburg four years later **Peter Zadek** caused controversy by making his Othello wear a King Kong costume in an attempt to shock audiences out of their complacency. But in retrospect probably the more influential production was the 1971 RSC version by **John Barton**, which pitched the play in a nineteenth-century colonial outpost and emphasized its barrack-room bravado; **Brewster Mason**'s stolid Othello played second fiddle to **Emrys James**'s energetic Iago. By that time, though, it was nearly the end of an era: the last two white Othellos in major British productions, **Donald Sinden** (RSC, 1979) and **Paul Scofield** (National, 1980), both opted for light brown makeup rather than trying to convince audiences (as Olivier did) that they were actually of a different ethnicity.

**Janet Suzman**'s production at Johannesburg's Market Theatre in 1987 did not have the luxury of disengagement. South Africa was still under apartheid rule and the play (rarely performed) became highly political: **John Kani**, playing Othello, thought that audiences divided along racial lines in their response. In a different way ethnicity was also crucial for **Terry Hands**'s production at the RSC two years earlier: Hands tried to stress the dangerous affinities between the Othello of **Ben Kingsley** (himself of Indian descent) and **David Suchet**'s Iago, but it was Suchet's decision to play Iago as obviously gay that proved most influential. **Ian McKellen** hinted something similar in **Trevor Nunn**'s 1987 production – with **Willard White** a statuesque and commanding Othello to **Imogen Stubbs**'s girlish Desdemona – as did **Simon Russell Beale** under **Sam Mendes** at the Old Vic in 1998. While Nunn once more drew on the nineteenth century for his production, Mendes opted to set *Othello* in the 1930s, drawing out the play's militarism with Russell Beale's bully-boy villain dominating **David Harewood**'s youthful hero – an approach emulated at **Michael Attenborough**'s RSC in 1999, with **Ray Fearon**'s Othello in thrall to **Richard McCabe**'s bluff Iago. Conceivably the boldest attempt to redefine *Othello* in recent years, however, was the Washington Shakespeare Theatre production by **Jude Kelly**, which staged a "photonegative" version of the play in 1997: **Patrick Stewart** played a white Othello surrounded by blacks, among them **Patrice Johnson**'s moving Desdemona and the hefty Iago of **Ron Canada**. Many critics were unconvinced, though, arguing that Kelly's approach created more problems than it solved.

In 2004 two major UK productions graced the stage, testament not only to *Othello*'s continuing popularity, but also to a new generation of black actors willing to take the role. **Declan Donnellan**'s touring production for Cheek By Jowl had a gentle, almost boyish hero from **Nonso Anozie**, utterly bewildered by **Jonny Philips**'s brilliant, cooing Iago. His equivalent at the RSC was **Antony Sher**, who took the role opposite **Sello Maake ka-Ncube**'s Othello. Gregory Doran's production was much hyped for its South African connections – the stars grew up on the different sides of apartheid – but it was its near-operatic intensity that most captured reviewers, embodied in Sher's defiantly energetic villain as much as ka-Ncube's histrionic downfall.

Until the TV adaptation of Nunn's production (1990) no footage existed of a black actor playing Othello in a mainstream version. A 1922 silent film by **Dmitri Buchowetzki** (with **Emil Jannings** as Othello and **Werner Krauss** as Iago) and **Sergei Yutkevich**'s 1955 Russian version aside, the dominant English-language productions are those by **Orson Welles** (1952), **Stuart Burge** – a 1965 rendering of the Dexter–Olivier staging – and **Oliver Parker** (1995), the last with **Laurence Fishburne** as Othello. **Jonathan Miller**'s much-criticized BBC/Time-Life production initially (1981) tried to secure James Earl Jones as Othello, but in the end cast **Anthony Hopkins** opposite **Bob Hoskins**'s Iago.

# Screen

## Othello

### O. Welles, S. Cloutier, M. MacLiammóir; Orson Welles (dir.)

Morocco/Italy, 1952/1993 ▷ Second Sight / Academy **DVD** ▭

Welles's recently reconstructed *Othello* – like pretty much everything he did – has divided audiences. Some have junked it as eccentric bilge, others consider it a masterpiece in the best traditions of *film noir*. Whichever camp you find yourself drawn into, when you consider the terrible labours of production, it's a wonder anything got made at all: with funding practically non-existent, shooting took, on and off, four years – two weeks for every minute of film. Though there is much that will offend purists (not least the savage cuts, which shrink the action to a hurtling 87 minutes and render the immaculately paced onset of jealousy all but nonsensical), it's the shards of brilliance that remain lodged in the memory: Welles's sturdy Othello, sunlit at first but trapped in cloying shadow as he descends into madness; Micheál MacLiammóir's febrile Iago; superbly inventive flashes of cinematography and stage business. While it may not comply with the letter of Shakespeare's play, this *Othello* is a loving tribute to its spirit.

## Othello

### L. Olivier, M. Smith, F. Finlay; Stuart Burge (dir.)

UK, 1965 ▷ British Home Entertainment **DVD** ▭

Anyone expecting a noble, Robeson-like Moor will be shocked by Laurence Olivier's portrayal, which presents a vividly unsympathetic Othello, an arrogant fraud only tolerated in Venice because of his usefulness to the state. This is interesting and radical stuff, much indebted to Leavis (see p.272), but Olivier, characteristically, goes too far. Quite apart from his colour, which makes Othello look as if he's been dipped in antique wood-stain, Olivier's efforts "to *be* black" (in his words) by lowering his voice, altering his gait and attempting a Jamaican accent seem offensive in all the wrong ways. In striving for "blackness" as a mark of "otherness", this interpretation veers too close to racist caricature – and is often too embarrassingly comic – for its many insights to be taken seriously. Almost as importantly, it doesn't allow Othello's character to go anywhere: what Shakespeare scores as a series of infinitesimal psychological fractures become variations on a theme, and Frank Finlay's smirking, NCO Iago barely has to lift a finger to return his master to savagery.

## Othello

### W. White, I. Stubbs, I. McKellen; T. Nunn (dir.)

UK, 1990 ▷ Metrodome **DVD** ▭

Qualities that marked out Nunn's 1978 filming of *Macbeth* – pared-down setting, taut atmosphere, excellent casting – are very much in evidence here, in what remains probably *Othello*'s best translation to video. Shakespeare's domestic tragedy feels naturally at home on the small screen, and particularly so when Nunn's claustrophobic sets and dour nineteenth-century staging, originally designed for the RSC's tiny The Other Place, begin to do their work. Willard White, better known as an opera singer, has the stature and the voice to make a superb Othello, and Imogen Stubbs brings an appealingly fragile quality to Desdemona. Zoë Wanamaker's Emilia, too, deserves praise for her blend of strength and neediness. But in Nunn's hands the play belongs throughout to Ian McKellen's restless Iago, as impressively flexible as the play needs him to be yet always teetering on the brink of sanity.

## Othello

### L. Fishburne, I. Jacobs, K. Branagh; Oliver Parker (dir.)

UK, 1995 ▷ Columbia / Warner **DVD** ▭

A film starring Kenneth Branagh in which he isn't the director? True enough, though you could get through watching this picture without realizing it: some of the old crew are here (Tim Harvey's lush designs are unmistakable) and Oliver Parker's debut film is solidly in the style of Hollywood Shakespeare *à la* Branagh. Its gorgeously shot Italian settings will be an antidote to too many studio-bound versions, though in most other respects this film simply fails to come alive. Laurence Fishburne's Moor did not deserve the critical mauling it received upon release, but despite Fishburne's impressive screen presence he sorely lacks depth and often seems rudderless in the verse. That might be Parker's fault: everyone attempts to keep the dialogue naturalistically low-key, and with the play's melodrama pumped up (most famously for fantasy sequences in which Othello imagines Desdemona's infidelity) the results are oddly imbalanced. Branagh himself looks uneasy playing his first Shakespearian villain, and with about half the script gone (including Iago's crucial final lines), this *Othello* is more lightweight than it needed to be.

# Audio

## Othello

### P. Robeson, J. Ferrer, U. Hagen; Godard Lieberson (dir.)

USA, 1944 ▷ Pearl ⊙

Paul Robeson's life was intimately bound up with *Othello*: the role itself became a vocal part of his struggle for civil rights, and gave him a much-valued opportunity to extend his acting skills beyond the stereotyping confines of Hollywood. For that reason alone this 1944 recording is unique testament to a man who has still perhaps to receive his full due. Unfortunately it doesn't hold many other attractions: José Ferrer's unruffled Iago barely breaks into a trot, Alexander Scourby sounds insipid as both Cassio and Brabanzio and while the script is quite heavily trimmed this taping somehow lacks any real tension. The goods are delivered, however, by the lead couple (who were having an affair at the time): Uta

The distinguished bass Willard White came to Trevor Nunn's RSC *Othello* (1989) fresh from the operatic stage, and made a dignified and expressive hero. Ian McKellen's paranoid Iago was a dangerously perfect foil.

Hagen is passionate and persuasive as Desdemona, and opposite her Robeson is calmly adamantine. While he doesn't find the fire in the role you might expect, the detailed modulation of his astonishing voice offers its own rich insights – particularly as the play develops and Othello disappears into the depths of his inner soul (the final scene is extraordinarily intense). In addition, three of Robeson's song recordings close disc two of this set.

### Othello

#### H. Quarshie, A. Lesser, E. Fielding; David Timson (dir.)
UK, 2000 ▷ Naxos ⊙ ⊡

Hugh Quarshie presents an entirely different hero to Fearon (see below): older, cooler, oakier in vocal tone, somewhat more thoughtful, yet alert to the quiet humour of the role. Quarshie – who has written about the play – has looked at Othello long and hard, and his breakdown, when it occurs, is like watching a building subside, but brick by brick. Anton Lesser as Iago might struggle to persuade that he's a career soldier, but nevertheless his is a versatile high-wire performance, one that might almost convince you (as Othello is convinced) of Iago's bluff but hard-edged honesty. Emma Fielding makes a mature and searching Desdemona, resigning herself to the wreckage of her marriage (like that of Patience Tomlinson's wry Emilia) with clear but saddened sight. Supporting parts are also well filled: John McAndrew whines delightfully as Roderigo, and Peter Yapp is surprisingly sympathetic as Brabanzio. Not as searing an experience as the BBC version, but this is a mature and well-rounded production.

### Othello

#### R. Fearon, J. Frain, A. Hille; Jeremy Mortimer (dir.)
UK, 2001 ▷ BBC ⊙ ⊡

A few years before recording this, Ray Fearon provided one of the most memorable of recent Othellos at the RSC. On tape he is less vocally resonant than some (Hugh Quarshie, above, offers strong competition) but nevertheless manages to deliver an interpretation of the role which is both intelligent and terrifyingly sad – particularly in the scenes with James Frain's bully-boy Iago, which are so intimately recorded that Frain merely has to whisper to tighten the screws on his master's sanity. Fearon's hero is young and virile, but comes to pieces with almost startling ease: listening to the bleached-out monotone of his voice in the latter stages of the play you sense that his revenge will be terrible and unstoppable – that of a man who has confronted his devils and will not return. Anastasia Hille's rather quiet Desdemona is sensitively done and Lindsey Coulson pulls out all the stops as Emilia.

## Editions

### Arden Shakespeare (third series)
#### E.A.J. Honigmann; 1999 ▷ Thomson Learning

This *Othello* was one of the first third-series Ardens to be commissioned, and given the approach of the second series editor, M.R. Ridley (who cheerfully attempted to defend Desdemona's choice of husband by explaining that Othello didn't necessarily have to be seen as "sub-human"), it's easy to understand why. By the time this edition appeared, however, it was some eleven years late and Honigmann had been forced to write another book, *The Texts of "Othello"* (1996), en route. This extended gestation has delivered mixed results: though a troublesome text is handled with insight and comes up afresh, Honigmann's critical views on the play veer towards eccentricity. The skimpy stage history is also frustrating, though could be cross-referenced with Lois Potter's recent book on *Othello* in the Cambridge *Shakespeare in Performance* series (2002). A more serious concern is that Honigmann is not free from the obsession with ethnicity that still infects some commentators: perhaps it is best left to the reader whether s/he thinks the editor's views on Othello's "primitive" drives and the role of "ancestral voices" in his psychological makeup are interesting or plain offensive.

# Some criticism

### The Common Pursuit
**F. R. Leavis; 1952** ▷ Penguin [o/p]

Fearless as well as ferocious, F.R. Leavis trampled on many toes during the course of a distinguished and provocative academic career. One of the leading lights of the so-called "Cambridge" school, Leavis set up his own journal, *Scrutiny*, to publish his views and those resembling it, and many of the essays in *The Common Pursuit* appeared there first. Though they cover plenty of non-Elizabethan ground (Milton, Gerard Manley Hopkins, Johnson, Henry James), Shakespeare was always integral to Leavis's literary pantheon and three pieces confront him directly. The essay on *Othello* is the most famous, not least for the fact that it relegates the hero to a subtitle: "Diabolic Intellect and the Noble Hero: or The Sentimentalist's Othello" describes the dignified Moor of legend but insists that he figures nowhere in the play. Instead Othello has "a habit of approving self-dramatization", is fatally "self-centred" while also lacking in "self-knowledge", and, in short, has it coming to him. Plenty to disagree with, but that's the point: if Leavis doesn't make you livid there's little point in reading him.

### The Masks of Othello
**Marvin Rosenberg; 1961** ▷ Delaware UP

First published in the early 1960s but helpfully reprinted by Delaware, generations of readers have had their views on *Othello* refined and developed by Marvin Rosenberg's terrific work. Like later examples in his "Masks" series – notably *Lear* (1972), *Macbeth* (1978) and his immense *Hamlet* (1992) – *The Masks of Othello* goes straight to the heart of the play's appeal, tracking what Rosenberg's subtitle calls "the search for identity of Othello, Iago and Desdemona by three centuries of actors and critics". Examining how some of the greatest practitioners in history have approached the play provides rich rewards for a tragedy with such power to woo audiences, and this study is as enlightening about *Othello*'s deep themes as it is about its extensive life on stage. Leavis would pour scorn on Rosenberg's conclusions about Othello's essential "nobility" (built on the theories of A.C. Bradley and many after him), but Rosenberg has history on his side.

# Pericles

P ericles embodies a new mode of work for Shakespeare – away from the grand run of tragedies capped by *Antony and Cleopatra* and *Coriolanus*, and towards the world of romance. The playwright's source was the medieval poet John Gower, a figure who actually appears on stage to relate the story of the Tyrean hero, his numerous adventures and his hardships – all experiences comparable to those of wanderers in classical epic such as Odysseus and Aeneas. *Pericles* itself, excluded from the all-important First Folio, has had an equally difficult time of it, facing criticism from scholars and still rarely performed. No one is quite sure why Heminges and Condell decided not to include the play, but their reasoning probably had little to do with its literary or theatrical merit, for even in the text we possess, which appears to be corrupt or otherwise unpolished (some think it was co-written with a minor dramatist named George Wilkins), it contains moments of outstanding beauty. And as those who have been fortunate enough to have seen it in the theatre can testify, *Pericles* delivers a finale which is among Shakespeare's most intensely moving.

**[DATE]** *Pericles* was seen by the Venetian ambassador probably in 1608, and was most likely written the previous year – the earliest of Shakespeare's "romances".

**[SOURCES]** The Greek story of Apollonius (Pericles) of Tyre was widely known, but John Gower's version in *Confessio Amantis* (1390s) is the central source – the poet even stars as the play's narrator. Laurence Twine's novella *The Pattern of Painful Adventures* (1576) also furnished some details.

**[TEXTS]** *Pericles*'s sole text was printed in 1609 in an unauthorized edition, perhaps reconstructed from memory. Because it was not included in the 1623 Folio, it has been argued that *Pericles* is a collaboration with the poet George Wilkins, whose novella, *The Painful Adventures of Pericles Prince of Tyre* (1608), recalls the play. Some modern editions divide the play into scenes, but not acts.

## Interpreting the play

*Pericles* never allows us to forget that it is a story – an old tale worked up anew. The first person on stage, and a recurrent presence thereafter, is Gower, medieval poet and author of the *Confessio Amantis* ("The Lover's Confession"), Shakespeare's main source for the play. "To sing a song that old was sung / From ashes ancient Gower is come," he jauntily begins,

> Assuming man's infirmities
> To glad your ear and please your eyes.
> It hath been sung at festivals,
> On ember-eves and holy-ales,
> And lords and ladies in their lives
> Have read it for restoratives.
>
> [Sc. 1, 1–8]

## Major Characters & Synopsis

**Gower**, the narrator
**Pericles**, Prince of Tyre
**Marina**, Pericles's daughter
**Helicanus** and **Aeschines**, counsellors of Tyre
**King Antiochus** of Antioch
Antiochus's **Daughter**
**Thaliart**, a villain
**King Simonides** of Pentapolis
**Thaisa**, Simonides's daughter
**Cleon**, governor of Tarsus
**Dionyza**, Cleon's wife
**Leonine**, a villain
**Lychorida**, Thaisa's nurse
**Cerimon**, a physician from Ephesus
**Philemon**, Cerimon's servant
**Lysimachus**, governor of Mytilene
Various brothel characters, including a **Bawd**, a
   **Pander** and **Boult**, the Pander's servant
**Diana**, goddess of chastity

[This synopsis retains traditional act
divisions, but follows the scene numbering
of the Oxford *Complete Works*]

**SCENES 1–4** Gower relates an old story: how
King Antiochus has had an incestuous affair with
his daughter, and tries to keep her for himself by
setting her many suitors an impossible riddle.
When each one fails to solve it, he sentences them
to death. Antiochus enters with Pericles, who
intends to woo the princess, and sets him the riddle; when Pericles astutely works out the correct
answer, Antiochus secretly orders him to be murdered. But before Thaliart can poison the Prince,
Pericles arranges with Helicanus to escape to
Tarsus. Thaliart arrives in Tyre, but misses Pericles,
who has meanwhile arrived in Tarsus and delivered
its citizens from famine by bringing corn.

**SCENES 5–9** As news arrives about Thaliart's
plot, Pericles leaves once more but is shipwrecked in a storm. He is washed up on the
shore near Pentapolis, and is looked after by a
group of kindly fishermen. When they drag his
armour from the sea, Pericles decides to travel
incognito to the court of King Simonides and take
part in the tournament there, which is intended to
test the prowess of his daughter's suitors. The
mysterious knight wins the jousting, and also the
princess's heart, but refuses to divulge his identi-

ty. Back in Tyre, Pericles's own knights complain
about his absence and try to persuade Helicanus
to take the crown in his place – but Helicanus
nobly refuses. In Pentapolis, Simonides tests
Pericles's feelings for his daughter by showing
him a forged love letter to Thaisa; after hearing
Pericles's protestations of virtue, the King grants
the couple permission to marry. Their wedding is
described by Gower with the aid of a dumb
show.

**SCENES 10–14** Pericles and his pregnant
bride sail for Tyre, but during a terrible storm
Thaisa seemingly dies in childbirth and the super-
stitious sailors insist that her body be thrown
overboard. Horrified and grief-stricken, Pericles
complies but resolves to transport their newborn
daughter, Marina, to Tarsus, where her upbringing
will be entrusted to the governor Cleon and his
wife Dionyza. Thaisa's coffin, meanwhile, has
washed ashore at Ephesus, where the physician
Cerimon manages to revive her from a deathlike
sleep. Unable to remember the birth, Thaisa is
taken to join the temple of Diana.

**SCENES 15–19** Gower narrates Marina's
development into a beautiful young woman, and
how Dionyza grows jealous of her charge, arranging to have the girl murdered by Leonine. Before
Leonine can succeed, however, Marina is kidnapped by pirates and sold into prostitution at
Mytilene. There she stoutly refuses to co-operate
with customers – to the Bawd's despair – and
when the governor Lysimachus appears, she persuades him to help. Pericles has meanwhile
returned to Tarsus and is told that Marina has
died in his absence; he sadly vows to spend the
rest of his life in mourning.

**SCENES 20–23** Pericles's ship arrives at
Mytilene, and – not knowing of their relationship –
Lysimachus sends Marina to sing to the grief-
stricken Prince and ease his sorrow. Pericles
does not recognize his daughter immediately, but
after a heart-stopping pause they are reunited.
Moments later, the goddess Diana appears to
Pericles in a vision and persuades him to go to
Ephesus, where he discovers Thaisa. All are joyfully brought back together, and Lysimachus is
betrothed to Marina.

Unlike the Chorus of *Henry V*, who apologizes for the theatre itself, "this unworthy scaffold", "Ancient Gower", like all the best storytellers, begs forgiveness for his tale by simultaneously advertising its pedigree. That apology goes for *Pericles* as a whole, the first of Shakespeare's so-called "romances", which draws attention to its artifice while secretly celebrating the fact. Rejuvenating the long-dead Gower from his grave – which was just around the corner from the Globe in what is now Southwark Cathedral – and putting him on stage is the first of the miracles the play will perform.

Not that this impressed Ben Jonson, the first of *Pericles*'s many enemies. On the point of abandoning the stage entirely, and no doubt anxious to distance himself from the fashion for romance in the Jacobean theatre, he sullenly dismissed it as a "mouldy tale ... and stale / As the shrieve's crusts, and nasty as his fish- / Scraps". Though other critics have agreed – many conjecture that the play is lacking in quality and possibly co-written – it is hard not to think that this misses the point. *Pericles* has that "once upon a time" quality: it is *meant* to seem old, meant to be magical.

## Unknown travels

Gower's expedition through the centuries is merely the first of many journeys in *Pericles*, which moves restlessly from place to place, "bourn to bourn, region to region", as Gower himself puts it (Sc. 18, 4). Though Shakespeare himself had no use for the word "romance", like many of his contemporaries, *Pericles* is his fullest expression of romance motifs, themes that ultimately have their root in ancient epics such as Homer's *Odyssey* but became formalized during the early medieval era and flowered for at least another three centuries. Integral to romance tales, narratives of adventure and love, is the idea of the quest – the task that the hero (there are few romance heroines) must perform, and the adventures he encounters along the way. In this sense *Pericles* has all the right ingredients: a questing hero, a story of love and loss, seemingly impossible feats, multiple tragedies averted only by the most magical of realizations. All these are experienced by the play's eponymous hero, Pericles, who is compelled by mischance to take up what seems like an endless journey across the eastern Mediterranean. Like Odysseus in Homer's epic – and indeed like Egeon and Antipholus of Syracuse in *The Comedy of Errors*, which also uses Gower as a source (see p.33) – he becomes an adventurer, nomadic, rootless.

Pericles enters the play on the first of many quests, to win the hand of King Antiochus's beautiful daughter, but is compelled to flee when he discovers a dark secret at the heart of the Syrian court. This sets up a chain of transit that takes in such exotic centres of the ancient world as Ephesus, Tarsus and Myteline. The restlessness that lies at the heart of *Pericles*'s source material has often attracted comment. What Laurence Twine, the sixteenth-century author of *The Pattern of Painful Adventures* (1576), which Shakespeare seems to have used, billed the "delectable variety ... chances and changes" of his story has been less well received nearer the present day. The critic G. Wilson Knight, though one of *Pericles*'s champions, famously described its plot as "merely a succession of happenings linked by sea-journeys", while editor J.C. Maxwell catalogued what he saw as the "fantastic and often irrational narrative" on the page before him. But *Pericles* is dominated by vast, almost fairy-tale, struggles between good and evil; and it is one of the play's most telling themes that in the face of powerful natural forces humans have little opportunity to control their own fates. Even ending other people's lives can prove a problem, as Thaliart (the assassin hired by Antiochus to murder Pericles) finds to his cost when he arrives at Tyre in hot pursuit, only to discover that the King has "betook himself to unknown travels" (Sc. 3, 35), already en route elsewhere.

## Tragical-comical-historical-pastoral

It's obvious enough that Shakespeare's plays defy easy categorization, and commentators these days often fight shy of affixing labels. The playwright's colleagues Heminges and Condell had few such anxieties, however, cheerfully dividing the 36 works included in the First Folio into "**Comedies, Histories, and Tragedies**", as the title infamously puts it. Occasionally their decisions have raised eyebrows. *Cymbeline*, although it ends happily for the major characters, appears among the tragedies, while some of the Folio's "histories", among them *3 Henry VI* and *Richard II*, were originally published as "tragedies".

That said, sixteenth-century audiences would know what to expect with a **comedy**: laughter, yes, and probably stock characters, but also varieties of satire – the world gone mad or held up to ridicule. Renaissance theorists and their classical forebears did come up with more complex definitions based on Roman dramatists such as Plautus and Terence, yet although Shakespeare learned extensively from classical precedents he crafted an idiosyncratic comic world. His comedies use witty wordplay, ingenious plotting and have satiric elements (often via clowns; see p.27), but they invariably deliver some kind of social resolution, usually sealed by marriage between his protagonists – a device that hints at festive modes of renewal and reconciliation.

Critics have spent more time thinking about the serious business of Shakespearian **tragedy**, often comparing it to the work of the revered Greek tragedians Aeschylus, Sophocles and Euripides. **Aristotle**'s fragmentary musings on the genre in his *Poetics* received much attention after they were rediscovered in the sixteenth century, but Shakespeare's own tragedies don't draw directly on Greek traditions and often operate quite differently, not least in their penchant for inserting comedy where neoclassical writers, following Aristotle, felt it vulgar. The definition of the Elizabethan translator **John Florio** is Aristotelian but workmanlike: he wrote in 1598 that "a tragedy or mournful play" was "a lofty kind of poetry and representing personages of great state and matters of much trouble, a great broil or stir: it beginneth prosperously and endeth unfortunately or sometimes doubtfully, and is contrary to comedy". Closer to home is the observation that, in many of Shakespeare's plays – to reverse the famous aphorism – tragedy equals comedy plus time.

Though a majority of Shakespeare's plays could convincingly be called "tragicomic" (a term of abuse until his colleague John Fletcher attempted to write a tragicomedy), another genre pops up in critical jargon: that of the **romance**. This has the least claim to authenticity, and was invented by the nineteenth-century scholar Edward Dowden, who attempted to isolate what was unique about Shakespeare's final group of plays (often just called the "last comedies"). In this group, so Dowden thought, "the dissonances are resolved into harmony; the spirit of the plays is one of large benignity; they tell of the blessedness of the forgiveness of injuries; they show how the broken bonds between heart and heart may be repaired and reunited; each play closes with a victory of love". But Shakespeare never used the word "romance", and his contemporaries would have found it hard to comprehend what modern critics mean by it. And whether we even accept Dowden's sentimental opinions is another – and much larger – critical question.

The reasons behind Pericles's decision to travel to Tarsus near the beginning of the play remain unexplained – a mysterious start to his many mysterious voyages – but the famine-struck city provides a gruesome instance of humanity brought low by Fate. A city "whose tow'rs bore heads so high they kissed the clouds, / And strangers ne'er beheld but wondered at," is now in the depths of misery, its ruler, Cleon, laments:

> Those mothers who to nuzzle up their babes
> Thought naught too curious are ready now
> To eat those little darlings whom they loved.
> So sharp are hunger's teeth that man and wife
> Draw lots who first shall die to lengthen life.

**[Sc. 4, 24–46]**

Cleon's exclamation moments earlier – "see what heav'n can do by this our change" – fore-shadows the trials of Pericles himself.

The dangers that the play's characters face are starkly presented by the all-encompassing role of the sea in *Pericles*. Even more so than *The Tempest* (written perhaps two years later), the play is obsessed with the risks of the voyage, which separate the hero not just from his homeland but wrench him away from his wife and daughter. Two terrible storms occur in the course of the action: in the first Pericles is shipwrecked and all his possessions drowned; in the second he loses his wife to the flood. Though in one sense these tempests enable the plot to develop and turn in unexpected directions – *Twelfth Night*, too, relies on the shipwreck that separates the heroine Viola from her brother – in *Pericles* the sea often features as a malevolent dramatic force: a fearful barrier rather than a liberating medium. By heading to Tarsus, Helicanus frets that his friend Pericles "puts himself unto the ship-man's toil, / With whom each minute threatens life or death" (Sc. 3, 24–5), and indeed the frustrated assassin Thaliart contents him-self that the King has done his job for him by opting to travel by water, grimly noting that "he scaped the land to perish on the seas" (Sc. 3, 29). Though these dark forebodings will not prove quite accurate – Pericles will not die during this first storm – other troubles soon strike.

For although Pericles will survive the second tempest, too, it is at appalling cost. When his new wife, Thaisa, appears to have died in childbirth, the sailors insist that "the ship be cleared of the dead", that her body must be dumped overboard; the "venomous" ocean will not be sat-isfied until it has swallowed her corpse. Pericles's moving farewell speech to his wife carries the play to its first climax, and in it he attempts to negotiate with the vast forces that surround them both. "A terrible childbed hast thou had, my dear," he murmurs,

> No light, no fire. Th'unfriendly elements
> Forgot thee utterly, nor have I time
> To give thee hallowed to thy grave, but straight
> Must cast thee, scarcely coffined, in the ooze,
> Where, for a monument upon thy bones
> And aye-remaining lamps, the belching whale
> And humming water must o'erwhelm thy corpse,
> Lying with simple shells.
>
> **[Sc. 11, 55–63]**

Passionately simple and movingly homely in tone, Pericles's obsequy attempts to find a human, personal space in the "great vast" for his dead wife. Though the play's language is not always this fine (the text as we have it may be faulty or otherwise incomplete), here it calls down themes that resonate with the great tragedies. And yet Pericles does not, like Lear, rant against the elements – as he later admits, "Should I rage and roar / As doth the sea she lies in, yet the end / Must be as 'tis" (Sc. 13, 9–12).

## This great sea of joys

Into the sea, Thaisa's immense grave, go Pericles's hopes: this is the play's bleakest moment. Yet the "ooze" – both the end of life and its source, a word that becomes densely suggestive in Shakespeare's late plays – will not swallow her body for ever, and in fact it will deliver her. Lord Cerimon, the virtuous doctor, speaks of "the disturbances / That nature works, and of her cures" (Sc. 12, 34–5), describing the inherent balance that lies at the heart of creation. Sure enough, out of the "turbulent and stormy night" arrives Thaisa's casket, presenting Cerimon with the opportunity to revive its living but unconscious cargo; a miraculous reawakening that proves the first of several in *Pericles*. Calling for "still and woeful music", Cerimon observes how, as it works, Thaisa "'gins to blow / Into life's flow'r again" (Sc. 12, 92–3) – both a breathtakingly theatrical moment and a figurative rebirth for the Queen, herself just free from the pangs of childbed. When she exclaims breathlessly, "Where am I? Where's my lord? What world is this?" (Sc. 12, 104) it is as if she begins to relearn what it is to live.

Thaisa's recovery from the clutches of the storm echoes that of her husband after the first tempest just a few scenes before. "Cast up" (vomited) by the "drunken" sea after his shipwreck (and with all his possessions drowned), Pericles is on the verge of collapse when he comes across a group of fishermen by the shore:

PERICLES
What I have been, I have forgot to know,
But what I am, want teaches me to think on:
A man thronged up with cold; my veins are chill,
And have no more of life than may suffice
To give my tongue that heat to crave your help,
Which if you shall refuse, when I am dead,
For that I am a man, pray see me burièd.
*He falls down*

MASTER Die, quotha? Now, gods forbid't an I have a gown here! Come, put it on, keep thee warm. Now, afore me, a handsome fellow! Come, thou shalt go home, and we'll have flesh for holidays, fish for fasting-days, and moreoe'r puddings and flapjacks, and thou shalt be welcome.

**[Sc. 5, 112–24]**

Again, humanity intervenes. Though this scene has none of the magical splendour of Thaisa's reawakening, the fishermen's homespun generosity is powerful enough. A stranger and a survivor, Pericles is warmly welcomed into their society. And as if in response to their kindness, the "rough seas" that provide their livelihood suddenly disgorge the King's armour – giving Pericles the opportunity to prove his heroic worth at King Simonides's court and ultimately win Thaisa's hand in marriage.

Perhaps the most expressive example of the sea's changefulness appears on the dreadful night of Thaisa's loss – indeed, is the reason for her apparent death. Marina, "born in a tempest" and named after the ocean that carries away her mother, is less rooted even than her father, as she exclaims mournfully to the wicked Dionyza:

The world to me is but a ceaseless storm,
Whirring me from my friends.

**[Sc. 15, 71–2]**

After being forced to flee from the court of Cleon and Dionyza (recalling her father), and suffering "death" (shades of her mother), she is kidnapped by pirates before ending up in a brothel. Cast once again to the mercy of fate, she is nevertheless able to talk her way out through sheer strength of personality: sending her would-be clients away with prayers on their lips and charity in their hearts, she is so chaste, her baffled pimp exclaims, that she would "undo the whole of generation" if she could (Sc. 19, 13).

Marina's radiant virtue saves her from the depredations of "lewdly inclined" clients, but it also prepares for the play's emotional summit. Brought unknowingly to meet the woebegone Pericles – who thinks that his daughter, like his wife, is dead and buried – it seems at first that the King is too catatonic in grief to be saved. But the fractured, sea-borne story of Marina's life ("If I should tell / My history," she exclaims, "it would seem like lies" (Sc. 21, 106–7)) begins to work at his curiosity until the truth about her parentage steadily – and incredibly –

becomes clear. Beginning to realize that she is his child (a fantasy too improbable to be true), Pericles cries out, "Give me a gash, put me to present pain,"

> Lest this great sea of joys rushing upon me
> O'erbear the shores of my mortality
> And drown me with their sweetness!

[Sc. 21, 179–82]

"Thou that begett'st him that did thee beget," he continues, a wonder-struck father addressing the daughter who has given him life once more. The sea has delivered more than pain and death: it has metamorphosed into the bringer of "joy". It seems only fitting that the goddess Diana should descend from the heavens to crown the event, as Shakespeare (perhaps assisted by new technology at the Blackfriars playhouse, a likely early venue for the play) makes her do just moments later.

> *As [Pericles] elaborates, feature by feature, on the similarity he senses, the remembered past merges with the perceived actuality, until the images of the wife who "was" and that of the daughter who "might have been" dissolve … into the girl before him.*
>
> Inga-Stina Ewbank, "'My name is Marina': the language of recognition" (1980)

Once daughter and father are together once more, all that remains for the story to have worked itself through is for Thaisa, too, to be recovered. Shakespeare does not try his audience's patience: in the very next scene Pericles announces that he will give thanks to Diana when one of her attendant nuns suddenly swoons. "Voice and favour—" she exclaims, "You are, you are—O royal Pericles!" (Sc. 22, 33–4). The recognition this time is immediate, but no less astonishing. "O, let me look upon him," Thaisa begs,

> If he be none of mine, my sanctity
> Will to my sense bend no licentious ear,
> But curb it, spite of seeing. O, my lord,
> Are you not Pericles? Like him you spake,
> Like him you are. Did you not name a tempest,
> A birth and death?

[Sc. 22, 48–54]

As with Marina, it is the story that tells all: the tempest, birth and death that are the lineaments of Pericles's tale reunite him with his family. In the first of these romance plays, Shakespeare steers a way through tragedy – the storms, the long-lost child, the death – and finds something new and miraculous at his journey's end.

## Stage history and adaptations

Amid the shifting sands of theatrical taste, *Pericles*'s fate seems especially cruel. Unquestionably an immense hit in the first years of its life (nearly Shakespeare's largest), during the late seventeenth century it sunk into almost total obscurity, disappearing from the stage altogether for nearly two hundred years. Even now, haunted by doubts about its authenticity, it is one of the most rarely revived of the plays.

We know it was initially popular because of the runaway success of **printed editions** – the 1609 quarto was reprinted five times, despite being massively error-strewn – and it was performed at James I's **court** that same year (though not in front of the King, whose wife had

Yukio Ninagawa's production of *Pericles*, which visited the UK in 2003, was a stunning visual experience. Masaaki Uchino played the long-suffering hero, seen here about to be reunited with his wife Thaisa.

recently died and who therefore had good reasons for staying away). A poem published in 1646 describes *Pericles* as one of Shakespeare's finest achievements, and that seems to have been the view of Restoration actors and managers too. The young **Thomas Betterton**, then a trainee bookseller, performed it at the Cockpit Theatre in London in 1659, making the play one of the earliest to feature after the reopening of the theatres under Charles II.

But after the official licensing of London drama – and the carving up of Shakespeare's repertoire between impresarios William Davenant and Thomas Killigrew – *Pericles* disappeared from favour. The playwright **George Lillo**, better known for an original piece called *The Merchant* (a morality tale about a man who falls in love with the wrong woman and murders for her sake), put together an adaptation he dubbed *Marina*, which debuted at Covent Garden in 1738. Lillo cut the first two acts of Shakespeare's romance in order to focus on Pericles's daughter and added a moralizing prologue apologizing for the original's "rude wild scenes" (which, naturally, he had done his utmost to smooth over).

It was over a hundred years before *Pericles* proper appeared again. The great **Samuel Phelps**, once described as "a diligent labourer in the vineyard of old plays", revived it at Sadler's Wells in 1854 in a lavish production costing around £1000 – and gained little but condescension from *The Times*, who noted "the paucity of the dramatic interest". The only other British nineteenth-century production on record was another adaptation put together by **Frank Benson** at Stratford. Benson wrote to a friend that in veteran actor **John Coleman**'s acting version there was "nothing objectionable" (the brothel scene was cut, along with much else), and it duly appeared at Stratford in 1900 to some acclaim – one reviewer declared that "the production of such a work filled me with wonder". *Pericles* was staged only twice more before World War I, both times in Germany.

**Robert Atkins** put on a production during 1921, early in the Old Vic's glory days, noted for its simplicity, directness and use of an uncut text. Just before World War II **Robert Eddison**

appeared as Pericles at London's Regent's Park Theatre, and his success was matched after hostilities ceased by **Paul Scofield** and **Daphne Slater**, who appeared in a heavily cut Stratford version of 1947. Another Stratfordian leading couple, **Richard Johnson** (Pericles) and **Geraldine McEwan** (Marina), wowed audiences in a spectacular staging directed by **Glen Byam Shaw** in 1958, particularly noted for its fairytale magic and moving recognition scene.

Stratford-upon-Avon has in fact proved *Pericles*'s most assiduous host, particularly after the creation of the subsidized RSC in 1961. **Terry Hands** put it on in 1969 in a production that emphasized the hero's place in the action by putting a vast copy of Leonardo's famous sketch of a naked man on the front curtains, but savagely cut the script. By contrast, **Ron Daniels**, directing at The Other Place a decade later, retained some of the so-called "Wilkins" text and drew attention instead to the role of **Julie Peasegood**'s impassioned Marina. But the English Stratford has not been the play's only champion: its Canadian cousin presented an enthusiastically received production (1973) directed by **Jean Gascon** and starring **Nicholas Pennell** and **Pamela Brook**, while the same year **Toby Robertson**'s Prospect Theatre company presented a carnivalesque reading of the play at the Edinburgh Festival.

For all that, however, *Pericles* remains one of Shakespeare's least popular plays. **Declan Donnellan**'s Cheek By Jowl staged a touring production in 1984 that was a model of narrative clarity using the simplest of means, but many remained unconvinced. The play was excluded from Peter Hall's survey of the romances at the National Theatre in 1987, though at the Ontario Shakespeare Festival the previous year it had appeared in an acclaimed production by **Richard Ouzounian** starring **Geraint Wyn Davies** as Pericles and **Goldie Semple** as Thaisa. **David Thacker**'s RSC version of 1989 attracted notice for casting **Helen Blatch** in the male part of Cerimon as well as its experimental approach to the text, and the production's refreshingly low-tech staging also gained plaudits. The same could not be said for **Adrian Noble**'s recent RSC production (2002), which involved plenty of high-wire theatrics – not least a breathtaking descent from the lighting rig by Diana. **Ray Fearon**'s Pericles was noble yet searching and **Kananu Kirimi** shone as Marina, though Noble's self-consciously "Oriental" staging gained mixed reviews.

In contrast, genuine excitement greeted the arrival of **Yukio Ninagawa**'s Japanese company at London's National Theatre in 2003. Ninagawa's overall approach tended towards the symbolic, seeing in *Pericles* a "restorative" message (as Gower puts it) for refugees across the world – the action was framed by a crowd of dispossessed people shambling across the stage to the sound of gunfire and helicopters. Exploiting the Olivier Theatre's large space, the production was designed around a series of standpipes which communicated the water-bound message of the play. Brilliantly executed stage effects, like the human puppet shows illustrating Pericles's adventures, created a fairytale world, but it was the strength of the cast – notably **Masaaki Uchino**'s forceful Pericles and the delicate **Yuko Tanaka** who doubled Thaisa and Marina – that made the play so captivating and genuinely moving.

It seems that *Pericles* has little chance of appearing on the silver screen in the imminent future, and the only production in existence is that for the BBC/Time-Life series (1983), directed by **David Hugh Jones** and featuring **Mike Gwilym**'s Pericles opposite **Juliet Stevenson**'s Thaisa.

# Screen

### Pericles

**M. Gwilym, J. Stevenson, E. Petherbridge; David Hugh Jones (dir.)**
UK, 1984 ▷ Ambrose Video `DVD`

The great selling-point of the BBC Shakespeare series was

that it would explore the further reaches of the canon as well as the better-known plays. Unfortunately, with *Pericles* their heart doesn't seem to have been in it: this version is timid rather than adventurous. Given Pericles's incessant travels, lack of access to any kind of exotic location is a major shortcoming (the studio-bound fishermen scene, complete with added-in coastal background, is disastrous, while the shipwreck scene is little better), and the whole thing feels more than slightly lukewarm. Mike Gwilym's callow Pericles struggles to impress, although the women surrounding him are better: Juliet Stevenson is poignant as Thaisa while Amanda Redman's clear-eyed Marina is strong – if somehow a bit spooky. Recently rereleased in the US, along with the rest of the BBC series, by Ambrose Video Publishing.

## Audio

### Pericles
**N. Terry, S. Gonet, J. Cox; Clive Brill (dir.)**
UK, 1998  ▷ Arkangel ⊙ 📼

This 1999 *Pericles* was one of the final projects John Gielgud ever did, and his august tones – a throwback to a lost age of Shakespearian verse-speaking – make him ideal (in all sorts of ways) as Gower. In fact on audio all of *Pericles* comes across very strongly, more strongly than critics of its verse style would have you believe, and it often has a wonderfully exotic tang. Nigel Terry speaks particularly well, presenting a rounded interpretation of the hero, and Stella Gonet's womanly Thaisa is also fine. Julie Cox sounds youthful as Marina but produces extensive reserves of inner strength – especially during some vigorously realized brothel scenes. It may be the only spoken-word *Pericles* available, but this Arkangel version is genuinely compelling.

## Editions

### New Cambridge Shakespeare
**Doreen DelVecchio & Antony Hammond (eds); 1998**  ▷ Cambridge UP

To say that DelVecchio and Hammond are protective of *Pericles* is some understatement: they are scandalized by everything from the market in art dealing (when making a point about intrinsic artistic value) to a duff video recording of a recent Stratford production. They give short shrift to notions floated by the *Oxford Shakespeare* and others about Shakespeare's possible collaboration with the unappealing George Wilkins, and are thus sometimes too eager to defend what is, in the text we possess, hardly outstanding theatrical

writing. But ultimately *Pericles* needs someone to fight its corner, and the editors do a fine job, offering a sympathetic analysis of its key themes along with more contentious issues.

## Some criticism

### The Crown of Life
**G. Wilson Knight; 1947**  ▷ Routledge

The book that finally put *Pericles* on the critical map, *The Crown of Life* is subtitled "essays in interpretation of Shakespeare's final plays" and is every bit as lapidary as its quasi-biblical title suggests. "Interpretation" in the grandest sense of the word is what concerns Knight, who remains splendidly aloof from debates about authorship, preferring instead to probe the play's artistic merits – what he terms its "organic" qualities, the sense that (despite the textual problems) everything is imaginatively coherent. Unabashedly Christianized though his philosophical framework is (Pericles's discovery of sin at Antioch is seen as an Adam-like Fall), Knight avoids the sentimentality that afflicts many later studies of the romances and is refreshingly upfront about the play's attractions – and limitations.

### Shakespeare and the Sea
**Alexander F. Falconer; 1964**  ▷ John Constable [o/p]

It is strikingly hard to think of a Shakespeare play in which the sea does not play some kind of role (he even grafts a sea-coast onto *The Winter's Tale*'s landlocked Bohemia), and often its involvement is crucial. While among the romances *The Tempest* most obviously enshrines the playwright's mistrust of the ocean, in *Pericles* it provides, as well as destruction and separation, ultimate resolution. Written by a naval officer, *Shakespeare and the Sea* doesn't deal with these themes upfront, but what it does provide is utterly absorbing: a study that adeptly mingles historical detail and literary interest to describe the role of the sea in the lives of Elizabethans. Falconer's portrait is of a nation proudly conscious of its island status, and while this sometimes makes Shakespeare's work seem like naval propaganda, the insights offered by *Shakespeare and the Sea* (everything from tides to ship-boys) more than outweigh its occasionally gung-ho tone.

# Richard II

For his fifth foray into English history, Shakespeare turned to the roots of the feud whose consequences are played out in the three parts of the early *Henry VIs*: the deposition of Richard II by his cousin Henry Bolingbroke in 1399. That event ignited a slow-burning conflict, the Wars of the Roses, that destabilized British politics for the next ninety-odd years and fragmented England's ruling class. In *Richard II* these fissures lie mostly beneath the surface, though the play's central quandary – how a country can be ruled by a rightful but weak monarch – must have engaged Elizabethan audiences, well aware that their own Queen (sometimes compared to Richard) faced both criticism and rebellion in her last years in power. The play is uniquely experimental among Shakespeare's histories: it contains not a word of prose, and its rich verbal texture closely resembles baroque comedies such as *Love's Labour's Lost*. At the centre of this operatic drama stands King Richard himself, whose preternatural skill with words is matched by his limitations as a ruler, a polar opposite to his efficient but chilly replacement. Obsessed with the performance of his own life, Richard – and his downfall – make for utterly compelling theatre.

[DATE] Probably 1594–95. *Richard II* has stylistic similarities to the "lyrical" comedies, including *Love's Labour's Lost*, *Romeo and Juliet* and the *Dream*.

[SOURCES] Shakespeare worked closely with Holinshed's *Chronicles* (1587), and also used Edward Halle's *Union* (1548). Samuel Daniel's epic *Civil Wars* (1595) is a key source, as is the anonymous play *Woodstock* (c.1592). Marlowe's *Edward II* also had an influence.

[TEXTS] The quarto (Q1) of 1597 sold well, and was reprinted twice. Q4 (1608) restores several politically sensitive sections cut from Q1, and was itself reprinted as Q5 in 1615. The 1623 Folio text is based mainly on Q3, but includes Richard's abdication scene.

## Interpreting the play

In real life, the reign of Richard II was marred by popular revolt and bitter aristocratic feuding, and he was ejected from the English throne not once but twice. To succeeding generations, his flaws as a leader attracted widespread condemnation, and by the nineteenth century his rule had become a byword for incompetence and cronyism. The Elizabethans appear to have thought likewise: no fewer than three plays concerning the king (not including Shakespeare's) appeared on the London stage during the dramatist's career, and all were harshly unforgiving – dwelling on Richard's culpability for the murder of his uncle, the Duke of Gloucester, and satirizing his notorious weakness for flatterers.

Behind this thriving trade in portrayals of a long-dead monarch was the example of his very much alive (though somewhat elderly) successor, Elizabeth I, who was herself accused of being misled by her favourites, and about the matter of whose succession – given her childlessness – there was continued anxiety throughout the 1590s. Elizabeth herself recognized the resemblance only too well, remarking acidly to the antiquarian William Lambarde a few years

## Major Characters & Synopsis

**King Richard II** of England
**Queen Isabel**, Richard's wife
**John of Gaunt**, Duke of Lancaster, Richard's uncle
**Harry Bolingbroke**, Duke of Hereford, Gaunt's son (later King **Henry IV**)
**Duchess of Gloucester**, widow of the murdered Duke (Gaunt's and York's brother)
**Duke of York**, Richard's uncle, and his wife, the **Duchess of York**
**Duke of Aumerle**, the Yorks' son
**Thomas Mowbray**, Duke of Norfolk
**Green**, **Bushy** and **Bagot**, intimates of King Richard
Percy, **Earl of Northumberland**
**Harry Percy**, Northumberland's son
**Lord Ross**
**Lord Willoughby**
**Earl of Salisbury**
**Bishop of Carlisle**
**Sir Stephen Scrope**
Other nobles, including **Lord Berkeley**, **Lord Fitzwalter**, the **Duke of Surrey**, the **Abbot of Westminster** and **Sir Piers Exton**
A **Groom** from King Richard's stable

**ACT 1** The old Duke of Gloucester is dead and the English court is riven by faction. On one side Harry Bolingbroke accuses his enemy Mowbray of the murder, but Mowbray denies the charge. They are eager to prove themselves in combat, and King Richard eventually consents. But when the day of the duel arrives, Richard suddenly changes his mind, deciding to banish the two troublesome lords instead – Bolingbroke for ten years, Mowbray permanently. This does little for Richard's popularity, nor does it dampen suspicions (held by the widowed Duchess of Gloucester and John of Gaunt) that the King himself is implicated in Gloucester's death. Back at court, Richard and his favourites carp about Bolingbroke's departure from England and his ballooning popular support when news arrives of a rebellion in Ireland.

**ACT 2** Joined by York, the dying Gaunt bemoans the state of the country, which is struggling under Richard's unpopular rule – a point that Gaunt makes to the King personally. Richard is unmoved, however, and as soon as Gaunt expires makes a point of seizing his estates. Rumour has it that Bolingbroke is gathering forces to return home, and, sure enough, as soon as Richard departs for Ireland he lands at Ravenspurgh. Richard's supporters panic, while York (made regent in Richard's absence) finds his loyalties divided, and when Bolingbroke and his army reach Berkeley Castle he reluctantly allows them to enter.

**ACT 3** Returning in emergency from Ireland, Richard faces a terrible situation: his army has dispersed, three of his closest friends have been executed by Bolingbroke and York has defected. In despair he travels to meet his enemies at Flint Castle. Despite Bolingbroke's protestations that he has no wish to seize the throne, Richard admits he is powerless. A coup begins to seem inevitable when the Queen overhears her gardeners discussing Bolingbroke's intentions towards the throne.

**ACT 4** As Bolingbroke attempts to search for the truth behind Gloucester's murder in Parliament, Richard's abdication is announced. Carlisle warns that civil war will break out if Bolingbroke becomes king, but Northumberland has him arrested. When Richard arrives to abdicate in public, he succeeds in upstaging his successor with a histrionic and self-pitying performance in which he refuses to acknowledge the legitimacy of his deposition. Carlisle, Westminster and Aumerle are persuaded by his cause and vow to fight back.

**ACT 5** York and his wife are discussing Bolingbroke's huge popular support when they discover that none other than their son Aumerle is guilty of plotting against Bolingbroke. York rushes to plead with the new King that his son should be punished, but Aumerle is pardoned. Richard is less lucky. Believing that Henry has ordered the ex-king to be murdered, Exton heads to Pomfret Castle, where Richard is imprisoned, and stabs him to death. Hearing the news, King Henry vows to go on a penitential pilgrimage.

before her death that "I am Richard II, know ye not that?", and observing that a "tragedy" of the king had been "played forty times in open streets and houses".

Whether Shakespeare's play was the "tragedy" to which Elizabeth alluded we will never know. But elsewhere the part it took in her life seems more definite. On the eve of his rebellion against the Queen in 1601, supporters of the Earl of Essex paid the Lord Chamberlain's Men to revive a play about "the deposing and killing of Richard II", possibly Shakespeare's. Though the performance at the Globe went ahead as arranged on February 7, Essex's attempted coup foundered the following day and he was captured, then beheaded, before the end of the month.

## This realm

The parallels between *Richard II* and Elizabeth's reign were sensitive enough for the scene depicting the King's abdication to be blue-pencilled by the censors (or cut before they got to it), only being restored in the 1608 text, published five years after the Queen's death. And those resonances are distinctly unflattering. Much is made of Richard's political mismanagement and unpopularity: the Earl of Northumberland accuses him of financial largesse and being "basely led / By flatterers"; Ross laments the "grievous taxes" he has imposed; Willoughby grumbles how "daily new exactions are devised" (2.1.242–250). Nahum Tate, whose adaptation of the play briefly graced the Restoration stage, observed that Shakespeare's Richard was "painted in the worst Colours of History".

Furthermore, England itself – as critic E.M.W. Tillyard suggests, the ever-present "hero" of Shakespeare's histories – seems to be in mortal danger. Close to death at the start of Act Two, Gaunt gives impassioned voice to his nephew's fickle betrayal of "this royal throne of kings, this sceptred isle,"

> This earth of majesty, this seat of Mars,
> This other Eden, demi-paradise,
> This fortress built by nature for herself
> Against infection and the hand of war,
> This happy breed of men, this little world,
> This precious stone set in the silver sea,
> Which serves it in the office of a wall,
> Or as the moat defensive to a house
> Against the envy of less happier lands;
> This blessèd plot, this earth, this realm, this England …
>
> **[2.1.40–50]**

Though this speech is often (too often) quoted as a patriotic celebration of England and Englishness – it was anthologized as one of "the Choicest Flowers of our English Poets" as early as 1600 – its dramatic purpose is markedly different. Gaunt underlines everything that England should be under Richard's command but conspicuously isn't. The nation is, Gaunt objects, "leased out … Like to a tenement or a pelting farm", "bound in with shame" (2.1.59–63); the King is its "landlord", not its ruler. And Richard's betrayal of England is compounded by a personal betrayal. Just moments after Gaunt's death, the king coolly announces that he will seize his "plate, coin, revenues, and movables" in order to fund the Irish wars – in effect disinheriting Gaunt's banished son, Bolingbroke, and setting in train events that will culminate in Richard's own deposition.

Up to this point in the play, the case against Richard seems watertight – particularly because Bolingbroke, his opponent and eventual successor, is presented in terms starkly antithetical to those of the King. Banished by Richard, ostensibly for challenging Mowbray (but in reality because Richard seems anxious about his growing power), his response to the news is calm rather than histrionic; although he expresses pain at bidding England farewell, he promises to carry consoling thoughts of its "sweet soil" with him:

> Whe'er I wander, boast of this I can:
> Though banished, yet a trueborn Englishman.
>
> [1.3.271–2]

Bolingbroke astutely plays the patriotic card, a successful strategy underscored just a scene later by reports of his mounting popular support – and Richard's rancorous jealousy at it. Though Bolingbroke is never that outspoken, the play has begun to present him as England's saviour, a "trueborn" liberator who will combat the (French-born) King. As Northumberland puts it, it is Bolingbroke who will "shake off our slavish yoke",

> Redeem from broking pawn the blemished crown,
> Wipe off the dust that hides our sceptre's gilt,
> And make high majesty look like itself …
>
> [2.1.293–7]

But, in the event, things are not so straightforward. Bolingbroke's own views on the progress of his career rarely receive a public airing. His main attraction – that he is utterly different from Richard – is also his most enigmatic quality. Shakespeare never permits him to speak in soliloquy, and his motives remain consistently in shadow. For all that, his opportunism is undeniable: as soon as Richard is out of the country, Bolingbroke stages a surprise reappearance with several thousand men. The question of precisely what he will do once he arrives is left open: the return from banishment takes place off stage, and it is left to Bolingbroke's ally Northumberland to insist that "the noble Duke hath sworn his coming is / But for his own" (2.3.147–8), in effect that he has come to reclaim the property illegally seized from his father. Nearly everyone else suspects that he is after the throne itself, however, and when the King disappears to Ireland during the crucial centre of the play, the balance of power suddenly shifts. York, left in control of England, cannot resist the invading army; Richard's favourites, "the caterpillars of the commonwealth" (2.3.165) fall into Bolingbroke's hands and are summarily dispatched; the King's Welsh troops melt away as the rest of the country rebels. Yet Bolingbroke's own words on his intentions sound more opaque the closer he gets to power. Warned by York to "Take not … further than you should, / Lest you mistake the heavens are over our heads", Bolingbroke's reply is elegant doublespeak:

> I know it, uncle, and oppose not myself
> Against their will.
>
> [3.3.18–19]

If the "will" of the heavens reads two ways, then so can Bolingbroke's intentions towards the King in the first climax of the play, when they finally meet at Flint Castle after Richard's hurried (and disastrous) return from Ireland. Urging his cousin not to kneel in front of him, Richard cries, "Up, cousin, up,"

> Your heart is up, I know,
> Thus high at least, although your knee be low.
>
> BOLINGBROKE
> My gracious lord, I come but for my own.
>
> KING RICHARD
> Your own is yours, and I am yours, and all.
>
> [3.3.192–5]

## Kinged again

It seems astonishing that an entire kingdom can be resigned in words of such painstaking ambiguity (it may be that Shakespeare didn't dare risk anything more politically overt), but a reaction against this seemingly unstoppable procession of events is not long in arriving. Moments after Bolingbroke accepts Richard's resignation, the Bishop of Carlisle retorts, "Marry, God forbid!"

> Worst in this royal presence may I speak,
> Yet best beseeming me to speak the truth.
> Would God that any in this noble presence
> Were enough noble to be upright judge
> Of noble Richard.

**[4.1.104–10]**

Carlisle identifies the central conundrum of *Richard II*: how can mere subjects condemn their monarch? Landing in Wales, Richard boldly insisted that "Not all the water in the rough rude sea / Can wash the balm from an anointed king" (3.2.50–1), and his assertion, articulating the so-called "divine right" of monarchy, was a commonplace of Tudor political theory. But it was not uncontested, and Shakespeare makes it plain just how vulnerable a king can be. The irony of Richard's metaphor proves sharp: Bolingbroke (whose name, spelt "Bullingbrooke" in the early texts, could mean "boiling brook") will find it all too easy to wash away the King's political foundations.

Unusually self-conscious about its use of language, *Richard II* is in fact filled with poetic images identifying both protagonists with the elements. Richard begins the play as a "sun-king of fire" opposed to Bolingbroke's flood, but as the action progresses the two steadily change place. On his way to surrender, Richard casts himself as "glist'ring Phaethon" (Apollo's doomed son, who stole his father's sun-chariot and drove it too close to the earth), but before long he imagines his body as "a mockery king of snow, / Standing before the sun of Bolingbroke" (4.1.250–1). The balancing-point occurs when Richard is called upon to hand over his crown "in common view". He pictures it as "like a deep well / That owes two buckets filling one another,"

> The emptier ever dancing in the air,
> The other down, unseen, and full of water.
> That bucket down and full of tears am I,
> Drinking my griefs whilst you mount up on high.

**[4.1.174–9]**

Rewriting Bolingbroke's coronation into his own "unkinging", Richard takes charge of the event. But the speech also marks a decisive shift in the tone and focus of the play. Once Bolingbroke actually takes the crown (Richard wittily insists he "seize" it), the focus moves decisively away from him. Bereft of political power, meanwhile, Shakespeare makes Richard free to express himself on stage. His *coup de théâtre* in front of his enemy occurs when he requests a "mirror" to "show me what a face I have". Looking into it, he exclaims, "No deeper wrinkles yet?"

> *I cannot believe that Shakespeare looked on his Richard II with any but sympathetic eyes, understanding indeed how ill-fitted he was to be King, at a certain moment of history, but understanding that he was loveable and full of capricious fancy.*
>
> William Butler Yeats, *Ideas of Good and Evil* (1903)

                    Hath sorrow struck
So many blows upon this face of mine
And made no deeper wounds? O flatt'ring glass,
Like to my followers in prosperity,
Though dost beguile me!

[4.1.268–71]

Richard's examination of his reflection – which reaches a peak when he dashes the mirror to pieces – is a persuasive gesture, and despite his narcissistic tastes, like all solo performances it reverberates strongly in the theatre.

The question of just how to perceive Richard is one that Shakespeare makes remarkably difficult for his audiences. Put simply, it changes as the play develops. Critics have been divided in their response to his character (Coleridge dismissed Richard's "constant flow of emotions from a total incapability of controlling them … a waste of that energy which should have been reserved for action"), but few have questioned that in this second phase of the action Shakespeare displaces our sympathy for Richard's victims and redirects it instead to Richard himself. Doing so, his play becomes less a history and more what its first printed title promises, "The Tragedy of King Richard the Second", with Richard the hero at its centre.

Though to some extent the form of *Richard II*'s title is conventional – the history plays *Henry VI Part III* and *Richard III* are also described as "tragedies" in early printed texts – here Shakespeare makes us aware that responding to the King in this way is not merely forced by events, but enshrined in his personality. Following Aristotle's use of the term, Richard really is a tragic hero: a man who (like Sophocles's Oedipus or Ajax) blunders and is culpable, and who suffers terribly for his mistakes. Richard's awareness of his own experience is more solipsistic, but no less solemn: he repeatedly compares himself to Christ and his enemies to Judas, exclaiming during the climactic deposition scene that "[Christ] in twelve / Found truth in all but one; I, in twelve thousand, none" (4.1.161–2), tragically aware of the gulf between them – a gulf all the more obvious because of Richard's supposedly godly role. In fact like Gaunt, who declares (for all his criticisms of his nephew's reign) that "God's is the quarrel" (1.2.37) and that humans should not intervene, in the first half of the play Richard believes that his royal status – sanctioned by the King of Heaven – exerts quasi-divine powers. Newly arrived on the coast of Wales after returning from Ireland, Richard gives short shrift to Aumerle's warning that Bolingbroke threatens the realm. "Discomfortable cousin," Richard cries,

                    know'st thou not
That when the searching eye of heaven is hid
Behind the globe, that lights the lower world,
Then thieves and robbers range abroad unseen
In murders and in outrage bloody here;
But when from under this terrestrial ball
He fires the proud tops of the eastern pines,
And darts his light through every guilty hole,
Then murders, treasons, and detested sins,
The cloak of night being plucked from off their backs,
Stand bare and naked, trembling at themselves?

[3.2.32–42]

Richard talks here of the "eye of heaven": a metaphor for the sun (one of his favourite self-images, as we have seen), but also a literal representation of God – the ferocious Old Testament God who will scourge "thieves and robbers" like Bolingbroke and bring their sins to light. Yet Richard's sense of divinity changes with his experience through the play: in his last

At Stratford in 1951 Michael Redgrave played Richard as an unworldly and effeminate monarch, tragically unable to halt the march of events against him, but powerfully expressive in the play's final scenes.

minutes alive he will recall the New Testament teaching of Christ, which insists that Heaven will house those who are powerless and impoverished – the "seely [simple-minded] beggars" rather than the great monarchs, as Richard touchingly observes (5.5.25). Richard's new awareness of a consoling God adds an unexpected pathos to his deposition, a fate that God himself has apparently done little to prevent.

As soon as Bolingbroke takes power it is clear that Richard's liberty is at an end, and that he can no longer be free – and indeed it won't be long before he is dead, murdered by Exton (who believes, perhaps rightly, that Bolingbroke set him on). Sent under guard to Pomfret Castle after an emotional farewell from his wife, Richard is left to contemplate his shattered being. Alone on stage once more, he eloquently ruminates, "Thus play I in one person many people, / And none contented."

> Sometimes am I king;
> Then treason makes me wish myself a beggar,
> And so I am. Then crushing penury
> Persuades me I was better when a king.
> Then am I kinged again, and by and by
> Think that I am unkinged by Bolingbroke,
> And straight am nothing. But whate'er I be,
> Nor I, nor any man that but man is,
> With nothing shall be pleased till he be eased
> With being nothing.
>
> **[5.5.31–41]**

Richard has sometimes been called an actor rather than a monarch, but if so he is unable to relinquish his key role – or is perhaps trapped inside it. Though his speech calls attention to the uniqueness of his own position (he cannot separate his official persona from his human identity, cannot sever what some critics have called "the king's two bodies"), his words embrace something larger. "Any man that but man is" – anyone alive – needs to realize that "nothing" is where we come from, and it is to nothingness that we return. Richard's flawed journey to this difficult self-knowledge anticipates, however partially, that of King Lear.

Towards the end of *Richard II*, it is impossible not to think that Richard's weaknesses have somehow become strengths: he makes a finer victim than he does a king, arranging the tragic spectacle of himself with impressive aplomb. His last long speech is in some ways his most candid, but it is also the most rhetorically beautiful of many in this intensely poetic play. "I wasted time, and now doth time waste me," he reflects,

> For now hath time made me his numb'ring clock.
> My thoughts are minutes, and with sighs they jar
> Their watches on unto mine eyes, the outward watch
> Whereto my finger, like a dial's point,
> Is pointing still in cleansing them from tears.
> Now, sir, the sounds that tell what hour it is
> Are clamorous groans that strike upon my heart,
> Which is the bell. So sighs, and tears, and groans
> Show minutes, hours, and times. But my time
> Runs posting on in Bolingbroke's proud joy,
> While I stand fooling here, his jack of the clock.
>
> **[5.5.49–60]**

Having earlier compared himself to Christ, Richard's image here is touchingly rueful. Haunted by the absurdity of his position, the only self-image he can find is that of a "fool".

# Stage history and adaptations

*Richard II* has long been one of Shakespeare's most frequently revived plays, almost his only native history to achieve a defining stage tradition, ironically enough, outside of "this sceptred isle". It was popular initially (among Shakespeare's top five hits), possibly at the Shoreditch **Theatre**, and also thrived in print, with six editions appearing before its author's death. It may have been performed at the residence of **Sir Edward Hoby** in 1595, and was perhaps the "play of King Henry the Fourth, and of the killing of Richard the Second" put on by Shakespeare's company and paid for by the **Earl of Essex**'s supporters in 1601, just as he rebelled against Elizabeth I (though some historians question this theory). In addition to being played in London and perhaps on tour, *Richard II* even reached the coast of West Africa in 1607, when it was performed alongside *Hamlet* on board the *Dragon*, a ship belonging to the East India Company.

Though the *Dragon*'s Captain Keeling rubber-stamped that staging, the authorities would not look so kindly on **Nahum Tate** in 1680. Though Tate did his best to disown historical parallels between King Charles II and his ancestor – insisting in his preface that "why a History of those Times should be suppressed as a Libel upon Ours, is past my Understanding" – the authorities banned it almost immediately, Tate's newly blameless Richard notwithstanding. This was the first of several adaptations, among them **Lewis Theobald**'s (1719) and **Francis Gentleman**'s (1755), designed to answer contemporary disquiet with *Richard II*'s orotund dramatic style and subject matter. Although **John Rich** staged an unadapted version at Covent Garden in 1738, it would be the century's last.

The way lay clear for the Romantics to rediscover the play's soloistic potential, which in **Edmund Kean**'s hands they did. Kean's 1815 text – in a version by company member **Richard Wroughton** – emphasized the King at the cost of much else. Interestingly, Kean played Richard as a courageous figure; an interpretation that Hazlitt took issue with: "Mr Kean made it a character of *passion*, that is of feeling combined with energy; whereas it is a character of *pathos*, that is to say of feeling combined with weakness." Where Edmund went for naked emotion, his son **Charles** (a lesser actor) kept the box-office of his Princess's Theatre humming with the most lavish production of *Richard II* yet seen, debuting in 1857. Though again the plight of Kean's own King was underscored, audiences flooded in to see the spectacular sets, chiefly the triumphal procession of Bolingbroke with the defeated Richard – an event only described in Shakespeare's play, but which in Kean's vision became "one of the most gorgeous and effective scenes that we have ever witnessed on stage" (*The Illustrated London News*). By then *Richard II* had become popular in the US, which saw a steady stream of productions mounted throughout the nineteenth century by **Junius Brutus Booth**, then his American-born son **Edwin**.

Back in England, **Frank Benson**'s Stratford productions (from 1896), with himself as a sympathetic but weak-minded Richard, kept old traditions alive, but soon afterwards the revolutionary **William Poel** staged an "authentic" version in London with the young **Harley Granville-Barker** as the King (though it still lasted a reported four hours). Fashions were changing by the time **Herbert Beerbohm Tree** mounted his spectacular version in 1903 – boasting real horses – and at first *Richard II* foundered. Only after **Harcourt Williams**'s 1929 Old Vic version, with **John Gielgud** in the lead, did the play's actorly potential become truly apparent, and **George Hayes** and **Maurice Evans** later excelled in the role. The year 1937 saw two defining productions: **Margaret Webster**'s on Broadway, with Evans's Richard (America's most successful *Richard II* to date); and Gielgud's own Queen's Theatre production in London. As with his Hamlet, Gielgud relished the poetry of the role, and was well supported by an enviable cast that included **Michael Redgrave** as Bolingbroke and **Peggy Ashcroft** as the Queen.

At Stratford in 1951 **Anthony Quayle** directed a production most notable for Redgrave's insistence on playing Richard as "an out-and-out pussy queer" (as Laurence Olivier put it). **Paul Scofield**'s Richard, directed by Gielgud at the Lyric, Hammersmith the following year, on the other hand, possessed a chilly hauteur that made him seem fatally detached from what was happening. The concept of a homosexual Richard was reinforced in **Richard Cotterell**'s 1969 Prospect Theatre production, which played Shakespeare's tragedy in parallel with Marlowe's *Edward II*. **Ian McKellen** acted both monarchs with show-stopping theatricality, while **Timothy West** was contrastingly gruff as Bolingbroke and Mortimer. By then **John Barton** and **Peter Hall**'s "Henriad" cycles of 1964 had come and gone – **David Warner** playing an overtly Christian Richard to **Eric Porter**'s Bolingbroke – but Barton would return in 1973 with an RSC *Richard* that shocked as many audiences as it delighted. In the first of many conceits Barton had **Ian Richardson** and **Richard Pasco** alternate as Richard and Bolingbroke on successive nights to underline the ritualized similarities between them, and also featured escalators representing their relative positions on the treadmill of power – even a snowman literalizing Richard's "mockery king of snow" metaphor. A byword for director's theatre, this version more than any other united academic theory with theatrical practice (Barton's wife Anne, a Cambridge don, wrote the programme notes).

Since then RSC Richards have included **Alan Howard** (1980), **Jeremy Irons** (1986) and a youthful **Sam West** (2000), while away from Stratford *Richard II* has appeared in some strikingly different incarnations. In 1981 **Ariane Mnouchkine** stressed the play's ritualistic aspect in a Kabuki- and Noh-influenced production at the Théâtre du Soleil in Paris. At the National Theatre in 1995 **Deborah Warner** daringly cast **Fiona Shaw** as a de-sexualized King, literally cocooned in his medieval world, in stark contrast to **David Threlfall**'s pragmatic, modern Bolingbroke. Compared to these two, the painstaking "original practices" theatre seen at Shakespeare's Globe in summer 2003 – "original" even down to the costly Italian velvet sported by **Mark Rylance**'s Richard – seems positively conservative. What was unusual was Rylance's interpretation, which found a surprising degree of comedy in Richard's capriciousness and, as with Fiona Shaw, emphasized the character's childishness.

Not unfittingly, the BBC has a near-monopoly on screenings of *Richard II* – initially with its 1960 *Age of Kings* television extravaganza; then with a Prospect-based version from 1970 featuring **Ian McKellen** and **Timothy West**; and most recently tapings of Warner's 1995 staging. The 1978 Time-Life production was directed by **David Giles** and starred **Derek Jacobi**, **Jon Finch** and **John Gielgud**.

## Screen

**Richard II**

**D. Jacobi, J. Finch, J. Gielgud; David Giles (dir.)**
UK, 1978 ▷ Ambrose Video (BBC) `DVD`

It's about as theatrically radical as an episode of *The Archers*, but this version of *Richard II* brings out many of the play's essential qualities, studiously avoiding innovations such as those exhibited by John Barton's contemporary RSC production. It is primarily an actors' vehicle, strongly differentiated between Jacobi's arrogant, camp, often histrionic – but finely spoken – King and Jon Finch's guarded Bolingbroke; while Gielgud, who made the play his own in the 1930s, delivers a fine "This England" speech as a convincingly emaciated Gaunt. The studio setting is if anything a boon, adding to the sense of rigidity and stylization, and Giles's camerawork is effective and unobtrusive – even if his decision to have Richard gossip with his favourites in what looks suspiciously like a Turkish bath could hardly be described as a subtle commentary on his sexuality. Not a masterpiece, but very watchable nevertheless. Recently rereleased in the US as part of the entire BBC Shakespeare set by Ambrose Video Publishing.

## Audio

### Richard II
**S. West, J. Ackland, D. Lewis; Jeremy Mortimer (dir.)**
UK, 2000 ▷ BBC ⊙ ▭

Sam West's devil-may-care Richard II gained plaudits at Stratford in 2000, and so it's good that he had an opportunity to record it for the BBC just beforehand. On audio he is every bit as impressive as the stage critics would have you believe, making the character less effete and tougher than is customary, while injecting a touching humanity into the play's closing scenes. Damian Lewis brings hauteur and impetuosity aplenty to Bolingbroke (a welcome change from more inscrutable interpretations), and Joss Ackland is finely grained as Gaunt. Jeremy Mortimer's decision to have Richard's nobles playing billiards isn't going to shock anyone these days – why does modern-dress have to be visual, after all? – but his re-ordering of the play's opening scenes might raise eyebrows. Even so, this is one of the most impressive audio Shakespeares currently available, creatively directed and utterly absorbing.

## Editions

### Arden Shakespeare (third edition)
**Charles Forker (ed.); 2002** ▷ Thomson

Arden 3 editions keep on getting fatter, and Charles Forker's *Richard II* is one of the fattest yet – nearly six hundred pages all told. What you get for your money is impressive: 170-odd pages of critical introduction, extensive "longer notes" presenting mini-essays on various phrases in the text, an extensive textual analysis along with various other appendices, and detailed footnotes quoting liberally from Halle and Holinshed. Some may feel that Forker's eagerness to cover every possibility produces more heat than light, but his treatment of the text is admirably clear – passages unique to the Folio version are enclosed by superscript "F"s.

## Some criticism

### The King's Two Bodies
**Ernst H. Kantorowicz; 1957** ▷ Princeton UP

The anniversary edition of this classic work, first printed forty years earlier, appeared in 1997. Essentially it's a study of medieval political theology and much of Kantorowicz's argument will be of interest only to the most devoted of students, but his insistence that *Richard II* "has always been felt to be a political play" gives him the opportunity to uncover some fascinating detail on the historical symbols behind the play as well as contextualize its markedly ritualized tone and stagecraft. The "bodies" of the title are the king's "body natural" (real body) and his "body politic" (the symbolic essence of his kingliness); Richard's problem, Kantorowicz suggests, is that in being deposed his very identity is snapped in two.

### Shakespeare and the Idea of the Play
**Anne Righter; 1962** ▷ Chatto / Vintage [o/p]

While Kantorowicz's sober study is sometimes heavy going, Anne Righter's slimline and very readable *Shakespeare and the Idea of the Play* (published before she married director John Barton) is emphatically not. Righter's broad thesis is that Shakespeare's peculiar self-consciousness about the business of the theatre is both an inheritance and a break from his medieval and early Tudor precursors, one that produces a quite different approach to the drama of power. According to Righter, plays such as *Richard II* weave dramatic awarenesses so tightly into the fabric of the action that, as she puts it, "the image of the actor pursues Richard relentlessly" on his path to infamy. The book covers nearly all the plays in varying amounts of detail as well as providing plenty of background on older dramatic traditions, making it a fine introduction not just to Shakespeare's work but to the theatre that provided him with employment and inspiration.

# Richard III

**S**hakespeare's first great villain and his lengthiest early role, the part of Richard III has long been a gift for actors. All the greats have played him, and each has made the irresistibly evil king their own. To many, it's Richard's breathtaking theatricality that makes him what he is: the smiling murderer, the seductive humpback, the man who engages with the audience outside the action yet nevertheless controls it until almost the last moment. In some ways Richard is a stock villain, a fusion of the medieval "Vice" character and the Elizabethan "Machiavel" of Marlowe and others, but he is a chillingly convincing one – so much so that Shakespeare's creation has been accused of obliterating the real King Richard from the historical record. Stepping out from the carnage of the *Henry VI* plays and the devastation wrought by the Wars of the Roses, Shakespeare makes him embody a new and brutal age of politics, one on which the laws of society (even God) seem to have no purchase. And even though we know that Richard's brutal and violent reign will come to an end – that "The Tragedy of King Richard the Third", as the play was first printed, will culminate in England's deliverance – it proves more difficult to lay Richard's ghost to rest, as the play's lively stage history testifies, than the Tudor chroniclers can ever have suspected.

[ DATE ]   Presumably written once *1 Henry VI* was finished, *Richard III* is likely to have been completed 1592–93 (the same period as *Titus*), perhaps for the newly formed Lord Pembroke's Men.

[ SOURCES ]   As with the *Henry VI* plays, two Tudor historical accounts – Holinshed's *Chronicles* (1587) and Halle's *Union* (1548) – provide the basic matter and many of its colourful details. Both sources reprint Thomas More's unflattering *History* of Richard (c.1513), and Senecan tragedy must also have been in Shakespeare's mind.

[ TEXTS ]   Notoriously complicated. A quarto edition (Q1, 1597) was reprinted seven times, but it's likely to be a later version of the play than the 1623 Folio one – possibly revised for touring.

## Interpreting the play

As *Richard III* opens, some of its audience could be forgiven for feeling a sense of *déjà vu*. The brilliant, twisted Richard of Gloucester is alone, centre-stage – acting like a malevolent chorus on the action even though it is yet to begin, and even though it will involve him too. It isn't long before his warm praise of King Edward's victory over the Lancastrians, "Now is the winter of our discontent / Made glorious summer by this son of York", dissipates. He is possessed solely by an obsessive lust for power:

> I that am rudely stamped and want love's majesty
> To strut before a wanton ambling nymph,
> I that am curtailed of this fair proportion,
> Cheated of feature by dissembling nature,
> Deformed, unfinished, sent before my time

## Major Characters & Synopsis

**Richard, Duke of Gloucester** (later **King Richard III**)

Richard's brothers: **King Edward IV** and **George, Duke of Clarence**

**Duchess of York**, their mother

**Queen Elizabeth**, Edward IV's wife

Anthony Woodville, **Lord Rivers**, Queen Elizabeth's brother

The two young princes: **Edward, Prince of Wales** and **Richard, Duke of York**, sons of King Edward and Queen Elizabeth

**Marquis of Dorset** and **Lord Gray**, Queen Elizabeth's sons by her previous marriage

**Lady Anne** (later **Anne, Duchess of Gloucester**), widow of Henry VI's son, Edward

**Queen Margaret**, Henry VI's widow

**William, Lord Hastings**, the Lord Chamberlain

**Lord Stanley**, Earl of Derby, Hastings's friend

**Henry, Earl of Richmond** (later **King Henry VII**)

Richmond's followers: **Earl of Oxford, Sir James Blunt, Sir Walter Herbert**

Richard of Gloucester's followers: **Duke of Buckingham, Duke of Norfolk, Sir Richard Ratcliffe, Sir William Catesby, Sir James Tyrrel**

**Cardinal Bourchier**, Archbishop of Canterbury

Archbishop of York

**Lord Mayor of London**

**Sir Robert Brackenbury**, Lieutenant of the Tower

**Ghosts** of King Henry VI, Prince Edward, Clarence, Lady Anne, Buckingham and Hastings

[▶▶ **action continued from** *Henry VI Part III*]

**ACT 1** Edward Plantagenet is now King, but already his brother Richard is plotting against him. Having turned Edward against Clarence, Richard now proceeds to woo Lady Anne, widow of the Lancastrian Prince Edward – despite having a hand in her husband's murder, he manages to seduce her over the coffin of her father-in-law. With the King now ill, Queen Elizabeth fears that Richard will seize the throne if he dies. Richard and Elizabeth are arguing when Queen Margaret arrives, denouncing her Plantagenet usurpers. In the Tower, Clarence's nightmares turn to reality when two murderers in Richard's pay appear.

**ACT 2** Having ordered Clarence's execution to be revoked, Edward is recovering when Richard coolly announces that he has been killed after all.

Everyone is appalled and King Edward dies shortly afterwards. When Richard and Buckingham imprison Lords Rivers and Gray, Queen Elizabeth's family, she decides to seek the sanctuary with her youngest son, the Duke of York.

**ACT 3** As Prince Edward arrives in London, Buckingham persuades the Archbishop of Canterbury to remove the Duke of York from sanctuary. Richard then conveys both princes to the Tower. Attempting to build support, Richard sends Catesby to sound out Hastings and promises Buckingham high office when he becomes King. Hastings refuses to support Richard, and after arriving in London (to plan Prince Edward's coronation), he is summarily executed on Richard's orders. Buckingham and Richard then convince the Mayor of London that Hastings was a traitor and suggest that Edward IV and his heirs are illegitimate. In front of the Mayor and various citizens, Richard feigns devoutness and seems reluctant to accept the throne when Buckingham insists it is his by right.

**ACT 4** At his coronation Richard suggests to Buckingham that the two Princes should die. When Buckingham hesitates, Richard turns on him and gets Tyrrell to arrange the deed. Richard also plans the murder of his wife so that he can marry his niece Elizabeth. Buckingham reminds Richard of his promise of high office, but Richard stalls and Buckingham flees. Queen Elizabeth and the Duchess of York meet with Queen Margaret and all three bewail the loss of their loved ones. Richard enters and is cursed by his mother; he then asks Queen Elizabeth for help in wooing her daughter and she pretends to agree. As news arrives of Richmond's invasion, Richard's grip on power begins to falter.

**ACT 5** Buckingham is captured by Richard's allies and is executed. Meanwhile, Richard, marching to meet Richmond, pitches camp at Bosworth. The night before battle, he is visited by the ghosts of those he killed on the way to power. Richard's forces are defeated in battle when Stanley switches to Richmond (his son-in-law). Richmond kills King Richard in single combat and Stanley presents him with the crown. Richmond promises to restore peace and unite the Houses of York and Lancaster by marrying Elizabeth, Edward IV's daughter.

Into this breathing world scarce half made up—
And that so lamely and unfashionable
That dogs bark at me as I halt by them—
Why, I in this weak piping time of peace
Have no delight to pass away the time,
Unless to spy my shadow in the sun
And descant on mine own deformity.
And therefore since I cannot prove a lover
To entertain these fair well-spoken days,
I am determinèd to prove a villain …

**[1.1.14–30]**

All this might seem familiar to audiences who have witnessed *3 Henry VI* and heard Richard declaring, in strikingly similar terms, that "love foreswore me in my mother's womb" and resolving

since this earth affords no joy to me
But to command, to check, to o'erbear such
As are of better person than myself,
I'll make my heaven to dream upon the crown …

**[3 Henry VI, 3.2.165–8]**

Gloucester's repeated statement of ambition is more than a link between *Richard III* and its "Henriad" predecessors – it is the keynote of Richard's own personality.

Not surprisingly, critics have seized on these lines. Led by Freud, who famously saw in Richard the archetype of a personality bruised by childhood experience and bent on revenge, psychoanalytical commentators have worried away at the connection between Richard's deformity and his lust for power – "to o'er bear such / As are of better person than myself". The French critic René Girard suggests, on a symbolic level, that "Richard's deformed body is a mirror for the self-confessed ugliness of his soul", making a strikingly similar point to that proposed several centuries earlier by Francis Bacon, who argued in his essay "Of Deformity" that "all deformed persons are extreme bold … [I]t stirreth in them industry … to watch and observe the weakness in others that they may have somewhat to repay".

Other writers have been disturbed by what this seems to imply, that Richard's character is the result of his deformity, and much psychological effort has gone into diagnosing what drives him. Is it hatred of his mother? envy of his brothers? anything at all? What such critics have been reluctant to notice, though, is that Richard himself makes the link. In fact, his own account of himself ("Cheated of feature", "Deformed, unfinished", "scarce half made up") produces such monstrous reflection that it cannot help but be an exaggeration. Richard is, as he says, "descanting" on his own deformity – playing with it, spinning it out, drawing us in. Though – in Bacon's terms – he is "extreme bold" in his determination to wreak revenge (something that inflicts and impels Iago too), it is clear that Richard seizes on the monstrous aspects of his appearance and makes them into a source of malevolent power.

## Change shapes with Proteus

In another speech from *3 Henry VI* so closely identified with Gloucester that, from Cibber onwards (see p.301), it has often found its way into versions of *Richard III*, the Duke trumpets his skill as an actor, turning his unusually mutable identity to his own advantage:

Why, I can smile, and murder whiles I smile,
And cry 'Content!' to that which grieves my heart,

And wet my cheeks with artificial tears,
And frame my face to all occasions ...
I can add colours to the chameleon,
Change shapes with Proteus for advantages,
And set the murderous Machiavel to school.
Can I do this, and cannot get a crown?
Tut, were it farther off, I'll pluck it down.

**[3 Henry VI, 3.4.183–95]**

Though he is "disproportioned", "Like to a chaos", this offers him the opportunity to recast himself at a moment's notice. Richard is the first of Shakespeare's great villains, all of them able to bend the characters around them to their will by fitting themselves to their purposes. Shakespeare stresses Richard's theatricality so much that even as we gasp at his deeds, we are astonished by his control over events. The strength of that power is revealed by the fact that other people think him honesty incarnate: Clarence attempts to persuade his very murderers that Gloucester "loves me"; Hastings is dispatched just moments after declaring confidently that "by his face straight shall you know his heart". Only to himself (and, importantly, to the audience) does Richard admit that he is backed by "the plain devil and dissembling looks" (1.2.224). It has long been recognized that Richard is a great role which was almost certainly designed for Shakespeare's most celebrated star, Richard Burbage, who would go on to play Hamlet, Othello, Malvolio and Lear. It's surely no accident that Burbage was himself described as a "Protean" talent: both Richards fit that billing.

"Mr Kean as Richard the Third". A popular print ("penny plain, tuppence coloured") produced by William West reflects the huge popularity of Edmund Kean – the greatest English actor of the early nineteenth century. Of Kean's enactment of Richard's death, the critic of the *Examiner* wrote: "we never felt stronger emotion, more overpowering sensations, than those kindled by the novel sublimity of the catastrophe."

Richard's success on the stage is also due to his descent from a long pedigree of Vice characters in medieval "Morality" plays, whose task it is to persuade good characters to stray from the path of righteousness; it is a pedigree Richard himself revels in. But equally important is Richard's relationship to one of Shakespeare's main sources, Thomas More's *History of King Richard III*, which was influential enough to be partly reprinted by both Tudor chroniclers, Holinshed and Halle, in their own histories of the period. In More's text, "ill-featured", "crook-backed" Richard is "close and secret, a deep dissembler, lowly of countenance, arrogant of heart, outwardly companionable where he inwardly hated, not letting to kiss whom he thought to kill" – a diabolical description which does its best to desecrate his reputation. But where More, Halle and Holinshed produce (and reproduce) an image of Richard which is nothing but evil – for reasons that have much to do with their Tudor affiliations – Shakespeare realizes the sheer attraction of his character in all its twisted genius. A man who is that good at being bad must be fascinating to watch; he unites dramatic energy with political power.

## Some tormenting dream

Richard's skill at remaking himself transforms political events just as rapidly. His wooing of Lady Anne over her father-in-law's coffin is a sublime example of theatrical daring – and in fact a literalization of the argument put forward by the real-life Machiavelli in his book *Il Principe* ("The Prince"), that "fortune [*fortuna*] is a woman, and if you want to control her, it is necessary to treat her roughly". We watch as Richard's power over words remakes Anne's terms of abuse – again, dwelling on his physical deformity – into flirtatious banter, reworking a situation in which he cannot win into one that he has no chance of losing:

> LADY ANNE
>> Never hung poison on a fouler toad.
>> Out of my sight! Thou dost infect mine eyes.
> RICHARD GLOUCESTER
>> Thine eyes, sweet lady, have infected mine.
> LADY ANNE
>> Would they were basilisks to strike thee dead.
> RICHARD GLOUCESTER
>> I would they were, that I might die at once,
>> For now they kill me with a living death.
>
> **[1.2.147–52]**

When Lady Anne enters the play, it is as the mourner of her husband and her father-in-law, one of the female voices of lamentation and remembrance that dominate *Richard III*. But in persuading Anne to be his wife, Richard rewrites her role. Instead of defusing the situation, he redirects its power by casting her as scornful mistress, himself as wounded lover. His creative potential even redefines the ring he instructs her to wear: "Look how my ring encompasseth thy finger; / Even so thy breast encloseth my poor heart" (1.2.191–2). The conventions are twisted around – Richard claims that she is in control, but it is *his* ring on her finger and *his* heart in her breast. Despite Richard's malign persuasiveness, Anne's capitulation, gruesome as it is, has infinite capacity to shock – as of course Shakespeare intended. It is as if Richard's willpower – and here his will is sexual too – simply overcomes all opposition, no matter how righteous and strong. Only with Queen Elizabeth's double-crossing of Richard later in the plot will events (and the women that surround him) produce any kind of effective revenge.

Richard's dealings with another woman in the play – Margaret of Anjou, who makes a spectral but powerful appearance (particularly spectral because she is historically dead at the time the action takes place) – have comparable transformative electricity. Like Anne, she bitterly denounces the usurping Plantagenets before cursing Richard himself:

> No sleep close up that deadly eye of thine,
> Unless it be with some tormenting dream
> Afrights thee with hell of ugly devils.
> Thou elvish-marked, abortive, rooting hog,
> Thou that wast sealed in thy nativity
> The slave of nature and the son of hell,
> Thou slander of thy heavy mother's womb,
> Thou loathèd issue of thy father's loins,
> Thou rag of honour, thou detested—

**[1.3.222–30]**

But Richard does not give her the opportunity to finish. He breaks in by shouting out "Margaret", turning the curse back on the curser. It is a moment of élan and wit, but a revealingly ironic one too. While Margaret's call for vengeance on the Plantagenets ("God I pray him, / That none of you may live his natural age" (1.3.209–211)), certainly bears fruit, it is Richard's agency that brings it all about.

> *That this play has scenes noble in themselves and very well contrived to strike in the exhibition, cannot be denied. But some parts are trifling, others shocking, and some improbable.*
>
> Samuel Johnson, commentary to *The Plays of William Shakespeare* (1765)

Some critics have pointed to Margaret's threat of "some tormenting dream" and noted that *Richard III* is the play of Shakespeare's in which the word "dream" occurs most often. Many characters express the sense that, as events take new and agitating turns, their whole experience is being turned into a waking nightmare. Nowhere is this truer than with Clarence, who is sent to the Tower because of King Edward's "prophecies and dreams" (in fact Richard's prompting) and whose description of the eerie nightmare he suffers occurs just moments before his execution. Bemoaning his "miserable night, / So full of fearful dreams", he describes how he dreamt he was voyaging away from imprisonment with his brother:

> As we paced along
> Upon the giddy footing of the hatches,
> Methought that Gloucester stumbled, and in falling
> Struck me—that sought to stay him—overboard
> Into the tumbling billows of the main.
> O Lord! Methought what pain it was to drown,
> What dreadful noise of waters in my ears,
> What sights of ugly death within my eyes.
> Methoughts I saw a thousand fearful wrecks,
> Ten thousand men that fishes gnawed upon,
> Wedges of gold, great ouches, heaps of pearl,
> Inestimable stones, unvalued jewels,
> All scattered in the bottom of the sea.

**[1.4.16–28]**

Clarence's words come from any number of sources, but the Tudor commonplace that drowned riches represent worldly vanity is perhaps strongest here – and yet "simple, plain"

Clarence has no vanity, just naive faith in Richard. He doesn't deserve a dream like this, and yet it plots the outline of his downfall and that of Richard's route to the throne. In a similar (if less appalling) way to Lady Anne, it is as if the play makes him complicit in his own fate.

Ultimately, though, Richard loses control over what he himself has set in motion: almost as soon as he gains the crown, that long-held obsession, things start to unravel – and, during Act Four, do so with frightening rapidity. Richard's process of decline reaches its nadir the night before battle at Bosworth as, with eerie inevitability, Margaret's curse comes true. Richard's victims, quite literally, come back to haunt him: the ghosts of the young princes, King Henry, Clarence, Rivers, Gray, Vaughan, Hastings, Anne and Buckingham troop through Richard's sleeping mind, sending him into chaotic confusion:

> O coward conscience, how dost thou afflict me?
> The lights turn blue. It is now dead midnight.
> Cold fearful drops stand upon my trembling flesh.
> What do I fear? Myself? There's none else by.
> Richard loves Richard; that is, I am I.
> Is there a murderer here? No. Yes, I am.
> Then fly! What, from myself? Great reason. Why?
> Lest I revenge. Myself upon myself?
> Alack, I love myself. Wherefore? For any good
> That I myself have done unto myself?
> O no, alas, I rather hate myself
> For hateful deeds committed by myself.
> I am a villain. Yet I lie: I am not.

**[5.5.132–45]**

"Richard loves Richard … I am I", the self-possessed mantra of isolation, first voiced at the end of *3 Henry VI* (see p.133), has left him friendless, just as his effortless skill at changing shape leaves him uncertain about what he is. As Richard's psychology spills out once more on stage, these ghosts become both imaginary and real, a blurred distinction that mirrors the final breakdown in his mind. Not in full control for the first time in the play, Richard simply collapses. The consummate actor has created a world so fluid and changeable that he himself cannot survive it; and far from being able to master Fortune, he is ultimately her victim.

## Stage history and adaptations

*Richard III* is unusual among Shakespeare's oeuvre in having been almost continually on the stage – in one form or another – ever since it was written. The first quarto of 1597 describes it as having been "lately acted" by the **Lord Chamberlain's Men**, and it survived the transition to the indoor Blackfriars theatre in 1609. The play was a star vehicle from its inception: **Richard Burbage**, the greatest actor in the company, created the part of Richard; and it was taken by **Ellyaerdt Swanston** in the next-generation King's Men. It remained in the repertoire, and was performed at court before Charles I and his French wife, Henrietta Maria – both of whom had an abiding interest in theatre – in 1633. Nor did it die after the reopening of the theatres in 1660: several performances are recorded (one, in 1690, had **Samuel Sandford**, an expert in playing villains, in the lead role), though it was apparently not popular, despite productions which played up Richard's apparent resemblance to Oliver Cromwell.

In 1700, the enterprising actor-dramatist **Colley Cibber** put together an adaptation that would become the most popular play on the English stage for the next two centuries. Cibber cut over three-quarters of Shakespeare's text, added a thousand lines and deleted Margaret and Clarence entirely. This version made the career of **David Garrick**, who debuted in the title role in 1741 and acted it continually thereafter. Garrick was naturalistic but mercurial in the lead – Fanny Burney caught a performance in 1772 and declared him "sublimely horrible" – but his crown would be challenged by a new generation of stars, most notably **George Frederick Cooke**, who stressed the character's sarcasm at the expense of the nobility so admired in Garrick, and **Edmund Kean**, whose Drury Lane debut as Richard in 1814 caused a sensation. The diminutive Kean conveyed a vitality and a casual menace which mesmerized his audience; the battle scenes, in particular, were singled out by critics as a thrilling depiction of a disintegrating and desperate personality who yet retained a core of regality.

While both Cooke and Kean stuck with Cibber, as did the Kean imitator **Junius Brutus Booth**, Shakespeare's stock was on the rise. **William Charles Macready**, whose 1819 debut in the part was a daring challenge to Kean's supremacy, used the original text in his 1821 performance, as did **Samuel Phelps** at Sadler's Wells in 1845, but the script was still doctored to throw more limelight onto the lead role (Phelps played Richard to **Mary Amelia Warner**'s Margaret). The situation was more enlightened in Germany: full translations of Shakespeare's play had been performed for years, and **Bogumil Dawison** excelled as Richard at the Dresden Court Theatre in the 1850s (and might well have been witnessed by the young Henrik Ibsen). US audiences wanting a comparably authentic experience had to wait until **Edwin Booth**, the son of Junius Brutus Booth, performed in New York in 1878.

**John Barrymore** brought a dynamic physicality to Richard in an otherwise conventional 1920 Broadway production (his performance was partly inspired by the movements of the tarantula spider). In the same year **Leopold Jessner** mounted an expressionistic staging in Berlin, in which the set was dominated by a huge flight of stairs, that was to inspire Jan Kott's "Grand Mechanism" view of history (see p.112). Jessner's reading would provide the inspiration for another innovative Berlin production, that by **Jürgen Fehling** in 1937, which bravely outlined parallels between Shakespeare's play and totalitarianism (**Berthold Brecht**'s 1941 *The Resistible Rise of Arturo Ui*, loosely based on *Richard III*, preferred to draw upon gangsterism). The notion of parodying Hitler himself had occurred to **Donald Wolfit** in wartime England, as it had **Laurence Olivier**, whose startling personification of the hunchback – complete with false nose and wheedling, sanctimonious voice – was first aired at the New Theatre in 1944. Touring widely and preserved in his 1955 film, Olivier's Richard was highly idiosyncratic but in the star pedigree of Cibber and Garrick: the consummate actor playing the consummate actor.

Successors attempted to escape from Olivier's shadow. In 1953 **Alec Guinness** played Richard with a light touch at the brand-new theatre in Stratford, Ontario; **Marius Goring** opted for subtle madness in **Glen Byam Shaw**'s pared-down version at Stratford in 1953; while eight years later, also at Stratford, **Christopher Plummer** presented a weary and neurotic Richard. But the most successful break with the past was masterminded by directors **John Barton** and **Peter Hall**, whose politicized *Wars of the Roses* of 1963 melded the *Henry VI* plays with *Richard III*. **Ian Holm**'s insinuating Richard had the energy of a coiled spring but in the greater scheme of things was just another monarch on the treadmill of power; and it was **Peggy Ashcroft**'s tragic Margaret who really dominated.

The best recent productions of *Richard III* have found new things to say. **John Hirsch** drew upon Brecht's theatre of alienation at Stratford, Ontario in 1967, while at the Nottingham Playhouse in 1971 **Leonard Rossiter** (a brilliant Arturo Ui the year before) invested the role

Ian McKellen played Richard as a fascist dictator in Richard Loncraine's 1996 film, a Turkish cigarette continually clamped beneath his pencil moustache. This adaptation drew closely on Richard Eyre's National production six years earlier.

with his own unique brand of twitchy grotesquerie – often to highly comic effect. A heavily stylized Georgian-language production toured by **Robert Sturua** in 1980 also used Brechtian techniques leavened by Mikhail Bakhtin's theories of the carnivalesque. Perhaps the most widely admired English portrayal of Richard of the 1980s, though, was that by **Antony Sher** in **Bill Alexander**'s RSC production of 1984. Sher was a charismatic "bottled spider", scuttling with crutches in a highly physical but intelligent performance; in a reversal of tradition, he faltered as the play went on. **Ian McKellen**, in **Richard Eyre**'s 1930s vision at the National Theatre (1990), was a stylish and powerful man of action – every inch the fascist tyrant – who met his end with valour. In the same year, **Andrew Jarvis** played a pinstriped, power-crazed and impeccably Thatcherite monarch in **Michael Bodganov**'s ESC *Wars of the Roses*. **Simon Russell Beale** made a heavyweight, toad-like but slightly camp Richard in **Sam Mendes**'s RSC version of 1992, while **David Troughton** emphasized the hero's comedy, but also his vulnerability, at Stratford three years later. **Kenneth Branagh** has provided one of Richard's most successful recent incarnations: in **Michael Grandage**'s 2002 production at the Crucible Theatre in Sheffield he was described by the *Times Literary Supplement* as a "villain for the era of smile politics". A novel twist (but one not without historical precedent) was aired the following summer at the London Globe, **Barry Kyle**'s all-female troupe taking on a play not noted for its open-minded portrayal of women; **Kathryn Hunter** excelled as a mischievous monarch who clearly revelled in acting up for the groundlings.

   *Richard III* has been well-represented on celluloid: in addition to the two stage-inspired films of Olivier (1955) and McKellen (1996), the play provides the earliest example of American cinematic Shakespeare, courtesy of **Frederick B. Warde** in 1912. Another silent movie was made by **J. Stuart Blackton** (1908), and **Frank Benson**'s Stratford version is preserved in a 1911 film. **Al Pacino** remixed the play in his 1996 *Looking for Richard*, framing his own powerful performance in the title role with a documentary in which he pounded the streets of New York searching for the play's essence. *Richard III* has also made good TV: a segment was broadcast by the BBC in 1937 – one of the earliest transmissions of Shakespeare – and the play was incorporated into **Jane Howell**'s BBC production of 1982.

# Screen

### Richard III

**F. Benson, M. Carrington, M. Johnston; Frank Benson (dir.)**
UK, 1911 ▷ on Silent Shakespeare (BFI) 📀 📼

The British Film Institute's terrific *Silent Shakespeare* compilation fills a large gap in the market, including early versions of seven plays – among them the *Dream* (see p.246), *Twelfth Night* (see p.378) and *The Tempest* (see p.335). Most were adapted specially for the silent screen, but Frank Benson's 23-minute *Richard III* is a condensation of his infamous Stratford production; less engaging cinematically but historically priceless. What makes this film of more than antiquarian interest, though, is Benson himself: he reveals more with one malicious gesture than many lesser actors manage with an entire script – gleefully snatching up an apple after sending Hastings to his doom, momentarily unsteady on his feet as combat with Richmond looms. It's worth keeping this film silent, however – Laura Rossi's music is desperately poor.

### Richard III

**L. Olivier, J. Gielgud, R. Richardson; Laurence Olivier (dir.)**
UK, 1955 ▷ DD Video / Criterion 📀 📼

This *Richard III* encapsulates what many people probably dread about Shakespeare on film: affected acting, kitschy sets, bad wigs. Indeed, Olivier's crookback king was so successfully parodied by Peter Sellers that it's sometimes hard to take this movie entirely at face value. For all that, it is one of *the* Shakespeare classics, perhaps best appreciated as an eighteenth-century star vehicle (complete with Cibber and Garrick interpolations) which has somehow survived into the Technicolor age. Olivier is mesmeric in the lead – both repellent and fatally irresistible – and declaims the verse with a panache that would simply be impossible nowadays. He flirts with the camera, guiding the viewer through the play with malevolent glee and often shot in close-up as the grim tableau of his deeds unfolds behind him. When the central performance is this strong, it's even possible to understand how Claire Bloom's quiescent Anne feels she has no options left. Unmissable, particularly in the Criterion DVD version, which includes lots of extra features.

### Richard III

**I. McKellen, N. Hawthorne, J. Carter; Richard Loncraine (dir.)**
UK, 1996 ▷ MGM / Pathé 📀 📼

A full forty years after Olivier's version, Ian McKellen and Richard Loncraine's film steers a very different course to its illustrious predecessor. No medieval trimmings here: the setting is upper-crust 1930s England (with *arriviste* elements courtesy of Americans Annette Bening and Robert Downey, Jr), enlivened by a Cole Porter-ish soundtrack and intelligently shot in megalomaniacal locations including Brighton Pavilion, and London's St Pancras Station and Shell-Mex House. Though hardly the first actor to sense fascistic overtones in Richard's character (Donald Wolfit and indeed Olivier, both performing in wartime England, made a similar imaginative leap), McKellen makes a persuasive dictator and conveys a carefully judged balance between suaveness and menace. He is quieter than Olivier, but every bit as fine – full of sardonic humour and gleeful glances to camera. This *Richard III*'s only flaw – and it is a fairly major one – is that visual style and postmodern wit smother most of the play's brute nastiness, which makes it feel curiously shallow at times. It will make you smirk rather than quake.

### Looking for Richard

**A. Pacino, K. Spacey, W. Rider; Al Pacino (dir.)**
USA, 1996 ▷ Fox 📼

"Ya know Shakespeare?" Pacino bawls amiably to a surprised six-year-old on a Manhattan sidewalk. "We're peddling Shakespeare on the streets." That's probably the best description of this perplexing but personable film, which chronicles Pacino's efforts to get on speaking terms with *Richard III*. The project occupied three years and saw Al and pals criss-cross not only New York but the Atlantic too – paying homage at Stratford and London, getting the lowdown from a couple of academics, and chin-wagging with Famous English Thesps. Everything is woven around preparations for an abbreviated film version of the play starring Pacino as a mafioso-style Richard, a smirking Kevin Spacey as Buckingham and Penelope Allen's awesome Queen Elizabeth. If this sounds like a jumble it's intentionally so, and while *Looking for Richard* has its dire moments, it is redeemed by its insights into the mysteries of rehearsal, its frankness about American inhibitions concerning the Bard, and its genuine eagerness about Shakespeare's many wonders.

# Audio

### King Richard III

**K. Branagh, M. Maloney, S. Gonet; David Timson (dir.)**
UK, 2001 ▷ Naxos ⊙ 📼

Perhaps it's fitting to recommend an audio version starring the actor–director who's done more to manhandle Shakespeare into the popular cultural mainstream than anyone since Olivier – Kenneth Branagh. In fact, his CV has little to do with it: Branagh puts in a genuinely involving performance, sometimes surprisingly moving, and his distinctive voice is here disconcertingly varied – so much so that you'll be hard-pressed to recognize him in the infamous opening soliloquy.

No less impressive are Geraldine McEwan's commanding and well-spoken Margaret and Celia Imrie's sharply authoritative Elizabeth. Only Michael Maloney's slightly hysterical Clarence fails to evoke any sympathy. Under David Timson's direction the pace never slackens and – a rarity in audio Shakespeare – the music works well.

## Editions

### Oxford Shakespeare
**John Jowett (ed.); 2000** ▷ Oxford UP

As Associate General Editor of the Oxford *Complete Works*, John Jowett has an excellent track record in the bibliographical nitty-gritty of Shakespearian scholarship, and his edition of *Richard III* is typically scrupulous. Jowett's control text is the 1597 quarto, an unusual choice but selected on the basis that it represents something close to the play as first performed. With Folio additions listed in an appendix, the result is an unusually complete picture of the script and its various forms (including plenty on Cibber's adaptation). These are further complemented by detailed appendices, among them excerpts from More's *History* – otherwise surprisingly tricky to get hold of – and an index of directors and actors.

## Some criticism

### Angel with Horns
**A.P. Rossiter (ed. Graham Storey); 1961**
▷ Longman [o/p]

In this wide-ranging collection of fifteen lectures delivered at Cambridge University by Rossiter and published after his death, the "Angel" of the book's title is the gloriously paradoxical Richard III, the brutal tyrant who is also irresistibly alluring. The opening essay was one of the first studies of the play to challenge critical orthodoxy and propose what theatregoers have known all along – that Richard is a great deal more exciting than anyone else who surrounds him. In doing so, it offers a reading of the play that sits quite happily with its customary role as a star vehicle, though which perhaps undervalues its wider political arguments – critics such as Jan Kott, who famously proclaimed that Richard "has no face", find fault with this character-based brand of interpretation. Despite these shortcomings, Rossiter's charm and off-hand brilliance are likely to win you over.

### Engendering a Nation
**Jean E. Howard & Phyllis Rackin; 1997**
▷ Routledge

Subtitled "A feminist account of Shakespeare's English histories", Howard and Rackin's study, completed twenty or so years after feminist analysis of Shakespeare first took hold, leaves little to the imagination – though is none the worse for that. Their examination of the role of women in the first tetralogy under the heading "Weak kings, warrior women, and the assault on dynastic authority" is bracing and instructive. If at times tendentious, this approach works particularly well for *Richard III*, and throws useful light on women characters manipulated and victimized (and all too often obscured) by their celebrity king. An interesting comparison – perhaps even corrective – to Rossiter and much male-centred criticism.

# Romeo and Juliet

t's perhaps the most timeless Shakespearian image of all: the star-crossed lovers in the balcony scene, united by their passion yet doomed to separation. But *Romeo and Juliet* is all about time, and the fact that the lovers are given so little time with each other lends their love affair a volatile and dramatic intensity. Shakespeare's Juliet and Romeo fall in love on the instant, they're married almost immediately, and they are allowed just one precious night together before their feuding families drive them apart. They are not permitted to grow old, and *Romeo and Juliet* describes better than any other Shakespearian work what it feels like to be young. The play draws its power from violent conflict: between youth and age, life and death, fate and free will. Some have felt this makes it too schematic; the work of a man still learning his craft. Yet *Romeo and Juliet* is also a bold experiment, one that Shakespeare would never quite repeat. It begins in a world of bantering comedy and teenage rebellion, but when danger and death intervene, full-blooded tragedy consumes the action. The lovers may attempt to transcend their fractured world, but they are in the end unable to escape it – the play at once portrays the power of romantic ideals and their fragility in the face of crushing social forces.

[DATE] Given its stylistic similarities to *Love's Labour's Lost* and *A Midsummer Night's Dream*, probably 1595 or 1596.

[SOURCES] Arthur Brooke's poem *The Tragical History of Romeus and Juliet* (1562) is the play's largest source (*The Two Gentlemen of Verona* also uses it), though the basic tale exists in many versions – one of which, William Painter's *Palace of Pleasure* (1566–67), Shakespeare may have consulted.

[TEXTS] Trading on *Romeo*'s apparent popularity, an unlicensed text (Q1) was pirated in 1597, probably reconstructed from memory. Q2, seemingly set from Shakespeare's papers, appeared two years later and was reprinted in 1609 (Q3), c.1622 (Q4) and 1637 (Q5). The 1623 Folio version uses the third, 1609 printing.

## Interpreting the play

It is testament to the immortal power of what is frequently billed as the greatest love story ever that, each year, thousands of love-struck correspondents write to "Juliet" in Verona asking for her blessing; so many, in fact, that there is a municipal organization dedicated to replying on her behalf. That appeal to universality is part of *Romeo and Juliet*'s attraction. The couple are overwhelmingly in love yet fatally divided; conjoined in what Juliet achingly calls "my true-love passion" (2.1.146) yet separated by destiny. Their relationship, it's been said, taps into some mythic vein – it is one example of the kind of "separation romance" that animates ancient tales such as those of Hero and Leander, Troilus and Cressida, Tristan and Isolde. Richard Wagner, whose opera *Tristan und Isolde* magnifies the myth to earth-shattering proportions, called it *Liebstod* ("love-death"), and *Romeo and Juliet* has frequently been interpreted in similarly totalizing terms.

Shakespeare, like countless writers before him, found inspiration in separation: that's why the balcony scene, with its gorgeous speeches between the divided lovers, works so powerfully

## Major Characters & Synopsis

### THE MONTAGUES

**Romeo**, a young man from Verona
**Montague**, Romeo's father, head of the household
**Lady Montague**, Montague's wife
**Benvolio**, Romeo's cousin and friend
**Abraham**, Montague's servant
**Balthasar**, Romeo's servant

### THE CAPULETS

**Juliet**, a young lady from Verona
**Capulet**, Juliet's father, head of the household
**Lady Capulet**, Capulet's wife
**Tybalt**, Juliet's cousin
Juliet's **Nurse**
**Peter**, **Samson** and **Gregory**, the Capulets' servants

### OTHERS

**Escalus**, Prince of Verona
**Mercutio**, a young nobleman related to the Prince, Romeo's friend
**Count Paris**, a young nobleman related to the Prince
Paris's **Page**
**Friars Laurence** and **John**, Franciscan monks
An **Apothecary**
**Chorus**, introducing the action

**ACT 1** Verona is riven by a feud between the Capulets and the Montagues, powerful local families. Even a minor skirmish between servants rapidly escalates into a full-scale riot, halted only by the arrival of the Prince. After order is restored, Montague asks Benvolio to find out why his son Romeo is so melancholy; when Romeo reveals that he's in love with a woman who has sworn never to marry, Benvolio suggests he finds another lover. The Capulets, meanwhile, have agreed to let Paris, the Prince's kinsman, woo their daughter Juliet, and invite him to a feast to be held that night. Learning of the feast from a servant, Benvolio persuades Romeo that the two of them should attend. Despite Romeo's misgivings that it will end badly, they put on masks and – joining up with their friend Mercutio – succeed in getting in. Romeo catches sight of Juliet while dancing, and is immediately captivated. Though recognized by Tybalt, Romeo succeeds in speaking to her and they exchange kisses before Juliet is called away.

**ACT 2** Romeo is hiding in Capulet's orchard when Juliet appears on her balcony; the two exchange loving words and agree to marry as soon as possible. The next morning, Romeo rushes to Friar Laurence, who undertakes to marry them in the hope of ending the feud. After meeting up with Mercutio and Benvolio (who are relieved to find him in good humour), Romeo arranges with the Nurse for Juliet to join him at Friar Laurence's cell that afternoon.

**ACT 3** Benvolio and Mercutio are walking through the streets when they are approached by an aggrieved Tybalt, who is looking to challenge Romeo. Arriving from his marriage, Romeo fails to placate Tybalt, who then fights with Mercutio, fatally wounding him. Enraged by the death of his friend, Romeo fights and kills Tybalt. When the Prince hears of the murder, he banishes Romeo. The news reaches Juliet, but the Nurse and Friar Laurence arrange for the lovers to spend the night together before Romeo flees to Mantua. No sooner is Romeo gone, though, than Capulet insists that Juliet must marry Paris.

**ACT 4** Friar Laurence outlines a solution to the desperate Juliet: she will agree to marry Paris, but on the evening of the wedding take a drug which will put her into a death-like sleep. When she is laid in the family tomb, Romeo will be waiting there and the two can elope. Juliet takes the potion as planned, and Friar Laurence takes charge of the funeral arrangements.

**ACT 5** But the message explaining the plan never reaches Romeo, and the first he hears is that Juliet is dead. Grief-stricken, he rushes to Verona to Juliet's tomb. Paris is lying in wait, though, and the two fight – Paris is killed and Romeo enters the tomb. There he finds the unconscious Juliet, kisses her one last time and takes poison. As Juliet begins to awaken, Friar Laurence arrives, but is frightened away by the appearance of the Watch. Seeing Romeo's body, Juliet resolves on suicide and stabs herself. As the Capulets and Montagues arrive, the Prince reflects that the lovers' deaths are punishment for the feud, and the two families finally resolve to be reconciled.

– and perhaps why it has become the play's most potent image. Nor does *Romeo and Juliet* discourage its audiences from thinking of it as a kind of myth. As the play prepares to close, the Prince instructs the assembled citizens of Verona to "have more talk of these sad things":

> Some shall be pardoned, and some punishèd;
> For never was a story of more woe
> Than this of Juliet and her Romeo.

[5.3.306–9]

"Never was a story of more woe" transforms the couple into something beyond themselves, like the "statue[s] in pure gold" that Capulet and Montague undertake to raise in their memory. They and their story have become examples, models, precedents – and for Shakespeare, who based his play on several retellings of this old story, perhaps they already were.

## In a name

All of which might make it surprising that Shakespeare's main source interprets the tale in quite a different light. *The Tragical History of Romeus and Juliet* was published in 1562 by Arthur Brooke, poet, translator and soldier (he drowned the following year while travelling to fight abroad), and his 3000-line poem provided Shakespeare with the most accessible narrative version of an old story. Like the play's Prince, Brooke is eager to impose a strict way of interpreting the story he is about to tell, as his note "To the Reader" attests:

> And to this end (good Reader) is this tragical matter written, to describe unto thee a couple of unfortunate lovers, thralling themselves to unhonest desire, neglecting the authority and advice of parents and friends, conferring their principal counsels with drunken gossips, and superstitious friars (the naturally fit instruments of unchastity) attempting all adventures of peril, for the attaining of their wished lust … abusing the honourable name of lawful marriage, to cloak the shame of stolen contracts, finally, by all means of unhonest life, hasting to most unhappy death.

Brooke intends to make an example of the lovers, but in the darker sense of that phrase. Far from being caught up in fateful events far beyond their control – still less being tragic victims whose only sin, as Othello says of himself, is to love "not wisely but too well" – the damning fault of the lovers is their selfishness. They reject the sensible advice of "parents and friends", allow themselves to be overtaken by "unhonest desire" – and get their just deserts. Brooke pits the lovers against the rest of the city, but they are decisively on the wrong side.

Reading Brooke, Shakespeare evidently noted that the same story could be told in the same way – and yet quite differently. Instead of providing a cautionary tale addressed to young lovers, warning them to buckle under or face the penalties, he demonstrates in graphic terms where the "will" of senior Capulets and Montagues has actually landed Verona. His Chorus sketches out the terms:

> Two households, both alike in dignity
>     In fair Verona, where we lay our scene,
> From ancient grudge break to new mutiny
>     Where civil blood makes civil hands unclean.

[Prologue, 1–4]

In those remorseless puns on the word "civil", the Chorus prepares the ground for the "new mutiny" that immediately and brutally follows, the argument between servants from the two opposing houses which rapidly spirals into a full-blown brawl. Aggression is total in Verona: the city's streets are war zones. At pains to emphasize this, Shakespeare has the play open with Capulet servants Samson and Gregory, clearly spoiling for a fight:

GREGORY  The quarrel is between our masters
and us their men.
SAMSON  'Tis all one. I will show myself a
tyrant: when I have fought with the men
I will be civil with the maids—I will cut
off their heads.
GREGORY  The heads of the maids?
SAMSON  Ay, the heads of the maids, or their
maidenheads, take it in what sense thou
wilt.

**[1.1.18–25]**

Spranger Barry (Romeo) and Maria Nossiter (Juliet) were lovers in life as
well as on stage. This engraving, after a painting by Robert Pyle, depicts
their celebrated 1753 Drury Lane performance.

Even though both are Capulets, the instinct to vie is inveterate – and in striving to out-brag each other, Gregory and Samson further twist that word "civil" into still darker realms, those of sexual violence. Raping and killing Montague women is just another way to get one over on the enemy.

Some commentators have taken this harshly masculine world as the keynote of the play. Men are the driving force behind the violence – and engaging in violence, as Samson and Gregory idly reveal, becomes synonymous with proving masculinity. Confronted with Benvolio's protestation that he is simply trying to "keep the peace", Tybalt angrily declares that "I hate the word / As I hate hell, all Montagues, and thee" (1.1.65–8): violence and family territory are locked inescapably together. This is not society in any real sense of that word: it is a world in which the masculine "name" swamps everything else. Juliet astutely realizes that much in her much-quoted lines on the balcony:

O Romeo, Romeo, wherefore art thou Romeo?
Deny thy father and refuse thy name,
Or if thou wilt not, be but sworn my love,
And I'll no longer be a Capulet.

**[2.1.75–8]**

Calling upon Romeo to refuse his "name" will force him to "deny" his father and the legacy of his family. Protesting that "'Tis but thy name that is my enemy", Juliet attempts to separate the name from the object – or, rather, to restore the name to some true sense of what it really is. "What's in a name?", she questions,

That which we call a rose
By any other word would smell as sweet.
So Romeo would, were he not Romeo called,
Retain that dear perfection which he owes
Without that title. Romeo, doff thy name,
And for thy name—which is no part of thee—
Take all myself.

**[2.1.85–91]**

Juliet offers to replace Romeo's name with her own body, but the irony this speech introduces is not just that Romeo and Juliet will not eventually be able to transcend their surnames (at least not in life), but that Romeo's first name – which means "a roamer, a wanderer" – points towards his banishment and their ultimate separation. The irony is compounded as soon as Romeo is banished, when he begs Friar Laurence, "tell me, friar, tell me, / In what vile part of this anatomy / Doth my name lodge?" so that he can "sack / The hateful mansion" (3.3.104–7). This realization that his name has become a death sentence is one of the play's sharpest. There is a further irony, too, in the site of the lovers' death: they end up in the Capulet family tomb, along with all the feud's previous victims.

## My love as deep

As the great twentieth-century actor and director Harley Granville-Barker commented in his perceptive *Preface* to the play, "this is a tragedy of youth, as youth sees it", and some have argued that *Romeo and Juliet*, with all its turmoil and extremes, is about nothing less than the process of adolescence. Romeo enters the play every inch the moody teen, mooning distract-edly over Rosaline. Significantly, she never appears – she doesn't need to, for Romeo is clearly in love with love itself, and his passion for Rosaline evaporates as soon as her Capulet kinswoman, Juliet, arrives on the scene. "O brawling love, O loving hate," he exclaims to Benvolio,

> O anything of nothing first create;
> O heavy lightness, serious vanity,
> Misshapen chaos of well-seeming forms,
> Feather of lead, bright smoke, cold fire, sick health,
> Still-waking sleep, that is not what it is!
> This love feel I, that feel no love in this.

[1.1.173–9]

Romeo has yet to understand a love which is anything more substantial than oxymorons – one reason, perhaps, why Benvolio urges him to look elsewhere. Juliet is similarly on the cusp of maturity: though her father initially considers her "yet a stranger in the world" (her four-teenth birthday is two weeks away at the play's opening), at the lovers' breathless initial meeting she is more than able to hold her own, calmly parrying Romeo's flirtatious words – and in fact Shakespeare makes their first exchange into a fourteen-line love sonnet, as if urging Juliet that, despite her youth, she has not a moment to lose. The fact that the lovers speak a poem almost without realizing it also acts as a kind of miraculous confirmation that their des-tinies are fatefully tied to each other, yet in its very intensity it also hints that, like poetic lovers before and since, they are doomed to separation.

> *Romeo is Hamlet in love. There is the same rich exuberance of passion and sentiment in the one, that there is of thought and sentiment in the other. Both are absent and self-involved, both live out of themselves in a world of imagination.*
>
> William Hazlitt, in *Characters from Shakespeare's Plays* (1817)

Again, speed dominates: just a handful of lines after encountering each other, the lovers exchange their very first kiss. They will be married in just five scenes' time; Mercutio and Tybalt will be dead a few scenes later; and in that brief period this comedy of romantic love will have become a full-blown tragedy. But though the couple's time together is agonizingly short,

Shakespeare refuses to make it one-dimensional. Juliet, if anything, matures faster than Romeo. In the balcony scene, as he vows to love her "by yonder blessèd moon", she urges him: "O swear not by the moon, th' inconstant moon … Do not swear at all", fearing that "if thou swear'st / Thou may prove false". For her, their love lies not in immediate vows, but is organic, ever-growing:

My bounty is as boundless as the
    sea,
My love as deep. The more I give to
    thee
The more I have, for both are
    infinite.
                                **[2.1.175–7]**

But of course the sea is controlled by the moon, and their love, while it will not become shallower, will eventually be betrayed. The lovers often attempt to alter the fabric of the universe, to push on time when apart but arrest it when together. Yearning for her wedding night, Juliet cries, "Gallop apace, you fiery-footed steeds, / Towards Phoebus' lodging" to the heavens,

Johnston Forbes-Robertson as Romeo and Mrs Patrick Campbell as Juliet in the 1895 production of the play at London's Lyceum Theatre, which ran for 79 performances. Though admired for her Pre-Raphaelite beauty, Mrs Campbell's Juliet divided critics; George Bernard Shaw called it "an immature performance at all the exceptional points…"

                    Such a waggoner
As Phaëton would whip you to the west
And bring in cloudy night immediately.
Spread thy close curtain, love-performing night,
That runaways' eyes may wink, and Romeo
Leap to these arms untalked of and unseen.

                                        **[3.2.1–7]**

Juliet here is trying to manipulate the passage of time, just as she is attempting to uproot convention by calling for night instead of day (a theme that much concerns the lovers); furthermore, her sexual language displays her as a woman – so much so that many nineteenth-century actresses refused to perform this speech altogether, regarding Juliet's description of "love-performing night", and, later, "amorous rites" unfitting for a girl not yet fourteen. In yet another irony, Juliet's wish is partly granted – time does fly – but so urgently that the lovers' rush to death rapidly becomes unstoppable.

    Given the fact that the lovers don't escape their fate – and the ways in which we're constantly reminded they won't – some have even wondered whether *Romeo and Juliet* even counts as tragedy. If they are predestined by "some consequence yet hanging in the stars" (1.4.107), if Friar Laurence is right that "these violent delights have violent ends" (2.5.9), do they ever reach tragic greatness? Or are they, as Capulet sadly notes, "Poor sacrifices to our enmity" –

blameless, "star-crossed" victims? Perhaps the answer is that, in this early tragedy, Shakespeare wants to have it both ways. He constantly reminds the audience of the hastening inevitability of betrayal, while presenting us with the couple's growing maturity and the deepening of their love. Romeo and Juliet try to seize control, but ultimately they cannot – and in that juxtaposition lies the tragedy.

# Stage history and adaptations

It seems probable that *Romeo and Juliet* was put on initially at the **Theatre** in Shoreditch, then perhaps at the nearby **Curtain** after Shakespeare's company moved there temporarily in 1597, but all we can really be sure of is that its use of contrastive theatrical spaces (especially the gallery "aloft" and the curtained-in area behind the main stage) will have stretched the resources of both theatres. It's likely that **Richard Burbage** took the part of Romeo and **Master Richard Goffe** Juliet. It even achieved international popularity, being performed early in the seventeenth century by German companies touring Europe.

The next we know is of a version prepared by **William Davenant** (who liked to boast that he was Shakespeare's love child, but was most likely his godson). This appeared in 1662 at Lincoln's Inn Fields, and was witnessed by Pepys – who couldn't decide which he detested more, the play or the actors. The latter were **Mary Sanderson** as Juliet, possibly the first woman to play on the English public stage, her future husband **Thomas Betterton** as Mercutio and **Henry Harris** as Romeo. But help was at hand: just over fifteen years later, **Thomas Otway** decided to rejig Shakespeare's play and set it in ancient Rome; the finished work, *The History and Fall of Caius Marius*, was premiered in 1679 with Betterton in the title role. Underscoring the drama's political dimensions, it was a timely arrival given the crisis over Charles II's succession then gripping the nation.

The next significant production, that undertaken by **Theophilus Cibber** in 1744, claimed to be the real *Romeo and Juliet*, but retained Otway's revised ending – in which Juliet awakes before Romeo's death and the lovers are allowed a frenzied parting dialogue. Its success was muted, however, and it took the theatrical genius of **David Garrick**, who mounted a revival at Drury Lane four years later, to make the play into a sure-fire hit – which it certainly was, being performed some 329 times before 1776, even more than Garrick's *Hamlet*. It was not without competition, however: Garrick's original Romeo, **Spranger Barry**, jumped ship to Covent Garden in 1750 and forced Garrick to act the role himself, igniting a showdown between the two productions that lasted eight years. While Barry was considered better in the love scenes, Garrick's forte was tragedy – so, when both versions were performed on the same night, many theatregoers simply swapped venues halfway through. The era also saw a succession of fine Juliets grace the stage: **Susannah Cibber, Anne Bellamy, Isabella Nossiter** and **Hannah Pritchard**.

While the big names of the early nineteenth century – **John Philip Kemble, Edmund Kean** and **William Charles Macready** – all played Romeo in Garrick's version, it was commonly felt that the part lacked virility. Ironically, the actor responsible for changing that was the iconoclastic American **Charlotte Cushman**, who caused a sensation when she played Romeo to her sister's Juliet at the Haymarket in 1845. The critics were unanimous in their praise: *The Athenaeum* declared it "one of the most extraordinary pieces of acting, perhaps, ever exhibited by a woman", while *The Times* gushed that "Miss Cushman's Romeo is a creative, a living, breathing, animated, ardent, human being" – and, furthermore, not at all bad with a sword. The great Italian actress **Eleonora Duse** had one of her earliest successes in 1872, when, at the age of 14 (the "correct" age for the role), she played Juliet in the vast amphitheatre at Verona.

Trailing rose petals whenever she met Romeo, and smothering his corpse with them, an idea she dreamt up just before the first performance, her complete identification with the character created a sensation. The chief fixation of late-nineteenth-century performers – pictorial realism, the grander the better – touched *Romeo* relatively late on, most magnificently in **Henry Irving**'s monumental production of 1882. Irving played Romeo to **Ellen Terry**'s Juliet (she would act the Nurse at the other end of her career, in 1919), but it was his double set for the final scene that really made audiences gasp: after slaying Paris in the churchyard, Romeo descended a set of steps and, following a miraculous scene-change, reappeared in an eerie Gothic crypt. In 1895 **Johnston Forbes-Robertson** took over the management of the Lyceum, and scored a notable success with a dreamily romantic account of the play, starring himself as Romeo and **Mrs Patrick Campbell** as Juliet.

Into the new century, **William Poel**'s pioneering attempts at quasi-Elizabethan staging were well-received, but that didn't stop his 1905 performance of *Romeo and Juliet* coming to a halt after just four performances. It was **John Gielgud**'s sprightly production at the New Theatre (1935) that pushed the play into the frontline. Selecting an Italian Renaissance setting and costumes that emphasized the division between old and young, Gielgud alternated the roles of Romeo and Mercutio with **Laurence Olivier**. As with the Garrick–Barry contest, the two actors were acclaimed for the differences they brought to the lead role: Olivier later commented (with a hint of a sneer) that Gielgud was "all spiritual, all spirituality, all beauty, all abstract things; and myself … all earth, blood, humanity". **Peggy Ashcroft** played Juliet, while **Edith Evans**'s Nurse was memorably described as "earthy as a potato, as slow as a cart horse and as cunning as a badger".

Peter Brook staged a markedly unsentimental *Romeo* at Stratford in 1947 with the youthful **Laurence Payne** and **Daphne Slater** taking the leads. On a virtually bare stage, Brook emphasized the play's violence and contrasted the lovers' youthful idealism with suffocating Veronese society; the mood was further darkened by **Paul Scofield**'s intense Mercutio, and the fact that the closing reconciliation between the Capulets and Montagues was cut. **Franco Zeffirelli**, directing at the Old Vic in 1960, administered an injection of *Zeitgeist* – commissioning a set that looked like a real Italian street, cutting about a third of the lines and encouraging his actors to speak naturalistically. **Judi Dench** (and later **Joanna Dunham**) played Juliet to **John Stride**'s teenagey Romeo, while **Alec McCowen**'s Mercutio was applauded as an "angry young man".

Since these ground-breaking productions *Romeo and Juliet* has become a massive big-hitter, revived over 350 times internationally in the half-century following World War II. That it continues to offer real possibilities for contrast is indicated by the RSC over recent decades: **Terry Hands** foregrounded the play's masculine violence – **Bernard Lloyd**'s misogynistic Mercutio dismembered a life-size doll on stage (1973); **Trevor Nunn** and **Barry Kyle**'s production (1976) had a similarly dangerous feel, with **Ian McKellen**'s Romeo more neurotically than erotically charged; **Michael Bodganov** interpreted the play as a capitalist tragedy – though ironically his production was nicknamed "Alfa-Romeo and Juliet" for its sharp Italian tailoring (1986); **Michael Attenborough** chose a sun-baked Sicilian setting (1997). But perhaps the most adventurous productions have appeared in locations where conflict has been dangerously real – from **Otomar Krejča** and **Josef Svoboda**'s acclaimed Prague production, which caught the disaffection of Cold War Czech youth (1964); to the Romany company **Pralipe** (Brotherhood), forced into exile from their native Macedonia, who set the play in Bosnia with a Muslim Juliet and a Christian Romeo (1994).

No fewer than 61 film versions of *Romeo* have been counted over the century or so following the appearance of the earliest, directed by **Clement Maurice** (1900). The 1936 film directed by **George Cukor** is probably the least loved of the major versions, stymied by the casting of **Leslie Howard** (aged 44) and **Norma Shearer** (aged 36). John Gielgud claimed that "for unspeakable vulgarity, appalling hammery, and utter silliness, I have seen nothing worse." **Renato**

Castellani's 1954 neo-realist version won plaudits, but was soon eclipsed by **Franco Zeffirelli**'s 1968 movie, chock-full of youthful sex appeal and Italianate passion. Zeffirelli's hold on the youth market has been challenged by **Baz Luhrmann**, whose 1996 *Romeo + Juliet* made the play comprehensible (and appealing) to the MTV generation. Rejoicing in a different kind of anachronism, **John Madden**'s *Shakespeare in Love* (1998), written by **Marc Norman** and **Tom Stoppard**, played *Romeo and Juliet* autobiographically, with **Joseph Fiennes**'s Bard bidding for the manicured hand of **Gwyneth Paltrow**, his aristocratic, boy-actor-impersonating inamorata.

# Screen

### Romeo and Juliet
### L. Whiting, O. Hussey, J. McEnery; Franco Zeffirelli (dir.)
Italy/UK, 1968 ▷ Paramount DVD 🔲

Zeffirelli's film takes his 1960 stage production to its logical extreme: much of the text is eradicated in the name of "visual eloquence", the quest for realism leads him to the Tuscan hill-town of Pienza, and the story is angled from the lovers' perspective as they battle against mean old parents. All this is risky, given the limited resources of the teenage leads, Olivia Hussey and Leonard Whiting, and the fact that Zeffirelli's cuts render their roles atoms away from two-dimensional. Any hint at Juliet's emotional maturity, for instance, is airbrushed out, and for all the sultry passion ostensibly on display, the film feels surprisingly chaste. And though the couple are undeniably gorgeous, they're really not very good: Hussey's

balcony speech is delivered as if to a favourite puppy, while Whiting's Romeo often sounds as if he's trying to paper over barrow-boy origins. John McEnery's emotionally tormented Mercutio is much more successful, as is Michael York's pouting Tybalt. In some ways the scenes without the lovers – and the soupy, overblown music that accompanies them – are the ones that really work: Zeffirelli distils the "mad blood" of the play with typical verve, his cat-calling young men purring with aggression and *machismo*.

### Romeo + Juliet
### L. DiCaprio, C. Daines, H. Perrineau; Baz Luhrmann (dir.)
USA, 1996 ▷ Fox DVD 🔲

"Shakespeare has never been this sexy", screamed *Rolling Stone*, and after watching Zeffirelli you can see where they're coming from. But that does a disservice both to Shakespeare and to Luhrmann, whose adaptation is sharper

"Two blushing pilgrims": Romeo (Leonardo DiCaprio) steals a kiss from Juliet (Claire Danes) in the freshest and sparkiest Shakespearian film of recent times, Baz Luhrmann's *Romeo + Juliet* (1996).

than the shoutlines have you believe. It centres on the fictional Verona Beach, a half-futuristic US city suspended somewhere between Miami and Mexico – violent, trashy and brash. The feud is fought out at gas stations and policed by helicopters, while the lovers meet to the strains of Des'Ree at the Capulets' gated mansion and woo each other in a swimming pool. Though the visuals are pure Luhrmann – channel-surfing, freeze-framing, jump-cutting – the real surprise is how well this suits Shakespeare's own restive depiction of a society at war with itself. *Romeo + Juliet* is consistently smart without being earnest: Elizabethan wit effortlessly becomes punchy street-speak, while the film's in-your-face Catholicism brilliantly animates an aspect of the play many have thought irretrievable. Neither DiCaprio nor Danes were ever going to win Oscars, but that doesn't matter: Luhrmann does all the work for them, crafting an intense – and tense – denouement that actually, amazingly, has the power to shock.

# Audio

### Romeo and Juliet
**D. Henshall, S. Dahl, S. York; Peter Kavanagh (dir.)**
UK, 1999  ▷ BBC ⊙ ▭

Douglas Henshall and Sophie Dahl are the excellent leads, albeit ones who might struggle to convince you that they are in their teens. No matter: Henshall is persuasive as Romeo while Dahl (more familiar as a supermodel) brings an appealing innocence to the role of Juliet. Elsewhere Kavanagh's production is more mixed: its modern-day Veronese setting sounds a bit props-department (roaring Vespas and Italian cursing) and other cast members are not so strong – Milo O'Shea's Friar Laurence is breathless and Freddie Jones's Capulet is almost too plummy for words. At least the lovers don't sound as if they're unblocking a sink when kissing (as they do in the rival Naxos version).

# Editions

### New Cambridge Shakespeare
**G. Blakemore Evans (ed.); rev. 2003**  ▷ Cambridge UP

Evans's edition of *Romeo and Juliet* (1984), one of the best in the New Cambridge series, was revised in 1997, but has now been more thoroughly overhauled. The editor's careful treatment of the text remains the same, as do his informative but level-headed notes, and his excellent introduction – organized along conventional lines, but helpful nonetheless –

remains the same. But a full 21 pages has been added covering the latest trends in criticism and performance, all the way from gender studies to Baz Luhrmann. If you're interested in the differences between various incarnations of *Romeo and Juliet*, Jill Levenson's Oxford edition (2000) reprints the first quarto text in appendix.

# Some criticism

### Shakespeare's Mercutio
**Joseph A. Porter; 1988**  ▷ North Carolina UP [o/p]

Though the play's title might not admit it, there's much more to *Romeo and Juliet* than the fresh-faced lovers. Among its more intriguing residents is Mercutio, one of Shakespeare's most astonishing characters yet whose untimely death at the hands of Tybalt shifts him decisively out of the action (Dryden thought that Shakespeare was forced to kill Mercutio lest he take over the play). Joseph Porter's study takes an extended look at Romeo's incendiary companion across theatrical and critical history, beginning with the merest of hints in Brooke's *Romeus* and underpinning this with an insightful exposition of Mercutio's most important facet – his name, derived from the god Mercury. Porter also has some intriguing thoughts on Marlowe, suggesting that in Mercutio Shakespeare might even have been celebrating the work of his recently dead rival.

### Young Hamlet
**Barbara Everett; 1989**  ▷ Oxford UP [o/p]

*Young Hamlet: Essays on Shakespeare's Tragedies* is in two parts, its first section a group of lectures delivered at University College London in 1988 on Bradley's "big four" (*Hamlet*, *Othello*, *Lear* and *Macbeth*), its second bringing together older pieces from a variety of sources. All are informed by Everett's wit and wisdom, as well as her commitment to what is sometimes thought to be a dying art – the skill of intensely close reading. As the book's title indicates, *Hamlet* is the centrifugal force here, but Everett's early article "*Romeo and Juliet*: The Nurse's Story", which looks carefully at Juliet's Nurse and what less intelligent critics have dismissed as her wasteful prattle, is exemplary and involving, suggesting that she (like Mercutio) is utterly central to the human story of the play. Everett can be cryptic at times – her most resonant statements often have an air of mystery about them – but her ability to pick up tiny details and work them into  rich patterns is invaluable. Though Everett's work isn't included, other essay-length pieces on the play can be found in John F. Andrews's excellent Garland anthology, *Romeo and Juliet: Critical Essays* (1993).

# The Taming of the Shrew

t is difficult not to feel, at least on the face of it, that *The Taming of the Shrew* is a problem in need of solving. It depicts an unruly and strong-willed woman forced into marriage, then "tamed" into obedience by her new husband, who employs violent means to get his way. While some commentators have simply written off the *Shrew* as a delinquent farce, since the rise of feminist criticism it has attracted growing attention – albeit much of it unsympathetic. Opinion still remains sharply divided: one leading theatre critic has described it as "totally offensive … barbaric and disgusting"; elsewhere, it has been held up as an Elizabethan celebration of wifely triumph. On stage, where solemn rules rarely function, Shakespeare's most deliberately outrageous drama can be all of those things at once – and more. In his hands a didactic and brutal folk tale becomes something infinitely richer, and the relationship between Katherine (the play's spirited "shrew") and her gold-digging suitor Petruccio suggests that love can blossom from the most unlikely of ingredients. Above all, perhaps, the *Shrew* is a play about playing: itself an experiment in dramatic form (the main action is a play-within-a-play), in performance it can be one of the most challenging and surprising of all Shakespeare's works.

[DATE] Although it is undeniably one of Shakespeare's earliest comedies, the play's precise date is complicated by its textual history (see below). It was probably written in 1590 or slightly later, close to *The Two Gentlemen of Verona*.

[SOURCES] The main story probably derives from folk tale or ballad. The subplot appears in George Gascoigne's drama *Supposes* (1566), while some parallels recall the anonymous play *A Knack to Know a Knave* (1592).

[TEXTS] Two versions exist: one printed in anonymous quarto in 1594 as *The Taming of a Shrew*, the other in the 1623 Folio as *The Taming of the Shrew*. Their relationship remains puzzling, though most scholars believe *A Shrew* is not directly Shakespeare's work.

## Interpreting the play

Tales about "taming" women whom society deems to be unruly have a long and fairly grim history. The misogynistic archetype of the shrewish woman crops up repeatedly in oral story-telling, and tales about taming apparently difficult wives were a staple of the early modern world – as indeed they had been for centuries. One broadside ballad from 1635 even has the same name as Shakespeare's play, though its subtitle "The only way to make a Bad WIFE Good: At least, To keep her quiet" suggests that its function is less to entertain than to advise. Another, entitled "A Merry Jest of a Shrewd and Curst Wife Lapped in Morel's Skin for Her Good Behaviour", is different again – it relates the tale of a defiant wife whose husband makes her behave by beating her violently, then wrapping her in the skin of a dead horse.

Though the "shrew" of Shakespeare's title, Katherine, is described by Hortensio as "intolerable curst, / And shrewd and froward so beyond all measure" (1.2.88–9), she is not made to

## Major Characters & Synopsis

**THE INDUCTION**
**Christopher Sly**, a drunken tinker
**Hostess** of an alehouse
A **Lord**
**Bartholomew**, the Lord's page
**Players** acting the play-within-the-play

**THE PLAY-WITHIN-THE-PLAY**
**Katherine** (**Kate**) **Minola** of Padua, the "shrew"
**Bianca**, Katherine's younger sister
**Baptista**, Katherine's father
**Petruccio**, a gentleman from Verona,
  Katherine's suitor (later her husband)
**Grumio** and **Curtis**, Petruccio's servants
**Gremio**, a rich old man from Padua, Bianca's suitor
**Hortensio**, another suitor for Bianca (later
  disguised as **Licio**)
**Lucentio**, a gentleman from Pisa (later
  disguised as **Cambio**, a teacher)
**Tranio** and **Biondello**, Lucentio's servants
**Vincentio**, Lucentio's father
A **Merchant** from Mantua (later disguised as
  **Vincentio**)

**INDUCTION** Christopher Sly, a drunken tinker,
is thrown out of an alehouse and falls asleep. He
is discovered by a Lord, who gets his servants to
play an elaborate trick on him. Taking him to their
master's house, they convince Sly that he has
been insane for the last fifteen years and is actually a Lord. After much ado he eventually believes
them, and settles down to watch the players perform an Italian play, in which …

**ACT 1** Hortensio and Gremio both seek the
hand of the lovely Bianca, the younger daughter
of Baptista. Unfortunately Baptista has vowed
that she cannot marry until her sister, the
shrewish Katherine, has done so. All this is overheard by Lucentio, newly arrived in Padua, who
– having seen Bianca – falls for her himself.
Knowing that Baptista is seeking tutors for his
daughters, Lucentio concocts a plan – he will
gain access to her by disguising himself as a
schoolteacher while his servant Tranio impersonates him. Petruccio has also arrived in town;
hearing from Hortensio about Katherine's substantial dowry, (and undeterred by her reputation), he resolves to win her – much to the relief
of Bianca's numerous suitors.

**ACT 2** Katherine is bullying Bianca into reveal-
ing which suitor she prefers when the men arrive.
Petruccio offers himself as a suitor for Katherine,
and presents Hortensio (disguised as Licio) as a
music master for the two sisters. Gremio
responds by introducing Lucentio (disguised as
Cambio) as a teacher, while Tranio (disguised as
Lucentio) presents himself as a third suitor for
Bianca. Hortensio/Licio immediately suffers at
Katherine's hands, but Petruccio defiantly gives
as good as he gets in their first meeting.
Meanwhile, Gremio and Tranio (still disguised as
Lucentio) attempt to win Baptista's consent by
boasting of their respective riches.

**ACT 3** Bianca is already under siege from
Hortensio and Lucentio, both of whom covertly
reveal their identities in an attempt to win her.
Petruccio turns up late for his wedding to
Katherine, shocking Baptista by his bizarre and
unkempt dress. After the ceremony, Petruccio
insists that he and his wife cannot attend the
wedding dinner but must leave straightaway.

**ACT 4** After an awful journey, during which
Katherine falls off her horse and is covered in mud,
the newlyweds arrive at Petruccio's house.
Petruccio denies his wife food and prevents her
from going to sleep, intending to tame her by making her life miserable. Bianca, meanwhile, has chosen Lucentio – to the feigned disgust of Tranio and
the disappointment of Hortensio (who marries a
widow instead). However, Lucentio still lacks funds,
so Tranio is forced to trick a passing Merchant into
imitating Vincentio, Lucentio's father, in front of
Baptista. All goes well, and Lucentio and Bianca
rush off to marry. Petruccio continues to break
Katherine's will, forbidding her to contradict
anything he says.

**ACT 5** When the real Vincentio turns up at
Lucentio's lodgings, he is amazed to meet the
impostor Merchant; and when Tranio emerges in
Lucentio's clothes, Vincentio fears the worst. He
is about to be arrested when Lucentio (and wife)
appear; begging forgiveness, he reveals everything. All are reconciled, but Petruccio has one
final test in store for Katherine: at a banquet that
evening he wagers Lucentio and Hortensio that
his wife is more obedient than theirs …

Petruccio (Jasper Britton) and Katherine (Alexandra Gilbreath) often saw the funny side of the *Shrew* in Greg Doran's RSC production (2003).

suffer anything quite so violent as her counterparts in ballads and broadside tales. But in telling the story of Katherine's taming by Petruccio, a man who freely admits that he wants to marry her simply for her money, Shakespeare deploys motifs his audiences would be easily and deeply familiar with. Some of them would probably approve of the hero's actions, which include forcing her into marriage, then denying her food and sleep. Newly arrived in Padua, Petruccio's servant Grumio promises that if Katherine attempts to resist, his master will not be sparing. "An she stand him but a little," he chortles,

> he will throw a figure in her face and so disfigure her with it that she shall have no more eyes
> to see withal than a cat.
>
> **[1.2.111–4]**

While the subplot of *The Taming of the Shrew*, the wooing of Bianca by several disguised suitors, has an unimpeachably literary source – ultimately from Ariosto's *I Suppositi* via George Gascoigne's witty comedy *Supposes* – the main "taming" story comes straight out of low culture, and it has the brutality to prove it.

## Right supremacy

It's tempting to dismiss the play as a simple-minded farce – not as physically fierce as ballads such as the "Merry Jest", but every bit as emotionally violent. Those who do dismiss it point to scenes such as the one in which Petruccio's servants nervously describe the fearful behaviour of their master towards his new wife. Petruccio, says his man Curtis, is at that moment

> In her chamber,
> Making a sermon of continency to her,
> And rails, and swears, and rates, that she, poor soul,
> Knows not which way to stand, to look, to speak,
> And sits as one new risen from a dream.
>
> **[4.1.168–72]**

There is a bitter kind of irony here: Petruccio rails on "continency" (restraint or self-control) while he himself indulges in unrestrained aggression.

Petruccio's harsh words follow hard upon Katherine's very public humiliation at her wedding, where Petruccio offends everyone by turning up late, wearing hideously inappropriate clothing and boasting that his new wife is his to order around as he wishes. Nor is Katherine's re-education complete at this. Confronted by her habit of talking back and refusing to stay quiet, Petruccio decides to repossess nothing less than her language. Over the course of several scenes he forces her to follow his every verbal whim, especially when doing so flies in the face of reason, and she complies. Near the end of the play, he takes advantage of the daytime to impose a bizarre demonstration, exclaiming, "how bright and goodly shines the moon!":

PETRUCCIO
    I say it is the moon.
KATHERINE
    I know it is the moon.
PETRUCCIO
    Nay then you lie, it is the blessèd sun.
KATHERINE
    Then God be blessed, it is the blessèd sun,
    But sun it is not when you say it is not,
    And the moon changes even as your mind.
    What you will have it named, even that it is,
    And so it shall still be for Katherine.

**[4.5.16–23]**

By imposing this doublethink, Petruccio bends to his will not just his wife, but the physical universe they share. It's little surprise to note that, when describing his relationship to his wife in this phase of the play, Petruccio reaches most often for the language of hawking – Katherine is, he claims, a "falcon" trained to respond to "her keeper's call" (4.1.180), and he is even prepared to literalize the metaphor by starving her into obedience. Katherine is simply not permitted to contradict the view of the world he demands – and it's interesting to note in passing that his diminutive nickname for her, "Kate" (she herself sticks resolutely to "Katherine"), is one most critics of the play unthinkingly use.

Katherine's trials climax in the closing scene of the play, when Petruccio, Lucentio and Hortensio set up a wager to see which of their wives is the most compliant. Both Hortensio's newly found Widow and Lucentio's Bianca fail to appear when called, but the apparently reformed Katherine dutifully turns up on cue, wins her husband the bet and so confirms what he gloatingly calls his "aweful rule and right supremacy" (5.2.114). And Katherine goes still further, lecturing the other two wives on the obedience a true wife should display. Describing "a woman moved [angered]" as "like a fountain troubled, / Muddy, ill-seeming, thick, bereft of beauty," she piously continues,

    Thy husband is thy lord, thy life, thy keeper,
    Thy head, thy sovereign, one that cares for thee,
    And for thy maintenance commits his body
    To painful labour both by sea and land,
    To watch the night in storms, the day in cold,
    Whilst thou liest warm at home, secure and safe,
    And craves no other tribute at thy hands
    But love, fair looks, and true obedience,
    Too little payment for so great a debt.

**[5.2.147–59]**

Whether she is actually pious, still less sincere, is a moot point, and some actresses have deliberately played up the irony of this speech – perhaps noting that Lucentio, exclaiming in the very last line of the play that "'Tis a wonder … she will be tamed so" (5.2.194), apparently finds her conversion difficult to credit. Other actors and directors have seen the darker side of Katherine's "taming", having her mumble this final speech like a victim of torture, her spirit visibly crushed. After all, she has been told to call the "sun" the "moon", and then on a whim the "sun" again; she has been forced to accept a rigidly hierarchical view of marriage – one in which it is only natural that a woman obey her husband. It is genuinely difficult, nearly impossible, to come to a firm view on this issue: as a glance at its stage history testifies, the *Shrew* can be played in countless different – and entirely contradictory – ways, perhaps more so than any other Shakespeare play.

> *Depending on how we take her tone, Kate is seriously tamed, is ironic at Petruchio's expense, has learned comradeship and harmonious co-existence, or will remain a shrew till her death.*
>
> Lisa Jardine, *Still Harping On Daughters* (1983)

And less brutalizing possibilities certainly exist, all of them tenable. Some have seen Katherine's journey away from shrewishness as a good thing: a humanizing process that reflects her sincere love for Petruccio, and perhaps too his love for her – a genuine relationship shared by two damaged and difficult people. Others prefer to interpret Shakespeare's indulgence in extremes as a kind of knowing nod-and-wink to audiences (or readers) who know better – *Shrew* as satire. Others go even further, arguing that what Katherine actually declares in this infamous speech is more radical than we might suspect. As she goes on, they point out, her words become more intriguing:

> Such duty as the subject owes the prince,
> Even such a woman oweth to her husband,
> And when she is forward, peevish, sullen, sour,
> And not obedient to his honest will,
> What is she but a foul contending rebel,
> And graceless traitor to her loving lord?
>
> **[5.2.159–65]**

It is not too much to say that there is an implicit contract in action here: the wife is bound to obey, but her husband must be "loving" and "honest" too; Katherine may be publicly toeing the line, but she does so in her own terms – and it's notable that of the other couples competing in this final scene, only Katherine and Petruccio seem, albeit roughly, to have got the measure of each other. As some critics have commented, what Katherine actually declares to the other wives is on a par with arguments put forward by sixteenth-century Protestant reformers, who held that marriage should be a union of like-minded belief, not domestic tyranny. An early response to the play, John Fletcher's seventeenth-century sequel *The Woman's Prize*, makes something of the same point: the newly widowed Petruccio decides to marry again but is put through a sequence of trials by his new wife – all in the name of making him reject male supremacy and learn the importance of marital harmony.

## Dreamed till now

But perhaps there is a danger of becoming too serious about this. A comedy is what the *Shrew* is, and many of its most worrisome moments for readers (particularly twenty-first-century readers) come across in performance as rather more tongue-in-cheek. In the event, most of the violence presented by Shakespeare's play is rhetorical – a battle of wit and spirit which, though it is hard-fought, is often very funny. Responding to Katherine's incessant put-downs at their first ever meeting, Petruccio chuckles, "Come, come, you wasp, i'faith you are too angry":

KATHERINE  If I be waspish, best beware my sting.
PETRUCCIO  My remedy is then to pluck it out.
KATHERINE  Ay, if the fool could find it where it lies.
PETRUCCIO  Who knows not where the wasp does wear his sting? In his tail.
KATHERINE  In his tongue.
PETRUCCIO                    Whose tongue?
KATHERINE  Yours, if you talk of tales, and so farewell.
PETRUCCIO  What, with my tongue in your tail?

[2.1.209–16]

Beneath the sharp-edged competitiveness a flirtatious current seems to ripple, and though Petruccio here succeeds in silencing Katherine with an obscene pun (she goes on to slap him, infuriated), he will by no means have the last word. Shakespeare hints that sexual attraction can blossom from this kind of banter, and indeed in later comedies including *As You Like It* and *Much Ado* (whose own Beatrice and Benedick owe much to Katherine and Petruccio) it forms a witty component of the wooing process, enabling characters to sound each other out without risking their feelings. The *Shrew* is certainly more unsparing in that respect, but it is not necessarily "barbaric" (as one theatre critic insists). Katherine, though she later chooses to conform, can more than hold her own; and in that way she is not that different from a Rosalind or a Beatrice.

One of the things that makes it difficult to take the story of Katherine's reformation entirely at face value, however, is that she doesn't actually exist – and nor do any of the characters in the so-called "taming" story. Though few productions acknowledge the fact, the main subject of the *Shrew* (indeed, the subject of its title and what most people mean when they talk about the play) is actually a play-within-a-play. Its characters are presented as fictions, acted by hired players in front of a beggar called Christopher Sly. At the farcical opening of the action, Sly crashes in halfway through a fight with the hostess of an inn, and soon collapses drunkenly on stage. While he sleeps, a nameless Lord happens by and decides to play a bizarre trick on the slumbering beggar – arranging for Sly to wake up and be persuaded that he is wealthy beyond his wildest dreams. The Lord's servants are primed by their master to fool Sly, and when he awakens everything goes to plan. Astonished to hear that he is not a beggar after all, but a great lord, Sly is thrown into bewildered confusion. "Am I a lord?" he cries,

Or do I dream? Or have I dreamed till now?
I do not sleep. I see, I hear, I speak.
I smell sweet savours, and I feel soft things.
Upon my life, I am a lord indeed,
And not a tinker, nor Christopher Sly.

[Induction 2.67–72]

Shakespeare is fond of experimenting with ever-receding dramatic perspectives: *Love's Labour's Lost* ends with a farcical pageant of the "Nine Worthies", while its successor among the lyrical comedies, *A Midsummer Night's Dream*, closes with the play put on by the hard-handed artisans. Still later, *Hamlet* binds its own play-within-the-play, "The Mousetrap", tightly within the main plot when its princely protagonist makes his father-in-law confess to murder by having a reconstruction of the deed performed in front of him. But the *Shrew* is the only drama of Shakespeare's in which he allows the interior action to become dominant, in which the story of Katherine and Bianca and their suitors takes over.

It takes over so completely, in fact, that once Sly settles down to watch it – and, after nodding off in boredom, wishes anxiously that "would 'twere done" (1.1.252) – he utterly disappears from the text. This really is baffling: a competing version of the play, the anonymous quarto published in 1594 as *The Taming of a Shrew*, finishes with a conclusion in which Sly is risen from his drunken slumbers to exclaim that "thou has waked me out of the best dream / That ever I had in my life" – an ending that at least matches up with the beginning. But the Folio *Shrew*, apparently Shakespeare's text, has nothing of the kind. There are any number of reasons why this might be so, ranging all the way from mechanical cock-up to staging difficulties – or even a conscious artistic decision. The *Oxford* single-volume edition tidies things up by printing "Additional passages" from *A Shrew*, but there is no denying that Shakespeare's play as it stands is reluctant to conform in this way.

The effect is intriguingly open-ended, and in the end it makes *The Taming of the Shrew* surprisingly difficult to pin down. Even if Sly's disappearance from the text is a simple mistake, the very fact that the taming plot is presented as a fit entertainment for a bewildered drunkard makes it hard to take in the soberest of terms. And while *A Shrew* ends with Sly declaring that he has learnt his lesson, that "I know now how to tame a shrew", Shakespeare's play conspicuously avoids making any such easy judgement. Near the end of the action, Petruccio admits that his approach might not in fact be the most effective. "This is a way to kill a wife with kindness," he muses,

> And thus I'll curb her headstrong humour.
> He that knows better how to tame a shrew,
> Now let him speak.
>
> [4.1.195–7]

Trusting to his actors and the dramatic moment, the playwright dares his audiences to make up their own minds.

# Stage history and adaptations

*The Taming of the Shrew* has been widely performed, in one form or another, until relatively recently – when anxieties about its "message" have made many directors think twice. Although we know little about the play's early stage history, it appears to have remained in repertoire for at least two decades. But doubts about the ending seem to have existed even then: **John Fletcher** (Shakespeare's collaborator on *Henry VIII* and *The Two Noble Kinsmen*) wrote a sequel entitled *The Woman's Prize, or The Tamer Tamed*, which gives the recently widowed Petruccio a new wife, Maria, who proves to be more of a handful than Katherine ever was. In its attempt to prove that husbands "should not reign as Tyrants o'er their wives", it even has Maria revenging herself by persuading Petruccio that he is dying of the plague. Shakespeare's play and this were performed within a few days of each other at **court** in 1633.

Fletcher's eagerness to tamper would prove prophetic. In 1667 it was seized on by **John Lacy**, who cut the last act and played Grumio himself – or, rather, "Sauney", Lacy's name for the character. This offshoot was published in 1698 as *Sauney the Scot: or, The Taming of the Shrew*. Though it was still being performed thirty years later, en route it had been challenged by three other pretenders. In 1716, two farces entitled *The Cobbler of Preston* appeared, one by **Charles Johnson**, the other by **Christopher Bullock** – both were loose adaptations

Lily Brayton was a formidable Katherine at the start of the twentieth century, playing the role opposite her husband Oscar Asche.

emphasizing Sly. These were followed in 1735 by **James Worldale**'s *A Cure for a Scold*, a two-act "ballad-farce" that again revised the ending and erased most of Shakespeare's text. But the most influential spin-off would be one of **David Garrick**'s successful Shakespeare redactions, *Catharine and Petruchio*, which was first aired in 1754. Despite claiming that not "one drop" of Shakespeare was lost, Garrick cut extraneous material – including Sly and the subplot – and removed much of the play's moral ambiguity. Garrick also initiated a venerable tradition by issuing himself as Petruchio with a whip (the prop would remain obligatory well into the twentieth century). **Hannah Pritchard** played Catharine in the debut production before **Henry Woodward** revived it a few years later with himself in the lead; **Kitty Clive** later took over from Mrs Pritchard. That great theatrical dynasty, the Kembles, kept Garrick's version in the family as well as on the stage: **Sarah Siddons** played Catharine to her brother, **John Philip Kemble**, as Petruchio in 1788, who was still playing the role opposite his wife in 1810. Both **Henry Irving** (playing Petruchio to **Ellen Terry**'s Catharine in 1867) and **Herbert Beerbohm Tree** (1867) used Garrick. *Catherine and Petruchio* was also a success in America; it had been premiered in Philadelphia in 1766.

But all was not lost for Shakespeare. In 1844, **J.R. Planché** mounted a production of the uncut *Taming of the Shrew* in the "Elizabethan manner", with just two sets and simple placards announcing locations. Clearly impressed by Planché's resurrection, **Samuel Phelps** played Sly in his own production at Sadler's Wells in 1856, but was less happy with the final act, which he edited heavily. The American **Augustine Daly** also made cuts in his 1887 version of Shakespeare's play, but with conspicuously more success than Phelps: it ran for over 120 nights, **Ada Rehan** being especially acclaimed for a Katherine who was, in Rehan's own words, "high-strung and nervous, though at the same time strong and thoroughly healthy".

One of the first twentieth-century productions to create a real impact was that mounted by husband-and-wife team **Oscar Asche** and **Lily Brayton** at the Adelphi Theatre, London in 1904 and again at the Aldwych in 1908. Asche was a populist and his approach was direct and irreverent: "we played it as a jolly farce and it always went with a scream" was his own rather dubious description. From then on, the *Shrew* entered one of its most popular periods, being performed at Stratford-upon-Avon every year for nearly a decade – in the view of one 1930s reviewer, in reaction to the militant activities of "vote-hungry viragoes" at the time. But it took the mischievous modern-dress production by **Barry Jackson** in 1928 – complete with a Ford car, fashionable tailoring and press photographers – to remind audiences of the play's up-to-the-minute resonances. Jackson's version had the young **Laurence Olivier** supporting, though **Ralph Richardson** stole the show as a cheeky cockney Tranio. Katherine was a popular apprentice part throughout the twentieth century: she was played by **Sybil Thorndike** (1927), **Edith Evans** (1937), **Sian Philips** (1960), **Vanessa Redgrave** (1961), **Janet Suzman** (1967) and **Joan Plowright** (1972). It was also **John Barton**'s first production at the RSC in 1960, with **Peter O'Toole** as Petruccio and **Peggy Ashcroft** as Katherine – who relented gracefully, prompting

Kenneth Tynan to declare that her performance "almost prompts one to regret the triumph of the suffragette movement". **Clifford Williams**'s version of 1973 also played it safe by dissolving any hint of gender struggle and concentrating on the play's farcical qualities. **Michael Bodganov**'s RSC staging of five years later made an apposite contrast: its first audiences were terrified by what appeared to be a football hooligan breaking into the auditorium, only for him to turn into **Jonathan Pryce**'s Sly (and later his supremacist Petruccio). Viewing the play as a "male wish-fulfilment dream of revenge upon women", Bogdanov had **Paola Dionisotti**'s Katherine utter her final sermon in unreal, ironic tones – to the discomfort of many critics. Both **Barry Kyle**'s exuberant 1982 production (with **Sinead Cusack** and **Alun Armstrong**) and **Jonathan Miller**'s chillier version of 1987 (with **Fiona Shaw**) created less divided reactions. By common consent, though, one of the most interesting productions of the last twenty years was that directed by **Di Trevis** for the RSC regional tour in 1985, which underlined connections between the subjection of women and that of the *Shrew*'s players in a shabby Victorian setting.

Back in the RSC's main house in 1992, **Bill Alexander** preferred to focus on the play's social divides, as did **Stephen Unwin** for the English Touring Theatre seven years later. **Phyllida Lloyd**'s Globe staging from 2003 gained points for novelty as well as ensemble acting. By having an all-female company, headed by **Janet McTeer** as Petruccio (a wonderful caricature of swaggering *machismo*) and **Kathryn Hunter** as Katherine, the violence of the play was largely dissipated and it emerged as less ideologically problematic and more an out-and-out comedy. Also offering new insights was **Gregory Doran** at the RSC a few months later, who took the brilliant move of setting the *Shrew* alongside Fletcher's *The Tamer Tamed* with the same cast. The thought-provoking conclusion of Shakespeare's play was, **Alexandra Gilbreath**'s Katherine and **Jasper Britton**'s Petruccio reminded us, not quite the end. The carefully psychologized nature of their relationship emphasized that this remained a continuing narrative, though Doran's production refused to take itself too seriously with plenty of punchy comedy.

The play has inspired a number of spin-offs – some political, many less so. **Charles Marowitz**'s savage adaptation of 1973, *The Shrew*, presented the unrelenting brutalization of Katherine (**Thelma Holt**) culminating in her rape. Less contentiously, Shakespeare's play has also inspired numerous composers: at least six musical versions exist, the most famous of which is probably **Hermann Goetz**'s opera of 1874. Better known is **Cole Porter**'s enduringly popular musical, *Kiss Me Kate* (1948), which sets its action around a staging of Shakespeare's play. But it is in the cinema that the *Shrew* has been most well-served: at least eight films have been made in countries as far afield as Italy, Denmark and India. **D.W. Griffith**'s 1908 silent version (shot in just two days) is now too fragile to be shown, and **Sam Taylor**'s adaptation of 1929, with **Mary Pickford** and **Douglas Fairbanks** – the first Shakespeare "talkie" – is rarely screened. More familiar is the film by **Franco Zeffirelli**, starring a couple renowned for offstage fireworks on a par with the script – **Richard Burton** and **Elizabeth Taylor**. The play's newest big-screen incarnation is perhaps the most unexpected: the teen-movie spin-off *10 Things I Hate About You* (1999), which translates elements of the play to a high school in present-day Seattle. On TV, the BBC production (1980) was directed by **Jonathan Miller**, who took the unusual step of casting comedian **John Cleese** as Petruccio opposite **Sarah Badel**'s Katherine.

## Screen

### The Taming of the Shrew (La Bisbetica Domata)

**E. Taylor, R. Burton, M. York; Franco Zeffirelli (dir.)**
USA/Italy, 1966 ▷ Columbia 🆅 ▭

A mere pit-stop for the Burton–Taylor bandwagon it may be,

but Zeffirelli's carnivalesque *Shrew* offers many of the attractions – and flaws – of his *Romeo and Juliet*. Large chunks of the text are nowhere to be seen (our playwright gets a minor writing credit), and all the limelight illuminates the lead couple – cast for their offscreen shenanigans as much as their onscreen talent. That said, Taylor brings some depth to Katherine and Burton could do Petruccio in his sleep (the drink presumably helped). Theirs are big, physical performances, matching Zeffirelli's operatic style: the screen is cluttered and the comedy, little of it Shakespeare's, is broadly done. While this makes for amenable cinema, the film's view of women leaves a bitter taste in the mouth: Katherine's metamorphosis from fierce-eyed vixen to placid wifey is uncomfortably managed, and her simpering sister (Natasha Pyne) is hardly an admirable role model.

### 10 Things I Hate About You
**J. Stiles, H. Ledger, L. Oleynik; Gil Junger (dir.)**
USA, 1999 ▷ Touchstone 𝐃𝐕𝐃 ▭

Spin-off, schminoff. *10 Things I Hate About You* stands as an interesting alternative to the Taylor and Burton vehicle – and arguably it's only as much (or as little) an adaptation as Zeffirelli's film. In Karen McCullah Lutz and Kirsten Smith's script, the narrative of the play – troublesome woman brought into line, social norms reinforced – becomes its modern analogue, the teen romance movie. The tomboyish Kat (Julia Stiles) hates men because she's had bad experiences, while oddball newcomer Patrick Verona (Heath Ledger) is happy to be bribed into dating her. There's no attempt to keep the text, but cute Shakespearian references are smuggled in nonetheless. One girl is so smitten with the Bard that she has his picture in her locker; the "10 things" of the title concerns a homework exercise to rewrite Sonnet 141 ("In faith, I do not love thee with mine eyes") in modern language. Kat's rendition of her poem proves the film's emotional climax, but, unsurprisingly, there's no attempt to replicate a sermon on obedience: that would be too, like, *uncool*. Not as satisfying as Luhrmann's *Romeo + Juliet*, but fun nonetheless.

## Audio

### The Taming of the Shrew
**G. McSorley, R. Mitchell, J. Ford; Melanie Harris (dir.)**
UK, 2000 ▷ BBC ⊙ ▭

Few stage producers opt to retain the Christopher Sly scenes, so it's not entirely surprising to see the same policy here – though it is disappointing, as they are certainly easier to get around without the problems of visual staging. Melanie Harris's decision was swayed by her determination to "get more immediately to the heart of the play", though, and this she undeniably does. Ruth Mitchell as Katherine brings plenty of energetic unruliness to the role without making her unsympathetic. Gerard McSorley could perhaps do with a touch more energy as Petruccio, but his Irish burr has plenty of appeal and the scenes between the couple are nicely done. Perhaps this production's best recommendation is that it refuses to moralize: despite the callowness of the men's bar-room barracking, Katherine speaks her famous speech with fervour and leaves them in stunned silence – a victory of sorts.

## Editions

### New Cambridge Shakespeare
**Ann Thompson (ed.); rev. 2003** ▷ Cambridge UP

Perhaps it's a sign of modern angst about the *Shrew* that until 2003 its newest mainstream edition was nearly twenty years old. But Ann Thompson's 1984 text has recently been updated, following New Cambridge policy, accommodating a busy two decades for the play in theatre and lecture hall alike. Thompson has a refreshingly no-nonsense approach to the play's moral challenges – asking why it is that many of us are driven to make excuses for it (and Shakespeare), and suggesting that we redefine it as a "problem play". Whether or not you agree with this, an appendix including excerpts from *The Taming of a Shrew* – a drama which is noticeably less enlightened than Shakespeare's – might help you make up your mind.

## Some criticism

### Clamorous Voices
**Carol Rutter; 1985** ▷ Routledge [o/p]

*Clamorous Voices* corrals together five influential British actresses (Sinead Cusack, Paola Dionisotti, Fiona Shaw, Juliet Stevenson, Harriet Walter), who among them played nearly all Shakespeare's heroines in landmark RSC productions dating from the mid-1970s onwards. The format is that of a round-table discussion – for the *Shrew* the speakers are Dionisotti, Shaw and Cusack – held together by comments by theatre historian Carol Rutter. While the views of the panel offer sometimes stray into luvviedom, their contrasting thoughts on the *Shrew* in particular (often sharpened by their own commitment to feminism and conflict with male directors) bespeak not just the problems the play presents but the different solutions they found. As theatrical history this book is enlightening enough, but *Clamorous Voices* offers a great deal more; the kind of close reading and interpretive sanity on offer here should make academics green with envy.

### Shakespeare and the Nature of Women
**Juliet Dusinberre; rev. 1996** ▷ Macmillan

Sometimes described as the first major feminist work on Shakespeare, Dusinberre's study (originally published in 1975) makes a revolutionary claim for its subject – as feminist *avant la lettre*. Her reading of the *Shrew* makes much of Shakespeare's rejection of convention and sees him siding with radical elements in Elizabethan society, particularly Puritan marriage reformers, in their bid to equalize the balance between the sexes. This progressive approach is not without its problems – her claim that Katherine's sermon is actually a libertarian document seems hard to sustain for many modern readers – but it's sympathetic and engaging. Despite some tweaks in the second edition, the main body of Dusinberre's thinking remains intact.

# The Tempest

I f *The Tempest* is one of Shakespeare's most cherished works, it can also seem his most abstruse, even unfathomable. It recounts the story of an exiled Italian ruler who inflicts revenge upon his usurpers by calling up a magical "tempest" that shipwrecks them on his island; a story that is apparently of the playwright's own devising, and which has tempted any number of competing analyses. Some have seen the plot as an allegory of divine learning, as the mage Prospero uses his celestial powers to conquer evil and restore the forces of good. Others have been engaged by *The Tempest*'s dissident colonial themes, its depiction of an island colonized by white Europeans who enslave its indigenous inhabitants. Still others interpret it as the veteran playwright's bewitching swansong, Prospero "drowning" his book at the play's end just as Shakespeare turned his back on the stage and entered retirement soon afterwards. Though that last theory is sentimental – not least because there would be three more co-written plays to come – it is true that *The Tempest* dwells more than any other Shakespearian work upon the vivid transformations wrought by dramatic poetry and spectacle, and some of its most astonishing moments harness Prospero's magic to the illusions conjured in the theatre. Though all the author's plays are dazzling in their way, *The Tempest* holds a special charge for audiences and readers alike.

[DATE]  The first recorded performance of *The Tempest*, almost certainly the last play that Shakespeare wrote on his own, was at court in November 1611. It's likely to have been written earlier that year, or possibly late in 1610 – around the same time as *The Winter's Tale*.

[SOURCES]  *The Tempest*'s plot seems to be original – uniquely among Shakespeare's plays – but may have been inspired by reports of an actual shipwreck in 1610 (see below). It quotes Michel de Montaigne's essay "Of the Cannibals" (translated by John Florio in 1605), and the influence of Virgil's *Aeneid* and Ovid's *Metamorphoses* has also been identified.

[TEXTS]  The 1623 Folio version provides the only authoritative text, and contains unusually detailed stage directions – suggesting that the person who typeset it might have seen the play performed.

## Interpreting the play

In 1607, four years into James I's reign, the Virginia Company, dedicated to investing in the recently colonized Americas, founded a settlement they called "Jamestown" in his honour. Two years later, the Company attempted its boldest venture yet, the settlement of no fewer than four hundred colonists, shipped across the Atlantic during the summer of 1609. But disaster struck: caught in a hurricane, the fleet was broken up, one of the ships was sunk and another, the *Sea Venture*, driven onto the rocky coast of the Bermudas. Soon afterwards news began to filter back to Britain that the *Sea Venture*'s human cargo had lived to tell the tale, and in September 1610 a sensational real-life story by one of the survivors, William Strachey, began circulating among London's chattering classes. Strachey's "True Reportory of the Wreck" breathlessly described how the passengers and crew had encountered a miraculous and exotic island, its seas bursting

## Major Characters & Synopsis

**Prospero**, the deposed Duke of Milan, living in banishment on an island
**Miranda**, Prospero's daughter
**Antonio**, Prospero's brother, the usurping Duke of Milan
**Alonso**, King of Naples
**Sebastian**, Alonso's brother
**Ferdinand**, Alonso's son
**Gonzalo**, an honest old counsellor from Naples
**Adrian** and **Francisco**, lords
**Ariel**, a spirit attending on Prospero
**Caliban**, a wild "savage" enslaved by Prospero
**Trinculo**, Alonso's jester
**Stephano**, Alonso's drunken butler
**Master** of a ship and his sailors

**ACT 1** Antonio, Alonso and his son Ferdinand are travelling by sea when their boat is caught in a terrible storm. Shipwrecked, they and their party are cast ashore on a strange and apparently deserted island – unaware that the tempest has been caused by the magic of Prospero, their former duke and now the island's ruler. Responding to questions from his daughter Miranda, Prospero relates how they arrived on the island twelve years earlier: as Duke of Milan he had handed some duties to his brother Antonio who, gaining a taste for power, usurped Prospero with the aid of Alonso, King of Naples. Cast adrift in a boat, Prospero and the young Miranda eventually landed on the island, where they took as servants the spirit Ariel and the savage Caliban – whose island it originally was. When Ariel reveals to Prospero that his enemies are where he wants them, the magician initiates the next stage of his plan. Enticing Ferdinand to them by magic, he encourages him and Miranda to fall in love, while pretending to disapprove.

**ACT 2** Alonso and his companions are searching for Ferdinand. Ariel, who remains invisible, sends everyone to sleep except Antonio and Sebastian, Alonso's brother. These two then plot to murder Alonso and the courtier Gonzago, but before they manage it Ariel wakes the others. On another part of the island, Trinculo comes across

Caliban, to their mutual shock; when the drunken Stefano arrives, Caliban thinks he must be a god and offers to serve him in the hope of escaping Prospero's control.

**ACT 3** Prospero has enslaved Ferdinand and made him carry logs, but the young man does so willingly in order to serve his beloved Miranda. Watched secretly by Prospero, the two pledge to be married. Caliban tells Trinculo and Stephano that he is Prospero's slave; he proposes that they murder the magician, and that Stephano marry Miranda and rule in Prospero's stead. When the voice of Ariel interrupts, Caliban and Stephano think that it is Trinculo speaking, and the two men argue. Alonso and his party have given up hope of finding Ferdinand when, to the sound of strange music, spirits materialize in front of them and produce a banquet. Before they can eat, Ariel appears, and makes the banquet vanish before condemning Alonso, Antonio and Sebastian for their part in deposing Prospero.

**ACT 4** Prospero admits that the tasks he set Ferdinand were to test his love for Miranda, and he now blesses their marriage with a masque performed by spirits. Suddenly remembering Caliban's plot against his life, Prospero angrily halts the performance and calls Ariel to him. Ariel tells how he has beguiled the would-be murderers into losing their bearings; when they finally arrive at Prospero's cell, Stephano and Trinculo are distracted by Prospero's regal robes before all three are chased away by spirits disguised as hunting dogs.

**ACT 5** Ariel reports how the spirits of Alonso and the other Neapolitans have been broken, and Prospero instructs him to release them. Ariel leads the group in by magic, and to their amazement Prospero appears and reveals who he is. Prospero then produces Ferdinand and Miranda, and all are reunited and reconciled. Ariel is guaranteed freedom, Caliban is forgiven and Prospero renounces his magical arts and declares that he will return to Naples as Duke once again.

with fish, its skies filled with strange but luscious birds, its forests teeming with massive wild boars. Unlike their unlucky and ill-prepared compatriots in Jamestown itself (who had been all but wiped out the previous winter by starvation and disease), the Bermudan colonists stayed for nine relatively tranquil months. Two of their members voted to stay behind when the rest set sail for Virginia, and became the islands' first permanent settlers.

On November 1, 1611 – just over a year after the "Reportory" reached England – a partial reconstruction of some of those events was performed in front of the same King who had chartered the Virginia Company four years earlier. That play was *The Tempest*. Scholars agree that Shakespeare probably read Strachey's account and others that drew upon the chaotic experiences of the fledgling American colonies, and the *Tempest*'s subject matter had never been more topical. In what has been called Shakespeare's "American play", a group of Milanese voyagers are shipwrecked by a storm every bit as wild as that experienced by Strachey. Washed ashore on a mysterious and apparently "uninhabited" island, they begin to confront the idea that they, too, are colonists – and might be stuck there for the rest of their lives. "Had I plantation of this isle, my lord," begins the counsellor Gonzalo,

> All things in common nature should produce
> Without sweat or endeavour. Treason, felony,
> Sword, pike, knife, gun, or need of any engine,
> Would I not have; but nature should bring forth
> Of its own kind all foison, all abundance,
> To feed my innocent people.
>
> **[2.1.165–70]**

Gonzalo's fantasy echoes those of many seventeenth-century Europeans, eager to read about the apparently infinite liberties promised by the New World. Though Shakespeare's reliance on colonial literature for *The Tempest* is difficult to pin down (even with Strachey, supposedly a key source, the resemblances are fleeting and unspecific), his dramatization of colonial desires – the utopian wish to return to an older, simpler life, unfettered by the advances of civilization and nourished by all-giving Nature – shows just how seductive those dreams can be.

## This thing of darkness

But Gonzalo and his aristocratic companions do not, in fact, have the place to themselves. Elsewhere on the island, two other survivors from the wreck, the jester Trinculo and the drunken butler Stefano, are making their own groping – and alcohol-hazed – explorations of their new environment. Trinculo is first on the scene, and espies what he initially assumes to be a "fish", then "an islander that hath lately suffered by a thunderbolt" (2.2.35–6). After a fair amount of comic ado (in which Trinculo clambers in under the islander's coat, making Stefano believe that he is looking at a creature with "four legs"), the two Italians recognize each other and confront the "scurvy monster", who kisses Stefano's foot and promises to serve them both. "I prithee," the monster cries, "let me bring thee where crabs grow,"

> And I with my long nails will dig thee pig-nuts,
> Show thee a jay's nest, and instruct thee how
> To snare the nimble marmoset. I'll bring thee
> To clust'ring filberts, and sometimes I'll get thee
> Young seamews from the rock.
>
> **[2.2.166–71]**

This is Caliban, a "savage and deformed slave" (as the First Folio's list of parts expresses it) whose very name – a near-anagram of "cannibal" – identifies him as something far outside most

"Mercy on us! We split, we split!" The opening scene of *The Tempest* as depicted by engraver Elisha Kirkall for Nicholas Rowe's 1709 edition of Shakespeare, with Ariel hovering over the main-mast and Prospero directing the action from his island.

Europeans' experience. The riches he offers, too, are wild and exotic, the dramatic equivalent of those that William Strachey described on Bermuda. But whereas Strachey and his companions had to unlock the island's assets for themselves, Caliban promises to do it all.

The scene is obviously meant to resemble those enacted in real life by colonists who found that the world they thought of as "new" in fact belonged to other people, with all the horrendous consequences that invited (not least the smallpox virus, introduced by European colonists, whose devastating effects on indigenous communities on the East Coast of America were recorded by English settlers). But Shakespeare's replay is satirical: here the wannabe colonists are from the dregs of society, their offerings alcoholic, their ambitions simply to get what they can out of Caliban (perhaps by shipping him to England and showing him off for money, as Trinculo speculates). The tragic farce of the encounter is captured by Trinculo: "A most ridiculous monster," he sniggers, "to make a wonder of a poor drunkard" (2.2.164–5).

> *In Caliban it is that Shakespeare has risen, I think, to the very height of creative power, and, by making what is absolutely unnatural thoroughly natural and consistent, has accomplished the impossible.*
>
> Horace Howard Furness, in the New Variorum *Tempest* (1892)

Shakespeare was well-acquainted with writing that expressed discomfort about the colonial enterprises of ambitious Europeans (and the assumptions they carried with them to far-flung corners of the globe), and in fact he culled Gonzalo's dreamy speech about "plantation" from an essay by the French sage Michel de Montaigne, in which Montaigne argues that the native inhabitants of what is now Brazil are not "savage" or "barbarous" – and that in thinking so we are blind to our own faults. In Shakespeare's play, the Milanese are not the first to try and exploit Caliban: he is already enslaved by the all-powerful Prospero, the mysterious magician who seized control of the island when he was desposed from office in Milan. Having made the mistake of uncovering the island's riches to the exiled Duke – just as he does to Stefano and Trinculo – Caliban naively helped bring about his own displacement. Forced into menial service for Prospero and his daughter, Caliban ("this demi-devil … this thing of darkness", Prospero disgustedly calls him (5.1.275–9)) finds that the island's wonder now only entraps him. "Be not afeard," he advises Stefano and Trinculo,

> The isle is full of noises,
> Sounds, and sweet airs, that give delight and hurt not.
> Sometimes a thousand twangling instruments
> Will hum about mine ears, and sometime voices
> That if I then had waked after long sleep
> Will make me sleep again; and then in dreaming
> The clouds methought would open and show riches
> Ready to drop upon me, that when I waked
> I cried to dream again.
>
> [3.2.138–46]

The magical occurrences on the island confirm that it is Caliban's prison, as this heartbreaking and unexpectedly beautiful speech, in which "dreaming" becomes a kind of solace, attests. Caliban is a collection of contradictions, far more complex than the innocent "noble savage" imagined by neoclassical philosophers such as Voltaire and Rousseau – he is cheerfully unrepentant about his attempt to rape Miranda, for instance – but coming into contact with "civilization" has only made things worse for him, even as it attempted to mould him to its needs. "You taught me language," he snarls at Prospero, "and my profit on't / Is I know how to curse" (1.2.365–6). Perhaps it is no surprise that Caliban, the character in *The Tempest* who most often steals the show, has sometimes been taken as its tragic hero.

## No mortal business

But the play is not in Caliban's hands, and his one attempt to control its outcome – his plot, with the ineffective aid of Stefano and Trinculo, to topple Prospero and win the island back for himself – is doomed to failure. With the aid of the spirit Ariel, Prospero exerts absolute control, able through his "potent art" to summon up everything from a tempest to a pack of snarling dogs in order to baffle and torment the shipwrecked royal party. Though the comedy is, famously, the only one of Shakespeare's to fit the so-called "unities" of neoclassical drama (the law, supposedly derived from Aristotle, that a play should occupy real-time and a single location), Prospero's story began twelve years earlier, and a world away. As he tells Miranda:

> I, thus neglecting worldly ends, all dedicated
> To closeness and the bettering of my mind
> With that which but by being so retired
> O'er-priced all popular rate, in my false brother
> Awaked an evil nature; and my trust,
> Like a good parent, did beget of him
> A falsehood, in its contrary as great
> As my trust was, which had indeed no limit,
> A confidence sans bound.

**[1.2.89–97]**

"Rapt" in secret studies in Milan, Prospero fails to realize that his position there is under threat. This "evil" transformation in Antonio begins what Prospero calls his "sea sorrow": his romance-like ejection from power and flight to the island with the infant Miranda. But Prospero's magic enables him to set up his own poetic justices: Antonio and his retinue have fallen into his lap, and the fearsome sea storm he raises brings them once again under his control. In this sense, *The Tempest* is a story of revenge: Prospero shipwrecks his brother on the island in order to get his own back (quite literally, given that he succeeds in regaining the Milanese throne).

It is also a story that uses the full resources of Shakespeare's dramatic skill, to such an extent that Prospero has frequently been interpreted as a kind of stand-in for the poet himself, the magician's art and the playwright's merging into one. To an extent, it's undeniable that they resemble each other. The tempest that begins the play – which gives it its name – would have been strikingly presented in its first performances at the candlelit Blackfriars theatre, *The Tempest*'s unusually elaborate stage directions calling first of all for "a tempestuous noise of thunder and lightning" (created either by offstage fireworks or perhaps cannon-balls rolled around a drum). The fierceness of the storm, and the peril the ship is in, is represented by the "Mariners" who appear on stage soaked to the skin – and who shout to each other in jargon that makes little sense to landlubbers. All is hyper-realistic. And yet the whole thing, as we soon find out, is doubly make-believe – it is Prospero's play-within-a-play, and, as he comforts Miranda, for all the shipwrecking horror, "there's no harm done" (1.1.15). Though the sailors' clothes have been stained by saltwater, the courtiers arrive on shore magically dry; "on their sustaining garments not a blemish," Ariel eagerly explains, "but fresher than before" (1.2.218–20). Gonzalo is quite right to urge Alonso to be "merry"; "You have cause," he says, "so have we all, of joy,"

> for our escape
> Is much beyond our loss. Our hint of woe

Is common; every day some sailor's wife,
The masters of some merchant, and the merchant,
Have just our theme of woe. But for the miracle,
I mean our preservation, few in millions
Can speak like us.

[2.1.1–8]

Amid the grinding, daily "woe" of life on the sea, their survival does seem extraordinary; it is still more so because Prospero plays the same tricks on the baffled Milanese as Shakespeare does on his audiences. They are spared, even as they are hoodwinked, by the miracles of theatre.

For, though Prospero brings the party to his island to achieve some kind of revenge – which he exacts by taunting them with spirits, culminating in Ariel's appearance as a scourging harpy to make them "mad" (3.3.58) – his treatment of them is ultimately beneficent. His cruellest trick is to make Alonso think that his son Ferdinand has perished in the shipwreck. Yet far from Sebastian's morbid certainty that Ferdinand cannot be "undrowned", undrowned is precisely what he is: a fact that Prospero reveals in the most impressive sleight of hand in the play, the sudden appearance of Miranda and Ferdinand innocently playing chess (staged in the so-called "discovery space" at the back of the stage) while the visitors to the island stand goggle-eyed at the front.

Despite his initial fierceness at Ferdinand's interest in Miranda, Prospero in fact encourages the young couple to fall in love, a redemption which, enshrined in their marriage, reaches out to involve nearly everyone in the play. It is the kind of strange metamorphosis captured in Ariel's haunting song "Full fathom five":

Full fathom five thy father lies.
 Of his bones are coral made;
Those are pearls that were his eyes;
 Nothing of him that doth fade
But doth suffer a sea-change
Into something rich and strange.

[1.2.399–404]

The words remind a puzzled Ferdinand of his "drowned father", little knowing that their reunion will be as "rich and strange" as the lyrics predict. "Full fathom five" is a song about transformation, about finding new life where none seemed possible. It is, as Ferdinand says, "no mortal business" (1.2.409).

With the lovers married and all reconciled, Prospero swears to "abjure" his "rough magic" and travel back to Milan – a promise of retirement that has been seen to foreshadow Shakespeare's own. But the transformations Prospero talks of are not unmingled in their happiness. "Be cheerful, sir," he tells Ferdinand after the magical masque celebrating the wedding, "our revels now are ended."

> These our actors,
As I foretold you, were all spirits, and
Are melted into air, into thin air;
And like the baseless fabric of this vision,
The cloud-capped towers, the gorgeous palaces,
The solemn temples, the great globe itself,
Yea, all which it inherit, shall dissolve;
And, like this insubstantial pageant faded,
Leave not a rack behind.

[4.1.147–56]

## Rough magic

So powerful that it keeps the cast of *The Tempest* utterly in thrall – so powerful, in fact, that it dominates the experience of watching the play – Prospero's "so potent art" (5.1.50), his skill at magic, has long been a source of fascination. In placing a magician at the centre of his drama, Shakespeare wasn't doing anything particularly unusual: medieval and early Tudor plays often employed sorcerer-like figures, mostly evil, but these were succeeded in the Elizabethan era by more complex creations. Marlowe's **Doctor Faustus** (c.1588), in which a scientist conjures up the devil and agrees to trade his soul for divine knowledge, is now the most famous, but other examples include Robert Greene's comedy **Friar Bacon and Friar Bungay** (c.1594), which retells the life of medieval philosopher Roger Bacon with lashings of lurid necromancy, and Ben Jonson's **The Alchemist**, a satirical tale concerning a con man who uses "magic" to make a fast buck, which was performed by Shakespeare's company the year before *The Tempest*.

All these plays warn of the dangers of meddling in magic: its potential for evil, its power to pervert. Shakespeare often presents witchcraft in this light, notably in *1 Henry VI* and *Macbeth*. Not quite so in *The Tempest*, however, where Prospero's "Art" (the Folio script capitalizes it throughout) has often been seen as a benign force, perhaps like the "secret art" of the physician Cerimon in *Pericles*, which awakens the heroine Thaisa from a deathlike slumber. Both have been interpreted as so-called "**white magic**", which in the Renaissance became linked to Neoplatonic thought – a philosophical movement that sought to transcend earthly things and touch the divine, and which found in the rediscovered texts of Plato and his followers a model for mystical and spiritual intellectual exploration. German Neoplatonist **Cornelius Agrippa** (1486–1535) authored a survey entitled *De Occulta Philosophia* ("Of Occult Philosophy") that defended magic as being on the side of the angels. Later in the sixteenth century, the English mage **John Dee** (1527–1608) expounded what sounds strikingly like Prospero's "secret studies", describing how the contemplative mind should "deal speculatively in his own Art, and by good means mount above the clouds and stars". Dee first gained a reputation for sorcery at Cambridge, where his ultra-realistic stage effects for a performance of Arisophanes's *Peace* scandalized audiences, and later became astrologer to Queen Elizabeth. As well as being credited with the victory over the Armada in 1588 (he is supposed to have cursed the Spanish fleet), the most famous occultist of his age has also been interpreted as Shakespeare's original for Prospero.

But where Dee protested to hostile commentators that these powers were used – like Cerimon's – simply to cure, Prospero's motives are more complex. Though he claims that his "prosperous" government of the island is better than that of the "damned witch" Sycorax, the previous ruler, Prospero nevertheless keeps her son Caliban enslaved, torturing him with delusions, cramps and biting aches – symptoms that have been compared to **ergotism**, a form of rye-grain poisoning caused by fungus and commonplace in early modern Europe. Like Sycorax, too, Prospero forces Ariel to serve him, despite the spirit's repeated appeals for liberty. And the main role for Prospero's magic in *The Tempest* is to enact revenge on his usurping brother Antonio, first raising the storm that seems to wreck his ship, then pursuing him across the island with a series of hallucinatory visions. As interest in the play's colonial dimensions has grown, Prospero and his magic have come to seem exploitative as well as violent, and his hunger for absolute power on the island has been compared to that of the Stuart monarchs (James I dabbled in witchcraft and had a taste for Prospero-like masques). And if the ideal ruler should become expert in natural sciences, as philosopher **Francis Bacon** argued, Prospero is at best an ambiguous role-model: neglecting his Milanese dukedom for contemplative study, he was banished and left to lord it over a scantly populated island.

Perhaps that is why Prospero ultimately renounces his "Art", "drowning" his book and breaking his magical staff before returning to Milan – a decision that has puzzled those who have tried to present him as a Neoplatonist philosopher renouncing earthly cares. At the play's end Prospero heads not into retreat, but back to the daily grind – another reason why we should beware of reading *The Tempest* as Shakespeare's retirement note. The metatheatrical "revels" of this great and experimental play may be ended, "melted into air, into thin air" (4.1.148–50), but for playwright as much as for Prospero there was still great deal of work to be done.

"We are such stuff / As dreams are made on," he continues, "and our little life / Is rounded with a sleep" (4.1.156–8). If this is Shakespeare announcing retirement, even looking towards death – and another three plays, though co-written, lay in front of him – the tone is not indulgent. Leaving the magic of the stage, the "great globe itself", will be a painful and irrecoverable loss.

# Stage history and adaptations

It's possible that *The Tempest* was specially written for the **Blackfriars** theatre, where Shakespeare's company began performing in 1609; in any case the only surviving text (that in the 1623 Folio) has unusually detailed stage directions and requires a great deal of music. It was also acted several times at **court**: once for James I in 1611, again during the celebrations for his daughter's wedding in 1613.

However spectacular those early performances, however, they would be trumped after the Restoration with the appearance of **William Davenant** and **John Dryden**'s adaptation *The Tempest, or the Enchanted Island* (1667), which featured impressive stage machinery but less than a third of the original text. Davenant introduced several new characters – among them "Hippolito", an innocent male counterpart to Miranda – and emphasized the piece's comedy (to the delight of Pepys, who saw it several times). Capitalizing on its runaway popularity, **Thomas Shadwell** mounted an "operatic" version of the same in 1674, with music mostly by **Matthew Locke** which was so successful that remnants were still being performed in the nineteenth century.

Making the most of *The Tempest*'s popularity, **David Garrick** launched another operatic version in 1756, though he returned to Shakespeare's text the following year (albeit with savage cuts) and acted it frequently afterwards. **Thomas Sheridan** kept Garrick's text when he took over Drury Lane, but **John Philip Kemble** reinstated some of Davenant's changes in his productions of 1789, 1806 and 1815 (much to Hazlitt's outrage). During this period Prospero was presented as unwaveringly noble, at first by **Robert Bensley**, then the "majestic" Kemble himself, but even so **John Emery** was allowed to present a sympathetic, near-tragic Caliban.

The most influential production of the nineteenth century would prove to be **William Charles Macready**'s at Covent Garden in 1838, which finally restored most of Shakespeare's script (if not his opening scene, replaced by a "grand panoramic spectacle" depicting the ship-wreck); **George Bennett**'s heart-rending Caliban appeared alongside the radiant Miranda of **Helen Faucit** and **Priscilla Horton**'s jaunty Ariel. **Samuel Phelps**'s productions at Sadler's Wells from the 1840s were also praised, *The Times* observing that they offered "the best combination of Shakespeare and scenery", but for sheer ostentation it would be hard to outdo **Charles Kean**'s 1857 staging at the Princess's Theatre. This opened with a storm scene so magnificent that the visiting Hans Christian Andersen was overawed (at least until his host Charles Dickens explained how it worked), and Kean's own "mysterious" Prospero was widely praised.

But in the high Victorian era *The Tempest* became more than ever Caliban's play. **Frank Benson** took on the part during his numerous touring productions in the last decades of the century and later at Stratford, basing an athletic interpretation on chimpanzees he had observed at the zoo (and making a habit of appearing on stage with a real fish in his mouth). Also pursuing the theory that Caliban was a Darwinian "missing link" was **Herbert Beerbohm Tree**, whose portrayal from 1904 became infamous – not least because he expanded it to make the character more appealing, closing the play with a newly "civilized" Caliban waving farewell to the Milanese ships.

By this time **William Poel**'s radical productions with his Elizabethan Stage Society had come and gone, and innovation was all the rage. **Ben Greet**'s performances at the Old Vic from 1915 lasted just two hours and starred **Sybil Thorndike** as Ferdinand; while **John Drinkwater**'s Birmingham Rep production from the same year was designed by **Barry Jackson** and featured **E. Stewart Vinden** as Ariel, the first man in the role for some two centuries. **William Bridges-Adams**, a Poel disciple, put on a 1919 *Tempest* designed to look as it might have done in 1613, and staged it again at Stratford in 1934 with **Neil Porter** as Prospero, who dared to present the character as both irascible and distinctly unpleasant (contravening a stage tradition insisting that he must be kindly).

The most influential Prospero of the era – perhaps of the century – was **John Gielgud**, who first acted him under **Harcourt Williams** at the Old Vic in 1930 to **Ralph Richardson**'s Caliban. Gielgud, then just 26, dispensed with the flowing robes and beard of yore and instead created a man "rich in … melancholy", according to one witness. In **Peter Brook**'s 1957 production Prospero was an essentially noble figure, returning in triumph to his dukedom in the play's closing moments; whereas for **Peter Hall**, at the National in 1974, the interpretation had hardened into brusque aloofness – a reading partly inspired by the Elizabethan magician and natural scientist John Dee (see p.332). **Michael Benthall**'s celebrated 1951 Stratford staging, by contrast, went the other way – initially featuring **Michael Redgrave**'s forceful Prospero, later replacing him with the more approachable **Ralph Richardson** (not to mention a conventionally female Ariel, **Margaret Leighton**, for **Alan Badel**).

If there is a single thread connecting postwar *Tempest*s, it is that of concern with the play's colonial politics. Unsurprisingly, much of the impetus behind this re-evaluation has come from North America, where Shakespeare's "American play" was performed in New York as early as 1854 by **William Burton**. In 1945 **Canada Lee** was the first black actor to play Caliban, in a New York production directed by **Margaret Webster**, while **Nagel Jackson**'s 1970 staging in Washington had both Ariel and Caliban played by black actors (**Darryl Croxton** and **Henry Baker** respectively) in order to draw parallels with America's slave history. Over in the UK, **Jonathan Miller** directed a fiercely anti-colonialist production at the Mermaid Theatre in London, also in 1970, inflected by the director's reading of Octave Mannoni's *Prospero and Caliban*, a study of the French colonization of Madagascar. Miller cast a black Ariel and Caliban to **Graham Crowden**'s neurotic Prospero. Even more didactic was **Aimé Césaire**'s rewriting, *Une Tempête* (1969), which posited Caliban as a revolutionary hero. Earnest approaches such as these were intriguingly mirrored in 1990 by **Peter Brook** with a touring multiracial troupe, among whose number were **David Bennent**'s boyish Caliban and **Sotugui Kouyate**'s benevolent Prospero. Nine years earlier, **Giorgio Strehler**'s Milanese version stunned audiences with its theatrical virtuosity – much, one suspects, as Shakespeare would have wanted.

Plurality of approach as well as of casting has, naturally enough, characterized recent productions of this much-seen play. In just one year, 1988, British audiences saw **Peter Hall**'s second National Theatre production, with **Michael Bryant**'s grizzled Prospero; **Declan Donnellan**'s typically impious Cheek By Jowl version; a modern-dress production from **Nicholas Hytner**'s RSC, focused on **John Wood**'s all-too-human Prospero; and a Noh-influenced Japanese version directed by **Yukio Ninagawa**. Ariel finally got his moment under **Sam Mendes** at the RSC in 1993, with **Simon Russell Beale**'s haughty sprite allowed to spit at his master (**Alec McCowen**) after being granted freedom. In **Jude Kelly**'s 1999 West Yorkshire Playhouse production, **Ian McKellen**'s Prospero attracted comment (some condemnation) for his unrepentant grumpiness; wearing a plastic raincoat and a battered hat, he presented an essentially introverted figure, and it was **Claudie Blakely**'s powerful Miranda who provided the play's heart. In an even more radical approach to the play's interpersonal relationships, the London Globe witnessed **Vanessa Redgrave** play Prospero in 2000, directed by **Lenka Udovicki**, though, like McKellen, Redgrave gave a pointedly gruff and unlyrical performance.

Directed by Sam Mendes at the RSC in 1993, Simon Russell Beale's Ariel reversed some of the *Tempest*'s traditional power polarities, often treating Alec McCowen's Prospero with icy disdain.

On screen, *The Tempest* has inspired numerous tributes. The earliest, a filming of the shipwreck from **Herbert Beerbohm Tree**'s touring production, appeared in 1905; while other film adaptations range from the relatively faithful (**Derek Jarman**'s 1979 *Tempest*) to the ostentatious (**Peter Greenaway**'s *Prospero's Books*, 1991) and the wonderfully bizarre (the sci-fi *Forbidden Planet*, directed by **Fred McLeod Wilcox** and released in 1956). The 1979 BBC/Time-Life production was directed by **John Gorrie** and saw **Michael Hordern**'s Prospero opposite **Warren Clarke**'s Caliban.

# Screen

## The Tempest
### Percy Stow (dir.)
UK, 1908 ▷ on Silent Shakespeare (BFI) **DVD** ⅴ

Though not quite twelve minutes long, this silent *Tempest* from 1908 feels like a veritable odyssey, packing the play's highlights and parts of its back story otherwise absent from Shakespeare's plot into a succession of swift-flowing scenes. Details of the cast have long since disappeared, and although its members share equal screen-time the elfin little girl playing Ariel and an exaggeratedly hirsute Caliban (shown munching on roots, Timon-style) especially catch the eye. It's a charming version, made all the more appealing by its deft mixture of set-based footage and adventurous location shots (Ariel dances around a sun-dappled wood, Ferdinand literally clambers out of the sea), cinematography that comes together in one impressive split-screen shot in which Prospero is shown conjuring a real storm – with waves, pyrotechnics and a flock

of real doves for good measure. It's available on the BFI's excellent *Silent Shakespeare* anthology along with intriguing versions of *Twelfth Night* (see p.378), *Richard III* (see p.303) and the *Dream* (see p.246).

## Forbidden Planet
### W. Pidgeon, A. Francis, L. Nielsen; Fred McLeod Wilcox (dir.)
USA, 1956 ▷ Warner **DVD** ⅴ

Esoteric plotting, an improbable love story and sometimes impenetrable dialogue? That's just the original. But this cult re-rendering of Shakespeare's final solo riff has many of those features too, translating Prospero's potent art into twenty-third-century sci-fi wizardry. We're beamed down to the green-skied planet of Altair-4, where a scientific colony has long since lost contact with Earth. A military team headed by Commander John J. Adams (Leslie Nielsen) heads into space to locate the problem, and ends up encountering the mysterious Dr Morbius (Walter Pidgeon) and his daughter Altaria (Anne Francis) – not to mention their dutiful servant,

Robby the Robot. The film's borrowings from *The Tempest* pretty much halt there, though in its influential special effects *Forbidden Planet* has surprisingly intimate affinities with the theatrical innovations of the play. What keeps it earthbound, unfortunately, is the lumpen and hilarious script, which largely hobbles the cast (a pre-*Naked Gun* Nielsen rarely has a smirk off his lips). And in its lurching final twist, the film ditches any connections with Shakespeare and invests rather too much in 1950s American paranoia. Entertaining nonetheless.

### The Tempest

**H. Williams, T. Wilcox, K. Johnson; Derek Jarman (dir.)**

UK, 1979 ▷ Second Sight / Kino **DVD**

*The Tempest* may well be the most conspicuously unified play in the canon – all its action takes place in one location during the space of one day – but watching this idiosyncratic adaptation you'd hardly guess. Jarman hacks and rearranges the text, reflowing its narrative into a series of brief and disjunctive scenes, while the "island" is a series of firelit interiors in which rocking-horses, baroque furniture and straw liberally mingle. Though in a strange kind of way this emphasizes the play's bespoke originality, the film's successes are fragmentary – a series of vignettes rather than a satisfying composition. The mix of different performing styles adds to the oddness: poet Heathcote Williams's youngish but gruff Prospero seems strangely disengaged, but Toyah Wilcox's Miranda fizzes with quizzical energy, while Jack Birkett (a blind performance artist) very nearly steals the show as Caliban. Jarman reserves his greatest coup for a wonderfully camp finale, which succeeds in trumping even Shakespeare's magical masques with the help of elderly jazz diva Elisabeth Welch and a chorus of wheeling sailors.

### Prospero's Books

**J. Gielgud, I. Pasco, M. Rylance; Peter Greenaway (dir.)**

UK, 1991 ▷ 4 Front / Allied Artists

*Prospero's Books* takes Shakespeare's mage quite literally at his word. Greenaway's central conceit is familiar enough, equating Bard and Prospero, but his way of broaching it is characteristically esoteric. The "books" of the title are those that tempted Shakespeare's rightful Duke away from the day-job, and Greenaway imagines them to cover the panoply of Renaissance knowledge – from cosmology to pornography. These volumes structure the film, producing a series of meditations on aspects of *The Tempest* rather than a fully fleshed-out narrative. It's as much a paean to John Gielgud as anything else, and until the very end his spry but sober Prospero speaks all the play's lines as well as solemnly inscribing them in the last book of all, *The Tempest* itself. With most of the cast able to communicate only through body language, this often feels like a dance piece, and alongside Gielgud its other star is dancer Michael Clark's stunning Caliban. As an idea the film is attractive, but *Prospero's Books* ultimately feels hollow: too exclusive a concept, and for all its display of learning pretty vapid intellectually.

# Audio

### The Tempest

**P. Madoc, N. Wadia, C. Rhys; David Hunter (dir.)**

UK, 2001 ▷ BBC

Listening to recordings of *The Tempest* can be an odd experience: on audio the isle "full of noises" has a unique power to charm – and also a unique habit of going awry at the hands of over-enthusiastic sound engineers. This version sits firmly in the first category (despite some odd silvery tinklings around Nina Wadia's giggly Ariel), and makes for excellent listening. Philip Madoc's rumbling Prospero has a voice to die for, as do many of this predominantly Welsh cast, who lend a rugged sonority to Shakespeare's late verse (particularly Joshua Richards's Caliban). The audio mix lends real intimacy to this production, although interpretatively it's hardly radical: Madoc stresses the inscrutable but benign aspects of the character, Wadia's Ariel is eager to please and the play's feel-good conclusion has reconciliation aplenty.

### The Tempest

**I. McKellen, S. Handy, E. Fox; John Tydeman (dir.)**

UK, 2005 ▷ Naxos

A burst of thunder, and we're in – on the groaning deck of a soon-to-be-sunk ship, creaking and groaning amid the waves. The sound of this Naxos *Tempest* is realistic and vibrant, and magic is most often signalled by Renaissance music rather than gee-whiz sound effects (though there is some nifty digital fading accompanying Scott Handy's cooing Ariel). Pulling the levers is Ian McKellen's Prospero, though it's the quiet subtleties of his performance that impress most. Some might wish for a more dynamic approach to the miraculous poetry of the part – McKellen's growling "our revels now are ended" is almost thrown away – but it's effectively done, and suits this restrained and pensive production. Emilia Fox sounds a little prim as Miranda, though Benedict Cumberbatch makes a winningly earnest Ferdinand; and the colonial dimensions of the play are registered here by the dignified Caliban of black actor Ben Onwukwe.

# Editions

### Oxford Shakespeare

**Stephen Orgel (ed.); 1987** ▷ Oxford UP

Students (and playgoers) wanting access to recent intellectual approaches to *The Tempest* – many of which have overturned long-cherished verities about the play – should turn immediately to the Oxford Shakespeare and Stephen Orgel's terrific edition. Orgel is a distinguished writer and critic, also the Oxford editor of *The Winter's Tale*, and particularly expert on the lavish seventeenth-century royal entertainments known as masques (many of his essays on these and other topics are collected in *The Authentic Shakespeare*, published in 2002). Given that *The Tempest*'s virtuosic staging contains elements of masque, Orgel is well-placed to offer insights into its theatrical practice, but he is equally informative on a range of topics, ranging from the play's involvement with the New World to its use of history. No fewer than six appendices – one devoted to Montaigne – add formidable range to this edition.

# Some criticism

### Shakespeare's Caliban
**Alden T. Vaughan & Virginia Mason Vaughan; 1991**
▷ Cambridge UP

In the days when *The Tempest* was widely understood as a serene retirement note from Shakespeare, critics still found time to investigate the play's most puzzling and troubling component – Caliban. *Shakespeare's Caliban: A cultural history* joins (and describes) a long tradition of engagement with the "savage and deformed slave" of the Folio's job description. It was assembled in partnership by the Vaughans, literary critics both, who also edit the excellent Arden 3 edition of the play (2003). Their work is predictably engaging, following Caliban's tracks from the historical contexts that most likely spawned him to recent concerns with the play's colonial ramifications. It also looks at his history on stage and screen as well as in visual art. In that sense *Shakespeare's*

*Caliban* is partly a history of changing cultural taste, but the Vaughans' wider observation – that Caliban has been "endlessly transformed yet always recognizable" – underlines the extent to which his mutating shape reveals as much about us as about Shakespeare's play.

### The Tempest and its Travels
**Peter Hulme & William Sherman (eds.); 2000**
▷ Reaktion / Pennsylvania UP

It doesn't have much truck with traditionalist approaches to *The Tempest*, but in every other way this newly commissioned collection goes in for plurality: it includes poems and excerpts from theatrical reworkings of the play along with a welcome focus on visual art (there's a fine piece by David Dabydeen on Hogarth's well-known painting of Act One, scene two, showing Prospero, Miranda and Caliban). Many of the essays here touch on colonial and post-colonial topics located in the New World (somewhat *de rigueur* these days), but others go off in more unusual, if less exotic, directions – among them Robin Kirkpatrick's terrific article on the Italian background to the play and Donna Hamilton's piece on English versions of that great travelling epic, Virgil's *Aeneid*. An illuminating anthology.

# Timon of Athens

The fable of the big-spending man who uses, then loses, all his wealth – with it his wits and everything he owns – is probably as old as money itself, but Shakespeare's variation on the theme ranks as one of his most neglected works. Clearly indebted to the morality plays that toured medieval England, with all their stern warnings about the dangers of avarice, *Timon of Athens* also has certain affinities with Marlowe's *Dr Faustus* in its portrayal of an (anti)hero who risks it all for supreme glory – in Faustus's case by trading his soul for knowledge of the divine, in Timon's by losing his vast Athenian fortune via a lifestyle of sensationally hedonistic proportions. Other contexts for *Timon* could be offered: some have suggested that the play is a philosophical debate between epicurianism and cynicism; others have seen in its bitter, hard-bitten tone shades of *King Lear*, which may have been written soon beforehand (Coleridge suggested that it was "a *Lear* of domestic life"). But where *Faustus* and *Lear* are tragic masterpieces, *Timon of Athens* is less certain in tone, and more puzzling to understand. As it was possibly co-written, the play's place in the canon is still earnestly debated, but audiences have had little opportunity to decide for themselves: it remains one of Shakespeare's least popular works, and is still infrequently revived.

[DATE] Conjectural: some critics argue for a date prior to *King Lear* (c.1605); others put *Timon* close to *Antony and Cleopatra* and *Coriolanus* (1606–08); still others regard it as one of Shakespeare's very last plays – if it is, indeed, fully by him. Thomas Middleton, among others, has been suggested as a collaborator.

[SOURCES] As with the Roman plays, Plutarch's *Lives* in Thomas North's 1579 translation is a key source – enough to feature word-for-word in places. An anonymous play, *Timon* (c.1602), seems to have had some influence, as does William Painter's collection of tales, *The Palace of Pleasure* (1566), the basis for numerous other works by Shakespeare.

[TEXTS] *Timon* first appeared in print in the 1623 Folio (F1) – seemingly in the place where *Troilus and Cressida* was originally meant to go.

## Interpreting the play

The sixteenth-century essayist and philosopher Michel de Montaigne, observing that "what we hate we take to heart", chose Timon of Athens as an example of the kind of man who becomes so possessed by hatred of the world that he flees it. Timon's predicament – in Shakespeare's play he is driven to madness by his own insane generosity and the stinginess of his friends – has a tragic ring to it, but there is also something savagely comic about his story. Forced into poverty, Timon digs for roots but, to his rage, unearths gold coins; abandoning the city, he becomes a hermit who has to deal with an unending stream of greedy visitors. In fact Montaigne mentions Timon while discussing another famous philosophical paradox: whether one should weep over mankind's tragic situation; or, better still, simply laugh at the futility of it all.

## Major Characters & Synopsis

**Lord Timon** of Athens
**Lords** and **Senators** of Athens
Timon's false friends: **Lucius**, **Lucullus**,
 **Sempronius** and **Ventidius**
**Alcibiades**, an Athenian soldier
**Apemantus**, an ill-tempered philosopher
**Servants** of Timon's various creditors
**Flavius**, Timon's steward (head servant)
Timon's other servants: **Flaminius**, **Lucilius** and
 **Servilius**
**Phrynia** and **Timandra**, prostitutes with
 Alcibiades
**Thieves**
A **Poet**, a **Painter**, a **Jeweller** and a **Merchant**,
 all in Timon's pay
An **Old Athenian**
A **Fool**

**ACT 1** Timon's immense wealth – and, more
importantly, his generosity – is talked of throughout Athens, and artists and tradesmen queue up
to gain his favour. Though the Poet has written a
fable warning his patron that Fortune is fickle,
Timon accepts his work, and that of all the others, without blinking, pausing only to pay his
friend Ventidius's bail and to give his servant
Lucilius money so that he can marry his wealthy
sweetheart. Timon has even invited the churlish
philosopher Apemantus to a great banquet for
his fawning friends. Apemantus hurls insults at
the assembled guests and is particularly
incensed when Timon insists on giving expensive
gifts to all and sundry. The fact that Timon is
heavily in debt is known to one man alone – his
steward Flavius.

**ACT 2** Timon's creditors are getting restless
and send their servants to request that he pay his
debts. Flavius is attempting to stall them when
Timon appears and demands to know what is
going on. Flavius informs him that he has squan-
dered his estate by his extravagance and that
there is nothing left to pay off even half of what he
owes. But Timon is undaunted, confident that his
friends will help him out.

**ACT 3** One by one Timon's so-called friends
refuse to assist him, all citing the feeblest of excuses. As the servants of Timon's creditors pursue
their claims, Timon enters enraged, but instead of
paying them invites their masters to dinner one last
time. His guests assemble (thinking that Timon's
good fortune is restored), but when the meal is
served it turns out to be nothing but warm water,
which Timon throws at them as he rails against
their falsity. Meanwhile the soldier Alcibiades has
been banished from Athens for pleading for one of
his soldiers, who is under sentence of death for
manslaughter. Alcibiades storms out, swearing to
have his revenge on the city.

**ACT 4** Though his servants stay loyal to him,
Timon is now insane with anger; he curses the
city and its inhabitants, and departs to live in the
woods. While digging for roots in the forest, he
discovers gold, but still remains implacable in his
hatred – even when Alcibiades appears with two
whores and offers to help him. Timon gives gold
to Alcibiades for his campaign against Athens,
and also to the whores, encouraging them to
spread disease among the citizens. Timon is also
visited by Apemantus, who insists that his misanthropy is just another kind of pride. Only the visit
of Flavius touches his humanity, but Timon dismisses even him.

**ACT 5** The Poet and Painter head to the forest
in the hope of payment, but Timon drives them
away. By this time Alcibiades is threatening
Athens itself, and two Senators, accompanied by
Flavius, hasten to Timon in the hope that he can
help. But Timon, dreaming only of death, is
unmoved, and proclaims that he does not care if
the city is destroyed. As Alcibiades enters Athens,
the senators plead with him to spare the innocent, and he agrees to punish only his enemies
and those of Timon. As the gates of the city are
opened to him, news arrives that Timon has died,
leaving an epitaph that curses his enemies and
exhorts all others to pass by and ignore the
gravestone in front of them.

"A pretty mocking of the life": a debonair Timon (David Suchet) clutches the fruits of his patronage in Trevor Nunn's 1991 production at the Young Vic.

*Timon of Athens* treads a similarly wild territory to *King Lear*, a play to which it has often been compared (and with which it is often dated) since Samuel Taylor Coleridge suggested that it was a kind of "after vibration" to that great tragedy. Both have heroes who descend into insanity in response to the unkindness of others, yet who are themselves tragically culpable; both, too, expose the painful fact that, when it arrives, there is nothing noble about madness. *Coriolanus*, also, with its own hero who is unable to adjust to his place in society, resembles *Timon*; but perhaps its closest Shakespearian cousin is the playwright's earliest tragedy, *Titus Andronicus*, which counterpoises comic and tragic themes with such unsettling effect that even now audiences can struggle to take it all in. Where Titus's sufferings are so unbearably intense that he bursts out laughing, exclaiming that "I have not another tear to shed", Timon's bitter misanthropy expresses itself in brilliantly scabrous insults against anyone – or anything – who has the misfortune to get in his way. It is difficult to know whether to laugh, cry or rant with him.

Like *Titus*, *Timon*'s status as genuine Shakespeare has frequently been questioned. Dr Johnson, noting "perplexed, obscure, and probably corrupt" stretches of text, was among the first to query whether it was in fact unfinished, though he approved of its moral value (a quality he felt all too deficient in Shakespeare). By doing so he unleashed two large questions that still dominate critical discussion about the play: if *Timon* is finished; and whether it was co-written, perhaps with the young and brilliant Thomas Middleton. As Karl Klein, one of its most recent editors, goes to some lengths to demonstrate, even with the aid of computerized statistical analysis it is almost impossible to prove that Shakespeare did *not* write significant sections of the play – so the question, for many, remains open. Though for many years critics found it tempting to assume that the playwright suffered some kind of nervous breakdown during this phase of his career (Shakespeare-as-Timon, it might be said), as *Timon* has been more widely read – if not necessarily more frequently performed – it has been appreciated as a work of art in its own right.

# Without price

Not that the play itself has unmixed thoughts about the status of art. *Timon* begins with a Poet, Painter and various other craftsmen and salesmen, all gathering to pay their respects to the "worthy lord" Timon – and of course to advertise their work in the hope of selling it to him. The importance of patrons like Timon was a fact of life for jobbing playwrights and poets (Shakespeare himself had dedicated two poems, *Venus and Adonis* and *The Rape of Lucrece*, to the Earl of Southampton, and the 1623 Folio was addressed to two starry aristocrats), but nowhere else in Shakespeare's drama is the paradoxical place of art in the fiscal economy so openly explored. Commending the Painter's piece as "admirable", insisting that "it tutors nature", the Poet explains that his own work will do something similar. It warns Timon to beware of the "great flood of visitors" who cluster around him in the hope of material reward. Should Fortune decide to look the other way, the Poet insists, those crawling admirers will be the first to desert Timon:

> When Fortune in her shift and change of mood
> Spurns down her late belovèd, all his dependants,
> Which laboured after him to the mountain's top
> Even on their knees and hands, let him fall down,
> Not one accompanying his declining foot.

**[1.1.85–9]**

Timon's fall, when it does come, will be horribly lonely: his fawning "dependants" will not hesitate to make themselves scarce as soon as trouble arises.

But the Poet's stark warning is not by any means disinterested. For one thing, Timon accepts the poem without even reading it, warmly inviting the author to dinner without a second thought. For another, as Apemantus sourly jibes, the Poet is as bad as the rest – poetry, like painting or jewellery, is a flattering art, and the Poet writes in order to earn a living. Furthermore, as the Jeweller observes of the costly gem he presents to Timon,

> My lord, 'tis rated
> As those which sell would give; but you well know
> Things of like value differing in the owners
> Are prizèd by their masters.

**[1.1.172–5]**

Which is to say that everything is relative: value has no value when money is involved. What something is worth depends entirely on what someone else is prepared to pay for it. That goes for poetry too; and Timon is prepared, as with everything else, to pay the highest of prices. One question that the play poses is whether a Jeweller and a Poet can be thought of as the same type of salesman: one selling precious stones, the other pleasing words.

Another problem in *Timon* – in fact Timon's own problem – is that, contrary to the Jeweller's assertion, the hero doesn't "well know" the value of possessions at all. Or rather, his apparently boundless munificence blurs the meanings of value so grossly that it becomes impossible to know the real worth of anything, as gifts of astronomical price exchange hands between his intimates as liberally as if they were free. The word "priceless" does not appear in this play (Shakespeare seems to have invented it, but used it just once in his entire career, in *The Rape of Lucrece*) but the concept of something that is worth everything and yet nothing hovers over it continually. At the lavish banquet thrown for his friends at the end of Act One, Timon receives extravagant gifts from his acquaintances – "Four milk-white horses trapped in silver" from Lucius, "two brace of greyhounds" from Lucullus – but no sooner are they delivered than Timon demands that other, costlier, presents be returned to them in compensation. As he declares to Ventidius, "there's none / Can truly say he gives if he receives" (1.2.9–10). In this way the workings of gift exchange become as debased as those of the financial economy: Timon's friends give him things not out of "free love" (as Lucius obsequiously declares) but because they hope they will get something even more valuable in return. A concept familiar to cultures around the globe, for *Timon*'s first audiences this competitive gift-giving may also have played on contemporary anxieties about inflation, which had sky-rocketed throughout the 1590s to the point that indebtedness had become more commonplace than ever before.

> *The act of giving is for Timon its own aesthetic thrill; a man who will bestow anything on anybody is as superbly indifferent to particular persons and use values as the most mean-spirited miser ... His munificence is thus rather like money itself, perturbing all particular values in its restless expansiveness.*
>
> Terry Eagleton, *William Shakespeare* (1986)

There is more than a touch of fantasy to Timon's unstoppable largesse, and he is as free with his promises as he is with his possessions. "Methinks I could deal kingdoms to my friends, / And ne'er be weary," (1.2.220–1), he exclaims, and his friends no doubt hope that he will. But watching helplessly as his lord liberally dispenses jewels to his dinner guests, his steward Flavius knows that Timon's spectacular behaviour is just that – a spectacle. "What will this come to?" he frets,

> He commands us to provide and give great gifts,
> And all out of an empty coffer;
> Nor will he know his purse, or yield me this:
> To show him what a beggar his heart is,
> Being of no power to make his wishes good.
> His promises fly so beyond his state
> That what he speaks is all in debt, he owes
> For every word.

**[1.2.191–9]**

"He is so kind," Flavius mournfully continues, "he now pays interest for it." Behind the appearance of infinite wealth lurks the spectre of poverty: despite acting as if nothing has a price-tag (if you need to know, after all, you can't afford it), Timon is himself without worth, his very "words" indebted to his creditors.

## The yellow slave

Despite Flavius's nerves, when those creditors begin circling the steward is forced to tell all. Apprising his master about the state of his balance sheet – to Timon's utter disbelief – Flavius sets in train events that will occupy the rest of the play. To his credit, Timon springs into action with impressive resolution, at first demanding that his land be sold (Flavius reveals it has already gone) and then suggesting that his "friends" will of course help him out. But Timon's judgement of character is even less finely attuned than his awareness of his accounts: one by one, over three extraordinary scenes, those friends decline to assist a man who has given them so much. Lucullus has the cheek to claim that Timon had it coming to him, and offers a far tinier amount than Timon had requested; Lucius is free with his promises but, when pushed, pleads poverty; and Sempronius affects to be offended that Timon did not come to him first – and then refuses altogether.

In a seemingly fateful echo of the events of *Titus Andronicus*, Timon decides to get his revenge by inviting them all to dinner. But his approach will be less grisly than his Roman counterpart, Titus, who famously bakes a pie from the sons of his guest-of-honour. Timon decides to give his former friends food for thought instead: serving them with bowls full of stones and warm water, he shouts, "Uncover, dogs, and lap":

> May you a better feast never behold,
> You knot of mouth-friends. Smoke and lukewarm water
> Is your perfection. This is Timon's last,
> Who, stuck and spangled with your flattery,
> Washes it off, and sprinkles in your faces
> Your reeking villainy.
>
> **[3.7.87–92]**

It is fitting that events come to a head at dinner, given that at the play's previous feast – one sufficiently opulent to boast a chorus of dancing girls and a boy dressed as Cupid – the play's resident cynic, Apemantus, had exclaimed: "O you gods, what a number of men eats Timon, and he sees 'em not! It grieves me to see so many dip their meat in one man's blood" (1.2.38–40).

As Timon's situation worsens, images of cannibalism begin to reverberate in his language too. Though the bloody events of *Titus* are not repeated, his words continually hark back to the earlier tragedy – and of course to a tragedy narrowly averted, that of Antonio in *The Merchant of Venice*. Facing baying demands for his creditors' "bills", Timon offers the messengers nothing less than his body in repayment:

TIMON
    Knock me down with 'em, cleave me to the girdle.
LUCIUS' SERVANT  Alas, my lord.
TIMON  Cut my heart in sums.
TITUS' SERVANT  Mine fifty talents.
TIMON
    Tell out my blood.
LUCIUS' SERVANT         Five thousand crowns, my lord.
TIMON
    Five thousand drops pays that.

**[3.4.88–93]**

If comparisons with Antonio seem obvious, for some critics Timon's betrayal by his so-called "friends" is nothing less than an analogue to Christ's betrayal by Judas, especially so given that images of them drinking his blood and eating his body seem to tally with the flesh-and-blood substance of the Christian Eucharist, which itself replays Christ's final supper with his disciples. Other commentators, however, find it difficult to squeeze that much nobility out of the situation – particularly given that Timon's tragic mistake is, strictly speaking, his reluctance to confront the accountants.

That is not quite how Timon sees it, perhaps understandably enough. In his view it is not his own behaviour that is at fault, but money itself – a conclusion that is reinforced by a bitter irony, for when he attempts to dig the ground for roots he somehow turns up gold. Counting it out in his hands, he addresses the "yellow slave" wonderingly:

> O, thou sweet king-killer, and dear divorce
> 'Twixt natural son and sire; thou bright defiler
> Of Hymen's purest bed; thou valiant Mars;
> Thou ever young, fresh, loved, and delicate wooer,

Whose blush doth thaw the consecrated snow
That lies on Dian's lap; thou visible god,
That sold'rest close impossibilities
And mak'st them kiss, that speak'st with every tongue
To every purpose; O thou touch of hearts:
Think thy slave man rebels, and by thy virtue
Set them into confounding odds, that beasts
May have the world in empire.

**[4.3.384–95]**

Karl Marx quoted Timon's words in his early *Political Economy and Philosophy* (1844), describing the way in which money acts as "the universal whore ... the alienation of human capacity" in early capitalist societies, but it is tempting to say that in doing so he missed (or chose to ignore) Shakespeare's larger suggestion. Timon diagnoses money as the root of his woes – the alienating effect of money, which perverts good things into evil – when in fact it is his alienation from himself and others that initiates his downfall. Even in pouring scorn on the "sweet king-killer", in fact, Timon is unable to get away from its glistening allure. Blaming money for everything, like giving vast quantities of it away, has no meaning: the no-holds-barred totality of both acts strips them of any significance. As Apemantus declares to Timon on a trip to the forest, "the middle of humanity thou never knewest, but the extremity of both ends" (4.3.302–3).

In fact Timon's attack on money seems to express a kind of terrible poverty of spirit. While Lear's ravings, expressing in a convoluted way the king's own terrible guilt at his personal failings, have a kind of savage grandeur, Timon's are passionate only in their absolute hatred of absolutely everything – himself excluded. Handing gold to a group of thieves who come across his den in the forest, he promises to "example you with thievery", but his philosophy is limited in its scope:

The sun's a thief, and with his great attraction
Robs the vast sea. The moon's an arrant thief,
And her pale fire she snatches from the sun.
The sea's a thief, whose liquid surge resolves
The moon into salt tears. The earth's a thief,
That feeds and breeds by a composture stol'n
From gen'ral excrement.

**[4.3.437–44]**

We can all understand Timon's feelings, but his problem is that he doesn't learn or change. Longing for death, he fails to repent or acknowledge his mistakes. All that is left is a curse, as his self-written epitaph records: "Here lies a wretched corpse," it begins,

'Of wretched soul bereft.
Seek not my name. A plague consume
  You wicked caitiffs left!
Here lie I, Timon, who alive
  All living men did hate.
Pass by and curse thy fill, but pass
  And stay not here thy gait.'

**[5.5.71–8]**

Laid out like a morality play it may be, but in the end *Timon of Athens* denies there is anything to learn.

# Stage history and adaptations

From a twenty-first-century perspective it seems apt that, in theatrical terms at least, *Timon of Athens* disappeared as soon as it was written. There is no evidence that the play was performed in Shakespeare's lifetime – cannon-fodder for critics who argue that it was unfinished or somehow suppressed for political reasons. But *As You Like It, All's Well, Antony and Cleopatra* and others are in a similar position, so it is difficult to draw firm conclusions, just as it's difficult to say whether **Thomas Middleton** was involved in writing it, as some believe, or not.

In any event, the first performance on record is that of an adaptation, **Thomas Shadwell's** *The History of Timon of Athens, the Man-Hater*, which first appeared in 1678 and lasted for the next half-century. Shadwell adjusted the dramatis personae as well as adding a love story, catering for the new fashion for actresses by giving Timon two mistresses. At least he had good personnel: **Thomas Betterton** took the lead with his wife **Mary** as the faithful Evandra, while **Henry Purcell** put together the music. This adaptation was among the most popular of its time, but when in 1771 **David Garrick** wanted to put on the play at Drury Lane in 1771 with **Spranger Barry** in the lead, he commissioned **Richard Cumberland** to come up with a more modern version, which further moralized Shakespeare's play. This saw twelve performances, but by this stage *Timon* was on the way out: another adaptation from 1786, this time by **Thomas Hull**, achieved only one performance before being pulled. One great might-have-been of the period is a translation by **Catherine the Great** of Russia, left unfinished at her death in 1796.

**George Lamb** put together a text somewhat resembling Shakespeare's for performance at Drury Lane in 1816, but it was his lead, the perfectly cast **Edmund Kean**, who stole the show: with a script skewed to flatter Timon's better parts, Kean was described by one witness (with a newly fashionable adjective) as "electrical", but he gave a mere seven performances of the play. **Samuel Phelps** put on *Timon* in a more Shakespearian text at Sadler's Wells in 1851, and achieved a surprise hit – he staged it again five years later, this time with an impressive panorama of Athens dominating the set. Even so, this would be the last London production of the century, and *Timon* would not be staged again in Britain until **Frank Benson**'s three-act redaction at Stratford in 1892. Benson continued the time-honoured tradition of playing Timon nobly, but the play was not one of his triumphs.

Several stagings were put on in the interwar period, but all of them struggled to find audiences. **Robert Atkins** at the Old Vic (1922) and **William Bridges-Adams** (1928) up in Stratford attempted to find new angles on the play, while in 1935, directing for London's Westminster Theatre, **Nugent Monck** simply decided to cut those parts of the text he assumed not to be by Shakespeare. Monck also inserted a ballet scene and employed the young **Benjamin Britten** to follow in Purcell's footsteps and write the music. All these versions would be thrown into relief, however, by **Willard Stoker**'s Birmingham Rep production of 1947, which opened its doors to a war-weary city by setting the play in modern-day Athens and making Timon's cave a bomb crater.

Productions since have been distinguished by their contrasting presentation of Timon himself – all the way from **Tyrone Guthrie**'s harshly satirical Old Vic version (1952), which painted the hero in an unflattering light, to **Paul Scofield**'s sensitive interpretation for **John Schlesinger** at the RSC in 1965. As with Peter Brook's *Lear* a few years previously (see p.180), Schlesinger drew out the Beckettian images in Shakespeare's text, representing a society eating itself alive in corruption. Brook himself directed *Timon* in 1973 at the Bouffes-du-Nord complex, employing a French translation by **Jean-Claude Carrière** for his Parisian audience. Notable for its cheerful breaking of theatrical taboos (not least that of the stage's imaginary "fourth wall"), Brook's was a Marxist-inflected production that has been described as the play's finest twentieth-century incarnation. **Richard Pasco** sensed a defining humanity in Timon when he played him for **Ron Daniels** at Stratford's The Other Place ten years later, but the Japanese setting of Daniels's production was ridiculed by many critics.

Oddly, perhaps, for a play that seems so in touch with latter-day cynicism about conspicuous consumption, productions of *Timon* have remained few and far between. It has had some success in Germany (**Frank Patrick Steckel**'s 1990 production, heavily influenced by Brecht, attracted international attention), but to date only two major British stagings have made it past the drawing-board. **Trevor Nunn**'s version at the Young Vic in 1991 looked askance at a newly post-Thatcherite London – money-obsessed and bitterly divided between rich and poor – but attracted criticism for being over-literal in its detailing and its ironing-out of the play's oddities, although **David Suchet**'s impressively characterized Timon was applauded by many. **Gregory Doran**'s 1999 RSC version was perhaps a more rounded achievement, emphasizing *Timon*'s links with the homosocial world of James I's court as well as its contemporary resonances. **Michael Pennington** was widely praised for his performance in the title role, as was **Duke Ellington**'s musical score (composed for **Michael Langham**'s 1963 production at Stratford, Ontario) – just the latest in a series of starry musical connections for one of Shakespeare's oddest plays.

## Screen

### Timon of Athens
**J. Pryce, J. Welsh, N. Rodway; Jonathan Miller (dir.)**
UK, 1981 ▷ Ambrose Video (BBC) `DVD` `▭`

The rarely produced *Timon* is one of those plays the BBC Shakespeare was designed to showcase to posterity, but its making proved unhappy: Michael Bogdanov was initially hired to direct, but his insistence on doing it in modern dress (an option ruled out by series policy) guaranteed his ignominious exit. Miller took over the project, and despite those early troubles what emerges is persuasive, especially in the first half of the action – where Timon's spendthrift house is a forest of wealthy ruffs and conspicuous quaffing reminiscent of Dutch militia paintings. There are problems after this, however: Jonathan Pryce plays Timon as sympathetic and wronged throughout, and correspondingly struggles to present the crazed dementia the play demands. Miller's conclusion attempts tragedy, but *Timon* itself is reluctant to go that far. Recently rereleased in the US by educational publishers Ambrose Video.

## Audio

### Timon of Athens
**A. Howard, N. Rodway, D. Lewis; Clive Brill (dir.)**
UK, 1998 ▷ Arkangel `⊙` `▭`

A shame that Alan Howard never got to play Timon on stage – the full-throttle reading he produces for this audio version makes you wish you had a chance to see him do the part. In contrast to Pryce, this Timon is petulant and misdirected from the off, and while Howard gives little hint of insecurity or eagerness to please, it's a strategy that delivers impressive results in the crazed latter stages of the play. In early scenes Norman Rodway's abrasive and embittered

Apemantus forms an unlikely duet with John McAndrew's youthful and anxious steward Flavius in attempting to put on the brakes, but Howard's descent into madness is too much a juggernaut for that. The rest of the cast is mixed – those in supporting roles (and there are a fair few) sound a bit uninspired and there is some over-enthusiastic chortling in the crowd scenes. That said, the giddy pace of Timon's court forms a vivid contrast with the wilderness outside Athens, and the role of Damian Lewis's commanding and impressive Alcibiades provides some kind of catharsis, as well as a surprisingly moving finale.

## Editions

### Oxford Shakespeare
**John Jowett (ed); 2004** ▷ Oxford UP

John Jowett's impressive edition is a recent addition to the Oxford stable, and it continues the series policy of editorial radicalism: this *Timon* is boldly credited to "William Shakespeare and Thomas Middleton". Jowett's presentation of the text, as with his *Richard III* (see p.304), is meticulously done, but before getting to the script itself you're offered over 120 pages of introductory material. This might seem excessive, but Jowett uses thematic headings – "Misanthropy", "Giving and Sacrifice", "Debt" and so on – to break the flow, so the whole thing feels like a series of insightful and interlinked mini-essays. There's plenty to think about here, not least Jowett's verdict on the involvement of Middleton, based on textual analysis that purports to identify the playwrights' separate linguistic fingerprints. Not that you have to delve into bibliography to connect with the play: Jowett's introduction moves smoothly from critical questions on *Timon* to the most detailed stage history currently available. His appendices include a list of major productions and Shakespeare's major source materials.

# Some criticism

## The Structure of Complex Words
**William Empson; 1951** ▷ Penguin / Michigan UP [o/p]

One of the most brilliantly independent critics in the history of English studies, William Empson remained as cheerfully iconoclastic at the end of his career as at its outset, when he switched from studying maths at Cambridge to focus on literature. Though the concept behind *Complex Words* is less esoteric than elsewhere (other studies include *Seven Types of Ambiguity* and *Some Versions of Pastoral*), Empson's rich insights do require navigation through tables and equations – his way of notating the relationships between certain words. Algebra-phobes would do best to skip to the tiny but terrific cadenzas on keywords in works from Pope, Milton, Wordsworth and many others. As Empson notes in *Seven Types*, "it is impossible to avoid Shakespeare in these matters", and words such as "honest" in *Othello* and "sense" in *Measure for Measure* bring into focus extended lines of enquiry. But it's the discursive nature of his approach that proves the most fun: his quizzical analysis of the strange permutations experienced by the word "dog" in *Timon* sees the author at his best. Also worth looking at is Empson's *Essays on Shakespeare* (1986), which collects his late work with some earlier pieces.

## Timon of Athens
**Rolf Soellner; 1979** ▷ Ohio State UP [o/p]

Though it may be difficult to get hold of, Soellner's *Timon* is the only book-length survey of the play (it is bulked out with various appendices, including a stage history by Gary Jay Williams, useful enough but obviously not up to date) – an interesting contrast with Empson's nine brilliant pages. Subtitling his study "Shakespeare's pessimistic tragedy", Soellner lays his cards decisively on the table, arguing that *Timon* deserves full tragic status and taking issue with those – like Wilson Knight in *The Wheel of Fire* (see p.182) – who defend the play solely by reading it in providential terms. Soellner persuasively insists that, instead of succumbing to such idealizations, we should understand the play as a study in pessimism and materialism. Though it's worth keeping your mind open as you read, Soellner's detail on the philosophical background to the play is engaging and instructive.

# Titus Andronicus

B y some distance Shakespeare's most wilfully grisly play, for most of its history *Titus* has been written off as a sensationalistic excursion into the kind of blood-spattered drama that thrived on the 1590s stage – video nasty rather than *film noir*. Commenting on the fact that several of its characters end up cooked in a pie, the eighteenth-century editor George Steevens gaily proclaimed that in this play "*justice* and *cookery* go hand in hand", while his twentieth-century equivalent, John Dover Wilson, simply thought the whole thing "a huge joke". But in recent years critics have begun to take *Titus* more seriously: its exposition of the themes of tragic madness and cyclical revenge have been seen to foreshadow the grander achievements of *King Lear* and *Hamlet*; interest in the classical origins of this most fiercely well-read of tragedies has uncovered its inventiveness with source detail; and powerful productions by Peter Brook (1956) and Deborah Warner (1988), among others, have demonstrated that *Titus* has much to offer engaged – and open-minded – audiences.

[DATE] *Titus Andronicus* was an instant success when it hit the stage in January 1594, and was probably written shortly before – perhaps in collaboration with the dramatist George Peele.

[SOURCES] The play has no direct sources, yet classical motifs predominate: a copy of Ovid's *Metamorphoses* actually appears on stage, and the story of Lucrece (employed in *The Rape of Lucrece*) is another analogue. The success of Thomas Kyd's *The Spanish Tragedy* (1592) and other Elizabethan blockbusters indicates that blood-and-guts Senecan tragedy was all the rage in the 1590s.

[TEXTS] A quarto (Q1) was printed in 1594, and went through two more editions – 1600 (Q2) and 1611 (Q3). The Folio version (1623) is based on the last.

## Interpreting the play

The bad reviews are impossible to ignore. T.S. Eliot declared *Titus* "one of the stupidest and most uninspired plays ever written", complaining of "a wantonness, an irrelevance about the crimes". Much the same thing was said four hundred years earlier by one Jacques Petit, a French tutor who witnessed a private performance and was sufficiently unimpressed by it to record that "the spectacle had more value than the theme". Edward Ravenscroft, whose own version of *Titus* replaced Shakespeare's on the Restoration stage, was equally ungracious about his source, condemning it as "a most incorrect and undigested piece … rather a heap of Rubbish than a Structure". Editors have been, if anything, more damning: J.C. Maxwell wrote in 1953 that "*Titus* is neither a play with a complicated staging nor one which will ever be widely read"; a few years earlier, John Dover Wilson thought it "like some broken-down cart, laden with bleeding corpses from the Elizabethan scaffold". As Stanley Wells wryly remarks, "Shakespeare's earliest tragedy was a great success in its own time and has been regarded as a terrible mistake almost ever since."

On the face of it, the criticisms are easy enough to understand. *Titus* contains horrors. One of its characters is raped, then grotesquely mutilated to keep her quiet. The action culminates in a cannibalistic banquet, itself capped by a killing spree. It requires some of the grisliest props in the

# Major Characters & Synopsis

## THE ROMANS

**Saturninus**, eldest son of the late Emperor of Rome, later Emperor himself

**Bassianus**, Saturninus's younger brother

**Titus Andronicus**, a Roman general

**Marcus Andronicus**, Titus's brother, a tribune of the Roman people

**Lucius**, **Quintus**, **Martius** and **Mutius**, sons of Titus

**Lavinia**, Titus's only daughter

**Young Lucius**, Lucius's son

**Publius**, Marcus's son

**Sempronius**, **Caius** and **Valentine**, relations of the Andronici

**Aemilius**, a Roman

## THE GOTHS

**Tamora**, Queen of the Goths (later Saturninus's wife)

**Alarbus**, **Demetrius** and **Chiron**, Tamora's sons

**Aaron**, a Moor in Tamora's service and her lover

**ACT 1** The Emperor of Rome is dead and his sons, Saturninus and Bassianus, vie for the succession. A third candidate, Titus Andronicus, is nominated as the people's choice, but must bury those sons who have died fighting the Goths. As part of the rites, the son of Tamora, Queen of the Goths, is sacrificed – despite his mother's pleas. Titus then rejects the crown in favour of Saturninus, who offers to marry Titus's daughter Lavinia. But Lavinia is betrothed to Bassanius, and – with the aid of Titus's remaining sons – the two escape. Titus is outraged, and kills his son Mutius who attempts to defend them. Saturninus denounces the Andronici family and decides to marry Tamora instead. Tamora appears to reconcile the quarrelling parties, but plans to wipe out the Andronici with Saturninus.

**ACT 2** Tamora's sons, Chiron and Demetrius, are arguing over Lavinia. Aaron interrupts and suggests that they take her by force rather than woo her. Titus, meanwhile, has organized a hunt in the forest for Saturninus, during which Tamora (now Empress) slips away to find Aaron. Discovered by Bassianus and Lavinia, Tamora gets her two sons to murder Bassianus, after which they drag off Lavinia. Aaron then lures two of Titus's sons, Quintus and Martius, into the pit where Bassianus's body has been

dumped, and fetches Saturninus. The brothers are further implicated by a letter (fabricated by Aaron), and Saturninus orders their execution. In another part of the forest, Lavinia, who has been raped and had her hands and tongue cut off, is discovered by her uncle Marcus.

**ACT 3** Titus vainly pleads for Quintus and Martius, and another son, Lucius, is banished for trying to rescue them. Marcus then enters with the mutilated Lavinia, and Titus and Lucius are filled with horror. Aaron interrupts with a message from the Emperor: he will release Quintus and Martius on condition that either Titus, Lucius or Marcus cut off one of their hands. Titus agrees, but for nothing – his hand is returned with the heads of his two sons. Titus's response is to laugh, crazed by shock. Later that evening, when Marcus kills a fly, Titus denounces it as murder.

**ACT 4** Lavinia identifies her attackers by pointing to the tale of Philomel in Ovid's *Metamorphoses* and inscribing their names in the sand. Titus responds by sending a gift of weapons with a message to Chiron and Demetrius, knowing they will be unable to decipher it. Aaron alone realizes that Titus means revenge, but he is distracted by the arrival of a nurse with his newborn baby by Tamora, which she wants killed because of its dark skin. Aaron saves the baby's murder but kills the nurse to stop her talking. Titus, meanwhile, is apparently mad; he bemoans the absence of Justice and orders arrows to be shot into the sky with messages for the gods. At the palace, Saturninus is alarmed to hear that Lucius is marching on Rome at the head of a Goth army.

**ACT 5** Thinking that Titus is mad, Tamora, Chiron and Demetrius appear at his house dressed up as Revenge, Rape and Murder. Realizing who they are, Titus agrees to summon Lucius to dine with the Emperor and Empress. But after Tamora leaves, Titus unleashes a gruesome plan. First he kills Chiron and Demetrius and bakes them in a pie, which he offers to Tamora and Saturninus. He then kills Lavinia; reveals the ingredients of the dinner; and stabs Tamora. Titus is immediately killed by Saturninus, who is himself killed by Lucius. Elected Emperor, Lucius orders that Aaron be executed and Tamora's body be thrown to wild beasts.

canon ("*Enter a Messenger with two heads and a hand*", one notorious stage direction instructs). And, as one recent editor points out, *Titus* still manages to push the boundaries of taboo. Following their rape of Lavinia, Chiron and Demetrius first cut out her tongue, then amputate her hands. Then they torment her (and the audience) with appalling wisecracks about it:

CHIRON
Go home, call for sweet water, wash thy hands.
DEMETRIUS
She hath no tongue to call, nor hands to wash …

**[2.4.6–7]**

The gouging-out of Gloucester's eyes in *King Lear* barely compares – that is perplexing and brutal, this is a craziness way beyond. So it is, too, when Titus finds out that cutting off his hand in order to save his imprisoned sons' lives has been pointless (they are already dead). He responds not with tears, but with laughter:

MARCUS
Why dost thou laugh? It fits not with this hour.
TITUS
Why, I have not another tear to shed.

**[3.1.264–5]**

## It fits not

"It fits not" could stand as an epigraph for *Titus Andronicus*; it specializes in squeezing distressing events into beautiful patterns. Shakespeare uses classical sources throughout his career, but in *Titus* (if the play is solely by him; some think it is a collaboration with the minor dramatist George Peele) he often breaks them down, forces them into gruesome new settings. To many critics (audiences have rarely been given the opportunity to see it), the most glaring disjunction occurs when Marcus catches sight of his mutilated, speechless niece. Instead of going to Lavinia's aid – instead, indeed, of being struck dumb by horror – he addresses her in bizarrely stylized rhetoric:

> Why dost not speak to me?
> Alas, a crimson river of warm blood,
> Like to a bubbling fountain stirred with wind,
> Doth rise and fall between thy rosèd lips,
> Coming and going with thy honey breath.
> Be sure, some Tereus hath deflowered thee
> And, lest thou shouldst detect him, cut thy tongue …
> Fair Philomel, why she but lost her tongue
> And in a tedious sampler sewed her mind.
> But, lovely niece, that mean is cut from thee.
> A craftier Tereus, cousin, hast thou met,
> And he hath cut those pretty fingers off
> That could have better sewed than Philomel.

**[2.4.21–43]**

It is one of the most difficult points in the play. Marcus's first reaction is not to deal with the primacy of Lavinia's (horribly real) injuries, but to reach for a classical precedent, that of Philomel's rape by Tereus in Book 7 of Ovid's *Metamorphoses*. Furthermore, the way in which Marcus aestheticizes her anguish – comparing her bleeding mouth to a "bubbling fountain", her amputated limbs to "sweet ornaments" – is deliberately confrontational. Marcus's lengthy speech does more than make us gaze in horror at the spectacle (much as we gaze in wonder at the climax of *The Winter's Tale*): it forces us to consider a terrible gulf between florid words and theatrical reality, made even more striking here by the play's otherwise clear and direct language.

Yet Marcus is quite right: Lavinia's suffering is in conscious imitation of Philomel's, as becomes still clearer when Lavinia is attempting to explain what has happened by the most efficient means possible – by finding a copy of the *Metamorphoses* and pointing to the relevant passage. Titus realizes what she is trying to communicate:

> Lavinia, wert *thou* thus surprised, sweet girl,
> Ravished and wronged as Philomela was,
> Forced in the ruthless, vast, and gloomy woods?
> See, see. Ay, such a place there is where we did hunt—
> O, had we never, never hunted there!—
> Patterned by that the poet here describes,
> By nature made for murders and for rapes.

**[4.1.51–7]**

Ovid provides Shakespeare's "pattern", even the woods play out their preordained role. Lavinia, it might be said, is sacrificed to her source. Even her death at her father's own hands is modelled on the classical hero Virginius, who slew his own "enforced, stained, and deflowered daughter" to spare her shame – "a reason mighty, strong, effectual," as Titus grimly exclaims:

> A pattern, precedent, and lively warrant
> For me, most wretched, to perform the like.

**[5.3.42–4]**

It is not enough that Titus kills his daughter like a character in Livy; he provides reasons for his action like a good Renaissance schoolboy. Lavinia is hardly the only abused woman to appear at Shakespeare's behest – *The Rape of Lucrece*, using many of the same sources, also dates from this period – but it is interesting to note how bookishly he treats her.

Critics have noted other classical parallels at work in *Titus*. In this, his earliest tragedy, Shakespeare adopts the motifs of revenge drama, then doing the rounds on the Renaissance stage. Like Kyd's *The Spanish Tragedy*, a lurid and popular example of the genre, this play contains a cycle of revenge which involves three protagonists, Tamora, Aaron and Titus – all done along the lines of the Roman tragedian, Seneca, whose own retellings of revenge exerted a powerful influence on Renaissance drama. Again, though, Shakespeare doesn't go for subtle remodelling. As with Lavinia's much-stressed parallels with Philomel, Tamora attempts to trap Titus (murderer of her sons) not by acting out her revenge, but by actually *acting* Revenge, thinking him mad enough to believe her. Disguised in her "strange and sad habiliment", she announces: "I am Revenge,"

>               sent from th'infernal kingdom
> To ease the gnawing vulture of thy mind
> By working wreakful vengeance on thy foes.
> Come down, and welcome me to this world's light.
> Confer with me of murder and of death.
> There's not a hollow cave or lurking-place,
> No vast obscurity or misty vale
> Where bloody murder or detested rape
> Can couch for fear, but I will find them out,
> And in their ears tell them my dreadful name …

**[5.2.30–39]**

She has read the script, it seems, as has her paramour Aaron, who in one of his most cartoonishly villainous moments threatens "murders, rapes, and massacres, / Acts of black night, abominable deeds" (5.1.64–5).

## O, vengeance!

The tragedy of revenge is probably as old as drama itself. The Greek tragedian Aeschylus produced in around 458 BC what remains Western theatre's most ancient dramatic cycle: the **Oresteia**. This sequence of three plays tells the story of the hero Orestes, who is set on a murderous path to revenge when his mother Clytemnestra kills his father Agamemnon (itself an act of vengeance for Agamemnon's sacrifice of their daughter Iphigenia, Orestes's sister). Driven by fierce hatred and a command from Apollo, Orestes hunts down Clytemnestra and brutally butchers her – whereupon Furies rise up and pursue him. They are called off only after the intervention of Athena, goddess of justice and patroness of Athens.

This is both the problem and the – literally – fatal attraction of revenge: the cycle of violence is potentially inexhaustible. The attraction for dramatists is obvious, and in the work of the Roman playwright **Seneca** (d. 65 AD), much influenced by the Greeks, the genre became gorier than ever. Seneca's most famous revenge tragedy is *Thyestes*, which sees the eponymous hero seducing his brother Atreus's wife and stealing his kingdom. Calling upon vengeance to harden his heart, Atreus gets his own back in the grisliest way imaginable, by tricking Thyestes into eating a banquet prepared from the flesh of his own sons.

Elizabethan writers knew their Seneca, and in the first years of Shakespeare's career revenge tragedy was all the rage. The bestselling play of the 1590s was *The Spanish Tragedy*, written by trained legal clerk **Thomas Kyd**. Watched over by a character actually named "Revenge", the *Tragedy* tells the lurid tale of a Spanish official named Hieronimo whose son is killed in cold blood. Though crazed by grief, Hieronimo manages to uncover the identities of the two murderers by putting on a play in which he himself stars, before killing them. Standing over their bodies, he declares that the revenge cycle has come full-circle (before biting out his tongue rather than explain his actions):

My guiltless son was by Lorenzo slain,
And by Lorenzo and that Balthazar
Am I at last revenged thoroughly,
Upon whose souls may heavens be yet revenged,
With greater far than these afflictions.
Methinks since I grew inward with revenge,
I cannot look with scorn enough on death.

[4.4.191–9]

The end of Kyd's own life was nearly as sensational as his play: after being imprisoned following the arrest of Christopher Marlowe in 1592, Kyd denounced his former room-mate to the authorities and died soon afterwards, broken by his experiences in jail.

Closely modelled on Kyd's Hieronimo is Shakespeare's Titus. Though there is no obvious source for *Titus Andronicus*, revenge co-writes its plot: Titus executes Tamora's sons; she and Aaron arrange for Bassianus to be murdered and Lavinia raped; and Titus retaliates by capturing Chiron and Demetrius and cooking them in a pie. This gruesome finale glances back to *Thyestes*, but it also prepares the way for Shakespeare's later experiments with revenge motifs, which work their way into many of his works. Shakespeare's most famous revenge tragedy is of course *Hamlet*, but here it is the hero's difficulties acting as a revenger that dominate the tragedy. Although he puts on a play, just like Hieronimo, Hamlet misses his opportunity to kill Claudius in its aftermath. And by the time that he brings himself to act, Hamlet's own death – itself an act of revenge for the murder of Polonius – has already been arranged for him.

# A wilderness of tigers

But *Titus* does more than investigate classicism; its human actions point forward to Shakespeare's greatest dramatic achievements. Titus is the most developed character in the play, and his journey as a father forms its emotional centre. His mourning farewell to his sons is moving (not least because of its pre-echoes of the extraordinary song from *Cymbeline*, "Fear no more the heat o'th' sun"):

> In peace and honour rest you here, my sons;
> Rome's readiest champions, repose you here in rest,
> Secure from worldly chances and mishaps.
> Here lurks no treason, here no envy swells,
> Here grow no damnèd drugs, here are no storms,
> No noise, but silence and eternal sleep.

**[1.1.150–5]**

But there is more than emotion at stake here. In Shakespeare's first dramatic exposition of the self-sacrificing severity of Rome, it is Titus's early mistake not to realize that, as he puts it later, the city has become a "wilderness of tigers" and "affords no prey / But me and mine" (3.1.53–5). The tomb in which his sons reside, standing centre-stage throughout this extremely long first scene, is in fact where most of Titus's family is located; like the tomb in *Romeo and Juliet* (written a year or two later), it actually comes to replace his family. Titus's faltering awareness of the importance of his family is strongly counterpointed in the play by the behaviour of his sons – one of whom, Mutius, he hacks to death after the young man defends his brother Bassianus. That brotherly solidarity is also embodied in the figure of Marcus, who stands alongside Titus throughout his sufferings and is one of the few survivors left on stage at the play's end, movingly promising his fellow Romans that they will come together once more as a people and a family, knitting "this scattered corn into one mutual sheaf" (5.3.69–70). It doesn't say a great deal for Titus that even the villainous Aaron is a more loving, if no less bloody, father to his newborn child: seizing the boy from (then stabbing) the Empress's Nurse, he refuses to let him be killed – something insisted on by Tamora, who will not tolerate the "treacherous hue" of the baby's black skin.

Notably, when Titus uses the word "love" first, it is to describe his service to his ruler. His journey towards a fuller understanding of the concept foreshadows that of Lear – both are driven to the point of madness, both suffer for their lack of emotional understanding. As Titus struggles to comprehend the "reason for these miseries" (he can see none), his horrified empathy with his daughter gives way to powerful liquid imagery in one of the play's most impressive soliloquies:

> When heaven doth weep, doth not the earth o'erflow?
> If the winds rage, doth not the sea wax mad,
> Threat'ning the welkin with his big-swoll'n face?
> And wilt thou have a reason for this coil?
> I am the sea. Hark how her sighs doth blow.
> She is the weeping welkin, I the earth.
> Then must my sea be movèd with her sighs,
> Then must my earth with her continual tears
> Become a deluge overflowed and drowned,
> Forwhy my bowels cannot hide her woes,
> But like a drunkard must I vomit them.

**[3.1.220–30]**

In this emotive speech – a sign of Shakespeare's growing dramatic skill – Titus describes himself conjoined not only with his daughter ("She is the weeping welkin [heavens], I the earth"), but with the distant memory of his sons, themselves insulated from "storms" like these.

> [Titus Andronicus] *shows a pitilessness, a sharp predilection for the ugly, a titanic quarrel with the gods, such as we find in the first works of the greatest poets.*
>
> Heinrich Heine, *Shakespeare's Girls and Women* (1838)

But this speech propels Titus into the only expression of love the play allows him – he must "vomit" revenge. In one sense, his tragedy is also the play's grimmest joke: his father's love is ridiculous in its futility. Titus cuts off his hand to save his surviving sons, but to no avail; love for his daughter eventually forces him to kill her. In this company, it is ironic but "fitting" that his sincerest expression of familial love concerns a fly killed by Marcus:

> How if that fly had a father, brother?
> How would he hang his slender gilded wings
> And buzz lamenting dirges in the air!
> Poor harmless fly,
> That with his pretty buzzing melody
> Came here to make us merry—and thou hast killed him!

**[3.2.60–5]**

Just as the play's bizarre use of classicism makes its audiences think again, so this tender lament for a dead insect is counterpointed with the fact that its human characters are often treated like meat (literally so, given that two of them are baked in a pie). Even Lucius's closing promise, as he stands over the "poor remainder of Andronici", to "knit again … These broken limbs into one body" (5.3.69–71), is a kind of bitter joke. Far from being moronic, it might be said that *Titus* ranges across the extremes of human emotion – all the way from black humour to genuine sorrow and back again. Titus laughs because he has "not another tear to shed"; if we find some elements of the play difficult to understand, it is because it explores so much.

## Stage history and adaptations

The first mention of the performance history of *Titus Andronicus* appears courtesy of **Philip Henslowe**, the owner of the Rose theatre, who noted in his book of accounts that the play was "new" (probably completely new, rather than revived) in January 1594, and that it had done well at the box-office. **Richard Burbage**, who had already played Titus's model Hieronimo in *The Spanish Tragedy* and would later play Hamlet and Lear, presumably created the lead role. But what would probably have been a successful and long run for *Titus*, such as the *Henry VI* plays enjoyed, was cut short by an outbreak of plague at the end of the month, when the theatres were shut down. The play was rushed into print in February, in all likelihood to avert a financial crisis for the players. It was revived later in the year when Shakespeare's company toured outside the city, transferred to the Blackfriars – when the "fly scene" (3.2) was perhaps added – and was popular up to and beyond the closure of the theatres in 1642. (**Ben Jonson** was sufficiently jealous of its success that he inserted a barbed reference to it in *Bartholomew Fair*.)

*Titus* was also performed privately at the house of **Sir John Harington** in Rutland in 1596, though from the comments of his tutor (see p.348), it appears to have been less suited to that exclusive audience. Its early life is further illustrated by the existence of a pen-and-ink drawing, supposedly by the draughtsman **Henry Peacham**; though it conflates several different episodes from the play, it reveals that Elizabethan actors made little effort to costume in "Roman" attire. Early on, *Titus* was also popular outside England: it was translated into German by **Frederick Menius** as *Eine Sehr Klägliche Tragaedia von Tito Andronico* and printed in 1620. A work by the Dutch dramatist **Jan Vos** as *Aren en Titus*, published first in 1641 then in no fewer than 28 editions by 1726, is more than likely an adaptation of Shakespeare's play.

Following the Restoration reopening of the theatres, Shakespeare's version continued to be acted but was shunted off the boards in 1678 by **Edward Ravenscroft**'s adaptation, *Titus Andronicus; or, The Rape of Lavinia*. This gave Aaron a beefed-up role and had his young child killed by Tamora in yet another revenging twist, but was in other respects remarkably faithful to the original – particularly when compared with other Restoration remakes (see p.176). It was revived frequently, with the famously declamatory **James Quin** – an actor who insisted on performing only tragic parts – playing Aaron in the 1720s.

Equally enthusiastic about Aaron's potential was the African-American actor **Ira Aldridge**, who commissioned in the 1850s what would turn out to be the only nineteenth-century British revival of *Titus*. Basing his interpretation on his other celebrated Shakespearian role, Othello, Aldridge made Aaron an essentially noble character whose relationship with Tamora was consciously legitimized. Aldridge's adapter, **C.A. Somerset**, was careful to omit anything that might offend squeamish audiences – including Lavinia's rape and mutilation – resulting in "a play not only presentable but actually attractive", as one reviewer put it. Another American, the actor-playwright **N.H. Bannister**, had introduced the play to Philadelphian audiences back in 1839. Though Bannister claimed that "the language of the Immortal Bard" was retained, he took pains to assure audiences that his text cut "every expression … calculated to offend the ear".

Difficulties of decorum also confronted **Robert Atkins** at the Old Vic in 1923, but he bravely dusted off Shakespeare's full text nonetheless – the first time it had seen the stage for nearly 250 years. Though some theatregoers fainted, Gordon Crosse thought the production "thoroughly enjoyable in spite of the horrors". In contrast, the Japanese writer **Shoyo Tsubouchi** seems, if anything, to have revelled in the play's horrors when he translated *Titus* in 1926, comparing it to the notorious brutalities of Kabuki theatre.

But the play's potential was most radically realized by **Peter Brook** at Stratford-upon-Avon in 1955, where abstract stylization was employed to dignify its subject: **Vivien Leigh**'s glamorous Lavinia entered following her rape with ribbons, not blood, trailing from mouth and hands (Brook was accused of "squeamishness" by Evelyn Waugh, never a man to avoid nastiness), and some seven hundred lines were cut overall. The visual impression was similarly emblematic: Brook's enormous set was lit in visceral colours which advanced unremittingly towards a blood-red finale. **Anthony Quayle** played Aaron to **Maxine Audley**'s hyper-exotic Tamora, but it was **Laurence Olivier**'s haggardly lyrical Titus which most impressed the reviewers: Kenneth Tynan described how "a hundred campaigns have tanned his heart to leather, and from the cracking of that heart there issues a terrible music … the noise made in its last extremity by the cornered human soul"; J.C. Trewin thought that Olivier's cry of "I am the sea!" made "its surge beat on the world's far shore". It was all the more remarkable an achievement given that Leigh and Olivier were splitting up at the time – she would take advantage of her costume and whisper insults to her soon-to-be-ex-husband while they were actually performing.

Despite Brook's success, *Titus* has remained on the margins: along with *Timon of Athens*, it has featured on the RSC's list of productions guaranteed to make a loss – perhaps the

"What book is that she tosseth so?" The mute and mutilated Lavinia (Sonia Ritter) uses Ovid to communicate with her father (Brian Cox). Deborah Warner's 1987 production at the RSC pummelled audiences with the grim realities of Shakespeare's text.

only reason why **John Barton**'s bizarre double-bill of *Titus* and *The Two Gentlemen of Verona* (1981) actually made it past the drawing-board. But **Deborah Warner**, who directed the play at Stratford's Swan Theatre in 1987 in its most successful recent incarnation, demonstrated that the play could be trusted in its own terms. Where Brook stressed abstraction, Warner went for grim violence: **Sonia Ritter**'s bruised, groaning Lavinia had the stumps of her arms covered with clay to stem their bleeding and **Brian Cox** Titus's cut off his own hand on stage with a cheese wire – though Warner carefully avoided the use of fake blood until the deaths of Chiron and Demetrius in order to maximize the shock. The text remained intact, Warner deliberately courting the audience's laughter by Cox's chef's-hatted hero, who whistled an infamous tune from *Snow White* while preparing his grisly banquet.

Surprises lay in store for the cast of **Gregory Doran**'s 1994 touring production to Johannesburg (*Titus* was memorably described by Doran as "Shakespeare in Tarantino mode"), which saw Aaron applauded for his defiance by a predominantly black audience. The play's most recent mainstream production on home turf, that directed by **Bill Alexander** at Stratford, garnered praise for its unflinching representation of violence – even if most headlines were generated by the RSC's decision to team up with the National Blood Service, who parked a donation van outside the doors.

Out of the theatre, as within it, *Titus* has not featured largely. Two screen versions have been made, both directed by women. **Jane Howell** directed the BBC TV version of 1985, with **Trevor Peacock** in the lead, in a warmly received production which attempted to position the action from the viewpoint of the play's sole innocent, Young Lucius. **Julie Taymor** attempted a similar strategy in her Hollywood version of 1999 (which starred **Anthony Hopkins** as Titus and **Jessica Lange** as Tamora), but with far zanier results; her film enthused some critics but confused others.

# Screen

## Titus
**A. Hopkins, A. Cumming, J. Lange; Julie Taymor (dir.)**
USA, 1999 ▷ Fox 🔲 ▭

You can't but admire Julie Taymor's courage: fresh from transferring Disney's cuddly *The Lion King* to the Broadway stage, she decided to do her first movie – basing it on Shakespeare's grisliest play. And, though the studios wouldn't touch it, she got it made. Whether you admire her film might be a different matter: the play's precarious balance between crazed brutality and crazed comedy is tilted decisively in favour of the latter, and Taymor's decision to go for high camp could be regarded as an easy way out of its moral ambiguities. But the excellent cast redeems their director's excessive eclecticism: Anthony Hopkins is superbly cast as Titus, putting in a persuasively grizzled performance – somewhat in the mould of Olivier – which illustrates well his character's naivety about matters political (even if it's difficult not to think of the inimitable Dr Lecter as the play approaches its flesh-munching climax). Alan Cumming, the campest of the lot, is also excellent as a ravingly extreme Saturninus, and Laura Taylor's poignant Lavinia is very finely done.

# Audio

## Titus Andronicus
**D. Troughton, H. Walter, P. Joseph; Clive Brill (dir.)**
UK, 1998 ▷ Arkangel ⊙ ▭

So how *do* you stage this most visually violent play on audio? If this Arkangel version is anything to go by, with plenty of sickening sound effects. But to concentrate on these would be entirely unfair, for producing *Titus* must be like juggling with high explosives, and this is a very well-cast and serious-minded version. Troughton sounds perhaps surprisingly young in the lead, but that's all to the good: his mad scenes have a touching tenderness about them that tougher actors might miss; while Harriet Walter, too, proves that there is plenty more to Tamora than wicked witch. Paterson Joseph is good as Aaron, but is perhaps missing that last ounce of dangerous sarcasm. The rape of Lavinia (Emma Gregory) is traumatically presented – her noisy weeping is a bitter counterpoint to the scenes afterwards – and in fact the whole middle section of the play makes for raw and uncomfortable listening. This is the way it should be, of course, but you are warned: *Titus* is upsetting, somehow especially so without the visuals.

# Editions

## Arden Shakespeare (third series)
**Jonathan Bate (ed.); 1995** ▷ Thomson

As the Renaissance man behind *Shakespeare and Ovid* (1993), a *tour-de-force* analysis of Shakespeare's transformation of classical forms, Jonathan Bate proves the perfect guide to *Titus Andronicus*, perhaps the most perverse yet classically influenced play in the canon. A troublesome text receives sympathetic and scrupulous treatment, and Bate helpfully reprints some of its "patterns and precedents" – the material Shakespeare plundered to assemble his earliest tragedy. What emerges from this stout defence of *Titus*'s virtues is, in the editor's words, a drama which is a "complex and self-conscious improvisation upon classical sources". What it doesn't spend much time on, however, is the notion that the play is co-written – a topic on which Bate has recently shifted his ground, suggesting that George Peele may have been involved after all.

# Some criticism

## Shakespeare and Classical Tragedy
**Robert S. Miola; 1992** ▷ Oxford UP [o/p]

Like Jonathan Bate, Robert Miola has written extensively on Renaissance reworkings of classical material. This slim study traces what T.S. Eliot called, rather too elegantly, "the penetration of Senecan sensibility" into the work of Shakespeare and his colleagues. Despite Eliot's loathing of the play, *Titus Andronicus* is an obvious calling-point, and Miola's chapter on it is especially interesting both as a defence of *Titus* and of Seneca himself – perhaps the most maligned tragedian of all. Moving between the twin poles of "Heavy Seneca" (serious responses) to "Light Seneca" (comic and tragic-comic retellings), the book also covers *Hamlet*, *Richard III*, *Macbeth*, *King Lear* and *A Midsummer Night's Dream*.

## Titus Andronicus: Critical Essays
**Philip C. Kolin (ed.); 1995** ▷ Garland

It has been the fate of *Titus Andronicus* to be sat awkwardly at the fringes: interesting things have been said about the play, but all too often in the esoteric, out-of-the-way crannies of Shakespearian scholarship. This makes Philip Kolin's labours in bringing together a substantial (518-page) slab of criticism on the play especially worthwhile. The essays here are cast into two sections, "*Titus* and the critics" and "*Titus* on stage", prefaced by Kolin's own detailed analysis of the critical legacy. They vary in quality, but there are some real gems – Heather James on cultural disintegration in the play, Robert Miola (see above) on "Rome and the Family" and David Bevington's analysis of stagecraft. The lack of an index is irritating, however.

# Troilus and Cressida

O nce memorably described as "the work of a man whose soul is poisoned with filth", *Troilus and Cressida* has consistently scandalized critics over the four centuries or so since it was first produced. Audiences have had less opportunity: a cleaned-up version by Dryden notwithstanding, it was regarded as unperformable until the very end of the nineteenth century, and only in modern times has this most cynical and nihilistic of plays found a welcoming environment. Written as Shakespeare approached his forties, *Troilus and Cressida* is the earliest of his so-called "problem plays", and it nearly didn't make the First Folio due to copyright issues – in the event it was squeezed in between the Comedies and the Tragedies. And if ever there were a play that made those generic labels difficult to believe in, it's *Troilus and Cressida*. Not a history, comedy or full-scale tragedy, despite having elements of all three, this story of a futile love affair trapped in the middle of an apparently endless conflict is also a scathing satire on the glory and chivalry of the Trojan War, which in this play often seem to be little more than a front for lust, vanity and misogyny. Or, as Thersites – the play's most cynical character – sums it up: "Lechery, lechery; still, wars and lechery: nothing else holds fashion."

[DATE] Though certainly penned after 1598, *Troilus and Cressida* resists more accurate dating: on the basis of internal style, 1601–02 seems most likely.

[SOURCES] Chaucer's poem, *Troilus and Criseyde* (1385–87), is the most direct source – Shakespeare possibly recalled it from memory – but numerous others influence the play: Robert Henryson's fifteenth-century *Testament of Cresseid*, Chapman's *Homer* (1598), William Caxton's *Recuyell of the Histories of Troy* (1475).

[TEXT] Perplexingly, two slightly variant quarto texts – Qa and Qb – were published in 1609 (see p.364). Despite copyright snags, it was squeezed into the 1623 Folio in a version perhaps based on a revised quarto text, including a Prologue not otherwise present.

## Interpreting the play

The story of the Trojan War is one of the defining legends of Western literature. It was canonized in the *Iliad*, the great Greek epic credited to Homer and written down some time in the eighth century BC. Poem and poet alike were regarded with supreme reverence by the ancient Greeks, and the tale of Troy, along with the flamboyant manner of its telling, filtered down to Virgil, who took it as the basis for his founding Roman epic, the *Aeneid*, composed some eight hundred years later. It was another millennium and a half before the works of Homer made it into English, via the poet George Chapman – a masterly translation that took him eighteen years to complete.

By the early seventeenth century, when Shakespeare was in his late thirties, reworkings of the Troy story had begun to stack up. In addition to Chapman's *Homer*, the first chunk of which was published in 1598, there had been several plays on the subject and a number of poems – all of which makes it hard to pin down precisely what the playwright drew upon

## Major Characters & Synopsis

**Prologue**, dressed as an armed man

### THE TROJANS
**Priam**, King of Troy
Priam's sons: **Hector**, **Deiphobus**, **Helenus** (a priest), **Paris**, **Troilus** and **Margareton** (a bastard)
**Cassandra**, Priam's daughter, a prophetess
**Andromache**, Hector's wife
**Aeneas** and **Antenor**, Trojan commanders
**Pandarus**, a lord
**Cressida**, Pandarus's niece
**Calchas**, Cressida's father (who has defected to the Greeks)
**Alexander**, Cressida's servant

### THE GREEKS
**Agamemnon**, commander-in-chief of the Greeks
**Menelaus**, Agamemnon's brother
**Helen**, Menelaus's wife (now living with Paris)
Greek commanders: **Nestor**, **Ulysses**, **Achilles**, **Diomedes**, **Ajax**
**Patroclus**, Achilles's companion
**Thersites**, an ill-tempered wit
A **Servant** attending on Diomedes

**ACT 1** Seven years on, the Trojan War is locked in stalemate. Inside Troy itself, however, Troilus is more concerned with wooing Cressida via her uncle Pandarus. Although Cressida affects disdain, it is a ploy and she is already in love with him. In the Greeks' camp, meanwhile, their commander Agamemnon bemoans the war's lack of progress. Ulysses blames a breakdown in control, intimating that their finest warrior, the arrogant Achilles, is undermining Agamemnon's authority. When the Trojan warrior Aeneas arrives with a message from Hector challenging any of the Greek warriors to single combat (a challenge clearly meant for Achilles), Ulysses and Nestor resolve to humble Achilles by choosing the doltish Ajax instead.

**ACT 2** Ajax is questioning Thersites about what is going on, but is answered by insults. Achilles arrives (with his friend Patroclus) and tells Ajax of Hector's challenge, about which Achilles then feigns indifference. Back inside Troy, King Priam and his sons are angrily debating whether they should return Helen to the Greeks and end the war. Hector argues that she is not worth fighting for, but Troilus defends her, at which point

Cassandra bursts in raving and predicting the destruction of Troy unless Helen is given up. Paris justifies his original abduction of her, and the brothers are temporarily reconciled – the war goes on.

**ACT 3** Pandarus has finally arranged a meeting between Troilus and Cressida, but fails to make himself scarce. Initially nervous, the couple make a vow of mutual constancy before retiring to the bedroom – unaware that Cressida's father, the defector Calchas, has arranged for his daughter to be ransomed for the Trojan prisoner Antenor. As Ajax prepares for the fight, the other Greek commanders cold-shoulder Achilles and Ulysses explains to him that his reputation is in decline.

**ACT 4** Aeneas breaks the news to Troilus: Diomedes has arrived with Antenor, who is to be exchanged for Cressida. With little time left, the couple tearfully exchange love tokens, and Troilus begs Cressida to remain faithful to him. In the Greek camp, meanwhile, preparations for the combat have been finalized; Cressida and Diomedes arrive, closely followed by Hector, Aeneas and Troilus. Ajax and Hector begin to fight, but Hector calls a halt on the grounds that the two are cousins. Hector is then welcomed by the Greeks as an honourable foe, but the mood is soured when the piqued Achilles rashly challenges him to combat.

**ACT 5** During the feasting on the eve of battle, Ulysses takes Troilus to Calchas's tent to find Cressida. As they approach, they witness Cressida flirting with Diomedes and giving him one of Troilus's love tokens. Troilus cannot believe his eyes, but is soon beside himself with rage and vows to kill Diomedes. Back inside Troy, Hector arms himself for the fight – despite his wife and sister's attempts to dissuade him. Troilus also prepares for battle, tearing up an unread letter sent by Cressida. As battle commences, personal vendettas take precedence: Troilus fights both Diomedes and Ajax, and Achilles demands vengeance when his beloved Patroclus is killed. Though beaten back by Hector, Achilles sneaks up on him with a group of soldiers and has him brutally murdered, even though he is unarmed. As news reaches the Greeks, they become convinced that victory will be theirs. Troilus mourns the loss of Hector and plans revenge; when Pandarus appears, he curses him.

when writing *Troilus and Cressida*. His title points to one major source, Chaucer's *Troilus and Criseyde* (1385–87), an elegant and poignant version of a fragment from the tale also related by Boccaccio, but it seems likely that Shakespeare also knew the very first book printed in English, William Caxton's *Recuyell* [Anthology] *of the Historyes of Troye* (1471–76), as well as John Lydgate's *Troy Book* (1412–21). These last provided him with a narrative which simply doesn't appear in Homer – the tale of the lovers Troilus and Cressida, whose tragic separation over the battle lines at Troy provides an eloquent inset to the nine-year war for the city.

## All the argument

But in Shakespeare's hands that story is not, as we might expect, all that noble. Troilus enters the play almost literally incapacitated by love, unable to fight or even sleep. Where Rosalind in *As You Like It* winningly admits that she is "fathom deep" in love, Troilus describes despairingly to his go-between Pandarus how it is his "hopes" that lie "drowned":

> I tell thee I am mad
> In Cressid's love; thou answer'st 'She is fair',
> Pourest in the open ulcer of my heart
> Her eyes, her hair, her cheek, her gait, her voice;
> Handlest in thy discourse, O, that her hand,
> In whose comparison all whites are ink
> Writing their own reproach, to whose soft seizure
> The cygnet's down is harsh, and spirit of sense
> Hard as the palm of ploughman. This thou tell'st me—
> As true thou tell'st me—when I say I love her.
> But saying thus, instead of oil and balm
> Thou lay'st in every gash that love hath given me
> The knife that made it.

**[1.1.51–63]**

Love is abject, painful – in the first of the play's many haunting images of disease, Troilus describes how his heart is made such an "open ulcer" by love that even Pandarus's description of Cressida's beauty (especially her white hands, softer than the "cygnet's down") is a "knife" that wounds him. In Troilus's eyes there is nothing liberating, still less pleasurable, about passion: it is illness and injury, aptly enough given that the cause for which the Greeks and Trojans have fought so long is the retrieval of Helen, wife of the Spartan king, who has been abducted by the Trojan prince Paris.

Pandarus's advice is merely to "tarry", and as the play develops it becomes apparent why Troilus is being left to wait – because of Cressida's conviction that only by waiting do men learn the value of what they are after. "Women are angels, wooing," she pointedly observes,

> Things won are done. Joy's soul lies in the doing.
> That she beloved knows naught that knows not this:
> Men prize the thing ungained more than it is.

**[1.2.282–5]**

Perhaps she is right: surrounded by men (Shakespeare never puts her on stage with the play's few other female characters), Cressida is keenly aware that she must retain her value in the sexual marketplace. That those same men, having "gained" Helen and thus triggered the Trojan War, are now debating whether the queen is "worth what she doth cost", as Hector sourly puts it (2.2.50), only makes Cressida's position seem more fragile.

If there is one thing in this play that the Greeks and Trojans have in common, ironically enough, it is disgust for Helen and the war they are compelled to fight in her name. Though Troilus joins Paris in defending Helen's beauty and reputation, it is no accident that he describes her as a commodity, twisting Marlowe's infamous lines from *Doctor Faustus* to emphasize the "price" of the woman who has "launched above a thousand ships / And turned crowned kings to merchants (2.2.81–2). The Greek Diomedes, discussing the same subject with his enemy Paris later in the play, is not convinced by Troilus's sense of Helen's value: "She's bitter to her country," he spits:

> For every false drop in her bawdy veins
> A Grecian's life hath sunk; for every scruple
> Of her contaminated carrion weight
> A Trojan hath been slain. Since she could speak
> She hath not given so many good words breath
> As, for her, Greeks and Trojans suffered death.

[4.1.70–6]

In Diomedes's cruel analysis it is Helen's body, "contaminated" by the frank sexuality that has led her to desert her husband, that is the root of their trouble. Thersites, perhaps the most cynical voice of all in the play, boils down still further what he thinks the war over Troy is really about: "All the argument is a whore and a cuckold," he remarks sarcastically; "a good quarrel to draw emulous rival factions and bleed to death upon" (2.3.71–3).

> *Troilus and Cressida* has no story, or is as near to having none as a Renassaince play can be.
>
> Barbara Everett, *Young Hamlet* (1989)

Thersites's point would perhaps have little force (he is, as he admits to Hector, "a rascal, a scurvy railing knave, a very filthy rogue" (5.4.26–7)) were it not for the fact that when we do get to see Paris and Helen together a scene later, as Pandarus tries ham-fistedly to prepare the ground for Troilus and Cressida, it becomes only too obvious that there is nothing even faintly ennobling in their relationship. While Helen acts the skittish schoolgirl, petulantly demanding attention – and Pandarus is ordered to sing a grimly obscene song to amuse the court – Paris muses, to the best of his shallow abilities, on some insights into love. Troilus "eats nothing but doves, love," he nudgingly informs Helen,

> and that breeds hot blood, and hot blood begets hot thoughts, and hot thoughts beget hot deeds, and hot deeds is love.

[3.1.124–6]

Every bit as obsessed with the body as Diomedes (or other of the play's male characters), Paris regards love and lust as entirely interchangeable. Perhaps Thersites is right: in *Troilus and Cressida* there is little to show for so much sacrifice. Blood – the blood of war as much as what Hector calls the "distempered blood" of passion (2.2.168) – is much of what the play is about.

Paris is not the only one of Shakespeare's characters to prove a disappointment – the play's subplot rests upon a tawdry attempt to undermine Achilles, the Greeks' greatest warrior but so insufferably arrogant that his compatriots Ulysses and Nestor agree to teach him a lesson. When the Trojan Hector sends a challenge to the Greeks to single combat, they deliberately exclude him from the competition and support the "blockish" Ajax instead, hoping to rile Achilles in the process. When the day for the combat arrives, Ajax and Hector begin fighting, only to stop when Hector realizes they are cousins. As a lull in the fighting beckons, the two sides seem, momentarily, to come to an understanding – until Achilles manages to puncture the bonhomie by turning up and challenging Hector to fight. In the bitter final battle of the play, Achilles even arranges to have his enemy murdered in cold blood. So much for chivalry.

## No sooner got

The fraught issues that crowd the relationship between Paris and Helen – and which also touch Hector's macho scorn for his wife Andromache – do not bode well for the play's pivotal love affair. On hold for what seems like an eternity, by the time Troilus and Cressida finally manage to meet, over halfway into the play, the tension between them is embarrassingly painful. Waiting (yet again) for Cressida to arrive at their assignation, Troilus cannot stop thinking about death, comparing himself to "a strange soul upon the Stygian banks / Staying for waftage" (3.2.8–9). When Cressida does appear, the couple seem unable to find the right things to say, let alone understand what the other is thinking. Troilus exclaims, "You have bereft me of all words, lady," and the confusion between them does not dissipate:

CRESSIDA  Will you walk in, my lord?
TROILUS  O Cressida, how often have I wished me thus.
CRESSIDA  Wished, my lord? The gods grant—O, my lord!
TROILUS  What should they grant? What makes this pretty abruption? What too-curious dreg espies my sweet lady in the fountain of our love?
CRESSIDA  More dregs than water, if my fears have eyes.

**[3.2.53–65]**

Cressida's first words can – and have – been interpreted in a bewildering multiplicity of ways, and acted in just as many. Her "will you walk in?" sounds disturbingly like a prostitute calling to her client, but it could just as easily be a plea to escape from the omnipresent Pandarus, who, as ever, is doing his utmost to ruin the occasion by hanging around and making leering wisecracks (the word "pander", meaning "pimp", is rooted in his name).

The point is that Shakespeare leaves it open, much as he leaves Cressida's character open to diametrically opposed interpretations. She has been characterized (usually by male critics) as a sex-hungry vixen; as an emblem of female independence in a misogynistic world; and as someone who is herself betrayed by actions over which she has no control. Though Cressida seems clear-eyed about the difficulties surrounding their relationship – far more so than Troilus, who is content to trot out patronising clichés about the "fountain of our love" – just a few lines later she is fumbling to explain why she played hard to get for so long:

But though I loved you well, I wooed you not—
And yet, good faith, I wished myself a man,
Or that we women had men's privilege
Of speaking first. Sweet, bid me hold my tongue,
For in this rapture I shall surely speak
The thing I shall repent.

**[3.2.123–8]**

Cressida's fear that her words will betray her is a haunting pre-echo of the play's conclusion, further intensified by the vows that the lovers take almost immediately afterwards. While Troilus swears, awkwardly, that he will be "as true as truth's simplicity, / And simpler than the infancy of truth", Cressida rushes to seal her side of the bargain:

> If I be false, or swerve a hair from truth,
> When time is old and hath forgot itself,
> When water drops have worn the stones of Troy
> And blind oblivion swallowed cities up,
> And mighty states characterless are grated
> To dusty nothing, yet let memory
> From false to false among false maids in love
> Upbraid my falsehood. When they've said, 'as false
> As air, as water, wind or salty earth,
> As fox to lamb, or wolf to heifer's calf,
> Pard to the hind, or stepdame to her son',
> Yea, let them say, to stick the heart of falsehood,
> 'As false as Cressid'.
>
> [3.2.180–92]

People did say "as true as Troilus" in the Renaissance, just as they did "as false as Cressida"; the lovers confront the historical aftershocks of their actions without realizing it. The dramatic irony here is so extreme as to be bitterly absurd. While Chaucer's Criseyde frets that her behaviour towards Troilus will "shende" (ruin) not only her reputation but that of women everywhere, Shakespeare's Cressida blindly ensnares herself without even knowing it. Far from being a perfect relationship cruelly broken off by fate – as Chaucer and others present it – in this play it seems stillborn from the first moment.

The morning after the lovers spend their one and only night together, news arrives that Cressida's traitorous father and the Greeks want to swap her – a literal exchange in a play full of metaphorical ones – for the Trojan prisoner Antenor. She must leave at once for the Greek camp, and their affair will be, as Pandarus exclaims in an uncomfortable echo of Cressida's words about wooing, "no sooner got but lost" (4.3.1). The Trojan leadership's eager consent to the deal – Antenor is militarily useful – is a compound betrayal, but Troilus, ever the loyalist, greets the news with a stiff upper lip. Yet his response to Cressida's apparent flirtation with Diomedes, which comes (though he does not know it) just after a welcome by the Greek generals in which she is required to kiss each in turn while they banter about her attractiveness, is less restrained. Watching in hiding as she surrenders to Diomedes the love token he gave her just a few scenes earlier, Troilus cannot believe what he sees:

> This, she? No, this is Diomed's Cressida.
> If beauty have a soul, this is not she.
> If souls guide vows, if vows be sanctimonies,
> If sanctimony be the gods' delight,
> If there be a rule in unity itself,
> This is not she.
>
> [5.2.140–5]

"This is and is not Cressid," he continues, battling to overlay his fantasized vision of her with the new reality. Far from believing that he and she are indissoluble, he is agonized by the fact that Cressida might have a life separate from his thoughts of her. As Troilus is coming to realize, there is in fact no "rule in unity itself".

Except that this lack of unity is not by any means new, as Cressida herself explained to him at their first, anxious, meeting:

> I have a kind of self resides with you—
> But an unkind self, that itself will leave
> To be another's fool.
>
> [3.2.144–6]

Though her words are simple (a rarity in a play noted for its difficult, knotty language), Cressida's thoughts are densely intricate. She means – if she entirely knows what she means – that while part of her "resides", and wants to reside, with Troilus, she also despises herself for becoming "another's fool". That sense of internal dislocation goes some way to explaining why she acts as she does, and in so doing why she lives up to the reputation for which she had become notorious by the time Shakespeare's play reached the stage. Her betrayal of Troilus is also a betrayal of herself – but so was her getting-together with Troilus in the first place.

Once Troilus is jilted – if he truly is (Cressida writes him a letter, but he dismisses it out of hand and we are not permitted to hear its contents) – the play brings to an end its cycle of betrayals. Despite Andromache's misgivings, and Cassandra's lurid premonitions of disaster, Hector is determined to fight and heads out to battle. Though he soon faces his arch-enemy Achilles, their first fight is inconclusive and they separate. But when news arrives that Patroclus, Achilles's favourite (and perhaps lover), has been killed, Achilles orders, then carries out, Hector's death – unarmed and in cold blood. This epic betrayal, so immense that it touches even *Hamlet*'s players, who act Hecuba's lament over Hector's corpse in front of the Prince, effectively ends the action of the play, which closes with Troilus's bitter insistence that "no space of earth shall sunder our two hates" (5.10.28).

But Troilus is not permitted to have the last word. In the earliest text of the play it is the bawd Pandarus who closes the action, ruminating on the betrayal of his own reputation. After being struck by Troilus for his behaviour, he complains:

> O world, world, world!—thus is the poor agent despised. O traitors and bawds, how earnestly are you set a work, and how ill requited! Why should our endeavour be so desired and the performance so loathed?

**[Additional Passage B]**

Pandarus's final words are as grimly punning as ever, and they provide a troubling ending to the play. The impression the audience is left with is hardly one of epic tragedy – the kind of tragedy enshrined in Hector's death – but nor are Pandarus's jokes about "endeavour" and "performance" easy to laugh at, given the horrendous separation endured by the lovers. *Troilus and Cressida* ends, like its position in the First Folio, stuck somewhere uncomfortable between tragedy and comedy.

# Stage history and adaptations

Mystery hangs over the early years of *Troilus and Cressida*, mainly because it was published in quarto in 1609 with two sets of front matter – one claiming that the play had never been "stal'd with the stage", the other insisting that it had been performed at the Globe by the King's Men, Shakespeare's regular troupe. The latter seems more likely, but for many years scholars believed (and some still do) that the play was written for performance at an **Inns of Court** (law school), as with *The Comedy of Errors* and *Twelfth Night* – though neither of these plays shows much sign of being customized for a legal audience.

The play's life in the following century is not much clearer: it possibly resurfaced at Dublin's Smock Alley Theatre in the 1670s, then was heavily adapted by **John Dryden** in 1679. Like Dryden's other rewritings, his approach in *Troilus and Cressida; Or, Truth Found Too Late* was invasive: expressing his determination to save the play's "many excellent thoughts" from a "heap of rubbish", the playwright rewrote it almost entirely, transforming Cressida into a virtuous victim who only pretends to fall in love with Diomedes before conveniently committing suicide. In the first cast were **Thomas Betterton**'s Troilus alongside the Andromache of his wife **Mary**.

Aside from infrequent revivals of Dryden up to the 1730s, *Troilus and Cressida* genuinely disappeared from the stage until the very end of the nineteenth century – a fate not suffered even by *Timon of Athens* or *Pericles*. Initially translations of Shakespeare's text appeared in Germany and elsewhere in Europe (Berlin saw productions in 1899 and 1904, Munich one in 1898), and on home turf audiences had to wait until 1907 and **Charles Fry**'s London staging. In the event most critics were baffled, though in **William Poel**'s Elizabethan production five years later they were won over, not least by a milliner turned actress called **Edith Evans**, then making her debut. By this time, **Frank Benson** had put on all Shakespeare's plays up at Stratford with the exception of *Titus Andronicus* and *Troilus*, though Poel eagerly accepted the invitation to remedy half the deficit by touring it there in 1913.

It was no accident that interest in so world-weary (and war-weary) a play as *Troilus* began to boom after the horrors of World War I. **Robert Atkins**'s Old Vic production from 1923 failed, mounted as the last in his series of plays put on to celebrate the tricentary of the First

Troilus (Denholm Elliott) and Ulysses (Eric Porter, far right) catch Cressida (Dorothy Tutin) succumbing to Diomedes (David Buck). This 1960 *Troilus and Cressida*, co-directed by Peter Hall and John Barton, set the action on an expanse of glittering white sand.

Folio, but **Ben Iden Payne** encountered more success with an Elizabethan staging at Stratford in 1936. Yet probably the play's defining production in this era was **Michael Macowan**'s at the Westminster Theatre in 1938, just a year before war was declared once again. Macowan put *Troilus* in a smart-set 1930s context, immortalized by **Max Adrian**'s dissolute, bow-tied Pandarus.

**Anthony Quayle**'s 1948 Stratford production captured some of the exhaustion of postwar Britain, though **Glen Byam Shaw**'s 1954 successor was more openly cynical about conflict, starring Quayle as a fussy and wearisome Pandarus. The growing fashionability of the play is attested by **William Walton**'s opera from the following year, and in 1955 Shakespeare's text would receive infamous exposition in **Tyrone Guthrie**'s Old Vic production. This knowingly set the play just prior to World War I in decadent Edwardian society; the Trojan warriors were described as "callow specimens of a privileged caste".

The 1960s proved to be the play's busiest decade yet. The connection began early at Stratford, with **Peter Hall** and **John Barton**'s infamous "sand box" *Troilus* of 1960, focused on the sensual allure of **Dorothy Tutin**'s Cressida. **Peter O'Toole**'s acidic Thersites also gained glowing reviews, however, as did Max Adrian's return as Pandarus, and the political resonance of the production was underscored when the cast members scrawled "Ban The Horse!" in the sand at the height of the CND anti-nuclear rallies. Political campaigning was the hallmark of many 60s and 70s productions, particularly in the United States during the Civil Rights conflict and then the Vietnam years, and gender politics was also explored in **Joseph Papp**'s 1965 production in New York, which played Cressida against recent type by displaying her as a victim of male aggression. That approach would have its most influential recent incarnation in **Juliet Stevenson**'s fragile yet eloquent heroine at the RSC for **Howard Davies** in 1985. Although she raised hackles among conservative commentators, Stevenson was acclaimed for bringing to the role qualities many had thought absent – much like **Corinna Harfouch**'s Cressida with the Berliner Ensemble the following year, who repeatedly stressed her fragile position within a patriarchal community. By way of contrast, further productions by John Barton in 1968 and 1976 stressed the *Troilus*'s male sexualities; **Alan Howard**'s Achilles and **Richard Jones Barry**'s Patroclus were shown as openly gay in 1968.

Directors more recently have frequently seized on the play's ambiguous tone to offer any number of eclectic interpretations. The Citizens' Theatre under **Philip Prowse** brought to 1972 Glasgow an all-male *Troilus* played for dangerous and somewhat crazed comedy, an approach mirrored more recently by **Sam Mendes** at the RSC (1990), which was dominated by **Simon Russell Beale**'s acerbic Thersites; **Ralph Fiennes**'s nervy Troilus and **Amanda Root**'s emotive Cressida conducted their courtship with his scabrous insults ringing in the audience's ears. Mendes's approach was effectively postmodern (his Trojan War referenced many different eras), as was that by **Mark Wing-Davey** at the Delacorte Theatre in New York five years later, which spliced excerpts from CNN over Ulysses's famous speech on "degree". **Ian Judge**'s 1996 version, back at the RSC, was too tricksy for many critics, but its concern with **Victoria Hamilton**'s Cressida was one of its strongest features. The 1999 National Theatre production by **Trevor Nunn** steered a markedly different course, instead sketching *Troilus* as an intimate and painful psychological study. **Sophie Okonedo**'s Cressida won plaudits for her depth of character, and the *Guardian* claimed that the whole thing was "a breakthrough".

*Troilus and Cressida* has yet to appear on the large screen, though several TV adaptations have been made. Only **Jonathan Miller**'s BBC/Time-Life version from 1981, with **Anton Lesser**'s Troilus opposite **Suzanne Burden**'s Cressida, is still readily available.

# Screen

## Troilus and Cressida

**A. Lesser, S. Burden, C. Gray; Jonathan Miller (dir.)**
UK, 1981 ▷ Ambrose Video (BBC) 📼

Jonathan Miller's decision to get involved with the BBC Shakespeare halfway through turned around its artistic fortunes, and under his stewardship some of its finest achievements appeared. This *Troilus and Cressida* is perhaps not among them, but its rather serious-minded reading of the play nevertheless has virtues – and it is the only one available. Staging is Elizabethan, but less busily than elsewhere in the series and Miller cleverly contrasts the Renaissance world of Troy and the grim muddle of the Greek camp. Suzanne Burden's Cressida is coolly measured, only hinting at the troubled passions beneath but registering her character's genuine lack of power; and opposite her Anton Lesser is painfully earnest as Troilus. Charles Gray is a bit too hammy as Pandarus, although Thersites receives a lively (if somewhat bizarre) performance at the hands of blind performance artist Jack Birkett (aka "The Incredible Orlando"), who also stars in Derek Jarman's *Tempest* (see p.336). Recently rereleased in the US by Ambrose Video Publishing.

# Audio

## Troilus and Cressida

**I. Pepperell, J. Ford, D. Troughton; Clive Brill (dir.)**
UK, 1998 ▷ Arkangel ⊙ 📼

There's plenty to like in this Arkangel *Troilus and Cressida*, if you discount the unpleasant events of the play. Despite the large size of the cast, there are many excellent performances: particularly worthy of note are David Troughton's superlatively sarcastic Thersites; a swaggering Achilles from Julian Wadham; an excellent Pandarus in Norman Rodway; and Gerard Murphy's dyspeptic and sanctimonious Ulysses. But if the play is to be anything more than bitter satire it needs a convincing couple in the lead, and Ian Pepperell and Julia Ford rise to the challenge. Ford makes it clear that Cressida's slightly shallow cynicism is a tactic forced by male locker-room posturing, and Pepperell's urgent but ultimately naive Troilus is effortlessly outmanoeuvred by almost everyone else – most notoriously Duncan Bell's suave Diomedes. These carefully considered touches are assisted by Clive Brill's clear and unsentimental production.

# Editions

## Arden Shakespeare (third series)

**David Bevington (ed); 1998** ▷ Thomson

As the newest and most comprehensive edition of *Troilus*, Bevington's Arden 3 makes an obvious top choice. As with his Oxford edition of *1 Henry IV*, his work is comprehensive, ranging through competing views of it at a pace that can sometimes be as dizzying as the play itself, but what emerges is consistently intelligent and informative, and amplified by Longer Notes at the back. On the tricky issue of text Bevington provides copious detail but leans towards the Folio (he includes Pandarus's epilogue, possibly cut from some productions). Only his decision to entitle sections of his introduction with wordy epigraphs from the play, some of which "strain" (a key word in *Troilus*), might perplex rather than inform.

# Some criticism

## Shakespeare and the Common Understanding

**Norman Rabkin; 1967** ▷ Chicago UP [o/p]

While not exclusively concerned with *Troilus and Cressida*, the broad point of Norman Rabkin's masterful study – that it is the buried complexities within Shakespeare's work, not their surface appeal, that guarantees them resonance among our "common understanding" – means that he seems particularly sympathetic to the warts-and-all (or perhaps pox-and-all) world of this play. And although Rabkin covers nearly all Shakespeare's works in the course of this study, his half-chapter on *Troilus*'s contradictory views on worth and value is especially engaging. We have no need to apologize for this play, Rabkin argues, nor find a form of special pleading: its moral ambivalence and complex metaphysics are marks of a genius.

## The Swan at the Well

**E. Talbot Donaldson; 1985** ▷ Yale UP [o/p]

Shakespeare used Chaucer quite sparingly but the medieval poet does crop up in intriguing places – as is witnessed by Feste's impersonation of a cleric called "Sir Thopas" in *Twelfth Night* (the name comes from one of the *Canterbury Tales*, although the play otherwise has little connection with Chaucer). E. Talbot Donaldson deals with more obvious connections, concentrating on the *Dream*, *The Two Noble Kinsmen* and *Troilus and Cressida* alongside various analogues. The strongest part of this slightly patchy book deals with the last of these: *Troilus and Criseyde* underpins every aspect of Shakespeare's play, and Donaldson's expert exposing of Chaucerian motifs demonstrates just how intimate the dialogue between the two masterpieces is.

# Twelfth Night

Lyrical, emotional and bittersweet, *Twelfth Night* has long been regarded as perhaps Shakespeare's most perfect comedy. Written soon after *Hamlet* and *As You Like It*, its mood is delicately poised: while its title promises carnival misrule, what the play delivers is grave and searching as well as riotously funny. It also stands at the very centre of Shakespeare's dramatic career, looking back to the twinned chaos of *The Comedy of Errors* and the boisterous laughs of Falstaff as well as anticipating the miraculous resolutions of *Cymbeline* and *The Winter's Tale*. As so often in Shakespearian comedy, here romantic love is both plague and cure – at the climax of the action nearly everyone on stage is in love with the wrong partner, and unscrambling the mess takes formidable, not to mention mischievous, dramatic skill. The insanity of desire is a major theme in *Twelfth Night*, and so is its potential to humiliate: never more so than in the subplot of a household servant who is gulled into falling for his employer, a story the playwright does not allow to end happily. The only play of Shakespeare's to be equipped with an alternative title, *What You Will*, this comedy teases its audiences with dizzying implausibilities alongside searching insights into human nature.

⟦DATE⟧  Performed at London's Middle Temple (a law college) on February 2, 1602, *Twelfth Night* was probably written the preceding year – soon after *Hamlet*. Numerous allusions tie it to this date, though an independent record of an unnamed entertainment performed before Elizabeth I on Twelfth Night 1601 is unlikely to be this one.

⟦SOURCES⟧  *Menaechmi*, by the Roman comedian Plautus, ultimately provides the twins story (it's also the main source for *The Comedy of Errors*), while the love interest derives from a titillating sixteenth-century Italian play called *Gl'Ingannati* ("The Deceived"), which Shakespeare could have read in a number of Italian and English versions.

⟦TEXTS⟧  The play was first printed in the 1623 Folio (F1) in an unusually trouble-free text, probably set from a scribe's copy.

## Interpreting the play

Like Shakespearian comedies before and after it, *Twelfth Night* begins sadly. There has been a shipwreck – one of Shakespeare's ever-malevolent tempests – with just a handful of survivors. The lady Viola, her sea journey cruelly interrupted, finds herself in a strange and possibly hostile land. Apart from the captain and sailors who accompany him (none of them reappears in the play), she is alone. And she is bereaved:

> VIOLA
> What country, friends, is this?
> CAPTAIN                        This is Illyria, lady.
> VIOLA
> And what should I do in Illyria?
> My brother, he is in Elysium.

[1.2.1–3]

## Major Characters & Synopsis

**Orsino**, Duke of Illyria
**Valentine** and **Curio**, Orsino's servants
**Viola**, a shipwrecked lady (later disguised as
   **Cesario**)
**Sebastian**, her twin brother
A **Sea Captain**
**Antonio**, another sea captain
**Olivia**, a countess
**Maria**, Olivia's servant
**Sir Toby Belch**, Olivia's uncle
**Sir Andrew Aguecheek**, Sir Toby's companion
**Malvolio**, Olivia's steward
**Fabian**, Olivia's servant
**Feste**, Olivia's clown
A **Priest**

**ACT 1** The Illyrian court is at a standstill – Duke
Orsino is in love. But the object of his affections,
Olivia, is in mourning for her brother and remains
aloof. Orsino is not the only one in pursuit of
Olivia: her uncle Sir Toby Belch has persuaded his
friend, the rich but dim-witted Sir Andrew
Aguecheek, to present himself as a suitor.
Meanwhile on the coast of Illyria, two survivors of
a shipwreck, Viola and the Sea Captain, are discussing what to do. Convinced that her twin
brother Sebastian has drowned, Viola decides to
disguise herself as a young man, Cesario, and
serve at Orsino's court. She rapidly becomes a
favourite of the Duke, who employs her as a go-
between in his courtship of Olivia. The plan goes
awry, however, when Olivia finds herself more
charmed by the messenger than the message.

**ACT 2** Sebastian has survived – rescued by
Antonio – although he, too, thinks his twin is dead
and resolves to head for the court of Orsino.
Meanwhile Viola/Cesario has fallen in love with
Orsino. Over at Olivia's house, Sir Toby and Sir
Andrew are carousing with Feste, despite a warning from Maria, Olivia's maid. The revelry comes
to an abrupt end, however, when Malvolio,
Olivia's steward, storms in, complaining about the
noise and threatening to throw them out. As soon
as he leaves, the assembled company plans its
revenge. Maria devises a scheme whereby, with
the help of forged love letters, Malvolio will think
that Olivia is in love with him. The plan works:
Malvolio discovers the anonymous letters and,

assuming they are addressed to him, begins to
fantasize about life as Olivia's husband.

**ACT 3** Olivia confesses her love to
Cesario/Viola but Viola tells her that it cannot be
returned. Noting Cesario's apparent success
with Olivia, the frustrated Sir Andrew is persuaded by Toby to challenge him to a duel. But Olivia
now has another suitor: Malvolio, who hopes to
win her by following the bizarre instructions supplied by the letters. Olivia, however, believes him
to be mad and asks Sir Toby to keep an eye on
him. The duellists are about to begin their fight
when they are interrupted by Antonio, who has
arranged to meet Sebastian. Mistaking
Cesario/Viola for Sebastian, Antonio cannot
understand when his friend fails to recognize
him.

**ACT 4** Sebastian is talking with Feste, who
believes him to be Cesario, when he is attacked
by Sir Andrew – who is under the same impression. Sebastian retaliates and Sir Toby joins in,
before Olivia arrives and puts a halt to the fighting. Making the same mistake, and by now completely smitten, Olivia proposes to Sebastian that
they marry; though bewildered, Sebastian falls in
love on the instant and accepts. Things go from
bad to worse for Malvolio – by now locked up for
his own safety – when the fool Feste is persuaded by Maria and Sir Toby to imitate a priest and
exorcize Malvolio's "demons".

**ACT 5** Confusion mounts when discussion
between Cesario/Viola and Orsino is interrupted
by Olivia. As the Duke attempts to win his lady
one last time, she triumphantly announces that
she's already married to Cesario, who promptly
denies it. Olivia then summons the priest, who
seems to confirm the news, when Sir Andrew
and Sir Toby limp in followed by Sebastian, who
admits to having fought them both. After a few
moments of astonishment, the twins joyfully recognize each other, Sebastian is reunited with
Olivia (and Antonio), and Orsino proposes to
Viola. All that remains is for the release of Malvolio
who, when told of the trick that has been played
on him, stomps off – vowing revenge on everyone
present.

## Boy meets girl

While the public theatre of other European countries allowed women to act, in Renaissance England they did not. No one is quite sure why: Spain, France and Italy had similar medieval, male traditions of academic and guild-sponsored theatre, but from around the middle of the sixteenth century women began to perform in public there. In England, however, boys and men continued to be employed in transvestite roles until 1642 and the closure of the theatres. The term "actress" did not become current until after the Restoration.

Most writers who attacked the theatre singled out the "wanton" practice of stage transvestism for especial vitriol, arguing that theatre – already dangerously sexual – encouraged its audiences to indulge in homoerotic fantasies. **Philip Stubbes**, one of the most prolific and compulsive pamphleteers during the period, screeched in his *Anatomy of Abuses* (1585) that people who had been to see plays were tempted to "play the sodomites or worse", while his fellow Puritan **John Rainoldes** reminded readers that Scripture outlawed precisely this kind of "beastly filthiness".

Yet wider society had ambivalent feelings about male homosexuality (the word itself is a nineteenth-century invention). Sodomy was a crime technically punishable by death, but on the other hand passionate friendships between young men seem to have been relatively commonplace. The position of the boy players themselves (and "boys" might be as old as 17; adolescence seems to have occurred later in the sixteenth century) was correspondingly ambiguous: apprenticed to adult players, they were thought by some to be exploitable youths working in an exploitative industry. And yet the idea of males pretending to be females on stage seems not to have bothered too many theatregoers – pretending to be a member of the opposite sex just took skill in acting, like anything else. The late Elizabethan fashion for women with small breasts and narrow hips can only have helped.

It is with these multiple ambiguities that Shakespeare's comedies teasingly flirt. Most often the device of swapping gender accomplishes a fixed purpose – allowing female characters to roam at large without attracting what *The Two Gentlemen*'s Julia calls "the loose encounters of lascivious men" (2.7.41). But in later plays the capacity for cross-dressed double entrendres becomes wickedly playful. *Twelfth Night*'s Viola finds her "masculine usurped attire" presents only problems: falling for her master Orsino, she realizes that the countess Olivia has also fallen for her disguise. *As You Like It*'s Rosalind, by contrast, employs her new identity more mischievously, renaming herself "Ganymede" – recalling not just Jove's cup-bearer in Roman mythology, but also Elizabethan slang for a homosexual youth. And she uses that sexual camouflage to winning advantage: first escaping to Ardenne, then teasing herself (and us) by pretending to be Rosalind so that Orlando can polish his wooing technique – the most dizzying Shakespearian transformation of all, in which a boy pretending to be a girl pretends to be a boy pretending to be a girl.

Though she is terrified to think of it (and the Captain tenderly tries to convince her otherwise), Viola's brother is apparently drowned; although he may be in a better place, she is stuck here on earth. Like the brothers Antipholus in *The Comedy of Errors*, Viola and her brother – his name is Sebastian – are identical twins, and from this impossible fact Shakespeare spins one of his most moving comedies. Though she cannot know it yet, Viola's similarity to her sibling (something that causes her such pain in this scene) is something that will deliver her from sadness and ultimately reunite them both. Opting to "conceal" herself by dressing as a youth – a youth who inevitably resembles her brother – Viola travels to the Illyrian court, like many a hero of romance before her, to seek her fortune. It is as though she leaves the mourning, solitary sister behind: donning her costume, Viola propels herself into a comic world of mysterious disguises, capricious love and crazy topsy-turvydom.

*Twelfth Night*, as befits its place in Shakespeare's canon (it was written around the same time as *Hamlet*), continually bridges worlds that are comic and those that are tragic. Soon after Viola arrives we are shown the household of the Illyrian countess Olivia, likewise in mourning. Shakespeare means the parallels between the two heroines to be uncanny: just as

Olivia's name is a near-anagram of Viola's, she too is grief-stricken for a dead brother. Yet her long-absent fool Feste gently reminds his mistress that perhaps it is time to rejoin the living. "Good madonna," he asks, "why mournest thou?"

> OLIVIA  Good fool, for my brother's death.
> FESTE  I think his soul is in hell, madonna.
> OLIVIA  I know his soul is in heaven, fool.
> FESTE  The more fool, madonna, to mourn for your brother's soul, being in heaven.
>
> [1.5.62–7]

Feste tries to laugh his mistress out of her sadness: comedy has the potential to heal grave emotional wounds, and with the clown's reappearance in Illyria the cast of *Twelfth Night* discovers, with Olivia, that to find happiness you first have to make yourself happy. The irony is that, before the play is out, more will be exposed as "fools" than they think.

## Excess of it

Not all the sadness at the opening of *Twelfth Night* strikes such grave notes. Elsewhere in Illyria Duke Orsino is mournful with love – worse, he is mournful with love for Olivia, who will not listen to his pleas for mercy. In fact the play begins with Orsino (though there is a long stage tradition of opening with the shipwreck), and with some of the most-quoted lines in Shakespeare. "If music be the food of love," he calls to his musicians, "play on,"

> Give me excess of it that, surfeiting,
> The appetite may sicken and so die.
> That strain again, it had a dying fall.
> O, it came over my ear like the sweet sound
> That breathes upon a bank of violets.
> Stealing and giving odour. Enough, no more,
> 'Tis not so sweet now as it was before.
>
> [1.1.1–8]

Orsino wants nothing less than too much: he demands "excess" in the hope that somehow it will cure his "appetite" for tears by killing it. Although he is in love, he begs to be out of it; though he listens to music, he wants it to stop. "So full of shapes is fancy," Orsino reflects to himself, "that it alone is high fantastical" (1.1.14–15). Orsino is in love with love itself – and with the power of his own "fantastical" imagination.

> *An improbable world of hair's-breadth rescues at sea, romantic disguises, idealistic friendships and sudden, irrational loves. This is not quite the country behind the North Wind, but it approaches those latitudes.*
>
> Anne Barton, "*As You Like It* and *Twelfth Night*: Shakespeare's sense of an ending" (1972)

Before long both he and Olivia find themselves more authentically in love, but the consequences are unexpected. Both fall for Viola – someone who is, in the strange logic of Shakespearian comedy, both "maid and man" (5.1.261). Before *Twelfth Night* gets there, however, other craziness ensues. Also bent on maximizing their own experience – though in grosser terms than Orsino – are the aptly named Sir Toby Belch, Olivia's boozy cousin, and his companion Sir Andrew Aguecheek. Perpetually short of money because of his riotous lifestyle (in this he echoes Falstaff), Sir Toby cultivates the rich Sir Andrew for the very reason that he is embarrassingly dim: persuading him to make a doomed attempt for Olivia's love, Toby hopes to sponge off Sir Andrew for as long as possible. After all, as he patiently explains, there is a great deal of revelry to do:

> SIR TOBY   Not to be abed after midnight is to be up betimes, and *diliculo surgere*, thou knowest.
> SIR ANDREW   Nay, by my troth, I know not; but I know to be up late is to be up late.
> SIR TOBY   A false conclusion. I hate it as an unfilled can. To be up after midnight and to go to bed then is early; so that to go to bed after midnight is to go to bed betimes.
>
> **[2.3.1–9]**

"Let us therefore," Toby robustly continues, "eat and drink" (2.3.12). In doing so he draws attention to the spirit caught in the play's title: "Twelfth Night" was the closing feast of the Christmas season and its crazed climax. Historically, it was a medieval celebration that survived until the eighteenth century, an occasion upon which "misrule" (the inversion of social hierarchies) and carnivalesque licence were allowed full voice. Turning night into day with drinking and dancing, Sir Toby does his utmost to turn *Twelfth Night* the play into Twelfth Night the festival.

## That is and is not

Not everyone here is willing to let that happen. When Sir Toby's midnight revelry threatens to spin out of control, Olivia's puritanical retainer Malvolio bursts in and furiously demands that they call a halt. Sir Toby is appalled that a jumped-up "steward" should presume to say anything of the kind, but it is Malvolio's fellow servant Maria – egged on by Sir Toby – who hatches a satisfyingly cruel revenge: she will write a letter to Malvolio, purportedly from Olivia, hinting that she wishes to be more intimate with him. The plot catches fire immediately, and the letter itself is a comic masterstroke. Casually coming across it while out taking the air, Malvolio thinks that his chance for glory has finally come. "By my life, this is my lady's hand," he exclaims – then begins to puzzle away at the cryptic message it expresses:

> 'I may command where I adore.' Why, she may command me. I serve her, she is my lady. Why, this is evident to any formal capacity. There is no obstruction in this. And the end—what should that alphabetical position portend? If I could make that resemble something in me. Softly—'M.O.A.I.'
>
> **[2.5.113–8]**

Malvolio has come across the central riddle of the letter: the mysterious phrase "M.O.A.I":

> 'M.O.A.I.' This simulation is not as the former, and yet to crush this a little, it would bow to me, for every one of these letters are in my name … I do not now fool myself, to let imagination jade me; for every reason excites to this, that my lady loves me.
>
> **[2.5.135–60]**

Malvolio does not "fool" himself, at least not entirely, but he does make a fool *of* himself by being convinced so easily – and on such implausible grounds – that Olivia loves him. Like Orsino, he has fallen in love with a reflection of his own figure: as Olivia astutely realized, he is "sick of self-love" (1.5.86).

The joke had real attractions for Shakespeare's contemporaries, themselves keenly aware of how "serving" in someone's household could, and sometimes did, encompass a suggestive range of possibilities. The error Malvolio makes is to mix up his mistress (his boss) with his mistress (his lover), and it is one that a seventeenth-century spectator of *Twelfth Night*, a lawyer named John Manningham, who saw one of its earliest performances, was particularly impressed by. Noting that "a good practice in it [was] to make the steward believe his lady widow was in love with him", Manningham relates in his account of the play that Malvolio's embarrassment does not stop at this. Instructed by the letter to don ridiculous yellow stockings in order to signal to Olivia that he has understood her message, Malvolio does so – and is promptly locked up because everyone "took him to be mad". The incarcerated Malvolio attempts to right the situation by insisting on his sanity, but the omnipresent Feste (Olivia's "allowed", or professional, fool) neatly turns it back on him:

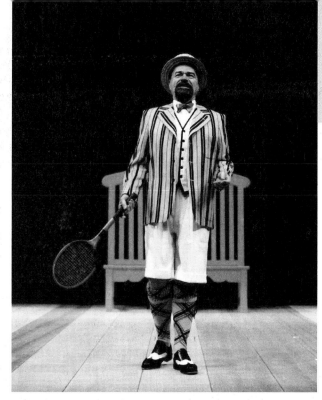

Malvolio (Philip Voss) making a fool of himself. Adrian Noble's 1997 colourful RSC production of *Twelfth Night* emphasized the broad humour of the play and ignored its darker side. While most critics were dismissive, audiences loved it.

MALVOLIO  Fool, there was never man so notoriously abused. I am as well in my wits, fool, as thou art.
FESTE  But as well? Then you are mad indeed, if you be no better in your wits than a fool.

**[4.2.89–92]**

Malvolio passionately retorts that "I am as well in my wits as any man in Illyria" (4.2.109–10), but by the time he says it the claim is beginning to look double-edged, for he is not the only character exhibiting signs of insanity. Having turned down Orsino, Olivia finds that she has become attracted to Cesario, his page (in other words, the disguised Viola), while Viola herself – resisting Olivia's impassioned advances – is sick for the sight of Orsino. "How will this fadge [turn out]?" Viola wonders at one point:

> My master loves her dearly,
> And I, poor monster, fond as much on him,
> And she, mistaken, seems to dote on me.
> What will become of this? As I am man,
> My state is desperate for my master's love.
> As I am woman, now, alas the day,
> What thriftless sighs shall poor Olivia breathe!
> O time, thou must untangle this, not I.

**[2.2.33–40]**

Time will indeed unscramble things, though Malvolio's treatment is hard to forgive (he leaves the play vowing to be "revenged on the whole pack of you" (5.1.374)) and, in the shorter term, it will make Viola's life considerably more complicated. By this stage of *Twelfth Night* we know that her grief at the beginning of the play has been too hasty: though Sebastian has been separated by the shipwreck, he has in fact survived and is at this moment also wandering around Illyria. In a throwback to the perplexities of *The Comedy of Errors*, it is only inevitable that confusion between them will result – first when Sebastian's companion and rescuer Antonio mistakes Viola for her twin, again when Sir Andrew, emboldened by love for Olivia (and plenty of prompting by Sir Toby), attacks Sebastian in the belief that he is Cesario/Viola. In the play's most startling moment, however, it is Olivia's inability to tell the twins apart that has the most far-reaching consequences. Protecting Sebastian from his assailants, she begs, "Go with me to my house":

> Do not deny. Beshrew his soul for me,
> He started one poor heart of mine in thee.
>
> SEBASTIAN
> What relish is in this? How runs the stream?
> Or I am mad, or else this is a dream …

[4.1.53–60]

Neither is quite true, though madness is certainly in the air when the love-struck Sebastian agrees to be "ruled by" (and very rapidly married to) Olivia. Despite her best efforts – and the convolutions of Shakespeare's gender-bending plot – she has succeeded in getting wed to a man.

Although in *Twelfth Night* it frequently seems as if everyone has fallen in love with everyone else (even Sir Toby ends up marrying Maria, albeit as a reward for her scheme against Malvolio), the play allows these tangles to be untied, as so often, in a climactic final scene. It begins darkly: captured by Orsino's men, Antonio is stunned that the "ingrateful boy" Cesario (whom he thinks is Sebastian) should now pretend not to know him. "His life I gave him," he bitterly reflects,

> and did thereto add
> My love without retention or restraint,
> All his in dedication.

[5.1.76–8]

Again the languages of service and of love entwine – so closely that modern directors have sometimes played the relationship between Antonio and Sebastian as a homosexual one. Shakespeare is more ambiguous as well as more subtle: Antonio has given his all for Sebastian, a "love" that is among the play's truest. It is the kind of devoted service also expected by Orsino, the reason he is so appalled when Olivia arrives and announces that she has married Cesario (a marriage that, in a teasing Shakespearian joke, has seemingly not involved any exchange of names). Despite Viola's genuine protestations of innocence, for a few tense moments it looks as though her duplicity throughout risks turning into something much more serious. But then Sebastian appears, and the play's most complicated moment – the presence on stage of identical twins of different sexes – dazzlingly resolves into its simplest. The recognition between the twins is winningly easy, not so much a genuine surprise as a rehearsal of facts the audience already knows to be true:

> VIOLA
> My father had a mole upon his brow.
> SEBASTIAN  And so had mine.
> VIOLA
> And died that day when Viola from her birth
> Had numbered thirteen years.
> SEBASTIAN
> O, that record is lively in my soul.

[5.1.240–4]

From death Shakespeare conjures "lively" life: Sebastian's "sister ... whom the blind waves and surges have devoured" (5.1.226–7) is standing here in front of him. Though the pair have, as Orsino murmurs, "one face, one voice, one habit," they are also "two persons, / A natural perspective, that is and is not" (5.2.213–4). In this way Shakespeare adds a new dimension to his assertion in the Sonnets – many of which may have been written by the time *Twelfth Night* debuted – that "love is not love / Which alters when it alteration finds" (116, 2–3). What the play's characters discover is that love can "alter" and yet find truth: that Olivia can fall in love with a girl and yet marry a boy; that Orsino, deceived, can find himself "betrothed to both a maid and man" (5.1.261); and that twins can be the same as well as different, and different as well as the same.

## Stage history and adaptations

Unusually, we know a handful of facts about *Twelfth Night*'s early stage history: a 1602 performance at the legal hall the **Middle Temple** was recorded by a contemporary diarist (see p.373), and some have speculated that it might also have been the unnamed play acted at **court** the year before. It seems likely that Feste was written for the chief clown in Shakespeare's company, **Robert Armin** – noted for his thoughtful approach to comedic roles (see p.27).

The comedy remained popular up to the closure of the theatres in 1642, and after the Restoration it was revived in an adaptation by **William Davenant**. Pepys saw this version twice and pronounced it "silly", however, and within a few decades it had been supplanted by modernized reworkings. **William Wycherly**'s *The Plain-Dealer* held the stage from 1674, and **William Burnaby**'s *Love Betrayed* first appeared in 1703, its published text proudly insisting that while it used much of Shakespeare's plot, nearly all his lines were cut. But Burnaby's version only had a couple of performances, and afterwards *Twelfth Night* disappeared from theatres entirely.

Its fortunes would be reversed by **Charles Macklin**, who acted the comedy at Drury Lane in 1741 and made it one of Shakespeare's most popular. Macklin founded a theatrical tradition by seizing on the role of Malvolio, which he performed to **Hannah Pritchard**'s Viola and **Kitty Clive**'s Olivia. *Twelfth Night* was played in countless London revivals over the next half-century, and appeared in New York in 1804. Innovation would be attempted by **Frederick Reynolds** and **Henry Bishop** in 1820 with a musical version boasting songs "selected *entirely* from ... Shakespeare", but, as usual with Reynolds's productions, few of those came from the play in question. **Samuel Phelps** was more faithful to the text at Sadler's Wells in 1848, playing a frosty Malvolio, while two years later **Charles Kean** chose to open his series of spectacular Shakespearian revivals at the Princess's Theatre with the comedy.

Other producers found success with the play – among them the **Duke of Saxe-Meinigen**'s company, who toured to Britain in 1881 with *Twelfth Night*, *The Winter's Tale* and *Julius Caesar* – and it remained an integral part of the Victorian repertoire. **Henry Irving**'s Lyceum performances were lavishly staged and well cast (Irving played an emotive Malvolio to **Ellen Terry**'s Viola), but struggled to attract audiences – a problem not experienced by **Herbert Beerbohm Tree** in 1901, whose production was seen by many thousands of people over the years. Tree starred as Malvolio, but it was the impressiveness of his staging that struck audiences with wonder: the Italianate garden of **Maud Jefferies**'s Olivia was painstakingly copied from illustrations in *Country Life*, and took so long to set that the scenes there had to be run consecutively. Nearly as invasive were **Augustine Daly**'s various New York-based productions from 1894, which again rearranged the play's running-order; **Ada Rehan** starred as a buoyant Viola.

By this time the backlash against Victorian scenic overload was underway. **William Poel** staged *Twelfth Night* several times, first in 1895 with an amateur cast and Elizabethan music, and again in 1905. Many were unimpressed by Poel's attempts at historically informed staging, yet they laid the ground for **Harley Granville-Barker**'s ground-breaking production at the Savoy in 1912, often called the first truly modern version. **Norman Wilkinson**'s elegant black-and-silver design dominated and the staging was rapid and fluid, but it was Granville-Barker's cast that set *Twelfth Night* in fresh light: **Lillah McCarthy**'s Viola was passionate and **Henry Ainley**'s Mavolio a "dry puritan", but eyewitnesses were most struck by **Hayden Coffin**'s lugubrious Feste. The Paris-based production by **Jacques Copeau** two years later gained nearly as many fans (Granville-Barker was one), though the temptation to tinker got the better of **William Bridges-Adams** at Stratford in 1932 – he softened the play's conclusion by axeing the prison scene.

The difficulty of how best to reconcile *Twelfth Night*'s comic and tragic elements also caused problems for **John Gielgud**, directing at Stratford in 1955, though admittedly he wasn't helped by **Laurence Olivier**'s hysterically camp and hammy Malvolio (he insisted on falling backwards off a bench in the garden scene, though Gielgud begged him not to). Three years later **Peter Hall** produced a version at the same venue still often cited as a gold standard: it put **Dorothy Tutin**'s Viola into service at **Lila de Nobili**'s gorgeously designed Cavalier court, described by one critic as a "rich symphony in russet". Reviewers were ambivalent about **Geraldine McEwan**'s unusually youthful Olivia (one called her a "kittenish typist"), but **Max Adrian**'s melancholy Feste was warmly received. The production was revived in 1960 with a slightly reworked cast – among them **Ian Richardson** as Sir Andrew and **Eric Porter**'s Malvolio – and continued to attract plaudits.

Also much revived was **John Barton**'s 1969 version, with impressive personnel including **Judi Dench**'s powerful but level-headed Viola and **Donald Sinden**'s richly characterized Malvolio. Barton's reading of the play was Chekhovian – one witness commented that he couldn't recall a production "that held all the comedy's elements in such harmony" – and many audiences remembered its elegant staging, surrounded on three sides by a gauze box. **Peter Gill**'s 1974 version, again at the RSC, took a less romantic view of the play (Gill's theory that it was all about narcissism was represented by an image of Narcissus himself above the stage), and also emphasized its homosexual entanglements. **Terry Hands** took a literal-minded view of the play's post-Christmas setting, but as his 1979 production wore on green shoots sprung up beneath the snow; it wasn't an approach that convinced everyone, but **Cherie Lunghi**'s expressive Viola apparently did.

The RSC revival by **John Caird** from 1983 returned to the familiar theme of self-love (**Zoë Wanamaker** was unsettled rather than pleased by Orsino's advances), but a year previously **Ariane Mnouchkine** struck out in bold new directions with her Théâtre du Soleil production, which drew influences from Japan and India in order to construct a self-consciously exotic Illyria. Back at Stratford, **Bill Alexander**'s 1987 staging was dominated by **Antony Sher**'s striking Malvolio, who was driven literally mad after being chained to a stake. Elsewhere in the cast **Harriet Walter**'s Viola was acclaimed, as was **David Bradley**'s maudlin Sir Andrew. **Declan Donnellan**'s production with Cheek By Jowl the same year was utterly different, stressing instead the wild sexualities of the play along with its comic conclusion – Malvolio was brought back into the fold, and even Antonio and Feste paired off at the end.

It's difficult to generalize about a play which has had so rich a stage history as *Twelfth Night*, and recent approaches testify to the apparently endless ways of performing it. **Peter Hall**'s return to the comedy in 1991 at the Playhouse Theatre, 36 years after first doing it, impressed many critics with its "Shakespeare done straight" approach, but in general directors have searched for new angles – something Hall was reacting against. **Adrian Noble**'s 1997 RSC production was a case in point: creating a fantasy world of primary colours (reminiscent of Komisarjevsky's famous 1938 *Comedy of Errors*), Noble played it for laughs at the expense of the play's melancholy dimension – thus delighting audiences but upsetting the critics. And of the fifty-plus productions over the last ten years (in the UK alone), it's impossible to mention more than a few. Elizabethan approaches have been attempted by **Ian Judge** at the RSC (1994) and **Tim Carroll** at Shakespeare's Globe (2002), though Carroll's all-male production gained more good reviews; **Mark Rylance**'s Olivia was particularly excellent, bringing touching comic pathos to the character. In the same year as the latter **Sam Mendes** chose the play for his final season at the Donmar Warehouse, positioning it alongside Chekhov's *Uncle Vanya*. The pairing proved revealing and the cast, which included **Simon Russell Beale** as an especially fastidious and superior Malvolio, and **Helen McCrory** as a rather more sexy and wilful Olivia than is usual, captured the melancholic essence of the play as well as its riotous comedy – Malvolio's comeuppance was particularly cruel and humiliating. In 2004, at London's Albery theatre, director **Stephen Beresford** had the inspired idea of updating the play to contemporary India. Not all the critics were impressed, but most thought that the transfer worked well – **Paul Bhattacharjee**'s officious government-wallah Malvolio and **Kulvinder Ghir**'s Bollywood wannabe Feste were both singled out for special praise.

On screen, *Twelfth Night* has cropped up in various places. In addition to a number of BBC productions – the latest being the Time-Life collaboration starring **Felicity Kendal**'s Viola alongside **Alec McCowen**'s Malvolio (1980) – it has also appeared on commercial TV, most recently at the behest of Britain's Channel 4 with a production by **Tim Supple** that saw the play as a parable about multicultural society. On the big screen, **Yan Fried**'s Russian film (1955) has been joined by **Trevor Nunn**'s 1995 English-language version, set in Victorian Cornwall and starring **Imogen Stubbs** (Viola) and **Nigel Hawthorne** (Malvolio).

"Most wonderful!" Olivia (Mark Rylance), confronted by identical twins Sebastian (Rhys Meredith, left) and Viola (Michael Brown, far right), can't quite believe her luck. This all-male Globe Theatre production opened at Lincoln's Inn in 2002, four hundred years after the play first appeared there.

# Screen

## Twelfth Night
### F. Turner, C. Kent, J.S. Gordon; Charles Kent (dir.)
USA, 1910  ▷ on Silent Shakespeare (BFI) 🔲 ▭

Its over-literal redaction of the plot may well have left early audiences puzzled, but this Vitagraph *Twelfth Night*, like their *Dream* (see p.246) has oodles of charm. Like productions before and after it, this version begins in the sea – and with what appears to be a real shipwreck sticking out of the lapping waves, richly contrasted with the fussiness of Orsino's court. Florence Turner's expressive (and unbelievably tiny) Viola comes close to stealing the show, at first touchingly melancholy but responding quizzically to Olivia's advances. Director Charles Kent's lofty Malvolio provides stiff competiton, though, as does Turner's double for Sebastian – the scene where they appear together really does seem convincing on century-old film.

## Twelfth Night
### I. Stubbs, H. Bonham-Carter, N. Hawthorne; Trevor Nunn (dir.)
UK, 1995  ▷ Entertainment in Video / New Line ▭

Filmed a couple of years after Branagh's *Much Ado*, Nunn's rendering of *Twelfth Night* uses a similar formula: well-known names, picturesque locations, mellow interpretation. Nunn is a subtler director of actors, however, and his choice of period setting – stately-home Victorian, with the gloriously unlikely edifice of St Michael's Mount as Orsino's pleasure-dome – sets up some interesting collisions between gothicky fantasy and social reality, given further urgency by a played-up conflict between Illyria and Messaline. Thus it's a disappointment that the film's pace barely reaches a limp, the sound is pretty dreadful, and only a few performances really shine. Honourable exceptions are Nigel Hawthorne's tight-lipped Malvolio and Imogen Stubbs's Viola (Stubbs carries a moustache surprisingly well), while Helena Bonham-Carter gets the little-girl lunacy of Olivia very nearly right. Ben Kingsley's folkish, semi-Celtic Feste, however, may well make you want to wrap his accordion around his neck.

# Audio

## Twelfth Night
### S. Gonet, G. Murphy, L. Whybrow; David Timson (dir.)
UK, 1999  ▷ Naxos ⊙ ▭

There is much to recommend the Naxos *Twelfth Night*, certainly when compared with the somewhat leaden BBC offering. The cast are consistently excellent: high praise goes to Stella Gonet's mature (and appealingly world-weary) Viola, Jonathan Keeble's strongly spoken Orsino and Gerard Murphy's fruity Sir Toby, although the fussy Feste offered by David Timson – also the director – takes much of the danger out of the role. Olivia receives a persuasively humane performance from Lucy Whybrow, nicely set off by Christopher

Godwin's petty tyrant Malvolio. Most importantly, however, this recording has that spirit of mystery without which no performance of the play would be complete.

# Editions

## Oxford Shakespeare
### Roger Warren & Stanley Wells (eds); 1994
▷ Oxford UP

Few people have been busier in the service of Shakespeare than Stanley Wells, and Roger Warren is equally respected. This is that unusual thing, a truly collaborative edition: Wells prepared the basis of the text and Warren the introduction and notes, but both had input and what emerges benefits from the eagle eyes of two experts. All elements are of extremely high quality: the critical introduction is sensible without being bland, and nicely aware of *Twelfth Night*'s playful ambiguities and theatrical life, while the text itself is unusual among modern renderings in being very lightly punctuated – something that allows the lines to be spoken freely and clearly. A detailed appendix (prepared by yet another expert) covers the comedy's music.

# Some criticism

## Twelfth Night and Shakespearean Comedy
### Clifford Leech; 1965  ▷ Toronto UP [o/p]

Leech's slim book collects a series of three lectures given at Dalhousie University during the tercentenary of Shakespeare's birth. It's an elegant and urbane study that starts from the very beginnings of comedy before moving to more immediate sixteenth-century influences and an illuminating attempt to place *Twelfth Night* in the context of Shakespeare's development as a dramatist. Leech's subtle reading of the play is well-attuned to its discordances and careful intermingling of opposing forces, and in his second lecture he argues that its conclusion "gives over the comic idea", decisively returning us to the wind and rain of Feste's parting song – and eventually to the problem comedies themselves.

## William Shakespeare
### Terry Eagleton; 1986  ▷ Blackwell

Terry Eagleton is excessively proud of the fact that Prince Charles once described him as "dreadful", and during a long career as Britain's most loved/reviled/industrious Marxist literary critic he has turned controversy-making into high art. His polemical little book on Shakespeare is maddening and brilliant by turns, it being entirely in character for Eagleton to insist, with as much seriousness as whimsy, that "it is difficult to read Shakespeare without feeling that he was almost certainly familiar with the writings of Hegel, Marx, Nietzsche, Freud, Wittgenstein and Derrida". His article on the *Dream* and *Twelfth Night* appeared in a very early form back in 1968, and is in some ways the best in the book – the play perhaps being more suited to his Theory-led approach than others. You sense that he's particularly at home writing about Feste, a character with all the wily linguistic tactics of a university professor of English.

# The Two Gentlemen of Verona

T hough it was probably his first piece for the London stage, *The Two Gentlemen of Verona* sets out ideas that would interest and engage Shakespeare until the dying days of his professional career. Put simply, the problem explored in this comedy – a comedy that risks becoming far more serious – is what happens when male friends fall in love with the same woman, and how they reconcile that love with their friendship for each other: an almost identical storyline to his final work, *The Two Noble Kinsmen*. Like that play and many in between, Shakespeare's *The Two Gentlemen* is very much about growing up, and this test is one that both of the play's "gentlemen" come agonizingly close to failing. But it is also much more than this: although taking its cue from courtly Elizabethan comedies about the value of male friendship, the play exposes its two protagonists as shallow and selfish, contrasting them with a pair of female leads whose devotion to their menfolk is difficult to understand – a problem that becomes glaringly apparent in *The Two Gentlemen*'s troubling and bitter conclusion. But perhaps the play's most winning achievements are those it offers in light relief: it contains some excellent comic moments, not to mention the most coveted non-speaking role in the canon – that for a dog.

[DATE] In all likelihood the first of Shakespeare's plays to be penned, *The Two Gentlemen* was described in 1598 as encapsulating his talent for "Comedy". It was probably composed some time earlier, perhaps 1589–90.

[SOURCES] A version of Montemayor's pastoral romance, *Diana* (1559), describing the tale of "Felix and Felismena", provided the outline of the Proteus–Julia story. Thomas Elyot's 1531 version of the tale of "Titus and Gisippus" from Boccaccio's *Decameron* also had some influence, as did Ovid's *Metamorphoses* and Arthur Brooke's 1562 *Romeus and Juliet*.

[TEXTS] The 1623 Folio – a relatively clean job – is the first surviving text.

## Interpreting the play

When the Elizabethan schoolmaster and writer Francis Meres drew up a record of Shakespeare's plays (the earliest of its kind, and a unique testimony to the young poet's career), a play called "his *Gentlemen of Verona*" appears at the top of the list. For all that Meres might have been particularly impressed by the comedy, this is usually taken as evidence that *The Two Gentlemen* is Shakespeare's first surviving play. Many agree that it seems to be the work of a talented but relatively inexperienced dramatist, one who was still learning his craft. The comedy borrows from writers such as John Lyly – whose *Euphues*, a prose tale about two young gentlemen, was published in 1580 – as well as experimenting in a limited way with the resources of the stage. It employs a tiny cast (the playwright's smallest), often using just two

## Major Characters & Synopsis

**Proteus**, a gentleman from Verona

**Valentine**, another gentleman from Verona, Proteus's close friend

**Lance**, Proteus's clownish servant (accompanied by his dog **Crab**)

**Julia**, Proteus's beloved (later disguised as **Sebastian**)

**Lucetta**, Julia's waiting-woman

**Speed**, Valentine's page

**Duke of Milan**

**Silvia**, the Duke's daughter

**Thurio**, Silvia's rich suitor

**Antonio**, Proteus's father

**Panthino**, Antonio's servant

**Host** who lodges Julia

**Eglamour**, a Milanese courtier and Silvia's friend

A band of **Outlaws** living in the forest outside Milan

**ACT 1** Valentine and Proteus are best friends, albeit with contrasting views of the world – Valentine is anxious to leave Verona, while Proteus is content to remain at home with his beloved Julia (much to Valentine's disgust). Though Proteus loves Julia, she, so far, has shown little interest in him, and when her maid-servant Lucetta gives her a letter from him, she flies into a rage and tears it up. Just as things start to go right for Proteus – he has finally received a response from Julia – his father Antonio decides to send him to join Valentine at the Milanese court.

**ACT 2** In Milan, meanwhile, Valentine has fallen for Silvia – much to his servant Speed's amuse-ment – despite the fact that her father, the Duke, favours the dim-witted but rich Thurio. Silvia, in turn, loves Valentine, but will not say so; instead she persuades him to write a love letter suppos-edly for another suitor but actually intended for himself. Back in Verona, Julia and Proteus vow eternal fidelity and exchange rings, while Proteus's servant Lance parts sadly from his family. Arriving in Milan, Proteus is reunited with Valentine and meets Silvia; Valentine then discloses how he plans to elope with her and enlists Proteus's help. But Proteus is so struck by Silvia that he resolves to woo her himself. Meanwhile Julia is missing her lover and decides to follow him disguised as a page – despite Lucetta's misgivings.

**ACT 3** Proteus reveals his friend's plan to the Duke, who banishes Valentine upon pain of death. The Duke then asks Proteus to help Thurio find favour in Silvia's eyes by slandering Valentine and praising Thurio. Proteus eagerly agrees, hoping to win Silvia's affections for him-self. Lance, meanwhile, has fallen for a milkmaid and recounts to a bemused Speed her various attractions.

**ACT 4** Valentine and Speed are heading back to Verona through the forest when they are ambushed by outlaws. Impressed by Valentine's bearing, they ask him to lead them. Back at court, Proteus is troubled by his conscience but continues to woo Silvia, who is shocked at his betrayal of Valentine and Julia. When the dis-guised Julia arrives she immediately discovers what is going on, but bides her time. Silvia, on the other hand, has decided to act: she plans to escape her impending marriage to Thurio and, with the help of her friend Sir Eglamour, join Valentine in Mantua. In the meantime, Proteus has recruited Julia (renamed Sebastian) to deliver a letter and a ring to Silvia – the very ring that Julia had given him. But Silvia, out of sympathy for Julia, again rejects Proteus's advances. Lance, all this time, has been sorting out the problems caused by his troublesome dog, Crab.

**ACT 5** News has reached the Duke about his daughter's flight, and when Proteus, Thurio and Julia hear of it, they each determine to find her. Proteus succeeds first, rescuing Silvia from the outlaws who have captured her. When, however, she continues to reject him, he resolves to take her by force – unaware that Valentine is watching. Valentine intervenes, rescues Silvia and denounces the treachery of his friend. But when Proteus begs forgiveness, Valentine not only immediately con-sents but also declares that Proteus *can* have Silvia after all. At this, Julia/Sebastian, who has been present the whole time, faints – whereupon her real identity is uncovered and she is reunited with a penitent Proteus. The Outlaws enter with the captured Duke and Thurio, who initially claims Silvia but gives her up when threatened by Valentine. The Duke then consents to the marriage of Silvia and Valentine, and pardons all the Outlaws.

or three actors at a time, and the script is bedevilled by a number of narrative inconsistencies – among them a muddle between the various Italian locations it describes, suggesting that Shakespeare was struggling to get a tight grip on his plot.

*The Two Gentlemen* is also a comedy about what it feels like to be young. The "gentlemen" of the title, Valentine and Proteus, are youthful best friends at an emotional crossroads. Proteus is passionately in love, while Valentine longs to get out of Verona and see what he calls "the wonders of the world" (1.1.6). The play opens at a parting of the ways familiar to the wealthiest among Shakespeare's audience: while Proteus stays "sluggardized at home" (1.1.7), Valentine is off to exciting new places, the kind of destinations regarded by rich Elizabethans as sources of gentle-manliness. Some of their contemporaries, says Panthino, are sent "to seek preferment out,"

> Some to the wars, to try their fortune there,
> Some to discover islands far away,
> Some to the studious universities.
>
> **[1.3.7–10]**

Antonio, Proteus's father, agrees with this analysis. "Experience is by industry achieved," he observes, "and perfected by the swift course of time" (1.3.22–3). If Proteus is to achieve anything in life, he needs to get out there and see it.

## In love

But Proteus, like any teenager, is not exactly desperate to take his father's advice. Leaving Verona means abandoning his beloved Julia, and that for the young lovers means being separated from their very selves. It is a strong irony, then, that the absent Valentine – sent away to become the perfect gentleman – learns some unexpected lessons in Milan. He, too, falls in love, as his page Speed sarcastically explains:

VALENTINE  Why, how know you that I am in love?

SPEED  Marry, by these special marks: first, you have learned, like Sir Proteus, to wreath your arms like a malcontent; to relish a love-song, like a robin redbreast; to walk along like one that had the pestilence; to sigh, like a schoolboy that had lost his ABC; to weep, like a young wench that had buried her grandmam; to fast, like one that takes diet; to watch, like one that fears robbing; to speak puling [whining], like a beggar at Hallowmas … [Y]ou are metamorphosed with a mistress, that when I look on you I can hardly think you my master.

**[2.1.16–30]**

Valentine cannot find a way of expressing love which is anything other than ridiculous. Love – or at least his idea of it – has made him, as it also makes Proteus, into something less than a man.

This version of love, which receives unsparing scrutiny in *The Two Gentlemen* (as in many of Shakespeare's subsequent comedies), has a lot to do with words and not very much with reality. At first struck dumb by their mistresses, both Proteus and Valentine then talk themselves into mournful passion. In truth they have little excuse: unlike their counterparts in later plays, the two young men experience few problems having their feelings reciprocated. Julia, though at first she tries to hide it, rapidly finds herself in love with Proteus – as is obvious when, in a glorious piece of stage business, she rips up a letter from him in order to demonstrate that she couldn't care less, then spends the next few minutes trying desperately to reassemble the pieces. For his part, Valentine is so self-obsessed that he fails to realize his mistress Silvia has long since fallen for him too. Instructing him to write a letter (the play is full of them) to a "secret, name-less friend", she then orders the baffled Valentine to present it to himself:

SILVIA

A pretty period. Well, I guess the sequel.
And yet I will not name it. And yet I care not.
And yet, take this again.
*She offers him the letter*
                                And yet I thank you,
Meaning henceforth to trouble you no more.

SPEED (*aside*)

And yet you will, and yet another yet.

VALENTINE

What means your ladyship? Do you not like it?

SILVIA

Yes, yes. The lines are very quaintly writ,
But since unwillingly, take them again.

**[2.1.109–16]**

Silvia's "jest", wittily imitating the fickle mistress of Valentine's imagination, gently satirizes his self-absorption while also signalling that she is in fact interested – a message that Speed, unlike his obtuse master, quickly decodes. Silvia needs to operate in secret because her father wants to marry her to someone else, though it will be the end of the scene before Valentine realizes what she means.

This kind of high-bred game-playing is thrown into relief by Proteus's servant Lance, whose opinions on marriage are distinctly less elevated. Having met a likely match, a milkmaid, he first compiles a "catalogue of her conditions" (3.1.271) describing the things that are best – and worst – about her. Unlike the fantastical (though admittedly beautiful) song, "Who is Silvia? What is she?", written by Proteus on behalf of Thurio later in the play, Lance's list lives solidly in the real world. Among the "virtues" he mentions are the fact that his milkmaid can fetch and carry, milk, brew ale, sew, knit, wash and scour; among her "vices" are bad breath, talking in her sleep, having no teeth and being "slow in words". It's not exactly romantic, but then Lance saves his real love for his dog Crab, as he later reveals with a garrulous – and slightly bizarre – tale which is also one of Shakespeare's funniest comic speeches. "If I had not had more wit than he, to take a fault upon me that he did," Lance announces regarding Crab, "I think verily he had been hanged for't."

> Sure as I live, he had suffered for't. You shall judge. He thrusts me himself into the company of three or four gentleman-like dogs under the Duke's table. He had not been there—bless the mark—a pissing-while but all the chamber smelled him. 'Out with the dog,' says one. 'What cur is that?' says another. 'Whip him out,' says the third. 'Hang him up,' says the Duke. I, having been acquainted with the smell before, knew it was Crab, and goes to the fellow that whips the dogs. 'Friend,' quoth I, 'you mean to whip the dog.' 'Ay, marry do I,' quoth he. 'You do him the more wrong,' quoth I, ''twas I did the thing you wot of.' He makes me no more ado, but whips me out of the chamber.

**[4.4.13–28]**

"How many masters would do this for his servant?" he concludes, and it's undeniably true that the number would not be high. Lance's love for Crab inverts the relationship between dog and man, but also plays off the notion of male lovers (like Valentine and Proteus) blindly serving their mistresses. Those mistresses are always scornful, just as Crab is – as Lance earlier laments – "cruel-hearted" (2.3.9) in his reluctance to be properly doggish and worship Lance, instead of the other way round.

## Metamorphosed with a mistress

Every bit as devoted, it seems, is Julia, who decides with the kind of pragmatism also exhibited by Silvia that she cannot bear to stay in Verona while Proteus is absent seeing the world. The first in a long line of strong Shakespearian women – all markedly more in control of the situation than their menfolk – she takes the route chosen by heroines like Rosalind and Viola and dons male disguise in order to travel to Milan. Yet what she discovers when she arrives is horrendous: her beloved Proteus, "his heart as far from fraud as heaven from earth", has in fact fallen for someone else (2.6.78). And not just anyone else: Proteus's new target is Silvia. The parallels between Julia and Lance – slavish devotion to worthless dogs – are ever stronger, but the comedy has become bleached out from the situation. In one of the play's few soliloquies Proteus reflects grimly on where it leaves him. "Even as one heat another heat expels, / Or as one nail by strength drives out another," he begins,

> So the remembrance of my former love
> Is by a newer object quite forgotten.
> Is it mine eye, or Valentine's praise,
> Her true perfection, or my false transgression
> That makes me, reasonless, to reason thus?
> She is fair, and so is Julia that I love—
> That I did love, for now my love is thawed,
> Which like a waxen image 'gainst a fire
> Bears no impression of the thing it was.

**[2.4.190–200]**

That sickening change of tense – "I love" to "I did love" – shows Proteus shifting shape like the Greek god for whom he is named. Characteristically, he is unsure whether it is Silvia's apparent "perfection" or Valentine's description that has excited his lust: this is all about male competition, and dispensing with his "former love" is apparently done as easily as saying the words.

This is a dark and until now unexplored side of love. It puts under considerable pressure Proteus's insistence near the opening of the play that feelings for Julia have "metamorphosed" him (and equally Speed's obervation that Valentine, too, has been "metamorphosed with a mistress"): here Proteus is solely responsible for the swiftness of his alteration. Having resolved to forget Julia and pursue Silvia instead, he quickly realizes that Valentine – whose own name signposts him as the ideal lover – needs to be dispatched if he is to stand a chance. Exposing to Silvia's father the couple's plan to elope, Proteus ensures that Valentine is banished from Milan – for, as he coldly ruminates, "I cannot now prove constant to myself / Without some treachery used to Valentine" (2.6.32–3).

Fortunately Silvia is not so fickle, stoutly refusing the advances of this "subtle, perjured, false, disloyal man", as she boldly calls him to his face (4.2.92). And Julia is tragic in her constancy: shadowing Proteus disguised as a young man called Sebastian, she even agrees to deliver his messages of love to Silvia in order to get close to him. Although Proteus's actions do their utmost to make the women enemies, in fact Julia and Silvia end up reinforcing one another. When Silvia hears Sebastian/Julia recount the story of Proteus's "poor mistress", the affinity between them is touching. "Alas, poor lady, desolate and left," Silvia murmurs,

> I weep myself to think upon thy words.
> Here, youth. This is my purse. I give thee this
> For thy sweet mistress' sake, because thou lov'st her.

**[4.4.171–4]**

The final and most difficult test explored by *The Two Gentlemen*, however, is whether the warring men can ever be reconciled. As the plot builds to its climax, it looks as if they cannot: Valentine, forced into banishment, has become an outlaw in the woods while Proteus continues to chase Silvia. When she escapes Milan, he follows her into the forest; and when she refuses him for the last time, he bursts into terrifying violence:

PROTEUS
    Nay, if the gentle spirit of moving words
    Can no way change you to a milder form
    I'll woo you like a soldier, at arm's end,
    And love you 'gainst the nature of love: force ye.
SILVIA
    O heaven!
PROTEUS (*assailing her*) I'll force thee yield to my desire.

                                                  **[5.4.55–9]**

The attempted rape gets, thankfully, no further; the nearby Valentine has heard the commotion and bursts in to rescue Silvia, yelling, "Treacherous man, / Thou hast beguiled my hopes" (5.4.63–4).

While in Shakespeare's source for the play, a novella by the Portuguese writer Jorge de Montemayor, Silvia's equivalent dies so that the two men can be reconciled, in *The Two Gentlemen* the resolution is somehow even more grisly. Accepting Proteus's apology on the spot, Valentine gladly declares, "Then I am paid,"

    And once again I do receive thee honest.
    Who by repentance is not satisfied
    Is nor of heaven nor earth. For these are pleased;
    By penitence th' Eternal wrath's appeased.
    And that my love may appear plain and free,
    All that was mine in Silvia I give thee.

                                                  **[5.4.77–83]**

Rereading this scene while she waited anxiously for her lover George Henry Lewes to finalize his divorce, Marian Evans (better known as George Eliot) confessed herself "disgusted" by it, and even without external pressures like those, it is near-impossible not to agree. Before even accepting Proteus's skimpy apology Valentine does not so much as bother to check whether Silvia is all right after the attempted rape, then he promptly tries to hand her over. They exchange not another word for the rest of the play. It's hard to understand what Shakespeare means us to think here, and some have suggested that Valentine's bizarre and apparently indefensible move is simply the result of shallow dramatization – cardboard characters going through the motions. But perhaps we shouldn't rush to condemn Shakespeare's handiwork. Some of his contemporaries argued that male friendship was the summit of perfection, the kind of perfection described in Lyly's play *Endymion* (1588) as "the image of eternity in which there is nothing moveable, nothing mischievous", and which would always outweigh relationships between a man and a woman. In creating such a painful dramatic twist, Shakespeare asks his audiences bold and urgent questions: can any of us ever believe that? Would we want to? They are issues to which he would return in *Love's Labour's Lost*, and there too male comradeship is disastrously ill-equipped to deal with reality.

In this scene Valentine commits the same crass blunder that he and Proteus are guilty of all along: for all their talk of love, they are not mature enough for it. Valentine means his gesture to be a noble sacrifice, but in order to achieve this ideal he proves himself, like Proteus, capable of astonishing changes of face. As Julia says moments later, "it is the lesser blot, modesty finds, / Women to change their shapes than men change their minds" (5.4.107–8). While stereotype accuses women of changefulness, in this play at least it is the men who prove themselves muddled and inconstant.

> *The denouement is badly hurried and Valentine so far forgets his part as to offer Silvia to the penitent Proteus. Perhaps this fine gesture might be in accord with the code of honour for sworn friends, but it could scarcely be justified on a stage devoted to romantic love.*
>
> A.H. Thorndike, *English Comedy* (1929)

Typically, perhaps, the men do little to help the play find a more satisfactory resolution: it is only when Julia faints and her disguise is removed that Proteus is forced to rethink what has happened. "'Tis true," he admits after Julia's damning words.

> O heaven, were man
> But constant, he were perfect. That one error
> Fills him with faults, makes him run through all th' sins;
> Inconstancy falls off ere it begins.
>
> **[5.4.109–12]**

*The Two Gentlemen* seems to ask, at the very least, whether ideals purchased at this kind of price are worth their cost. Is Valentine's ideal of friendship worth abandoning the woman he is engaged to marry? Can Proteus's ever be trusted again? Ultimately the play stops short of demanding answers from its characters: Julia is dramatically unmasked, all is forgiven and two marriages are the result. But we in the audience don't have quite that luxury.

# Stage history and adaptations

The stage history of *The Two Gentlemen* makes for rapid reading. Although it was most likely Shakespeare's first play to be written (c.1589–90), we know nothing of its early years – aside from the fact that it may have still been among the King's Men's repertoire as late as 1606. The comic role of Lance was almost certainly written for the clown **Will Kempe**, though the identity of his sidekick, the dog Crab, has unfortunately passed into obscurity.

Only *Love's Labour's Lost* escaped revival longer than *The Two Gentlemen*, and it wasn't until 1762 that we can be sure a performance actually took place. This was in fact a free adaptation by **Benjamin Victor,** which softened the conclusion and straightened out the characters. The comic components were also beefed up in order to showcase **Richard Yates**, the most famous comedian of his day, but even though the singer **Joseph Vernon** also starred as Thurio, the production flopped.

It wouldn't reappear until 1784, this time at Covent Garden, in a production cheekily advertised as "SHAXESPEARE's, with alterations" (it including scenes from other plays). **John Quick** played Lance, but this time the comedy sank after only one performance. Six years later **John Philip Kemble**'s industrious Drury Lane adaptation did a little better (industrious not least because Kemble invented names for all the minor roles, Outlaws included), but it still followed Victor's lead by moralizing plot and characters alike: Valentine, played by Kemble himself in an 1808 revival over at Covent Garden, was a model of gentlemanliness.

Adaptations continued in 1821 with what proved to be *The Two Gentlemen*'s most popular nineteenth-century production: an "operatic" version by **George Reynolds** that employed Kemble's text alongside some awe-inspiring scenery. The following year **William Charles Macready** attempted a return to Shakespeare's script in Bristol, but it wasn't until 1841 that he staged a production in the capital. Although it was well received (mainly for its impressive sets), this version foundered – as did **Charles Kean**'s attempt at the Park Theatre in New York in 1846. Kean tried again in London two years later, and did somewhat better; among his cast were **Ellen Tree**'s Silvia and **Rob Keeley**'s Lance. But *The Two Gentlemen* was still a long way from being a favourite: when a London theatre chose the comedy for its debut production in 1849, *The Examiner* actuallly praised the audience for sitting patiently through until the final curtain. **Samuel Phelps**'s 1857 version at Sadler's Wells also stumbled, as did **Osmond Teale**'s at Stratford in 1890, though the great American actress **Ada Rehan** gained plaudits as Julia in 1895, directed by **Augustine Daly** in New York.

By the dawn of the twentieth century *The Two Gentlemen* was ripe for rediscovery. Two pioneers, **William Poel** and his disciple **Harley Granville-Barker**, both attempted it within a few years, but amid their experiments the play itself rarely attracted comment – reviewers were more struck by Poel's alterations to His Majesty's Theatre in 1910, which included covering the stalls with an apron stage and destroying most of the sightlines. **Frank Benson** put it on at Stratford that same year as his "revival play", casting his wife **Constance**, then in middle age, as Julia to **Norah Lancaster**'s Silvia; and the comedy appeared once again in Shakespeare's home town in 1916, this time directed by **Ben Greet** and with **Sybil Thorndike** as Julia.

"This cruel-hearted cur": Crab looks the other way while his master, Lance (Richard Moore), pours out his heart to the audience. From David Thacker's RSC *Two Gentlemen* (1992).

During the interwar years several productions appeared in both Stratford and London, but the play's nickname of "The Walking Gentlemen" (theatrical slang for a walk-on role) defeated its proponents. **Ben Iden Payne**'s colourful Stratford version from 1938, which name-checked Giotto and Palladio among its design influences, was reviewed more positively, if criticized for making the play too polite – a problem that didn't afflict **Hans Rothe**'s hugely popular German translation from five years previously, which eventually fell foul of Goebbels. Back in Britain, *The Two Gentlemen*'s turnaround came after World War II, with **Denis Carey**'s 1952 staging at the Bristol Old Vic. Carey employed a young cast (among them **John Neville**) and interpolated plenty of music, and found he had a surprise hit on his hands. **Michael Langham**'s 1957 production at the London Old Vic also gained plaudits, but this time for its Regency staging; among Langham's cast were **Barbara Jefford** and **Ingrid Hafner**, while **Keith Michell**'s Byronesque Proteus turned heads.

Unsurprisingly, Stratford-upon-Avon has hosted nearly all postwar productions of *The Two Gentlemen* – though even there it has done time on the company blacklist. **Peter Hall**'s 1960 version just predated the arrival of the RSC and state subsidy, and its autumnal setting failed to win hearts or profits. More divisive was **Robin Phillips**'s staging at the same venue ten years later, which transplanted the play to modern-dress and camped it up, with **Peter Egan**'s Valentine and **Ian Richardson**'s Proteus spending much of their time playing beach-ball while **Patrick Stewart**'s Lance formed the production's emotional touchstone. **John Guare** and **Mel Shapiro**'s musical adaptation, which debuted at **Joseph Papp**'s theatre in New York in 1971, was even more daring – and the critics loved it. The same could not be said of **John Barton**'s 1981 double-bill of *Titus* and *The Two Gentlemen* at Stratford, which opened to terrible reviews and never recovered.

More recently revivals have appeared more frequently than the ten-year postwar average. **David Thacker**'s 1992 RSC production was set in the 1930s, and had Cole Porter lyrics to prove it; while on Bankside in 1996 the comedy formed part of the Shakespeare's Globe "prologue" season in an enthusiastically received production by **Jack Shepherd**. **Edward Hall** also chose the play for a debut – this time his own first appearance at Stratford in 1998, 41 years after his father Peter made his own entrance. Hall's lively and youthful production was quickly headlined "cappuccino Shakespeare" for its sharply tailored Italian setting, and saw excellent performances from **Tom Goodman-Hill**'s sober Valentine and **Poppy Miller**'s Silvia in particular. **Rachel Kavanaugh** put on *The Two Gentlemen* at Regent's Park in London over the summer of 2003, but her production attracted less glowing notices – the *Guardian* called it "bland", though *The Independent* thought that Kavanaugh did as well as her material allowed.

On screen *The Two Gentlemen* has yet to make much of a splash – fleeting appearances in **Tom Stoppard** and **Marc Norman**'s 1998 *Shakespeare in Love* notwithstanding. The BBC/Time-Life version (1983) was directed by **Don Taylor**, featuring **Tessa Peake-Jones**'s Julia and **Joanne Pearce**'s Silvia opposite the Valentine and Proteus of **John Hudson** and **Tyler Butterworth**.

## Screen

### The Two Gentlemen of Verona

**T. Butterworth, J. Hudson, T. Peake-Jones; Don Taylor (dir.)**

UK, 1983 ▷ Ambrose Video (BBC) ▭

Don Taylor's *The Two Gentlemen*, the only version ever filmed, is bathed in what is presumably intended to be lustrous Mediterranean light – and, compared to the crepuscular interiors of other BBC Shakespeares, the effect is not unbecoming. Realism is a dangerous game in a TV studio, however, and elsewhere (for instance in hiring two cherubs, painting them gold and having them cavort between the lovers) Taylor attempts a more riskily stylized approach to the comedy. It's difficult to feel that either aspect of this production solidly works, though, and ultimately what makes it more than barely watchable is its youthful and energetic cast – top marks go to the women in particular, Tessa Peake-Jones's touching Julia and Joanne Pearce's vivacious Silvia. All too often, however, monstrous hair creates its own problems of credibility. Recently rereleased in the US as part of the full BBC set by Ambrose Video Publishing.

## Audio

### The Two Gentlemen of Verona
**M. Maloney, D. Lewis, S. Wickham; Clive Brill (dir.)**
UK, 1998 ▷ Arkangel ⊙ 〰

The relationship between Valentine and Proteus is crucial to any performance of the play – it's definitely rivalrous here, with plenty of aggression beneath the surface (sometimes not too deep) – but what listening to this recording makes you realize is that pace is all-important. *The Two Gentlemen*'s frequent wordplay needs to be fleet-footed if it isn't to stagnate, and fortunately old hand Clive Brill works his cast hard and edits rapidly. That said, speed (or Speed) isn't the only impression: John Woodvine's Lance is delightfully lugubrious, and more than takes his time, Lucy Robinson is a moving Julia, while Saskia Wickham provides a pert and persuasive Silvia.

## Editions

### New Cambridge Shakespeare
**Kurt Schlueter (ed.); 1990** ▷ Cambridge UP

This New Cambridge edition is the most recent since Clifford Leech's Arden 2 from 1969, implying that *The Two Gentlemen* has yet to make a journey from the critical margins to anything like the mainstream. Schlueter serves this early comedy well, presenting a clear text and sensible (if somewhat conventional) introduction – the latter enlivened considerably by C. Walter Hodges's characterful illustrations. Perhaps the only problem with this edition is Schlueter's limited annotation to the text: it would be good to have more detail on the play's language, particularly given that the editor is apparently not keen to dwell on Shakespeare's bawdier allusions.

## Some criticism

### Shakespearian Comedy
**H.B. Charlton; 1936** ▷ Methuen / Routledge [o/p]

This book is where modern understanding of Shakespearian comedy begins, so perhaps it's apt that it should be recommended for one of the playwright's very earliest works. A series of eight lectures, it was published to redress a critical trend (rooted in the eighteenth century) which insisted that only Shakespeare's tragedies were serious enough to be worth studying. While Charlton undoubtedly regards *The Two Gentlemen* as an apprentice piece and even something of a failure – it manifests, he argues, only the very first stirrings of Shakespeare's distinctive "comic idea" – his suggestion that in it Shakespeare makes love itself the butt of comedy has proved hard to shift, much as his developmental model of Shakespeare's growth as a dramatist still has much influence.

### Two Gentlemen of Verona: Critical Essays
**June Schlueter (ed.); 1996** ▷ Garland

It's not clear whether Schlueters Kurt and June are connected by anything other than shared enthusiasm for *The Two Gentlemen* – Kurt gets a credit in this book, but only as an editor – but the apparent coincidence is striking (and somehow quite Shakespearian). At any rate this *Critical Essays* volume is as useful as others in the series and particularly valuable for this often marginalized play. It unites classic essays, among them Harold Brooks's well-known "Two Clowns in a Comedy (To Say Nothing of the Dog)" from 1963, with some more recent fare, and closes with a helpful selection of theatre reviews from 1821 to 1991.

# The Two Noble Kinsmen

After the political intrigue of *Henry VIII*, it would be difficult to think of a play more different than that which followed it onto the stage. *The Two Noble Kinsmen* concluded Shakespeare's professional theatrical career, and although it was also co-written with John Fletcher, their collaboration seems to have been markedly less intimate than before. And despite being elegant and courtly – its source is Chaucer's "Knight's Tale", its dramatic language heavily influenced by elaborate Jacobean masques – the tone of *Kinsmen* is mixed, and often difficult to gauge. While the story of two men who fall in love with the same woman points back to Shakespeare's earliest comedies, most obviously *The Two Gentlemen of Verona*, in this play resolution proves strikingly difficult to achieve. The "kinsmen", Palamon and Arcite, claim to be closer to each other than anyone alive, but their conversion from extravagant devotion to bitter hatred undermines the chivalric ideals both claim to serve – and in the handful of professional performances the play has received they have often been quite outshone by another character, the nameless Jailer's Daughter, who falls hopelessly and tragically in love with Palamon. Dominated by loss and compromise – never more so than in its gruesome, troubling conclusion – *Kinsmen* feels a world away not just from *Henry VIII*, but from the renunciations and reconciliations offered by *The Tempest*, often assumed to be Shakespeare's cordial farewell to his art.

**[DATE]**   Featuring Shakespeare's last writing for the professional stage, *The Two Noble Kinsmen* was first performed in 1613–14, possibly at the indoor Blackfriars theatre.

**[SOURCES]**   Chaucer's "Knight's Tale" is the play's key source, as for *A Midsummer Night's Dream* – itself another influence. The masque in Act Three is lifted from Francis Beaumont's *Masque of the Inner Temple* (1613).

**[TEXTS]**   One of several Shakespeare plays not to make it into the First Folio (1623), *Kinsmen* was printed in a 1634 quarto edition proclaiming that it was co-written with John Fletcher – a plausible excuse for its earlier exclusion. Though regularly published in editions of Fletcher, it was not generally believed to be Shakespeare's work until the nineteenth century.

## Interpreting the play

*The Two Noble Kinsmen* is, it's been suggested, a kind of *Midsummer Night's Dream* part two: both plays draw upon Chaucer's "Knight's Tale", the graceful and courtly story told by the worthy, wise and "parfit gentil" Knight to the assembled gaggle of pilgrims as the first of *The Canterbury Tales*. But where the *Dream* merely takes up the Athenian setting of Chaucer's narrative and the wedding between the Duke Theseus and his bride Hippolyta, discarding the rest, *Kinsmen* is a full dramatization of the tale itself, that of two cousins, "yonge knyghtes" captured by Theseus as prisoners of war, who tragically fall for the same woman. That Shakespeare returned once more to a medieval author who had served him well before (most

## Major Characters & Synopsis

**Prologue** and **Epilogue**

**Palamon** and **Arcite**, cousins (the two "noble kinsmen"), both nephews of King Creon

**Theseus**, Duke of Athens

**Hippolyta**, Queen of the Amazons, later Theseus's wife

**Emilia**, Hippolyta's sister

A **Woman**, Emilia's attendant

**Pirithous**, Theseus's close friend

**Artesius**, an Athenian soldier

Three **Queens**, widows to kings killed at the siege of Thebes

**Hymen**, god of marriage

**Valerius**, a Theban

Six **Knights**, attending Arcite and Palamon

A **Jailer** of Theseus's prison

The **Jailer's Daughter** and her **Wooer**

A **Doctor**

Six **Countrymen**, led by the schoolmaster **Gerald**

**ACT 1** In Athens, preparations for the marriage of King Theseus and Hippolyta are disrupted by the sudden appearance of three queens, whose husbands have died fighting the evil King Creon of Thebes. Denied the right to bury their husbands – whose bodies still lie on the battlefield – the women demand that Theseus take up their cause and attack Thebes. At that moment, Palamon and Arcite (Creon's nephews) are debating whether to escape the corruption of Thebes when a messenger arrives with news that Theseus is threatening the city. Despite their disgust with their uncle, the two kinsmen decide to remain and fight. Theseus triumphs, however, and the wounded Palamon and Arcite are captured and imprisoned.

**ACT 2** In jail in Athens, Palamon and Arcite are consoling themselves with the closeness of their friendship when Palamon suddenly spots the beautiful Emilia (Hippolyta's sister) gathering flowers outside. Both men fall instantly in love, but Palamon claims precedence for having seen her first, and the cousins immediately begin to argue. Their quarrel is broken off only when Arcite is suddenly released. Though banished from Athens, Arcite takes the opportunity to appear in disguise at Theseus's games, where he impresses all with his wrestling skills and his noble bearing. His reward, fittingly, is to be bestowed on Emilia as a

servant. Meanwhile, the Jailer's Daughter has arranged Palamon's escape in the vain hope of winning his love.

**ACT 3** Separated from the royal party while out celebrating May Day, Arcite is suddenly confronted by Palamon. The two men argue over Emilia once more, before agreeing to fight a duel for her. At the same time, the Jailer's Daughter is desperately searching the woods for Palamon when she stumbles across a group of countrymen rehearsing an entertainment. Realizing that she has lost her mind, the performers include her in their masque, which they then present to Theseus and his companions. In another part of the wood, Arcite brings his cousin armour but no sooner do the two begin to fight than they are interrupted by Theseus and his party. When the Duke condemns them to death, Emilia pleads for the sentence to be commuted to banishment, but the kinsmen refuse this offer (both preferring to die rather than never see her again). Theseus then demands that Emilia choose between them, but when she is unable do so he agrees to supervise a final contest for her hand.

**ACT 4** The Jailer's Daughter, now completely mad, is reunited with her father. Observing her behaviour, the Doctor advises that the only possible remedy is that a former suitor (the Wooer) should simply pretend that he is Palamon. In the meantime, Emilia is still unable to choose between her two suitors – the contest between the rivals must go ahead.

**ACT 5** Palamon and Arcite, each accompanied by three knights, separately pray for success, while Emilia prays that whoever loves her best will be the victor. Back at the jail, the Doctor's treatment of the Jailer's Daughter seems to be working, and he encourages the Wooer to sleep with her. At court the contest begins, but Emilia refuses to attend and its progress is reported to her. Though at first it seems that Palamon will triumph, he is eventually defeated: Arcite wins Emilia's hand while Palamon and his knights are condemned to death. But just as Palamon is about to be executed, news arrives that Arcite has been fatally injured in a riding accident. As the cousins are briefly reunited, Arcite bestows Emilia on Palamon with his dying breath.

obviously in *Troilus and Cressida* as well as the *Dream*) attests not only to Chaucer's continued popularity – an expanded edition of his works appeared a decade or so before *Kinsmen* reached the stage – but also to a Jacobean taste for medieval romance. The small, indoor Blackfriars became the King's Men's winter house from around 1609, and the refined audiences who attended that theatre a few years later would surely have been flattered to hear that "Chaucer, of all admired" was providing their night's entertainment, as the Prologue announces. "If we let fall the nobleness of this," he goes on,

> And the first sound this child hear be a hiss,
> How it will shake the bones of that good man,
> And make him cry from under ground, 'O fan
> From me the witless chaff of such a writer,
> That blasts my bays and my famed works makes lighter
> Than Robin Hood'? This is the fear we bring,
> For to say truth, it were an endless thing
> And too ambitious to aspire to him,
> Weak as we are, and almost breathless swim
> In this deep water.
>
> **[Prologue 13–25]**

Begging its audience not to "hiss" – if only to preserve Chaucer's "sweet sleep" and keep him from spinning in his grave – the "child" play attempts a similar trick to the earlier *Pericles*, apologizing for, yet also showing off, its prestigious paternity. The authors keep their promise, too: while in previous scripts based on Chaucer Shakespeare reworks his material intensively (*Troilus and Cressida* is the most obvious example), in *Kinsmen* he and Fletcher are more restrained. This is to be a properly Chaucerian play.

## Dearer in love

Even so – and though the work of writing *Kinsmen* was shared with Fletcher – it will also be a convincingly Shakespearian one. As well as taking its cue from Chaucer, the story of cousins Palamon and Arcite gestures back to early comedies such as *The Two Gentlemen of Verona* and *Love's Labour's Lost*, in which intimate male friendships occupy a central position in the drama. In *Kinsmen* nowhere is this clearer than after the battle between Theseus and Creon that occurs in the middle of Act One. Despite the fact that the kinsmen have been captured by Theseus following the Theban defeat and thrown into prison, their Athenian jailer and his daughter are amazed by the prisoners' buoyant spirits. "They eat well, look merrily, discourse of many things, but nothing of their own restraint and disasters," the Jailer's Daughter wonderingly observes (2.1.38–40), and it soon becomes clear that what sustains the two men, "dearer in love than blood", is their own friendship (1.2.1). Arcite describes it extravagantly. "Even from the bottom of these miseries, / From all that fortune can inflict upon us," he declares,

> I see two comforts rising—two mere blessings,
> If the gods please, to hold here a brave patience,
> And the enjoying of our griefs together.
> Whilst Palamon is with me, let me perish
> If I think this our prison.
>
> **[2.2.56–62]**

Their intimacy is such that it overcomes mere physical hardship, and Palamon echoes not only his friend's thoughts but his high-flown way of expressing it. "Let's think this prison holy sanctuary," he agrees,

> To keep us from corruption of worse men.
> We are young, and yet desire the ways of honour,
> That liberty and common conversation,
> The poison of pure spirits, might, like women,
> Woo us to wander from. What worthy blessing
> Can be but our imaginations
> May make it ours? And here being thus together,
> We are an endless mine to one another:
> We are one another's wife, ever begetting
> New births of love; we are father, friends, acquaintance;
> We are in one another, families …

**[2.2.71–82]**

This doctrine of mutual self-sufficiency is incredible in every sense of the word. Rewriting their imprisonment as something they have chosen voluntarily, like life in a monastery, Palamon suggests that they provide the substance of each other's lives – friends, family, even spouse. Though it's undeniably more grandiose, this pact echoes the "deep oaths" signed at the outset of *Love's Labour's Lost* by the King of Navarre and his three lords, and like those ivory-tower fantasies it will prove utterly unsustainable. Palamon and Arcite, though they persuade themselves otherwise, are only this close because circumstance has brought them together, and when that changes so will everything else.

The transformation comes more immediately than anyone – even perhaps the audience – expects. Just a few moments later Palamon and Arcite are joined onstage by Emilia, Queen Hippolyta's sister, who appears outside the prison languorously picking flowers. "She is wondrous fair," says Arcite, and Palamon echoes him, sighing, "She is all the beauty extant" (2.2.148). So closely attuned to each other that they boast of being each other's "wife", the cousins, with the most ironic inevitability, fall for exactly the same woman. But it isn't long before the pair find themselves exchanging terms of high refinement for something less noble. "What think you of this beauty?" Palamon asks, suddenly suspicious:

ARCITE                 'Tis a rare one.
PALAMON
   Is't but a rare one?
ARCITE          Yes, a matchless beauty.
PALAMON
   Might not a man well lose himself and love her?
ARCITE
   I cannot tell what you have done; I have,
   Beshrew mine eyes for't! Now I feel my shackles.
PALAMON
   You love her, then?
ARCITE  Who would not?
PALAMON  And desire her?
ARCITE  Before my liberty.
PALAMON
   I saw her first.

**[2.2.154–63]**

Palamon's childish interjection is genuinely funny, but it also indicates how easy it has been for these two young men to renounce vows sworn so passionately just a few minutes earlier.

Palamon and Arcite are not alone in feeling the violent tremors created by love. When Arcite is suddenly banished from Greece, Palamon is left alone in prison – an arrangement that suits the Jailer's Daughter, who is earnestly trying to catch the stranger's eye. Acknowledging the social gulf between them, she admits that "to marry him is hopeless, / To be his whore is witless" (2.4.4–5) but can see no other way out. Then an idea strikes. "Say I ventured / To set him free?" she wonders,

> What says the law then? Thus much
> For law or kindred! I will do it,
> And this night or tomorrow he shall love me.
>
> **[2.4.30–3]**

The play does not make things that easy, however. Her lover remains aloof, seeming not to realize even when she helps him escape that she has fanciful ambitions of marrying him.

Shakespeare and Fletcher took the story of the Jailer's Daughter (they give her no other name) from the tiniest of hints in the "Knight's Tale" – there it is merely a mysterious "freend" who helps Palamon escape – but what they made out of it becomes utterly crucial to the play. Against the narrative of the two kinsmen, which becomes more contorted than ever – Arcite manages to work his way into Theseus's court in disguise, while Palamon hides in the forest – the playwrights set four haunting scenes that trace her emotional collapse. "Let not my sense unsettle," she begs when she is unable to find her beloved (3.2.29), but a scene later her fears have been realized. As she addresses the audience in soliloquy (almost the only person in the play to do so), it becomes apparent that her sanity is gone. "I am very cold," she shivers,

> and all the stars are out too,
> The little stars and all, that look like aglets—
> The sun has seen my folly. Palamon!
> Alas, no; he's in heaven. Where am I now?
> Yonder's the sea and there's a ship—how't tumbles!
> And there's a rock lies watching under water—
> Now, now, it beats upon it—now, now, now,
> There's a leak sprung, a sound one—how they cry!
> Open her before the wind—you'll lose all else.
> Up with a course or two, and tack about, boys.
> Good night, good night, you're gone.
>
> **[3.4.1–11]**

Shakespeare is usually credited with Act One of *Kinsmen*, the first two scenes of Act Three and three scenes in Act Five, including the play's very last – but even if this soliloquy is Fletcher's handiwork it reads like an assemblage of Shakespearian motifs. Mumbling scraps of folk ballads, the Jailer's Daughter resembles *Hamlet*'s Ophelia, though her habit of repeating words resembles that of King Lear. More tragically even than these, her rambling voice also resembles that of the equally nameless maiden in *A Lover's Complaint*, a poem of Shakespeare's likewise given over to the story of a grief-stricken and isolated young woman.

## For what we lack

Yet the plight of the Jailer's Daughter, in loving someone socially beyond her reach, is unusual in Shakespeare (Helen in *All's Well* is her closest relative), unusual enough for the Restoration dramatist William Davenant to enhance her status in his adaptation so that she can marry Palamon after all (see p.396). *The Two Noble Kinsmen* does not permit itself such a tidy conclusion, and in this play the remainder of the Daughter's experience is fairly wretched. A doctor persuades her father that the best cure for her illness is simply for the man who was

## Betwixt man and man

Though he is by no means so celebrated now, **John Fletcher**, Shakespeare's co-author of three plays, was one of the brightest stars in the Jacobean theatre and more prolific even than his mentor. Most often Fletcher worked in collaboration, and nearly fifty dramas have been attached to his name since his death in 1625.

Almost nothing is known of Fletcher's first years. He was born at Rye in Sussex in 1579, the son of a clergyman who rose to become Bishop of London but died in 1596 heavily in debt. By that time John had entered Bene't College, Cambridge – now Corpus Christi, also Christopher Marlowe's old college – but little evidence survives of his time at university and he next crops up a decade later in London, among the dramatists, poets and actors who used to drink at the **Mermaid Tavern** in London's Bread Street. Ben Jonson was a regular, and while tradition holds that Shakespeare also socialized there (in truth there's little evidence) it's more than possible that it was at the Mermaid that Fletcher met a man who would dominate his life: **Francis Beaumont** (1584–1616).

Despite their differing backgrounds – Beaumont was from a wealthy family and had trained as a lawyer – the two men began to write with each other, and seventeenth-century diarist John Aubrey reports (with a characteristic eye for gossip) that they became so close that they moved in together, dressed alike and "had one wench in the house between them". Fletcher never married, and whatever the precise details of his relationship with Beaumont, their professional partnership prospered. In the years before Beaumont's untimely death, the pair had written around six plays, although at least fifty would be ascribed to them subsequently. Among their joint creations is probably the hugely popular *Knight of the Burning Pestle* (1608), which lampooned Jacobean taste for high-flown courtly drama, relating the tale of a London grocer-cum-knight who takes part in a series of absurd adventures.

Fletcher also had connections with another man who died in 1616, William Shakespeare. Shakespeare was 14 years Fletcher's senior, and in the last few years of his career it seems that Fletcher was groomed by Shakespeare's company as his successor. They first came together for **Cardenio**, but that play has been lost (see p.186), making their earliest extant collaboration **Henry VIII**, written around 1613. Their only other work together was Shakespeare's last: **The Two Noble Kinsmen**, which dates from slightly later. It isn't clear how Fletcher and Shakespeare divided the writing of these plays, and attempts to separate their work on internal evidence haven't been massively convincing – hardly surprising, given that Fletcher in particular was used to writing in a variety of styles. The task of working out who wrote what is further complicated by the likelihood that each revised the other's material.

The most intriguing aspect of their collaboration is the most mysterious. Fletcher's play **The Woman's Prize, or The Tamer Tamed** continues where Shakespeare's *Taming of the Shrew* leaves off, getting rid of Katherine and supplying Petruccio with a new wife, whose task it becomes to administer some long-overdue humiliation. The play's date is not known, making it unclear whether *The Tamer Tamed* was the work that brought Fletcher to Shakespeare's attention, or was written after his death in 1616 – or even whether the older man gave it his blessing as a sequel. At any rate perhaps it was Fletcher's decision to bring male supremacist Petruccio down a few pegs that encouraged Dryden to utter the most famous summary of the difference between the two poets. "Shakespeare," he declared, "wrote better betwixt man and man; Fletcher betwixt man and woman."

---

wooing her previously (the script just calls him "Wooer") to seize advantage of her mental imbalance. "Take upon you, young sir," he tells the Wooer,

> the name of Palamon; say you come to eat with her, and to commune of love. This will catch her attention, for this her mind beats upon … Sing to her such green songs of love as she says Palamon hath sung in prison; come to her stuck in as sweet flowers as the season is mistress of, and thereto make an addition of some other compounded odours which are grateful to the sense. All this shall become Palamon, for Palamon can sing, and Palamon is sweet and ev'ry good thing.

**[4.3.72–84]**

"It is a falsehood she is in," the Doctor smartly concludes, "which is with falsehoods to be combated" (4.3.90–1), and many real-life Renaissance physicians would have agreed with his treatment. Even so the tone of the play is difficult here, balanced between comedy and something incalculably more perplexed – as it was a few scenes earlier, when the Daughter happened upon a group of country folk who took advantage of her insanity by getting her to join their chorus line and perform for Duke Theseus. While the rustic performance is of course another nod to the *Dream*, the suggestion in *Kinsmen* that it doesn't really matter whom the Daughter loves, Palamon or another man pretending to be him, also replays some of that comedy's concerns in a far more depressing key.

A little earlier the Jailer's Daughter is reported as having attempted to drown herself: death is a nagging theme in *Kinsmen*. Having opened on a scene in which three widowed queens plead with Theseus for their slaughtered husbands to be given a decent burial, the play has a finale, which resolves the conflict between Palamon and Arcite only in the messiest of ways, that is equally gruesome. Finding the two kinsmen fighting illegally in the woods, Theseus decides that unless Emilia can decide between them, they must face each other in combat one last time, with whoever loses facing execution. In what is probably a nod to the masques increasingly popular with the King's Men's royal employer, this climactic contest – like the queens' formal appeals to Theseus – will be performed with plenty of courtly, pseudo-medieval trappings. Each combatant is attended by three knights, and Theseus orders that whoever succeeds in touching a pyramid he sets up (an ancient symbol of success) will win the lady's hand. Yet at the heart of these intricate performances lies a stark emotional crisis. Emilia has no answer to the terrible quandary she faces, and in a later scene she is movingly depicted debating which of the two men is better (she cannot ultimately decide). Earlier Arcite had declared with characteristic fervour that to be removed from her sight would be "death / Beyond imagination" (2.3.4–5), but here the risk he and Palamon face is painfully real: Emilia's inability to choose between her suitors guarantees that one of them must die.

> *Palamon's unexpected salvation from execution is not the metaphorical resurrection of Shakespeare's other late plays, but just one more turning that will delay for a little his arrival in the marketplace of death.*
>
> Helen Cooper, "Jacobean Chaucer: *The Two Noble Kinsmen* and other Chaucerian plays" (1998)

As the tournament nears, the two rivals ready themselves for combat. Once again gesturing towards the stylized devices of masque, the play has them perform elaborate and lengthy rituals of preparation (rituals that also guarantee some impressive special effects): Arcite prays to Mars to the sound of clanging armour, Palamon invokes Venus accompanied by strains of mystical music – and even Emilia calls upon Diana for guidance, being rewarded with a blossoming rose tree that springs from the altar at which she kneels. Even when the competition finally arrives, though, the audience is kept guessing. The fight takes place off stage, with only background noise indicating what is going on. At first it seems that Palamon is winning, but then the cries for "Arcite" begin to filter through. When the news becomes more certain, the fretful Emilia greets the news with joy. "Half sights saw / That Arcite was no babe," she exclaims.

> God's lid, his richness
> And costliness of spirit looked through him—it could
> No more be hid in him than fire in flax,
> Than humble banks can go to law with waters

That drift winds force to raging. I did think
Good Palamon would miscarry, yet I knew not
Why I did think so.

[5.5.95–102]

She accepts Arcite gladly, and Theseus concurs, announcing that "the gods by their divine arbitrament / Have given you this knight" (5.5.107–8).

But in the play's lurching final move Shakespeare and Fletcher show that the gods' will is not always so easily interpreted. Palamon is about to be beheaded when a messenger bursts in, calling on the executioner to halt. Pirithous breathlessly follows, with news that it is Arcite who is on the point of death: the "hot horse, hot as fire" bestowed upon him by Emilia as a token of her love has bolted, and crushed the victorious knight. In a supreme but troubling sacrifice that directly recalls *The Two Gentlemen*, the dying Arcite insists that his kinsman should take his place: against all expectation it is Palamon, not his cousin, who is to marry Emilia. If the gods have declared their wish, as Theseus insisted before, their messages are achingly difficult to interpret. The Duke is permitted to address them one last time. "O you heavenly charmers," he calls,

What things you make of us! For what we lack
We laugh, for what we have, are sorry; still
Are children in some kind. Let us be thankful
For that which is, and with you leave dispute
That are above our question.

[5.6.131–6]

This scene is probably by Shakespeare, and as a conclusion to his career these halting words of Theseus are infinitely more painful than anything voiced by Prospero at the close of *The Tempest*. Everything is provisional, they imply – and the human condition is one in which comedy and tragedy are so closely entwined that we may never finally know which is which.

## Stage history and adaptations

About the first years of *Kinsmen* there is much speculation and precious little evidence. Given that it debuted around 1613, soon after the destruction of the Globe – the Prologue mentions "our losses" in what may be a reference to the fire – it's likely to have first been performed at the intimate **Blackfriars** playhouse. About casting we can only guess: both of the King's Men's star actors, **Richard Burbage** and **John Lowin**, were probably too long in the tooth, though some critics think the play may not have been performed by Shakespeare and Fletcher's troupe at all but another company. At any rate, we know it was considered for performance at **court** in 1619–20, but probably never staged, and the text (omitted from the First Folio) wasn't printed until 1634.

Exactly thirty years later it reappeared in the Restoration theatre in mutilated form, an adaptation by **William Davenant** entitled *The Rivals*. As with Davenant's other reworkings, this bulldozed many of the play's unsettling aspects and made it into a straight comedy. Arcite is spared death while "Celania" (equivalent to the Jailer's Daughter in the original play) is magically cured and married to "Philander", Davenant's Palamon, played by **Thomas Betterton** in the original production. **Moll Davies** took the part of Celania in a later revival, and caught the eye of Charles II – perhaps fittingly, she became one of his many mistresses soon afterwards.

In the eighteenth century, too, adaptation proved *Kinsmen*'s only path to staging. The playwright **Richard Cumberland** had limited success with his *Palamon and Arcite; or, The Noble Kinsmen* from 1779, which like Davenant's version sentimentalized the play but made it into a tragedy instead. In an altogether different vein was **Godolphin Waldron**'s *Love and Madness;*

Palamon (Gerard Murphy) and Arcite (Hugh Quarshie) come to blows over the same woman. A scene from Barry Kyle's *The Two Noble Kinsmen*, which opened the RSC's Jacobean-style Swan Theatre in 1986.

*or, The Two Noble Kinsmen*, which premiered in London in 1795. Unlike Cumberland's adaptation this ended happily, with Palamon cheerfully deciding to accept the advances of the mad "Hermia" on condition that his death will be stayed.

After these performances *Kinsmen* dropped out of the theatrical record entirely: its only verifiable stage history exists in the twentieth century. After over three centuries in abeyance, it was revived at the Old Vic in 1928 with **Eric Portman** as Arcite, **Ernest Milton** as Palamon and **Jean Forbes-Robertson** as the Jailer's Daughter. This staging played it safe by choosing a medieval setting ("an experiment in prettiness", according to one observer), although Milton found himself forced to play Palamon as a comic character after audiences tittered at his wig. The production sparked only mild curiosity, however, and for the next forty years *Kinsmen* became the preserve of academic and amateur productions. Many of these were impressive, however – an open-air staging by renowned Chaucerian and Shakespearian scholar **Neville Coghill** in the gardens of Merton College, Oxford in 1957 attracted attention – and bravely kept its spirit alive.

Its next foray into professional theatre came under **Richard Digby Day** at York's Theatre Royal in 1973. This presented a beautiful but skewed version of the play, cutting the rustics along with much of the comedy and concentrating instead on its timeless qualities. A French adaptation by **Véronique Réand** from 1979 offered a tragic view of its material, while an English-language Edinburgh Fringe production the same year by **Andrew Visnevski**'s Cherub Company stressed the intimate homosocial ties between the two kinsmen with an all-male cast. Despite heavy cutting and confrontational staging, many reviewers were struck by the emotional Jailer's Daughter of **Anthony Best**. Other performances followed, several in the US: **Walter Scholz**'s Los Angeles-based Globe Playhouse production was well reviewed, **Suzanna Peters**'s Jailer's Daughter again a centrepiece.

The production with the greatest impact to date, however, appeared in 1986, and in fact opened the RSC's brand-new Swan Theatre (itself based on Jacobean models). **Barry Kyle** used Japanese-influenced staging and costumes to draw out the play's stylized qualities, but it was the calibre of his cast that really shone through. **Gerard Murphy**'s white Palamon played opposite the black Arcite of **Hugh Quarshie**, while **Imogen Stubbs** very nearly stole the show as an uninhibited and hugely affecting Jailer's Daughter. Elements of Kyle's staging – notably the suspended cage in which the prison scene was played – irritated some, but his interpretation of *Kinsmen* has gone down in theatrical history as perhaps the finest yet.

Not that there has been much competition since: fewer than a handful of professional productions have made it past the drawing board, among them **Nagle Jackson**'s medieval staging for the Oregon Shakespeare Festival in 1994. British audiences had a rare chance to see *Kinsmen* courtesy of **Tim Carroll** at the rebuilt Shakespeare's Globe in summer 2000, but Carroll's cast – to its director's irritation – fell into the trap of playing the play for laughs. Despite powerful performances from **Will Keen** (Palamon), **Jasper Britton** (Arcite) and **Kate Fleetwood** (Jailer's Daughter), it struggled to convince audiences it was serious and faced heavy fire from theatre critics. Few such problems appear to have bedevilled a recent staging by **Darko Tresnjak** at New York's Public Theater (2003), which received plaudits from reviewers impressed that so obscure a play had such power to move. Acting in Tresnjak's "crisp" production were **David Harbour** and **Graham Hamilton** as the Kinsmen, while **Doan Ly** attracted positive notices for a spirited Emilia.

Not admitted into the BBC/Time-Life series due to queries about its authorship (and presumably anxieties about recouping the cost), *Kinsmen* has yet to find a producer willing to capture it on film or TV.

## Audio

### The Two Noble Kinsmen
**J. Firth, N. Cooke, H. Schlesinger; Clive Brill (dir.)**
▷ Arkangel ⊙ 🎞️

Employing Simon Russell Beale to speak the Prologue elevates expectations, and – even considering the lack of competition – this production of *Kinsmen* does not disappoint. The masques and songs come across surprisingly well, with Dominique Le Gendre's vibrant music evoking well the kinds of spectacle your mind's eye might supply. The interplay between Jonathan Firth's Palamon and Nigel Cooke's Arcite is effectively intimate, and while they don't always relish the more arcane corners of the play's verse, these Kinsmen never run the risk of blurring into each other – Firth seems youthful and open, Cooke more reserved and shadier. Sarah-Jane Holm makes a poignant Jailer's Daughter, while Helen Schlesinger's wistful Emilia also communicates the character's emotional resilience. Only the obtrusive sound effects (chain-rattling in the jail scenes) occasionally weaken this recording's appeal.

## Editions

### Arden Shakespeare (third series)
**Lois Potter (ed.); 1997** ▷ Thomson

It's pleasing that Arden has expended effort in attempting to cover the lesser-known areas of the Shakespearian canon before going for the really major works, and Lois Potter's edition of *Kinsmen* demonstrates what a first-rate version can do for the play. Potter covers the question of authorship without getting in the least bogged down by it, and likewise her analysis of its tragicomic genre is sensitive and subtle. Glancing at this book, too, you'd have little sense that the play's stage history is sparse – Potter's detailed coverage fills more than thirty pages.

## Some criticism

### Shakespeare's Chaucer
**Ann Thompson; 1978** ▷ Liverpool UP / Rowman & Littlefield [o/p]

Thompson's was the earliest study to look in detail at what (surprisingly) had been a comparatively understudied area, the relation between Shakespeare and one of his most famous of literary antecedents. What emerges is evidence that Shakespeare not only knew his Chaucer well (the fact that he wrote two plays, *Troilus and Cressida* and *Kinsmen*, on Chaucerian models makes that clear) but that Chaucerian echoes permeate his work – all the way from half-remembered asides to large-scale liftings. *Shakespeare's Chaucer* devotes plenty of space to *Kinsmen*, travelling through the play scene by scene and comparing it with the "Knight's Tale"; and although some of Thompson's conclusions about the different intentions of Fletcher and Shakespeare might not suit everyone's taste (she argues that Fletcher was writing for the market, Shakespeare for all time), the book is thoughtful as well as helpful.

### Shakespeare, Fletcher and The Two Noble Kinsmen
**Charles H. Frey (ed.); 1989** ▷ Missouri UP [o/p]

It testifies to the interest in *The Two Noble Kinsmen* following the RSC's production of 1986 that a few years later a Shakespeare Association of America conference devoted itself entirely to the subject of the play. The convenor of that seminar, Charles Frey, decided to bring together the papers given there and the result is this book. It's a valuable collection covering everything from textual compositors (prepare yourself for lots of tables and signature marks) to the role of the sadness in the play (a slightly whimsical essay by Frey himself), plus a particularly intriguing article by Hugh Richmond on *Kinsmen*'s performance history. There's also a detailed bibliography.

# The Winter's Tale

To call something a "winter's tale" was Jacobean slang for something fanciful, something unreal – a fireside story. The tale told by the play itself has sometimes been called that, too, but initially at least it promises little in the way of light-hearted entertainment. It relates the story of a king whose jealousy is so strong, yet so without ground, that it loses him not only his wife but his young son and his baby daughter. In this *The Winter's Tale* closely resembles an earlier play of jealousy, *Othello*, and for over half its length it seems to be an even bleaker remake – until, that is, the mystical appearance of Time (himself personified on stage) and the shift to a mysterious new location, one where a cure for the play's romantic ills gradually blossoms. Shakespeare's source, a novella by his long-dead theatrical rival Robert Greene entitled *Pandosto: or, The Triumph of Time*, suggests that time can heal even the most violent of fractures, and therefore that the tale doesn't have to end in disaster; and after an improbable sequence of events, the play delivers a powerful, almost mythical, resolution. Its final scene, which can still astonish unprepared audiences, is justifiably famous and marks a decisive transformation from tragic winter into reviving spring.

[DATE]   Difficult to pinpoint – a version of the play was performed on May 15, 1611, but much of it may have been written several years earlier.

[SOURCES]   Shakespeare reworked Robert Greene's popular tragic novella, *Pandosto* (pub. 1588), changing its characters' names and modifying its plot. Passing references to other sources have been identified, Puttenham's *Art of English Poesie* and Ovid's *Metamorphoses* among them.

[TEXTS]   The play seems to have been squeezed into the First Folio (1623) at the last minute by the scribe Ralph Crane, and his text forms the basis of all subsequent editions.

## Interpreting the play

The title of *The Winter's Tale* seems to announce a return to the kind of throwaway, whimsical phrases that predominate in Shakespeare's middle comedies. Along with *Twelfth Night; or, What You Will* and *As You Like It*, it has a kind of take-it-or-leave-it quality – perhaps a kind of built-in defence against audiences reading everything too seriously. But the "tale" of this play's title is of more than symbolic importance: it appears within the action itself. Early in Act One, the heavily pregnant Queen Hermione and her attendants are idly amusing themselves at Leontes's court when Hermione hits upon an idea. "Pray you sit by us," she calls to her son Mamillius, "and tell's a tale":

MAMILLIUS   Merry or sad shall't be?
HERMIONE   As merry as you will.
MAMILLIUS
    A sad tale's best for winter. I have one
    Of sprites and goblins.

## Major Characters & Synopsis

**Leontes**, King of Sicily
**Hermione**, Leontes's wife
**Mamillius**, their son
**Perdita**, their daughter
**Camillo, Antigonus, Cleomenes** and **Dion**,
  lords at Leontes's court
**Paulina**, Antigonus's wife
**Emilia**, Hermione's attendant
**Polixenes**, King of Bohemia
**Florizel** (initially disguised as the countryman
  **Doricles**), Polixenes's son
**Archidamus**, a Bohemian lord
**Autolycus**, a con-man
**Old Shepherd**, Perdita's foster father
**Clown**, the Shepherd's son
**Mopsa** and **Dorcas**, shepherdesses
The figure of **Time**, acting as a chorus

**ACT 1** King Polixenes is staying at the court of his close childhood friend, Leontes, but after nine months away he has decided to return home to Bohemia. When Polixenes reluctantly refuses all entreaties to stay another week, Leontes asks his wife to intercede – but then interprets her success as evidence of an adulterous relationship between the two of them. Convinced that he is right, Leontes orders Camillo to poison Polixenes, but instead Camillo tips him off and both of them leave, in secret, for Bohemia.

**ACT 2** Hermione is with her son Mamillius when Leontes rushes in, having heard of Polixenes's and Camillo's flight. Taking this as proof of his former friend's guilt, Leontes confronts Hermione and accuses her of adultery. Though she vehemently denies it, he has her imprisoned, ignoring the pleas of those who defend her. Leontes then announces that he has sent messengers to Apollo's oracle at Delphos, in the expectation that it will confirm her guilt. When Hermione gives birth to a daughter in prison, her friend Paulina takes the child to Leontes, hoping to persuade the King that the baby is his. He is outraged, however, and orders that Paulina and the baby be burnt to death. When his lords refuse, he relents and instructs Antigonus to abandon the child in a deserted place outside the kingdom. As news arrives that the messengers are returning from Delphos, Leontes orders Hermione to stand trial.

**ACT 3** Leontes formally accuses Hermione of adultery and plotting to kill him, but she remains firm and declares that Apollo will be her judge. But when the oracle's words – which describe Hermione as utterly blameless – are read out, Leontes declares them to be false and orders the trial to continue. Everything is thrown into disarray, however, when news arrives of Mamillius's sudden death: Hermione collapses and is carried away, as Leontes begins to regret his terrible mistake. Paulina arrives and bitterly renounces Leontes before announcing that the Queen has died. Antigonus, meanwhile, has abandoned the baby (whom he calls Perdita) in Bohemia, where she is discovered by the Shepherd and his son, who take her home.

**ACT 4** The figure of Time restarts the action some sixteen years later, during which time Perdita has grown up in Bohemia as the daughter of the Shepherd. More recently, she has been wooed by Florizel, Polixenes's son. Hearing of this, Polixenes and Camillo decide to attend the shepherd's shearing feast in disguise in order to spy on the couple. When Florizel (known to Perdita as Doricles) admits that he intends to marry her, his father angrily reveals himself, condemns the Shepherd to death, and threatens to disinherit his son. After he departs, Camillo hatches a scheme whereby the young couple will elope to Sicily and present themselves to Leontes. In the meantime, the Shepherd and his son are on the way to plead with Polixenes, when they are fleeced by Autolycus, the local con man.

**ACT 5** In Sicily, Leontes, still in mourning for Hermione, vows not to marry again without Paulina's consent. When Florizel and Perdita arrive Leontes is captivated by the young couple, but Polixenes has discovered their flight and has pursued them to Bohemia. The truth is revealed, however: the Shepherd relates his discovery of the infant Perdita, and father and daughter are happily reunited. All then go together to Paulina's house to view the statue of Hermione recently erected there. While the company marvels at its life-like qualities, Paulina commands the statue to descend. The living Hermione steps forward.

HERMIONE                    Let's have that, good sir.
   Come on, sit down, come on, and do your best
   To fright me with your sprites.

[2.1.23–30]

Though she calls for a childish ghost story to while away the time, there is in fact more than enough to "fright" Hermione – and the audience – right here. Her husband, Leontes, is in the process of persuading himself that his wife has been unfaithful, and his instinct has hardened into deadly conviction. Leontes has invented his own "sprites and goblins": his jealousy is terrifyingly groundless. But though, like Mamillius's story, it is nothing but a "winter's tale" – a fairy story – its consequences will be brutally real. As she sits down to listen to her son's tale, Hermione has not an inkling of the danger she, or her unborn child, are in.

## A spider steeped

The story of a king who becomes convinced that his wife has slept with his best friend, and is about to give birth to an illegitimate child, was an old one, and Shakespeare encountered it – if not at his mother's knee – in a wildly successful collection of tales by Robert Greene, the playwright's long-dead theatrical rival (see p.128). In Greene's version, *Pandosto*, the king of that name is happily married to Bellaria (Hermione in the play) when his good friend Egistus (Polixenes) arrives to stay. After they have spent hour after hour in each other's company, enjoying what Greene calls their "secret uniting of affections", Pandosto begins to suspect that all is not as it should be. Wrestling with his conscience, he finally concludes that they have been unfaithful with each other, and is driven to seek revenge.

But in Shakespeare's play there is nothing whatsoever to back up Leontes's jealousy, so sudden and brutal in its onset that, when he demands that she hand over their son just a few lines later, Hermione at first thinks he is joking:

LEONTES  Give me the boy. I am glad you did not nurse him.
   Though he does bear some signs of me, yet you
   Have too much blood in him.
HERMIONE                         What is this? Sport?
LEONTES (*to a Lord*)
   Bear the boy hence. He shall not come about her.
   Away with him, and let her sport herself
   With that she's big with, (*to Hermione*) for 'tis Polixenes
   Has made thee swell thus.

[2.1.58–64]

Barely a scene after he first announced his suspicions, Leontes has become utterly possessed by the belief that he has been cuckolded – a change so abrupt that actors often struggle to present it convincingly, as if in having written about jealousy so often before Shakespeare felt at liberty to represent it here in brutal shorthand. Hermione's pregnancy, coming to term nine months after Polixenes's arrival in Sicily, instead of being a joyful celebration of married love, becomes evidence of adultery, and as becomes clear in the humiliating trial scene to which he subjects her later in the play, the King has not one scintilla of proof.

As numerous critics have proposed, Leontes's jealousy is, fairly obviously, rooted in hatred – and fear – of women, apparently brought on by reminiscing about his childhood companionship with Polixenes, an era before the females that would separate those "two twinned lambs" were even dreamt of. "Temptations have since then been born to's,"

Polixenes laughingly tells Hermione when they are all together, "for / In those unfledged days was my wife a girl."

> Your precious self had then not crossed the eyes
> Of my young playfellow.

[1.2.79–82]

Polixenes's tone is playful, but – as Hermione immediately picks up – this description of an Edenic boyhood existence, free from "tempting" females, casts the two queens as "devils", a pair of corrupting Eves to their husbands' sinless Adams. Yet Shakespeare, characteristically, shades things even more subtly. Hermione's position in this scene is complex: she clearly feels close to Polixenes, and in her fervent attempts to make him stay (prompted, of course, by Leontes) she uses all the resources she can. The words exchanged by them stray momentarily into off-limits territory: "Force me to keep you as a prisoner," she laughingly offers Polixenes, sounding for an instant less like a hostess and more like a mistress (1.2.53). And we also find out that things have not always been easy between Hermione and Leontes; it took him "three crabbèd months", he claims, to convince her to love him (1.2.104), and the image of his wife speaking so warmly with his best friend – so warmly that Polixenes relents and agrees to stay in Sicily, though Leontes himself could not make him – clearly begins to eat away at the King's mind.

Leontes, like Shakespeare's other jealous males, is unable to shake off the idea that sexuality itself is a kind of loss of innocence. Though one might wish for blissful ignorance, Leontes muses ("Many thousand on's / Have the disease and feel't not" (1.2.207–8)), that sin only lies dormant, waiting to poison its victim. "How blest am I in my just censure, in my true opinion!" he congratulates himself, appallingly, hearing of Polixenes's terrified flight from Sicily:

> Alack, for lesser knowledge—how accursed
> In being so blessed! There may be in the cup
> A spider steeped, and one may drink, depart,
> And yet partake no venom, for his knowledge
> Is not infected; but if one present
> Th'abhorred ingredient to his eye, make known
> How he hath drunk, he cracks his gorge, his sides,
> With violent hefts. I have drunk and seen the spider.

[2.1.38–47]

Knowledge itself, Leontes reflects, is the danger: it is the real "venom". The irony here is that the King thinks that he is looking the truth squarely in the face, swallowing the terrible reality; but, of course, the "spider" he sees, like Macbeth's ethereal dagger, proceeds entirely from his own brain.

In one of the most famously difficult of his speeches in the play, jealousy has a kind of clotting effect on Leontes's tongue. Calling his little son to him, he stutters, "Affection, thy intention stabs the centre":

> Thou dost make possible things not so held,
> Communicat'st with dreams—how can this be?—
> With what's unreal thou coactive art,
> And fellow'st nothing. Then 'tis very credent
> Thou mayst co-join with something, and thou dost—
> And that beyond commission; and I find it—
> And that to the infection of my brains
> And hard'ning of my brows.

[1.2.140–48]

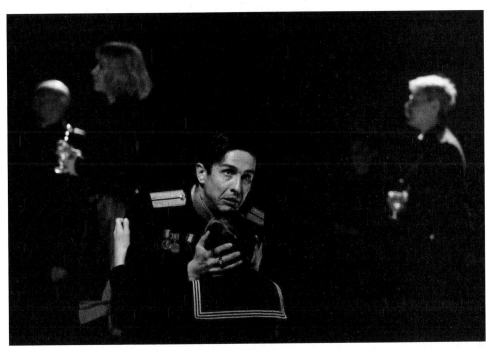

Leontes (Pyotr Semak) clutches his son Mamillius (Nikolai Zakharov) as jealousy consumes him. A scene from Declan Donnellan's harrowing production for the Maly Theatre, St Petersburg in 1999.

Leontes is almost impossible to understand here, as broken thoughts race through his mind, and not just for the young son he addresses – Shakespeare's first audiences, too, would surely have stumbled to unscramble his words. If "affection" means sexual passion, he seems to be communicating the idea that if sex can "co-join" (or "breed", since breeding is on his mind) with "dreams", then it will certainly do so with realities. He could also mean that his own jealousy is eating away at his sense of what is real, or that his state of mind ("affection") is wildly out of control. But the central thought is that "nothing" is as dangerous as "something" – and so Hermione is guilty whether she has done anything or not, because Leontes suspects as much (his brows "harden" in the expectation that cuckold's horns will shoot out of his head, a fear that also afflicts Othello). Over all this, the unmistakeable impression is of a man spewing diseased thoughts from a mind which is struggling to work out how realities can be made to fit fantasies.

Yet the problem is not so much that everyone believes Leontes's version of events, as in *Othello*: where in that earlier play the rest of the cast are taken in by Iago's brilliant improvisation, Leontes has to fight tooth and nail to assert his belief that Hermione is guilty. After threatening to dismiss his advisers if they so much as speak in her defence, Leontes answers Antigonus's scalding criticism that he has tried her "only in [his] silent judgement" (2.1.173) by publicly humiliating Hermione, who has just given birth to their daughter, under the pretence of testing her in court. As she lucidly announces at her trial, she is caught in a terrible catch-22, attempting to defend herself with herself. "My life," she explains to Leontes, "stands in the level of your dreams" (3.2.80): her husband, and his brittle fantasies, have seemingly absolute power.

## A course more promising

But Leontes's "dreams", unlike Othello's, also encounter resistance. Despite doubting the paternity of his daughter, who is born while Hermione is imprisoned, the bustling energy of the girl's arrival (she is, says Emilia, "lusty, and like to live" (2.2.29)) offers promise. When good news arrives from the Delphic oracle, which Leontes has consulted in the hope of silencing his critics, it seems as if everything, finally, will be resolved. "Hermione is chaste," it proclaims,

> Polixenes blameless, Camillo a true subject, Leontes a jealous tyrant, his innocent babe truly begotten, and the King shall live without an heir if that which is lost be not found.
>
> **[3.2.132–5]**

In language of crystalline clarity (Shakespeare copies it almost verbatim from his source), the oracle dismisses the King's crabbed fantasies in an instant. Redemption beckons. But Leontes, crying out that it is "mere falsehood", will not accept a verdict which differs from his own, and by this time he has already ordered that the newborn child should be taken out of the kingdom and exposed to the elements, "where chance may nurse or end it" (2.3.183). Upon that "chance" – and with the oracle's challenge of dire consequences if "that which is lost be not found" – the rest of *The Winter's Tale* will hang.

The next shock is sudden: Mamillius is announced to have died. Hermione collapses at the news, then it is declared that she, too, is dead. Paulina, her steadfast defender, is terrifyingly outspoken in grief. "I say she's dead," she screams at Leontes, "I'll swear it."

>                     If you can bring
> Tincture or lustre in her lip, her eye,
> Heat outwardly or breath within, I'll serve you
> As I would do the gods. But O thou tyrant,
> Do not repent these things, for they are heavier
> Than all thy woes can stir. Therefore betake thee
> To nothing but despair. A thousand knees,
> Ten thousand years together, naked, fasting,
> Upon a barren mountain, and still winter
> In storm perpetual, could not move the gods
> To look that way thou wert.
>
> **[3.2.203–13]**

The barriers to any kind of resolution seem as impenetrable as any futile penance Leontes could trouble himself with. The play seems trapped in tragedy.

Yet *The Winter's Tale* does not, like Mamillius's story (or even *Pandosto*), end sadly. Antigonus has abandoned the child in Bohemia – she is called Perdita, "lost" – whereupon, in the middle of a furious storm, she is discovered by a kindly shepherd. Like the fishermen in *Pericles* who haul the hero from the ocean and cheerfully promise to care for him, the Old Shepherd proves an unstoppably kindly force. "What have we here?" he exclaims:

> Mercy on's, a bairn! A very pretty bairn. A boy or a child, I wonder? A pretty one, a very pretty one. Sure some scape. Though I am not bookish, yet I can read 'waiting-gentlewoman' in the scape. This has been some stair-work, some trunk-work, some behind-door-work. They were warmer that got this than the poor thing is here. I'll take it up for pity …
>
> **[3.3.68–74]**

Assuming the child has been abandoned because it is illegitimate (conceived, he chuckles, on the stairs, perhaps, or in a trunk, behind a door), he converts at a stroke what has been Leontes's public nightmare into something entirely unexceptional. It doesn't matter if the baby is a bastard – but it does matter that it is looked after. Hearing of the terrible storm at sea, the Shepherd tells his son, "Thou metst with things dying, I with things new-born" (3.3.111).

Those "new-born" things turn the play around. Following the intercession of Time, a personification of whom appears on stage to advertise (and apologize for) a sixteen-year gap in the action, *The Winter's Tale* continues with a fully grown Perdita who, like Guiderius and Aviragus in *Cymbeline*, somehow manages to exude royal breeding despite her humble upbringing with the Shepherd. But then Bohemia, like Ardenne in *As You Like It*, is an exotic and pastoral location, complete with a real bear (possibly from a Southwark bear-baiting pit) that in an infamous stage direction chases away and kills Antigonus; a con man, Autolycus, straight out of Jacobean city comedy; and a fictional sea-coast, all of which seem to announce that Shakespeare has no intention that his location be taken too literally. In Bohemia there are in fact hardly any mentions of the main plot: people apparently spend their time in revelry, with Florizel casually wooing the strangely beautiful girl in his land (without revealing his royal blood). Nothing, it seems, can dent their joy. When Perdita promises to "strew" her "sweet friend" with garlands, he is momentarily shaken:

> FLORIZEL    What, like a corpse?
> PERDITA
>      No, like a bank, for love to lie and play on,
>      Not like a corpse—or if, not to be buried,
>      But quick and in my arms.
>
> **[4.4.129–32]**

The wonderfully vibrant sexuality implicit in Perdita's words hints that death can be banished by love, and that the play's winter can be transformed into a flower-filled spring. Bohemia contains everything the play needs to become a comedy: Perdita herself, her sweetheart Florizel and the kindly Camillo. Even the tall tales of the con man Autolycus, who roams the Bohemian countryside relating fantastical stories to the country's open-mouthed inhabitants, have a certain bizarre charm. Though Florizel's father Polixenes is displeased that his son has fallen for (he thinks) a shepherdess, it is not long before Camillo persuades the lovers to elope. All they have to do, he explains, is trust in providence, follow "a course more promising / Than a wild dedication of yourselves / To unpathed waters, undreamed shores" (4.4.565–6).

Yet the couple's destination is not "undreamed" – it is Sicily, and the play is very nearly home. But though we are not shown on stage what seems to be the point of the action, the long-lost daughter's reunion with her father (as we are in *Pericles*), Shakespeare has a yet more impressive *coup de théâtre* up his sleeve. Grieving for his dead wife, Leontes has been promised a commemorative statue of her, commissioned by Paulina. The time for it to be unveiled drawing near, Perdita joins her father to witness her first-ever sight of her mother, but as the curtain is drawn it is Leontes who seems most moved by what he sees in front of him. Then something incredible happens. Paulina calls out to the statue, "'Tis time. Descend."

> Be stone no more. Approach.
> Strike all that look upon with marvel. Come,
> I'll fill your grave up. Stir. Nay, come away.
> Bequeath to death your numbness, for from him
> Dear life redeems you.
>
> **[5.3.99–103]**

The theatrical moment is near-impossible to reproduce on the page, not least because Hermione's apparent reawakening from the dead is as much a shock for the offstage audience as it is for the dumbstruck Leontes. The last we heard, Hermione fainted, apparently fatally – yet here she is, alive and (as Leontes breathlessly observes) "warm". "If this be magic," he exclaims, "let it be an art / Lawful as eating" (5.3.110–1). Paulina's earlier threat to the King, that only if he could give the dead Hermione "heat outwardly or breath within" would she serve him, has come mystically true. The moment is astonishing not merely because it is unlooked-for, but because it is undeserved: Leontes has no right to expect his wife to be restored, just as there is no reason Hermione should want to go back to the husband who destroyed everything they shared. But Shakespeare, preparing his audience for an improbable "winter's tale", lets us – if we want to – believe in something infinitely more wondrous. Paulina's words to Leontes address the audience too. "That she is living," she proclaims,

> Were it but told you, should be hooted at
> Like an old tale. But it appears she lives …
>
> **[5.3.116–8]**

*The real world [at the end of* The Winter's Tale*] has none of the customary qualities of reality. It is the world symbolized by nature's power of renewal; it is the world we want; it is the world we hope our gods would want for us if they were worth worshipping.*

Northrop Frye, *A Natural Perspective* (1965)

# Stage history and adaptations

Astrologer Simon Forman saw the first recorded performance of *The Winter's Tale* in May 1611 at the **Globe**, and the play was also popular at **court**: no fewer than six performances across two decades are in the records and when Charles II saw it in 1634 it was apparently "liked" by spectators. For all that, it didn't survive past the Restoration and remained off the stage well into the next century. **Henry Giffard** staged a performance at Goodman's Fields in 1741, and later that same year it appeared at Covent Garden with **Samuel Stephens** as Leontes and **Christiana Horton** as Hermione. The production foundered, though – despite a rural "Grand Ballet" in the Bohemia scenes – and when the play next appeared it was in an adaptation by **Macnamara Morgan**. This was named *The Sheep-Shearing; or, Florizel and Perdita* (it cut the first half of Shakespeare's script entirely) and opened at Covent Garden in 1754 with the magnetic **Spranger Barry** as Florizel opposite **Isabella Nossiter**'s Perdita. Hot on Morgan's heels was **David Garrick**'s own adaptation, also called *Florizel and Perdita*, which appeared in direct competition later that year. Both versions excised nearly all the tragedy and concentrated instead on the play's magical reunion, acted movingly for Garrick by **Hannah Pritchard** as Hermione, though lighter fare was offered in the form of **Richard Yates**'s Autolycus (Yates apparently excelled in "characters of low and vulgar mould"). It was Morgan's adaptation that lasted, however, and forty years later it was still being performed in preference to Shakespeare as far away as New York.

The man responsible for bringing *The Winter's Tale* back from the dead was **John Philip Kemble**, who produced it several times in the first years of the nineteenth century. These productions were grand affairs – the prison scene was designed after Piranesi – with Kemble playing a dignified Leontes to **Sarah Siddons**'s passionate Hermione (one critic gushed that Siddons "towered beyond all praise"). **William Charles Macready** took on the play in 1823 but tried to inject it with more life: his own Leontes expressed such passion in the recognition scene that **Helen Faucit**, playing Hermione, was nearly overcome. **Samuel Phelps**'s Leontes (from 1845) was more restrained as well as more prudish: he dropped some of the play's "indelicacies". Phelps's Sadler's Wells boasted impressive sets, but they were soon outdone by

Charles Kean, who built his 1856 production around spectacular designs by **William Grieve** – to the extent that the script was pruned to remove any references that contradicted the Grecian setting. Kean's success even sparked a burlesque by **William Brough** entitled *Perdita; or, The Royal Milkmaid* that poked fun at the producer's serious-minded staging; in it the bear was instructed to be "respectably dressed".

English audiences were won over by the arrival of the **Duke of Saxe-Meiningen**'s company with *The Winter's Tale* in 1881, which set standards for ensemble performance far exceeding those of home-grown troupes. The 1887 staging at the Lyceum was a case in point, being a star vehicle for the American actress **Mary Anderson**, who starred as both Hermione and Perdita opposite **Johnston Forbes-Robertson**'s Leontes. Many loved it, though, and the production had over 160 performances and transferred to New York. **Frank Benson** attempted to draw on insights learnt from the Saxe-Meiningen approach, but his 1903 Stratford staging was still dominated by his own Leontes. **Herbert Beerbohm Tree**, as so often, produced a version that took to an extreme the indulgences of Victorian actor-managers: his 1906 production reduced the play to three acts so as not to distract from the grandiloquent staging.

The turnaround for *The Winter's Tale* came in 1912, with **Harley Granville-Barker**'s avant-garde production at the Savoy. Granville-Barker restored a full text and played it at lightning speed (too fast for many critics to keep up). **Henry Ainley** brought new life to Leontes by playing him with frightening psychological realism, while the elegant and simple designs by the fashionable **Albert Rutherston** were strong on atmosphere rather than straightforwardly realistic. **Jacques Copeau** would go still further eight years later in Paris, setting the play on an entirely bare stage, but in England Granville-Barker's ideas were too radical for many: his production was a critical failure. **Michael McOwan**'s Old Vic staging (1936) went for a softer, Italianate style while **Anthony Quayle**'s postwar Stratford version (1948) harked back to the spectacular tastes of the nineteenth century. Nevertheless **Esmond Knight**'s raging Leontes impressed, as did **Claire Bloom**'s fragile Perdita.

Quayle's Hermione was the alluring **Diana Wynyard**, who returned to the role under **Peter Brook** in a famous Phoenix Theatre production of 1951. Opposite Wynyard's flaxen Queen was **John Gielgud**'s swarthy Leontes, who brought a brooding intensity to the role that reached its climax in the recognition scene. Brook muted the play's laughter – his bear was tragic, not comic – and was rewarded with commercial success. In North America two productions from 1958 offered fresh insights as well as bringing the play to new audiences: the staging by **John Houseman** and **Jack Landau** at Stratford, Connecticut was modern (Time wore a business suit and carried an umbrella); while at Stratford, Ontario **Douglas Campbell** encouraged **Christopher Plummer** to play Leontes as victim rather than villain. Back in Stratford-upon-Avon two years later, **Peter Wood**'s production was blessed with an enviable cast, among it **Eric Porter** (Leontes), **Elizabeth Sellars** (Hermione) and **Peggy Ashcroft** (Paulina), but it was Wood's attention to detail that most impressed audiences: the small scenes were carefully staged, while the dances in Bohemia were full-bloodedly rural.

By contrast **Trevor Nunn**'s production at the same venue in 1969 emphasized the otherworldly qualities of *The Winter's Tale*: set wholly in a white box, it used props prompted by the play's language and enacted Leontes's perverted fantasies in dumb-show. **Barry Ingham** played a cool King to **Judi Dench**'s Hermione and Perdita (shades of Mary Anderson), but **Alton Kumado** came close to stealing the show as Time and a rural Green Man – a doubling intended to cast doubt on the innocence of the play's Bohemia. Less obviously an example of director's theatre was the **John Barton** and **Trevor Nunn** production from 1976, dominated by **Ian McKellen**'s dangerously unstable Leontes. It wasn't without meaningful design touches, though: the pastoral landscape of Act Four was overshadowed by a single bare tree. Hall returned to the play at the National Theatre in 1988 as part of his triple-bill of romances. This latter staging was darker than before, featuring **Tim Pigott-Smith** as a nervy Leontes to **Sally Dexter**'s Hermione and hinting that the reconciliation between the pair might be merely provisional. **Adrian Noble**'s 1984 touring production for the RSC had a claustrophobic intensity and boasted powerful performances from **Alan Armstrong** as Leontes and **Lynn Farleigh** as Hermione.

The small number of major productions since have also emphasized the play's unsettling qualities. **Annabel Arden**'s Complicite version (1992) allowed itself to conclude peacefully, but hinted that not all that much had changed between **Simon McBurney**'s Leontes and **Gabrielle Reidy**'s Hermione. That same year **Adrian Noble**'s second RSC version presented a set dominated by a large gauze box, representing perhaps the play's fantasy world, in which characters – including **Samantha Bond**'s Hermione – eerily appeared; for all that, Noble's Bohemia was a resolutely English vision, complete with village band. **Gregory Doran**'s 1998 version pitched Sicily as stuffily Edwardian, but it was **Antony Sher**'s clinically psychologized Leontes, not the staging, that attracted the warmest reviews. A collaboration between **Declan Donnellan** and the St Petersburg Maly Theatre debuted the same year: making no concessions to redemption, it ended in what the *Guardian* called "as great a piece of theatre as you are ever likely to see", with **Natalia Akimova**'s Hermione visibly destroyed by her long years in isolation. The 2001 National Theatre production, directed by **Nicholas Hytner**, was praised for **Alex Jennings**'s finely nuanced portrayal of Leontes, in which the character's fluctuating mental states were communicated with extraordinary precision. Not every critic welcomed Hytner's decision to make the rustic Act Four a Glastonbury-type festival, but **Phil Daniels** convinced as a Cockney wide-boy Autolycus.

No film of *The Winter's Tale* later than World War I exists: it appeared in a 1910 silent adaptation by **Theodore Marston**, followed by foreign-language versions in 1913 and 1914. Two television productions have been made: one in 1960, another in 1981. The latter, directed by **Jane Howell** and featuring **Jeremy Kemp** (Leontes) alongside **Anna Calder-Marshall** (Hermione), was part of the BBC/Time-Life project. More recently, tapings of Gregory Doran's 1998 staging have become available.

## Screen

### The Winter's Tale
**J. Kemp, A. Calder-Marshall, M. Kendall; Jane Howell (dir.)**
UK, 1980 ▷ Ambrose (BBC) **DVD**

The most immediately striking thing about this *Winter's Tale* is probably its set, a stark space tinted a blinding white in Sicily, moody gray at the Bohemian coasts and a rich gold in Bohemia itself. More stylistically ambitious than elsewhere in the series, Howell's inventive production did much to rescue the BBC project from its reputation for turgidity, though whether her work has dated well is more open to question (watch out for the bear and you'll understand). At any rate Howell's aim was to focus attention on the cast, and here we are well rewarded: Jeremy Kemp, an inky-coated King in a sea of white, responds to the intimacy of the camera well and produces a memorable first phase of the play with Anna Calder-Marshall's intense Hermione and Robert Stephens's

somewhat louche Polixenes. Kemp is perhaps too cool in the finale and Howell's staging is less effective here than elsewhere, but Margaret Tyzack's Paulina is powerful and the ending works – just.

### The Winter's Tale
**A. Sher, A. Gilbreath, E. Kohler; Gregory Doran (dir.)**
UK, 1998 ▷ Heritage **DVD**

Though undeniably traditional, Greg Doran's 1998 *The Winter's Tale* for the RSC made persuasive sense of the text and was quietly intelligent throughout. That it works less well on film is largely due to Antony Sher – after quizzing psychologists about Leontes's behaviour, Sher became convinced that the character was suffering from a condition called "morbid jealousy" and on stage he produces a full menu of symptoms. This approach makes for a somewhat jagged interpretation, and some may feel (especially in close-up) that Sher doesn't succeed in joining all the dots. But he is ably supported by a poignant Hermione from Alexandra Gilbreath, Estelle Kohler's gimlet-eyed Paulina is close to perfect, and the rest of the cast is strong. Also available from Heritage is a fascinating "Casebook" version, which places excerpts from the production alongside interviews with its key personnel.

## Audio

### The Winter's Tale
**C. Hinds, S. Cusack, J. Gielgud; Clive Brill (dir.)**
UK, 1998 ▷ Arkangel ⊙ 📼

John Gielgud contributed to this recording just a month before his death in May 2000, and his near-operatic performance as the magical healer, Time, is perhaps fitting testament to a career lasting some sixty years. By the time he appears half the play is done, but fortunately there are plenty of other highlights along the way. Ciaran Hinds makes a high-quality Leontes, exploding with fearsome power in the jealousy scenes and audibly aged at the end, but he is more than equalled by Sinead Cusack's passionate Hermione. Other parts are well-filled: especially charming is Alison Reid's rustic and uninhibited Perdita, while Alex Jennings's Autolycus rightly dominates the Bohemian part of the play. The statue scene is almost unbearably moving here – on audio you realize how the final miracle moves the lead characters to dumfounded silence, Paulina (wonderfully voiced by Eileen Atkins) incanting this spellbinding metamorphosis in a wonderful solo aria.

## Editions

### Oxford Shakespeare
**Stephen Orgel; 1996** ▷ Oxford UP

Nearly a decade after publishing his Oxford *Tempest* Stephen Orgel followed it up with this equally impressive *Winter's Tale*. Again it's Orgel's sympathy with the play's spirit that is his most memorable contribution, though the technical work of this edition is typically excellent: he resists the temptation to emend tricky readings in the text (particularly an issue in Leontes's knottier speeches) and makes a strong case that the Folio script is right in most instances. This sits comfortably with his

arguments for the Jacobean context of the play, though there is also some interesting detail on the performance history of key scenes – among them the statue's reawakening, played (as Orgel demonstrates) with intriguing differences between the seventeenth century and the nineteenth.

## Some criticism

### Shakespeare's Wordplay
**M. Mahood; 1957** ▷ Routledge

More than equal to the task of decoding the fractured workings of Leontes's mind, Mahood's classic study closely examines how Shakespeare used – or misused – words in *Romeo and Juliet*, *Richard II*, the Sonnets, *Hamlet*, *Macbeth* and *The Winter's Tale*. Though his language zips past in the theatre, in the late plays especially, it consistently manages to hit its audiences "at or very near the unconscious level", as Mahood observes, and thus rewards careful and nuanced analysis. What emerges in *Shakespeare's Wordplay* is not merely the richness of the playwright's aural craft but the sheer joy with which he puts language into service – an enthusiasm matched by that of Mahood, who is always lively and illuminating.

### A Natural Perspective
**Northrop Frye; 1965** ▷ Columbia UP

Frye was one of the earliest critics to move the study of myth and its themes towards the centre of Shakespearian studies, and in *A Natural Perspective* he argues that the romances are, in some deep sense, the summation of Shakespeare's work – plays which return to ancient traditions of storytelling in order to repair the devastation of the major tragedies. Despite bucket-loads of recent cynicism about Frye's work (it's easier to see the cracks in Shakespeare's miraculous conclusions than he allows), his argument that the world of the romances is "symbolized by nature's power of renewal; it is the world we want" is a compelling one. It seems particularly pertinent to a play such as *The Winter's Tale*, which ends as much in death-suspending fantasy as any kind of conventional reality.

# The Poems

# A Lover's Complaint

O riginally published as the final part of the volume entitled *Shakespeare's Sonnets, A Lover's Complaint*, a narrative poem some three hundred lines long, engages with many of the same themes as the sonnet sequence – love, lust, betrayal, sorrow. In a broader historical context, the poem is perhaps best understood as Shakespeare's idiosyncratic contribution to an English tradition of "complaint": the haunting and dark tale told by this poem is one of desolation in the ancient sense of that word – from the Latin *desolatus*, "left alone, forsaken". It relates the enigmatic confession of a woman betrayed by her lover and discovered in grief-stricken solitude. Though it is one of Shakespeare's most poignant and beautiful poems, its critical history is almost as gloomy as the story it relates – neglected for centuries, only recently has it come to enjoy anything like the attention it deserves.

[ **DATE** ]   On the basis of parallels with *All's Well* and *Measure for Measure*, some commentators plump for a date of c.1600, while stylometric tests (see p.516) suggest that the *Complaint* was completed up to a decade later. Others have it both ways, arguing that the poem was begun early, but revised prior to publication.

[ **SOURCES** ]   Though no sources as such exist, the poetic form of a "complaint" was well used – enough to be getting elderly by 1609. In the 1590s, poets Samuel Daniel, Thomas Lodge and Richard Barnfield all wrote sonnet sequences capped by "complaints".

[ **TEXTS** ]   First printed as part of the 1609 quarto *Shakespeare's Sonnets*, the *Complaint* was excluded from the plays-only Folio.

## Interpreting the poem

Commentators have given the impression of being puzzled – even embarrassed – by the 329-line poem entitled *A Lover's Complaint*, which is written in a markedly different style from much of Shakespeare's other work. Many have doubted whether he had a hand in it at all – or if he did, why the poem reads quite like it does. Criticisms of its "pedantry", "artificiality" and "ill-digested" scholarship (the words are those of the early twentieth-century scholar J.W. Mackail) have been legion, and the *Complaint* was widely assumed to be the work of an inferior contemporary until the 1960s. The poem's subsequent acceptance into the canon has proved grudging, and the march to respectability has been slow: no more than a few articles have been published on the poem in recent years. For the critic Hallett Smith, writing recently in the popular one-volume *Riverside Shakespeare*, the poem had no tangible value whatsoever. "If it is by Shakespeare," he wrote, the *Complaint* "neither detracts from his achievement nor adds anything to it."

Such studied (not to say meaningless) neutrality reflects the fact that the *Complaint* has not won many to its cause. This may be because it doesn't make things easy. While the Sonnets are uniquely intense and demand a great deal from their readers, they do allow glimpses of shared intimacy – of love, anger, paranoia, fear, delusion, ecstasy. The *Complaint* is difficult in a quite different way: it is oblique, even deliberately perplexing. It is expressed in dense language and riddling, tightly packed syntax. "From off a hill," the poem begins,

While out in the countryside, the poet-narrator describes hearing the voice of a crying woman echoing from the hillside. Tracing the sound, he comes across a once beautiful "maid" seated by the edge of a river. Highly distraught and with her hair dishevelled, she is reading and tearing up letters, and throwing love tokens into the water. The poet then observes the approach of a "reverend man" who sits down near the woman and asks her the cause of her unhappiness.

She relates that she has been ruined after falling for a beautiful and brilliant youth, so handsome that both men and women find him utterly irresistible. At first she held out, but gradually her resistance was broken down by the power of his eloquence. Despite his callous behaviour towards previous lovers and an appalling reputation, the young man flatters her that she is the only woman he really cares for – arguing that, though he has seduced others, they meant nothing to him. He even shows her the tokens they sent, boasting that a nun was once so desperate for his love that she promised to renounce her vows. Moved by his tearful entreaties, the maid confesses that, despite herself, she slept with him. She goes on to suggest that no one, least of all someone as inexperienced as her, could resist the sheer subtlety of his advances. And though she regrets it, she wonders whether she would be able to refuse him were he ever to try again.

> whose concave womb re-worded
> A plaintful story from a sist'ring vale,
> My spirits t'attend this double voice accorded,
> And down I laid to list the sad-tuned tale;
> Ere long espied a fickle maid full pale,
> Tearing of papers, breaking rings a-twain,
> Storming her world with sorrow's wind and rain.

**[1–7]**

A breathtakingly mysterious opening prepares the reader for what is to follow. While out walking in the countryside, the poet hears a "double voice" resounding off a hill – "double" because it is an echo of the desperate cries of a young woman standing by a river, the "fickle maid", whose weeping catches the poet's ear and tempts him to sit down and eavesdrop on what she has to say. Her story turns out to be as distressing as her appearance: joined on the riverbank by another figure, a "reverend man" who acts as her confessor, the maid tearfully relates how a beautiful but treacherous youth used all his persuasiveness to woo her – and how, despite knowing of his reputation, she surrendered her virginity. Thus seduced, she was cruelly, and inevitably, abandoned.

Despite the simplicity of the tale – it doesn't take long to describe the plot of *A Lover's Complaint* – this opening scene is weirdly theatrical: the "maid" seems to inhabit not a real-life landscape but a terrain of the mind, where hills "re-word" her sorrow and her own tears and sighs are every bit as destructive as storms and rain. To that extent she resembles King Lear, but even closer is the mad Ophelia in *Hamlet*, whose "untucked" hair and distracted manner she seems to echo. And in the *Complaint* the very experience of reading is made to feel somewhat delusional. The poem is complex structurally: it is ostensibly voiced by an eavesdropping poet – apparently unseen by both maid and reverend man – but after setting up the framing narrative (a form borrowed from medieval pastoral verse), he falls out of view, saying nothing more and simply relaying the maid's confession as if from the margins. The reverend man, too, remains all but silent, becoming just another pair of ears; a few of his words are reported by the poet, but no other response is recorded. And although it is the maid's lament that dominates *A Lover's Complaint* and brings it to a close, much of her speech quotes the young man's words to her. The poem is an echo-chamber of different voices, all of them nameless and bewilderingly blurred together.

But critics who condemn the *Complaint* on the grounds that it is too unfathomable or eso-teric to be Shakespeare's are blind to the poem's troubling brilliance. Arguably, the old-fashioned language and archaic style of *A Lover's Complaint* are designed to make it look older than it is – a 45-year-old author's tribute to the kind of poetry he was reading in his twenties, even (if he came across similar kinds of poems at school) much earlier. And the *Complaint* also looks back in the sense that it is Shakespeare's final narrative poem, published long after the pair that made his name as a poet, *Venus and Adonis* and *The Rape of Lucrece*. Though up to fifteen years, and nearly twenty plays, separate the *Complaint* from these early works, it returns to similar themes – and one theme in particular, that of frustrated desire. In *Venus and Adonis* the poet plays this subject mainly for laughs: the poem tells the tale of Venus, the eternally desirable love goddess, who nevertheless fails to bed the beautiful mortal Adonis – despite her enthusiastic attempts at wooing (at one stage she simply grabs him and pulls him on top of her), he remains indifferent. In *Lucrece*, however, the theme becomes grimly tragic: when the eponymous Roman heroine resists the advances of one of her husband's military colleagues, he viciously rapes her, leaving her to commit suicide in despair at the loss of her honour and the shame to her family.

## Gilded in his smiling

In *A Lover's Complaint*, it is as if Shakespeare attempted what seems like the impossible – to unite the contrasting experiences of his two early heroines. The "maid" who is his protagonist in this poem has, like Lucrece, been violated and bitterly regrets it; but, like Venus, she keenly wanted to be, seduced by the "youthful suit" of a divinely handsome young man. "His browny locks did hang in crookèd curls," she swoons,

> 'And every light occasion of the wind
> Upon his lips their silken parcels hurls.
> What's sweet to do, to do will aptly find.
> Each eye that saw him did enchant the mind,
> For on his visage was in little drawn
> What largeness thinks in paradise was sawn.'

[85–91]

This youthful, even androgynous, figure is a close relative of the boyish/girlish Adonis, but where Adonis was insistent that he was far too young to be tempted by Venus, *A Lover's Complaint* reverses those polarities: its nameless youth is rapaciously eager to take advantage of the maid, and does everything he can to persuade her to sleep with him.

After spending several tantalizing stanzas describing his beauty, the maid reveals that she was far from the only person susceptible to his charms: "maidens' eyes stuck over all his face", she claims (81); and this paragon of loveliness was so perfect that "sexes both" fell under his spell (128). A major component in that shimmering attraction appears to have been the young man's eloquence, which reputedly wins over everyone who encounters him. "On the tip of his subduing tongue," she claims, sensually linking his sexual appeal with his oratorical prowess,

> 'All kinds of arguments and question deep,
> All replication prompt, and reason strong,
> For his advantage did wake and sleep.
> To make the weeper laugh, the laugher weep,
> He had the dialect and different skill,
> Catching all passions in his craft of will …'

[120–6]

## Lovers make moan

While our understanding of "**complaint**" is nowadays fairly impoverished – it carries connotations of criticizing, grumbling, moaning – for Shakespeare's first readers the word would have been richly resonant, and possessed of serious literary credentials. Writing in the late fourteenth century, Chaucer was one of the first English figures to use "complaint" to describe a kind of poetry that voiced mourning and lament: his *The Book of the Duchesse*, probably written at the prompting of John of Gaunt, Duke of Lancaster, to commemorate his wife's death in 1368, uses complaint as a touching way of dealing with the horrors of bereavement. Employing a familiar device in medieval poetry, Chaucer's poet describes a strange dream encounter in which he meets a knight clad "al in blake", "ful pitous pale and nothyng red", mourning the loss of his lady. "I stalked even unto hys bak", the poet says,

> And ther I stood as stille as ought,
> That, soth to saye, he saw me nought;
> For-why he heng hys had adoune
> And with a dedly sorwful soun
> He made of rym ten vers or twelve
> Of a compleynte to hymselve—
> The moste pitee, the moste rowthe [sorrowful],
> That ever I herde; for, by my trowthe,
> Hit was gret wonder that Nature
> Myght suffre any creature
> To have such sorwe and be not ded.

**[458–69]**

The poet goes on to relate the knight's desperate "compleynte" in full, before awakening in his bed and discovering that the whole thing was a dream, but nevertheless promising to write it down as a poem – the poem being, of course, *The Book of the Duchesse* itself. Though this complainant is male, his resemblances to the pale and tearful "maid" in *A Lover's Complaint* are obvious enough, and this poet, like Shakespeare's, is (at least initially) invisible to the speaker.

For in Shakespeare's period, six or seven generations later, "complaints", more commonly listing the grievances of female speakers disappointed in love, had begun to shoot up in anthologies of poetry such as Richard Tottel's *Songs and Sonnets* (1557), George Gascoigne's *Hundredth Sundry Flowers* (1573) and John Flasket's collection *England's Helicon* (1600). Despite the sixteenth-century popularity of the genre, however, some critics have traced the roots of female-voiced complaint back even earlier, to Ovid (see p.240), whose *Heroides* is a collection of passionate imaginary letters written by the most famous women of classical mythology (Dido, Hero, Helen of Troy, Medea), many of which rebuke their lovers for abandoning them. Edmund Spenser, the most famous writer of the generation preceding Shakespeare's, certainly knew Ovid, and also translated a series of complaints by the French poet Du Bellay that lament the impermanence of civilization and the grinding erosions of time. Spenser's *Amoretti* (1595), a collection of love sonnets, closely influenced Shakespeare's own, as did several other sonnet sequences – two of which, Samuel Daniel's *Delia* (1592) and Thomas Lodge's *Phillis* (1593), were published with "complaints" which relate the sorrows of abandoned women closely resembling the "maid" in Shakespeare's poem.

Someone who has mastered all these different "dialects" rather resembles the figures mentioned in one of Shakespeare's most intriguing but riddling sonnets, number 94, which describes a kind of ideal people "who have power to hurt and will do none … who moving others are themselves as stone" (94, 1–3). Such as these, the sonnet claims, "rightly do inherit heaven's graces" (5), but the youth of *A Lover's Complaint* makes that assertion sound jaggedly ironic: far from embodying Christian virtue, he is callously deceitful and shamelessly immoral – worse, the maid knew it even before she relented. "For further could I say this man's untrue," she goes on,

'And knew the patterns of his foul beguiling;
Heard where his plants in others' orchards grew,
Saw how deceits were gilded in his smiling,
Knew vows were brokers to defiling,
Thought characters and words merely but art,
And bastards of his foul adulterate heart.'

**[169–75]**

The young man is entirely able to separate himself from the "true" meaning of "characters and words", as if they, too, were the illegitimate children that he has so callously sired and abandoned. This chilling coldness is most graphically illustrated by one of his seductive ploys, which is nothing less than to boast and exhibit how many "tributes" he has received from previous lovers. Among the "pallid pearls and rubies red as blood" (198), the locks of hair "with twisted mettle amorously impleached" (205), the "deep-brained sonnets" (209) that have been sent by lovelorn admirers, another "device" even came from a "nun, / A sister sanctified of holiest note", lured into renouncing her religious vows and joining the young man's cult (233). Despite his apparent perfection, it is only too clear that this devilish tempter exemplifies a particular kind of evil, one that does indeed, as Sonnet 94 has it, possess the "power to hurt" precisely because of his stony separation from others. He would, Shakespeare insinuates, make a dangerously good actor – or indeed a poet.

> *The young maiden's unrepentant, unfinished testimony reveals Shakespeare's interest in both the elusiveness of confession and the narrative instabilities involved in recording it.*
>
> Katherine Craik, "Shakespeare's *A Lover's Complaint* and Early Modern Criminal Confession" (2002)

For although the young man of the *Complaint* resembles the "lovely boy" of the first sequence of Sonnets (who has likewise been unfaithful), he also calls to mind the alluring but duplicitous Bertram in *All's Well That Ends Well*, who refuses to consummate his marriage so that he can sow his wild oats elsewhere. In fact, though commentators have so often been reluctant to allow it into the canon, *A Lover's Complaint* seems compellingly Shakespearian in its concern with the sweet temptations and bitter realities of sexual passion, the kind of concerns that lie close to the surface in the poet's middle period (the *Complaint*, published in 1609, is often sometimes thought to have been written earlier in the decade). Another play morbidly interested in these themes, *Measure for Measure*, betrays intriguing similarities with the poem: it, too, contains a nun, Isabella, repeatedly pressured to leave her novitiate; it, too, features a mysterious "reverend man" well acquainted with the "ruffle ... Of court, of city" (56–9), the Duke of Vienna, who dons the disguise of a friar apparently in order to spy out his city's corruptions, but ends up fatefully implicated in them. And, most strikingly, the play also offers a woman bitterly betrayed in love – Mariana, betrothed to the Duke's deputy but abandoned by him when she lost her fortune. He "left her in her tears," the Duke claims, "and dried not one of them with his comfort" (3.1.227).

But where Mariana wins back the man she loves (her total devotion is one of the play's many puzzles), no such consolation is offered to the nameless maid of the *Complaint*. Her predicament is precisely that she is no longer a "maid" in the sense of "virgin", and although she spends more time describing the young man's beauty than listing her sorrows – it is perhaps impossible to separate them – it seems clear that the experience has left a physical as well as emotional mark. Her admission that she gave up her virginity is not only poetically gorgeous; it implies that she has, like those "other" lovers, become pregnant as a consequence:

'There my white stole of chastity I daffed,
Shook off my sober guards and civil fears;
Appear to him as he to me appears,
All melting, though our drops this diff'rence bore:
His poisoned me, and mine did him restore.'

**[297–301]**

This is the obverse to the early Sonnets' urging that the young man they address should seize the day and have children, thus leaving behind a record of his beauty. Responding to that suggestion, the *Complaint* points out that, from the perspective of a "poisoned" maid ruined in order to "restore" her vampiric lover, doing so can be cruelly destructive. It is clear that the maid, movingly described earlier as "the carcass of a beauty spent and done" (11), has sacrificed her own youth and beauty in order to preserve the young man's. The poem argues that love can imprison as much as it can emancipate: its protagonist is allowed no escape.

That is perhaps the *Complaint*'s final and most disturbing paradox, and the reason why its difficulties as a text are closely bound up with its brilliance. Despite being a confession, the poem's religious confessor does not absolve or counsel the maid, still less the long-departed youth; despite being a complaint, the poem's female complainer can find no way out of a brittle obsession with her former lover. In her closing words the maid tries to claim that she is desperate to be rid of him, but what at first seems like it will be a curse against his memory becomes – shockingly – something far more compromised. "O that infected moisture of his eye," she sighs,

'O that false fire which in his cheek so glowed,
O that forced thunder from his heart did fly,
O that sad breath his spongy lungs bestowed,
O all that borrowed motion seeming owed
Would yet again betray the fore-betrayed,
And new pervert a reconcilèd maid.'

**[323–9]**

Instead of condemning the youth's attractiveness, inseparable from his falsity, the maid persuades herself that, given the opportunity, she would fall for him all over again. There will be no cure; the poem ends where it began.

## Editions

### Oxford Shakespeare
**Colin Burrow (ed.); 2002** ▷ Oxford UP

The Oxford *Complete Sonnets and Poems* is easy to recommend, not least because it is the only single-volume edition to contain all the poems. In the case of the little-studied *A Lover's Complaint*, this broad context is especially valuable because it allows readers to come to their own conclusions about its teasing relationship with the Sonnets and the rest of Shakespeare's poetic output. Burrow's seven-page essay on the *Complaint* seems slender in a volume this thick – a wrist-snapping 750 pages – but it's lucid and sympathetic nonetheless, drawing attention to the *Complaint*'s links with the other narrative works and emphasizing its echoes of Spenser.

## Some criticism

### Motives of Woe
**John Kerrigan (ed.); 1991** ▷ Oxford UP [o/p]

Bookstore shelves are hardly groaning with criticism on the *Complaint*, and this title will almost certainly be hard to come by (not least because, frustratingly, it has never made paperback). That said, this really is worth the effort, and not just for the light it casts on Shakespeare. Though the book began life as an essay on the *Complaint*, it quickly expanded into an historical anthology of poems in the same mode. Kerrigan's selection is excellent, ranging from haunting medieval lyrics such as "Als i me rode" (c.1300) to gems such as Mary Sidney's wonderful sixteenth-century rendering of Psalm 137. In this setting, the *Complaint* begins to look less like a baffling oddity and more like the masterful expression of the genre it is.

# The Rape of Lucrece

lmost certainly the "graver labour" promised to his patron in the dedication to *Venus and Adonis*, Shakespeare's *The Rape of Lucrece* is a polished and ambitious follow-up, in every sense the more serious work of the two. Published just a year after that first narrative poem, *Lucrece* retells the anguished story of the Roman wife Lucretia, who is brutally raped by Sextus Tarquinius, son of her king, and who despairingly commits suicide soon afterwards, blaming herself for the attack. From the bare bones of this tale – which Shakespeare could have read in Latin versions by Ovid and the Roman historian Livy, as well as by medieval English poets Chaucer and Gower – the poet constructs a lengthy and brooding composition that does full justice to the gravity of its theme. And while its dense and rhetorically sophisticated style can be difficult to adjust to, *Lucrece* is much more than a display piece: in its fraught depiction of the heroine's trauma and self-loathing, the poem demonstrates astonishing and uncomfortable insights into human psychology. Though written for print publication rather than live performance, it is in many respects the most dramatic work of Shakespeare's early career.

[DATE]   Printed by summer 1594 (see below), *Lucrece* was most likely written soon beforehand, presumably after *Venus and Adonis*, published the previous year.

[SOURCES]   Ovid's *Fasti* ("Chronicles") is the main source for the story of Lucrece's plight, but Shakespeare also turned to Livy's account in the *Historia* (probably in a 1566 translation by William Painter) as well as Chaucer's version in *The Legend of Good Women* (c.1384).

[TEXTS]   Like *Venus and Adonis*, *Lucrece* was immaculately printed by fellow Warwickshireman Richard Field. His quarto text (Q1) was much reprinted subsequently and remains the basis for modern editions.

## Interpreting the poem

Fresh from the success of *Venus and Adonis* and still unable to work in the London theatres – which remained closed by plague for nearly two years – Shakespeare decided during the spring of 1594 to publish another narrative poem, around the same time that his first was being reprinted. This was "The Ravishment of Lucrece", as it was registered to be printed, simply *Lucrece* on its first title-page. Though there is some debate over precisely what the poem should properly be called (its traditional name, *The Rape of Lucrece*, might have been withdrawn and replaced with the less explicit *Lucrece* after the text was printed), there is no doubt that Shakespeare had the project in mind – and perhaps even on paper – for some time beforehand. In the dedication to the lighthearted *Venus and Adonis* he promised his patron, the Earl of Southampton, that he had every intention of turning himself to "some graver labour" as soon as he could, and *Lucrece* undeniably fits that bill. Indeed, readers not forewarned about its gravity might have got a shock if they were expecting a replay of the witty energy of *Venus and Adonis*: the tone of this poem, as befits its subject matter, is altogether different.

## Synopsis

[An abbreviated synopsis of *Lucrece*, perhaps by Shakespeare, is included in the "Argument" to the poem, following its dedication, but differs from the poem itself in a few details]

Sextus Tarquinius (Tarquin), son of the Roman king Tarquinius Superbus, is riding full-tilt to visit Lucretia (Lucrece), the virtuous wife of his friend Collatinus (Collatine). Tarquin does not have good intentions: having heard Lucrece's loveliness praised by Collatine, he is eager to experience her for himself in her husband's absence. Suspecting nothing, the beautiful and innocent Lucrece welcomes her royal guest before the two retire for the night.

Tormented by lust for Lucrece, however, Tarquin soon rises and debates in anguish what to do. Though acknowledging the terrible nature of the crime, he resolves to ravish her and steals to her bedroom. Once inside, he gazes upon Lucrece's sleeping body but she awakes and pleads with him not to go through with the attack. Deaf to her appeals, he gags and rapes her before escaping shamefully into the night.

Lucrece is devastated, at first hoping that morning will never come, then embarking on a lengthy sequence of laments. In despair she finally decides that suicide is the only way to safeguard her reputation and that of her husband, but resolves to tell Collatine what has happened beforehand. Dispatching a brief letter urging him to rush home, she burns with shame in front of her maid and the messenger, then sadly contemplates a painting of the fall of Troy, identifying herself with the grieving figure of Hecuba. As soon as Collatine arrives, in the company of her father Lucretius and other lords, she explains everything but holds back the rapist's name until the men have sworn to avenge the deed. Having secured their promises, to their shock she suddenly stabs herself. As she bleeds to death, Collatine's colleague Junius Brutus appeals to Collatine and the others to remember their vow. Lucrece's body is carried through Rome and – by popular consent – Tarquin and his family are banished.

Opening the volume as it was published, purchasers were confronted by a grand-sounding "Argument" introducing *Lucrece*'s narrative and explaining its historical ramifications. After relating the back story of the kings of Rome, the Argument goes on to describe how the son of the current incumbent, Sextus Tarquinius (Tarquin in the poem), was "enflamed with Lucrece' beauty" despite her "incomparable chastity" and marriage to Collatinus (Collatine). Abandoning his colleagues at their camp at Ardea, Tarquin heads surreptitiously for Lucrece's dwelling at Collatium, where she innocently welcomes him and encourages him to stay. She little suspects what will happen next:

> The same night he treacherously stealeth into her chamber, violently ravished her, and early in the morning speedeth away. Lucrece, in this lamentable plight, hastily dispatcheth messengers—one to Rome for her father, another to the camp for Collatine. They came, the one accompanied with Junius Brutus, the other with Publius Valerius, and, finding Lucrece attired in mourning habit, demanded the cause of her sorrow. She, first taking an oath of them for her revenge, revealed the actor and whole manner of his dealing, and withal suddenly stabbed herself. Which done, with one consent they all vowed to root out the whole hated family of the Tarquins, and, bearing the dead body to Rome, Brutus acquainted the people with the doer and manner of the vile deed, with a bitter invective against the tyranny of the King …

**[Argument, 19–30]**

Despite the horrifically personal nature of his crime, Tarquin's punishment proves political: his family is ejected from Rome and the city becomes a republic. It remained so until the series of events covered by Shakespeare in *Julius Caesar*, during which Caesar is offered the throne but murdered by conspirators led by another Brutus before he can accept it. The end of

*Antony and Cleopatra* coincides with yet another turning-point in Roman history: the accession of Augustus (Octavius Caesar), the first of the emperors.

Some have speculated that the poem's interest in republicanism might have well flattered the politics of Shakespeare's patron, and in other ways too *Lucrece* hints that it is addressed to a very specific audience. The poem's dedication resembles that to *Venus and Adonis*, but it is markedly warmer in tone, implying that the poet did indeed get some kind of reward for his labour from the Earl of Southampton – perhaps even the reward of his friendship. "The love I dedicate to your lordship is without end," the dedication begins, and continues more fervently,

What I have done is yours; what I have to do is yours, being part in all I have, devoted yours.

**[Dedication, 1–7]**

The poet hints at a special intimacy with his patron, and many readers of *Lucrece* have seized upon this as evidence that Shakespeare was emotionally close to the 20-year-old Southampton – perhaps close enough for him to be the "lovely boy" addressed in the Sonnets and the mysterious "M$^r$. W. H." mentioned in that text (Southampton's initials were "H.W.", though he was definitely not a mere "Mr"; see p.433).

## In time of sorrow

All that is to ignore the biggest questions raised by *Lucrece*, for what strikes most readers of this lengthy and introspective poem is its painful human dimension, focused tightly on its heroine and victim. The poem first depicts the harrowing experience of rape in ways that are poetically self-conscious but also so psychologically convincing that critics have compared it to real-life testimony. And Shakespeare makes the very experience of reading *Lucrece* recreate some of that pain. Written in a doleful rhyme royal (see p.423), the poem's sheer scale makes it difficult to confront (at 1855 lines, it is longer than *The Comedy of Errors*). The full text is something like twelve times as long as Ovid's version and was sufficiently drawn out and circuitous that when it was reprinted in 1616 the publisher added a list of contents so that readers would find it easier to follow the plot. In all sorts of ways, *Lucrece* is not easy to read, nor should it be.

And in this poem everything takes longer than it should; as Lucrece herself later notes, "how slow time goes / In time of sorrow" (990–1). After rising from his bed in Lucrece's house in the dead of night, Shakespeare depicts Tarquin holding frenzied "inward debate" with himself about whether he should go through with the rape or not. Although his mind is made up from the very first moment, Tarquin nevertheless fights with his conscience for twenty-three stanzas as he inches towards Lucrece's chamber. Once outside, time halts again as he pauses once more. "The locks between her chamber and his will," the narrator whispers,

Each one by him enforced, retires his ward;
But as they open they all rate his ill,
Which drives the creeping thief to some regard.
The threshold grates the door to have him heard,
    Night-wand'ring weasels shriek to see him there.
    They fright him, yet he still pursues his fear.

**[302–8]**

The task of opening Lucrece's door takes another age, and forty lines later Tarquin will still not be inside her chamber. Shakespeare would recall this eternal moment much later in his career, when he makes Macbeth think of "Tarquin's ravishing strides" while he too is stealing through the night, this time to King Duncan's bedroom (2.1.55). Here it is the poem's slow-

The frontispiece to John Quarles's 1655 edition of *The Rape of Lucrece*, engraved by William Faithorne. Quarles's own bombastic poem, *The Banishment of Tarquin*, appeared alongside Shakespeare's work as a sequel.

motion movement that is terrible to observe, as well as its depiction of a world where everything – the locks, the creaking door, the weasels outside, even a needle stuck in one of Lucrece's gloves – attempts to resist the rape, yet has no effect. Before long Tarquin will violate Lucrece just as unstoppably as he, the "creeping thief", has broken into her room.

This is the appalling certainty stressed again and again by *Lucrece*. Where *Venus and Adonis* makes light of Venus's inability to seduce the man-child Adonis – it is funny as well as touching that the goddess of love finds herself desiring someone beyond her reach – when reading the later poem we know only too well that physical force will count against the heroine. Tarquin is not only capable of forcing himself on his victim but he will, as the poem repeatedly puts it, have his "will". Shakespeare's narrator makes Lucrece's very womanliness conspire against her, because it opens her to Tarquin's predatory gaze. Standing over her bed, "rolling his greedy eye-balls in his head" (368), Tarquin takes in the view of the slumbering woman lying in front of him:

Her lily hand her rosy cheek lies under,
Coz'ning the pillow of a lawful kiss,
Who therefore angry seems to part in sunder,
Swelling on either side to want his bliss;
Between whose hills her head entombèd is,
    Where like a virtuous monument she lies
    To be admired of lewd unhallowed eyes.

[386–92]

Tarquin's look imposes on Lucrece an eroticism over which she has no control – to his mind the very pillows want to "kiss" her – yet in which she is fatefully implicated. This description implicates readers, too: our "unhallowed eyes" are also witnesses, forced to gaze on Lucrece just as Tarquin does. And our only option is to read on, able to do nothing but continue watching. Whereas in *Venus and Adonis* it is both fun and funny to eavesdrop on the titillating tussle between the two protagonists, in *Lucrece* the intimacy is grotesque and suffocating. Forcing us to act as mute audience to the terrible events of the poem, Shakespeare hints that we, too, will be tainted by what is about to occur.

## The same disgrace

Yet Lucrece herself proves stronger and more vocal than Tarquin appears to expect. Waking to find a stranger in her innermost chamber, Shakespeare's heroine does not dumbly accept her fate, as in other versions of the poem she does, but speaks up against her attacker with an eloquence that should surely prove winning (it is one of the anxieties explored by the poem that affecting words can end up having no effect). After she appeals to Tarquin's relationship with Collatine and urges him to be careful of his reputation, he cuts in with an angry exclamation that "my uncontrollèd tide / Turns not" (645–6). But Lucrece remains rhetorically in control, passionately turning his argument back on him:

## Rhyming it royal

In two of his narrative poems, *The Rape of Lucrece* and *A Lover's Complaint*, Shakespeare employs an unusual poetic form, **rhyme royal**. Analytically speaking, this form is made up of seven-line, decasyllabic stanzas in the rhyme-scheme *ababbcc* – that is to say, each stanza contains seven lines, and each line has ten syllables. The blueprint connecting each is visible in stanza 18 of *Lucrece*, for instance, where the poet describes Tarquin on his way to bed:

> For then is Tarquin brought unto his bed,
> Intending weariness with heavy sprite;
> For after supper long he questionèd
> With modest Lucrece, and wore out the night.
> Now leaden slumber with life's strength doth fight,
>   And everyone to rest himself betakes,
>   Save thieves, and cares, and troubled minds that wakes.
>
> [120–6]

Here the lines rhyme first in pairs across one another ("bed"/"questioned"; "sprite"/"night"), then conclude in a couplet ("betake"/"wake"). Between these, the fifth line brings the two kinds of rhymes together, introducing with "fight" another rhyme for "night" and making it, too, into a couplet – in other words, forcing line four in two directions at once and thus binding the whole stanza tightly together.

The effect of rhyme royal can be unsettling: it sets up a steady rhyming pulse for four lines which then falters in line five, anxiously treading water; and, though it does go on, the final couplet acts as a kind of conclusion (as in the Sonnets) which feels reluctant to travel anywhere further. Then, of course, the whole process begins again in the next stanza. Rhyme royal is a halting, limping way to tell a story – particularly given that, as some critics have suggested, it is a hobbled version of the elegant and courtly Italian *ottava rima* (literally "eighth rhyme"), an eight-line stanza form rhyming *abababcc*, which was deployed in Renaissance classics such as **Boccaccio**'s *Filostrato* (c.1335) and **Ariosto**'s *Orlando Furioso* (1516).

Furthermore, by the time Shakespeare turned to it, rhyme royal was sounding distinctly creaky. **Geoffrey Chaucer** pioneered its use in English, and it became so closely associated with his *Troilus and Criseyde* (early 1380s) that the form was initially known as the "*Troilus* stanza". Poets influenced by Chaucer frequently employed it in the years to come, notably **Hoccleve**, **Dunbar** and **Henryson** (who himself based his rhyme-royal *Testament of Cresseid* on Chaucer's poem). Its regal name seems to have appeared early in the next century, and by the time the poet, dramatist and sometime soldier **George Gascoigne** referred to it in 1575, the "royal" appellation had come to describe the way in which it was suited to grave, solemn subject matter.

But by the end of that century, the form was beginning to sound old-fashioned. While its use in *The Rape of Lucrece* presumably bears witness to Shakespeare's desire to provide a serious form for what he termed his "graver labour" after the erotic fripperies of *Venus and Adonis* (1593), by the time of the *Complaint*'s publication fifteen years later its antique patina would have been highly visible. Further into the seventeenth century, rhyme royal's days as a serious poetic option were numbered. Shakespeare's contemporary and fellow Warwickshireman **Michael Drayton** initially composed his historical poem *Mortimeriados* in the form, but, when revising it prior to 1619, decided to go for *ottava rima* instead.

'Thou art,' quoth she, 'a sea, a sovereign king,
And lo, there falls into thy boundless flood
Black lust, dishonour, shame, misgoverning,
Who seek to stain the ocean of thy blood.'

[652–8]

Lucrece appeals consistently to the good in her aggressor, to the sense that his innate nobility is being "stained" by forces from outside. Her words clearly catch a nerve, but Tarquin's response is not to back down: a moment later he stamps out the light, gags Lucrece and rapes her. Like Lavinia in *Titus Andronicus* (which Shakespeare may have written concurrently with *Lucrece*), whose tongue is cut out after she is raped, Lucrece's words are taken violently away from her.

One of the most distressing things about Lucrece's rape – Shakespeare does not describe it directly, but allows readers to imagine the worst – is that it begins to distort some of the moral certainties of the poem. We know (and are repeatedly told by the narrator) that Tarquin is evil and Lucrece blameless, but in the wake of the attack Lucrece herself begins to doubt that she is free from guilt. While Tarquin wishes for dawn to arrive so that he can forget about everything, Lucrece is desperate for it to remain dark so that she will not have to confront what she awkwardly terms "night's scapes" (747). Describing her "true eyes", she weeps to herself,

'They think not but that every eye can see
The same disgrace which they themselves behold,
And therefore would they still in darkness be,
To have their unseen sin remain untold.
For they their guilt with weeping will unfold,
    And grave, like water that doth eat in steel,
    Upon my cheeks what helpless shame I feel.'

[750–6]

Lucrece's words are painfully moving, but most troubling of all is perhaps her sense that her "eyes" – and by extension herself – have some culpability in what has just happened. Seeing "disgrace", she knows that others will see it too, and immediately transfers their assumption that she is guilty to herself. In a harrowing image Lucrece imagines her tears – marks of her innocence and terrible sorrow – visibly eating into her face, just as Tarquin has polluted her body.

Lucrece's response to her violation is as comprehensible as it is realistic (rape victims often relate that they feel blame, no matter how unfounded), but in Shakespeare's poem the heroine's sense of guilt sets her on a path to self-destruction. Unlike Tarquin, who has little problem adjusting to the thought of a crime that is both "shameful" and "hateful" yet utterly doable (239–40), Lucrece cannot accommodate a world in which, as Hamlet will later put it, "one may smile and smile and be a villain" (*Hamlet*, 1.5.109). Gazing later on a painting of the fall of Troy that decorates her bedchamber – itself ominous enough – she peers at the portrait of the treacherous Sinon (a Greek who persuaded the Trojans to take the wooden horse into their city) in disbelief, unable to comprehend that someone who looks so honest can have done something so horribly evil:

'It cannot be,' quoth she, 'that so much guile'—
She would have said 'can lurk in such a look',
But Tarquin's shape came in her mind the while,
And from her tongue 'can lurk' from 'cannot' took.
'It cannot be' she in that sense forsook,
    And turned it thus: 'It cannot be, I find,
    But such a face should bear a wicked mind.'

[1534–40]

Lucrece, still stunned, struggles to adjust to a world in which appearances do not map onto realities – and with the violent appearance of Tarquin's "shape" in her mind, it is as if her rape risks being committed all over again.

That is not the only way in which Lucrece fails to counter the chaotic complexity of her situation. Having been defiled, she appears to be certain that she must be at fault – not least of having betrayed her husband with "violated troth" (1059), a phrase that sounds as if it should come from someone guilty of adultery rather than a victim of rape. "Deep drenchèd in a sea of care" (1100), she becomes her own worst enemy in this latter section of the poem, railing helplessly against the various forces she sees as having conspired against her – night, time, even the "opportunity" that has allowed Tarquin to attack. These laments and complaints occupy a significant stretch of the action after the rape scene, and many commentators seem to agree that they are not poetically successful, too artificial and empty to have much impact. But that is Lucrece's sense, too, and if anything the wide range of her appeals succeeds in charting her utter desperation. "In vain I rail at opportunity," she insists, acutely conscious of the futility of it all,

> 'At time, at Tarquin, and uncheerful night.
> In vain I cavil with mine infamy,
> In vain I spurn at my confirmed despite.
> This helpless smoke of words doth me no right;
>    The remedy indeed to do me good
>    Is to let forth my foul defilèd blood.'

[1023–9]

Blood-letting was a common treatment in the Renaissance (used, sometimes disastrously, for all manner of illnesses), but here Lucrece is looking directly at suicide. Her decision to go through with it is unhappily ironic: to medieval commentators influenced by St Augustine's views on the matter, it was Lucretia's decision to take her own life that proved her guilt and thus condemned her. Lucrece's position, Shakespeare makes clear, is horribly unenviable: if she stays alive, she brings shame to her husband and risks giving birth to an illegitimate child (childbirth was itself a significant hazard); if she commits suicide, she stands being accused of complicity in the rape and even of arrogance in paying such heed to her reputation. Lucrece herself is tragically unaware of these complications, insisting to herself that

> 'To clear this spot by death, at least I give
> A badge of fame to slander's livery,
> A dying life to living infamy.'

[1053–5]

Like many things in the poem, this tugs two ways: Lucrece's death, too, will bring her "infamy". This theme is an insistent one in *Lucrece*, and history weighs heavily not only on the heroine, but also on Tarquin – who worries before the rape that going through with it will cause him "dishonour" (198), and later threatens Lucrece that if she resists he will simply ravish her anyway and leave her body lying incriminatingly with "some worthless slave" (515), thus poisoning not only her reputation but that of her husband. Shakespeare will not let his readers forget that posterity is a harsh judge, and his protagonists agonize with that knowledge too.

And it is Lucrece's loss of control over her identity that is perhaps the most tragic thing of all about this poem: in killing herself she also loses the ability to speak for herself. Although her speech continues until the last possible moment, once Lucrece is dead it is the responsibility of the men that surround her (no women are allowed into *Lucrece*'s conclusion) to interpret what has happened and act accordingly. Their solution, a "revenge" that turns out to be solely political, might be rational – but it utterly fails to take into account the emotional impact of Lucrece's suicide, an impact of which we as readers are only too aware. Their treatment of her corpse, like that of Julius Caesar in Shakespeare's play, seems like the final insult. "When they had sworn to this advisèd doom," the narrator sadly tells us,

> They did conclude to bear dead Lucrece thence,
> To show her bleeding body thorough Rome,
> And so to publish Tarquin's foul offence …

**[1849–52]**

Even in death, Lucrece's public humiliation is not over.

## Audio

### The Rape of Lucrece
**David Ian Davies**
US, 2001  ▷  One Voice ⊙

Though still often unthinkingly pigeonholed as the "non-dramatic" works, Shakespeare's narrative poems have plenty to offer in terms of drama, even if in *Lucrece* the effect is chiefly one of deliberate and extended dread. David Ian Davies does well to keep the poem moving (even on the page it can seem slow), and he makes for a thoughtful narrator. One sometimes wishes that he would be a little less straight-laced and register more of the text's varied ironies, but the world is hardly bursting with audio versions of *Lucrece*, and whatever quibbles there might be with this interpretation it's still excellent to hear the poem performed with such commitment. For listeners with a decent Internet connection, the recording can be downloaded from Audible.com (see p.500) for less than ten US dollars; alternatively, you can acquire a two-CD copy for $20.00 plus postage by emailing One Voice direct at: sales@onevoicerecordings.com.

## Editions

### Oxford Shakespeare
**Colin Burrow (ed.); 2002**  ▷  Oxford UP

As elsewhere with Shakespeare's poetry, our top recommendation for *Lucrece* comes in the recent (and bulky) form of Colin Burrow's single-volume edition of the *Complete Sonnets and Poems*. Burrow is particularly sensitive in his handling of this poem and the notes are extremely observant, particularly when dealing with what the printed realities of the poems offered to their early readers (an interest also dealt with at length in the introduction). He also provides plenty of insight into the different versions of the Lucretia tale that Shakespeare drew upon, and discusses the impact of Shakespeare's humanistic education on this early work.

## Some criticism

### Captive Victors
**Heather Dubrow; 1987**  ▷  Cornell UP [o/p]

The title of Dubrow's book is a quotation from *Lucrece* and, though she also deals with *Venus and Adonis* and the Sonnets, it is Shakespeare's tragic poem that dominates her imagination. Dubrow has a sharp eye for slippery, twisting language and she proves an expert guide to (and robust defender of) the apparent rhetorical excesses of *Lucrece*, arguing that its range of linguistic techniques is an index of its psychological insight rather than its greatest flaw. *Captive Victors* is also an impassioned and convincing response to those critics who have suggested Lucrece's own culpability in what she suffers, though some readers might wish that the further reaches of Dubrow's arguments were more grounded in the text.

# The Sonnets

Wordsworth thought them the key to Shakespeare's heart; Keats remarked that they were "full of fine things said unintentionally"; Ralph Waldo Emerson asked whether they did not speak of "the confusion of sentiments in the most susceptible, and, at the same time, the most intellectual of men?". More recently Shakespeare has been adopted (or outed) as a gay icon, the man who wrote over a hundred poems to a mysterious male lover. Despite the difficulties of trying to read the Sonnets as autobiographical testament, the temptation never really passes, so utterly believable do these rich, intense and passionate poems seem. They are the only works of Shakespeare in which the poet seems to speak in his own voice: to wonder about who is writing them, and to whom, and why, is part of the whole intimate encounter. Yet "SHAKE-SPEARES SONNETS. Neuer before Imprinted", as they were first published, guard their secrets well. As well as being a monumental poetic achievement – they may have taken two decades to reach their published form – the Sonnets are also some of Shakespeare's most difficult works to interpret, quite literally so given their concentrated and sometimes dizzyingly complex language. Yet they reward patient and careful reading, and, despite the best attempts of love-poetry anthologists, it seems impossible ever to exhaust their brilliance – one reason why they are among the greatest collections of poems ever written.

[DATE] The volume entitled *Shakespeare's Sonnets* was published in 1609, though the individual poems that make it up might have been composed nearly twenty years earlier. Stylometric analysis suggests that composition fell into four main groups between 1591 and 1604.

[SOURCES] Numerous sonnet sequences were published during the 1590s, of which Philip Sidney's *Astrophil and Stella* (first printed in 1591), Samuel Daniel's *Delia* (1592) and Edmund Spenser's *Amoretti* (1595) are only the most famous.

[TEXTS] Only one early edition, the 1609 *Shakespeare's Sonnets* (Q1), exists – poems were not printed in the plays-only First Folio (1623) – and is on the whole a good text with few errors. Unpopular compared with Shakespeare's narrative poems, it was not reprinted until a heavily revised version of 1640.

## Interpreting the poems

By the time that a book entitled *Shakespeare's Sonnets* was published in 1609, six years after Elizabeth I's death, the brief but brilliant fashion for sonnet sequences had waned. And along with love poetry in general, sonnets do not get a great press in Shakespeare's plays. In *Love's Labour's Lost* his Lords try frantically to woo their respective Ladies with a succession of cringeworthy verses; in *Much Ado* the quick-witted Benedick is stumped by his inability to write anything but "halting sonnets" to his newfound mistress Beatrice; and even the endlessly eloquent Hamlet, when he attempts to distil his feelings for Ophelia into verse, churns out what can best be described as doggerel. Not that Shakespeare is always so transparently cyn-

## Synopsis

There is no straightforward narrative connecting Shakespeare's 154 Sonnets, leading some scholars to conjecture that they were printed without the author's consent and not put into any kind of order. The last statement is not really accurate, and in fact there are two major groupings: Sonnets **1–126** appear to be addressed to a beautiful and anonymous young man; while Sonnets **127–152** mostly describe, or are addressed to, a similarly anonymous black-haired woman (**153** and **154** are poems on Cupid, the god of love).

The sequence addressed to the young man is the more carefully ordered of the two, and contains several mini-sequences relating to the relationship, some little more than a collection of related ideas. Sonnets **1–17** urge the young man to find a partner and have children; **41** and **42** hint that the poet's mistress has seduced him during the poet's absence; **78–86** describe a rival author who has apparently tempted the young man away from the poet; **87–90** worry that the young man has forgotten the poet altogether; **91–96** suggest that poet and young man have been reconciled; **100–103** describe the poet's struggles with his "truant muse"; **117–120** apparently apologize for the poet's own inconstancy to his subject; **126** brings an end to the "lovely boy" sequence.

**127–152** are more loosely organized, though many of the poems are addressed to a mistress described as black-haired (**130**), "tyrannous" (**131**) and unfaithful to the poet with his "friend" (**133–134**). Sonnets **135**, **136** and **143** pun on "Will" (Shakespeare's first name), while other sonnets in this section of the book dwell on the pain and humiliation of love.

ical. In *Romeo and Juliet* he achieves a heartstopping effect by having the lovers address each other for the first time in what turns out to be a sonnet:

ROMEO
    If I profane with my unworthiest hand
      This holy shrine, the gentler sin is this:
    My lips, two blushing pilgrims, ready stand
      To smooth that rough touch with a tender kiss.
JULIET
    Good pilgrim, you do wrong your hand too much,
      Which mannerly devotion shows in this.
    For saints have hands that pilgrims' hands do touch,
      And palm to palm is holy palmers' kiss.
ROMEO
    Have not saints lips, and holy palmers, too?
JULIET
    Ay, pilgrim, lips that they must use in prayer.
ROMEO
    O then, dear saint, let lips do what hands do:
      They pray; grant thou, lest faith turn to despair.
JULIET
    Saints do not move, though grant for prayers' sake.
ROMEO
    Then move not while my prayer's effect I take.
      *He kisses her*

**[*Romeo and Juliet*, 1.5.92–105]**

Shakespeare's lovers use a verse form often called the Shakespearian sonnet, though more correctly it was invented by his poetic ancestor the Earl of Surrey (see opposite). The fourteen-line pattern is simple and elegant: the first twelve lines rhyme across each other ("hand/stand", "this/kiss") before concluding in a two-line couplet in which the rhymes are identical ("sake/take"). Despite these taut formal constraints the effect here is betwitchingly fresh, because Juliet and Romeo produce the poem as it were without realizing it, sharing its lines in interweaving union. But the sonnet also has darker ramifications: though the moment is intense, it is also intensely short. These lovers will not be together for long.

## The only begetter

Delicately beautiful though it is, the solitary sonnet in *Romeo and Juliet* is dwarfed by *Shakespeare's Sonnets*, a volume containing not just 154 sonnets, nearly all in the same "Shakespearian" form – outrunning even Sidney's 108 in *Astrophil and Stella* – but the 329-line narrative poem *A Lover's Complaint* (see p.413). Yet some have doubted that the author even intended the volume so loudly published in his name ever to reach print. There is a long-standing theory that Shakespeare's Sonnets were stolen from the poet by an unscrupulous printer (like Sidney's) and published behind his back. The infamous title-page to *Sonnets*, which addresses the book "TO . THE . ONLIE . BEGETTER . OF . / THESE . INSVING . SONNETS.", a mysterious man called only "Mr. W . H .", does little to solve this puzzle: instead of being signed by Shakespeare, the initials of the printer, Thomas Thorpe, close this carefully typeset dedication. Some scholars have assumed as a consequence that Thorpe liberated these poems from Shakespeare's grasp and smuggled them into the press.

---

**KEY SOURCE**     Petrarch and Renaissance sonneteers

One of the most portable of poetic forms, the **sonnet** has been in Europe from the beginning of the Renaissance. Its name and origins are thought to be Italian: *sonetto* means "a small sound or song", and poems we think of as sonnets first started to appear in Italy as long ago as the thirteenth century. Though a variant on the form was used by Dante, the name of **Francesco Petrarca** (1304–74), Petrarch in English, always surfaces in connection with the sonnet. Petrarch formalized its delicate and intricate architecture (its metre and pattern of rhyme) and, building on medieval traditions of lyric, made the poem an expression of beautifully crafted but eternally unrequited love. Petrarch's sonnets are addressed to a mysterious figure named "Laura", who the poet claimed was a lady he met while living in Avignon but who suddenly died, perhaps killed by plague, leaving him grief-stricken and desperate for creative solace. It is not known whether Laura ever existed, but for the poems inspired by her it doesn't entirely matter. Petrarch uses the certainty of his mistress's absence – even the sense that she might be entirely imaginary – to construct an image of womanhood that rarely touches reality. His Laura is impossibly beautiful, unequalled in virtuousness, always just out of reach. She is an idea.

Writers influenced by Petrarch carried the form through the high Renaissance and into other countries: in France and Spain poets readily joined the cult, and by the first decades of the sixteenth century their counterparts in England had done so too. Two of the first home-grown exponents of the sonnet, **Sir Thomas Wyatt** (?1503–42) and **Henry Howard, Earl of Surrey** (?1517–47), travelled on the continent under Henry VIII, and were soon translating fashionable work by Petrarch and his successors. By the 1590s, when Shakespeare was making his name as a dramatist, poets such as **Sir Philip Sidney**, **Samuel Daniel** and **Edmund Spenser** had all seen sonnets published under their names (in Sidney's case a printer was responsible for publication, the poet himself being dead) and the concept of a "sonnet sequence" – a linked collection of sonnets, sometimes numbering fifty or more – had become entrenched. The sophisticated titles of these respective collections, *Astrophil and Stella* (first printed 1592), *Delia* (1592) and *Amoretti* (1595), reveals that, though the poems themselves are in English, being seen as continental was very much the thing. But the vogue for Elizabethan sonnets, brilliantly intense though it was, soon passed: no major sequences were published after 1600, and when the Jacobean poet **John Donne** revisited the form in his *Holy Sonnets*, what emerged – erotic verse linked with fervent Christianity – was shockingly iconoclastic.

Setting aside the equally long-running dispute over who exactly "W. H." really is (if anyone at all; see p.433), readers have unearthed other suggestions that Shakespeare never intended these poems to reach the reading public – something apparently believed by their earliest critic, who commented that the poet's "sugared Sonnets" circulated only "among his private friends". As if to confirm that claim, Sonnet 145 is one of the most intimately clandestine poems in the collection. It plays tenderly with the name of the poet's wife, married nearly thirty years earlier and usually supposed to be living at Stratford while her husband's career was down in London. "Those lips that love's own hand did make / Breathed forth the sound that said 'I hate' / To me that languished for her sake", it begins,

> But when she saw my woeful state,
> Straight in her heart did mercy come,
> Chiding that tongue that ever sweet
> Was used in giving gentle doom,
> And taught it thus anew to greet:
> 'I hate' she altered with an end
> That followed it as gentle day
> Doth follow night who, like a fiend,
> From heaven to hell is flown away.

**[145, 1–12]**

Adding "hate" to "away", as the sonnet suggests, makes something passably close to Anne Shakespeare's maiden name, Hathaway: without that knowledge, the poem makes little sense. Its audience might, rather wonderfully, be a private audience of one.

Just as this poem appears to glance at a real-life love affair (it is sometimes argued to be Shakespeare's first sonnet), readers of the Sonnets have long attempted to find similar biographical keys to the rest of the poems, which constantly open the way to a complex series of private narratives but teasingly refuse to go any further. Sometimes those readers have been baffled or even disgusted by what they have found: one nameless seventeenth-century commentator was sufficiently moved to scrawl "what a heap of wretched Infidel stuff" in his copy of the book, while the eighteenth-century editor George Steevens refused even to include them in his 1793 edition of Shakespeare's works on the basis that "the strongest act of Parliament that could be framed, would fail to compel readers into their service".

One basis for such heated vituperation may be the boldest and most intriguing fact about the Sonnets: most of them are written by a man to a man. More than that, they are often surprisingly frank about the appeals – and difficulties – of what we now call homosexuality (the word itself, a Victorian invention, was not known by Shakespeare or his contemporaries, though sodomy was technically illegal). Sonnet 20, for instance, toys with some gender-bending questions:

> A woman's face with nature's own hand painted
> Hast thou, the master-mistress of my passion;
> A woman's gentle heart, but not acquainted
> With shifting change as is false women's fashion ...

**[20, 1–4]**

The attractions of women, the poet continues, pale beside those of the young man to whom this sonnet (and over a hundred others) is addressed. Lest we should miss the point, he declares, "But since she pricked thee out for women's pleasure, / Mine be thy love and thy love's use their treasure" (13–14), punning rather heavily on the still-current slang for penis. The poem perhaps calls to mind the intimate male friendships described in plays including *The Two Gentlemen of*

*Verona* (from one end of Shakespeare's career) and *The Two Noble Kinsmen* (from the other): Palamon and Arcite, the paired "kinsmen" of the last play, declare that they may as well be "one another's wife", so close are they to each other (2.2.80). But this sonnet, mischievously, goes far further – flirtatiously insinuating that the poet and his addressee have shared, or desire to share, a good deal more than straightforward platonic companionship.

Not that all the Sonnets speak to a man. After Sonnet 126, which addresses "thou my lovely boy" for what appears to be the last time (the poem lacks two lines, as if the sonnet itself had exhausted its formal possibilities), there begins a second internal sequence apparently written to, and sometimes about, a female subject. Tradition calls this woman Shakespeare's "Dark Lady", but in the poems themselves the narrator is a good deal less refined. "Th'expense of spirit in a waste of shame / Is lust in action," Sonnet 129 begins, ferociously, and does not stop for another eleven lines,

TO.THE.ONLIE.BEGETTER.OF.
THESE.INSVING.SONNETS.
Mr.W. H. ALL.HAPPINESSE.
AND.THAT.ETERNITIE.
PROMISED.

BY.

OVR.EVER-LIVING.POET.

WISHETH.

THE.WELL-WISHING.
ADVENTVRER.IN.
SETTING.
FORTH.

T. T.

The sparse title-page of *Shake-speares Sonnets, neuer before Imprinted* (1609) offers a dedication signed by the printer, Thomas Thorpe, but no clue as to whom "Mr. W. H." might be – an unsolved literary enigma.

> and till action, lust
> Is perjured, murd'rous, bloody, full of blame,
> Savage, extreme, rude, cruel, not to trust,
> Enjoyed no sooner but despisèd straight,
> Past reason hunted, and so sooner had
> Past reason hated as a swallowed bait
> On purpose laid to make the taker mad;
> Mad in pursuit and in possession so,
> Had, having, and in quest to have, extreme;
> A bliss in proof and proved, a very woe;
> Before, a joy proposed; behind, a dream.

[129, 1–12]

"All this the world well knows, yet none knows well / To shun the heaven that leads men to this hell," the narrator finishes in a poisonous concluding couplet. Though many of the Sonnets are tricky to comprehend, even after repeated rereading, this poem is more difficult to untangle than most – yet its denunciation of "lust" takes on a clearer, and nastier, resonance if you listen to some of its puns: "spirit" can mean semen; "hell" was Elizabethan slang for vagina. What Sonnet 129 stops just short of declaring is that male "lust" for sex, a desire "enjoyed no sooner but despisèd straight", should be blamed solely on women. Though the Sonnets are sometimes thought of as the greatest love poems of all time, their dark and sometimes astringent tone seems to belie, or complicate, that reputation – or at least suggest they are impossible to pigeonhole.

It often seems that outright misogyny is rarely far away in the Sonnets, as indeed the dynamic of the Petrarchan tradition – all cruel mistresses and wounded males – somewhat encourages. In the poems addressed by Shakespeare's narrator to the young man, women are repeatedly cast as inferior, limited, changeable; in those to the female mistress, she is accused of adultery, tyranny, deceit, perhaps even of having contracted venereal disease. Her very appearance comes in for harsh criticism: "My mistress' eyes are nothing like the sun", declares Sonnet 130, famously drawing attention to her "dun"-coloured chest and wiry black hair. And yet this poem, like others in the final sequence of the Sonnets, also has more interesting and engaging things to offer. Part of Sonnet 130's argument is that verse extolling the beauty of matchless mistresses rarely has much time for imperfect human realities. "I love to hear her speak," the poet says,

> yet well I know
> That music hath a far more pleasing sound.
> I grant I never saw a goddess go:
> My mistress when she walks treads on the ground.
> And yet, by heaven, I think my love as rare
> As any she belied with false compare.

[130, 9–14]

The poet's mistress is not just "any she": her imperfections, what Sonnet 141 more brutally calls her "thousand errors" (141, 2), make her who she is, just as the narrator's own flaws (fleetingly catalogued in Sonnet 138) do the same for him. Read in this company, Sonnet 116's famous declaration that "love is not love / Which alters when it alteration finds," sounds more tentative than seems to be the case first time around. "O no, it is an ever fixèd mark / That looks on tempests and is never shaken," the narrator cries,

> It is the star to every wand'ring barque,
> Whose worth's unknown although his height be taken.
> Love's not time's fool, though rosy lips and cheeks
> Within his bending sickle's compass come;
> Love alters not with his brief hours and weeks,
> But bears it out even to the edge of doom.

[116, 2–12]

The poem is often interpreted as celebrating the eternal constancy of love – and it may indeed be so. But set alongside others in the sequence, the message is more surprising, and perhaps more insightful. Here the narrator speaks of noble ideals, but the poet of the sonnets to the dark-eyed mistress knows – as perhaps we all do – that ideals can go only so far. The Sonnets continually remind us that love is not fixed, or beyond time: it is something more human, and more mutable, and that is also what makes it so enduring.

## So long lives this

Attempting to read *Shakespeare's Sonnets* as a narrative about Shakespeare's own life is an engaging but ultimately frustrating occupation, and whether or not he was gay or straight in any modern sense of those words we should be wary of drawing any stable conclusions. For one thing, male sexuality in the Renaissance was an ambiguous and sometimes flexible reality, not easy to map onto modern-day values and beliefs. For another, these poems, no

## Mr Who He?

Even before the poems start, *Shakespeare's Sonnets* already plays with its readers. The book is dedicated to "THE . ONLIE . BEGETTER . OF . THESE . INSVING . SONNETS", a man only described as "Mr. W . H .". To understand the poems, this note implies, you might also have to figure out who the man behind those two initials really is; a heavy biographical hint that revelation awaits those in the know.

Though the temptation to crack the code seems largely to have passed Shakespeare's early readers by, interest awoke in the late eighteenth century. Edmund Malone's 1780 edition of the poems arrived at just the right time for the first generation of Romantic critics to discover the Sonnets, and to wonder afresh at what they revealed about Shakespeare's life and passions. Speculation over the identity of "W. H.", taken to be the "lovely boy" addressed in Sonnets 1–126, followed close behind. Two aristocratic candidates, both connected to Shakespeare's published work, jostled for pre-eminence. The first was proposed in 1817: he was **Henry Wriothesley**, Earl of Southampton, the man to whom *Venus and Adonis* and *Lucrece* were both addressed. The second was another Earl, this time of Pembroke: **William Herbert**, co-dedicatee of the First Folio and nephew of Sir Philip Sidney, offered as a possibility in 1823.

For much of the nineteenth century, arguments over the relative merits of these two bounced back and forth. Both are possible, though Pembroke perhaps has the edge: in addition to his initials being the right way round, his life story has been taken to support the genesis of the Sonnets. After refusing several times to marry women selected for him, the 20-year-old Pembroke succeeded in getting Mary Fitton, a maid of honour to Queen Elizabeth, pregnant – but refused to wed her, too, and was briefly imprisoned. The theory goes that Shakespeare was called in by Pembroke's exasperated parents and commanded to write a set of poems telling him to get on and marry before it was too late.

Even so, many readers were not convinced and the search for alternative "W. H."s raged on. Some suggested **William Harvey**, Southampton's stepfather; others **William Hathaway**, Shakespeare's brother-in-law; others even diagnosed a case of poetic narcissism, either on the basis of a misprint ("W. H." for "W. Sh.") or a cunning insertion ("W[illiam] H[imself]"). Easily the most creative theory to have appeared was dreamt up by **Oscar Wilde**, whose *The Portrait of Mr W.H.* (1889) spins the elegant story of a man claiming to own a portrait of the youth adored by Shakespeare, a boy actor called **Willie Hughes** for whom the playwright's greatest female roles were written. The echoes with Wilde's doomed love for the much younger Lord Alfred Douglas were acknowledged by Wilde and played a fateful part in his downfall: a letter to Douglas, described by Wilde as "like a little sonnet of Shakespeare", was produced at his trial in 1895 and helped to secure his conviction on counts of gross indecency.

Speculation as to the identity of Shakespeare's so-called "**Dark Lady**" has, if anything, been even more fevered – probably because many nineteenth-century scholars were unhappy confronting the notion that their idol might have loved a man. Lacking the evidence of even a pair of initials, theories have been remarkably ingenious. Mary Fitton, who carried Pembroke's child before being abandoned by him, has the attraction of fitting the most unimaginative biographical theory, that the Sonnets relate the story of their relationship with each other and Shakespeare. Fitton was fair (not "black"), however, and more exotic candidates have been lined up to compete – among them **Emilia Lanier**, herself well-known as a poet, who came from a family of Venetian musicians and has been linked with Sonnet 128 ("How oft, when thou, my music, music play'st"). Other rivals include the black-eyed **Lady Rich**, loved by Philip Sidney and ostensibly the "Stella" of his sonnets; **Jane Davenant**, mother of playwright William, who liked to claim he was Shakespeare's love child; and even a nameless black prostitute who caught the poet's eye.

matter the strength of their emotional feeling, continually remind us of their intense, often intricate, intellect. They are reluctant to take anything at face value – sometimes literally. "My glass shall not persuade me I am old / So long as youth and thou are of one date," begins Sonnet 22,

But when in thee time's furrows I behold,
Then look I death my days should expiate.
For all that beauty that doth cover thee
Is but the seemly raiment of my heart,
Which in thy breast doth live, as thine in me;
How can I then be elder than thou art?

[22, 1–8]

The poem (and the poet) play a complex philosophical and linguistic game with their young and beautiful subject, suggesting that because the poet's "heart" beats within the youth's breast (and vice versa) they are in fact the same age. Despite outward appearances – the older poet ruefully declares elsewhere that he is "beated and chapped with tanned antiquity" (62, 10) – love draws them together and makes them live as one.

> *I have long felt convinced, after repeated perusals of the* Sonnets, *that the greater number of them was composed in an assumed character, on different subjects, and at different times, for the amusement, and probably at the suggestion, of the author's intimate associates.*
>
> Alexander Dyce, in his edition of the *Poems* (1832)

Sonnet 22 develops into new territory the argument put forward in this first group of sonnets, that the nameless young man they address should get on and procreate lest his beauty be lost to the world – something also urged by the heroine of *Venus and Adonis*, who is eager to taste the joys of the young Adonis for herself. The Sonnets are rarely that explicit, though as the sequence builds the poet often returns to the promise that it is his words alone that can make the young man live for eternity. While held together by their address to the youth, Sonnets 1–126 range through an amazing variety of topics – from nobility of birth to the role of art, from the nature of inspiration to simple envy – and call upon a restless array of poetic locations. Sonnet 30 imagines love operating in a kind of "sessions", or law court; Sonnet 73 places the poet in a late autumnal world where "yellow leaves, or none, or few, do hang" (73, 2); Sonnet 23 sets its speaker in a position that must have been familiar to the poem's author, that of "an unperfect actor on the stage / Who with his fear is put besides his part" (23, 1–2). In a different world entirely, Sonnet 107 begins by gesturing towards recent historical events (many think it refers to the death of Elizabeth I in 1603 and the arrival of her successor James) but concludes with the resonant declaration that, because of this poem, the youth will outlast mere monarchs. Leaving "death" to "insult o'er dull and speechless tribes", the poet proclaims,

thou in this shalt find thy monument
When tyrants' crests and tombs of brass are spent.

[107, 13–14]

The idea that poetry conferred eternity on its subjects was not new, but Shakespeare makes it seem freshly minted, a gift of transcendent certainty in a world all too eager to forget. Much the same thing is argued by the most famous sonnet of all, number 18, which begins by asking "Shall I compare thee to a summer's day?" and concludes that it is only the poet's "eternal lines" that can make the young man known to posterity. "So long as men can breathe or eyes can see," the narrator exults,

So long lives this, and this gives life to thee.

[18, 13–14]

This sense that it is through poetry that the poet can himself triumph over what Sonnet 19 shudderingly calls "devouring time" is one of the most magnificent aspects of the book published as *Shakespeare's Sonnets*, and probably its most consistent single philosophy. Some evidence suggests that the poems printed in the volume were written over as much as a twenty-year period, so in that sense alone the work is a fitting testament to Shakespeare's career as a poet, a career that he appears to have continued even while his hands were full with writing plays. Revelling in its own power, sonnet 55 offers a brave challenge to the erosions of "sluttish time":

> Not marble nor the gilded monuments
> Of princes shall outlive this powerful rhyme,
> But you shall shine more bright in these contents
> Than unswept stone besmeared with sluttish time.
> When wasteful war shall statues overturn,
> And broils root out the work of masonry,
> Nor Mars his sword nor war's quick fire shall burn
> The living record of your memory.
> 'Gainst death and all oblivious enmity
> Shall you pace forth; your praise shall still find room
> Even in the eyes of all posterity
> That wear this world out to the ending doom.
>    So, till the judgement that yourself arise,
>    You live in this, and dwell in lovers' eyes.

**[55, 1–14]**

And so long as they go on being kept alive by readers, that pledge will seem true enough.

# Audio

## The Sonnets
### John Gielgud
UK, 1963 ▷ HarperCollins (Caedmon)

John Gielgud was widely acclaimed as having one of the most beautiful theatrical voices of his generation, perhaps even of the century. Even if the rest of his work perished, these 1963 tapings of the Sonnets would testify to his powers, for in them Gielgud is on transcendent form. What can in some other contexts seem like reserve or aloofness is here transformed into vivid urgency: when the speaker claims in Sonnet 147 that he is "past cure … past care", here you utterly believe him. These are gloriously full-bodied readings that express their emotions – and Gielgud's understanding of the poems' varied moods – intimately. The text followed is that of the 1609 first quarto, and really this recording's sole limitation is that it includes only 120 of the Sonnets, poems in the final part of sequence being among the chief casualties.

## The Sonnets
### Alex Jennings
UK, 1997 ▷ Naxos

Listening to an audio performance of the Sonnets can be an odd experience: poems that you're used to imagining one way are suddenly taken out of your control and made someone else's. It's as if Jennings addressed himself to this conundrum when recording these sessions, always striving for a quiet approach that doesn't indulge itself in extremes. Less ostentatious than Gielgud, he's also more interested in driving a narrative through the different sonnets. If at times you wish that Jennings gave more of himself to these recordings, his relatively downbeat style is subtly shaded and grows in appeal with repeated listening. And unlike Gielgud, he also reads the full set.

# Editions

## Oxford Shakespeare
### Colin Burrow (ed.); 2002 ▷ Oxford UP

The newest edition of the Sonnets to date, 750 pages long, is also by some way the fattest. Colin Burrow's *Complete Sonnets and Poems* includes not only *A Lover's Complaint* and the two major narrative poems but *The Passionate Pilgrim*, *The Phoenix and the Turtle* (though the editor doesn't call it that) and several poems Shakespeare's contemporaries thought might be his – a condition that gets Burrow off the hook of including the woefully bad "A Funeral Elegy" (see p.484). This collective context gives Burrow plenty of reason to reposition Shakespeare as a major poet in his own right rather than someone who tossed off the odd sonnet in his spare time. His treatment of the Sonnets is typically excellent, with insightful but sensible notes and an extended introductory essay that provides detail on biographical puzzles while refusing to get lost in them.

### New Penguin Shakespeare
**John Kerrigan (ed.); 1986** ▷ Penguin

Despite Colin Burrow's attempts to corner the market in Shakespearian verse, other editions of the Sonnets (there are many available) have plenty to offer. Kerrigan's version is particularly recommended, at least partly because of its different format. No on-page notes and glosses, for one thing, but in fact this apparent hindrance allows Kerrigan to exercise his intellect in an extended sequence of detailed mini-essays masquerading as notes. These take up nearly two-thirds of the book, but you have the option to ignore the lot and scan a clean text – as the first readers of *Shakespeare's Sonnets* did – instead. And Penguin have even reprinted this edition of the Sonnets in a slimline pocket format without notes, perfect whether you're reading them on the bus or slipping them under a lover's door. The narrative poem *A Lover's Complaint*, published following the Sonnets in the 1609 text, is also included.

## Some criticism

### The Art of Shakespeare's Sonnets
**Helen Vendler; 1997** ▷ Harvard UP

Whatever else *The Art of Shakespeare's Sonnets* is – and it offers much – this book is beautiful to use, in its hardback edition especially. Attractively designed and wonderfully printed, its format is also ingenious: each sonnet is printed both in original facsimile and a modernized text, with a long interpretative essay on the facing page. Vendler is one of the most perspicacious critics around, equally well-known for her writing on contemporary poetry as for historical work, and here she's in her element, teasing out the most intricate of meanings then zooming out for the long shot. Ultra-close readings of these poems have much to offer, and even if you find yourself quibbling with the details you will still find yourself in Vendler's debt.

### Shakespeare's Sonnets: Critical Essays
**James Schiffer (ed.); 1999** ▷ Garland

While single-author interpretations of the Sonnets have their merits – Stephen Booth's *Essay on Shakespeare's Sonnets* (1969) and Joel Fineman's *Shakespeare's Perjured Eye* (1986) are just two brilliant examples – to taste a fuller range of commentary on these poems it's worth digging out an anthology. The Garland one is typically excellent, though unlike some others in the series it includes historical criticism in overview rather than directly. Nevertheless Schiffer has some provocative recent work from contributors including Margreta de Grazia and Peter Stallybrass as well as fifteen specially commissioned essays. If you'd prefer to browse some older work, it's worth tracking down Peter Jones's fine (if long out-of-print) *Shakespeare's Sonnets: A Casebook* (1977).

# Venus and Adonis

E xuberant, sexy, funny, yet also tenderly sad, *Venus and Adonis* was Shakespeare's first work to be printed under his name – and it was a rapid and roaring success. Published in spring 1593, four or five years after the author first arrived in London, it was reprinted six times in the next seven years, making it by some margin Shakespeare's most popular and well-known work during his lifetime. The great scholar Muriel Bradbrook once suggested that the poet wrote this to thumb his nose at his competitor Robert Greene (see p.128), and even if the story has no basis in fact, it might as well be true. Shakespeare lifted the story of the goddess Venus and her frustrated love affair with Adonis from Ovid's *Metamorphoses*, but gave it a glorious new twist: in this poem Adonis simply will not be seduced, and Venus is driven to ever more ridiculous lengths to persuade him into it. Despite the tongue-in-cheek comedy that ensues, however, *Venus and Adonis* ends tragically, with a touching finale demonstrating a subtle and impressive shift in dramatic mood. Described by the poet in his dedication as "the first heir of my invention", *Venus and Adonis* is where Shakespeare's career – and not just as a poet – really began to take flight.

**[DATE]** On bookstands by summer 1593, *Venus and Adonis* was perhaps written shortly beforehand, during the poet's unemployment following the plague closures (see below).

**[SOURCES]** Ovid's retelling of the Venus and Adonis story in *Metamorphoses* was Shakespeare's main source, but other details creep into it from elsewhere in Ovid and perhaps even Christopher Marlowe's *Hero and Leander*, written around the same time.

**[TEXTS]** The poem was printed by Richard Field (also from Stratford-upon-Avon and possibly Shakespeare's schoolfellow) in a quarto text noted for its careful typesetting. It was immediately popular, with no fewer than sixteen editions appearing over the next half-century.

## Interpreting the poem

Most likely penned during 1592 or early the following year, *Venus and Adonis* arrived during a difficult time for its author. After plague struck London during the summer and the death-toll soared, the authorities quickly ordered that the playhouses be closed down. Ostensibly they posed a risk to public health, but there may also have been other motives at work. In the years to come Shakespeare and his colleagues found themselves locked in a bitter vendetta with the City fathers, who were continually trying to put the theatres out of business. The spiritual as well as physical health of the population was at stake: only a few years previously a London preacher had insisted in a sermon that "the cause of plagues is sin … and the cause of sin are plays", and many men in power agreed. The plague killed over ten thousand citizens in 1593, and it also caused devastation in the theatre industry: venues stood idle, actors died, companies were forced out on tour and fell apart. During these worrisome years it must have never been clearer, even for a man as gifted as Shakespeare, writing and acting plays was not a stable profession.

## Synopsis

As dawn breaks, the beautiful youth Adonis heads out hunting, little suspecting that the goddess Venus has him in her sights. Adonis is not remotely interested in love, however, as Venus discovers when she drags him from his horse and attempts to pin him to the forest floor with kisses. Although he manages to resist her – despite her many entreaties and her insistence that it's his duty to procreate – it is midday before he manages to spring free from her clutches. But just as he is about to get away, an in-heat mare gallops into view, prompting Adonis's steed to romp after her into the woods, leaving his master with no means of transport.

As Adonis sits down on the forest floor in a sulk, Venus again attempts to seduce him, but with the same lack of success. Appalled by his indifference, she faints, whereupon the shocked Adonis – thinking she might be dead – attempts to bring her round by kissing her. After Venus regains consciousness, Adonis agrees to a final kiss if they can then say good night, but the excited Venus

sees this as an opportunity to get as much of him as she can. Eventually separating, Venus attempts to make a date with Adonis for the following day, but he informs her that he plans to go boar-hunting with his friends. Alarmed at the idea, Venus grabs him and pulls him down so that he's sitting on top of her, but, to her frustration, still nothing much happens. Finally, she attempts to convince him of the terrible dangers of hunting, but he refuses to be moved, and – angrily accusing her of lust rather than love – heads off home, leaving Venus to weep the night away.

As dawn arrives once more, Venus hears the sound of the hunt and, rushing towards it, comes across a blood-stained boar. Wavering between fear and hope, her worst misgivings are realized when she discovers Adonis's mangled body lying in the woods. Initially stunned into silence, she pays a moving tribute to his beauty and predicts that love itself will be diminished by his loss. But as she watches over him, Adonis's body disappears and a purple and white flower springs up in its place.

It was only to be expected that he would explore other artistic avenues. *Venus and Adonis*, the first of Shakespeare's clutch of "narrative" poems (poems, simply, that tell a story), is sometimes written off as an irrelevance to a career otherwise spent in playhouses. But in the early summer of 1593, when the poem emerged from the press, most of Shakespeare's dramatic work still lay in front of him and, like many of his colleagues, he was not solely a man of the theatre. *Venus and Adonis* was written for the young and glamorous Earl of Southampton, known for his good prospects, literary taste and encouragement of artists (he was famously painted by Nicholas Hilliard at around this time). The poem's dedication addresses the Earl directly in an unashamed attempt to secure favour, some of it financial. "Right Honourable," the poet begins,

> I know not how I shall offend in dedicating my unpolished lines to your Lordship, nor how the world will censure me for choosing so strong a prop to support so weak a burden. Only, if your honour seem but pleased, I account myself highly praised, and vow to take advantage of all idle hours till I have honoured you with some graver labour. But if the first heir of my invention prove deformed, I shall be sorry it had so noble a godfather, and never after ear so barren a land for fear it yield me still so bad a harvest.

**[Dedication, 5–12]**

"Your honour's in all duty," he signs off with a flourish, "William Shakespeare". Whether poet and Earl ever met is not known – Shakespeare's tone, confident but properly deferential, gives little away – yet that is largely beside the point. The dedication to *Venus and Adonis*, the first ever appearance of Shakespeare's name in print, stakes his claim as a poet. Those "idle hours" may have been forced on him, but there is more here than a bitter joke at the theatre's expense. Shakespeare declares himself a man who is seizing control of his time and using it to his own professional advantage.

Shakespeare targeted his poem with some cunning. Southampton had an interest in fashionable Ovidian verse, but he was not by any means alone. Indeed, we don't know whether or not Shakespeare garnered any kind of fiscal reward from Southampton for his "labour" – the Earl ran into financial difficulties soon after the publication of *The Rape of Lucrece* and Shakespeare, with the possible exception of the Sonnets, never went near him again – but we do know that *Venus and Adonis* found a ready market at the booksellers. It raced through at least sixteen editions in the next half-century, many of which have simply not survived due to readers' enthusiastic thumbing. It's little surprise that this unabashedly erotic poem appears to have been popular with hormonal young men, particularly those studying at the universities or in London. Ironically enough, it was via some of those readers that Shakespeare's first full-time poetic venture even found its way onto the stage: it makes a fleeting appearance in a play put on at Cambridge around 1598, in which one of the characters promises to "worship sweet Mr. Shakspeare," and to "lay his *Venus and Adonis* under my pillow". Shakespeare's contemporaries were to make more reference to this work than any other he wrote.

## By law of nature

And if *Venus and Adonis* was written in anything approaching desperate circumstances (Shakespeare's income is likely to have collapsed with the closure of the theatres), this joyous and often very funny poem gives little hint of it. It gives little hint, too, of being written in a city – so convincingly rural that many commentators have assumed Shakespeare arrived from Stratford with a finished draft in his pocket, or else wrote it far removed from the squalor and clamour of London. Over two-thirds of the way into the poem the narrator describes in gorgeously vivid language the goddess Venus scampering through the forest in search of Adonis, the youthful object of her desire. "And as she runs," he remarks,

> the bushes in the way
> Some catch her by the neck, some kiss her face,
> Some twine about her thigh to make her stay.
> She wildly breaketh from their strict embrace,
>   Like a milch doe whose swelling dugs do ache,
>   Hasting to feed her fawn hid in some brake.

[871–6]

Here Venus is compared, half-humorously, to a "milch doe", or female deer who feeds her young, and elsewhere the poem teems with all the bustle of the natural world. The imagery of *Venus and Adonis* is noisy with nature: larks trill, hares scurry, water-birds dip and dart, hunting dogs bray – the narrator even spends eleven stanzas describing Adonis's "strong-necked" horse, who catches sight of a "jennet" (female horse) who takes his fancy and promptly races after her. This is of course the central joke of the poem, and one of the reasons it presents its bucolic setting with such helter-skelter glee: all around the forest nature is doing what it does best, renewing and reproducing, while at the centre of the action stand the lovers, one of whom resists the fertility and fecundity of the woods and refuses to do anything of the kind.

Shakespeare borrowed the story of the goddess Venus and her encounter with the youthful mortal Adonis from Ovid's compendium of tales and legends, *Metamorphoses*, but he made one crucial change. In Ovid Venus falls helplessly for Adonis ("She loved Adonis more / Than heaven", Ovid's narrator exclaims in the translation Shakespeare used), but her love is reciprocated and the two head off hunting together. Shakespeare, however, turns the story around: his Adonis is a moody but surprisingly frigid teen whose astonishing beauty is matched only by his conspicuous lack of interest in Venus's advances. Fertility goddess she may be – and lusted after by gods and mortals alike – but this poem presents her as a woman whose unembarrassed sexuality is something to run away from rather than succumb to. Attempting to seduce the youth as she reclines fetchingly on a bank of primroses, Venus tries to convince Adonis that "by law of nature thou art bound to breed," (171), and that, really, love is just a matter of doing as the plants do. "Things growing to themselves are growth's abuse," she urges,

> Seeds spring from seeds, and beauty breedeth beauty:
> Thou wast begot; to get it is thy duty.

**[166–8]**

## So bold with his name

By the late 1590s, Shakespeare had made his reputation as a published writer. His narrative poems *Venus and Adonis* and *Lucrece* were selling well, and 1598 saw the publication of editions of *Richard II* and *Love's Labour's Lost* with their author's name printed boldly on the title page. That same year a self-appointed critic named **Francis Meres** published a survey of Shakespeare's work that acclaimed him as one of the brightest stars of the London stage. Meres also noted that Shakespeare was a published poet, before adding enticingly that he was also the author of certain "sugared sonnets", which had never reached print and had only been seen by his "private friends".

Though Shakespeare must have been glad of the attention – yet another edition of *Venus and Adonis* followed soon afterwards – Meres's advert threw up unforeseen problems. Before 1599 was out, a publisher named **William Jaggard** had put out a collection of poems entitled ***The Passionate Pilgrim*** supposedly by "W. Shakespeare". Eager to cash in on that one name, Jaggard declined to mention that most of the works in *The Passionate Pilgrim* were by other people, Shakespeare's contribution being limited to early versions of Sonnets 138 and 144 and some reheated excerpts from *Love's Labour's Lost*. Alongside work by Marlowe and Ralegh, the rest of the book was padded out with vaguely Shakespearian verse by other writers.

It's highly unlikely that Shakespeare sanctioned *The Passionate Pilgrim*, and hints of his feelings on the matter are communicated by colleague **Thomas Heywood**, who complained heatedly after the book was reprinted in 1612 that Shakespeare was "much offended with M. Jaggard" for presuming "to make so bold with his name" (nor was Heywood impressed that "lines" of his own had been included). Perhaps unwilling to make more enemies, Jaggard backed down soon afterwards: a second version of the title-page for the 1612 edition drops Shakespeare's name entirely. Perhaps forgiven, a decade later Jaggard was given the commission to print the First Folio.

Conspicuously more Shakespearian than *The Passionate Pilgrim* is the lyric poem "**The Phoenix and the Turtle**", published under his name in 1601 alongside poems by "the best and chiefest of our modern writers", including Ben Jonson, George Chapman and John Marston. All these poems take up the theme of a rambling work by a painfully obscure writer named Robert Chester, entitled *Love's Martyr*, which describes the tale of the legendary phoenix bird and her love for a turtle dove. Shakespeare's response concentrates on the final moments of the story, the lovers' decision to commit suicide by immolating themselves in flames, although his work is sufficiently mysterious in tone that many have suspected that the poem is an allegory for something else, as yet unknown.

Nor does "The Phoenix and the Turtle" bring an end to the speculation over Shakespeare's poetic career. Later in the seventeenth century many people ascribed poems to him, the most famous of which is probably a short work beginning "**Shall I die?**", copied down in two poetic miscellanies from the 1630s and included (to much horror and disbelief) in the 1986 Oxford *Complete Works*. Another poem, the "Funeral Elegy" (see p.484), has generated even more friction among critics, but wasn't connected with Shakespeare until 1989. The hunger for Shakespeare's name, it seems, has only intensified in the four centuries after his death.

Anticipating many of the arguments put forward in the first sequence of the Sonnets (which urge the young man to whom they are addressed "to breed another thee", as Sonnet 6 has it), Venus tries to do what the forest later does to her – caress her lover and make him stay. "I'll be a park," she eagerly cries, "and thou shalt be my deer" (231).

> *If our poet had any moral design in view, he has been unfortunate in his conduct of it. The shield which he lifts in defence of chastity is wrought with such meretricious imagery, as cannot fail to counterpose a moral purpose.*
>
> George Steevens, note from *The Plays and Poems of William Shakespeare*, ed. Edmund Malone (1821)

Venus's somewhat frantic efforts to transform herself into a deer park – thereby making herself more attractive to a young man only too eager to get away and hunt with his friends – mine the rich seam of comedy that runs through *Venus and Adonis*. One of the multiple jokes played out by the poem is that Venus, goddess and irresistible embodiment of female love, finds herself stuck in a position conventionally assigned to men, that of the devoted but frustrated suitor held in thrall by his disdainful mistress. That dynamic (lovelorn man, cruel woman) animates much of the Italian courtly verse known in translation and adaptation by Shakespeare and his contemporaries, but here it is Adonis who refuses to become entangled in love, which is (as he nervously notes) reputed to be "a life in death" (413).

Nor is that the only inversion set up by *Venus and Adonis*. As in *A Lover's Complaint*, the poem smudges the boundaries separating man and woman in its loving description of the "sweet" Adonis, so boyish that he's all but girlish, with his "maiden" cheeks, "soft bosom" and "coral mouth" (50, 81, 542). Adonis's plight – and it is touchingly rendered – is that he's unable to be interested, and obviously somewhat puzzled by what Venus so eagerly proposes. With a virginal quiver he begs, "'Fair queen,'"

> 'if any love you owe me,
> Measure my strangeness with my unripe years.
> Before I know myself, seek not to know me.'
>
> [523–5]

It's not that he is knowingly disdainful or coy, Adonis pleads, simply that it isn't yet time. This poem is all about different kinds of "love", but the platonic variety the youth prefers just doesn't provide the sexual pleasure Venus so keenly desires – and it is left to readers to imagine how they would respond if they found themselves, quite literally, in his position. For if Adonis, "frosty in desire" (36), most often seems divinely unattainable, the same cannot be said for Venus, who is painted by Shakespeare in vivid and realistic colours. Though a woman, she takes charge of the situation like a "bold-faced suitor" (4); though a goddess, she is depicted in delightfully observant human detail. Early in the morning she is strong enough to pluck Adonis from his horse and fold him under her arm, and when midday arrives, it is she, not he, who begins to "sweat" in the heat (175). When Venus swoons a little later on, unable to cope with Adonis's harsh words, she simply flops onto the ground while he attempts some limp-wristed first aid. And when she is revived by his penitent kisses, she is eager not to let him go – and pulls him down onto her. "Now quick desire hath caught the yielding prey," the narrator greedily notes,

> And glutton-like she feeds, yet never filleth.
> Her lips are conquerors, his lips obey,

Paying what ransom the insulter willeth,
  Whose vulture thought doth pitch the price so high
  That she will draw his lips' rich treasure dry …

[547–52]

Not for the first time, Venus's attempts at seduction are described in frankly predatory terms: a few stanzas later, she has pulled Adonis on top of her, apparently in alarm at his plan to go boar-hunting. Yet she is also wonderfully chimerical: forceful one moment, weak-kneed the next; tender and gentle yet gifted with an iron grip; a touch voluptuous, yet airy enough to lie on "forceless flowers" and be drawn through the clouds by "strengthless doves" (152–3). It's difficult to think that when he came to write the part of the Egyptian queen in *Antony and Cleopatra* (herself associated with Venus by Antony's companion Enobarbus) Shakespeare didn't think back fifteen years earlier to his portrait of a goddess every bit as changeable.

## Variable passions

Mutability is a key component of *Venus and Adonis*, as in all Shakespeare's works influenced by Ovid, and Adonis's stubborn refusal to submit himself to the changes wrought by love commits him – as Shakespeare's readers would have known from the outset – to a grisly end. The poem races through time (it is dawn at the opening, midday soon afterwards, dusk when Venus faints and "dark night" by the time she warns her lover about hunting the boar), yet also makes it strangely elastic, pausing to digress or dwell upon a picturesque detail but always heading relentlessly towards its conclusion. The poem's comic high-point – the moment when Adonis ends up on top of Venus, but "will not manage her", as the narrator cheekily puts it (598) – foreshadows its mournful finale, in which Adonis is gored by the boar he himself has set out to hunt.

Although she does not see the connection between her attempts to pursue Adonis and the boar's own actions, Venus does sense that something terrible lies just around the forest corner. It shows Shakespeare's sensitivity to his material, though, that he resists making her plight seem ridiculous. As night falls, the poem too makes a decisive shift into a darker mood as Venus is left alone for the first time. Gazing forlornly after Adonis, the narrator movingly describes her "eye",

Which after him she darts, as one on shore
Gazing upon a late-embarkèd friend
Till the wild waves will have him seen no more,
Whose ridges with the meeting clouds contend.
  So did the merciless and pitchy night
  Fold in the object that did feed her sight.

[817–22]

As time and experience move on, so too does the forest. Instead of forming a fertile counter-point to her attempts to ensnare Adonis – as the woodland hums with life, it is almost as if it urges them both on – the "mistrustful wood" (826) now begins to compound Venus's misery, swallowing her lover, then making everything else disappear from sight. Like the "concave womb" of the hills at the outset of *A Lover's Complaint*, which echo the sound of the wailing female lover, in *Venus and Adonis* too the "neighbour caves" pick up the heroine's laments and amplify their grief:

'Ay me,' she cries, and twenty times 'Woe, woe!'
And twenty echoes twenty times cry so.

[833–4]

"With this, he breaketh from the sweet embrace, / Of those fair arms which bound him to her breast." An engraving (c.1560) by Giorgio Ghisi after a painting by his brother Teodoro.

As night shifts to dawn (again the change is accomplished speedily), that sound will soon be joined by the hunting dogs, whose "dismal cry", also resounding through the forest, seems to insist that something has gone tragically wrong. When Venus stumbles across the boar, whose "frothy mouth" is grotesquely "bepainted all with red" (901), she is right to fear the worst.

Shakespeare builds the poem's tension by refusing to clarify precisely what has gone wrong for another twenty-odd stanzas. The moment of Adonis's death remains unclear, and the heroine is plunged into terrible uncertainty, at one moment positive that he is gone (and cursing Death as a "hard-favoured tyrant"), at another confident that he has survived (at which point she asks Death for pardon). Change is yet again near the surface of the poem. "Variable passions throng her constant woe," the narrator remarks, not unkindly, "As striving who should best become her grief" (967–8). Even so, the instant of discovery still shocks – and Shakespeare startles his readers by focusing not on what Venus discovers lying on the forest floor, but her initial inability to contemplate the horror of the scene. As she faints with shock, her eyelids clamp shut as if flinching from the sight:

> her eyes, as murdered with the view,
> Like stars ashamed of day, themselves withdrew.
>
> Or as the snail, whose tender horns being hit
> Shrinks backward in his shelly cave with pain,
> And there, all smothered up in shade doth sit,
> Long after fearing to creep forth again;
>     So at his bloody view her eyes are fled
>     Into the deep dark cabins of her head …
>
> [1031–8]

What Venus cannot face is also withheld from us – Keats was so impressed by the effect that he copied it out in a letter to a friend. It is some lines before the narrator can bring himself to describe the gory sight of Adonis lying blood-stained on the ground with a "wide wound" underneath his ribs. As Venus faints for the second time in the poem, it is as if time has repeated itself, this time tragically: when she comes round it is to find her lover not alive in her arms but sprawled graphically on the forest floor.

But this is not quite an end: the poem's final and most amazing transformation is still to come. Returning to his Ovidian source, Shakespeare moves away from the earthy detail that characterized *Venus and Adonis*'s opening phase and shifts into the supernatural. As Venus stands by, bitterly complaining her loss, something quite astonishing occurs:

> By this, the boy that by her side lay killed
> Was melted like a vapour from her sight,
> And in his blood that on the ground lay spilled
> A purple flower sprung up, chequered with white,
>     Resembling well his pale cheeks, and the blood
>     Which in round drops upon their whiteness stood.
>
> [1165–70]

Shakespeare's contemporaries would have known that the flower associated with Adonis was the anemone, ravishingly described by the great English herbalist, John Parkinson, as "so full of variety and so dainty, so pleasant and so delightsome … that the sight of them doth enforce an earnest longing desire in the mind of anyone to be a possessor of some." But, intriguingly, Shakespeare engineers his own transformation here: the purple-and-white "chequered" species he describes is not an anemone at all but a Snake's Head Fritillary, a plant that flowers in early summer – around the same time that *Venus and Adonis* initially appeared. And if the poem's first readers paused to admire this beautiful and fragile plant, perhaps they, too, would have been tempted to imitate Venus in the last few lines of the poem. Plucking the flower from the blood-soaked ground, the unhappy heroine cradles it to her bosom, finally achieving the captive intimacy with Adonis that has eluded her all along:

> 'Here was thy father's bed, here in my breast.
> Thou art the next of blood, and 'tis thy right.
> Lo, in this hollow cradle take thy rest;
> My throbbing heart shall rock thee day and night.
>     There shall not be one minute in an hour
>     Wherein I will not kiss my sweet love's flower.'

**[1183–8]**

# Editions
## Oxford Shakespeare
**Colin Burrow (ed.); 2002** ▷ Oxford UP

During its author's lifetime *Venus and Adonis* was his most printed work, so it's good to be reminded – as Colin Burrow frequently states – that Shakespeare's efforts as a poet are integral to a complete understanding of his career. Comprehensiveness is very much the point of this Oxford edition of the *Complete Sonnets and Poems*, which brings together all the poetic work Shakespeare is known to have penned and some he almost certainly didn't – it also includes some hopeful seventeenth-century attributions. *Venus* is sensitively treated, Burrow's introduction capturing very nicely its rhetorical and intellectual innovation without losing sight of its fun.

# Some criticism
## Elizabethan Erotic Narratives
**William Keach; 1977** ▷ Harvester / Rutgers [o/p]

Part of the problem when studying *Venus and Adonis* and poems influenced by it (a kind of Jacobethan mini-genre) is what on earth to call them – hence the slightly catch-all title of this book, one of the first to consider them in relation to each other. Keach races neatly through poems such as Marlowe's *Hero and Leander*, Thomas Lodge's *Glaucus and Scilla*, Marston's *Metamorphosis of Pigmalion's Image* and others. He keeps in view the teasing ambiguities favoured by works like these, a kind of generic playfulness that goes back to Ovid – the poet in whose shadow they were written – but which also (as Keach says) has more serious things to say about "the turbulence and contradiction in erotic experience". Lest all that sound too serious, Keach's style is bright and interesting, and the book is attractively readable.

# Contexts

# Shakespeare's life

t's often said that all the facts we know about Shakespeare's biography fit onto a postcard (or, if you're feeling especially gloomy, a postage stamp). Not true. In fact, from contemporary records we have access to more information about Shakespeare than any of his playwright colleagues – except perhaps Ben Jonson, a man who did far more to preserve his own reputation for posterity. The problem for Shakespeare is that, for all the extensive documentary evidence, little gives us access to the man himself. There is plenty on his extensive land holdings, property investments and involvement with the law; but almost nothing suggesting what kind of person he really was – no manuscripts, none of his books, no diaries. Most of the portraits we possess are of questionable authority; even his few surviving signatures don't all match up. Jonson's famous declaration that Shakespeare was "not of an age, but for all time" actually points up something rather discomfiting – that in writing about his life it can be difficult to pin him down.

## A Midlands childhood [1564–70]

The story of William Shakespeare's life has its beginning and end in one place: the bustling market town of **Stratford-upon-Avon**, in an area where the surname is still relatively commonplace. Nowadays Stratford is in the shadow of nearby **Birmingham**, the industrialized capital of the West Midlands and Britain's second largest city, its sprawling suburban outskirts just twenty or so miles distant. Yet some two centuries before the Industrial Revolution, sixteenth-century Birmingham had a population of 1500 – merely "a good market town", as one contemporary historian described it. The most significant regional focus was **Warwick**, dominated by the medieval castle (seat of the Earls of Warwick, several of whom feature in Shakespeare's history plays), a trading centre for the area and the shire town that gives its name to the county. Stratford itself, eight miles to Warwick's southwest, began as a crossing point over the River Avon and became a planned settlement around 1200. By the mid-sixteenth century it was registered as a market town and became a thriving place to do business (it had three "very large streets" to Birmingham's pair), particularly for travellers on their way to the cathedral communities of **Coventry** and **Worcester** in the same area.

William Shakespeare was born directly into this mercantile Midlands environment. His father **John** (c.1530–1601) was most likely the son of a local farmer – John's brother **Henry**, the playwright's uncle, was one as well – but like many of his generation moved from the countryside into town, in John's case to train as a glover, wool-dealer and whittawer (skilled tanner of leather). William, too, might have taken up the family trade for a few years, and indeed memories of it intermittently appear in his written work. For his own part John seems not to have been able to write – a pair of compasses, a symbol of his trade, is one of the marks he used in place of a signature – and the same is apparently true for his wife **Mary** (born Mary Arden; only her death date, 1608, is known), who likewise used a cross to sign her name. Lack of writing skill might not mean illiteracy, however – many people in this period could read but not handle a pen – and in any case this limitation proved no barrier for the playwright's prosperous father. In 1558 John Shakespeare was sworn in as a town constable and rapidly ascended the corporate ladder, being made a burgess six years later and an alderman in 1567. The position of **chief alderman** (in effect mayor) followed a few years later.

By this time John and Mary had six of their eight children. The Shakespeares were typical in having a large family, and given that their first two daughters, **Joan** (b. 1558) and **Margaret** (b. 1562), both died in infancy, it is easy to comprehend why. **William** was their first son, followed by **Gilbert** (1566–1612), another **Joan** (1569–1646), **Anne** (1571–79), **Richard** (1574–1613) and **Edmund** (1580–1607). All except Anne made it into adulthood, but only Joan outlived her eldest brother – and then it was by thirty years.

All we know concerning William's arrival is that he was christened at Holy Trinity Church, Stratford, on April 26, 1564. Patriotic tradition holds that he was born three days earlier, on St George's Day (also the date on which he died), but it might as easily have been the 21st or 22nd. The Shakespeares were then living in a large house in **Henley Street** – we know because John was fined in 1552 for having an illegal rubbish-tip outside – and as a consequence the building is now known, reverentially, as the **"Birthplace"**. It's probable that John plied his trade at the same address, perhaps with his workshop downstairs, but soon after William's birth both work and family will have been overtaken by wider events. During the summer of 1564 **bubonic plague** hit Stratford, killing around two hundred people, perhaps a sixth of the town's population. As a member of the council, John was closely involved in dealing with the crisis, and is recorded as attending a meeting – held out of doors to avoid contagion – to arrange emergency financial assistance for those made destitute by the deadly outbreak.

## At school [1571–81]

It is not an overstatement to say that his father's position and influence in Stratford made Shakespeare's subsequent career possible. Though the records have since perished, it is almost certain that William attended the town's **King's New School**, a foundation dating from the fifteenth century, and as the son of an alderman he would have been guaranteed a place. Boys usually began there at the age of 6 or 7, having attended a "petty school" for two or three years where they were taught how to read, write and count (only a handful of schools accepted girls in the sixteenth century, and then just for the junior years; private tuition was the only other option). Though with some forty pupils Stratford grammar school was small, it was run by a university-educated master – Oxford graduates **Thomas Jenkins** and **John Cottom** are likely to have taught Shakespeare – who had an assistant to help with the younger boys.

The curriculum at Stratford Grammar will have been both difficult and impressive. Ben Jonson's waspish jibe that his colleague possessed "small Latin and less Greek" came from a man who was fiercely proud of his learning, and in fact the 15-year-old Shakespeare will have known as much Latin as a classics graduate today (see box opposite). As with any child growing up in the Elizabethan era, **Protestant Christianity** will have also played a significant part in Shakespeare's boyhood: he will have attended church twice every Sunday for morning and evening services – attendance was compulsory by law – and taken Holy Communion several times a year. Shakespeare's formal education will have also covered religious matters (he will have learnt the catechism in Latin as well as English, and spent time translating the Geneva Bible into Latin), each school day opening and closing with formal devotions. Despite the possibility that John Shakespeare had sympathies with the old Catholic faith (see p.454), it is all but certain that his son's education will have been in orthodox Elizabethan Protestantism.

## Unwillingly to school

The image evoked by *As You Like It*'s Jaques of "the whining schoolboy with his satchel / And shining morning face, creeping like snail / Unwillingly to school" (2.7.145–7), has become a cliché almost as weary as Jaques himself, but it presents an experience common to many Elizabethans. Though the records have since perished, it's overwhelmingly likely that Shakespeare attended the **King's New School** at Stratford, and if he didn't "creep", others certainly did. Lessons typically began at 6 or 7am six days a week, there was three hours' work before breakfast arrived, and the afternoons were long – most schools finished at 6pm, though pupils did get two hours for lunch, the main meal of the day.

Yet Shakespeare was incalculably lucky to benefit – however unwillingly – from a recent explosion of interest in the design of children's learning. Humanist thinkers such as Erasmus and Colet argued that school, not university, should be the top priority for educationalists, and Elizabethan treatises such as **William Kempe**'s *Education of Children in Learning* (1588) painstakingly laid out the curriculum. Between the ages of around 5 and 7 a child should attend a **petty school** for the rudiments of pro-nunciation and writing, practising with a "hornbook" that presented the alphabet, numbers and the Lord's Prayer. Then he – girls would usually stop here, unless they were lucky enough to have private tuition – would progress to one of the new **grammar schools** (nearly 150 were founded in Britain dur-ing the sixteenth century) to acquire the basics of Latin, frequently administered through the standard textbook, **William Lily** and **John Colet**'s *Grammar* (1567), which argued that Latin grammar was the "foundation and ground work" of all thought. Once this was mastered, pupils developed skill in read-ing and translating, and in the upper forms used some of the great Roman authors – Cicero and Quintilian were favoured, as were the poets Virgil and Ovid (see p.240) – to present arguments and test ideas. The practice of *imitatio* (creative imitation), was crucial: students often used books con-taining extravagant lists of *sententiae* (memorable phrases) for them to learn and regurgitate. The value of speaking – performing – was hard-wired into the humanist curriculum, and the use of play-texts such as those by Plautus and Terence would have given the young Shakespeare an early taste for the theatre.

Nevertheless, for all its benefits, what this added up to was up to ten years of extremely hard work, much of it based on learning by rote: an experience Shakespeare will hardly have recalled with unmixed pleasure. An entire scene in *The Merry Wives of Windsor* is devoted to the struggles of a small boy – knowingly named William – to master basic Latin, while *Henry VI Part II* sees Jack Cade, leader of a Kentish rebellion, threaten to execute Lord Saye, one of the King's aristocratic supporters, because he has "most traitorously corrupted the youth of the realm in erecting a grammar school" (4.7.30–1).

---

Aside from the teasing (and usually ironic) references to education in Shakespeare's plays, we don't know a great deal more about this period of his life. But in his last years at school his family circumstances were to change dramatically. During the mid-1570s the Midlands entered a prolonged **economic recession** that blighted Stratford especially hard: some records indicate that by the end of the century half of the town's population was living in poverty. John Shakespeare was not remotely close to being among them, but evidence of his debt and decline nevertheless accumulates in the records: he stopped attending council meetings in 1576, sold off part of his considerable land holdings in 1578 and began to owe money to a variety of creditors. An expensive and socially ambitious scheme to acquire a coat of arms, which John had begun a few years earlier, was likewise dropped, and in 1586 his colleagues at the council voted to replace him as alderman.

One source suggests that as a result of his father's financial difficulties William was taken away from school, but by then he would anyway have been close to the leaving age. Unlike Christopher Marlowe (who came from a background humbler than Shakespeare's but won a scholarship to Cambridge), William never attended either of the **universities**. John

Shakespeare's lack of funds might have stymied any ambitions his son had in that respect, but there is no reason to suppose that he wanted to attend. In the sixteenth century both Oxford and Cambridge were essentially prestigious theological colleges intended for well-connected young men, which also offered training in specialisms such as medicine and the law. University education might well have seemed a costly irrelevance; Ben Jonson, notably, did not experience it either.

## Wife and children [1582–85]

And there were soon to be other ties holding Shakespeare to Stratford. The strongest is also the most striking: his marriage in November 1582 to **Anne Hathaway**. Shakespeare was just 18; Anne was 26 at the time of her wedding, and she was pregnant. The ceremony was rushed through: the couple were forced to apply for a special licence because the date fell during the church season of Advent, when marriages were normally not performed, and had to travel to the bishop's court at Worcester in order to do so. The ceremony itself took place in late November, but we have no record as to where – one tempting suggestion is at the village of **Temple Grafton**, where the priest had a lax reputation, but the neighbouring **Luddington** and **Bishopton** could equally have played host. There is another puzzle, too: in the records at Worcester Anne's surname is given as "Whateley", not Hathaway, and the pregnant bride is described as a "maiden" (virgin). Though this divergence has encouraged some to guess that the young Shakespeare had somehow got himself betrothed to two women simultaneously, the prosaic likelihood is that the clerks simply made one of several slips – another Whateley had appeared in court that day – and were not too curious about her condition. Infinitely more certain is that the following May Anne gave birth to their first child, **Susanna**, who was christened in Holy Trinity, Stratford.

Anne is one of the most mysterious characters in Shakespeare's life story. The facts don't take us far: Anne was apparently the eldest daughter of a farmer – perhaps one of John Shakespeare's business contacts – from nearby Shottery, and from backdating her tombstone it is possible to work out that she was born in 1555 or thereabouts, making her seven or eight years older than her new husband. The sizeable farmhouse in which she grew up, now famously going by the name of **Anne Hathaway's Cottage**, stands around a mile away from the centre of Stratford and has since been swallowed by the growth of the town, but William would have passed through fields on the way to visit.

There are no records as to what Anne looked like – a pen-and-ink portrait, added in 1708 to a seventeenth-century edition of the *Works*, is highly unlikely to be authentic – and the nature of her relationship with William has remained similarly shadowy. Some biographers have guessed that the marriage, which began in straitened circumstances, was unhappy, but the truth is what little evidence we have points the other way – one of Shakespeare's Sonnets, number 145, plays tenderly with Anne's surname and might recall their courtship (see p.430). In marked contrast to William's parents, the couple had just two other children, the twins **Hamnet** and **Judith**, christened in February 1585, and when Hamnet died at the age of 11 just the daughters were left. At any rate the couple, who might well have moved in together with William's family in Henley Street, were not in the same place for long. Within seven years Shakespeare was in London, and making his name as a dramatist.

## Years lost [1585–92]

We don't know how Shakespeare landed himself a job writing for the London theatre, and indeed the period between the twins' christening (1585) and the first surviving reference to his work as a playwright (1592) – the biggest surviving blank in the documentary record of

Despite being known to visitors worldwide as a "cottage", the Shottery farmhouse in which Anne Hathaway grew up is a substantial structure, testament to her father's prosperity. Shakespeare would have crossed open fields to reach it; now pilgrims simply head up Shottery Road.

his adult life – is conventionally known as **"the lost years"**, although a 1589 court case mentioning him has since surfaced. In the absence of solid evidence, hearsay and tradition have supplied several options for Shakespeare's movements during this time. On the livelier end of the scale is the yarn that Shakespeare was punished for poaching the deer of **Sir Thomas Lucy**, master of nearby Charlecote (the playwright is meant to have got his own back by satirizing him in *The Merry Wives of Windsor*), but this story inconveniently fails to deal with the fact that Lucy didn't keep deer until 1618, two years after the supposed poacher's death. More workmanlike is the suggestion that Shakespeare was employed as a **lawyer's clerk** in Stratford or elsewhere, but again it is unlikely that no written evidence would have survived. Another option is even simpler: that he worked with his father in the **gloving trade** for a few years – by marrying he had excluded himself from an official apprenticeship – and thereby supported his young family.

Altogether more mysterious is a theory first mooted by seventeenth-century biographer John Aubrey, which is that Shakespeare left Stratford in order to work as a "schoolmaster in the country" (perhaps soon after leaving school himself). Investigation has uncovered mention of one "William Shakeshafte" among the household of **Alexander Hoghton** of Lea Hall near Preston in Lancashire, around a hundred miles from Stratford. If Shakeshafte is our Shakespeare he will have been there several years beforehand, in 1581 – just a year before he married Stratford-based Anne Hathaway and presumably less time still before he got her pregnant. Yet the connection remains intriguing, not least because the Hoghtons were **underground Catholics**, known as "recusants". According to a religious confession discovered by eighteenth-century workmen in the roof of the Henley Street house (but since lost), so was John Shakespeare, and it's not unlikely that the teenage William could have gained work in the Hoghton household through Catholic connections, perhaps involving his teacher at the King's New School, the Lancastrian John Cottom. Even more enticing is the possibility that William first gained experience of the theatre in Lancashire: the Hoghtons maintained players (the same will that mentions Shakeshaft describes musical instruments and "play-clothes"), and after Alexander's death his half-brother **Sir Thomas Hesketh** might have kept on the company – and was himself connected to **Ferdinando, Lord Strange**, patron of the London-based Strange's Men. If Shakespeare and his near-namesake are one and the same, this could have been a convenient route into a full-time theatrical career.

## To London [late 1580s]

One advantage of the Lancashire theory – though it has numerous flaws – is that it offers to solve the central conundrum of the "lost years": how Shakespeare came to be working in London. His interest in the theatre might well have been kindled back at home, however, for the Midlands were hardly deprived of theatrical spectacles (see p.468). Among the travelling troupes that visited Stratford during 1586–87 were the **Queen's Men**, a state-sponsored company led by the comedian **Richard Tarlton** but specializing in nationalistic English history plays. Before it reached Stratford one of the troupe's leading actors was killed by a fellow player in a brawl, and some have speculated that the 23-year-old Shakespeare was recruited to fill the gap – a seductive possibility, but unfortunately unprovable (and otherwise unheard of).

However he reached it, though, **London** was Shakespeare's eventual destination. Effortlessly the most important city in the realm, standing comparison with any in Europe, the capital had some 50,000 inhabitants by 1500 and four times that number just a century later. A bustling cosmopolitan metropolis, it became England's pre-eminent port through its position on the Thames and eventually stood at the hub of trade networks spanning the globe. Having left its medieval city boundaries far behind, the town migrated restlessly westwards during the sixteenth and seventeenth centuries, eroding the traditional distinction between the court based at Westminster and the City to its east, though the City still remained London's financial and religious heart, dominated by the towering Gothic cathedral of St Paul's, the brand-new Royal Exchange and the great markets of Newgate, Cheap, Leadenhall and the Stocks. It astounded and appalled visitors and residents alike – who repeatedly commented on its ever-increasing size, its fine houses, its slums, its bountiful opportunities, its squalid poverty.

London was also a young city (sky-high mortality rates and a constant influx of population from the countryside guaranteed that), and one that took its entertainment seriously. The first purpose-built, professional theatres had been erected north of the Thames in Shoreditch, but **Southwark**, across the river and outside restrictive City jurisdiction in the so-called "liberties" (see p.470), became the centre of London's burgeoning entertainment industry during the 1580s. It was around this time, presumably towards the decade's end, that Shakespeare first appeared in town. One tradition holds that he first got a job holding playgoers' horses before migrating inside the theatre, perhaps to the position of **prompter's assistant**. But all that we can be sure of is that by 1592 he was not merely acting, but writing.

## Young upstart [early 1590s]

We know this because someone tells us. It's somewhat ironic that the first recorded mention of Shakespeare as a playwright accuses him of plagiarism, but a vituperative attack published in the name of **Robert Greene**, referring knowingly to "an upstart crow" who "is in his own conceit the only Shake-scene in a country", parodies lines from *Henry VI Part III* to suggest that the non-university-educated writer was stealing tricks from his theatrical rivals. Greene died soon afterwards, but his colleague **Henry Chettle** (who transcribed and published the attack, and may even have authored it) soon published a retraction – indicating perhaps that Shakespeare, already well-known enough to be worth savaging in print, was also worth apologizing to.

If by that time *Henry VI Part III* had appeared – and done well enough to discomfit Greene and his fellow dramatists **Thomas Nashe** and **Christopher Marlowe**, two of the so-called "university wits" – the rest of the *Henry VI* cycle may have already been written, or at least sketched out. This three-part historical extravaganza was a bold feat for a young dramatist (Shakespeare was just 28 in 1592), and outpaced anything that the Elizabethan stage had yet seen. Shakespeare had already tried his hand at comedy in the mode of **John Lyly**, another university wit, with *The Two Gentlemen of Verona* (c.1598–90); and *Titus Andronicus*, his first attempt at high-style Roman tragedy, followed in around 1594. The exact chronology of his first professional plays is difficult to untangle, rarely more so than with *The Taming of the Shrew*: a stripped-down version of the script reached print in 1594, but was either a source for Shakespeare's comedy or an adaptation of it. *The Comedy of Errors*, an academic comedy to balance the learned tragedy of *Titus*, is also early, perhaps as early as 1591.

During the first few years of his professional writing life there is no evidence as to Shakespeare's involvement with theatrical companies, and he may well have worked, like many of his colleagues, as a freelancer. His earliest surviving collaborative work, additions to a play entitled *Sir Thomas More* mainly written by **Anthony Munday** and **Henry Chettle** (see p.140), probably dates from this period, while his own plays were acted by a variety of different companies. *Titus* was performed by **Sussex's Men**, *The Comedy of Errors* and *Henry VI Part III* by **Pembroke's Men**; and his work appeared at different venues – the Inns of Court for *Errors*, the Bankside Rose playhouse for *Titus*, and perhaps elsewhere for both. If Shakespeare hadn't joined

## Who wrote Shakespeare?

A seemingly perverse question, but one that has been asked time and again. Unable – or unwilling – to square the facts of Shakespeare's life with the soaring genius of his art, some have dared to think the unthinkable: is William Shakespeare even the right man?

As Shakespearian traditions go, the notion that he isn't is relatively modern. A stout book by the American writer **Delia Bacon** entitled *The Philosophy of the Plays of Shakespeare Unfolded* (1857) was the first to broach for a wide readership what others had been gossiping about for a decade or so: the theory that William from Stratford (a "stupid, ignorant, third-rate play-actor") was not the author of the works usually attributed to him. So-called **"anti-Stratfordian"** arguments multiplied as the nineteenth century wore on, fed by Victorian suspicions about the vulgarity of the popular stage and disbelief that a mere middle-class actor could have been the greatest poet England had ever produced. Unhindered by conventional scholarship – or the fact that many of Shakespeare's colleagues and successors testified to his identity – speculation about conspiracy theories and cover-ups had snowballed by the century's end, reaching their apogee in a fad for "cryptographic" analyses, each purporting to show by numerological keys buried in Shakespeare's works that he was not responsible. While **Henry James** was merely unsettled by these theories (remarking in 1903 that "I am … haunted by the conviction that the divine William is the biggest and most successful fraud ever practised on a patient world"), **Mark Twain** remains the movement's most famous literary convert. A century later, debates about authorship and conspiracy still have not died down; a conference on the subject was even staged at the London Globe during summer 2003.

So if not Stratford Will, whom? Before losing her sanity and being confined to an asylum, Delia eventually settled on her namesake **Francis Bacon** as her chosen candidate, this connection later strengthened by apparent resemblances between Bacon's works and the plays of "Shakespeare". Others prefer the claims of **Christopher Marlowe** or **Edward de Vere**, the Earl of Oxford, but the earliest proponent for the latter, the resplendently named **Thomas J. Looney**, failed to overcome the inconvenient fact that Oxford died in 1604, six years before *The Tempest* – the easiest late play to date – was written. Still others argue that a shadowy consortium was behind the plays, and an extreme sect have even argued that **Elizabeth I** somehow found time to pen them.

Whoever the playwright may have collaborated with over his long career, no serious authorities believe that Shakespeare was, well, anyone else (evidence enough for a conspiracy, say some). Arguments otherwise are distinguished mainly by their disregard for plain evidence, their intellectual naivety and their rank snobbery. Shakespeare didn't attend university, but neither did he need to: his grammar-school education gave him an enviable advantage (see p.451). Nor did he need to be a lawyer like Bacon or a noble like Oxford to work out how to reproduce a court on stage, any more than he needed to be black or a woman to find words for an Othello or a Rosalind. As the critic David Bevington observes, the amazing thing is not that a middle-class man from Warwickshire wrote Shakespeare's works – it's that anyone could have written them at all.

These and other arguments are eloquently put by Jonathan Bate in *The Genius of Shakespeare* (1997), which argues convincingly that conspiracy theories about Shakespeare's identity are closely related to his promotion to Romantic "genius". And if you're interested in finding out more, check out our list of websites (p.504) devoted to the subject.

the Queen's Men while they were on tour in 1586–87, he may well have been involved with them later on, given that a number of his plays – notably *Henry V*, *King John* and *King Lear* – draw upon scripts first performed by that company. In any case during the first years of the 1590s London theatres and companies were in a state of confusion and flux, not least because after the devastating appearance of **plague** in summer 1592 the Puritan city fathers seized the opportunity to close the theatres down, regarding them (inaccurately) as breeding grounds for pestilence as well as (more accurately) all manner of unwholesomeness. In the end they were closed for almost two years.

## Poems and patrons [1593–94]

Shakespeare's response, just a few years after beginning to write for the professional stage, was to seek other employment. Despite a legend that he took the opportunity to holiday in **Italy**, it's almost certain that the playwright spent this period transforming himself into a poet. *Venus and Adonis*, the first of his narrative poems, was published in 1593 by his fellow Stratfordian (perhaps schoolfriend) **Richard Field** and dedicated to **Henry Wriothesley**, the influential and cultured Earl of Southampton. Wriothesley supported numerous poets as well as being an enthusiastic playgoer, and so made an attractive target for Shakespeare's attempt to secure patronage. The titillating *Venus and Adonis* flew off the booksellers' shelves and gave Shakespeare's reputation a boost, and it was followed a year later by what he described as a "graver labour", a longer poem on the story of Lucrece, the celebrated Roman wife who commits suicide following her rape by a Roman prince. *The Rape of Lucrece* was again dedicated to Wriothesley, but seemingly did less well in the shops – though it sold respectably.

Yet if Shakespeare had any intentions of making a career as a poet, they seem not to have lasted. In addition to the publication of *Lucrece*, 1594 brought events that would alter the rest of his writing life. After plague had died down that autumn and the theatres reopened, Lord Hunsdon, Elizabeth's Lord Chamberlain, arranged for his theatrical troupe to be reformed as the **Chamberlain's Men**. Listed as among the consortium's members are Shakespeare, the great clown (and successor to Tarlton) **William Kempe** and **Richard Burbage**, who would become the company's star and take the lead in many of Shakespeare's subsequent plays. Also in the group were **George Bryan**, **John Heminges**, **Augustine Philips**, **Thomas Pope** and **William Sly**, all actor-sharers who had a stake in the company and supported it financially; other actors, notably **John Sincler**, were involved on a more informal basis.

The new Chamberlain's Men first played for the impresario and theatre-owner **Philip Henslowe** in June 1594, and then at court during the Christmas festivities, and seems to have been almost immediately successful despite the challenge offered by another company formed at the same time, the **Admiral's Men**. This was led by **Edward Alleyn**, famous for his leading roles in Marlowe's great tragedies *Tamburlaine* (1587), *Doctor Faustus* (c.1588), *The Jew of Malta* (c.1590) and *Edward II* (c.1592). Between them the Lord Chamberlain's and Admiral's Men, based respectively at the Shoreditch **Theatre** and the Bankside **Rose**, were given a near-duopoly over performances in London.

Now that Shakespeare's new company had a permanent home, it could get on with the serious business of theatre. Shakespeare's decision to join will have been a boost, for he seems to have brought his existing works to the group, forming a core repertoire which expanded by two plays a year, on average, for the rest of his working life. This unusually stable arrangement – Shakespeare was his company's "ordinary poet", its playwright-in-residence – ensured a steady source of income for both writer and company.

## Lyrical love [1594–99]

But that lay far in the future. *Richard III*, the sequel to the *Henry VI* trilogy, may have been performed as early as 1592–93, but became wildly successful in London after the plague re-openings, reaching print in a text of 1597. The first years of Shakespeare's involvement with the Chamberlain's Men are often known as the **"lyrical period"**, and represent the first flowering of his mature talent. Four works – *Love's Labour's Lost*, *Romeo and Juliet*, *A Midsummer Night's Dream* and *Richard II* – are usually assigned to this period, and their rich variety – two comedies, a love tragedy and a rhetorically sophisticated history – demonstrates that the playwright was exploring the art of theatre more fully than anyone of his generation. That at least was the view of **Francis Meres**, a schoolmaster and writer born one year after Shakespeare and the poet's first eulogist. Meres's *Palladis Tamadia* (1598) includes a head-by-head comparison of celebrated Latin, Roman and Italian authors with their English equivalents, among which Shakespeare is hailed as the "best" for comedy (with *The Two Gentlemen of Verona, The Comedy of Errors, Love's Labour's Lost, Love's Labour's Won, The Merchant of Venice*) as well as tragedy (*Richard II, Richard III, Henry IV, King John, Titus Andronicus* and *Romeo and Juliet*). He also garners praise for being a "mellifluous and honey-tongued" poet, the author of numerous "sugared Sonnets" – possibly the first mention of the works that would be printed as *Shakespeare's Sonnets* eleven years later.

Meres's list, invaluable to theatre historians, includes several plays Shakespeare composed after he had finished the lyrical comedies – *King John* and *The Merchant of Venice* seemed to have followed very rapidly – but also a ghost, the mysterious *Love's Labour's Won*. Satisfactory identification has so far eluded critics, but this may well refer to a lost work, possibly one of several that have failed to survive (see p.186). But the greatest theatrical hit of 1598 was another history play, *Henry IV*, which traced the story of Richard II's deposer Henry Bolingbroke. It was soon followed by a pair of sequels, *Henry IV Part II* and *Henry V*, to form the second of Shakespeare's historical tetralogies (often known, half-seriously, as his "Henriad"). *Henry IV* also provided what may have been the playwright's first brush with censorship: the runaway popularity of its dissolute antihero, Sir John Oldcastle, aroused the ire of the powerful descendants of a Protestant martyr of the same name, and Shakespeare was forced to rechristen him "Falstaff" and insert a public retraction (see p.82). Falstaff's fame was such that he seems to have spawned a suburban comedy, *The Merry Wives of Windsor*, though sections of this play were possibly performed for **Elizabeth I** as early as April 1597 (one story holds that they were commanded by her). *Henry V*'s connection with Elizabeth makes it far easier to date, in fact the easiest of all Shakespeare's plays – its description of "the General of our Gracious Empress", referring to the Earl of Essex, makes it almost certain to have been written while Essex was campaigning in Ireland, from March to September 1599.

## Around the Globe [1599–1602]

In the midst of this great run of triumphant productions, calamity struck the Chamberlain's Men. The lease to the Shoreditch Theatre had been due to expire in 1597, but when James Burbage (who had built the house in the first place), his actor son and colleagues attempted to renew it, **Giles Allen**, the landlord, proved intractable – first insisting on nearly doubling the rent, then pulling out of negotiations the following year. After performing sporadically at the nearby **Curtain**, the players were on the verge of securing a fresh deal when Allen suddenly decided to repossess his land and demolish the Theatre. With the play-hating authorities hardly likely to give them support, the Chamberlain's Men decided on a novel solution – to engage the carpenter **Peter Street** and have him supervise the dismantling of the building and its transportation elsewhere. This was accomplished overnight in December 1598, the timbers being moved to a new site across the river and rebuilt "in a new form" as the largest amphitheatre London had yet seen: the **Globe**. Though all this was legal – the far-sighted James Burbage had insisted on a clause allowing it in the original contract – Allen was furious and three years later was still doing his best to sue (to no avail).

The sizeable cost of doing all this was met by a **syndicate** of various partners, among them original members of the Chamberlain's Men including Shakespeare, but also Richard and his brother Cuthbert Burbage. Shakespeare's portion began as a tenth and fluctuated as new partners entered and old ones left, yet it testifies to his growing wealth and continued financial investment in the company. His artistic investment continued, too, though on Bankside the

As well as being one of Europe's most populous cities, London also became renowned for its entertainment districts during Shakespeare's lifetime. Bankside, depicted in this detail from Visscher's massive panorama (c.1625), tempted punters with bear-baiting, brothels and – of course – theatres.

playwright turned his back on the English histories that had prospered at the Shoreditch Theatre and headed back to Italian comedy and Roman tragedy. *Much Ado About Nothing* perhaps premiered in 1599, and *Julius Caesar* were seen by a Swiss tourist visiting the new Globe that same autumn. No such testimony describes early performances of the comedy *As You Like It*, which probably dates from that year or the next, but one theatrical tradition holds that Shakespeare himself took the role of Old Adam. Noting the small size of the part, some have assumed that the playwright was no great talent as an actor – a story apparently confirmed by his other starring role as the Ghost in *Hamlet*, a part he could well have performed silently with another actor's voice supplied from under the stage. (These stories may be unfair to him: Ben Jonson listed Shakespeare at the top of the list of "principal comedians" in his 1616 *Works*.)

*Hamlet* itself, Shakespeare's most adventurous work to date and for some audiences his finest of all, seems to have been written on the cusp of the new century; one version was onstage by 1600, though the revised play may not have appeared until the following year. It appears to have been a near-instant hit, being performed as far away as the coast of Sierra Leone within a few years (see p.73). The success of *Twelfth Night* (c.1601) might not have been correspondingly international, but it too was performed away from the Globe, in this case at the law inn of Middle Temple in February 1602.

## New places [1602–04]

Even at the apex of his London career, however, Shakespeare did not turn away from his family in Stratford. The years had witnessed changes there, too, notably the funeral of his only son Hamnet in August 1596 – an event that Shakespeare presumably attended, though no records survive. More positively, William's success seems to have had material benefits for the Shakespeare clan. John Shakespeare's application for a **coat of arms** was renewed later that year, probably at his son's behest, and was successful (in that respect at least John must have been content when he died five years later). In May 1597 William took an even larger social and financial step, buying one of Stratford's grandest premises, **New Place**. Though it has long since been demolished, this was a capacious five-gabled house of three storeys with at least ten rooms, reputedly the town's second largest structure. It also had gardens covering three-quarters of an acre with several outbuildings, and legend has it that Shakespeare himself planted a **mulberry tree** there. (The tree survived until 1758, when it was cut down by eager relic-hunters.)

It is not certain how often Shakespeare returned to Stratford to enjoy his new property, but it is usually thought that he made the journey at least once a year. Back in London, unpaid tax records – not uncommon – reveal that he had been living in the upmarket area of **Bishopsgate** (the Shoreditch Theatre was just up the road), but he seems to have relocated to **Southwark** when the Chamberlain's Men moved south of the river in 1599. He moved once again a few years later, this time to the middle-class area of **Cripplegate** in the northwest corner of the city, lodging with the French Huguenot wigmaker **Christopher Mountjoy** and his wife **Mary**. Though undoubtedly wealthy enough to buy a London house, Shakespeare preferred to rent; Stratford, perhaps, was still his home. Subsequent references to property in the sources generally relate to investments – two Stratford land-purchases in 1602, an outlay for Stratford tithes in 1605, the acquisition of a house in Blackfriars in 1614 – and point to the fact that Shakespeare's assets, and his willingness to invest, were steadily growing. He was also careful to hang on to what he accumulated: when a Stratford neighbour, **Philip Rogers**, defaulted on a payment he owed the playwright in 1604, Shakespeare promptly sued. While Ben Jonson's recollection of his rival, recorded long after Shakespeare's death, as "honest, and of an open and free nature" may well be accurate, it is clear that Shakespeare was not prepared to be taken for a ride.

Work continued, of course, with *Troilus and Cressida* (c.1601–02) and *All's Well That Ends Well* (1604–05), often grouped together as "**problem**" plays because of their uncertain and frequently bitter tone. The country's political mood was jittery around this time, too: the childless Queen was 69 and had yet to announce who would take the throne in her place. When she became ill in late 1602, many sensed that it was the end, and just a few months after seeing the Chamberlain's Men act for the last time (she had commanded a full round of performances that winter), Elizabeth died on March 24, 1603. Having waited until the last possible moment, the Queen had finally agreed that **James VI of Scotland** would be her successor, and he began the journey to London from Edinburgh soon afterwards.

## Royal Shakespeare [1604–07]

For Shakespeare and his colleagues there was near-immediate good news: James I, as he was crowned, munificently decreed that he would take the old chamberlain's company under his wing and rename them the **King's Men**. Whether *Measure for Measure*, performed for James at court in December 1604, was Shakespeare's way of repaying the compliment is a point as open to debate as the play itself (it does engage with the King's interest in justice and mercy), but in any case the company was now recognized as the country's finest, being guaranteed performances at court as well as at the Globe. Ironically, another outburst of **plague** closed the theatres once again soon afterwards and delayed the royal festivities, but the King's Men were there to parade in the postponed coronation procession in March 1604.

They also set about playing in earnest for their new patron. The court records indicate no fewer than eleven performances during the winter season of 1604–05, including seven plays by Shakespeare. Among them were old standards like *The Comedy of Errors*, *Love's Labour's Lost*, *Henry V* and *The Merry Wives of Windsor*, but the author had also penned a new tragedy, *Othello*, which was acted at Whitehall in November 1604. Another new play, *Macbeth*, seems to have been written around this time with the Scottish king expressly in mind (it unites the story of Banquo – believed to be the Stuarts' ancestor – and James's interest in witchcraft), and was also performed at the Globe.

Revivals of Shakespeare's earlier work might have given him more time to spend on writing new material, so perhaps this explains why his great series of tragedies, beginning with *Othello* and *Macbeth* and continuing with *King Lear* (c.1605) and *Antony and Cleopatra* (c.1606–07), appeared during this period. Perhaps, too, the 41-year-old Shakespeare felt freer to write what he wanted – an unbroken run of non-comic work might have been commercially risky earlier in his career. Though often regarded as a lesser piece, the bitterly pessimistic *Timon of Athens* is another product of this time, but unlike the earlier plays contains no starring role for the leading boy actor (we don't know his name) who presumably created the roles of Desdemona, Lady Macbeth, Cordelia and – most impressively – Cleopatra.

## Going private [1608–09]

While Ben Jonson had managed to secure himself the lucrative position of chief poet and masque-deviser to King James, Shakespeare's company also found themselves gifted with an opportunity to go upmarket, albeit on a less extravagant scale. Years earlier, while the lease of the Shoreditch Theatre hung in the balance, James Burbage had bought up a new property in **Blackfriars**, a well-to-do district on the north side of the Thames and just down from St Paul's. Intending to convert part of the former Dominican monastery there into an indoor playhouse, Burbage began work but was halted by an petition from local residents angered by the prospect of a common theatre in their midst. When Burbage died soon afterwards, the Chamberlain's Men opted for relocation instead, and the Blackfriars theatre was leased to a company of boy players run by **Henry Evans**.

But while the boys may have been upmarket enough for the good folk of Blackfriars, they specialized in satirical work and frequently aroused the ire of powerful figures at court. When in 1608 Evans's company produced **George Chapman**'s incendiary *Conspiracy and Tragedy of Charles, Duke of Byron*, King James stepped in to disband them. Though the Bankside playhouses were then closed due to plague, Richard Burbage swiftly moved to complete what his father had begun and set up another syndicate to regain control of the **Blackfriars theatre**, clearly hoping that his position as a King's servant would overcome any objections. It did. The indoor theatre became the King's Men's main winter home, catering for more select audiences than the great Elizabethan amphitheatres – though by no means did the company retire from large-scale public drama, keeping on the Bankside Globe for summer seasons until significantly later in the century.

Performances began at the Blackfriars in winter 1609, as soon as the plague (which had appeared once again) abated, but Shakespeare had not been standing idle while his theatres were unavailable. Earlier that year a slender quarto entitled *Shakespeare's Sonnets* had emerged from the press of **Thomas Thorpe**, containing a sequence of 154 sonnets capped by a longish poem, the "Complaint" of a nameless "Lover" about her seduction and abandonment by a handsome young man. A similar youth stalks the pages of the first group of Sonnets, the object of the poet's adoration and frustration, but a second internal sequence is addressed to a mysterious dark-eyed woman who is apparently unfaithful to the poet. This enigmatic set of characters, along with the sometimes haphazard printing, has led many to believe that Shakespeare was not involved in publication, and that these were private poems

## Look here upon this picture

The most familiar image of the playwright is just that, a portrait that commemorates his work in the theatre. This is the so-called **Droeshout engraving**, done by a young artist of Flemish descent named Martin Droeshout and placed conspicuously on the title-page of the monumental *Mr William Shakespeare's Comedies, Histories, & Tragedies*, the First Folio of 1623 (see p.466). As with all copperplate engravings, Droeshout's technique will have been simple: he inscribed lines into a sheet of copper with a metal stylus, the plate then being covered with ink and pressed onto dampened paper. The artist probably didn't work from life: Droeshout was just 15 when his subject died, and even in 1623 the engraving, perhaps copied from a long-lost miniature of the playwright, must have been an early commission. That fact is sometimes taken to excuse some of its apparent failings: Shakespeare's forehead (memorably described by one commentator as "that horrible hydrocephalus development") is awkwardly modelled, the head itself sits precariously on an enormous ruff, while the body seems far too small. Generally, too, the Droeshout portrait looks stiff and uncomfortable; this is a middle-aged Shakespeare in his Sunday best. Late printings of the Folio are even more unflattering to their subject: as the plate wore down it gave the poet a coating of stubble and a blotchy complexion to boot.

Even so, the Droeshout engraving was accepted by Shakespeare's theatrical colleagues and cannot have been that far from the real thing. More authenticated still is the **Janssen bust**, part of the funeral monument to Shakespeare in Stratford parish church. This time the artist, Geerhardt Janssen, was Dutch, though he was based around the corner from the Globe in Southwark. Despite the likelihood that Janssen knew Shakespeare personally – and that the monument was approved by the playwright's relatives – the bust has come in for even more flak than the Droeshout engraving: it's been slated as "incompetent", portraying a man who looks like "a self-satisfied pork butcher" (in the words of one critic) and who might have already been a corpse when Janssen did his preliminary sketches.

The problem with both Droeshout and Janssen for most bardolaters is that they aren't nearly romantic enough – they don't depict a man who looks like he wrestled with *Hamlet*, still less poached deer or had a covert affair with a dark-eyed lady. These legends, which gathered impetus during the eighteenth and nineteenth centuries, fed the need to find a likeness communicating more of Shakespeare's spirit. Newly popular in this period was the **Chandos portrait** (c.1610), an oil on wood painting that may have been painted in the flesh, and which has the advantage of capturing a more rakish poet, complete with ear-ring and open collar. Though its authenticity and authorship have been much debated, Chandos was endlessly copied in the nineteenth century and remains a popular alternative, particularly for publishers eager to illustrate a fashionably unconformist Shakespeare.

Other portraits – and there are many – range from the mildly spurious to the gloriously unlikely. Many are copies, some are copies of copies, legacies of the burgeoning trade in Shakespeare's image. Into this category come the **Flower**, **Ely Palace** and **Ashbourne** portraits, touted as long-lost originals but all in fact derivatives of Droeshout. Easily the most artistically accomplished candidate is a gorgeous

never intended to see print. Though not many credit that theory nowadays, debate still rages as to the identity of the various parties, particularly the "lovely boy" praised by the poet and (perhaps) addressed in a riddling dedication to "Mr. W. H.", signed not by Shakespeare himself but by the printer. Could "W. H." be **William Herbert**, Earl of Pembroke and co-dedicatee of the 1623 First Folio? Or (with the initials reversed) Shakespeare's former patron Henry Wriothesley? Or even anyone at all? (See p.433 for more.)

## Romantic tales [1609–13]

Shakespeare, however, did not renounce the stage (as the disillusioned Jonson would eventually do). In fact the Blackfriars inspired more new work, much of it in a different key. *Coriolanus* (c.1608–09) is in some ways a transitory play: composed at around the same time as *Antony and Cleopatra* (and having a common source in Plutarch's *Lives*), it is far less expanminiature of an unknown young man by **Nicholas Hilliard**. The connection with Shakespeare requires a lot of ingenious footwork – the scholar who suggested it, Leslie Hotson, devoted the whole of a somewhat bizarre book to it – and the obvious expense of the young man's garments (let alone the cost of employing Hilliard) pushes it further into the realms of implausibility. At this youthful age Shakespeare had a wife and children to worry about, and quite probably a very unstable income.

Somewhat more plausible, but not much more, is the **Sanders portrait**, discovered in 1908, rediscovered in 2001 and subject to a barrage of recent publicity. As a book on the subject, *Shakespeare's Face* (2003), argues at length, there is much to like about this portrait: its shyly smiling sitter has auburn hair, as Shakespeare is thought to have done (one minus point for Chandos, which has black), and does somewhat resemble the older man captured by Droeshout. Perhaps the best thing about Sanders is that it offers access to a Shakespeare well before the genteel and well-heeled retirement – a Shakespeare who looks like he is in the middle of work, perhaps eager to get back to it. Whether it *is* Shakespeare (the date of 1603, when Shakespeare was 39, counts against what appears to be a much younger man) remains pretty doubtful, however. Whether we like them or not, the handiwork of Droeshout and Janssen will be with us for a while yet.

"Supposedly we are to conceive of the poet as declaiming verses he has just composed," wrote one critic of Shakespeare's funeral monument, "but he appears for all the world to be struggling with indigestion." Even so, Janssen's bust is probably the most reliable representation we have.

sive in scope, focusing on one man and his fiery path to self-destruction. It was followed by the late tragicomedies, now often referred to as the **romances** because of their thematic connections (see p.276). These plays needed technology such as the ability to "fly in" actors, and shared a new kind of theatrical intimacy – both of which were provided by the small, candlelit theatre for which they were probably written. They appear to have been transportable, however: several were performed at the Globe, and the King's Men, called upon to join the court celebrations for the **wedding** of James's daughter in 1613, presented no fewer than fourteen plays including *The Tempest* and *The Winter's Tale* during the festivities.

The first play of Shakespeare's final phase was most likely *Pericles* (c.1607), the most romance-like piece of all with its tale of a wandering hero separated from – but eventually reunited with – his wife and daughter. Not included in the 1623 First Folio, *Pericles* is something of a mystery to scholars – perhaps co-written with the minor writer **George Wilkins**, or with a surviving text that is somehow incomplete. Few such puzzles surround *The Winter's Tale* (c.1610), though again its plot – climaxing in a theatrically astonishing recognition scene – challenges its audiences' capacity for wonder, and perhaps their credulity. More esoteric in terms of narrative is *Cymbeline* (c.1610), set in the distant British past and with a famously impressive conclusion in which apparent tragedy is repeatedly transformed into resolution. Yet the most famous romance is undeniably *The Tempest* (c.1610), almost certainly Shakespeare's final solo work and the one in which he is traditionally assumed to bid a graceful farewell to the stage, just as the magician Prospero swears to give up his "so potent art" at the drama's end.

Unfortunately for that theory, Shakespeare's art did not judder to a halt with *The Tempest*'s completion. He was to write two, perhaps three, more plays before retirement, but would not do so alone. His co-author was **John Fletcher** (1579–1625), an up-and-coming dramatist then being groomed to take over (see p.394). It's not known whether the decision to work together was part of the handover process or emerged because Shakespeare was attempting to lighten his workload, but at any rate the first of their collaborations seems to have been the enigmatic *Cardenio* (?1612), a play based on Cervantes's *Don Quixote* that left only scattered traces in the records and has long since vanished (see p.186).

The second, *Henry VIII* (also known as *All Is True*), made a greater impression in every way – it was included in the First Folio, but was also the cause of a **fire** which burnt down the Globe in June 1613. The blaze began when a piece of burning material from a stage cannon ignited the theatre's thatch roof, and although no one is known to have died, nothing was left of the building's fabric and the King's Men's investment. By the end of that year Shakespeare and Fletcher seem to have completed their final collaboration, *The Two Noble Kinsmen*, and as a consequence of the fire it probably opened at the Blackfriars. *Kinsmen* almost certainly contains Shakespeare's last writing for the stage, and it is tempting to feel that at least some of the tragicomedy's melancholy tone – a world away from the multiple miracles of the earlier romances – is the work of a man who felt death close at hand.

## Back home [1614–15]

Shakespeare turned 50 in April 1614. His last few years in London had been difficult. The death of his brother Richard in February 1613 was merely the latest in a sequence of funerals: Edmund (who became a player like his brother, but found little success) died at the age of just 27 in 1607, Mary followed in 1608, Gilbert in 1612. In just six years William and Joan had lost their mother and three of their younger siblings. The Globe fire might well have been the end for the playwright. Though his colleagues swiftly regrouped – they built a **second Globe**, this time with a tile roof, which opened within a few years – Shakespeare took no part in the venture and appears to have sold his shares soon afterwards. He returned one last time to Stratford.

Though it took place a few years earlier, one of his final recorded engagements in London was to testify in court during the 1612 **Belott v. Mountjoy suit** involving his old landlord, Christopher Mountjoy, and Mountjoy's former apprentice Stephen Belott. The dispute was fractious: after marrying Mountjoy's daughter Mary, Belott had set up a rival business and Mountjoy had failed to provide the agreed dowry, upon which Belott sued. Shakespeare, as the man who had arranged the marriage and acted as a go-between, was a crucial witness. But in the event his memory appears to have failed him, and he could not tell the court what had been originally agreed. The case ended inconclusively.

Back in Stratford, scandal would attach itself to Shakespeare's own family a few years later. In 1607 his eldest daughter Susanna had married the respectable and pious physician **John**

Hall (Hall's medical practice would later become known throughout the Midlands), but six years later she was publicly accused by one John Lane of having cheated on Hall – and of having caught gonorrhoea as a result. There seem to have been no grounds to the charges: Susanna immediately sued for slander, Lane failed to turn up in court, and the case was closed. Hall stood by his wife.

Susanna's sister Judith was less fortunate – particularly in her marriage. She wed, at the advanced age of 31, a wine merchant named **Thomas Quiney** in February 1616, but the match was deemed illegal because it had taken place during Lent and the couple had failed to acquire a special licence (unlike Judith's father all those years before). The offence was not serious, but Quiney was nevertheless excommunicated for failing to attend the hearing. He was far more unreliable in other ways, too: seven or eight months earlier he had managed to get another woman pregnant, and both mother and infant died in childbirth just a month after Judith and Thomas wed. Thomas was once more called upon to attend a church court, this time to admit charges of fornication. In the event he got off with a fine, but in a close-knit community such as Stratford the scandal will surely have blighted his and Judith's marriage.

## Wills and monuments [1616]

Some have suggested that the shock of all this also hastened their father's end. In March 1616 Shakespeare had just weeks to live, and may already have been ailing. Earlier that winter he had set about preparing a **will**: unlike his involvement with the Mountjoy suit, Shakespeare would not be forgetful of his own financial affairs. Though much of the testament, which organizes the sharing-out of his considerable estate, is conventional enough, there are a few surprising details. Shakespeare clearly had second thoughts about what to leave Judith, and was careful to ensure that Quiney would not defraud her. More celebrated – in fact notorious – is Shakespeare's treatment of his wife, which if not actively shabby is certainly equivocal. He does not mention her by name, and famously bequeaths her his **"second-best bed"**, a gift which most biographers have assumed to be insulting. It might not be: some believe that this was the marriage bed, the best being kept for guests, but in reality there is no way of knowing what Shakespeare intended here. Though no other specific bequests to Anne are made, it is fairly safe to assume that she would be provided for, presumably by Susanna and Dr Hall, who were left New Place.

Shakespeare signed each page of the will and stated (in a formulaic legal phrase) that it had been drawn up "in perfect health and memory", but on the final sheet his signature begins to break down: he was not a well man. He lingered for a few more months, but on April 23, 1616 – during an unusually temperate spring – he died. Though there is a seventeenth-century story that he contracted a "fever" while out drinking with old poet friends Ben Jonson and Michael Drayton, other diseases are more likely to have ended his life. **Typhoid**, virulent in warmer weather, is one possibility, but some have speculated that **syphilis** may have been a root cause. Again there is no evidence, and if Dr Hall treated his father-in-law (as he surely did) there is no record of it.

Shakespeare was buried two days later, on April 25, in the same place (and on nearly the same date) that he had been christened: Holy Trinity Church, Stratford. There is no surviving description of the funeral, but within a few years a sizeable **monument** was commissioned from **Geerhart Janssen**, an Anglo-Flemish sculptor based near the Globe in Southwark, which now stands in the church (see p.462). Although biographers have questioned the bust's accuracy (it does not look like any other representation), it was presumably paid for and sanctioned by Shakespeare's family, and thus has good grounds to be called authentic. There is no other way of guessing what he looked like: an inscription upon Shakespeare's **gravestone**

Mr. WILLIAM
SHAKESPEARES
COMEDIES,
HISTORIES, &
TRAGEDIES.
Published according to the True Originall Copies.

Martin Droeshout sculpsit London.

LONDON
Printed by Isaac Iaggard, and Ed. Blount. 1623.

"Published according to the True Originall Copies", Heminges and Condell's First Folio (1623) rescued the scripts of seventeen plays from almost certain oblivion; pristine examples now fetch anything up to $4 million at auction.

warns that anyone who "moves my bones" will be "cursed", a warning which has to date – despite a few close calls – been heeded.

But the poet's greatest monument was still to come. In his will Shakespeare bequeathed money to three of his closest theatrical friends, Richard Burbage, John Heminges and Henry Condell, and asked that they "remember" him. Heminges and Condell repaid the debt magnificently, collecting together nearly all of their dead colleague's plays and publishing them in impressive form: *Mr. William Shakespeare's Comedies, Histories & Tragedies*, the magisterial **First Folio**, appeared in print in the winter of 1623, just a few months after Anne's death.

# Reading on

### William Shakespeare: A compact documentary life
**Samuel Schoenbaum ; rev. 1987** ▷ Oxford UP

Distilled from his earlier, sumptuously illustrated *Documentary Life* (1977), this is Schoenbaum's answer to the solid scholarship laid down by E.K. Chambers's fine but now outdated two-volume *William Shakespeare: A study of facts and problems* (1930). Determined to "chasten speculative elaboration or romantic indulgence", Schoenbaum concentrates solely on what the records tell us about Shakespeare, and if you feel in need of hard facts, this is the place to come. Not that the author is dry: everything is written with the same flair and wry instinct for detail as Schoenbaum's monumental *Shakespeare's Lives* (see p.496). While other biographers can suffocate the reader under a weight of information, Schoenbaum never forgets to tell a story.

### Shakespeare: A life
**Park Honan; 1998** ▷ Oxford UP

Of the lives of Shakespeare able to take into account recent historical insights into the period, this is the most elegant, full and reliable. Many literary biographers have trouble aligning the life with the work, but Honan puts plenty of emphasis on Shakespeare's experience as a player and offers sophisticated critical judgement on his output. He also has a knack of making familiar details come up freshly scrubbed, suggesting supporting connections not specifically tied to Shakespeare but drawn from the wider social tapestry of his era. In attempting to put flesh on the bones of his hero, Honan undoubtedly engages in what Schoenbaum (see above) would term "speculative elaboration" – and some might find his conclusions too indulgent – but his approach delivers impressive insights nonetheless.

### Will in the World
**Stephen Greenblatt; 2004** ▷ Cape / Norton

If there's one thing that Shakespearian biographies demonstrate, it's that each generation remoulds him in its own image. Perhaps surprising, then, that Stephen Greenblatt – cast as the bad boy of Shakespearian scholarship ever since his unruly *Renaissance Self-Fashioning* (1981) emphasized the influence of power politics on Tudor writers – should produce a Life so utterly well-behaved. In fact *Will in the World*, dreadful title aside, is more intriguingly rebellious than might at first appear, chiefly in indulging those Shakespearian myths (deer-stalking, Catholic connections and all) that recent biographers have attempted to jettison. If the book has no new documentary evidence to offer, and is as ideologically conservative as Greenblatt's critics have always argued he is, it nevertheless scores highly for readability, friendliness and imagination, not to mention the author's keen and persuasive critical eye. An excellent introduction.

# Shakespeare's stages

S hakespeare wrote for the professional stage for twenty-five of the most eventful and exciting years English drama has ever seen. It's easy to forget that when he arrived in London, probably in the late 1580s, public theatre was still an astonishingly new medium – audiences nationwide had been living with it for less than half the time that we in the twenty-first century have had access to cinema. Renaissance drama melded aristocratic entertainments, academic theatre and the carnival of the street; and in the bustling and often cut-throat world of Elizabethan London, popular plays became an impressively versatile form. Moulded by talents such as John Lyly, Thomas Nashe, Thomas Kyd and Christopher Marlowe, then Shakespeare himself and his younger contemporary Ben Jonson, drama was not merely among the most successful entertainments of its time, but became one of the most revolutionary art forms in early modern Europe.

## Miraculous shows

No one is quite certain when Shakespeare first attended theatrical performances, and unlike several of his famous contemporaries – his star actor Richard Burbage being the most obvious example – he was not born into a theatre family. But as a boy growing up in the prosperous and cultivated West Midlands he had plentiful opportunity to see the distinct varieties of theatre Elizabethan England offered. At one end of the scale were the medieval **mystery** and **miracle plays**, performed at nearby Coventry during the festival of Corpus Christi (which generally falls in May or June) as late as 1579, when Shakespeare was 15 and may just have left Stratford grammar school. These epic religious narratives were usually put on by local craft guilds, who each took responsibility for one or more play in the sequence – so in the York mystery cycles, for instance, the Shipwrights acted the story of Noah and the Ark, while at Coventry the Shearmen and Taylors took on the Annunciation, the birth of Christ and Herod's Massacre of the Innocents. During their medieval heyday these appeared every few years or so, but by the late 1570s Queen Elizabeth's Protestant authorities were suspicious of pageants preserved from Catholic days and they appear to have been suppressed, or replaced with more religiously appropriate spectacles.

Elizabeth will have been more sympathetic to the spectacular festivities put on in her honour during her 1575 "progress" (one of her numerous summer tours around the nation), during which she visited Shakespeare's county, Warwickshire. For the twelve days she stayed with her close friend – gossip held him to be more than that – Robert Dudley, Earl of Leicester at **Kenilworth**, the Queen was honoured with numerous pageants and parties, some of which admitted the public. Dudley's impressive castle was just twelve miles from Stratford, and it seems more than possible that John Shakespeare took along his eldest son to be among the crowds. (*A Midsummer Night's Dream* contains teasing references to events strikingly like those at Kenilworth.)

Less rarefied theatrical occasions might also have been part of Shakespeare's youthful experience. Stratford itself frequently hosted travelling troupes of actors, never more frequently than during 1586–87, when no fewer than five companies performed in the town's Gild Hall as well as other venues. Among them were the state-sponsored **Queen's Men**, then the leading company of the day, who specialized in propagandistic and rambunctious English history plays. It has been suggested that Shakespeare may have joined the company at some point (several of his own plays, chiefly the histories, bear marks of their influence), but no evidence survives. The life of **travelling players** was hard: despite good rewards income was sometimes fitful, towns en route could be less than welcoming, the travelling itself was arduous – a company would need to carry all its props and costumes. On the road tensions within companies sometimes boiled over: soon before the Queen's Men visited Stratford, they lost their star actor, killed in a brawl with a colleague. It was little wonder that many troupes wanted a home in London, the theatrical capital of the nation.

## Outside the law

Theatre in London was well established, but so was the troublesome relationship between its practitioners and the rest of society. A government **Act** from 1572 announced that "Common Players in Interludes & Minstrels" who weren't affiliated to a patron (usually a nobleman) would be regarded as "Rogues, Vagabonds and Sturdy Beggars". Elizabeth's ministers were forever trying to regulate theatre, demanding that companies be properly licensed and even attempting to control what kinds of plays they performed. A royal proclamation of 1559 required that they steer clear of subject matter covering "either matters of religion or of the governance of the estate of the common weal", in effect anything that could be taken as criticism of Elizabeth's reign. The Queen's **Master of the Revels** – her events manager – was given powers in 1581 to license "players of comedies, tragedies, interludes, or what other shows soever", which involved hearing or reading whatever plays were to be performed publicly and, if necessary, censoring them. That **Edmund Tilney** (who stayed in the job from 1579 to 1610, covering nearly all of Shakespeare's career) took these responsibilities seriously is not in doubt: the manuscript of *Sir Thomas More*, in which Shakespeare probably had a hand (see p.140), shows marks of his interventions to tone down the script.

Theatre companies were more carefully regulated than ever before. When Elizabeth's ministers formed the Queen's Men in 1583, cherry-picking the finest actors in London (among them Robert Wilson, John Laneham, Richard Tarlton, John Dutton, John Bentley and John Singer), the intention was to keep a close eye on their activities. As well as giving the company's members the duty of acting at court and the right to tour during the summer months, this move also granted them a near-monopoly over performances in London. But that in itself guaranteed nothing: the City authorities took a consistently dim view of playing and players, and were always threatening to squeeze them out by whatever means possible. A 1585 declaration announced that entertainments would be "tolerated", but on strict conditions: that they should not play at night, nor on the Sabbath; that the authorities could close them down if bubonic plague threatened; and that only the Queen's Men were to be licensed. All other companies were effectively forbidden from playing in the City of London.

## Early playhouses

So where did the Queen's Men play? **Inns** were most likely the first venues for acting companies, and during the 1580s the troupe is on record as having performed at City pubs the **Bell** and the **Bull**, where makeshift stages will have been constructed for their performances. But the City fathers never approved of this arrangement, and in 1595 succeeded in banning companies from performing at inns altogether. In order to escape restrictive jurisdiction, there was only one option: to make a dash for the suburbs, which meant travelling outside the City's

SHAKESPEARE'S LONDON

○ Playhouse/
Bear garden
□ Inn
■ Law college
▦ Prison

SHOREDITCH
Theatre 1576
FINSBURY FIELDS
SPITAL FIELDS
Curtain 1577
Red Bull 1604
Fortune 1600
CLERKENWELL
Southampton House
Gray's Inn
HOLBORN
MOOR FIELDS
Fleet Prison
Lincoln's Inn
St Paul's Cathedral
Guildhall
Bull Inn
Clement's Inn
Inner Temple
FLEET STREET
COVENT GARDEN
Middle Temple
Blackfriars 1597
CHEAPSIDE
CANNON
Bell Inn
CORNHILL ST
FENCHURCH STREET
EASTCHEAP
STRAND
River Thames
THAMES STREET
CHARING CROSS
Whitehall Palace
KING STREET
Swan 1595
Bear Garden
Hope 1605
Rose 1587
Globe 1599
Clink Prison
St Mary Overies
Tower of London
Westminster Hall
Westminster Abbey
SOUTHWARK
HIGH STREET
LONDON BRIDGE
Lambeth Palace

Area of London under City administration
Area of London outside City administration (the "Liberties")
City wall

N

0    ½ mile

medieval walls. These extended from the Fleet River to the west all the way to Aldgate and the Tower of London on the eastern side; to the north they reached as far as Moorgate and Bishopsgate, with the Thames forming the City's southern border. Outside these boundaries (and in isolated pockets within) the authorities had little power over what went on, and in these so-called **"liberties"** theatres began to spring up.

London's first purpose-built theatre appeared in 1567 (three years after Shakespeare's birth, but twenty or so before he would make his way to the capital). This was the **Red Lion** at Stepney to the City's east, financed by a businessman named **John Brayne** and built with galleried seating and a large stage, but it might have been only a temporary structure lasting for no more than a few performances. Far more durable was Brayne's next venture, organized in collaboration with his brother-in-law, carpenter and entrepreneur **James Burbage**. Together they travelled north to Shoreditch, again outside the City walls, and in 1576 built an amphitheatre called the **Theatre** there, almost certainly the capital's first professional playhouse. With its impressive name (from the Latin *theatrum*), the Theatre would set the pattern for many subsequent houses – it was a "round" amphitheatre (actually polygonal, made up of angled bays in three vertical tiers) with a large internal stage jutting out from one set of bays and an open yard. Audiences could choose either to stand in the yard for a cheap fee, or sit in one of the galleries for rather more. One of the main incentives for designing a theatre like this seems to have been to offer a range of ticket prices – as well as ensuring that people paid before they could enter, a perennial problem in traditional venues – but the net effect was of a socially varied theatre dominated by the **"groundlings"** standing around the stage at the front.

The Theatre seems to have been an immediate success, able to draw audiences even to its comparatively remote suburban location, and a rival playhouse, the **Curtain**, went up nearby the following year. Both seem to have been available to whichever company could use them, and the Queen's Men are likely to have played there. But James Burbage seems to have been uncertain whether his theatrical risk would survive – he insisted on a clause in the original lease allowing him to dismantle the Theatre's structure and relocate it if need be. Presumably he anticipated problems with their landlord (which would indeed surface in 1597), or perhaps he foresaw the **plague closures** that dogged the London theatres on and off for the next thirty years. As part of their 1585 settlement the London authorities retained the right to close down public venues in an attempt to restrict contagion – the disease was believed to be spread through human contact – and were particularly harsh on the theatres. As one recent biographer has pointed out, it is a small irony that the hazelnuts munched by many theatregoers (remnants of which have been found by archeologists) may, if anything, have kept away the fleas carrying the bubonic bacillus. Nonetheless the authorities were unrelenting, and during closures many playing companies were forced back on to the road – assuming news of plague did not overtake them – to tour for their survival.

## On Bankside

By the time that a plague outbreak initiated the first major theatrical shutdowns of Shakespeare's London career, in 1592 and 1593, the Curtain and the Theatre had been joined by other London playhouses. Instead of being located to the north of the city, however, **Bankside** to the south of the Thames had become the destination of choice, encouraging Southwark's development into London's premier entertainment quarter. Here punters could be tempted by fishponds and bear-baiting, or prostitution, which was rife (none other than the Bishop of Winchester was the area's largest brothel-owner). In 1603 the Privy Council was told that the area was teeming with "thieves, horse-stealers, whore-mongers, cozeners, coney-catchers", and indeed most critics of the theatre seem to have regarded playgoing, too, as an all but criminal activity – partly because prostitutes tried to pick up trade outside the doors.

Right next to three of the largest brothels on Bankside, an impresario named **Philip Henslowe** built a playhouse he called the **Rose**, which opened for business in 1587. Although it followed the basic design of the Theatre and Curtain, the Rose seems to have been smaller than either, with a narrow, tapered stage. From archeological evidence we know that it was thatched, and Henslowe steadily built up its capabilities – extending the structure in order to squeeze in more spectators in 1592, fitting a "throne in the heavens", presumably a device to fly an actor onto the stage, a few years later. That we know so much about the operation of the Rose is due to Henslowe's *Diary* (really an account-book of his expenses and business dealings, logging most of the transactions involving the theatre), and also to the discovery in 1989 of the playhouse's foundations.

Henslowe's theatre became crucial to the story of London theatre in 1594, when the Queen's Men – who had dominated throughout the 1580s – broke up. They had been ailing for years, having struggled to overcome the death of Richard Tarlton in 1588, and several other companies (with actors moving freely between them) had emerged to fill the gap – among them **Lord Strange's Men**, the **Admiral's Men**, the **Earl of Pembroke's Men** and the **Earl of Sussex's Men**. But with the plague and through sheer competition it had been difficult for any of these to prosper, and in 1594 just two new companies emerged from the wreckage. They were the renovated **Admiral's Men**, and a brand-new troupe called the **Lord Chamberlain's Men**, sponsored by Elizabeth's Chamberlain, Lord Hunsdon (see p.457). Both initially performed at Henslowe's Rose, but as part of the new deal agreed with the court they were given separate venues at different ends of London – the Admiral's staying with

Elizabethan plays often ended with a "jig" performed by the company; at the Globe these were led by the clown Will Kempe (right), who once danced all the way from London to Norwich accompanied by his pipe and tabor player, Thomas Sly.

Henslowe on Bankside, the Lord Chamberlain's travelling to the Theatre at Shoreditch. Personal connections seem to have played a major role in this agreement: the Admiral's Men were led by **Edward Alleyn,** then the leading tragedian of his day, known for his "strutting" style and who had married Henslowe's stepdaughter; while their rivals were run by a consortium including James's son **Richard Burbage,** the famous clown **William Kempe** and **William Shakespeare** (Shakespeare's first appearance in the records as an actor).

## In rep

With their new duopoly in place the two companies were stable at last, and London theatregoers were rewarded with near-unbroken seasons for the first time ever – during the 1594–95 season the Admiral's Men played for a non-stop 49 weeks, six days a week, breaking only for Lent and some much-needed renovations to the Rose. Both companies adopted a furious pace of **repertory theatre,** with constant changes in their fare: during that same season alone the Admiral's Men acted 38 plays (equal to Shakespeare's lifelong output), of which 21 were new. Only eight plays would make it through to the next year, and it's reasonable to suppose that the Chamberlain's Men consumed material at a similar rate. Actors would have just a few weeks to rehearse a new piece while still performing older plays in the evenings, so it seems likely that **acting styles** will have been standardized and formulaic. Judging from the poor quality of so-called "reported texts" (see p.512), actors apparently had little time to concentrate on anyone's lines but their own.

In order to limit textual piracy as best they could, companies frequently gave their actors not whole scripts, but expurgated versions that contained just one part. Companies held copyright (such as it was) over an author's plays, and retained the right to **publish** them as they saw fit – as many did during the plague closures of 1592–93, when doing so created a valuable alternative stream of income. Playwrights themselves were initially used on a free-lance basis, but over time might become contracted as an **"ordinary poet"**, a writer-in-residence. These deals typically required the writer to produce a certain number of new works a year, in return for a steady salary as well as a fee each time a play was performed. Shakespeare seems to have begun as a freelance writer for a variety of companies (among them Sussex's and Pembroke's Men), but somehow managed to hang on to his early playscripts, perhaps offering them as collateral when he joined the Chamberlain's Men. After that date he seems to have become the new company's chief writer, producing an average of two plays a year during an exceptionally stable working relationship that lasted until the end of his career.

## Colleagues and rivals

Most playwrights were not that lucky – or that consistent. What has come down to us today is undoubtedly the cream of Elizabethan drama, and it's likely that much of what appeared during these fiercely busy years was hack work. Yet there were many brilliant stars in London, partly an effect of the lack of jobs for grammar-school-educated men like Shakespeare. Probably the most notable writers of the 1570s and 80s were those known as the **"university wits"**, a brilliant and correspondingly loud-mouthed group who are often credited with rev-olutionizing the early Tudor theatre pioneered under Henry VIII by **John Heywood** and **Henry Medwall**, two of the earliest "playwrights" (though the word does not appear until the late seventeenth century). Among the wits' number were **Thomas Lodge**, **Thomas Nashe**, **George Peele**, **Robert Greene** and **John Lyly**. As was customary in the competitive (and under-paid) world of Elizabethan theatre, none focused exclusively on writing plays – Lodge, Greene and Nashe penned sensational romances, satires and pamphlets, while Peele was known for his poetry.

But their most famous member was the brilliant **Christopher Marlowe**, whose iconoclastic dramas and dangerous private life were being talked about when Shakespeare arrived in London. Marlowe penned an unprecedented string of successes including the two-part *Tamburlaine* (1587–88), *Doctor Faustus* (c.1588), *The Jew of Malta* (c.1590) and *Edward II* (c.1592), all of which honed a famously grand, "mighty" style and sent up received notions about heroes and heroism (many of his most exciting characters are unapologetically evil). But Marlowe's career came to a brutal halt in June 1593 when he was arrested, then stabbed to death in a Deptford pub while on bail – killed, some said, because of his involvement with Elizabeth I's network of spies. Almost as notorious was Marlowe's former room-mate **Thomas Kyd**, who found himself caught up in the witch-hunt following his companion's death and was arrested soon afterwards. Kyd's most famous hit, *The Spanish Tragedy* (1592), became the must-see play of the early 1590s and launched a vogue for blood-soaked revenge drama that lasted well into the Jacobean period.

If Marlowe's and Kyd's careers make Shakespeare's seem pedestrian by comparison – at least in terms of intrigue – his near-contemporary **Ben Jonson** also enjoyed a taste for danger. Jonson once killed a fellow-actor in a duel (he put his classical skills to practical use afterwards by pleading "benefit of clergy" in court, gaining lenient punishment by demonstrating that he could read and write in Latin) and, never a man to be cowed by authority, was imprisoned no less than twice for his involvement in writing political satires that offended those in power, *The Isle of Dogs* (1597) and *Eastward Ho!* (1605). Jonson patched up his differences with **John Marston** in order to work on the latter play, for a few years earlier he became drawn into the

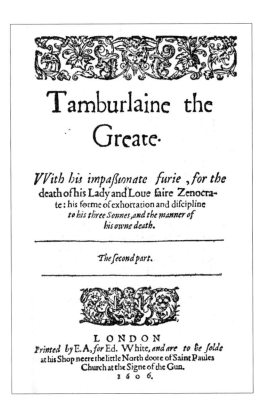

# Tamburlaine the Greate.

VVith his impaßionate furie, for the death of his Lady and Loue faire Zenocra- te: his forme of exhortation and difcipline to his three Sonnes, and the manner of his owne death.

The fecond part.

LONDON

Printed by E. A, for Ed. White, and are to be folde at his Shop neere the little North doore of Saint Paules Church at the Signe of the Gun.
1606.

Tamburlaine, the first of Christopher Marlowe's many power-crazed antiheroes, left an obvious impression on Shakespeare's *Henry VI* plays, just as *Richard II* probably paid homage to Marlowe's *Edward II*.

"Poet's War", in which Jonson vied for ascendancy with challengers including Marston and **Thomas Dekker**, noted for his romantic comedies. Jonson was initially involved with the Admiral's Men but flitted restlessly around, writing not only for the Chamberlain's but later for the all-boys' company run by **Henry Evans** based at the Blackfriars Theatre on the western tip of the City. Also writing for the boys' company was **George Chapman**, slightly older than Shakespeare and nowadays better known as a translator of Homer than for his classically influenced plays. Indebted to Shakespeare was the younger writer **Thomas Middleton**, who excelled in hard-bitten city comedy and appears to have revised parts of *Macbeth* for performance in the seventeenth century – testament to the continued taste for Shakespeare's work up to and after his death. Also linked with Shakespeare was **John Fletcher**, who collaborated on three of Shakespeare's last plays but was also known for his close writing partnership with **Francis Beaumont** (see p.394).

## The great globe itself

The Blackfriars was leased to the boys by none other than the Chamberlain's Men, who had been looking to relocate as early as 1597, when the landlord of the Theatre, **Giles Allen**, began to create difficulties about renewing their lease. Negotiations eventually broke down, but James Burbage's plan to develop a base in the City came off the rails when the wealthy inhabitants of Blackfriars protested about having a theatre in their midst. Burbage died soon afterwards, leaving the Chamberlain's Men with just one other option: to exercise their right to dismantle the Theatre and move it. With the aid of master carpenter **Peter Street**, this they duly did (to Allen's lasting chagrin), and transported the timbers of the old building through the City and across the Thames to a new site. They, too, were to have a Southwark playhouse, while the Blackfriars could be rented to Evans's boys.

What resulted was the most famous theatre of the age, enshrined in Prospero's metatheatrical reference to "the great globe itself" and (so a slightly suspect legend has it) with Jaques's "all the world's a stage" as its motto. This was the **Globe**, probably opened during the 1599 season and the theatre for which, despite its ignominious origins, Shakespeare wrote his most famous plays. In reality there was little new about the Globe – unless its timbers were reshaped it will have been structurally similar to the old Theatre – and yet by the time it was built the resources of the Elizabethan playhouse had been honed by long experience and offered sophisticated dramatic possibilities. No expense seems to have been spared on the job of rebuilding (the considerable cost had to borne by the Chamberlain's Men's "**sharers**", one of whom was Shakespeare; see p.458), and the theatre that emerged was probably larger than anything yet seen.

Its **dimensions** have been estimated at around 30 metres (100ft) in diameter at the outside walls, some 9 metres (30ft) larger than the Rose. Inside the walls, the yard must have been around 25 metres (80ft) wide, though some authorities have since scaled down all these estimates. No surviving evidence indicates the proportions of the Globe's stage, but scholars think that it might have been nearly square, perhaps with a width of around 12 metres (40ft). It will

## Staging old and new

From the little we know about costuming on the Elizabethan stage, Shakespeare's contemporaries had an eclectic and piecemeal view of history. The **"Peacham drawing"**, supposedly by writer and artist Henry Peacham, appears to illustrate Shakespeare's early Roman tragedy, *Titus Andronicus*. Though Titus himself is shown in a toga in deference to the play's classical setting, the soldiers accompanying him wear Elizabethan armour and carry halberds. As with the play's language (which is defiantly Elizabethan), there is little attempt at consistency of staging, a practice that predominated in theatre until well into the nineteenth century. **David Garrick** performed in modern dress, and though his competitor **Charles Macklin** introduced "Highland" costume in his productions of *Macbeth*, it wasn't until the extravagant productions of **Charles Kean** in the 1830s and later that "historical" staging (whether painstakingly researched Roman for *Julius Caesar* or beautifully constructed Tudor for *Henry VIII*) became the norm.

The notion of returning to "Elizabethan" theatrical practice – dismissed as primitive by succeeding generations – would not properly surface until the entry of a brilliantly innovative (and notoriously eccentric) actor named **William Poel** (1852–1934). Instead of employing the resources of Victorian theatre to create realistic period settings, Poel instead attempted to guess how Elizabethan companies had acted Shakespeare's plays. Later writing that "realism, so often thought healthy and natural, is with scarcely any exception only perverse sentimentality", he staged a watershed production of the so-called "bad" quarto of *Hamlet* at London's St George's Hall in April 1881. This employed a fit-up Elizabethan stage swathed on all sides by red curtains in order to block out the proscenium arch, while his cast wore scrupulously researched Elizabethan costume (his "Ofelia" even played the lute). Poel's passionately held views were controversial: his 1898 *Merchant* up-ended theatrical fashion by pitching Shylock as a snarling, fright-wigged villain, while a special apron stage for his *Two Gentlemen* (1910) covered most of the stalls in an attempt to recreate an authentic space. Following his founding of the **Elizabethan Stage Society** in 1895, Poel directed numerous productions that cast fresh light not only on Shakespeare but many of his contemporaries too. Not that audiences always got the point: Max Beerbohm once wrote to an actress friend that "poor William Poel's honoured name is a guarantee of badness".

And although he revolutionized theatrical approaches – partly through disciples like **Harley Granville-Barker** and **Robert Atkins**, who argued for fluid staging and fuller texts – Poel never lived to see a full-scale reconstruction of an Elizabethan playhouse. While replica Globes in various locations across Northwest America and more recently in **Tokyo** have prospered, Poel's shade would have to wait for the magnetic talents of **Sam Wanamaker**, American-born actor and director, and the moving force behind the project to rebuild "Shakespeare's Globe" as close as possible to its original Bankside location in London. The entire project took some thirty years' work and outlived its creator (Wanamaker died in 1993, just a few seasons before the new Globe opened its doors), but has since become a hit with visitors and theatre aficionados alike. Based on a combination of painstaking evidence and imaginative guesswork, the building is a replica closely modelled on the rebuilt post-1613 Globe but has seen much evolutionary tinkering – including manoeuvring the position of the pillars and reworking the balcony space as a music area. Under the stewardship of **Mark Rylance**, the Globe's artistic policy has proved itself every bit as eclectic as its historical namesake, mingling carefully historicized productions with *outré* experiments including, in 2003, a *Richard III* and *Shrew* with a cast made up entirely of women. Since London's Globe opened there have been several attempts to reconstruct new replicas elsewhere – most strikingly in **Gdansk**, Poland where troupes of touring English actors are reputed to have performed in a seventeenth-century playhouse modelled on the Fortune.

have been backed by a flat-faced *frons scenae* (stage wall), which probably had three doors – two smaller ones to the left and right, and a larger one in the centre opening into a **discovery space**. This was a room behind the stage and opening out onto it, suggesting an "interior" area into which a bed or other large prop could be inserted; Shakespeare calls for this kind of resource comparatively rarely, but the moment at which Ferdinand and Miranda are magically "discovered" playing chess near the conclusion of *The Tempest* shows him using it, as may Desdemona's bedroom scene in *Othello*.

Other kinds of transformations offered by the stage include **trap doors**, one down into the space underneath (colloquially known as the "hell") and perhaps another in the **"heavens"** above, a canopy covering the stage, richly painted (perhaps with the astrological signs of the zodiac) and supported by two huge pillars. The heavens originally protected the cast and their expensive costumes from the rain, but came to offer theatrical possibilities in their own right – one of which may have been some kind of **winch mechanism** via which personnel could be flown in from above. Players could also appear in the **"aloft"** space directly above the central doors, shallow rooms with open windows looking out over the stage (the balcony scene in *Romeo and Juliet* is Shakespeare's most famous use of this resource) which, later on, might have been adapted and expanded to contain **musicians**. Behind the stage and under the aloft spaces lay the **tiring house**, a room or complex of rooms in which actors could change and put on makeup, and where their costumes and promptbooks were most likely stored.

## Props and practice

Elizabethans talked of going to "hear" a play, not to see it, and they were far more used to using their ears – long weekly sermons guaranteed that – than most modern-day audiences. In a theatre so reliant on the transformative power of words, **scenery** at the Globe and other theatres like it was correspondingly sparse. The great pillars of the heavens could be used (hidden behind or clambered up), as could the aloft areas and other spaces – drapes and hangings could also be employed – but bulky props may have been avoided, particularly if a company was forced to take a play on the road. One exception would have been a chair of state upon which monarchs would sit, while beds and tents would also have been required. Judging by the inventory in Henslowe's *Diary*, small **props** – letters, books, candles and many more exotic things – seem to have been relatively commonplace. To make up for the lack of scenery, **costuming** at the Globe, as at other Elizabethan theatres, was magnificent – it's even been suggested that a ready source of ecclesiastical garb, repeatedly used in Shakespeare's history plays, would be real church robes flogged off at the Reformation. Much of a company's finance would be sunk into its costumes, though from surviving evidence the Elizabethan approach to representation was eclectic (see p.475).

Theatrical tricks such as blood, much in use during violent revenge plays like *The Spanish Tragedy*, will have probably used bladders filled with real pigs' or sheep's gore. **Swordplay** itself was likely to be impressive, especially because the young, male sections of the audience would have had a near-professional interest in the techniques of fighting, and the players themselves were likely to have plenty of physical skill (they also seem to have **danced** at the conclusion of each performance). **Sound effects** would include "thunder" – achieved, if the preface to Jonson's *Every Man In His Humour* is to be believed, by rolling a cannon ball around a drum or down a tin trough – and extend to noises off representing anything from armies massing to the sound of birdsong. **Music** could vary from trumpet flourishes and drum rolls to full-scale incidental compositions (especially after Shakespeare's company moved to the Blackfriars; see p.481). Other "realistic" effects seem to have become more commonplace and refined during Shakespeare's late career: one of *The Tempest*'s first stage directions calls for the entrance of sailors soaked to the skin by the storm, though whether Antigonus's famous exit "pursued a bear" in *The Winter's Tale* used a real animal from one of the baiting arenas nearby is still hotly debated.

In general plays were acted extremely rapidly and with no breaks between scenes, one group of characters entering as another left. In *Romeo and Juliet*, the Chorus's description of the "two-hours' traffic of our stage" might seem optimistic, but all the Globe's performances would have taken place in the afternoons and during **daylight**, night-time scenes being represented by actors dressing appropriately or carrying torches – or indeed discussing the prevailing conditions, as they do at the frosty opening of *Hamlet*. That play is something of a mystery, in fact, as in its longest incarnation (see p.62), it would have been near-impossible to perform before it became dark on all but a handful of days. This suggests that **cuts** to the script were probably a feature of theatrical life, though presumably the playwright would often have been involved with the process of trimming for performance. He may not have had the same luxury with **casting**, though in all likelihood a resident poet would have known who would take the main roles in a new play, as Shakespeare seems to have done with his star tragedian Richard Burbage.

Contexts

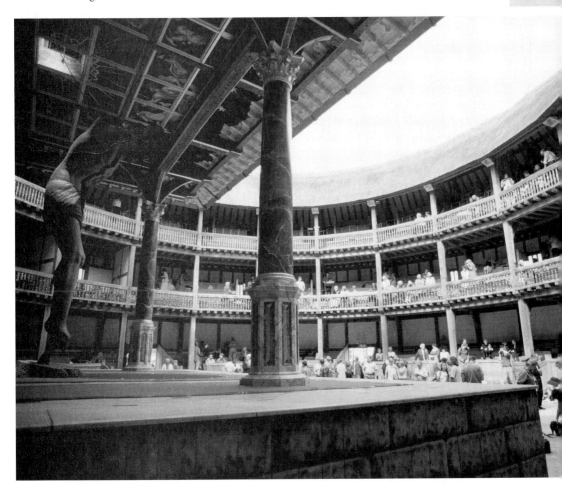

The reconstructed Bankside Globe was modelled using contemporary sources and painstakingly rebuilt with "original" materials. Fire regulations limit audiences to 1400, however – half the house Shakespeare might have hoped for.

477

The most obvious casting difference between Elizabethan practice and modern theatre was that companies were **all-male**; no women would act on the English public stage until after the Restoration, although they did so on the continent (see p.370). Boys took many of the female roles (there is some disagreement about what happened with older female characters), joining the companies young and staying with them until their voices broke – an event which often occurred later in the early modern period than it does now, perhaps as late as 16 or 17. Certain plays required plenty of extras, and there is some evidence that companies simply employed whichever boys they could find in non-speaking roles, luring them off the street with the promise of free admission.

## Plural playhouses

The Admiral's Men were seemingly irritated by the fact that their chief competitors had moved in to the Globe next door, and soon after Burbage and his company arrived on Bankside they upped sticks and moved – to Shoreditch. Edward Alleyn came out of retirement to lead them once more, leasing a plot and employing Peter Street to build a new house called the **Fortune**. Street had been the specialist carpenter who had moved the Globe, so it's not surprising that Alleyn commissioned a theatre very similar to that of their rivals – with the key difference that it was square rather than polygonal. It was slightly smaller, too, but the stage and other fittings were copied from those in the Globe. As a consequence it took Street only six months to get it up and running, and Alleyn's company were performing there by autumn 1600. The Fortune would stay in use past Alleyn's second and final retirement, but in the end he outlived it – the house burnt down in December 1621.

The Admiral's Men's departure did not leave their rivals with a monopoly on Bankside, however. Four years before the Globe appeared there, a goldsmith and minor court official named **Francis Langley** had bought a plot to the west end of Bankside and erected a theatre there that he called the **Swan**. Langley's sole connection with Shakespeare was an attempt to sue him in 1596, and it appears that the Chamberlain's Men never played there. Instead companies including the Earl of Pembroke's Men appeared there – unluckily, as it turned out, because after their performance of Jonson and Nashe's scandalous *Isle of Dogs* in 1597 the theatre was shut down by the authorities. When it reopened, a hoaxer named **Richard Vennar** conned an audience into paying for a non-existent show (one featuring women, no less), and though he managed to flee, the disgruntled punters took out their frustration on the building and destroyed much of its fabric.

The Swan's chief interest for theatre historians is a sketch of the building made soon after it opened by a Dutch scholar named **Johannes de Witt**. The original drawing has since disappeared – a copy by his friend **Arend van Buchell** is all that survives – and, though it is the only contemporaneous illustration of an Elizabethan playhouse's interior, it remains hotly contentious. While the basic details make sense, De Witt depicts a round building (the Globe and others like it were polygonal) and one in which the area under the stage seems open to the audience. There are only two stage doors, not three (no discovery space), and the "aloft" area, if it exists, appears not to be in use. Even more perplexing is De Witt's assertion in his notes that the Swan was built "out of a mass of flint stones", which seems highly unlikely.

Although Shakespeare is not known to have had personal dealings with them, two other later playhouses deserve mention, one in Bankside, the other north of the river. The first was the **Hope**, built by Edward Alleyn and Philip Henslowe near the Swan and replacing the old Paris Garden bear-baiting arena. Similar in design to the Fortune, it was completed in 1614. The other theatre, the **Red Bull**, had been converted from the remnants of a Clerkenwell inn ten years earlier. It lasted until the closure of the theatres in 1642, and even beyond, being employed by **Thomas Killigrew** for performances soon after the Restoration (although Pepys gave the house a damning review and Killigrew's company left for more commodious premises as soon as possible).

De Witt's drawing of the Swan, copied by a friend, is the only surviving image of an Elizabethan playhouse from an audience perspective –
apparently sketched mid-performance, and with the theatre's features helpfully labelled.

## Royal Shakespeare

The **Royal Shakespeare Company** can sometimes seem like a permanent part of the British cultural landscape (too much so, say its detractors), but in its present form it's less than a half-century old. It was the brainchild of artistic director **Peter Hall**, who had been involved with productions at Stratford's Shakespeare Memorial Theatre since 1957. Despite the theatre's many successes under its postwar artistic director, **Anthony Quayle**, Hall came to the conclusion that the theatre's management needed a serious overhaul if it was to survive. Inspired by continental models, Hall proposed a permanent company of actors tied to stable three-year contracts, based in Stratford but with a regular London home at the Aldwych. Most impressively, Hall also secured dramatically increased state funding via the newly forged Arts Council – and in 1961 the RSC was born.

Its first years were every bit as radical and exciting as Hall had planned. In addition to committing his company to the performance of new work, Hall commissioned directors willing to take the RSC in radical new directions. **Peter Brook**'s austere *King Lear* from 1962 immediately made waves (see p.180), and a year later *The Wars of the Roses*, a co-production of the English histories by Hall and **John Barton**, came close to defining a house style, with hard-hitting Brechtian theatre designed to leave Stratford audiences stunned in their seats. With the RSC boosted by cash injections from a newly elected Labour government, Hall's 1965 *Hamlet* (see p.75) located the *Zeitgeist* even more precisely, presenting David Warner's Prince as an undergraduate too cynical about politics to care.

Following Hall's withdrawal from the RSC in 1968, **Trevor Nunn** steered the company into its next phase, which saw the opening of a studio space called **The Other Place** (originally little more than a shed down the road from the main house) that debuted exciting and vivid productions of, among much else, his 1976 *Macbeth*. The company remained innovative, drawing in new directorial talent and continued to expand its operations when **Terry Hands** became involved in running things in 1978. In 1977 the RSC began touring to Newcastle; in 1982 it moved into a permanent London base at the **Barbican**; and four years later it opened yet another new Stratford theatre, a Jacobean-style playhouse called the **Swan**. Over all this time it has continued to be a hothouse for young stars, while each year the company maintains a company of seventy-plus actors plus many support staff. Its current turnover exceeds £32 million, around half of which is funded by the British taxpayer, and an estimated 850,000 visitors saw productions in 2001–02.

But at present big questions hang over the RSC's future. One perennial problem concerns the 1932 Shakespeare Memorial Theatre, whose Art Deco architecture came under fire from its opening night (locally it's known as the "jam factory") and still attracts criticism for its barn-like acoustics and poor sight lines. Another concerns the fact that actors are increasingly unwilling to be tied down to long-term contracts. In 2001 director **Adrian Noble** announced an ambitious plan to solve these difficulties at a stroke by abandoning old-style contracts, cutting ties from the Barbican and levelling the old RST to construct a £100 million "theatre village" designed by **Erick Van Egeraat** on the banks of the Avon. But after months of wrangling Noble departed in 2002, leaving the RSC at something approaching crisis-point. Although under his successor **Michael Boyd** (an RSC stalwart) the company has regained some of its artistic confidence, for the next few years – with no permanent London base, a sizeable financial deficit and the builders in at Stratford – the future looks uncertain.

# The private sector

During their years at the Globe the Chamberlain's Men played at a variety of other venues – among them law inns (as with *Twelfth Night* in 1602) and for other select gatherings. The "old" **Banqueting House** at Whitehall – "old" because after it burnt down in 1619 James I commissioned Inigo Jones to replace it with a sumptuous neoclassical edifice – was a familiar venue for Shakespeare's company; after James's accession in 1603 they played there more frequently than ever before. Though they had not been allowed in, the **Blackfriars**

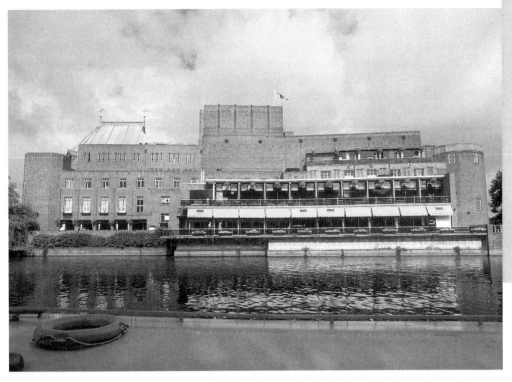

Built as a replacement for the Victorian original, burnt down in 1926, Elisabeth Scott's Art Deco Stratford Memorial Theatre opened six years later.

playhouse, too, had not been gathering dust: Henry Evans's children's troupe had been using it for their infamous – and increasingly scandalous – performances of satires. But when the boys acted **George Chapman**'s politically risqué *The Conspiracy and Tragedy of Charles, Duke of Byron* in March 1608, they went too far: James I took offence and shut them down.

The boys' downfall was a unique opportunity for Burbage, Shakespeare and their company. Recently adopted by James as the **King's Men**, they had acquired a powerful patron and at long last taking possession of the Blackfriars seemed possible. They moved in immediately, though because of more plague closures were unable to present their first plays there until the winter of 1609. But when they did, they acquired the holy grail of Jacobethan companies – an indoor winter venue. A Blackfriars address also offered enviable social cachet, and in a smaller, "private" theatre, with space for perhaps only 500 patrons, the company could charge higher ticket prices and attract a more exclusive clientele. Though they did not abandon the Globe – indeed, when it burnt down during a performance of *Henry VIII* in 1613 (see p.137), they rebuilt it on a grander scale than before – the King's Men began to move upmarket.

Little evidence survives of the Blackfriars interior, converted from part of the old Dominican monastery that gave the site its name, as the complex was demolished in 1655, thirteen years after the theatres had been closed by the Republican government. Nevertheless it's possible to make some educated guesses, not least about **dimensions**, which were considerably smaller than in the amphitheatres: around 20 metres (66ft) in length and 14m (46ft) wide, with the theatre itself rectangular rather than polygonal in shape. There will have been a **tiring house**, as before, though the **stage** was probably a lot smaller than at the Globe, edged with rails and cramped by audiences' boxes on both sides. These restrictions will have had a huge impact on **staging**, presumably ruling out all but the most small-scale swordfights and shrinking the number of personnel that could appear at any one time. Shakespeare's late plays especially make much of this intimacy – the bedroom scene in *Cymbeline* is a classic example – though they did continue to be performed at the Globe too. *Cymbeline* might also have been the play in which Shakespeare first used one of the most controversial props of his time. This took the form of a table with two head-shaped holes cut in it and called for two actors; one poked his head out, while the other's body lay on top with his head poking down and out of sight. The effect was of a decapitated body, though how convincing it was we can only guess.

In addition to seats in front of the stage equivalent to modern-day "stalls") there were perhaps three audience **galleries** at the Blackfriars, though some spectators got intimate with the action by paying a premium to sit on the stage itself – presumably desiring to lord it over their social inferiors as much as watch the play. As in a modern theatre, audiences paid more the closer they sat, and starting prices were in any case up to six times higher than at the Globe. The resources of the stage itself – trap doors, aloft and discovery spaces – would presumably have resembled the open-air theatres, and it is almost certain that flights would have been possible here. **Music** was a notable feature of the Blackfriars: the theatre's instrumentalists were famous, often accompanying theatrical special effects such as the use of the flight machine, and in fact the theatre was refitted to include a purpose-built music space on a balcony above the stage.

The last great innovation was, of course, **lighting**, though as yet this was unsophisticated, and many plays continued to be performed in the afternoons to make the most of daylight from the theatre's windows. Candles would have lit the space, but as the wicks had to be trimmed regularly in order to prevent them smoking, plays began to have several **intervals** during which the musicians would play. The upshot was that Shakespeare's late works began to use a five-act structure with breaks in between, his earlier plays being adapted to suit the new arrangements.

This brief survey of the theatrical environment in which Shakespeare and his colleagues worked can do little more than outline some facts (and guesses) about the busiest and most exciting period the English stage has probably ever seen. Within three decades of his death, the Jacobethan public theatre would be gone, banned in 1642 by Parliament because it offered "spectacles of pleasure, too commonly expressing lascivious mirth and levity", unfitting for a country then tearing itself apart through war. When drama re-emerged following the Restoration of Charles II, Shakespeare and his contemporaries would have had difficulty recognizing it: women were on the stage, theatrical technology was astounding, courtly fashions held sway. The era of adaptation and innovation was about to commence.

# Reading on

## The Shakespearean Stage: 1574–1642
**Andrew Gurr; rev. 1992** ▷ Cambridge UP

Andrew Gurr is the leading authority on the theatre of Shakespeare's time, and *The Shakespearean Stage* has remained the most useful textbook on the subject ever since it appeared in 1970. Though its slightly haphazard organization has remained, the book has been revised twice, a fact which is also its key attraction: Gurr is alert to the ephemerality of the Jacobethan theatrical enterprise as well as the ways in which

scholarship has evolved in response to new research (such as the chance discovery of the Rose Theatre's foundations in 1989). The same author's *Playgoing in Shakespeare's London* (rev. 1996) is an offshoot from the final chapter of the earlier book, and remains the fullest available survey of social attitudes to playing and playgoing.

## Shakespeare's Professional Career
**Peter Thomson; 1992** ▷ Canto

Instead of being a conventional biography or standard theatre history, *Shakespeare's Professional Career* takes the insights achieved by people like Andrew Gurr and puts them into practice. Practicality is in fact very much the focus of Peter

Thomson's lively and compact book, which looks at how Shakespeare's job developed and altered over the two and a half decades during which he wrote for the London stage. It provides a vivid sense of the rewards (few) and difficulties (numerous) of a career in the early modern theatrical business – all the way from patrons and printing to plague, punishment and Puritans. Much more dated, but nevertheless something of a classic, is Muriel Bradbrook's *The Rise of the Common Player* (1964).

## The Globe Restored
### C. Walter Hodges; rev. 1968 ▷ Oxford UP [o/p]

*The Globe Restored* unites Walter Hodges's considerable scholarship with his skills as an artist (although many illustrations here are taken from a variety of historical sources too) to provide an enthusiastic introduction to the stages that Shakespeare wrote for – and even if some of his conclusions have been superseded by subsequent research, this book remains a fine survey. Other titles by Hodges are also worth

seeking out: his more recent *Enter the Whole Army* (1999) brings together a range of his illustrations for the New Cambridge Shakespeare and looks pragmatically at how staging might have operated on a play-by-play basis.

## Shakespeare's Globe Rebuilt
### J.R. Mulryne & Margaret Shewring (eds); 1997 ▷ Cambridge UP

In 1995, on a London site next to the Thames, an Elizabethan-style theatre (nearly completed) opened its doors for the first time. The project was the rebuilt Globe, a painstaking reconstruction of the first London house to bear the name and the inspiration of the actor and director Sam Wanamaker, who fought tirelessly to get it completed but didn't live to see the opening season. *Shakespeare's Globe Rebuilt*, a collection of essays by many of those involved – from academic advisers to the master carpenter – retells the story with plentiful illustrations and lavish detail.

# Shakespeare's canon

For a collection of plays sometimes imagined to have been inscribed on tablets of stone, Shakespeare's canon has proved remarkably unstable in the years since his death. Though John Heminges and Henry Condell, actor-editors of the all-important **First Folio** (1623), have earned the gratitude of countless Shakespearians for reproducing seventeen texts – among them *The Two Gentlemen*, *Julius Caesar*, *Twelfth Night*, *Macbeth* and *The Tempest* – which would otherwise have disappeared, their decision to include just 36 plays (and no poems) has since proved massively controversial. Put simply, no one is entirely sure how much Shakespeare actually wrote, or even when he wrote it.

## Labour's lost?

In addition to Heminges and Condell's 36, two plays from other sources, **Pericles** and **The Two Noble Kinsmen**, are usually regarded as canonical, alongside the three major narrative poems and the Sonnets. Added to these are a pair of missing plays, **Cardenio** and **Love's Labour's Won** (see p.186), and the collaborative drama **Sir Thomas More**, which Shakespeare probably contributed to (see p.140). But a number of other works published during this time boast that they too were authored by Shakespeare. In addition to several minor poems, no less than six Jacobethan plays made this claim – *Locrine* (1595), *Thomas Lord Cromwell* (1602), *The London Prodigal* (first attributed in 1605), *The Puritan* (1607), *A Yorkshire Tragedy* (1608) and *Sir John Oldcastle* (1619) – and others followed before the century was out. Though their Shakespearian connections are vigorously defended in some quarters, most authorities believe the playwright never went near them, and they are most often grouped together as **"apocrypha"**.

Opinions change, however. A few years ago, the press was abuzz with news of a work entitled **A Funeral Elegy**, printed in February 1612 in order to rescue the reputation of a Devon man named William Peter, who had been stabbed in the back of the head a few weeks earlier during a drunken brawl. Computer-aided statistical analysis supposedly confirmed that the title-page's enigmatic "W. S." was in fact Shakespeare, and some scholars staked their reputations on the attribution – despite the fact that the poem lamented a man with no evident connection to the playwright, and appeared during weeks when Shakespeare was far more likely to have been attending to another funeral, that of his brother Gilbert. Most readers find the *Elegy* cringingly bad, too, and all but impossible to imagine as the product of Shakespeare's maturity. Sceptics have recently been gaining the upper hand: a recent writer on the subject, Brian Vickers, suggests that a more plausible author might be **John Ford**, whose later works include *'Tis Pity She's a Whore* (c.1628), and who sometimes imitated Shakespeare's style.

The hottest current contender for inclusion in the canon is the history play **Edward III**, which retells the exploits – both martial and marital – of the illustrious King Edward, his son the Black Prince (Richard II's grandfather and father) and their dual conquest of the French. In 1998 the play was included in the New Cambridge series in an excellent edition by Giorgio Melchiori, and was performed during 2003 by the Royal Shakespeare Company. The RSC christened *Edward III* "a new play by Shakespeare", and many critics agree that he wrote at least some of it, perhaps during the plague closures of 1592–94, but they disagree

## Minding your Fs and Qs

If you do even a little exploration in the texts of Shakespeare, sooner or later you'll have to confront the jargon – the F1s and Q4s, the ominous-sounding "foul papers" and "bad quartos". Although these terms sound cryptic and puzzling, in fact they're easy to decode.

A logical place to start is **F**, bibliographical shorthand for **Folio**. Folios (from the Latin *folium*, "leaf") are books made up of paper folded in half, creating two leaves or four pages. In the early modern publishing trade large folio volumes were grand and prestigious products, typically reserved for serious works of history, theology and philosophy such as the multi-million-word *Chronicles* (1587) edited by Raphael Holinshed, and Sir Walter Ralegh's *History of the World* (1614). Folios were not, in other words, for ephemera like playscripts – mere "tinsel", as one printer memorably described it.

Never a man to be cowed by convention, **Ben Jonson** bucked the trend in 1616 by publishing what he entitled (with typical audacity) his *Works*, the first time that plays had been printed in folio. And when the actors **John Heminges** and **Henry Condell** came to collect Shakespeare's plays after his death the same year, they decided on the same red-carpet treatment for their friend and colleague. What they produced in 1623 – a handsome volume entitled *Mr. William Shakespeares Comedies, Histories, & Tragedies* – has become known as the **First Folio**, or **F1** for short, and it's the earliest and most important collected edition of his work. The book was so popular that a corrected version was printed nine years later (**F2**), another appeared in 1663 (**F3**), one more in 1685 (**F4**), and a last edition (**F5**) made it in around 1700. Shakespeare used the word "folio" only once, in the mouth of Don Armado, *Love's Labour's Lost*'s preening show-off, so he would probably have been bemused by – or quietly amused at – such unremitting demand for his printed words.

**Quartos** (**Q**) were cheaper and smaller. Their name refers to the paper being folded in half twice to make four leaves (eight pages), which then had to be cut along one edge. Individual plays were printed in quarto, and around half of Shakespeare's appeared in this way while he was alive, with the narrative poems being printed in the even smaller **octavo** (**O**) format (in which the pages are folded three times). On the whole, however, printers preferred not to publish plays, which – then as now – didn't sell particularly well: gossipy broadsheets, almanacs, Bibles and sermons generally did a much better trade.

Each play was owned by the company that commissioned and performed it, or the publisher that arranged for it to be printed: writers exercised no legal rights over their text, and what we now call "intellectual copyright" did not emerge until nearly a century after Shakespeare's death. Partly as a consequence, in the publishing industry of the time there appears to have been a trade in **pirated copy**, where play texts were stolen and printed illicitly. So while some of Shakespeare's plays were printed from his **foul papers** (working manuscripts) or **fair copies** (transcripts), sometimes referred to as **"good quartos"**, others were not authorized and are frequently inaccurate – those so-called **"bad quartos"**. In recent years, however, many scholars have argued that such value-obsessed labels miss the point, and that many apparently "bad" (or "short") texts reveal things more polished or approved versions do not.

fiercely about the extent of his involvement – which might range from one scene to a whole act. Despite a fine production, the RSC failed to convince the sceptics, and *The Rough Guide to Shakespeare* doesn't (yet) include a drama that has still to have much of a life on stage.

## About time

**Dating** Shakespeare's output is still difficult and involves interpreting a complex set of data – records of performance, early texts, availability of sources, allusions by other writers, linguistic evidence and many more. The picture is further complicated by the likelihood that playscripts were performed or published in multiple versions, while the Sonnets may have been written over a fourteen-year period. If one thing is clear, it's that Shakespeare didn't have the luxury of dividing his time neatly – he was most likely juggling several projects at once, writing and revising almost continually for 25 industrious years.

This table follows the order suggested by Stanley Wells and Gary Taylor in *William Shakespeare: A Textual Companion* (1987), currently published by Norton; for more specific detail on each work, refer to the relevant chapter earlier in this book.

| [late 1580s–early 1590s] | The Two Gentlemen of Verona |
| | The Taming of the Shrew |
| | Henry VI Part II |
| | Henry VI Part III |
| | Henry VI Part I |
| | Titus Andronicus |
| | Richard III |
| | Venus and Adonis |
| [mid-1590s] | The Rape of Lucrece |
| | The Comedy of Errors |
| | Love's Labour's Lost |
| | Richard II |
| | Romeo and Juliet |
| | A Midsummer Night's Dream |
| | King John |
| [late 1590s] | The Merchant of Venice |
| | Henry IV Part I |
| | The Merry Wives of Windsor |
| | Henry IV Part II |
| | Much Ado About Nothing |
| | Henry V |
| | Julius Caesar |
| [early 1600s] | As You Like It |
| | Hamlet |
| | Twelfth Night |
| | Troilus and Cressida |
| | Sonnets and A Lover's Complaint |
| | Sir Thomas More [?never performed] |
| | Measure for Measure |
| [mid-1600s] | Othello |
| | All's Well That Ends Well |
| | Timon of Athens |
| | King Lear |
| | Macbeth |
| | Antony and Cleopatra |
| [late 1600s] | Pericles |
| | Coriolanus |
| | The Winter's Tale |
| [early 1610s] | Cymbeline |
| | The Tempest |
| | Henry VIII |
| | Cardenio [lost play] |
| | The Two Noble Kinsmen |

# Books

S omeone once estimated that a new book on Shakespeare is published every single day. The following clutch of titles isn't intended as a shopping list, still less is it complete (there are entire tomes dedicated to Shakespeare bibliography). It's merely meant to illuminate some pathways. Critical recommendations on specific works and themes are covered in the first portions of this book; this fills some remaining gaps with what is hopefully a lively mix of standard reference works and other reading. Classifying books on the Bard is a complex exercise, so it's worth skimming through the whole lot to find titles that interest you.

## Complete editions

Though the individual editions recommended earlier on are the best to go for if you're interested in, or studying, a particular play/poem in any depth, you'll soon want a *Complete Works*. Each is designed to provide an internally consistent approach to editing the text, which is why critical studies covering more than one work are frequently keyed to one of the standard editions (as this book is to the Oxford *Complete Works*). But each has its quirks, and none is ideal.

### Mr William Shakespeares Comedies, Histories, and Tragedies
**Charlton Hinman (ed.); rev. 1996** ▷ Norton

A pristine copy of the 1623 First Folio recently fetched over $4 million at auction, such is the fetish for a book produced seven years after Shakespeare's death and in which he had no involvement. *The Norton Facsimile* enables you to own a copy without mortgaging your grandparents, and to inspect the famous Droeshout portrait at close quarters. Other facsimiles are available, but this contains the standardized "Through Line Numbers" (line numbers without the act/scene divisions imposed by later editors) and uses several versions of the Folio to achieve a "perfect" copy. Understanding how a seventeenth-century book works is, as it happens, an education in itself.

### The Norton Shakespeare
**Stephen Greenblatt et al (eds); 1997** ▷ Norton

Recognizing that the *Oxford Shakespeare* (see below) lacked the reader-friendly equipment of other major editions and unwilling to invest in a revision, OUP gave permission to a team led by Stephen Greenblatt to use that text and construct a "full" edition around it. The result is extremely hefty (3420 Bible-thin pages), complete with one-word glosses; fuller notes at the bottom of each page; critical intros; and numerous appendices. The whole enterprise reads like an advertisement for new historicism – there's much on "Otherness" and censorship, for instance – and the hyper-student-friendly editorial matter may jar for some. But *Norton* offers many of the positive aspects of

*Oxford*, while taking a less take-it-or-leave-it approach: so you'll find a *Hamlet* which unites (by clever use of typography) the two main texts without conflating them; and no fewer than three *Lear*s.

### The Oxford Shakespeare
**Stanley Wells & Gary Taylor (eds); 1988** ▷ Oxford UP

The Oxford *Complete Works* caused a furore when it appeared, by rejecting a tradition of editing which strove to recreate "original" texts as Shakespeare "intended" them to exist. Pointing out that Shakespeare did not work as a published writer but as a full-time actor and director, the Oxford editors argue that each text has its own local value, as well as its own relationship with forces other than that of the playwright. Thus they generally print the "theatrical" versions of texts, producing two versions of *King Lear*, a play which seems to have been revised post-performance; *2 Henry VI* and others are known by their original titles; and they suggest that Shakespeare worked with collaborators as a matter of course. Two caveats: the editors are more creative than some would prefer; and editorial matter is scanty (there are no on-page notes). An old-spelling edition is also available.

### The Riverside Shakespeare (second edition)
**G. Blakemore Evans et al (eds); rev. 1997**
▷ Houghton Mifflin

Though not as textually avant-garde as *Oxford* and *Norton*, and utilizing traditions of scholarship now regarded with suspicion by some, *Riverside* may be more useful for many readers (and is the basis for Spevack's *Concordance*; see p.490). For a start it has explanatory notes and glosses, and each work is preceded by a sizeable critical essay – Anne Barton's introductions to the comedies and Frank Kermode's

to the major tragedies are particularly recommended. Then there is the rest: lavish colour sections; essays on critical trends and stage history; documents relating to Shakespeare; texts for the possibly apocryphal *Edward III* and "A Funeral Elegy".

## General reference and companions

With Shakespeare popping up on school and university curricula across the globe, it's little surprise that publishers have fought hard to get a foothold in the lucrative student market. The three books recommended below offer various different formats, and should also interest readers simply wanting to get hold of more information on the Bard.

### The Cambridge Companion to Shakespeare
**Margreta de Grazia & Stanley Wells (eds); 2001** ▷ Cambridge UP

If you're looking for someone to accompany your Shakespeare experience, Oxford and Cambridge have the market sewn up – with Stanley Wells playing for both teams. Actually the books are quite different: whereas *Oxford* (see below) is a large A–Z, the recently updated *Cambridge Companion* is a collection of undergraduate-level essays (19 in this volume) by academic contributors on various themes. It's something of a dream team: Anne Barton on "The London scene"; Ania Loomba on "Outsiders in Shakespeare's England", Michael Dobson on "Shakespeare on the page and stage"; John Kerrigan on the poems. They're mostly level-headed and spryly written, and the book contains a useful section on further reading.

### A Companion to Shakespeare
**David Scott Kastan; 1997** ▷ Blackwell

David Scott Kastan, general editor of the Arden Shakespeare, brings together an excellent collection of new essays in this chunky Blackwell *Companion*, all distinguished by their original

approach. At opposite ends of the volume David Bevington explores what Shakespeare might have been like as a man and Michael Bristol launches a hard-nosed (but not unsympathetic) examination of "Shakespeare: The Myth"; in between lie pieces grouped under "Living" (social and geographical history), "Reading" (education and detail on sources), "Writing" (contexts for Shakespeare's output), "Playing" (the Jacobethan theatre industry) and "Printing" (the realities of publication). All are readable, many are excellent, some are unique.

### The Oxford Companion to Shakespeare
**Michael Dobson & Stanley Wells (eds); 2001** ▷ Oxford UP

It is difficult to believe that a book like this didn't exist until a few years ago, so handy has this large and generously illustrated encyclopedia proved. Intelligent short articles from a wide range of contributors are punctuated by longer pieces on individual works, providing brief accounts of texts, sources, performance and critical history, and a scene-by-scene synopsis for each. It is a bold venture – and despite being on one level a supreme example of bardolatry, the *Companion* never takes itself too seriously.

## Shakespeare on stage and film

Shakespeare was an actor as well as a playwright for most of his working life, and so from the very first days his plays' performances have been integral to their development. Even so, looking at the stage histories of individual works – such as those provided earlier in this book – can provide a slightly fragmented impression of overall historical trends. Several books specifically to do with Shakespeare and his contemporaneous theatrical environment are recommended in the "Shakespeare's Stages" section on p.482. If you want to find out more about individual actors and directors, the *Oxford Companion* (see above) has many brief articles and suggestions for further reading.

### The Cambridge Companion to Shakespeare on Film
**Russell Jackson (ed.); 2000** ▷ Cambridge UP

Jackson's selection is an adroit and concise collection of essays, if occasionally a little too prone to film-studies jargon. It's well positioned to discuss the second renaissance in

Shakespeare film-making in addition to previous trends. The *Companion* is divided into four sections: "Adaptation and its Contexts"; a group of essays on genres and specific plays; pieces on specific directors (Olivier, Welles, Kozintsev, Zeffirelli and Branagh); and finally what the book calls "critical issues", including those involving Shakespeare's women on film and "filming the supernatural".

### The Oxford Illustrated History of Shakespeare on Stage
**Jonathan Bate & Russell Jackson (eds); rev. 2001**
▷ Oxford UP

Originally published as *Shakespeare: An illustrated stage history* but recently repackaged in paperback, this book is for the moment the definitive work in the area, though its rival *The Cambridge Companion to Shakespeare on Stage* (2002) also packs much of international interest into an essay-based format. Copious pictures make the Oxford book a pleasure to browse, and its contributors' consistently pithy and humane comments are always worth attending to. It also contains a detailed list of further reading on specific theatrical periods.

### Shakespeare from Betterton to Irving
**George C. Odell; 1920** ▷ Ayer Company

Odell's goliath two-volume study takes on over two centuries of staging, offering a compendious history of the changes and chances in Shakespearian theatre from the Restoration stage of Thomas Betterton to that of his Victorian successor Henry Irving. It's an elderly book and the style can veer towards the orotund, yet there's so much here – all the way from lighting and physical staging to commentary on individual acting styles, with plentiful eyewitness detail.

### Shakespeare in Performance
**Keith Parsons & Pamela Mason (eds); 1995**
▷ Salamander

*Shakespeare in Performance* glossily collects nearly four hundred images of influential productions, with a particular slant towards twentieth-century British stagings. It's a visual banquet, and the text, which provides potted stage histories linked thematically to the plays, is also good. Arguably the RSC is slightly over-represented, but that's a minor quibble when what's here is so good – it's revelatory to see images of historic productions you've only ever read about.

### Shakespeare in Production
**Various authors** ▷ Cambridge UP

Not one book, but an ever-expanding series. CUP is picking up where earlier publishers left off, producing a hugely useful collection of individual plays with on-page notes, using nuggets from promptbooks and reviews to piece together a strong sense of how different productions have handled the

text. Each also provides a detailed narrative stage history and illustrations, as well as tables saying who did what when. At the time of writing there are eleven titles available, including *Antony and Cleopatra, Hamlet, Henry V, The Merchant of Venice, Romeo and Juliet* and *The Tempest*; see their website at www.cambridge.org for more.

### Shakespeare in the Theatre
**Stanley Wells (ed.); 1997** ▷ Oxford UP

*Shakespeare in the Theatre* does exactly what it claims to and takes us inside the numerous theatres in which Shakespeare has been performed, from the age of Betterton up to a recent RSC *Comedy of Errors*. It's a collection of valuable snippets and reviews from such varied commentators as William Hazlitt, George Bernard Shaw and Virginia Woolf, and is as much a study of changing ways of reviewing performances as anything else. For all that, it provides a heady whiff of the greasepaint and a sense of what it might have been like to bitch with Evelyn Waugh over an interval drink.

### Shakespeare on Screen
**Daniel Rosenthal; 2000** ▷ Hamlyn / Sterling [o/p]

Academic essays such as those in Jackson's *Cambridge Companion* are all very well, but sooner or later they'll have you pining for the popcorn and the silver screen. If video doesn't fill the gap and your nearest art cinema is a continent away, perhaps a coffee-table tome such as this will suffice. Large-format, expensively illustrated, nicely printed and unquestionably specialist, it's little surprise that *Shakespeare on Screen* has already gone out of print, but it should be relatively easy to locate nonetheless.

### Shakespeare on the Stage
**Robert Speaight; 1973** ▷ Collins / Little, Brown [o/p]

Out of print but much worth tracking down, Speaight's "illustrated history" follows the story of performance from one Shakespearian titan (Richard Burbage) to another (Laurence Olivier), spending a refreshing amount of time out of Britain along the way. Speaight was a fine actor himself, and he handles his subject adroitly, giving a real sense of evolving trends in performance while providing plenty of colour on specific theatrical productions and their designs.

## Shakespeare's life and context

The paucity of hard evidence about Shakespeare's precise cultural milieu can make it rewarding to do some wider background reading, in addition to the conventional biographies recommended on p.467. Generalized historical and cultural studies have not been thick on the ground in recent years, perhaps because historians, more interested in particularities than ever, have fought shy of attempting to summarize entire swathes of Jacobethan life. The books recommended below deal – highly selectively – with aspects of this topic.

## A Companion to English Renaissance Literature and Culture
**Michael Hattaway (ed.); 2000** ▷ Blackwell

There are no fewer than sixty essays here from a large team of writers – many of them acknowledged leaders in their field – covering what seems to be everything from the Reformation (Patrick Collinson), travel writing (Peter Womack) and education (Jean R. Brink) to sexuality (James Knowles) and rhetoric (Marion Trousdale). The vast span of topics sometimes threatens to overwhelm the essay-based format, although Diana E. Henderson, to cite one example, does rather wellto introduce "love poetry" in just thirteen pages. On the whole, though, this is a usefully provocative volume that never threatens to become worthy.

## The Elizabethan World Picture
**E.M.W. Tillyard; 1943** ▷ Pimlico / Vintage

Though regarded with a mixture of scorn and horror by some, this remains an intriguing (and attractively slender) introduction to the period. Outlining a thesis grounded a few years later in *Shakespeare's History Plays* (see p.112), Tillyard suggests that the static elements in Elizabethan thought, which he terms the "chain of being" – order and degree, focused on God and mirrored by the four elements and the celestial spheres – ultimately governed Elizabethan society. At best this argument is selective, at worst it's hokum, but there is still much to learn – if you can stomach Tillyard's rather paternalistic tone.

## Religion and the Decline of Magic
**Keith Thomas; 1971** ▷ Penguin / Macmillan

Thomas's study still remains one of the finest and most suggestive introductions to a period which was less modern in many respects than we sometimes think. Thomas accomplishes the rather impressive feat of providing a lucid and illuminating guide to a dimly lit, sometimes little-documented world: one in which astrology, witchcraft, ghosts and fairies still loomed large in everyday life. It's fascinating both in terms of social history and anthropology, and has a very pragmatic resonance for students of Shakespeare, in whose work ghosts and the supernatural are frequently present.

## Shakespeare: The poet and his plays
**Stanley Wells; rev. 1997** ▷ Methuen

Originally published as *Shakespeare: A dramatic life*, this is now in its second incarnation. It's not a biography as such, but rather a critical introduction of each group of works in the order that they were probably written. The enviable breadth of Wells's experience makes this a pleasant (if slightly indulgent) read, spiced with detail from the countless productions he's witnessed and including an eloquent chapter on why Shakespeare should be seen as well as read.

## This Stage-Play World
**Julia Briggs; rev. 1997** ▷ Oxford UP

Julia Briggs explains that she wrote *This Stage-Play World* for English students interested in knowing more about the historical period as well as historians wanting access to literary texts. In truth anyone can learn something from this sophisticated and readable study of what is sometimes called the "high renaissance", the period from the second decade of Elizabeth I's reign to the last years of her successor James. Shakespeare's working life is neatly bounded by those dates, but there's also plenty on Bacon, Spenser, Marlowe, Dekker, Sidney and many others, making this the best introduction to Shakespeare's contemporaries as well as the cultural environment that nourished them all.

# Language and concordances

As a craftsman of the English language, Shakespeare has no peer – which is why it's worth exploring a little further into the words he used and had access to, and why he selected the ones he did. Words he didn't have access to were no barrier: he came up with over six hundred coinages in all, many of them drawn from Latin. The recommendations below cover both reference companions and discursive introductions.

## A Glossary of Shakespeare's Sexual Language
**Gordon Williams; 1997** ▷ Athlone Press

Contrary to what self-appointed guardians of public morality would have you believe, sex really does permeate the work of England's National Poet, and nowhere is that more evident than in his willingness to pun on sexual slang. Eric Partridge's *Shakespeare's Bawdy* (1955) was for generations the standard work in the area and still remains an engaging read, though Gordon Williams's more upfront and complete work provides a fine replacement. Also worth dipping into is the hugely fun *Shakespeare's Insults* (1991), edited by Wayne F. Hill and Cynthia J. Öttchen, which offers advice on Shakespeare-style abuse as well as a play-by-play compendium of insults.

## The Harvard Concordance to Shakespeare
**Marvin Spevack (ed.); 1973** ▷ Harvard UP [o/p]

Large (and pricey) enough in its present form, the single-volume *Harvard Concordance* is actually a redaction of Spevack's nine-part monster (1968–80), which contains all sorts of fascinatingly geeky extras. The slimmer version is certainly more useable, though, and will accommodate all but the most esoteric needs. It includes every single one of the 30,000-odd words Shakespeare used (with obvious functional exceptions) and the phrases in which they appear, with full references to locations in *The Riverside Shakespeare* (see p.487). Spevack also includes data on each word's absolute frequency, its relative frequency, and how often it appears in verse and prose.

### The Oxford English Dictionary (second edition)
**J.A. Simpson & E.S.C. Weiner (eds); rev. 1989**
▷ Oxford UP

Few will consider buying this new (the full-price twenty-volume edition is £2000/$3500), though it is also available via Web subscription, as a CD-ROM and in one-volume micrographic form for far less. It is unique: a historical dictionary that attempts to document not only the first citations of words but their meandering progress through the language from Anglo-Saxon texts to the near present day. Look up a wonderfully rich Shakespearian word such as "measure", and you're rewarded with an engrossing essay over three densely packed pages. Its grand flaw – that the Bard is cited with unrepresentative frequency – is only a blessing for Shakespeare scholars.

### Shakespeare and the Arts of Language
**Russ McDonald; 2001** ▷ Oxford UP

The last few years have been a boom time for Shakespearian reference works, spearheaded by OUP, whose selection of pocket-sized "Shakespeare Topics" books includes some real gems. One such is Russ McDonald's slim but juicy *Shakespeare and the Arts of Language*, which takes a less tendentious – if less complete – approach than Kermode's *Shakespeare's Language* and comes up with some real insights about the playwright (there's not much on the poems) and his linguistic toolkits. Very informative and a delight to read.

### A Shakespeare Glossary
**C.T. Onions, rev. Robert D. Eagleson; 1986**
▷ Oxford UP

Although to an extent succeeded by the Crystals' recent (and larger) *Shakespeare's Words* (see below), it would be churlish not to mention this long-standing favourite. Onions was one of the original editors of the *Oxford English Dictionary* and took it upon himself to produce a small guide to elucidate problematic and arcane words in Shakespeare, which first appeared in 1911 and was immediately popular because of the clarity of its explanations and range of reference. If you're interested in how the words fit together, Onions can be supported with another trusty Victorian reference, E.A. Abbot's *Shakespearian Grammar* (1869).

### Shakespeare's Language
**Frank Kermode; 2000** ▷ Penguin

Frank Kermode likes clarity – he attacks the playwright for unnecessarily "terse" moments in *All's Well*, criticizes *Cymbeline* for being "over-worked" – and is thus sometimes unwilling to hear that peculiarly Shakespearian trick of using words to frustrate as well as communicate, even for characters (like Macbeth) speaking to no one but themselves. But he is genuinely enthusiastic about language, as well as insightful about it, and if nothing else this book will make you listen and read more attentively.

### Shakespeare's Words
**David & Ben Crystal; 2002** ▷ Penguin

*Shakespeare's Words* is primarily a Shakespearian glossary, referring to the works and cross-checked with the *Oxford English Dictionary* (see above). As such its usefulness extends beyond being a replacement for C.T. Onions's standard *Shakespeare Glossary*: it can be employed as a stop-gap concordance, and in addition contains lists of names, synopses and engaging boxes on such topics as "Exclamations" and "Sounds". The only disappointment in this admirably clear book is that the Crystals didn't key everything to a standard *Complete Works*, such as Oxford or Riverside, but instead used Penguin's patchy New Shakespeare editions.

# Sources and influences

It can be a surprise to learn how much Shakespeare depended on sources and analogues for his plays and poems – all the way from sensationalist romances to serious tomes such as Holinshed's *Chronicles* and Plutarch's *Lives*. In addition to listing the key work in the field, Bullough's *Narrative and Dramatic Sources of Shakespeare*, we also review several other studies and modern editions containing some of Shakespeare's favourite reading. Single editions of the plays and poems often contain excerpts from key sources; see the individual reviews earlier in this book for details.

## Narrative and Dramatic Sources of Shakespeare
**G. Bullough (ed.); 1957–75** ▷ Routledge / Columbia UP [o/p]

Over a period of nearly thirty years, Geoffrey Bullough scoured libraries and archives for everything Shakespeare had access to when writing his plays and poems – and came up with some items he possibly didn't, classified here as "analogues". The result is the most complete collection of sources available, usually printed in generous excerpts with plentiful commentary. The series as a whole takes up eight volumes covering various groups of work (Roman plays, major tragedies and so on), and though out of print, it is possible to buy individual copies secondhand for around £20/$30 each. Bullough's tomes are supplemented by G. Harold Metz's *Sources of Four Plays Ascribed to Shakespeare* (1989), which covers *Edward III*, *Sir Thomas More*, *Cardenio* and *The Two Noble Kinsmen*.

## The Geneva Bible (1560 edition)
**Lloyd E. Berry (ed.); 1981** ▷ Wisconsin UP

So-called because of its translation into English by Protestant exiles based at the Academy there, the "Geneva" Bible, first published in 1560, was the version most Elizabethans grew up with. Shakespeare refers to it in the most varied (and oddest) of places, making it one of the major sources for his work (though his plays show that he was familiar with the 1568 Bishops' Bible too). Various facsimile editions of this hefty tome are available – none of them cheap – but an infinitely easier option is to get hold of the more familiar King James version, published a few years before Shakespeare's death, whose resonant, lapidary style owes much to Geneva.

## Ovid's Metamorphoses
**Arthur Golding (trans.); 1565** ▷ Penguin

Published in 2002, Madeleine Forey's edition of this Elizabethan classic is elegant, up to date and well presented, with endnotes and a handy glossary (Golding has a habit of relishing, sometimes inventing, colourful but obscure language). Golding himself is an engaging and never less than personable translator – it's Ovid, but he takes the task of "Englishing" his Latin very seriously. If what sometimes emerges struggles to sound as suave as you might expect, that's all part of the fun (and Shakespeare enjoyed it, too, as his version of "Pyramus and Thisbe" in *A Midsummer Night's Dream* shows; see p.237).

## The Riverside Chaucer
**Larry D. Benson et al (eds); 1987** ▷ Oxford UP / Houghton Mifflin

Although only the long and tragic poem *Troilus and Criseyde* and the "Knight's Tale" from *The Canterbury Tales* form large-scale sources (in *Troilus and Cressida*, the *Dream* and *The Two Noble*

*Kinsmen* respectively), we know that Shakespeare often turned to his copy of Chaucer, probably in Francis Thynne's sixteenth-century edition. While the relevant excerpts from these and other Chaucerian classics are readily available in Bullough, it's worth reading Chaucer in a deluxe (but not expensive) edition such as this one, with a full range of notes and appendices and so on.

## Shakespeare's English Kings
**Peter Saccio; rev. 2000** ▷ Oxford UP

It's been said that the English learn their theology from Milton and their history from Shakespeare. The perils of doing the latter are suggested by *Shakespeare's English Kings*, which provides plenty of facts to counterbalance Shakespeare's numerous excursions from historical truth. A manageable and useful book that offers plentiful detail from the chronicle sources, while also providing a convincing survey of each Shakespearian royal; only its slightly juiceless prose lets it down.

## Shakespeare's Plutarch
**T.J.B. Spencer (ed.); 1964** ▷ Penguin [o/p]

Spencer's anthology of Plutarch's *Parallel Lives*, which excerpts parts of Sir Thomas North's 1579 translation, is the most helpful book of its kind, containing the big four lives – Julius Caesar, Brutus, Antony and Coriolanus – that Shakespeare used intensively for his Roman dramas. Spencer helpfully prints snippets from the plays alongside relevant passages. Long out of print, but it's relatively easy to find a decent copy of this paperback on the secondhand market. If you can't, Wordsworth Classics has a more recent North's *Selected Lives* (1998).

## Shakespere's Smalle Latin and Lesse Greeke
**T.W. Baldwin; 1947** ▷ Illinois UP [o/p]

Not for novices and only available secondhand, Baldwin's monumental work is nevertheless the most complete survey of Shakespeare's education. It takes at face value Ben Jonson's snooty observation that Shakespeare had only "small Latin and less Greek" and demonstrates that, in fact, he had more than many modern-day classicists. Fascinating if somewhat suffocating.

## The Sources of Shakespeare's Plays
**Kenneth Muir; 1977** ▷ Methuen [o/p]

If you can't get access to Bullough and simply want an introduction to Shakespeare's sources and what he did to them, Muir's clear and concise survey takes you through the major texts for each play (but no poems) and explains what the playwright took from – and added to – his reading. Muir's eye is constantly on dramatic and literary effect, so this book also provokes thought about how someone like Shakespeare went about the business of writing; and the image that comes through is of an attentive, observant reader whose eye was caught by the most suggestively tiny of details.

# Shakespeare's work and texts

In the sections on Shakespeare's life and stages (see p.467 and p.482) we've already recommend studies that deal with the main fabric of Shakespeare's biography and work. But in recent years, encouraged by new scholarly interest in the materiality of texts and publishing practice, attention has focused on the environment in which he and his contemporaries actually wrote. Below you'll find reviews of some engaging academic studies that approach the issue from different perspectives – rehearsal, publication and revision.

## Rehearsal from Shakespeare to Sheridan
**Tiffany Stern; 2000** ▷ Oxford UP

Interpreting the term "rehearsal" broadly, Stern's enlightening study investigates how rehearsals were handled over two centuries of theatrical history – not just as preparations for performance, but try-outs of new work and even actors' private study. Stern's most contentious point is that players during this period were working exclusively from "parts" containing only their lines and had no idea about the rest of the play until it was performed. As the experimental work of Stern's uncle Patrick Tucker – who presents plays with Elizabethan-style rehearsal schedules – shows, if this lack of preparation is true, Burbage and his ilk must have been finer actors than we can imagine.

## Shakespeare and the New Bibliography
**F.P. Wilson, rev. Helen Gardner; 1970** ▷ Oxford UP
[o/p]

In a general sense, the so-called "new bibliography" of the mid-twentieth century steered a path through the chaotic conditions of early English publishing by attempting to reconstruct single, "ideal" texts as the author might have intended them to see print – a formidable task, particularly for Shakespeare (see p.485). Nowadays editors tend to scorn such ambitions, but even so *Shakespeare and the New Bibliography* is a lucid exposition of the subject, and an excellent introduction to the study of printed texts in the Renaissance.

## Shakespeare as Literary Dramatist
**Lukas Erne; 2003** ▷ Cambridge UP

Two interlocking theories about Shakespeare – that he was careless about publication during his lifetime and (narrative poems aside) wrote for the theatre rather than print – have been received wisdom for a few generations. Lukas Erne's provocative new book attempts to overturn convention by showing not merely that play-texts had a higher status in the booksellers' market than has often been supposed, but that Shakespeare managed his published image with some care. His further thesis, that the long and "literary" Folio texts represent scripts consciously worked up for publication, has caused controversy, but nevertheless makes for interesting reading.

## Shakespeare at Work
**John Jones; 1995** ▷ Oxford UP

Jones's account is a fascinating and lively study of what you might call Shakespeare the tinkerer – a playwright who can never resist playing around with his text, the kind of man we glimpse in the one surviving manuscript in his own hand, *The Book of Sir Thomas More* (see p.140), only too ready to cross things out and try another option. *Sir Thomas More* forms Jones's first chapter, and other plays – *Hamlet*, *Lear* and *Othello* – are a major part of the book, which tries to suggest that variant texts as they survive contain clues to Shakespeare's habits of revision and reworking. Some of this rests on shaky ground, but *Shakespeare at Work* makes for convincing reading.

## Shakespeare, Co-Author
**Brian Vickers; 2003** ▷ Cambridge UP

Brian Vickers's latest work heads purposefully into the much-fought-over territory of what actually Shakespeare wrote on his own. According to Vickers, it's less than many of us think: included in the "co-author" corpus are, he argues, *Titus Andronicus*, *Timon of Athens* and *Pericles*, alongside the usually acknowledged *Henry VIII* and *Noble Kinsmen*. What makes this approach persuasive is that it isn't based on snobbery or how "good" a work seems to be: Vickers spends time re-exploring the notion of what authorship implied both in theory and practice for Shakespeare and his contemporaries, and also provides a good introduction to the textual analysis that leads him to these conclusions.

## Unediting the Renaissance
**Leah S. Marcus; 1996** ▷ Routledge

The thrust of *Unediting the Renaissance* is that what kind of text you're reading matters a great deal: even supposedly minor issues can completely alter the way that people perform and write about Shakespeare. Marcus's initial illustration of this is Sycorax, the witch in *The Tempest* who is "blew ey'd" in the Folio text; despite the obvious enough meaning (that her eyes are blue), Marcus reveals how generations of editors have tried to claim almost everything else – that her eyelids are blue as a sign of pregnancy, that she has blackened eyes, that "blew" isn't really blue – in an attempt to water down Shakespeare's striking but shocking image of an Algerian witch with glittering cobalt eyes. A tiny instance, but suggestive and provocative – as indeed is the rest of the book.

# Shakespeare, music and art

Shakespeare's influence on visual and musical art has been every bit as profound as on the written word. As well as the many songs in his plays, set to music by succeeding generations of composers, nearly all the plays themselves have been turned into operas – notably the three by Verdi. Painters have been no less fired up by his writings, whether as recorders of the great performances of an age – as in the work of Zoffany – or as inspired interpreters in their own right – as in the case of Fuseli, Blake, Delacroix and Millais.

## Shakespeare and the Artist
### W. Moelwyn Merchant; 1959 ▷ Oxford UP [o/p]

Shakespeare's theatre employed a cornucopia of visual symbols, all the way from lavish costumes to the richly decorated stage canopy (and even the printed borders of texts). Merchant insightfully weaves together what evidence exists for the relationship between the visual arts and the Elizabethan theatre, and moves forward into an energetic history of the artist-as-designer, from Inigo Jones to John Piper. The second part of the book concentrates on specific examples – a post-Poussin illustration of *Coriolanus* by Kirkall (1709), John Runciman's *King Lear in the Storm* (1767) and the designs for Charles Kean's *Winter's Tale* (1856) among them.

## Shakespeare and the Dance
### Alan Brissenden; 1981 ▷ Dance Books / Prometheus

Alan Brissenden's *Shakespeare and the Dance* suggests among much else that dance was utterly central to the social fabric of Shakespeare's era. Building on an elegant chapter covering "Dance and the Elizabethans", which adopts some similar positions on harmony and order to E.M.W. Tillyard (see p.490), Brissenden then goes on to suggest ways in which dance in Shakespeare's plays offers an image of lively movement within overall cohesion: initially in the marriages of the early and middle-period comedies, then in the masques and pageants of his late work. The author even finds time for the (ostensibly dance-free) histories, presenting a subtle analysis of their imagistic concern with dance-like movement.

## Shakespeare and Music
### E.W. Naylor; rev. 1931 ▷ Best Books / AMS Press [o/p]

Although seventy-odd years old (even in its revised edition) and hard to find, Naylor's work is still a classic short introduction to the field. Well-known as a musical scholar, Naylor achieves a great amount in a short space: he outlines some of the social function of music in the Elizabethan era; introduces instruments and technical terms; contextualizes musical education; describes the differences separating communal song-making and dancing from musical "performance"; and even finds time to comment on musical stage directions. All this is closely tied to the plays with textual examples where appropriate, and everything is neatly done.

## Shakespeare in Art
### Jane Martineau (ed.); 2003 ▷ Merrell

Built around the excellent Dulwich Picture Gallery/Ferrara Arte Spa exhibition, this catalogue is gorgeously produced and contains much more than the curators had space to put on show. It discusses the whole range of visual representations of Shakespeare's work in the eighteenth and nineteenth centuries, including performer portraits, the eighteenth-century print market, the influence of Boydell's Shakespeare Gallery, and the set designs of the nineteenth-century Grieve Family. Plus, of course, the many pictures painted for exhibition, all lovingly presented and extensively contextualized.

## Shakespeare in Music
### Phyllis Hartnoll (ed.); 1964 ▷ Macmillan [o/p]

Still the most helpful single collection despite its date, *Shakespeare in Music* offers contributions from such specialists in the field as John Stevens (who provides a brilliant introductory essay reconstructing Shakespeare's musical environment), Charles Cudworth (writing on settings of the songs, 1660–1960) and Roger Fiske ("Shakespeare in the concert hall", a lively if somewhat tendentious essay that gets as far as Prokofiev). The book closes with a useful – if obviously not up-to-date – catalogue of musical works.

## A Shakespeare Music Catalogue
### Bryan N.S. Gooch & David Thatcher (eds); 1991 ▷ Oxford UP

This monumental five-volume resource attempts the ambitious task of listing every single musical composition related to or inspired by Shakespeare. The focus is on art music – operas, ballets, orchestral works and so on – but even so the editors find space to cram in details of incidental music and songs. Volume 5 may be of most interest to non-specialist readers who can afford it (at about two-thirds the price of the others, it's still around £60/$100 new): it contains useful articles on topics including Shakespeare's knowledge of music and his choice of titles.

## The Vocal Songs in the Plays of Shakespeare
### Peter J. Seng; 1967 ▷ Harvard UP [o/p]

The most complete study of a fascinating area, *The Vocal Songs in the Plays of Shakespeare* lists each lyric in the plays in old-spelling texts and gives plentiful information on each – general commentary, textual commentary, a description of its dramatic function and details of what music the song was originally set to (if any). Easier to get hold of, if less detailed, is Ross W. Duffin's *Shakespeare's Songbook* (2004), which has the nifty advantage of including an audio CD containing decent (if slightly earnest) performances of the songs.

# Critical trends

Individual works of criticism from all walks of life are recommended earlier in the book with reference to specific plays and poems (though most will have links to other works). But if you'd like to find out about some overall trends, ranging from Romanticism to post-colonialism, the works listed below offer some pointers – most are anthologies.

## A Feminist Companion to Shakespeare
**Dympna Callaghan (ed.); 2000** ▷ Blackwell

Including work by a number of well-known contributors – among them Juliet Dusinberre, one of the first critics to apply the "f"-word to Shakespeare with any seriousness – this collection of essays mounts an impassioned rearguard action on the notion that in recent years feminist critics have simply run out of steam. They haven't, says Callaghan, and moreover we need feminism now more than ever. The book helpfully covers the history of feminist criticism before moving off in more esoteric directions; not every essay is of equal quality (and some are considerably less well balanced than others), but all show that the movement continues to innovate and agitate within academia, as outside it.

## Johnson on Shakespeare
**Bertrand H. Bronson & Jean O'Meara (eds); 1986** ▷ Yale UP [o/p]

Among eighteenth-century critics Samuel Johnson was the most brilliant, able to distil views shared by his age and society yet make them his own. His largest contribution to Shakespeare scholarship was the monumental 1765 edition of the plays, the *Preface* to which remains perhaps the most lucid statement of its kind ever written. In it, Johnson's famous insistence that it is nonsense to claim (as Voltaire and other critics did) that Shakespeare's plays were jumbled and chaotic, rings true even now. Despite his distaste for Shakespeare's less moralistic moments and over-ingenious wordplay, Johnson is always an insightful critic, and this valuable collection brings together the *Preface* and the earlier *Proposals for Printing … the Dramatic Works of William Shakespeare* (1756) with the editor's numerous comments on specific moments in the plays, both textual and dramatic.

## Post-colonial Shakespeares
**Ania Loomba & Martin Orkin (eds); 1998** ▷ Routledge

It's the emphasis on plurality and contingency that makes this anthology so worth reading, and which enables it to escape beyond well-worn commentary on *Othello* and *The Tempest*. In Margo Hendricks's essay describing the 1996 Johannesburg conference on which the book is based we realize not merely that there are many different ways of approaching Shakespeare in many different cultural contexts, but that this matters a great deal. Kim F. Hall's "Literary whiteness in Shakespeare's Sonnets" is involving and surprising, and Michael Neill's "Post-colonial Shakespeare? Writing away from the centre" raises a sardonic eyebrow in the direction of the whole enterprise – while also suggesting some convincing ways in which it has meaning.

## Reinventing Shakespeare
**Gary Taylor; 1989** ▷ Oxford UP [o/p]

Gary Taylor knows plenty about reworking the Bard, having ruffled many feathers with his involvement with the *Oxford Shakespeare* (see p.487), an edition that restored to the canon the poem "Shall I die?", an attribution still resisted by many. This book is subtitled a "cultural history from the Restoration to the present day" and takes a view of Shakespeare's engagement with varied historical periods which is as combative (and occasionally facetious) as much of Taylor's other writing. Terrific fun to read.

## The Romantics on Shakespeare
**Jonathan Bate; 1992** ▷ Penguin [o/p]

Bate's anthology covers a solid chunk of one of the most exciting periods in Shakespeare appreciation. In this hefty paperback (571 pages) you'll find sizeable gobbets from contributors including Goethe, Schlegel, Hugo, Coleridge and Hazlitt – showing, as much as anything else, that by the late eighteenth and early nineteenth centuries Shakespeare had become a pan-European intellectual figure. If you feel like reading more from Coleridge, particularly his engaging marginalia, try R.A. Foakes's *Coleridge's Criticism of Shakespeare* (1989), which includes nearly everything of interest.

## Shakespeare and the Question of Theory
**Patricia Parker & Geoffrey Hartman (eds); 1985** ▷ Routledge

In the heady days of the mid-1980s essay collections appeared bearing fierce titles like *Political Shakespeare* and *Alternative Shakespeares*, all committed to annihilating dead-white-male readings of Shakespeare with brave new methods and theories (many imported from France and the US). *Shakespeare and the Question of Theory* is probably the scariest of the lot, but contains much work of interest and value, grouping separate essays under headings including "Language, rhetoric, deconstruction" and "Politics, economy, history". The book concludes with three essays on *Hamlet*, the most questioning play of all.

### Shakespeare Criticism in the Twentieth Century
**Michael Taylor; 2001** ▷ Oxford UP

Taylor's admirably slim book digests some stodgy fare well: he races through all the major critical debates over the past century, detailing their key exponents and signature works, quoting extensively, and highlighting the insights and limitations opened up by each. Probably the best introduction for beginners – or indeed anyone wanting to see wood rather than trees.

### Shakespeare's Lives
**Samuel Schoenbaum; rev. 1991** ▷ Oxford UP [o/p]

The great insight offered by *Shakespeare's Lives* is that what

people have written about the poet's life forms an uncanny obverse of what they think about his work. Shakespeare was applauded for his untutored wisdom by Johnson, lauded as a solitary hero by Coleridge and subject to endless conspiracy theories in the more suspicious reaches of the nineteenth century. Schoenbaum lollops freely across the lot, drawing together a lively narrative of Shakespearian life-writing from the moment the man was buried until the late twentieth century. The author's superlative scorn for scholarship he doesn't like is one of the book's most winning features.

### William Shakespeare: The critical heritage
**Brian Vickers (ed.); 6 vols, 1974–81** ▷ Routledge [o/p]

If you fancy getting more of a hold on the topic than a small study like Michael Taylor's allows, Vickers's six-volume beast will certainly show you the way. It contains lashings of criticism from all corners of the Shakespearian galaxy, all the way from (Margaret) Cavendish to Coleridge. Each volume covers a span of near enough a half-century, reaching from 1623 to 1801, and is able because of its size to quote at length.

## Shakespeare periodicals and journals

Reviews of major works on Shakespeare often make the mainstream press, and scholarly titles are frequently reviewed in the *Times Literary Supplement* and, less regularly, the *New York Review of Books* and the *London Review of Books* (see p.506 for their websites). But the journals listed below make a policy of catching pretty much everything Shakespearian in addition to carrying scholarly articles from the vanguard of research, so they're a good place to go if you want to find out what academics are debating at the moment.

### Shakespeare Quarterly
**Various editors; 1950–present** ▷ Folger

*Shakespeare Quarterly* has expanded immensely in the last few decades to cover not just standard fodder like special articles and book reviews, but scholarly exchanges and appraisals of Shakespearian performances across the globe. Like the Washington-based Folger Library, which publishes the journal, it's an entirely admirable, somewhat plush and enviably well-resourced American institution, and attracts high-calibre contributors. The *Quarterly* also publishes the annual *World Shakespeare Bibliography*, which attempts the remorseless task of tracking what's been published in the area that year.

### Shakespeare Studies
**J. Leeds Barroll (ed.); 1965–present** ▷ Farleigh Dickinson UP

Thirty years old in 2005, *Shakespeare Studies* has become an engaging and interesting annual forum for Shakespearian debate, one able to offer distinctive contributions (predominantly US-based) to the scholarly field. A few years

ago this saw the editors introduce "review articles", which identify and discuss recent critical trends and build round-table debate around it – so, for instance, a recent edition saw pieces focusing on theatre in the 1580s, while a later volume concentrated on "material culture" in the Renaissance (from texts to textiles).

### Shakespeare Survey
**Various editors; 1948–present** ▷ Cambridge UP

The brainchild of great Shakespearian scholar Allardyce Nicoll, *Shakespeare Survey* was set up as a British-based journal that would cover not only academic and critical work but pay close heed to Shakespeare in performance, something confirmed by its ties with what was then the Shakespeare Memorial Theatre (now the Royal Shakespeare Theatre and Company). The format has remained consistent over the years: each annual volume has a specified topic (among them "Shakespeare in his Own Age", "Characterization in Shakespeare" and "Shakespeare and Sexuality") with various essays tied to it, some one-off pieces, and reviews of productions in the UK and occasionally elsewhere.

# Reading even further

It's been the aim of this list to cover books that might be most immediately helpful to most readers, but – inevitably – it can only do so much. The bibliographies below contain many more suggestions for reading, and they should help you to chase down exactly what you're after, whether you know it yet or not …

## Garland Shakespeare Bibliographies
**William Godshalk (gen. ed.); 1980–** ▷ Garland

In addition to producing an excellent series of *Critical Essays* anthologies for individual plays, Garland also publishes a unique selection of in-depth bibliographies, again on a play-by-play basis. While these titles will be too specialized for many, they're an unparalleled reference if you want to dig deep into reading on a particular work or get a sense of what's around. Both full-length books and articles are reviewed, in areas including criticism, sources, textual history, music and stage/screen spin-offs; detailed one-paragraph articles describe each. To date some eleven plays or groups of plays have received this red-carpet treatment, but more are promised.

## Shakespeare: A bibliographical guide
**Stanley Wells (ed.); 1990** ▷ Oxford UP [o/p]

All the major companions to Shakespeare (see p.488) offer some suggestions for general bibliography, but Stanley Wells's contributors in this invaluable *Bibliographical Guide* helpfully recommend detailed reading for each and every play as well as putting that reading in context. The only problem is that the 1990s have been one of the busiest decades for Shakespeare publishing ever, so this guide really could do with an overhaul.

# Websites

W elcome to one of the busiest – and most useful – areas for Shakespeare studies. As with so many other things, the Web has revolutionized the process of finding out about Shakespeare: nowadays you can research Hamlet's motivations, check a quote, watch video footage of influential interpretations, try out your theories on a customized discussion group, find out some answers, read reviews of current productions, book tickets online – or just simply order the DVD to watch at your leisure. And all without straying from your Internet connection. This directory creams the best of what's currently available, but the Internet, like the universe, is continuously expanding, so keep your eyes peeled – perhaps at one of the online Shakespeare gateways (lists of interesting websites) listed below.

## Shakespeare gateways

Also sometimes called "portals" in Net-speak, these are websites about websites, offering lists of links put together and recommended by human beings rather than search-engine programs. Though if already you know what you're after it might be best to skip these and head to the destinations listed later on, these sites make it easy to browse – and marvel at the sheer amount of – Shakespearian content available online. They're a great way to get started. Another (constantly updated) option is to use a Web directory such as the Google Directory (dir.google.com) and drill down through its listings to find what you want.

### Internet Shakespeare Editions

ise.uvic.ca

Supported by the University of Victoria, the stated aim of Internet Shakespeare Editions is to create reliable and scholarly texts native to a Web environment. So far they've reached *Cymbeline, Romeo and Juliet, Troilus and Cressida* and some of the poems, but ISE is richer than just this, truly earning it gateway status: the list of Shakespeare sites compiled by supremo Michael Best is reason enough for visiting. At the moment it's something of a skeleton but has grand plans for the future, and its intelligent and thoughtful discussion documents on what the Web can do for Shakespeare give a taste of what's to come.

### Mr William Shakespeare and the Internet

shakespeare.palomar.edu

One of the best online Shakespeare resources around, Terry Gray's Mr William Shakespeare and the Internet must be high up the list of Shakespearian Web wonders. Not only terrifically comprehensive (covering all the major bases, from biographical and theatrical work to hand-picked texts), it's also

brilliantly annotated and laid out, making it ideal as a starting point – but one you'll come back to again and again. Compare Ken Bugajski's Shakespeare Web Links (www-english .tamu.edu/wsb/links.html) and the list at the German Shakespeare Society (see below).

### Sh:in:E – Shakespeare in Europe

www.unibas.ch/shine

An elegantly organized metasite, Shakespeare in Europe springs from an educational philosophy which promotes cultural cross-pollination – the Bard being selected because of his unique international appeal. (In an intriguing survey published here, Shakespeare featured as the most popular writer in France, Spain, Italy and Germany – though those surveyed were forbidden from voting for writers from their own country.) There are plenty of good sites recommended on these pages, and Sh:in:E's affiliation with the University of Basel links it to diverse academic content too.

### Touchstone

www.touchstone.bham.ac.uk

Touchstone is like a British equivalent of Sh:in:E, a newly

available research tool linking scholarly resources in the UK with those further afield, all based at Birmingham University. Its coverage is enviable, bringing together such things as a centralized catalogue for Shakespearian library resources, databases of British Shakespeare performances (Traffic of the Stage falls under the same umbrella; see p.503), links to global Shakespeare organizations and listings of scholarly and educational events.

## Shopping for Shakespeare

One of the purposes of this *Rough Guide* is to offer suggestions on what to purchase across a range of different media, so below we recommend some of the best and easiest ways to get your hands on exactly what you want – not always as easy as it may sound, with many Shakespeare-related products counting as specialist interest. But with these sites you should be able to track down even the most recondite recommendation. And if you fancy liberating your just-read tome and sharing it with the world at large, try Bookcrossing (www.bookcrossing.com) ...

### Amazon
www.amazon.com [.co.uk, .de., .jp, .fr, etc]

If you've been on the Web you're unlikely to have missed the gargantuan Amazon, which started off as a not-so-humble bookseller in the mid-1990s and now stocks products from gardening equipment to jewellery. Nevertheless books still account for a core component of their trade, and they have one of the fullest catalogues around – tap in the title of something published back in the 1960s, say, and it's likely to come up as easily as a paperback printed last spring. Helpful in this regard is their teamwork with secondhand partners, which lets you search through the main catalogue and order an out-of-print title from an affiliated retailer. Amazon's various country-specific sites do a brisk trade, so it's worth tracking down your local one first (the British Amazon.co.uk even has a Shakespeare Store).

### Abebooks
www.abebooks.com

If Amazon doesn't come up with the goods – likely if the book you're after is out of print – you may be best trying a specialist rare book website. Abebooks is probably the most impressive, renowned for its extensive network of affiliate booksellers across the globe, all accessible within a few clicks from the main search page: simply type in the title you want and a list of bookshops with relevant secondhand stock will rapidly appear. They provide detail about the condition of items, and if you have any further queries you can simply give the bookshop a call yourself. Also recommended is Alibris (www.alibris.com), who handle films and music too.

If neither Amazon nor Abebooks does the job, it's worth trawling through local booksellers (long lists at www.bookweb.org/bookstores in the US and www.books.co.uk in the UK):

| | |
|---|---|
| **Barnes & Noble** | www.barnesandnoble.com |
| **Blackwell's** | www.blackwell.co.uk |
| **Borders** | www.borders.com |
| **BOL** | www.bol.com |
| **Bookzone** | www.bookzone.co.uk |
| **Buy.com** | www.buy.com |
| **Country Books** | www.countrybookshop.co.uk |
| **Foyles** | www.foyles.co.uk |
| **Waterstone's** | www.waterstones.co.uk |
| **WHSmith** | www.bookshop.co.uk |

Another option is to search many stores simultaneously for availability and price by going to:

| | |
|---|---|
| **AddAll** | www.addall.com |
| **BookBrain** | www.bookbrain.co.uk |

## Ambrose Video

www.ambrosevideo.com

Educational publishers Ambrose feature in this list mainly because they've been responsible for rereleasing the complete set of BBC Shakespeare titles (recommended at certain points in this book; see individual play chapters for details) on DVD and VHS. These products are aimed at the US educational market rather than consumers and are correspondingly expensive – around $100 for individual titles in either format, though shop around for better deals.

## Audible.com

www.audible.com

Audible.com offers a neat idea that might appeal if you're fed up of ordering discs and tapes through the mail: computer software that converts audiobooks into digital files which can then be downloaded to your computer – and from there you can do what you want with them, whether that's shifting them to a portable MP3 player, sending them elsewhere or simply listening on your machine. You buy titles in the standard way (but with significant reductions), and the files you order are yours to keep.

## Moviemail [UK]

www.moviemail-online.co.uk

This mail-order supplier not only stocks art-house and world cinema titles, but follows up with some excellent prices. Set up in 1996 by film nut Carol Hunter, Moviemail has been expanding exponentially – recently into online rental – and

now offers thousands of hard-to-get titles, with their catalogue linked to the UK In-Print database, so you can see precisely what's available. And the Web interface, recently overhauled, is slick: you can browse not just by title and director but cast and geographical region too. They also do film rental (see below). See also Sendit.com (www.sendit.com), likewise based in the UK.

## Poor Yorick Shakespeare Catalogue

www.bardcentral.com

Really the first destination to check what's currently available in the field of Shakespeare media, and ideal for browsing Shakespeariana. Poor Yorick began life as an independent retailer based in Stratford, Ontario and migrated onto the Web, from where its founder, Tanya Gough, has been running an energetically updated database for over seven years. Coverage extends all the way from books and VHS/DVD to spoken word titles, soundtracks and Shakespeare for kids. Prices in US or Canadian dollars only, but they do ship internationally.

## Rob Wilton Theatricalia

www.phyllis.demon.co.uk/theatricalia

If you're at all interested in the history of the performing arts, Rob Wilton's online store is invaluable. Wilton stocks all manner of British theatre, music and opera programmes going back before World War I – you can get your hands on everything from a commemorative programme for Gielgud's celebrated 1930 *Hamlet* at the Old Vic to recent film memorabilia.

# Texts and concordances

Free online texts are an excellent quick fix: supremely handy for looking up quotations, saving you a trip to the library or the cost of a concordance (around £75/$100 for the latter at the time of writing). Despite the convenience – and it's undeniably easier to tap in a search term than thumb through a vast tome – any results should always be double-checked with a printed text if you're at all concerned about accuracy. Imperfect searching technology might also dampen your enthusiasm; if you're still stumped by the location of that mystery phrase after trying out this lot, it's always worth putting it in double-quotes and using a standard search engine such as Google (www.google.com).

## Open Source Shakespeare

www.opensourceshakespeare.com

New to the Net, but OSS is easily the most impressive free concordance we've come across – swift and seemingly accurate, and it contains the Sonnets and narrative poems too. The brainchild of US newspaperman Eric Johnson, the site is free from clunks and easy to use, the advanced search being particularly powerful. Texts are generally from that venerable Internet standard, the Moby Shakespeare, though a few are sourced from Project Gutenberg (there's no *Two Noble Kinsmen*, however). Even better for those of a techie disposition, its software runs on democratic open-source

principles and can even be built into other websites. Also recommended, but in development stage at the time of writing, is The Nameless Shakespeare (www.library .northwestern.edu/shakespeare), which promises to have more powerful search facilities than anything currently available.

## Oxford Shakespeare

www.bartleby.com/70

In case you're wondering, not the ultra-hip *Oxford Shakespeare* of 1988, but the more elderly incarnation of 1914 – so again no *Noble Kinsmen*. Haphazard search results might require some trawling, though the friendly interface makes it a doddle to use as an online text if that's what your after. All of Bartleby's other reference tools – from *Gray's Anatomy* to the works of Walt Whitman – are just a click away, and fully searchable.

### Project Gutenberg
www.gutenberg.net

The granddaddy of them all, Project Gutenberg has been putting copyright-free texts on the World Wide Web for what (in wired terms anyway) is ancient history – in fact since 1971, when its founder developed what we now know as "etexts" by sending a computerized US Declaration of Independence to some pals. Now Gutenberg has more than 10,000 ebooks online, all in low-tech, plain-text format so that as many people as possible have access. No frills, but that's the philosophy – you can either read these versions online or download the (super-tiny) files to your machine.

### Schoenberg Center for Electronic Text and Image
dewey.library.upenn.edu/sceti

With nearly every major research library in the world hurriedly

digitizing its collections and showcasing them online, there's never been a better time to get close to the holiest of holies, the 1623 First Folio. The University of Pennsylvania has come up with the glossiest version: an extensive collection of electronic Shakespeare editions residing in the Furness Library (see p.505), including a digital F1. You will need a broadband-speed connection to get the most out of it, though. Instead of gazing at lushly rendered images, if you'd rather browse (and search) text from the First Folio and early quartos laid out specially for the Web, the Electronic Text Center at the University of Virginia is terrific: etext.virginia.edu /shakespeare/folio

### Shakespeare Apocrypha
www.republicofheaven.org.uk /sh_apocrypha.htm

Does exactly what it claims to: brings together a list of all the plays that have ever been suggested as Shakespearian (all the way from *Noble Kinsmen* and *Pericles* to the wackier reaches of *George A Greene* and *Edmund Ironside*) and provides links to online texts, usually from Project Gutenberg. Unfussy and very helpful.

## Online DVD rental

The notion of renting DVDs through a website rather than via a bricks-and-mortar shop seems to have caught on in the last year or so, with even UK supermarket giant Tesco (www.tesco.com) recently getting in on the act. In theory it's a great idea – you're more likely to find the Shakespeare title you want from an online superstore than a corner-store – but it might be a while yet before you can taste a more varied menu than *Shakespeare in Love* and Baz Luhrmann's *Romeo+Juliet* (see p.313), partly because many Shakespeare titles still haven't made the leap to DVD.

### Love Film
www.lovefilm.com [UK]

Offering a good selection of art titles alongside standard Hollywood offerings, Love Film has got plenty going for it – including a great website that lets you browse for what you're after in an assortment of ways. Postage both ways is included in the price (around £10 per month at the time of writing), and you can hang onto discs as long as you like, with no late fees incurred. Moviemail (www.moviemail-online.co.uk), a

terrific mail-order store recommended above, also does UK rental.

### Netflix [US]
www.netflix.com

Working on a near-identical basis to Love Film, this US equivalent has been going since 1998 and comes recommended by nearly a million customers. They've got over 18,000 titles on offer and a flat subscription rate of $20 per month, for which you're able to order as many titles as you can bear to goggle at.

## Shakespeare theatres, companies and festivals

While Shakespeare can be – and, thankfully, is – performed anywhere from scout halls to factory floors, there are a number of theatres worldwide devoted to performing his plays and several Shakespeare festivals of international standing. So whether you want to nip to a production while you're in town or embark on a globetrotting tour of all the Stratfords in the world, research the options online. If you're simply interested in tracking what's on at the theatre centres of London's West End or Broadway, Official London Theatre (www.officiallondontheatre.co.uk) and Playbill (www.playbill.com) should do the trick, and they even have links so you can book tickets online. And for a full list of Shakespeare festivals worldwide, try Electronic Shakespeare (www.wfu.edu/~tedforrl/shakespeare).

## National Theatre, London

www.nt-online.org

Though its three theatres stage a wide range of plays, there have been many fine Shakespeare productions since the National Theatre first opened with *Hamlet*, starring Peter O'Toole, in 1963 (the website lists all subsequent Shakespeare stagings). The recent directorship of Nicholas Hytner has kept up the tradition, but given it a sharper edge. Recent highlights include a *Henry V* that drew parallels with the Iraq war (2003, see p.106), and a chillingly sleazy *Measure for Measure* in collaboration with Theatre de Complicite (2004).

## New York Shakespeare Festival

www.publictheater.org

Justly famous for its unique "Shakespeare in the Park" series, which runs every summer and attracts many thousands of spectators, Joe Papp's Public Theater began life in the 1950s as a workshop devoted to the Bard and has kept alive a strong Shakespearian tradition since. Many stars have graced its stage – James Earl Jones, Kevin Kline, Meryl Streep and Christopher Walken, among others – and the folk at the Public Theater continue to develop bright and interesting work.

## Oregon Shakespeare Festival

www.orshakes.org

In operation nearly nine months of the year (and it's been going nearly seventy), the OSF is the largest not-for-profit theatre organization in the US, with over 450 professional actors performing in its three houses at Ashland, Oregon. Repertoire is anchored in Shakespeare, naturally, but there's plenty else besides, both classic and contemporary – their 2004 season saw *Lear* and Lorraine Hansberry's *A Raisin in the Sun* rubbing shoulders with new writing from the likes of Frank Galati and Charlotte Jones.

## Royal Shakespeare Company

www.rsc.org.uk

One of the world's most famous classical companies has an excellent Web offering, allowing you to do all sorts of things: see what's on at Stratford, London or one of their UK (sometimes international) touring venues; buy tickets; look up the RSC's Web learning zone; or browse their extensive online archives (including photos from hundreds of historical productions). If you're planning a trip to the town, Stratford's web presence (www.stratford-upon-avon.co.uk) should provide some pointers – alternatively you could get the critical lowdown from *The Rough Guide to England*, freely online at: www.roughguides.com

## Shakespeare Festival of Canada

www.stratford-festival.on.ca

Based at the "other" Stratford – in fact Stratford, Ontario is just one of several in North America – the Canadian Shakespeare Festival has always been one of the most well-respected and artistically engaging set-ups of its kind in the world. Founded in the 1950s by a local journalist who decided that a gala devoted to Shakespeare was the best way for the town to stave off economic depression, the Festival has attracted a wealth of talent both international and home-grown, all eager to perform on Tanya Moiseiwitsch's famous open stage. Nowadays there's even a fringe.

## Shakespeare's Globe

www.shakespeares-globe.org

Though criticized by some as little more than a heritage tourist attraction when it opened in 1995, London's Bankside Globe (built just a few feet away from the site of the original) has proved to be very much more than that. It's true that productions can be patchy – not many Globe actors have the charisma and panache of its outgoing artistic director Mark Rylance – but at their best they provide unique insights into Shakespearian performance practice and involve the audience in a far more direct way than happens in more conventional spaces. Their website hasn't anything like the depth of content of other theatres', but there's enough here to tempt you into booking a visit.

## Shakespeare Theater, Washington DC

www.shakespearedc.org

Headed these days by internationally recognized artistic director Michael Kahn (a past head of Stratford, Connecticut), the Shakespeare Theater in the nation's capital was originally part of the Folger Library (see p.505), but split away in 1992 when it left to occupy the Lansburgh Theater in downtown DC. Generally regarded as one of the finest companies of its kind in the United States, the Shakespeare Theater has produced drama of international standing – most famously perhaps in 1997, when British director Jude Kelly presided over a "photonegative" production of *Othello* (see p.264). The company website is well maintained and contains plenty of detail on all their activities.

## Stratford Festival (Connecticut)

www.stratfordfestival.com

Not much going on at Stratford, CN at the time of writing (winter 2004): the theatre is closed for renovation and the State authorities are in the process of giving it back to the locals to run. Even so it's one of the most venerable and well-regarded of American Shakespeare festivals, and not just on the Northeast seaboard. It began life in 1951, built itself a permanent home a few years later and has become known for some excellent productions. Hopefully once things get going again that tradition will continue.

# Study guides & educational sites

There's lots of lowest-common-denominator Shakespearian content online, much of it catering for the market in homework hints and cheats. But if you know where to look there's some outstanding educational information out there, often served up attractively and with an eye to making learning as fun as possible. If none of the sites recommended below offers quite what you want, try combing reviews and recommendations at one of the big Shakespeare gateways (see p.498). And if you're looking for ideas on how to spice up your next English class, see what those folks at Cal Poly did on their big day out (cla.calpoly.edu/~smarx /Shakespeare/shakeswanton/shwanton.html).

## About Shakespeare
shakespeare.about.com

It's a sign that your subject has truly arrived on the Net when knowledge giants About.com begin to cover it. In these pages, authored by Amanda Mabillard (also the person behind Shakespeare Online.com), Shakespeare gets a typically thorough working over, with plenty of original, convincing articles, some fun diversions and links to useful sites elsewhere.

## Absolute Shakespeare
absoluteshakespeare.com

A handy and attractively built site, Absolute Shakespeare has won several awards for its content and layout. Here you'll find texts in easily browsable HMTL format, summaries and explanatory articles on some famous plays, excerpts from criticism by Coleridge and Hazlitt and plenty of Bardic trivia. The insights it offers aren't going to knock anyone's socks off, but this is a useful resource for first-timers nonetheless.

## The Globe: Then and Now
www.britannica.com/shakespeare

A typically impressive offering from info titans Britannica, this website commemorates the reconstruction of the London Globe. There's lots here (over 500 articles, in fact), all of it engaging and reliable – as you might expect, given that it was put together by well-respected Shakespeare academic David Bevington. In addition to information on the Globe itself, represented by animated digital views), there are biographies of Shakespeare and his contemporaries, information on the plays and some great "special features" – including a piece on Shakespeare and Opera supported by sound samples.

## OUP Shakespeare Centre
www.oup.co.uk/academic/humanities /literature/shakespeare

In recent years especially, Oxford University Press have become perhaps the foremost publisher of Shakespeare titles, and their various publications on the subject are brought together in this useful website. Though the content hasn't been refreshed for a while and at base it's promotional material, there are articles here from the likes of Stanley Wells (on the Oxford Shakespeare) and John Sutherland (on Shakespearian puzzles), as well as other stuff of interest. The OUP Reading Room (www.oup.co.uk/readingroom/literature) is also excellent: it provides tasters from recent titles, available as downloadable PDFs, so you can sample what's on the shelf at the moment.

## Shakespeare's Globe Research Database
www.rdg.ac.uk/globe

Though more scholarly in focus than other sites reviewed in this section, there's so much on offer here that anyone from schoolkids to professors could find something new. The site offers copious information on the sixteenth-century Globe (including archeological data and images taken from contemporary surveys by Hollar and Visscher) as well as its modern-day counterpart (there's loads here on the rebuilding project), and also a database of fascinating articles on performing Shakespeare from across the Web. If you're trying to find out details of a Shakespeare production that appeared anywhere in the UK after 1997, try the Shakespeare Institute's Traffic of the Stage database (www.is.bham.ac.uk /traffic).

## Shake Sphere
sites.micro-link.net/zekscrab

A US site aimed at schools, Shake Sphere brings nearly everything you want onto its extensive – and slightly daunting – front page, and is perhaps the best all-rounder in this category. There are essays on a wide range of topics (including one wittily comparing George W. Bush to Henry V), plot summaries and lists of characters for no fewer than 41 plays (*Edward III*, *Sir Thomas More* and *Cardenio* featuring too), study guides, glossaries of literary terms, biographies, texts – you name it. Reliable and intelligent, which is the best thing of all.

# Discussion groups

Feel the need to vent your opinions? To test-drive an extravagant new theory? Or simply to find out something from the experts? Then you might well be interested in that venerable Net concept, the online discussion group. Whether it's an old-style list, where subscribers communicate via email, or a newfangled Web-based forum, there's no better way to share Shakespearian news and views. Here are a brace of the best; you can track down others via a specialist gateway (see p.498).

## SHAKSPER

www.shaksper.net

The doyen of Shakespeare discussion groups, SHAKSPER is subscribed to by a large swathe of academics, experts and Bard enthusiasts – but even if you aren't admitted to join the party (applications to contribute are vetted by the moderator) every single thread is searchable on the Web, enabling you to comb the crop for whatever interests you most. Sanity sometimes gives way to fervour on SHAKSPER, but the standard of conversation is high, moderation is thoughtful and effective, and some genuinely interesting things get hammered out. Compare The Bard Online, a recently founded discussion group designed for graduate students but open to others; it's yet to get going properly at the time of writing (groups.yahoo.com/group/theBardonline).

## Shakespeare High

www.shakespearehigh.com

Aimed at a different target audience to SHAKSPER, Amy Ulen's impressive offering will suit high-schoolers across the globe as well as their teachers (there's a special "Faculty Lounge" to offer insight and support). At the heart of the site is the "Shakespeare High Cafeteria", a discussion zone allowing you to debate all sorts of interesting issues in a relaxed and inquisitive environment (hot topics at the time of writing include debates on Ariel's sexuality and a poll on Shakespeare's "greatest tragedy" with *Romeo and Juliet* and *Hamlet* currently neck-and-neck), but there are also links to fact-based educational resources. Only the editor's penchant for Shakespeare–*Star Trek* parallels might turn some surfers awry.

# The authorship debate

In common with most minority hobbies and conspiracy theories, the Internet has provided a cosy roost for devotees of the so-called "authorship debate" (see p.456), as the merest glance at an online directory will suggest. Despite the tangible air of derangement that attends most things in this area – and that goes for all sides of the argument – it can be intriguing to explore the options for yourself, and even to ask whether it really matters whether some of the greatest plays ever written were composed by a middle-class man from Stratford, or someone socially better connected. Even PBS's *Frontline* programme has expressed an interest (www.pbs.org/wgbh/pages/frontline/shakespeare).

## Shakespeare Oxford Society

www.shakespeare-oxford.com

Although better laid out than its Baconian adversary, the website of the Shakespeare Oxford Society – who suggest that Edward de Vere, Seventeenth Earl of Oxford, handed scripts to an actor called Shakespeare in order to preserve his courtly reputation – has significant mountains to climb. One is Oxford's surviving poems, which rarely rise above the level of doggerel; another is the fact that he died in 1604, well before about a third of the plays were written (including *The Tempest*, which is securely dated around 1610). Despite the yawning gaps in their case, though, the Oxonians scramble some precarious peaks with energy and occasional panache.

## Sir Francis Bacon's New Advancement of Learning

www.sirbacon.org

Behind the slightly lurid exterior lies one of the largest anti-Stratfordian sites on the Net, arguing that polymath Francis Bacon – a man whom everyone agrees to have been one of the great geniuses of his age (conspicuously unlike the Earl of Oxford) was behind Shakespeare. There's lots here, and it's not the easiest to browse through, but nevertheless it offers the sum total of Baconian arguments: if you're not persuaded by this, you won't be convinced by anything else.

### Shakespeare Authorship
shakespeareauthorship.com

A site "dedicated to the proposition that Shakespeare wrote Shakespeare": well-tempered and on the whole good-humoured, but nonetheless quite intent on its task. David Kathman marshals the standard arguments effectively, producing a range of bite-sized ripostes to every anti-Stratfordian suggestion under the sun, all linked to solid (if sometimes tendentious) scholarly foundations. Even super-sceptics might pause for thought.

# Libraries, organizations and other institutions

Many of the world's leading libraries contain work by Shakespeare, and a few are even built around his work. Some of these institutions have been at the forefront of Web presentation, offering sophisticated access to their enviable collections – particularly in the last few years, when new technology has made it easier than ever before to see digital texts and online exhibitions. We also include the sites of several Shakespeare-related organizations.

### British Library
www.bl.uk

The UK's national library has lots more than stuff from Britain's shores – among its "treasures" are Da Vinci's notebooks and a Chinese religious text that is the earliest printed book in the world. They have plenty of Shakespeare, too, even if you have to dig around the website to find it. And by that time you might have been distracted by some sumptuously presented digital collections including the Lindisfarne Gospels and Sultan Baybars' Qur'an – if you've got broadband, that is. The BL's recently overhauled master catalogue is easy accessible via the Web interface, and there are also plenty of online learning resources.

### Canadian Adaptations of Shakespeare
www.canadianshakespeares.ca

A unique resource, CASP attempts to track how Shakespeare has been accommodated into Canadian culture but has interest far beyond that – its tale of how an Englishman became an honorary Canadian has been replicated in countless countries worldwide. Proudly decorated with the Sanders portrait (recently rediscovered in Ottawa; see p.463) and a quote from Voltaire proclaiming that "Shakespeare is a drunken savage with some imagination whose plays please only in London and Canada", the site was originally built for students looking for unusual ways into Shakespeare but has since developed into a terrific storehouse of information on Canadian Shakespeariana – describing plays, songs, TV shows and films, much of it supported by multimedia backup.

### Deutsche Shakespeare-Gesellschaft
www.shakespeare-gesellschaft.de/english

The German Shakespeare Society goes all the way back to 1864, laying claim to be the oldest literary society in the world – fitting testament to a continuing special relationship between Shakespeare and Germany. The Society does all sorts of things, including running a well-regarded journal (*Shakespeare Jahrbuch*, which has contributions in English as well as German), supporting translation and editing activities, and holding international conferences. This bilingual site is constructed with impressive thoroughness, containing among much else a worldwide diary for Shakespeare events, reviews of productions and links to relevant German resources and institutions.

### Folger Shakespeare Library
www.folger.edu

The Folger is probably the hub for Shakespearian learning in the US (it's located, fittingly enough, on Capitol Hill), perhaps the world. On its shelves are over 250,000 volumes, including a remarkable selection of early printed books and early modern manuscripts. A shame more of this stuff isn't online, but there is at least plenty of information on the Folger's many events and real-life exhibitions. Plus you can take a walk-through of the building, and find out about the Folger Institute, a centre for advanced humanities study.

### Furness Library
dewey.library.upenn.edu/sceti/furness

There's plenty to learn at the website of the famous Furness Library, in fact just part of Penn University's gee-whiz Schoenberg Center for Electronic Texts (see p.501). As well as all those texts (many of them related to Shakespeare, whether it's work by Edwin Booth or Michel de Montaigne), there's the suavely named ERIC, a site devoted to putting the English Renaissance in context through multimedia tutorials and articles on early modern publishing. Undeniably the best introduction to the area current on the Web.

### Huntington Library
www.huntington.org

The Huntington has something of holy-grail status among research libraries – as well as containing all manner of wonderful books (among them the most famous Chaucer manuscript in existence, a Gutenberg Bible and copious Shakespeariana), the complex houses three art galleries and is surrounded by 150 acres of themed gardens. With the California beach only a few miles away, it's a wonder visiting scholars actually get any work done. The website contains plenty of interest, including selective images from their collection, and there's lots of information on events.

### Shakespeare Birthplace Trust

www.shakespeare.org.uk

The SBT guards the flame of Shakespeare in Stratford, maintaining the five properties associated with him as well as supporting a celebrated library (which boasts the RSC's archives, including an online database of productions, and local records going all the way back to 1879). Unsurprisingly the site is mainly aimed at those intending pilgrimage, but there's also some useful background and educational information. The Trust also has an excellent specialist bookshop, which offers to mail titles worldwide, with all profits supporting the SBT.

### Shakespeare Institute

www.shakespeare.bham.ac.uk

Affiliated to Birmingham University's English Department, the Shakespeare Institute was founded in the early 1950s by Renaissance scholar Allardyce Nicoll (also the first editor of the

journal *Shakespeare Survey*; see p.496) and now houses a fine library as well as running postgrad courses in Shakespeare studies. There's plenty going on both academically and with public events, so it's worth checking the site if you're planning to be in the area.

### Shakespeare's World

shakespeare.emory.edu

Based at Georgia's Emory University, this excellent site is run by Harry Rusche, a member of the English department there. It's in two main sections, both of them fascinating: "Shakespeare and the Players", an online exhibition of images commemorating American and British actors from the nineteenth and early twentieth centuries, many of them in postcard form; and the as-yet-incomplete "Shakespeare Illustrated", a compendium of nineteenth-century paintings and criticism. Both are great resources, intelligently and compellingly presented.

## Journals and criticism

Unsurprisingly, given that academic research formed the basis of the Internet, scholarly debate and discussion have prospered – in humanities as well as IT. All the major journals now have Web presences, and there are even a few that run solely online. We've selected the best Shakespearian ones and listed them below, along with other helpful resources if you're looking for critical writing in the area.

### Early Modern Literary Studies

www.shu.ac.uk/emls

*EMLS* is how an online journal should be done: it's a no-frills site but one offering an impressive range of content. Everything that appears here is peer-refereed, and there's also an active readers' forum enabling people to respond to anything that appears. Specialization is in sixteenth- and seventeenth-century literature, but there's understandably lots of focus on electronic publishing and online scholarship too. Plentiful reviews and some excellent original articles.

### London Review of Books

www.lrb.co.uk

An alternative to the *TLS* (see below), the biweekly *LRB* has a dedicated fan-base of slightly lunatic readers. Politically combative and painfully hip – in a tweedy sort of way – this journal offers more considered but esoteric reviews than are published elsewhere, many of them (though by no means all) to do with literature. The website is geared up for print subscribers, who have access to an archive dating back to 1998, but also offers a free taster of what's available.

### New York Review of Books

www.nybooks.com

The *NYRB* is difficult to sum up in a few words: it's a slightly-less-than-biweekly literary/political magazine with an all-star

selection of contributors. Only here could you find a review of a book about rats and an article on Nick Hornby nuzzling up to an earnest piece on the US involvement in Iraq. Most of it makes for a great and varied read, and the subscription rates for the website are fairly attractive – at the time of writing $20 a year if you're already a subscriber ($64 per annum), or you can pay a one-off fee of $4 for single articles.

### Shakespeare and His Critics

shakespearean.org.uk

Maintained by Shakespeare student and enthusiast Thomas Larque, Shakespeare and His Critics offers an excellent and expanding collection of critical work in the area, much of it nineteenth-century or earlier in origin. There's stuff here by usual suspects Coleridge and Samuel Johnson, but also some more unusual pieces – including an article by actress Helen Faucit on Ophelia and an electronic edition of Samuel Daniel's *Delia* (a sonnet sequence read by Shakespeare and probably a model for his own).

### Shakespeare Magazine

www.shakespearemag.com

Linked to the magazine *Shakespeare*, Shakespearemag.com is addressed primarily to those teaching the Bard in British and American schools. The website offers more than a support structure for the print version: its news section is particularly handy (freshly updated in the latest blogging fashion at shakespearemag.blogspot.com), and there are featured articles too.

## Shakespeare Quarterly
www.folger.edu/sq

*SQ*'s homepage offers little more than a list of what's currently in this well-respected journal (see p.496) and previous editions, but it can be worth dropping by every so often just to see what's going on. Text in every single issue is locatable via the JSTOR database (see p.508), but if you're not a subscriber or in an institution that is, knowing that will only make you jealous.

## Shakespeare Survey
www.cambridge.org

As with *Shakespeare Quarterly*, the website for the British *Shakespeare Survey* (see p.496), navigable via the main CUP

homepage, won't tell you much more than what's in the current edition, but makes a handy reference nonetheless – unlike many other journals it's easy to purchase single copies rather than having to subscribe.

## Times Literary Supplement
www.the-tls.co.uk

Published every week, the *TLS* is the UK humanities community's journal of record, reviewing nearly every significant scholarly title published on these shores and keeping an eagle eye on plenty else besides. Contributors are no longer anonymous, so messy hatchet jobs are rarer than they used to be, but nevertheless the standards set by the *TLS* are often severe. The website offers slim pickings to anyone not a subscriber to the print edition – a handful of articles – but if you do pay for full access you'll get your hands on a highly desirable archive.

# Renaissance gateways and tools

While Shakespeare may have the lion's share of online coverage, there are huge amounts of other stuff out there, and if you want to broaden your knowledge of the Renaissance – whether for school, university or just because you're interested – the Web offers plenty of routes to enlightenment (and ultimately to the Enlightenment). Here are some of the best.

## CERES
www.english.cam.ac.uk/ceres

Ceres is a classical nature goddess associated with fecundity and fertility; "CERES" stands for the Cambridge English Renaissance Electronic Service. Go figure. Despite a slight over-fondness for Latinate acronyms, this website, run by academics in the Cambridge University English department, is a fantastic resource, offering pointers to Renaissance material on the Web as well as regular email bulletins. The links page alone is worth a visit, and in recent years they've also started to put original scholarly work up on the site, both editions and critical writing.

## Humbul Humanities
www.humbul.ac.uk

A UK-based gateway aimed at those in further education, Humbul offers not just lists of links but a fully searchable database of educational resources in the humanities. It's set up rather like a hand-picked Web directory, and is a delight to use (it even lists British humanities jobs, if you feel like applying for a professorship or two).

## Perseus Digital Library
www.perseus.tufts.edu

Not a portal as such, but then it's pretty hard to say exactly what Perseus is – apart from supremely handy. At base it's a collection of electronic texts (a corpus that is geographically ever-expanding, as its innovative map on the homepage shows)

but has a series of invaluable research tools, among them online versions of Latin and Greek dictionaries and a digital archive devoted to the history and topography of London, as well as an area devoted especially to the English Renaissance.

## REED
eir.library.utoronto.ca/REED/

For nigh-on thirty years, the Records of Early English Drama team – internationally staffed but based at Victoria University in Canada – has been trawling dramatic texts and records referring to performances, aiming to construct a picture of what local drama was like in England between the middle ages and the closure of the theatres in 1642. As well as publishing their findings in scholarly editions, they also run this free pilot website, which enables you to search for specific events, performers and works – at the moment only in Lancashire, but coverage should be extended in future. An online exhibition available at the time of writing concentrates on "Shakespeare in the provinces".

## Voice of the Shuttle
vos.ucsb.edu

An old favourite but recently jazzed up with a glossy new design, Voice of the Shuttle (the term comes from Aristotle's *Poetics*) is a vast gateway for humanities research worldwide, with particular expertise in the opportunities offered by new media. Everything is searchable, but you can also drill down through specialist directories to find what you want.

# Subscription-only sites

It's an unpalatable truth that many of the serious literary research tools – the reliable texts, the facsimiles, the dictionaries – are not all free on the Web: they're costly to create and maintain, and inevitably that gets passed on to consumers (or, more usually, institutions who can afford to pay the subscription rates). Even so, we've listed the most impressive ones here in case you're lucky enough to have access – and in the forlorn hope that they become more democratically available in years to come.

### Early English Books Online

eebo.chadwyck.com

Another Chadwyck-Healey venture, EEBO is how all online databases should operate: it's nicely designed, a breeze to use and contains most of what you want. In this case the contents are electronic versions of the microfilm scans most research libraries undertook years ago to record and preserve their collections. What that boils down to is facsimile versions of 100,000 or so early English printed books in the Adobe Acrobat (PDF) file format, all a few clicks away and downloadable to your computer – so within seconds you can be scanning the Bodleian Library copy of *Venus and Adonis* annotated by Edmund Malone (or indeed browsing for some naughty sixteenth-century woodcuts). Even more exciting is the ongoing project to make each file text-searchable, so that you can find individual words and phrases.

### Electronic Short-Title Catalogue

www.rlg.org

This one really is for experts: a full-spec electronic database of every English book that appeared in print between 1475 and 1700, plus plenty more recent ones besides. Distilled from the hard-copy *Short-Title Catalogue* edited by Pollard, Redgrave and Wing, ESTC is uniquely useful if you're digging around in bibliographical history (and can work out how their slightly esoteric way of presenting information operates). RLG, the not-for-profit operators of the database and many others besides, will let you pay for individual searches rather than the full whack if you want to find out something specific; contact them for pricing details.

### Encyclopædia Britannica

www.britannica.com

Not quite fair to call this subscription-only: although for most of the deep content you'll have to fork out, information lying closer to the surface is yours for free. That's not much, so you'll soon get frustrated if you want to plumb *Britannica's* considerable depths on the cheap. Even so, rates aren't horrendous (about $10 a month), if you think you'll use it often, plus libraries are more likely to have this subscription resource than any other we've mentioned. But that's why free web encyclopedias (Bartleby's version of the *Columbia Encyclopedia* at www.bartleby.com/65 is as good as any) have their uses.

### JSTOR Archive

www.jstor.org

JSTOR collects over four hundred academic journals and publishes images of every page in every edition. Unwieldy at times (these can be quite large files), but this system enables you to read – or print off – text just as it originally appeared in the printed format, with footnotes, typos and all. Main attractions for Shakespearians are current and back issues of renowned journal *Shakespeare Quarterly* (see p.507), though other literary titles in the Renaissance area include *Representations*, *ELH* and *Studies in English Literature*. Subscription fees vary; contact JSTOR for details.

### Literature Online

lion.chadwyck.com

An enviable (and relatively non-specialist) resource for those wealthy enough to have access is Chadwyck-Healey's Literature Online, which boasts over 300,000 full-text English works in poetry, drama and prose. What this means is that you can search and browse literary works from Anglo-Saxon verse all the way up to contemporary fiction, for individual keywords if required. Both invaluable and very valuable – as Chadwyck-Healey know, as indeed will you after downloading the brochure and reading the pricing structure.

### Oxford English Dictionary

www.oed.com

Incredible to consider the energy, organization and resources that went into assembling the first versions of the *OED* all those years ago – slips of paper instead of computers for a start, although the *Dictionary* is nowadays updated digitally and a new print edition seems unlikely (the last in 1989 spanned 20 volumes). Especially because the advantages of the digital interface are considerable: as well as searching very precisely, you can sift through results in all sorts of creative ways and do lots of funky things besides. The downside, as ever, is the subscription: around £200/$300 per annum for individuals.

### World Shakespeare Bibliography

www.worldshakesbib.org

Much as it may seem as if there can be no method of keeping track of the rampant Shakespeare publishing industry, there is, and this is it: a regularly updated bibliography of every book, article and review from 1966 to the present, with plentiful other Shakespeariana besides. Even more astounding is the fact that the World Shakespeare Bibliography is truly global in reach, covering some 98 languages: altogether there are over 90,000 entries.

# Fun stuff

And if you're fed up of using it for work, the Web offers plenty of scope for Shakespearian-style time-wasting…

### Hamlet Machine
de.geocities.com/hamletmachine1

Erase the most famous soliloquy in the language word-by-word, with mad accompaniment from obscure popular culture as you go. Glossing *Hamlet* has never been this fun. Or so utterly batty.

### iPod Sonnets
www.westering.com/ipod

Transplant the Bard into the digital generation with this freebie from Westering, a simple file enabling you to upload all 154 Sonnets onto your shiny new 'Pod. See if you can memorize the lot before the battery dies.

### Proper Elizabethan Accents
www.renfaire.com/Language

Parley with the natives at this excellent site, which promises to teach you "faire Elizabethan". As a glance at the "Elizabethan insults" section will demonstrate, there's lots to learn – but get your lips round some "fies" and "zounds" instead of the usual effing and blinding and you'll be well on the way. Sound files linked to each word show you exactly how it's done.

### SCA Renaissance Dance
www.pbm.com/~lindahl/dance.html

Or of course you can forget the funny voices: learn how to impress by footing it featly here and there on this site dedicated to Renaissance dance. Includes a facsimile of a contemporary account of the "Nine Days' Wonder", the clown William Kempe's dance marathon from London to Norwich (see p.472).

### Shakespeare's Will
www.documentsonline.pro.gov.uk

You may have to mug up on your English secretary script in order to make sense of what's on offer (lots of squiggles; try the course at www.english.cam.ac.uk/ceres/ehoc if you fancy a bash), but for those able to decode it here's the famous Will's infamous will in PDF format.

# Glossary of useful terms

Although the *Rough Guide* tries to keep jargon to a minimum, on occasion we've used specialist technical terms, many of them drawn from Renaissance printing and theatre practice. This glossary lists and defines the most useful, supplemented by some relevant literary terminology. (If the word you're hunting for doesn't feature below, see our recommendations for further reading on p.517.) Cross-references appear in colour.

**Alliteration** ▷ The technique of repeating sounds that occur at the beginning of words, nearly always consonants. Shakespeare's Sonnet 12, which begins "When I do count the clock that tells the time", has two stressed alliterative patterns, one on *c* and the other on *t* (with three unstressed *th*s as well).

**Aside** ▷ Words spoken by a character when there are other people on stage but not meant to be heard by them – and thus addressed to the audience instead. Compare soliloquy.

**Autograph** ▷ When referring to text, "autograph" copy is a manuscript in the author's own hand – something that, with the exception of the collaborative play *Sir Thomas More* (see p.140), we don't possess for Shakespeare's work. Sometimes also known as "holograph".

**"Bad" quarto** ▷ A quarto with serious problems of some kind: from erroneous printing and poor layout to major omissions of the script, or obviously nonsensical text. "Bad" versions sometimes result when copy is stolen or pirated, or when text has been memorially reconstructed (see pirate(d copy) and memorial reconstruction), for instance in the 1603 quarto of *Hamlet*. Some argue against using such value-laden terminology, and that supposedly "bad" texts provide information that more polished ones don't.

**Blank verse** ▷ The overwhelming majority of Shakespeare's verse is in so-called blank verse or "iambic pentameter". In this metrical scheme, each line breaks down into five pairs of syllables, with the stress on the second (de-*dum*, de-*dum*, de-*dum*, de-*dum*, de-*dum*); the "blank" refers to the fact that lines are not rhymed. This basic pattern is clear enough in a line such as Romeo's "The precious treasure of his eyesight lost" (1.1.230). But Shakespeare continually experiments with the music of verse, often producing lines that break many of the apparent rules. "To be, or not to be; that is the question" is more famous than most: choppy rhythmically, it also has one syllable too many.

**Clown** ▷ See Fool.

**Comedy** ▷ As with tragedy, understanding what Shakespeare thought of as "comic" can be a full-time occupation. Laughs come into it, but so too does the expectation of social harmony, usually achieved through marriage between major characters. See p.276 for more.

**Commonplace book** ▷ Many educated people in the Renaissance – Hamlet is one – kept a notebook (sometimes called "tables") in which they jotted down aphorisms or useful quotes as practice for their own writing or speaking. This practice was encouraged by humanist educators, who argued that rhetorical skill was the foundation of civil society.

**Compositor** ▷ In a printshop, the person responsible for setting type within the grid laid out for each page in preparation for printing. Usually several compositors worked on a book at the same time; up to nine might have collaborated on the 1623 First Folio.

**Chorus** ▷ In Shakespearian plays, an individual who speaks before and sometimes during the performance, presenting and commenting on its action, and often describing events not shown on stage. Shakespeare's include the Chorus in *Henry V*, a character called "Rumour" in *2 Henry IV*, and the medieval poet John Gower in *Pericles*. See also Prologue and Epilogue.

**Deus ex machina** ▷ Literally "the god from a machine", a theatrical device, derived from ancient Greek drama, in which a god intervenes in the human action. Usually the deity is flown (lowered) on stage via some kind of mechanical device, and resolves the complications of the plot at a stroke. Shakespearian examples include the appearance of the marriage god Hymen in *As You Like It*, and of Jupiter, king of the gods, in *Cymbeline*.

**Discovery space** ▷ In sixteenth- and seventeenth-century theatres, an open room just behind the main stage and fronting onto it. Doors or a curtain usually hid the space from view, but could be opened to "discover" whatever lay within – sometimes a bed or other large prop, or even (in the case of *The Tempest*) two lovers silently playing chess.

**Doubling** ▷ The practice whereby one actor plays multiple parts. It's especially prevalent in Shakespeare's histories, where the list of characters often far exceeds the number of personnel that would have been available to him.

**Dramatis personae** ▷ List of characters in a play (from the Latin).

**Epilogue** ▷ A short speech concluding a play, usually spoken after its action has finished. Sometimes Shakespeare's heroes and heroines step outside the play to act as epilogues; Rosalind in *As You Like It* and Prospero in *The Tempest* are two celebrated examples.

**Fair copy** ▷ Before a text was published it had ideally to be copied out in neat, so that the printers could follow it accurately. This work might be done by a playwright, or (more likely) by a professional scribe.

**Farce** ▷ Since the eighteenth century farce has been categorized as a form (usually dramatic) designed to move the spectator to unreflective, simple laughter – as distinct from comedy, which also encourages thought. Samuel Taylor Coleridge claimed that "a proper farce is mainly distinguished from comedy by the licence allowed, and even required, in the fable, in order to produce strange and laughable situations. The story need not be probable; it is enough that it is possible."

**Feminism** ▷ Since the 1970s, supported by the growing political movement for women's rights, much academic criticism has focused on the place of women in literary culture – both within texts and as producers of them. Though much of this work has been banded together as "feminist", exploration of issues relating to gender and sexuality has taken a variety of forms and directions, especially in recent years.

**Folio** ▷ A large-format book, usually prestigious and expensive, for which each sheet of printer's paper was folded in half to make two leaves (*folium* is Latin for "leaf"), or four pages. See p.485 for more.

**Fool** ▷ In the Elizabethan and Jacobean theatre professional comedians were great stars, playwrights often tailoring roles specially for them. Fools (also known as "clowns") usually wore distinctive costumes, specializing in singing, dancing and witty wordplay as well as physical comedy – some powerful families even employed a jester for their own private entertainment. Shakespeare's fools (he writes parts for at least thirteen) are often given license to say things that other characters cannot, offering a sardonic perspective on the events of the play. See p.27 for more.

**Formalism** ▷ An academic movement that reached its apogee in the mid-twentieth century, which stressed the (internal) literary or aesthetic qualities of writing as opposed to their (external) placement in a historical or cultural setting. In Shakespeare studies, the term most often refers to "New" critics such as Cleanth Brooks (see p.206), who stressed the importance of looking past an author's "intentions" to what the text actually achieved.

**Foul papers** ▷ A playwright's rough manuscript(s), containing – as the name implies – redrafted and revised work rather than a finished or "fair" copy.

**Frons scenae** ▷ The wall forming the back of the stage in Jacobethan theatres, also the outside wall of the tiring house and into which stage doors were set. The *frons scenae* was often elaborately painted, and could have been decorated, for example with tapestries, for individual performances where required.

**Groundlings** ▷ Members of the audience who stood in the yard, closest to the stage in Jacobethan outdoor theatres. Because they had no seats, groundlings paid the lowest rate (usually a penny) to see plays.

**Heavens** ▷ The multi-functional canopy surmounting sixteenth- and seventeenth-century stages. It kept rain from spoiling expensive costumes and props, but also (in later, more sophisticated theatres especially) provided a room aloft from which actors or props could be "flown" in – descending, as if literally, from the sky. Like the frons scenae, often colourfully painted, perhaps with the signs of the zodiac.

**Holograph** ▷ See autograph.

**Humanism** ▷ There are many ways of understanding humanism, but in the Renaissance it is most closely identified with an educational movement, centred in northern Europe, that stressed the value of classical Greek and Roman culture and texts. Many reforming humanists set up schools – called "grammar" schools because of their emphasis on classical linguistic training – among them the King's New School in Stratford, which Shakespeare probably attended (see p.450).

**Iambic pentameter** ▷ See blank verse.

**Jig** ▷ A sprightly dance with folk roots. According to eyewitness testimony, Elizabethan actors danced and sang jigs at the end of a play, perhaps in order to show off the talents of their master dancer (the clown William Kempe took the lead in Shakespeare's company from 1594 to 1599; see p.472). Many surviving jig texts are bawdy, often involving adultery – so perhaps the romantic climaxes of Shakespearian comedy weren't originally as innocent as they now appear.

**Masque** ▷ A form of courtly entertainment that reached its extravagant height in the reigns of Elizabeth I, James I and his son Charles I. The Jacobean indoor masque combined music, dancing and poetry with lavish costumes and impressive stage effects, performed for (and by) courtiers, often in homage to the King. Masques usually included mythological or allegorical references, designed to flatter the learning and breeding of everyone involved. While Ben Jonson became chief masque writer to James I, Shakespeare restricted himself to writing public plays that occasionally reveal the influence of the form – *The Tempest* contains a wedding masque, for instance.

**Memorial reconstruction** ▷ Some plays appear to have been pirated and sold to printers by people claiming to have memorized the text – perhaps noted it down at a performance, or reconstructed it for themselves through their own involvement in the play (as with *Hamlet*; see p.68). Full scripts will not have been widely available to actors, perhaps in an attempt to forestall this practice; see p.472. Many of these texts were printed, producing what are sometimes called "bad" quartos.

**Metaphor** ▷ Literally "transference" in Greek, a metaphor is a figure of speech in which one thing is described in terms of another, usually by way of a comparison. The claim in Sonnet 116 that love is "the star to every wand'ring barque [boat]" (7) is a resonant example of metaphor. Compare simile.

**Miracle play** ▷ See mystery play.

**Morality play** ▷ A variety of religious drama that was especially popular in Europe in the late medieval period. Morality plays had a simple Christian message, often dramatizing the experience of man through temptation and sin (frequently personified by characters called, for example, "Vice" and "Pride") towards salvation. Shakespeare's Falstaff and Iago are descended from morality archetypes, both versions of the "Vice" character.

**Mystery play** ▷ Mystery plays were a familiar part of English popular culture for over three hundred years until the late sixteenth century. They were usually dramatizations of biblical scenes, sometimes part of extended "cycles" performed in large towns to celebrate major religious festivals. The cycles of York, Wakefield and Chester are perhaps the most famous, though only two plays from the Coventry cycle (which Shakespeare could have seen; see p.468) have survived. "Miracle" plays drew upon the lives of saints rather than directly biblical sources.

**Neoclassicism** ▷ Although significant swathes of Renaissance culture could be characterized as "neoclassical" in the sense that they gave new life to ideas derived from ancient Greece and Rome, here the term is commonly used to describe Restoration and early eighteenth-century approaches to Shakespeare. Influenced by continental models, neoclassical critics were united in distaste for Shakespeare's formal deficiencies (chiefly his reluctance to conform to Aristotle's Unities), lack of morality and "barbarous" phrases, and often resorted to

adaptation in order to make him fit their "enlightened" age (see p.176).

**New Criticism** ▷ A kind of criticism emphasizing the aesthetic importance of the text rather than its historical or cultural setting. See formalism.

**New historicism** ▷ A critical movement spearheaded primarily by American academics, which seeks to distinguish itself from the "old" historicism practised by critics such as E.M.W. Tillyard and Lily B. Campbell (see p.112). New historicism often attempts to throw light on canonical literary texts by reading them alongside more unconventional ones, arguing that historical culture is itself formed by texts of all varieties, from travel reports and works of history to marginal jottings and books of accounts.

**Octavo** ▷ A small-format book, exactly half the size of a quarto, in which the pages are folded three times to make eight leaves – hence the name – or sixteen pages. See p.485 for more.

**Part** ▷ For the theatres in which Shakespeare worked and wrote, an actor's role (sometimes several if he was "doubling" another part) was copied out individually, there being just one copy of the full-text promptbook. Parts would contain all a character's speeches as well as cues so that he knew when to appear and/or speak.

**Patron** ▷ In sixteenth- and seventeenth-century England (and indeed much later), patrons were an essential part of the cultural and economic environment. Poets would often look for patronage to support their work, and theatre companies were required by law to have an aristocratic patron who would subsidize and protect the players in exchange for whatever kudos they might gain by involvement.

**Pirate(d copy)** ▷ The concept of intellectual copyright largely being non-existent for authors in Jacobethan England (though Shakespeare was accused of plagiarism; see p.128), there was little to stop publishers from stealing text from writers and printing it without their permission. Sir Philip Sidney's sonnet sequence *Astrophil and Stella* reached print in a pirated edition of 1591 – Sidney himself was long dead – though debate rages as to whether Shakespeare's own Sonnets were lifted from their author and printed behind his back.

**Pit** ▷ The area directly in front of the stage in "private" theatres such as the Blackfriars (see p.481), which inverted the hierarchies of the Elizabethan outdoor theatres by containing the most expensive seats.

**Playbook** ▷ See promptbook.

**Printers (and publishers)** ▷ In Renaissance England printers owned type and a press on which to set it, while publishers acquired the rights to a text, registered it to be printed and arranged for distribution. Most title-pages from the period provide information about who was responsible: the first quarto of *Richard III* (1597) states that it was "printed by Valentine Sims [printer], for Andrew Wise [publisher]", though Shakespeare's own name does not get a mention.

**Problem play** ▷ Originally applied to the kind of drama pioneered by Ibsen and Shaw in the late nineteenth century, the term "problem play" was first used to describe Shakespeare in the 1890s. Its alternative, "problem comedy", points to a group of plays written in the first years of the seventeenth century – usually *Measure for Measure, All's Well That Ends Well* and *Troilus and Cressida*, though other works have been admitted too. These have in common an interest in sexual and social issues, but also a nagging sense that Shakespearian comic form – with its emphasis on social and sexual resolution in the finale – might be rendered problematic by the events of the plot.

**Prologue** ▷ A short speech introducing a play, usually spoken before its action begins. See also Chorus and Epilogue.

**Promptbook** ▷ Also known as a "playbook", this would have been in all probability the only full text of a play in the Jacobethan theatre – a valuable commodity, and usually kept in the playhouse itself. Actors' parts would be copied from it, although prompting in the modern sense (reminding actors of their lines during a performance) seems to have been uncommon.

**Publisher** ▷ See printers (and publishers).

**Pun** ▷ A literary trick in which a word is mistaken for another that sounds similar, so bringing into play their various meanings. As with Panthino's pun in *The Two Gentleman of Verona*, which exchanges "tail" for "tale" (2.3.45), the aim is usually to get laughs, and the pun often has bawdy undertones.

**Quarto** ▷ A medium-sized book format, half the size of a folio, in which each sheet of paper was folded twice to make four leaves (hence the name) or eight pages. When Shakespeare's works were printed during his lifetime, the portable quarto format was nearly always the one chosen. See p.485 for more.

**Rhetoric** ▷ Following the prompting of humanist educators, the study of oratory – chiefly as it was practised in ancient Greece and Rome – became an integral part of the curriculums of Renaissance grammar schools and universities. Rhetoric, the command of the spoken (and then written) word, was both prized and systematized, with students taught to use complex classical systems of schemes and devices in order to achieve eloquent and persuasive speech. As his works repeatedly show, Shakespeare put his schoolboy experience of rhetoric to good use – as a writer of plays and poems he employed it on a daily basis.

**Rhyme royal** ▷ A seven-line poetic form used by Shakespeare in his poems *Lucrece* and *A Lover's Complaint*; see p.423 for more.

**Romance** ▷ Although not to be confused with Romanticism, the term first appears in relation to Shakespeare in the nineteenth century. Generally it refers to his final comedies *Pericles*, *Cymbeline*, *The Winter's Tale* and *The Tempest*, which deploy motifs reminiscent of romance tales both ancient and medieval – they feature great journeys, wandering heroes, tempests and shipwrecks, separation and magical reunion – but add something particularly Shakespearian. Father-daughter reunions loom large in these plays, and spectacular staging is a highly visible part of their dramatic language (see p.276).

**Romanticism** ▷ A cultural, philosophical and political movement that eventually touched every corner of the creative arts, from painting and music to theatre and architecture, Romanticism is often traced to the late eighteenth and early nineteenth centuries, when artists and writers rebelled against what they saw as the rationalism and formality of the neoclassical period. In Britain Shakespeare was pressed into service by first-generation Romantics including Coleridge and Hazlitt, who alike stressed the importance of unfettered imagination and saw in Shakespeare's art a triumph of protean genius. Both were impressed by the acting of Edmund Kean, whose passionate and improvisatory performances as Richard III, Shylock and Othello became hallmarks of the Romantic style.

**Scribal copy** ▷ In dramatic work the phrase describes text – usually "fair" or neat – copied out by a professional scribe or "scrivener", perhaps for the purposes of printing. Much literature circulated in manuscript, however, and scribes were often employed to copy out these texts too; some of Shakespeare's Sonnets might well have been read in this form before they reached print in 1609 (see p.427).

**Signature** ▷ In Renaissance printing, the method of marking up groups of pages with alphabetical or numerical signs in the order that they were to appear in the book, designed to assist those responsible for assembling it to get everything in the right place (page numbers did not regularly appear until later in the period).

**Simile** ▷ While resembling metaphor in its transfer of the meanings of one word to another, simile keeps the distinction between them at greater distance, often with the formula "like" or "as", which can then be followed by "so". Sonnet 60, a poem which describes the inexorable passage of time, begins, "Like as the waves make towards the pebbled shore / So do our minutes hasten to their end." In *Romeo and Juliet*, Capulet reacts to the sight of the apparently dead Juliet by saying: "Death lies on her like an untimely frost / Upon the sweetest flower of all the field." (4.4.55–6).

**Soliloquy** ▷ In plays, a solo speech, usually spoken by a character alone on stage. By convention, a soliloquy is addressed by the character to him-/herself, as if thinking out loud. This makes it an important way of revealing a character's thoughts and feelings, and providing clues as to his/her motivation. However, a soliloquy can also be addressed directly to the audience, as in the opening speech of Richard III (see p.294). Shakespeare's master soliloquist is Hamlet, also the playwright's largest role. Compare aside.

**Sonnet** ▷ A fourteen-line lyric form popular in several European languages throughout the Renaissance, often associated with love poetry. Several versions exist, employing different patterns of rhyme, but in the kind of sonnet preferred by Shakespeare the lines are ten syllables long and rhyme in the pattern *ababcdcdefef*, before closing with a final couplet *gg*. See p.429 for more.

**Speech prefix** ▷ A cue in a dramatic script identifying who is speaking, an often haphazard system in early printed texts – in fact some of Shakespeare's plays were printed with the name of the actor appearing by mistake.

**Stage direction** ▷ As with speech prefixes, a sometimes chaotic system for cueing players to perform actions outside the spoken text, or informing readers that a particular device was used in performance. Many printed versions of Shakespeare's earlier plays have few stage directions (modern editors often opt to insert them), although others – particularly his last plays – have very detailed cues describing how particular moments should be staged.

**Stationers' Register** ▷ The detailed accounts of the Stationers' Company, which licensed printers and (theoretically) ensured who had rights to publish a particular text. Everything printed was meant to be recorded in the Register, making it a valuable resource for modern scholars.

**Staying order** ▷ An entry in the Stationers' Register designed to assert ownership of a particular text, and thus prevent it from being published illegally by others. Although an entry theoretically declared an intention to print, publishers did not always go ahead and do so.

**Stylometrics** ▷ An analytical technique that tries to identify which stylistic forms (such as vocabulary, syntax, metre) are characteristically employed by a particular author, usually in an attempt to work out precisely what s/he wrote. Since the nineteenth century many different stylometric tests have been applied to Shakespeare, recently with the aid of sophisticated computer-aided statistics, but it is notoriously hard to prove anything beyond doubt without drawing on other evidence.

**Tiring house** ▷ The "attiring" or dressing-room space of the Jacobethan theatre, traditionally located directly behind the stage and leading onto it via several doors.

**Tragedy** ▷ Understanding (and defining) the concept of tragedy has been an obsession in Western culture at least since Aristotle, and Renaissance theorists had many views – chief among them that a tragic play should end sadly, usually with the death of a princely protagonist. See p.276 for more.

**Trap** ▷ The door in the floor of many Renaissance stages, colloquially known as the "hell". Actors could climb out of the trap, bodies could be buried in it and sound effects could be supplied by someone standing underneath the stage.

**Unities, the** ▷ The theory that for drama to be convincing it should be "unified" in place, action and time – that a play should take place in one location, have one plot and possess a time-frame corresponding to the literal time of performance. The idea was developed by neoclassical critics from Aristotle's fragmentary treatise on *Poetics*. Shakespeare had no such concerns, as he repeatedly demonstrates (only *The Tempest* fits this description, and even then has sub-plots), and his plays were frequently adapted to make them more neoclassical from the Restoration onwards.

**Yard** ▷ In Jacobethan outdoor theatres, the space surrounding the stage in which groundlings were allowed to stand for the cheapest entrance fee. Its origins lay in the inn-yards where temporary stages were erected, an arrangement that continued with touring companies well into the seventeenth century.

# Reading further

This glossary cannot hope to cover everything, and it may prompt more questions than it answers. More detailed discussions of literary terms can be found in Chris Baldick's *Oxford Concise Dictionary of Literary Terms* (2001), but perhaps the ultimate resource in this field is *The New Princeton Encyclopedia of Poetry and Poetics* (1993), edited by Frank J. Warnke, O.B. Hardison and Earl Miner, which contains extensive essays on technical topics and literary genres.

Questions on matters of Renaissance staging might be answered by *The Oxford Companion to Shakespeare* (see p.488), perhaps in collaboration with a general theatre encyclopedia such as Martin Banham's *Cambridge Companion to Theatre* (1995) or *The Concise Oxford Companion to the Theatre* (rev. 1992), edited by Phyllis Hartnoll and Peter Found.

If you want to find out more about rhetoric, the system of codifying and shaping speech that Shakespeare will have learnt at school, head to the World Wide Web, where an excellent website called The Forest of Rhetoric at http://humanities.byu.edu/rhetoric/silva.htm should answer your queries and direct you to further resources. See p.498 for an extensive directory of Shakespeare-related websites.

# Picture credits

Rough Guides would like to thank all those who have given permission for the use of the following illustrations (listed by page number). Every effort has been made to trace copyright holders, but we will be happy to correct any errors that may have arisen.

10 Courtesy of the Stratford Festival Archives
(photo: Peter Smith)

17 Private collection

20 © Donald Cooper/Photo*stage*

26 © Donald Cooper/Photo*stage*

30 Shakespeare Centre Library, Stratford-upon-Avon
(photo: Angus McBean)

36 © Donald Cooper/Photo*stage*

40 Shakespeare Centre Library, Stratford-upon-Avon
(photo: Ernest Daniels)

49 © Donald Cooper/Photo*stage*

54 Private collection

59 © Donald Cooper/Photo*stage*

65 Shakespeare Centre Library, Stratford-upon-Avon
(photo: Tom Holte)

71 The Moviestore Collection

75 Private collection (photo: Bertram Park)

86 Shakespeare Centre Library, Stratford-upon-Avon
(photo: Angus McBean)

95 International Films Espanola/Alpine
Productions/The Kobal Collection

102 © Donald Cooper/Photo*stage*

107 The Moviestore Collection

116 Shakespeare Centre Library, Stratford-upon-Avon
(photo: Tom Holte)

125 Shakespeare Centre Library, Stratford-upon-Avon
(photo: Tom Holte)

134 © Donald Cooper/Photo*stage*

141 Private collection

146 Private collection

153 MGM/The Kobal Collection

157 © Donald Cooper/Photo*stage*

164 Private collection

173 Private collection

179 Shakespeare Centre Library, Sratford-upon-Avon

187 © Donald Cooper/Photo*stage*

190 Shakespeare Centre Library, Stratford-upon-Avon
(photo: Angus McBean)

196 The Garrick Club, London/The Art Archive

200 © Donald Cooper/Photo*stage*

205 Toho/The Kobal Collection

214 © Donald Cooper/Photo*stage*

222 Private collection

227 © Donald Cooper/Photo*stage*

232 © Donald Cooper/Photo*stage*

242 London Theatre Museum/V&A Images
(photo: JW Debenham)

246 © Donald Cooper/Photo*stage*

252 The Moviestore Collection

256 Private collection

264 Manchester City Galleries

268 London Theatre Museum/V&A Images

271 © Donald Cooper/Photo*stage*

280 The National Theatre

289 Shakespeare Centre Library, Stratford-upon-Avon
(photo: Angus McBean)

297 Collection of David Robinson

302 The Moviestore Collection

308 Private collection

310 London Theatre Museum/V&A Images

313 The Moviestore Collection

317 © Donald Cooper/Photo*stage*

322 Private collection

328 London Theatre Museum/V&A Images

335 © Donald Cooper/Photo*stage*

340 © Donald Cooper/Photo*stage*

356 © Donald Cooper/Photo*stage*

365 Shakespeare Centre Library, Stratford-upon-Avon
(photo: Angus McBean)

373 © Donald Cooper/Photo*stage*

377 © Donald Cooper/Photo*stage*

386 © Donald Cooper/Photo*stage*

397 © Donald Cooper/Photo*stage*

403 © Donald Cooper/Photo*stage*

422 Private collection

431 By permission of the Shakespeare Birthplace Trust

443 © Philadelphia Museum of Art/CORBIS

453 Rob Reichenfeld © Dorling Kindersley

459 © Bettmann/CORBIS

463 Rob Reichenfeld © Dorling Kindersley

466 © Historical Picture Archive/CORBIS

472 © Dorling Kindersley

474 Private collection

477 © Nik Wheeler/CORBIS

479 Private collection

481 Rob Reichenfeld © Dorling Kindersley

# Index

For ease of reference, Shakespeare's major works are listed individually as part of the alphabetical sequence; the main chapter on each is highlighted in colour. Entries highlighted in **bold** indicate that the subject is covered in a feature box. Non-Shakespearian works are generally indexed under the author's name.

# H

Hack, Keith 214
Hackett, James Henry 85
Hafner, Ingrid 387
Hagen, Uta 270
Haig, David 215, 257
Halio, Jay L. 182
Hall, Edward (director) 106, 117,
  126, 135, 246, 387
Hall, John 464–465
**Hall, Peter** 50, 59, 60, 75, 96, 105,
  116, 125, 135, 180, 202, 225, 245,
  292, 301, **334**, 366, 376, 387, 480
Hallam, Lewis 156, 224
Hallam, Nancy 58
Halle, Edward (chronicler) 79, 98,
  100, 109, 112, 119, 123, 124, 128,
  137, 283, 294
Hamilton, Graham 398
Hamilton, Victoria 366
*Hamlet* 27, 62–78, 149, 212, 258,
  309, 320, 348, 368, 414, 424, 459
  **"bad" quarto of 68**
  audio versions 77–78
  characters and synopsis 63
  criticism on 78
  date 62
  editions of 78
  screen versions 76–77
  sources 62
  stage history and adaptations 73–76
  texts 62, 68
  and the "*ur-Hamlet*" 62, 64
Hammond, Antony 282
Hands, Terry 50, 86, 96, 105, 117,
  126, 135, 235, 256, 269, 281, 312,
  376, 480
Hanson, Alexander 226
Harada, Mieko 181
Harbour, David 398
Hardwicke, Cedric 59
Hardy, Robert 86, 87, 96
Harewood, David 269
Harfouch, Corinna 366
Harington, Sir John 354
Harris, Henry 311
Harsnett, Samuel 170
Hart, Joseph C. 82
Hathaway (later Shakespeare), Anne
  25, 452, 465, 467
  Anne Hathaway's "Cottage" 452
Hattaway, Michael 32
Havergal, Giles 20
Havilland, Olivia de 246
Hawke, Ethan 76, 77, 87, 96
Hawkins, William 58
Hawthorne, Nigel 303, 377, 378
Hayes, George 291
Hazlitt, William 44, 170, 224, 267,
  309
Heine, Heinrich 354
Helpmann, Robert 167, 245
Heminges, John 85, 111, 234, 254,
  457, 467, 485
Henderson, John 73, 85, 213

*Henry IV Part I* 79–88, 89, 91, 94,
  149, 160, 228, 458
  audio versions 88
  characters and synopsis 80
  criticism on 88
  date 79
  editions of 88
  screen versions 87
  sources 79
  stage history and adaptations 85–87
  texts 79
*Henry IV Part II* 42, 89–97, 98, 103,
  149, 160, 228, 248, 458
  audio versions 97
  characters and synopsis 90
  criticism on 97
  date 89
  editions of 97
  screen versions 96
  sources 89
  stage history and adaptations 94–96
  texts 89
*Henry V* 22, 42, 98–108, 109, 140,
  149, 160, 248, 456, 458, 461
  audio versions 106
  characters and synopsis 99
  criticism on 108
  date 98
  editions of 108
  screen versions 106
  sources 98
  stage history and adaptations
    104–106
  texts 98
*Henry VI Part I* 109–118, 119, 121,
  160, 197, 294
  audio versions 117
  characters and synopsis 110
  criticism on 118
  date 109
  editions of 118
  screen versions 117
  sources 109
  stage history and adaptations
    115–117
  texts 109
*Henry VI Part II* 111, 119–127, 132,
  160
  audio versions 127
  characters and synopsis 120
  criticism on 127
  date 119
  editions of 127
  screen versions 126
  sources 119
  stage history and adaptations
    124–126
  texts 119
*Henry VI Part III* 111, 128–136, 276,
  288, 296, 300, 455
  audio versions 136
  characters and synopsis 129
  criticism on 136
  date 128
  editions of 136
  screen versions 136
  sources 128
  stage history and adaptations
    133–135
  texts 128

*Henry VIII* 137–148, 160, 389, 394,
  464
  audio versions 147
  characters and synopsis 138
  criticism on 148
  date 137
  editions of 148
  screen versions 147
  sources 137
  stage history and adaptations
    145–147
  texts 137
Henry, Guy 168
Henryson, Robert 358, 423
Henshall, Douglas 314
Henslowe, Philip 115, 354, 457, 471
Henson, Nicky 26
Herlie, Eileen 76
Hesketh, Sir Thomas 454
Heston, Charlton 20, 21, 158
Hewitson, Ian 40
Heywood, John 473
Heywood, Thomas 139, 140, 440
Hicks, Greg 51
Hille, Anastasia 271
Hilliard, Nicholas 438, 463
Hinds, Ciaran 409
Hirsch, John 301
Hoby, Sir Edward 291
Hoffman, Dustin 225
Hoffman, Michael 247
Hoghton, Alexander 454
**Holinshed, Raphael** 52, 79, 82, 91,
  98, 100, **100**, 109, 112, 119, 123, 124,
  128, 137, 160, 193, 196, 283, 294
Holland, Joseph 157
Holland, Peter 247
Hollander, Tom 31
Holloway, Baliol 10, 268
Holm, Ian 96, 105, 135, 180, 246,
  301
Holt, Thelma 323
Homer 358
Honan, Park 467
Honigmann, E.A.J. 271
Hooper, Ewan 51
Hope theatre 478
Hopkins, Anthony 20, 50, 269, 356,
  357
Hordern, Michael 181, 335
Horton, Christiana 406
Horton, Priscilla 333
Hoskins, Bob 269
House, Gordon 88, 97
Houseman, John 407
Houston, William 87, 106
Howard, Alan 19, 50, 51, 86, 96,
  105, 117, 126, 135, 180, 245, 255,
  292, 346, 366
Howard, Jean E. 304
Howard, Leslie 312
Howell, Jane 117, 126, 135, 303,
  356, 408
Hudson, John 387
Hughes, Ken 204
Hull, Thomas 39, 345

Index

Index

Index

Index

Index

# Y

# Z

Index